Her story

This book chronicles the author's own childhood, growing up in a dysfunctional community called Trench Town in Kingston, Jamaica. It outlines the beginning of the two main political parties and their competitiveness to the point where human beings were slaughtered like animals to ensure politicians their ultimate ambition (power). Read about the worst year of her life.

1 9 8 0

Jamaica witnessed its longest and most violent election campaign. Over 900 people were killed, including her brother who was gunned down at the age of seventeen by a political activist. Read about the rapes, murders and corruption in Trench Town. 'The Green Bay Killings', 'Gold Street Massacre' and the vicious political motivated arson attack on the Evening Tide Home. Over 150 elderly disabled women perished in the fire. Jamaica's shame they all want us to forget.

TRENCH TOWN

CONCRETE JUNGLE KILL OR BE KILLED

PAULINE EDWARDS

Copyright 2001
by
Pauline Edwards

All rights reserved. No part of this book may be reproduced, in any form or by any means electronic, mechanical or otherwise including photocopying, information storage and retrieval systems without the written permission of the publisher.

ISBN 0-9541682-0-8

Published By Pauline Edwards

For information about this book call 07960 261296

patsyedwards@talk21.com

TRENCH TOWN

This book is dedicated to my brother Carlton Tomlinson who was brutally gunned down in July 1980, and to all the other victims of political and gang warfare in Jamaica.

Carlton Tomlinson 4th June 1963 - 11th July 1980.

Also in memory of the one hundred and fifty-three elderly women who died in the Evening Tide Home fire on 20th May 1980.

Acknowledgments

It has taken six years to complete this book and during this time I have come to know my purpose. I am now wiser and stronger so my journey through earth will be more positive despite all the negative forces I have to encounter. I would like to say a special thanks to a wonderful cousin, Tony Brown, you were my main support through it all. Kabura, thanks for the help and information. Also, a big thank you to Jean Sogbodjor and everyone who has contributed to this book, this is as much your story as it is mine.

FOREWORD

Trench Town, Jamaica....Three words that are recognised the world over and conjure up so many images - poverty, vitality, a thumping reggae bassline with an endless stream of wannabe deejays and singers riding the rhythm, police brutality, political corruption and open gang warfare.

Trench Town's most famous exports are the musicians and singers that carry reggae music and its message to the ears of true music lovers. The Wailers - Bob Marley, Peter Tosh and Bunny Wailer - are the ghettos eternal international ambassadors. But back at home the area they come from has been divided into garrison communities where to talk to the wrong person, even if they are your blood relatives could cost you and your family very dear.

The divisions are stark. A road, sports field or school playground mark out the territory. The police are either ineffective or involved in the disputes between armed groups who sometimes sport more high-calibre artillery than them. The army is ill-disciplined and ill-equipped to deal with the crime and violence and soldiers are trained to understand only total war which brings the obvious response from the 'ghetto sufferahs'. The business class want to make money at any cost and so long as the problems stay away from those who live 'up in the hills' then they will indulge in any practice that makes them an extra dollar (preferably US). The church leaders are fighting a losing battle (if they haven't already lost it by slipping into their own personal corruption and pervasion) and yet Jamaicans boast that they are a Christian nation and have more churches per head of the population than any other country on the planet. As for the politicians they started the whole thing by shipping guns and drugs to aid their election campaigns over three decades ago. Now they couldn't get the guns and criminal mentality out of society, even if they wanted to.

This is the backdrop for this autobiographical journey through the tenement yards and lanes of western Kingston. Jimmy Cliff's Ivan ruled here in the film 'The Harder They Come', but rather than glorify the guns and machismo of the male rebel, Trench Town (Kill or be Killed) is one woman's story of her struggle to survive against all odds in an environment where 'born fi dead' is one of the most common slogans uttered by the massive.

This is a true story of where Jamaica has come from and where it is heading told from the view, not of the aristocrat or textbook sociologist, but by someone who grew up in the heart of the ghetto amongst some of the most callous and depraved human beings, yet there is also a strong streak of humanity and endless fight for justice for the down-pressed.

Kubara Zamani
October 2001

INTRODUCTION

My purpose for writing this book is to break the silence of conspiracy by speaking out against the tyranny of a corrupt political system in Jamaica. This book is based on my own experiences growing up in the politically volatile community Trench Town in the capital city of Kingston. It will also cover some of the other places I have journeyed to. I aim to reveal some of the murders, rapes, genocide and exploitation of certain groups of people who have no voice. I will explain the impact of poverty on those of us who were children and the ways in which my family became dysfunctional, leaving us vulnerable to suffering and pain.

My story begins in the pre-colonial era when the people were disempowered and fighting for justice. Two political parties were formed and their founding leaders Norman Manley and his cousin Alexander Bustamante promised to bring the long awaited liberation, pride, equal rights, but most of all the right to choose. What we inherited instead was a corrupt political system that encouraged the murders of thousands of people in Jamaica.

In the late 1960s politics changed for the worse. Older veterans were stepping aside making way for younger radical men, who wanted power by any means necessary. The dynamic socialist Michael Joshua Manley took over the leadership of the People National Party from his father, Norman. He was seen as a champion of the oppressed and won the 1972 and 1976 elections. Edward Seaga, born and educated in America, went to Jamaica where he started his political career but always stayed loyal to his birth country. The US financed his 1980 election campaign which he won after taking over the leadership of the Jamaica Labour Party from Bustamante and Shearer.

Our country was a class-ridden society where the gap between the rich and the poor was very wide. Everyday we were fed the poisonous cocktail of racial prejudice courtesy of our school curriculum and the white biased media. This did not kill our bodies, but 'My God' it did eat at our souls making us believe that white was right and black was wrong every time. Middle and upper class people lived in posh neighbourhoods such as Red Hills, Meadow Brook Gardens, Sterling Castle, and Cherry Gardens. People from the elite classes fed their dogs with expensive food whilst the young children in Trench Town lived on the mercy of God. The elite classes looked down on their poorer compatriots and blamed them for their poverty and the high crime rate. This was easier for them to do, because if they were to put the blame where it really belonged, many would have to start looking closer to home as they were the policy makers, the teachers, the lawyers, the bankers, the politicians and the contractors of killers.

The country was divided into uptown and downtown, rich versus poor and whites versus blacks. In Kingston most of the houses uptown were posh while downtown most were run-down. My maternal grandparents lived in Trench Town a poor community where most of the homes were old dilapidated board houses. Unemployment was high, the people were poorly educated and poverty stricken. Peer group pressure was hard to ignore and most of the homes were headed by single mothers. There were very few role models to emulate. The culture and norm was that, young men would steal and women would be dependent on them. Men who were brave and daring were known as 'dons'. They were the role models for young men in Trench Town. The dons had many young men following behind them who were not afraid to carry out some atrocious crimes in the hope that they would one day be dons too. The dons would rob banks, post offices, supermarkets and any other places where they could get fast money. Young men who were not as brave as the dons, picked pockets and attacked other easy targets such as corner stores or broke into houses. The price of a donship was very high, yet it was the most sought after and prestigious position in Trench Town. To be on the bus of the dons you have purchased a one way ticket en route to prison, the mortuary and the cemetery. The dons had many baby-mothers who would fight openly in the streets for their affections. The men were divided into gangs and fought amongst each other. Those wars, however, only involved gang members. Young men who were not members of gangs were more or less invisible as you had to belong to a group to be accepted in Trench Town.

The residents of Trench Town could be loving and caring, yet cruel and selfish. They had a tribal instinct coupled with poverty that made them vulnerable to exploitation.

The two main political parties came about when Jamaica was going through many changes and the people wanted something different from white colonialism. The two party leaders went head to head for votes at any cost. They were so competitive it was not long before they found their way into the dysfunctional community, Trench Town. The place was divided into garrison areas loyal to PNP or JLP. The border between a PNP and a JLP garrison was called 'no man's land,' no one walked or lived there. Politicians identified the different gangs in the community and armed them with guns to intimidate residents to vote for them. Dons were promoted to area leaders, those who did not play ball were eliminated while others ran away to other places to live. It was suicidal to live in a PNP garrison and vote JLP. The people of Trench Town became predators with PNP supporters hunting JLP supporters and JLP hunting PNP. The residents became sworn enemies hating each other in the name of politics. Trench Town became Concrete Jungle and the rule was 'Kill Or Be Killed.'

Most of the names of the characters have been changed to protect the identity of the people who were involved. The analysis' are my own thoughts and perception of events and are not the views of any of the characters in this book.

Chapter One

For you to understand my story I have to take you back to the time before I was born. Most of the information came from relatives and friends but I can still remember some of the stories my grandfather used to tell us about the early years before Jamaicans got their independence from Great Britain.

There was a district in Kingston, Jamaica by the name of Trench Town where people lived in hard times. The physical appearance of the place has changed since the pre-colonial days but the mental scars of the people remain the same. They did not have proper drainage and when the rain fell the water settled in potholes, ponds and gullies for weeks until they became stagnated and infected. Children would play in the infected water in the streets as they had no playgrounds. In fact they had no toys and Santa never visited them at Christmas. Garbage was not collected regularly, due to this, piles of refuse were all over the place and articles from them would often be used as weapons in street fights. The houses were mostly board shacks usually shared by several families. On some occasions five different families shared a five-bedroom house as there were more people than accommodation. Many families living together in one place created a tenement yard environment where families would be at each other throats most of the time. There was constant backbiting, stabbing, obeah (witchcraft) and competitiveness. The whole atmosphere was dysfunctional. Children lost their innocence at an early age having to share a one bedroom with their parents and witnessed sexual acts much too early. Some children had to go on the streets to hustle a living for themselves and in some cases their families. Teenage girls as young as twelve were getting pregnant by much older men.

Pepe, as my maternal grandfather was affectionately called, was born and bred in Trench Town. Not much is known about his parents and where they came from and I have never met any of his siblings. He was a tall, dark-skinned man with distinguished features. Pepe was a strong-minded individual who had to be in control and accepted no bullshit. He met Lily, my maternal grandmother in the early 1930s. She was living in the parish of Clarendon with her parents and siblings but visited downtown Kingston frequently to sell ground provisions from their land as a means to survive. Lily was short, stocky and a subservient woman who was taught to serve her man. Pepe was working at the Jamaica Flour Mill operating the machinery. Lily was impressed with him as people from the rural parishes hero-worshipped

Kingstonians. In those days everyone in rural parishes of the island wanted to live in Kingston as they thought they would get good jobs and a better standard of living. The truth was they were living in a healthier environment with just one family to one home but the other side looked greener and Lily wanted to be on the greener side.

Pepe became Lily's passport out of Clarendon and she gladly traded her secured home and her part of the family land for an old tenement yard in Trench Town. She had a child who was two years old by a previous relationship and Pepe had children before he met Lily and continued having them during the union. The relationship was abusive from the start. Pepe had a reputation as a womaniser and a bad man. He did as he liked and bullied Lily when she spoke out about his behaviour. The women she could put up with, but the beatings were getting out of control. The other problem was as soon as she had one baby she was impregnated again. There was no way of preventing this as Pepe demanded sex whenever he wanted it and contraceptives were not easily available to them at the time.

Lily was oppressed and lost all control of her life. She was Pepe's slave and a baby factory. This was not healthy for her and the children she was bringing into the world. She had no one to turn to in the vicious cut throat tenement yard and the 'country bumpkin' girl from Clarendon was not as street-wise as the more in the know Trench Town ghetto mamas. The children were dropping fast from their mother's womb and she was too preoccupied with her next pregnancy to pay attention to the ones running about fighting with neighbouring children. Pepe thought a good father was one who provided food on the table. No boundaries were set so everyone was left to their own devices.

Pepe was also preoccupied with outside activities. He and his friends were campaigning for justice and staged regular road blocks in protest at the poor living and working conditions of the people in Jamaica. They had gained inspiration from past freedom fighters like Paul Bogle and Sam Sharpe who had given up their lives for the betterment of the people. My grandfather and his friends were freedom fighters and even though history forgot them, they helped to liberate the island. Pepe was more interested in liberation than what was happening at home and a lot of people remember him as a fighter and not a father. What he had was a slave plantation mentality. He wanted freedom and knew only one way to get it (even though he was no longer on the plantation; blood would spill for any injustice).

He worked with Fred, Sonny and Dorothy (who was one of the women cleaners at the flour mill). Dorothy was recognised by her big arse and very short mini skirts that made her a hit with the men she worked with. They worked long and unsociable hours for low wages. The beneficiaries of their hard labour were the colonial masters who did not care if they died on the job, as there was always someone else willing to replace them at anytime. The atmosphere at home and work was tense. Many nights Pepe did not go home to Lily and the children, as he and his colleagues were busy planning strategies against their employers. It was the general climate of the entire country. Rebellions were infectious and once it started in one area it quickly spread to other places.

Rebellions in our society can be traced back to the 1500s when slavery was introduced to the Caribbean by Europeans. Christopher Columbus will always be an integral part of our past and no story about the history of the island can be told without him being mentioned. He was on his way to India on the orders of the King of

Spain when he lost his way and ended up in the Caribbean. He claimed the islands for Spain and renamed them the West Indies. He arrived in Jamaica in 1494. The Arawak Indians the indigenous people of the islands, were welcoming and friendly to the Europeans but were tricked out of their land. They were used and abused in the worst possible way and started dying en-masse.

British pirates, on orders of their monarch, fought Spain for the islands and seized control of some including St Kitts, Trinidad, Antigua and of course Jamaica. The Arawak Indians were eventually wiped out by enslavement, the gun and European diseases such as common cold. East Indians and poor whites were brought in to work the land but they could not deal with the harshness on the plantations so Africans were then imported for use as slaves. The first set of African slaves arrived in Jamaica in 1517 and trouble was brewing from day one. The slaves were treated badly but were well fed to make sure they had enough energy to carry on working the plantations. The island was never developed to any decent living standard as the only interest the Europeans had in it rested on the sugar plantations. There was no such thing as a black family on plantations as the people were the property of plantation owners who could divide a family by selling a member at anytime. Young men and women were used as breeders to ensure that their masters had a steady growing slave population and it was a well known fact that Europeans who bred slaves could be just as rich as any other entrepreneur. Young men were forced to have sex with strange women just for the sake of breeding, then they would move on to the next.

The slaves were not content with life on the plantations and rebelled against it, but the plantation owners had devised strategies to keep them in their place. Their most effective weapon was the divide and rule tactic and it worked every time. Some slaves were given privileges over others in order to inform or police their fellow slaves so there was a division in the midst that would help to keep them in bondage for more years than any amount of guns the Europeans had. Plantation owners invested heavily in keeping the rebellions at a tolerable level and made sure that what was happening in Jamaica was kept quiet in case the slaves in neighbouring islands caught the rebellion fever. This was not hard to do as the islands were divided by miles of water.

The first serious uprising in Jamaica happened in 1673 in the parish of St Ann when three hundred slaves murdered their masters, several other white people and some well trained house slaves who went to the rescue of their beloved masters. The runaway slaves fled to the hilly parts of the island where they hid and came out only at night to run terror on the white population, they became famous as the mighty Maroons. They not only killed their oppressors; their main aim was to destroy the slave trade so that they could return home to Africa and so they torched the cane fields whenever they could. Several years later four hundred slaves in the parish of Clarendon escaped from a plantation and left behind dead bodies and burning cane fields. With so many slaves on the run plantation owners were getting nervous and had to come up with a plan swiftly.

Cudjoe and his cousin Nanny were leaders of a group of Maroons who were running Jamaica red with terror. Their names alone sent shivers through the spine of plantation owners. Cudjoe led his army and was on the run for over fifty years when the slave masters finally came up with a formula to silence him forever. If they could not beat him then they would recruit him. Cudjoe was getting old and wanted to settle somewhere in his old age so he accepted a peace treaty offered to him by the ruthless plantation barons. He was given land for his followers and himself and the right to their own laws and freedom, but in return he and his followers had to police runaway slaves. That divided the Maroons as Nanny would not agree to such a treaty and continued to wage war against slave owners. She believed no slave was free until all slaves were freed. She was feared. Many people said she worked African witchcraft to help her defeat her foes and as usual the black woman stood firm in the fight for justice. On the battlefield she led her army from the front with the cry to her people: 'No retreat, no surrender'.

As time went by the number of slaves who took part in rebellions grew. Sam Sharpe led a revolt in 1831 to 1832, which involved over fifteen thousand people. Over a thousand died on the battlefield. Sharpe was hunted down and hanged in a square that was later named after him. Paul Bogle spearheaded the Morant Bay rebellion in 1865 when more than four hundred slaves perished. Bogle was caught by the Maroons loyal to Cudjoe and handed over to the white establishment. He was hanged along with other freedom fighters including George William Gordon. The British historians wrote that it was sympathetic English men who fought for the abolition of slavery but the above mentioned people should never be excluded as their blood was spilled for freedom. Slavery could no longer be profitable with so many rebellions, slaves on the run and burning plantations.

Our fore-parents who fell in battle did so with us in mind. They knew they would not be around to reap the rewards of freedom but died in the hope that one day we would be free. Marcus Garvey, another great son of the island summed up the role of our fore-parents in one of many inspiring speeches he made to a group of people in the USA in 1922 when he said:

'We are descendants of the men and women who suffered in this country for two hundred and fifty years under the barbarous, that brutal institution known as slavery. You who have not lost trace of your history will recall the fact that over three hundred years ago your fore-bears were taken from the great continent of Africa for the purpose of using them as slaves. Without mercy, without any sympathy they worked our fore-bears. They suffered with their blood which they shed in their death, they had hope that one day their posterity would be free and we are assembled here tonight as children of their hope'.

Sister Nanny, Paul Bogle, Sam Sharpe, George William Gordon and Marcus Garvey were given national hero status except for Cudjoe who sold out.

The African slave trade was abolished in 1808 but it was not until August 1834 that emancipation was proclaimed. Colonialism took over from slavery. The ex-slaves were expected to work long unsociable hours for little or nothing. Exploitation became a way of life for colonial masters and rebellions became a way of life for the ex-slaves in Jamaica.

Jamaicans never accepted that they were slaves and moreso, they never came to terms with the fact they were stolen from Africa and used as such, neither could they accept the degradation of colonialism. You can hear it in their songs up to the present day, Bob Marley sang:

> Old Pirates yes they rob I,
> sold I to the merchant ships.
> Minutes after they took I
> from the bottomless pit,
> but my head was made strong
> by the hand of the almighty.
> We forward in this generation
> triumphantly.

This might be the reason why Jamaica had more uprisings than anywhere else in the slavery and colonial era. The two most well known uprisings I am aware of outside Jamaica were the one led by the African-American Nat Turner in the United States, in 1830 and the other one in Haiti from 1791-1804 and even though both of them helped pave the way to freedom, the numbers were very small compared to those rebellions on the tiny island of Jamaica, which involved hundreds of slaves at any one time. Any black person who got close to a white man would be called an informer and we still have that mentality in us by labelling people who report crimes to police as informers.

Colonialism brought out the worst in Jamaicans, they did not accept slavery and colonialism was slavery in disguise. By the mid 1930s the fire was heavily lit and the people were on heat. Everything was ready to explode. In 1937 there was a worldwide recession which adversely affected Britain and as they were our colonial masters Jamaica suffered also. The sugar industry was taken over by another British firm and they started to reorganise to save money. Some of the recommendations were to lay off workers and cut wages and they did just that without consulting the workers. This was the last straw to be broken for many people who were waiting for the right time to act. Some workers on a sugar plantation in Westmoreland set fire to the cane fields and went on strike. This set a precedent for other workers all over Jamaica, everyone from the window cleaner to the priest went on strike. The workers at the Jamaica Flour Mill also seized the opportunity to walk out. The black people in Jamaica were united on the grounds of oppression but the old slavery mentality was embedded in their soul and this would eventually lead to their destruction.

Jamaicans danced to the tune of the old slavery ode "If you are brown stick around, if you are white you are all right and if you are black stay back". There were many capable grassroots black leaders who came up through the ranks but were overshadowed by the mulatto class (mixed race) in Jamaica. The mixed race people knew they were in a privileged position at the time as the masses were black and would not trust a white leader. They certainly would not have any confidence in another black man and a woman leader of any colour would be a big joke. Two men from the mulatto class who were aware of their privileged position and watching the story unfold used the turbulent period of the 1937 uprising to make their move, they were Norman Washington Manley and Alexander

In his speech Garvey said:

'If the white man has the idea of a white God, let him worship his God as he desires. If the yellow man's God is of his race let him worship his God as he sees fit. We, as Negroes, have found a new ideal. Whilst our God has no colour, yet it is human to see everything through one's own spectacle, and since the white people have seen their God through white spectacle, we have only now started out (late though it be) to see our God through our spectacles. We Negroes believe in the God of Ethiopia, the everlasting God - God the Father, God the Son and God the Holy Ghost, the one God of all ages. That is the God in whom we believe, but we shall worship Him through the spectacles of Ethiopia'.

Through that speech Rastas chose the living being Emperor Haile Selassie to be their Messiah and Garvey their Prophet. Today Selassie means to Rasta what Moses means to the Jews. He became immortal in their sub-consciousness when he gave them Shashamene land in Ethiopia. Rastas see Shashamene as their promised land.

Amongst Rastas there was black pride. They vowed vengeance against colonial masters, but were not keen on a two political party Jamaica either and campaigned tirelessly against it but their words were ignored. They were marginalised by both black and white people and were called "The Black Heart Man". For many years I misunderstood the meaning of the label and so did many Jamaicans including my relatives. We were told they were dangerous. My mother told me never to speak to a "Black Heart Man" on the street, as they would rape me. In fact she was saying they were child molesters and had no good in them. I later worked it out for myself that when the slave masters gave the Rastas the name "Black Heart" what they meant was Rastas were too black in spirit and too strong to brainwash. They used parents to indoctrinate the children into believing Rastas were bad so that the "The Black Heart" would not pass on to the younger generation.

Jamaica went to the polls for the first time in 1944, the JLP won by a landslide, everyone could see it coming. JLP supporters celebrated in the streets and taunted their friends who voted for the losing party. Rather than joining together and building the island the losers were busy plotting how they would undermine the ruling party and the ruling party was too busy trying to hold on to power. Sonny was uneasy and on edge. All the time he told his friends Bustamante and Manley did not really care for the people, but only for power. He said the two parties would only divide the people and he could not support such a move. He was always looking for the opportunity to get out of Jamaica. Young men were stowing away frequently on boats to go to Britain in search of a better life for themselves and their relatives so Sonny was always on the look out for his chance. The sad story about those who left the island was that many of them never returned or were ever heard of again. Those who kept in touch sent most of their hard earned money to loved ones back home so relatives in Jamaica were not in touch with the realities of the living and working conditions in Britain. They took it for granted that life in the so-called 'Motherland' was easy and were not aware of the sacrifices made by their loved ones who kept them afloat with ready cash month after month. Every month money

away with the old board huts they once called homes. The PNP were not to be outdone so they too started to build houses for their supporters to live in, but their plan was to keep as many people in one place so that they could always have a large constituency.

Dudley Thompson, a lawyer educated in Britain, joined the political arena and ran against Seaga for the seat in Western Kingston. He thought being black could help dethrone the 'white god' who was not even born in Jamaica but Seaga proved too hot to handle in every way and saw him off. His henchmen moved in quickly on the people and secured the votes for their leader as they were already in the wings waiting. Thompson was taken by surprise and the small amount of followers he mustered up in his election campaign, were no match for Seaga's multitude. They crushed Dudley's boys on the battlefield and at the polling station. Dudley Thompson was wounded but not down. A man who runs today, lives to fight another day and that was exactly what he did. He went home to assess his loss and regroup with his PNP colleagues. He had also learnt some new strategies from his rival Seaga and was ready to return to Western Kingston. He was bad but not mad. He knew he could not return to Seaga's patch.

He turned his eyes to Trench Town instead and he would do there what Seaga did to Back-o-wall. 'If a badness Seaga dealing with, then prepare fi blood run'. With the two don daddas, Bustamante and Seaga in the JLP the party was more popular than ever. Thompson felt no white man should have such a privilege in Jamaica that his people fought and died for. Securing a garrison constituency was a direct disrespect to black grassroots leaders. Seaga threw down the gauntlet and Thompson took up the challenge. No-one was going to get in the way of him challenging the 'white god' not even the original gangsters of Trench Town. Seaga drew first blood but Thompson was out for revenge and he was 'Rambo tough'.

The PNP stepped up a gear in Trench Town to seize control of the area. Those who opposed tribal politics were hounded by the police and some gang members were found dead in trenches and gullies under mysterious circumstances. Some of the deaths were not even picked up by the media but those that did were quickly forgotten. Dirty cops were also recruited by politicians to keep disobedient gang members under control. Everyone had their job to do. The cops could not be seen intimidating citizens to vote for their undercover politician bosses, so gang members would have to be used for this as they were criminals already. When some mainstream newspapers got on to the story of irregularities at the polling stations by gang members the general public saw it as part of their criminal behaviour rather than the work of unscrupulous politicians. The police would be needed if a gunman was getting too big for his boots or if his service was no longer needed. This was not hard to do as the man would have already been known as a lawbreaker and it would appear that he got what he deserved.

Trench Town was getting too hot for gang members so some were giving in to tribal politics while others were going to jail. Quite a few OGs ran away to England in the mid 1960s. Those who had nowhere to go had to stand up and fight. Young men who became gunmen for politicians were allowed to carry on with their criminality with added protection from their powerful bosses. Law abiding police were not allowed to do their jobs properly due to interfering politicians. Prince and Steve were PNP supporters but seemed to be the enemy of the PNP politicians and also

I was a bore but my grandfather entertained me every time. He looked so interested I wanted to share my new found knowledge with him. I had to sleep with him or else all hell would break loose. I slept so badly sometimes when my grandfather woke up and found my bum in his face, he used to say 'what a piece a liberty' but he would always be smiling at me.

Pepe was my world, I put all my trust in him. With him around I felt no pain, no hunger and no sadness. Prim came around but she was almost invisible as all I cared about was Carl and Pepe. Pepe cooked for us, made our beds and sometimes washed our clothes. The apartment we had was a bed-sit with a small kitchen at the front and a much smaller bathroom at the back. We managed to fit two single beds and a double bed in the main room along with a small dining table. It was home to me, Moses, Carl, Pepe and Prim when she visited us. Pepe was more than grateful to Bustamante for giving him his first concrete home, for all his life he had lived in board and zinc shacks. Even though we were living like sardines in a tin that did not matter to him. What was important was that we had a roof over our heads. People like Pepe did not want much and would make do with very little but politicians wanted much more. The cornmeal and flour they were giving away to the people was not securing enough votes so they started assessing the different groups in Trench Town and testing the integrity of the people by giving away free money to see who could be bought.

They targeted gang members, as they knew they were the backbone of the community. Their plan was to get the gang members to intimidate people to vote for them but this did not go down well with some of the original gangsters. To the politicians surprise not everyone in Trench Town had a price or at least not the way they thought. They were thieves with principles and were willing to defend those principles. Two men from Trench Town who would not sanction such a move to intimidate people to vote and could not be bought at any price were Prince and Steve. Prince said it was downright wrong and he could not look the people in the face again not after many of them hid him in their homes when the police were after him. Steve's pain went much deeper for he had a bigger family than Prince and most of them were JLP supporters at the time. He was the only PNP supporter in his family. How could he turn on his own flesh and blood and friends he grew up with and what about Pepe his own father who was a staunch Bustamante follower? For those reason he could not do it.

Some gang members were taking bribes but not on a scale to make a difference. The stronger men were against tribal politics and as long as they were around people were free to vote for who they wanted and walk anywhere in Trench Town whenever they liked. Some gang members would just take the money and do nothing but the situation in Tivoli was different. Edward Seaga was the Member of Parliament for that area, secured a stronghold in the community and never lost his seat in a general election since 1962, that record speaks for itself. The people in Tivoli had no choice but to vote JLP. To do otherwise was like signing their own death warrants. The very poor, oppressed and hot-tempered people were targeted by politicians who encouraged a dependency culture amongst their constituents. The people were given just enough for them to sing praises to the politicians but never enough for them to be independent of them. Seaga later rebuilt Back-o-wall, and rewarded his faithful servants with new concrete apartments and did same politicians.

Pepe and Fred were in good spirits now that their elected Prime Minister led the country to independence, but were still mourning the death of Dorothy who died in 1957. She went on a train trip early September 1957 and was never seen alive again. The train she was on had twelve coaches. It derailed near Kendall in Manchester, killing one hundred and ninety three passengers, her body was never found amongst the remains. One month after the train crash a taxi driver turned up at a betting shop where Pepe and his friends used to hang out, asking for a woman fitting the description of Dorothy. The taxi driver said he picked up a lady from Constant Spring Road and that she had asked him to take her home to Trench Town but changed her mind and told him to drop her off at the betting shop downtown instead, as her friends would be waiting for her. He saw her walked into the shop to get money from someone inside but when she did not come back out he decided to go and find her. When asked, nobody in the shop saw her come in. It was only when he described her, the regulars at the shop became suspicious and paid the taxi driver before he left. Pepe said he did not have the guts to tell the driver that it was a duppy (ghost) he had carried in his taxi. Months after the train crash in Kendall, people reported sightings of victims who perished in the disaster. Pepe and Fred used the excitement of the political fever hitting the island to deal with the loss of Dorothy and Sonny who had gone to the United Kingdom.

Jamaica was fast becoming a two tier society the rich versus the poor, the strong versus the weak and JLP versus PNP. The people who were fighting the most for the politicians were benefiting the least. Political warfare took over where colonialism left off, friends and families became political enemies. Bustamante appeared to be a rough scout and the people from the ghettos loved him for that. He also had the emerging Edward Seaga in his corner who played a vital role in the history of Jamaica's political system. Seaga was born in Miami, USA to a Syrian family who lived in Jamaica. He came to the island in the early 1950s after finishing his college education and joined the JLP but had to settle in the wings while Bustamante was reigning supreme as the party leader. Edward Seaga ran for the Western Kingston seat, which he won and was appointed a Minister with portfolio. He managed to secure a stronghold in the community called Back-O-Wall, later renamed Tivoli Gardens. He, like his party leader, had a sophisticated gangster appearance and was never liked by Norman Manley who saw straight through his polished exterior.

At a memorial service at the National Heroes Circle where many dignitaries gathered to pay tribute to our heroes who fell on the battlefield for liberation, Seaga let his true colours show to the public for the very first time. Many PNP supporters from nearby Trench Town attended and booed Seaga. He lost his temper and threatened the crowd that he could go to Western Kingston (his own constituency) and get men to come and deal with them any time. All those who were present were shocked as that was not the time or place for such vulgarity and they could not believe it was coming from such a public figure. Seaga had no respect for us or our heroes who died on the line of duty. He dishonoured their memory in front of our eyes there and many other times to follow and we just allowed him to get away with it. After that many politicians made similar comments and no one called for their resignation as the precedence was already set. Anyone from any sordid background could join any of our political parties and say or do whatever they liked no matter how offensive and get away with it.

Manley was so angry by the threat he rebuked Seaga and referred to him as an alien amongst us, trying hard to be one of us. Manley senior sent out a message to the people warning them of the danger of having Seaga in Jamaican politics but his words fell on thorny grounds. In a speech to the nation in 1966 Norman Manley addressed the nation with these words:
"**With what language does this man speaks, this highly educated and sophisticated man? What language does he use? Do we recognise the voice of Jamaica, or do we hear the voice of an alien to our ideals, our practice, and our faith? One side cannot quiet this ugly turmoil. Both sides must meet and honestly agree. I hate to see Jamaica divided and torn. I hate to see Jamaicans killing and maiming Jamaicans while the leaders roll around in comfort. I hate to see the spirit of nationhood broken and destroyed, Who will join me, for Jamaica sake"?**

No one joined him, moreso no one heard his words. The people were into one mind set and the quiet voice of Manley Snr was too soft to be heard.

Political rivals used broken bottles as weapons against each other during election campaigns and at rallies. Party leaders never used the rallies to discuss the agendas of the parties but as an exercise to excite the crowd with violent speeches. Pepe and some of his friends left a JLP rally on fire one night, the fire was lit by an electric and violent speech by Bustamante. They went downtown where a PNP rally was taking place and threw a home made petrol bomb in the crowd which injured some people. It was a miracle no one was killed. They threw the bomb with no real intention to kill or harm anyone as none of them had any grudges or had any enemies attending the PNP meeting but the powerful words of Bustamante was enough for them to commit criminal acts. PNP supporters decided to fight fire with fire and started attacking people attending JLP rallies, this was just a start of things to come.

The politicians were fighting for supreme power what the people wanted was no longer important, some of them made it very clear that there would be bloodshed if they were opposed. Somewhere along the long rocky road from slavery the people lost their way and were heading down a dead end road being led by their blind leaders. Those with eyes who could see were either silenced or stayed silent.

At work one day Fred told Pepe that he received a letter from a cousin who went to England a few years before Sonny. His cousin informed him that she was working as a cleaner in a mental institution in London where Sonny was an in patient. Pepe and Fred shed many tears for their boyhood friend. Pepe said the only explanation he had for Sonny ending up in a madhouse (mental institution) was that white people obeah him or the cold got to him, after all Sonny never had any mad genes in him. They were wondering how they could get Sonny back to Jamaica but Fred lost contact with his cousin and England was a far and cold place. They never heard about Sonny again, nor did they bother to tell Sonny's wife about his breakdown. She often accused Sonny of abandoning her and the children for white women in England. They thought it was best for her to think he abandoned her rather than her knowing the truth. She became a broken woman. The man she loved and cared for left her to suffer along with their eight children. She was unemployed and without a skill who was going to give her a job. Depravation forced Sonny's children to fend for themselves. His daughters had sex with much older men for money and his sons took up stealing as a career. They had no welfare system or social workers to help and the police only got involved when they committed a crime. Sonny's wife died aged forty-nine of a broken heart and some of their children were killed violently in the harsh ghetto of Trench Town.

By 1963 Lily had twelve children with Pepe, they were all growing up in Trench Town and adapting to the lifestyle of their community. All the children were involved in activities in Trench Town but three of them moreso than the others, they were Prim, Peaches and Steve. All the children were identified as Pepe's children and never Lily's (in fact some people didn't even know her). Pepe's popularity overshadowed her and some of the children were walking in his footsteps. The children were never called by their proper names they were all given pet names either by their parents or by their friends. Lily got tired of the abuse and Pepe's womanising and left him in 1964. She had to move addresses several times as Pepe always found where she was living and forced her to return to him. The final straw came when she was living in Thompson Avenue with some of the children. Pepe was on his way to see her and their off-springs one Friday evening when he saw her talking to man. The man saw Pepe coming towards them in a temper, so he ran away and left Lily to face the music on her own. Pepe took a piece of stick from a nearby garbage heap and started to beat her with it, Sam one of their sons was on his way home and saw the fight. He took a broken bottle from the garbage heap and threw it at Pepe, the bottle went straight through his left cheek. Blood poured from his face like a running tap and Pepe screamed out at his son who ran away to hide. The other children heard the noise from their home and came out to intervene. Some took Lily's side and surprisingly some were on their father's side. Even though Pepe was abusive to Lily they did not want to see another man with their mother.

Prim accompanied her father to the Kingston Public Hospital in downtown where he received eleven stitches. The hospital staff called in the police who asked Pepe if he wanted to press charges. He said yes, but could not remember Sam's full name to the officers' amusement. He asked Prim who told him that she did not know it either. He gave her a dirty look as if she should have known even if he did not. The investigating officer who knew Pepe was in tears of laughter. He asked Pepe, 'yu waan fi tell me dat yu no know yu own pickney name'? Pepe's explanation was that they were too many to remember. He left the hospital without speaking any further to the police.

That fight almost split the family, as some of the children were loyal to Pepe and some to Lily. One son swore he was going to kill Sam for injuring his father while a daughter swore vengeance and said it was going to be blood for blood. Sam wisely stayed out of sight until things calmed down. The children who were on Lily's side were the younger and weaker ones so they were more silent but prepared to fight if they had to. Prim, Peaches and Steve commented but stayed out of it. They did not agree with Pepe beating Lily but were upset about what Sam did to their father. That was the last beating Pepe handed out to Lily. He knew he had to let go because the children were no longer prepared to ignore the abuse on their mother and also he was getting older and could not handle himself the way he used to.

Chapter Two

Peaches and Prim were very close - Peaches was older by two years. Prim did not get on with her mother. Lily gave her away to strangers twice but on both occasions her eldest sister went for her and brought her back home. Lily was having the children so fast it was not surprising she did not bond with them but she did favour some over the others and made her feelings known. The children were shown very little love and affection so it was inevitable that they were going to do the same to their children one day. Peaches and Prim were ghetto girls and played by the rules. They started going to dances from an early age and had boyfriends without their parent's knowledge. They stole out of the house at night sometimes going through the windows when Lily was in bed. They pressed their hair with Lily's hot pressing comb and acquired money from men they met at dances to buy new clothes. They were both fat, rounded and had big arses which were a definite hit with the young men in their community. They looked good and knew it.

The inevitable happened, Peaches became pregnant at seventeen and like many teenage pregnancies the father disappeared before the baby was born. Peaches had a baby girl who Lily took from her as she was not ready to raise a child. This gave Peaches the opportunity to go back to her old lifestyle and she soon met a new lover and moved in with him. Prim was having an affair with Dan who was quiet and reserved and she became pregnant at fifteen. She was too young and poor to be a parent, much too young to sustain a loving relationship and he was too young to know anything either. Her mother found out about the pregnancy and turned her out on the streets. She had no job, no social skills and nowhere to live. Dan was living with his relatives and did not have anywhere to put her so bewildered and frightened she went to her father who was still living at Ninth Street and asked him if he could take her in. For the first time in his life Pepe took responsibility for someone like a real conscientious father should. Maybe being on his own he had time to reflect on the mistakes of the past and now he was ready to do the right thing by his daughter and grandchild.

Dan and Prim were still seeing each other in the first half of the pregnancy but broke up before she gave birth due to family interference. Pepe gave Prim money to buy things to prepare for the baby and made sure she was eating healthily. In June 1963

Prim gave birth to a baby boy at the Victoria Jubilee Hospital, North Street. She named him Carl and he became Pepe's pride and joy.

Several months after the birth of her son Prim started going to dances again and sleeping out. She knew that Pepe would not allow her to bring men into his house so she went to live with Peaches in Jones Town. She left baby Carl behind because she wanted to court again and a baby would only get in the way. Pepe became mother and father to Carl, which was very hard on him as he was working full time and advancing in age. Prim visited them from time to time but the bulk of the responsibility rested with Pepe. Prim had a new man in her life, Tom who hailed from the parish of St Mary. He had no ties in Trench Town but adopted the area as a second home and squatted with his new friends. Most of the time he had no-where to sleep so he tented out under the cellar of a house. The family who lived in it felt sorry for him and took him in their home. Where else but Trench Town would a family take in a complete stranger feed and shelter him as if he was one of their own? A friend once told me that poor people have the richest heart and in this case it was true. The relationship between Prim and Tom was erratic and unhealthy but made sense to them. Tom was possessive and ignorant and it would not take much for Prim to get a beating. The beatings came from his fists, feet or any objects he could lay his hands on but she encouraged his aggression and said it was his way of showing affection for her. His friends did not waste anytime showing him the tricks of the trade. They had him stealing shortly after his arrival to the area. He had learnt a trade as a furniture maker but stealing was a quicker way of making easy money. Like all newcomers to Trench Town Tom had to impress his new colleagues that he was up to the job, so he had to take the lead in some of the robberies and that was no problem for Tom who wanted to fit in.

One day Prim was walking with her mother home when she saw Tom and his friends standing at one of their regular hang outs. He called her but she ignored him and continued walking. His pride got in the way so he walked after her and grabbed her from behind. She turned around to face him and he slapped her in the face. She tried to defend herself and Lily took off one of her shoes and hit him in the head with it, while shouting at him to leave her daughter alone. He took the shoe out of Lily's hand and threw it into an over grown plot where it could not be found. Lily had to take off the other one and walked home barefoot. After that incident everyone told Prim to leave Tom because he was no good but she ignored their advice.

In mid 1965, Tom went on the run because he was wanted by the police for questioning about an armed robbery. He went to hide in his native St Mary with Prim's best friend Icilda. Icilda's boyfriend found where they were hiding and led armed police to them and Tom was apprehended. Icilda lost an eye in a fight with her boyfriend. Tom was too busy with the cops to help Icilda fend off her possessive jealous lover. Tom was later tried and sentenced to nine years imprisonment at hard labour, Prim was six months pregnant, once again she was pregnant without the support of a baby-father.

Peaches was also pregnant by her live in boyfriend but the relationship was deteriorating. For some reason relationships did not really last in Trench Town. Lenny, Peaches boyfriend, was not happy with her as he was fed up with her partying all the time and spending very little time at home. A friend told Prim that Lenny was

15

planning to leave Peaches as soon as the baby was born. He was only staying because of the baby. Prim knew they were going to end up on the streets if Lenny left as he was the one paying the rent so she went back to Pepe.

A few months later Peaches gave birth to a son. Lenny took him and went abroad with him and he was never seen again. The only thing that is known about the baby is that he too was called Lenny. In a funny sort of way Lenny proved to be the most responsible man in Peaches life as he was acting in the child's best interest. Peaches was left on the streets with just her clothes and she too had to go and ask Pepe to put her up. Moses and Steve were also staying with Pepe as Lily sent them to live with their father due to her inability to control them. Pepe now had Moses, Carl, Steve, Prim (who was pregnant) and Peaches living with him and none of them able to contribute to their keep.

Pepe was given one of the new apartments in Rema (Fourth Street) built by the Bustamante government as a thank you to his supporters, (of course Pepe would be one of the first to be rewarded as he was a staunch supporter). He took Carl and Moses with him and left the others in the board house on Ninth Street. Pepe visited them every Friday to deliver groceries and money as he was particularly concerned about Prim who was still carrying her second child without the father's support. Everywhere Pepe was seen, so was Carl. The grandfather loved his grandson more than his own life and it showed so much that neighbours even started calling Carl 'Pepe Carl'.

Pregnancy slowed Prim down, she was mostly at home desperate to drop her burden. Peaches stayed away from dances as her sparring partner was too heavily pregnant to go with her. She would not take the chance going out alone at nights as the notorious serial rapist Big Sid was on the prowl. He became the bogey man in the area. No girl or woman was safe at nights with him running loose in Trench Town. The police were looking for him for several counts of rape so most of his activities were at night-time in order to elude arrest. People in the community said that girls as young as nine years old were raped by Sid who was an amateur boxer and muscular in built. A woman on her own stood no chance of defending herself against him. Women walked in twos or more armed with ice picks and acid so they could at least have a fighting chance against the perverted rapist. If ghetto girls said they were going to defend themselves they would, so when Sid saw them dressed in their fancy dresses going to dances in groups he had no choice but to hold down his urges until he caught one by herself off guard. If he had ever made the mistake and attacked a group of girls they would have cut him out of his clothes.

Rumour was rife that Big Sid was also raping men but no one knew who the male victims were. This was a major cover up in Trench Town as it was something of a taboo. Male sex was not the done thing there and anyone who was found guilty of such an act would be severely dealt with. The men in Trench Town were macho and would not admit to being one of Sid's victims so by staying silent they allowed him to get away with his criminal behaviour. Some women who came forward were stigmatised as rape victims so many others stayed silent like their male counterparts to avoid the stigma. Big Sid was not alone when it came to raping women as it was a well known fact that some gang members raped young girls in the area. It was a gang culture to 'battery' (group rape) young girls. These men see it as part of every day life and part of growing up. The reason why batteries were not seen as rape and reported was that a young girl might have agreed to have sex with one man who set up his friends to get a piece of the action and because of that many girls blamed themselves and kept it quiet. Young women who escaped rape in Trench Town were those who stayed away from dances, kept off the streets at night or those who had brothers or rude boys as boyfriends to defend them.

Big Sid was finally apprehended and sent to prison for only a small portion of the rapes he did, due to lack of evidence and the tardiness on the part of the police, who trivialised crimes committed in Trench Town as the victims were usually poor. Big Sid did his time in the General Penitentiary Prison (GP) home to Jamaica's most dangerous criminals. In GP Big Sid became infamous as Jamaica's most feared sodomite preying on the weak and the greedy. To the prison authorities he was a model prisoner but to fellow inmates he was their punishment. It was well known on the outside that Sid was still raping in prison. That was the crime he was doing time for, so why did this crime continued in a place where he should not have been a risk to other people?

Big Sid became institutionalised after several years behind bars. He knew it was in his best interest being in prison as he developed a strong appetite for male sex and where else in Jamaica could he rape young men openly without being punished, so GP became his home. Whenever he was released from prison it would not be long before he was back again. It was obvious that such punishment was not working for this criminal but there was no alternative. Some of his victims were traumatised by their ordeal but had no one to turn to. Big Sid targeted new prisoners as he liked fresh blood and was powerful in GP. The wardens allowed him privileges as he did not give them any trouble and it was rumoured that some of them were sexually involved with him.

Sid always had cigarettes, toiletries and other necessities that were a luxury in prison. He enticed the greedy with gifts and those who were not drawn by his luxuries were gang raped by him and his cronies. He was a rapist but no fool, he chose his victims carefully as GP housed some dangerous murderers who would slit his throat in the twinkle of an eye and he knew it. Category A Prisoners, outlaws like Silver, Prince and Manny showed their contempt for his actions by licking blank shots after Sid and shouting 'batty man fi dead' whenever they saw him on their wings. For many it was not the crime of rape they were against, but the act of homosexuality. Many prisoners had to lie to fellow inmates that they were in prison for murder to escape being skivvies in prison. In GP if you are a murderer or armed robber you get maximum respect. Rapists and paedophiles were way down the pecking order in fact a paedophile was safer on the outside and if you ended up in prison for incestuous rape, beg God that was your best kept secret and that you did not confess in your sleep at night. For if your fellow inmates found out you were in prison for raping your own relative you were long dead. In GP the only real criminal was a paedophile, they did not see stealing as criminality but a way of life.

Prim gave birth to her second child on the sixteenth day of August 1965. It was a baby girl she named Patsy. That baby was me. I arrived in Trench Town to the Smith clan and I had no say in the matter. I am the result of the turbulent affair between Prim and Tom, I could not choose my family, but thank God I can choose my friends. Do not get me wrong I have grown to like some members of my family but I am not blind to their actions. Prim found out that Tom had two other women who had baby girls earlier that year including a set of twins. In all he had four children born without the support of a father as he was behind bars. One of the twins and I were given the same first name. With Pepe around Carl and I might just have a fighting chance to break the dreaded cycle of Trench Town but the odds were against us. There was no positive role models to inspire us and with the limited resources we would have to dig deep to find our inner strengths. It was clear that our parents could not help or protect us at least not the way we should be protected, in fact most of our ordeals were to come from the hands of our parents.

One Friday night well after ten o'clock Pepe visited Prim and the others at the Ninth Street house. He heard me crying my head off from way down the street. His blood started to boil as he was sure that Prim was beating the baby out of frustration but when he got into the house his mood changed from that of anger to homicidal intentions and pity at the same time - Pity for his grandchild and murderous intentions towards his daughter for leaving a defenceless baby by herself. I was lying in bed alone in the house with a kerosene lamp burning. Without hesitation he wrapped me up in a towel and took me home with him. Pepe not only punished Prim but everyone who had lived in the house at Ninth Street by stopping his money and food. They stayed out of his sight (especially Prim who knew she had to wait until the dust was settled before she could see her children again). Pepe also had to give in for the sake of his grandchildren, especially me who was still on breast milk. Prim came to see us but returned to the streets to enjoy her life. Pepe had to juggle childcare with his full-time job but carried out his duty for us out of love. He knew he had to be strong and continue working in order to buy the necessities for his son, Moses, and two grandchildren. We had no future without him.

With their children out of the way and no man in their lives Prim and Peaches were young, free, single and ready to mingle. Their experiences on the streets meant that they were now ready for the big league. Steve joined up with some local boys in the area and started to steal as a way of life. Lily could not afford to support him and the little money Pepe gave her every week was not enough to sustain them especially since the arrival of Carl and I her weekly maintenance money had been reduced. Lily was not happy with this and showed direct resentment towards Prim. She said Pepe was forsaking his own children for other men's children. It became a war of words between her and Pepe with Prim in the middle. On one occasion Lily was so angry she told Prim, Pepe was the biological father of her children. Prim always thought Lily hated her but that confirmed it to her, she would never forget that statement until the day she died.

Lily's statement was wrong and partial because she was the sole carer for Peaches' first child without any interference from Pepe but did not want him to help us. He felt sorry for us and Prim because Lily supported her other children and grandchildren but not Prim and us. Someone had to care for us and he chose to do it but maybe Lily would have preferred to see us starving and living on the streets. Well, Pepe was not going to stand by and let that happen to us. He thought it was too late for some of his children who were already showing signs of being in the fast lane, but felt he could do right by Carl and me and if it meant forsaking his own children so be it.

He continued buying shares in the Jamaica Flour Mill each week for he thought they would be our ticket out of Trench Town.

Poverty was strangling my uncle Steve who was not getting much support from Pepe and even though he was no stranger to hunger his ribs were starting to show due to lack of nourishment. Now he had two choices die or rob, he chose the latter. Steve and Scully, his sparring partner, went on a stealing rampage. They had to survive somehow but knew people were prepared to defend their properties and belongings and would not just hand them over without a fight. They decided to get a gun as a weapon because people were ready to take on a robber with a knife. Steve saw his opportunity to get a gun one day when he and Scully were standing idly on the sidewalk on Collysmith Drive. A lone police man was riding on a bicycle with a gun sticking out of his back pocket, Steve crept up behind him, grabbed the gun and ran off with it. He had no intention of ever using it but thought it would intimidate his victims to hand over their belongings without any resistance.

The local Chinese shops and supermarkets were targeted by local gangs. Everyday one would get robbed. Many of the Chinese entrepreneurs decided to defend themselves and applied for license guns. Mr Chin who operated a store off Spanish Town Road was robbed several times by different gangs. He got a licensed gun and prepared himself for the next hit. Steve and Scully ignorant of the previous robberies at Mr Chin's store chose him to be their next victim. Scully who was the most daring of the two, took the gun and went in front. He pointed the gun at Mr Chin and told him to hand over the days sales, Mr Chin bowed his head in compliance and bent down to get something. Scully and Steve thought it was the money and carelessly waited for him to come with it. What he had in his hand instead was a revolver and he fired several shots so quickly the boys were taken by surprise. They crawled out of the shop on their hands and knees in fright. They were amateurs at their new job and it showed but they had time to mature and master it.

They made their escape in a nearby gully. Both young men were confused by the incident, they were not aware that the gully led straight to the sea and that was exactly where they ended up. They had to swim for their lives, luckily for them they were both strong swimmers. Neither of them knew what happened to the gun they had. Scully seemed to have dropped it somewhere in the shop during the excitement. After that incident they knew they had to be more careful. The news of the attempted robbery spread like wild fire in Trench Town so they were being recognised as gangsters. Trench Townians liked that and started bigging (praising) them up. The young men's new found fame went to their heads and they became mean. Their popularity in the area was not good as the police too were hearing about them. Scully a well known policeman's brother was medium built and dark in complexion. His popularity grew due to the fact he was a thief and the brother of a policeman and also because he was the front man in the robberies. Steve the more handsome of the two friends was popular with the ladies. He had a wart on his left cheek which he tried to get rid of mainly due to vanity and also because the police remembered him by it.

They became familiar to the special crime squad members who were onto them, so they laid low for a while and even tried to walk the straight and narrow but with no income coming in from anywhere the hunger started to buck and bite. They both enjoyed horse racing and would walk four miles to the Caymanas Park Race Track. They had no money so they had to beg the security guard to let them in. They waited for punters to throw away their half eaten food and drink then they would feast on them. After the races they walked back home to Trench Town. No one asked those fourteen-year-old boys where they were and in truth they were not missed at all. Life dealt them a lousy hand of cards and their destiny was to lose. The pinch of poverty was bruising them so they had to start stealing again. Other gang members were wearing fancy clothes and they too wanted to brag. Clothing was a sign of wealth in Trench Town. As everyone was more or less living in the same type of houses status had to be measured somehow. Like many places class was an important feature in everyday life and Trench Town was not an exception to the rule. They determined class by the clothes they wore. One would exhibit their finest garments at dances and on Sundays, those who could not afford to buy nice clothes would just look on with envy while others could not wait for their dressmakers to come up with something hotter (nicer).

Scully and Steve lived in a material environment and wanted the things that their environment encouraged so they started robbing again. Once they made a big hit and it was easy it became a habit. Steve liked only the finest Jamaica had to offer, he wore suits daily in the hot sunshine. It was a big joke amongst his friends to see Steve walking around Trench Town immaculately attired with nowhere to go. The first time Steve was seen in one of his suits a friend asked him if he was going to court; Steve caused a humorous uproar when he told them he was only visiting them. What made the joke even funnier he just lived across the road from them. Everyday he changed clothes to keep up appearances so he had to continue robbing big bucks. He became popular and well liked amongst his peers and his women only wore the best. One day Steve was pointed out to a police officer by a woman who knew him well. The copper saw Steve in his suit and asked the woman if she was mad to point on a lawyer going about his business, calling him a thief. Steve heard what was said and felt like a million dollars if only he could be a real lawyer instead of a thief.

Scully was picked up off the streets one day by some police officers who had a warrant out for his arrest. They took him to Hunts Bay Police Station and were interrogating him when Scully decided to use his connections to get out of his predicament. He told the investigating officer that he was the brother of officer Cole. He made the biggest mistake of his life. Five police officers jumped on him and gave him the beating of his young life. They used their feet, batons and fists on him, he was screaming for dear life but they only stopped when they got tired. They later freed him as they did not have any evidence against him but they knew he was up to no good. No one was talking so they had to let him go but not until they had given him a good hiding.

After that incident Scully was in and out of jail and young offender's institutions. His mother was in England. She had left Jamaica a couple of years earlier in search of a better life for her and her children. News reached her that Scully was living rough and was wanted by the police. Scully was lying low to keep out of jail. The police wanted something to stick so he was afraid that he would go to prison for a long time like some of his friends. Then one day one of his aunts came to see him and told him to pack his clothes and follow her. He was not allowed to tell anyone where he was going and the next time Steve heard about Scully he was in England.

Steve was not happy that his good friend Scully left without saying goodbye but he understood why he did it. Steve linked up with new friends from the Vikings gang and was particularly close to gang members Prince and Jim Bob who both became his brother in laws. Jim Bob and Prince made regular visits to the yard at Ninth Street so it was inevitable that they would come in contact with the glamour girls, Peaches and Prim. Peaches started dating Jim Bob and Prim dated Prince. Prince was feared by some and loved by many. Along with the Vikings there were other rival gangs like Saigon, Zulu and Pigeon. They were the original gangsters of Trench Town and all the others who came afterwards were cold-blooded murderous imitations. The original gangsters did not intimidate and terrorise innocent people and prided themselves on this. Gang members moved around Trench Town on bicycles. Each gang had up to twenty members armed with machete and knives sharpened back and front. They did not tolerate crimes against children and with Big Sid out of the way children could be seen on the streets on their own all hours of the day and night. They had gang wars but only fought amongst themselves. Women and children were not harmed intentionally but sometimes got hit in cross fire. A gangster could 'lose his stripe' if he was to fight a woman because his friends and rival gang members would take the mickey by calling him a sissy and see him as weak. A woman was mainly beaten by her man an action some of the women encouraged as they said it was an act of love.

For some unknown reason a lot of young women and girls were attracted to gang members and made themselves available to them. Prim and Peaches knew Prince and Jim Bob had other women but that did not stop them from going out with them in fact Prim was hell bent on being Prince's number one even though he had a long standing relationship. One day Prim was on her way to visit Prince at his mother's home when she saw him outside his gate with his long time girlfriend Sonia. Instead of turning back she went straight up to them and started giving the other woman dirty looks. They traded insults for sometime before Prince stepped in and said that they should fight and the winner would get to go home with him. Prim did not wait for anymore encouragement she jumped on her rival like a lioness and started beating the hell out of her, Prince had to pull her off before any damage was done. He then lived up to his promise and went off with the victorious one who felt like a queen. Prim and her rival had many other fights over Prince. Sonia was adamant she was not going to give up her man without a fight as they were coming from far and Prim wanted him real bad for he was dangerously good looking. Prim told Sonia that Prince wanted her badly because her body was good and Sonia's one needed fixing. Prim must have been doing something good because Prince even rented a room and moved in with her and left Sonia on the side. Whenever Prim and Peaches saw their rivals on the streets and at dances they would swing their backsides at them and laugh out loud. This would antagonise them to respond and then there would be a war of words and sometimes fist fights.

The Vikings gang was well known in the area and so were its members. They stole as a way of life and shared their loot amongst each other. They also gave elderly people money from their take, which made them popular and well liked. The police were always on the look out for them and due to this they were constantly on the move. Prim and

Peaches were also on the road with the gang members. Steve, Prince and their friends were in and out of prison and approved school. They were even going to adult prisons before they turned sixteen. Time in the house of correction however, seemed to have made little impact on them for as soon as they were released, they would be back to their old ways. Some of them would even commit a robbery on their way home from jail. For them prison was a university and Steve graduated with an MA honours in 'how to rob a post office'. Politics was the last thing on his mind.

Pepe was worried about them as his health was fading and he was constantly going to Kingston Public Hospital for tests. He came home with a wound on his tummy one day. I thought he was in a fight and a man cut him, but he said the doctor did it. I did not understand why the doctor had to cut Pepe but nothing was explained to me so I thought everything would be all right in a couple of days. Pepe looked weaker everyday and sometimes he looked as if he would fall over, but despite all the tell tale signs that Pepe was dying I could not recognise them. I thought he was invincible and that he would be there for me as long as I wanted him.

Carl started attending Father basic school when he was four and I went with him as this was a means of childcare and respite for Pepe. After the first few weeks Carl was able to take us to and from school which was not too far from our home. As for me I did not know where I was going I was just following Carl my beloved older brother but when he upset me I used to bite him. At school we played in the water and drew with crayons I could not wait for Father to go outside to look at the sun and announce it was lunch break. Sometimes, he had to look twice at the sun to make sure as this was how he read the time because he did not have a watch or a clock. Some occasions the lunch break took so long to come I wondered if Father was reading the time right or the sun was playing up. In the evening I wanted to go home to Pepe but Father kept saying it was not time. I got bored and ate the chalks. Father must have been wondering where the chalks were going but whenever he asked if anyone saw the chalks I looked away. One little girl saw me once eating the chalk and when Father asked what happened to the chalks she looked at me as if she wanted to inform on me, but she smelt a rat by the look I gave her that I would have bitten her after school so she kept quiet.

My grandfather transferred us from Father school to Miss Kelly's basic school, as he said we were not learning anything there. I think he was talking about me more than Carl as all I was interested in was eating the crayons and chalks. Miss Kelly sussed me out quickly and put me to sit down in the front just to keep an eye on me with the chalks and crayons. We teased her behind her back and called her Miss Kelly with electric belly. I joined in the fun but up to this day I do not know why they called her that I cannot even remember if Miss Kelly's belly was big or not. Anyone who came from our community even if they did not attend her school should know about the educator Miss Kelly she was an institution and I am proud that I was one of her students. At Father school I learnt nothing but at Miss Kelly I learnt about Brother Anancy and the song 'Sammy plant piece a corn dung a gully and bear till it kill poor Sammy'. I also learnt to count from one to a hundred and to say the letters of the alphabet. I was so proud of myself that I could not wait to go home to Pepe each evening to tell him what I had learnt.

I was a bore but my grandfather entertained me every time. He looked so interested I wanted to share my new found knowledge with him. I had to sleep with him or else all hell would break loose. I slept so badly sometimes when my grandfather woke up and found my bum in his face, he used to say 'what a piece a liberty' but he would always be smiling at me.

Pepe was my world, I put all my trust in him. With him around I felt no pain, no hunger and no sadness. Prim came around but she was almost invisible as all I cared about was Carl and Pepe. Pepe cooked for us, made our beds and sometimes washed our clothes. The apartment we had was a bed-sit with a small kitchen at the front and a much smaller bathroom at the back. We managed to fit two single beds and a double bed in the main room along with a small dining table. It was home to me, Moses, Carl, Pepe and Prim when she visited us. Pepe was more than grateful to Bustamante for giving him his first concrete home, for all his life he had lived in board and zinc shacks. Even though we were living like sardines in a tin that did not matter to him. What was important was that we had a roof over our heads. People like Pepe did not want much and would make do with very little but politicians wanted much more. The cornmeal and flour they were giving away to the people was not securing enough votes so they started assessing the different groups in Trench Town and testing the integrity of the people by giving away free money to see who could be bought.

They targeted gang members, as they knew they were the backbone of the community. Their plan was to get the gang members to intimidate people to vote for them but this did not go down well with some of the original gangsters. To the politicians surprise not everyone in Trench Town had a price or at least not the way they thought. They were thieves with principles and were willing to defend those principles. Two men from Trench Town who would not sanction such a move to intimidate people to vote and could not be bought at any price were Prince and Steve. Prince said it was downright wrong and he could not look the people in the face again not after many of them hid him in their homes when the police were after him. Steve's pain went much deeper for he had a bigger family than Prince and most of them were JLP supporters at the time. He was the only PNP supporter in his family. How could he turn on his own flesh and blood and friends he grew up with and what about Pepe his own father who was a staunch Bustamante follower? For those reason he could not do it.

Some gang members were taking bribes but not on a scale to make a difference. The stronger men were against tribal politics and as long as they were around people were free to vote for who they wanted and walk anywhere in Trench Town whenever they liked. Some gang members would just take the money and do nothing but the situation in Tivoli was different. Edward Seaga was the Member of Parliament for that area, secured a stronghold in the community and never lost his seat in a general election since 1962, that record speaks for itself. The people in Tivoli had no choice but to vote JLP. To do otherwise was like signing their own death warrants. The very poor, oppressed and hot-tempered people were targeted by politicians who encouraged a dependency culture amongst their constituents. The people were given just enough for them to sing praises to the politicians but never enough for them to be independent of them. Seaga later rebuilt Back-o-wall, and rewarded his faithful servants with new concrete apartments and did away with the old board huts they once called homes. The PNP were not to be outdone so they too started to build houses for their supporters to live in, but their plan was to keep as many people in one place so that they could always have a large constituency.

Dudley Thompson, a lawyer educated in Britain, joined the political arena and ran against Seaga for the seat in Western Kingston. He thought being black could help dethrone the 'white god' who was not even born in Jamaica but Seaga proved too hot to handle in every way and saw him off. His henchmen moved in quickly on the people and secured the votes for their leader as they were already in the wings waiting. Thompson was taken by surprise and the small amount of followers he mustered up in his election campaign, were no match for Seaga's multitude. They crushed Dudley's boys on the battlefield and at the polling station. Dudley Thompson was wounded but not down. A man who runs today, lives to fight another day and that was exactly what he did. He went home to assess his loss and regroup with his PNP colleagues. He had also learnt some new strategies from his rival Seaga and was ready to return to Western Kingston. He was bad but not mad. He knew he could not return to Seaga's patch.

He turned his eyes to Trench Town instead and he would do there what Seaga did to Back-o-wall. 'If a badness Seaga dealing with, then prepare fi blood run'. With the two don daddas, Bustamante and Seaga in the JLP the party was more popular than ever. Thompson felt no white man should have such a privilege in Jamaica that his people fought and died for. Securing a garrison constituency was a direct disrespect to black grassroots leaders. Seaga threw down the gauntlet and Thompson took up the challenge. No-one was going to get in the way of him challenging the 'white god' not even the original gangsters of Trench Town. Seaga drew first blood but Thompson was out for revenge and he was 'Rambo tough'.

The PNP stepped up a gear in Trench Town to seize control of the area. Those who opposed tribal politics were hounded by the police and some gang members were found dead in trenches and gullies under mysterious circumstances. Some of the deaths were not even picked up by the media but those that did were quickly forgotten. Dirty cops were also recruited by politicians to keep disobedient gang members under control. Everyone had their job to do. The cops could not be seen intimidating citizens to vote for their undercover politician bosses, so gang members would have to be used for this as they were criminals already. When some mainstream newspapers got on to the story of irregularities at the polling stations by gang members the general public saw it as part of their criminal behaviour rather than the work of unscrupulous politicians. The police would be needed if a gunman was getting too big for his boots or if his service was no longer needed. This was not hard to do as the man would have already been known as a lawbreaker and it would appear that he got what he deserved.

Trench Town was getting too hot for gang members so some were giving in to tribal politics while others were going to jail. Quite a few OGs ran away to England in the mid 1960s. Those who had nowhere to go had to stand up and fight. Young men who became gunmen for politicians were allowed to carry on with their criminality with added protection from their powerful bosses. Law abiding police were not allowed to do their jobs properly due to interfering politicians. Prince and Steve were PNP supporters but seemed to be the enemy of the PNP politicians and also of the state. Vikings' members were hounded by the police like never before so they were always on the move. Prim was also on the run with her brother and boyfriend. The pressure was getting to Pepe who was getting paler everyday. He was constantly visiting the Kingston Public Hospital and taking medication but I was not aware of what was going on.

Prince continued to resist the notion of segregation and distressed those who supported it. Prince and Steve thought they were tough enough to keep Trench Town united but the heat was on. The police were after them night and day. They could not sleep in their beds at night; they were always on the run. The politicians knew Prince and Steve were the two main thorns in their sides so with them out of the way the others would have to conform or leave the area. Many of the bad eggs were already dead. Some men in the area wanted to take control of the community but they had to keep their cool until Prince and his crew were cut down. One thing was for sure, the PNP wanted a garrison community with henchmen they could call upon in times of trouble and Trench Town was going to be it by hook or crook. Time was running out for Prince and Steve.

Steve was on his way from Jungle to Rema one day when some young men rushed him and called him a PNP boy. They were acting territorial and said Steve was riding through their town. Someone recognised Steve as one of Pepe's children and ran to his home to call him, he had just arrived from work. When Pepe heard that his son was being attacked by men with knives he grabbed his old kitchen bitch (knife) and rushed to where his son was. Pepe ran up to the men and pulled out his knife. He stood between his son and the gangsters tempting them to make a move. Steve knew his father was ill so he begged him please to go home with him but Pepe was in fighting spirits. People who knew the old timer were drawing near so the young men walked away. In front of everyone present Pepe told his son that if more than one man attacked him, he should find a wall put his back against it and cut out the belly of the first one he could get hold of. Steve laughed at his father's advice and took him home. Pepe's neighbours thought the whole thing was funny but his words were heard by Steve more than they thought.

A few days later Steve and two friends were rushed by another set of gang members loyal to the JLP. They were outnumbered by the ten strong men who had knives. They ran off to get away but one of his friends was caught and kicked to the ground, a knife was used to slice through his left cheek. The gangsters wanted to leave their mark on him as a sign of victory. Steve heard his friend's cry and heroically went back to help him. He rushed down on the men, and put his blade right in the first person's belly he got hold of and turned it before pulling it out. Steve and his friend were surrounded by the angry young men who were thinking if they should kill both of them or take their bleeding friend to hospital. Steve was also concerned about his friend who was bleeding heavily. Then their rescue came in the form of the third friend who returned to help them. He came around the corner with a crate of empty bottles stolen from someone's back yard. He threw the bottles at the group of men like a man possessed by demons, even his own friends had to seek cover, but it also gave them the opportunity to escape from their enemies. The fights in Trench Town were slowly moving away from rival gang warfare to political.

Prim came to stay with us during the summer break from school while Pepe was at work. Prince, Steve and John (another uncle of mine) were at our apartment cooking. Someone shouted from downstairs that some police men were on their way up to our place. It was too late for them to run outside so they all looked for a hiding spot indoors. One chose under the bed another went in the closet and John grabbed the pot of food from the fire without any protective cloth and ran into the toilet with it. The first person the police found was John still holding the hot pot of food in the toilet. That was what saved them that day for the police officers were too amused to search any further. They laughed at the sight of a grown man hiding with his food in his hand. In front of my brother and I one of the cops swore at him, 'how yu so bloodclaat craven' (greedy) and then left. Steve and Prince took the mickey out of him for the rest of the day.

I was told by grandmother Lily that my uncle Steve was my favourite uncle. He used to buy me sweets and teased me when I was eating, 'Patsy please give some of your dinner'. Sometimes I gave him and other times I told him, 'yu na get none'. He enjoyed our game more when I said no as he did not really want to eat what I had been playing in for some time. I cried when he had to leave, Steve did not have any children at least none that we knew of, so he was particularly close to Carl and me.

Late 1967 Steve was walking along 13th street lost in his thoughts unaware of the activities that were happening around him. He was immaculately attired as usual. Some youths were teasing a mentally ill man who was ranting and raving. Steve decided to stop at one of his usual hang out spots on 13th street close to where the insane man was. The man was hiding behind a wall waiting for his tormentors. He saw Steve and thought he was one of the youths troubling him and decided to act. He closed in on the unsuspecting Steve and cut him in the face with the cover of a used rusty blade he got from a nearby dumped heap. Steve was bleeding heavily but knew he could not go to hospital for assistance as he was wanted by the police. He was getting disoriented from the loss of blood so he bent over in the street to rest. He did not see the policeman who came up behind him, besides he was too weak to do anything. He was hurt and unarmed but the police shot him down in the street like an animal. He died on the spot. He was nineteen years old.

The news hit Pepe like a nuclear bomb. I never saw my uncle Steve again in fact I forgot about him for many years and it was my grandmother who reminded me of him. She was talking about him one day when I asked her who he was. She was very surprised that I had forgotten about my favourite uncle who I was always talking to long after he died. My grandmother said the family was concerned when I was talking to an imaginary person calling him Steve and saying, 'yu na get none a mi dinner', this she said continued for quite some time and then stopped.

The news of Steve's death affected Pepe a great deal. He did care more than we thought and he aged in a short space of time. Carl and I were following him to the hospital but did not know how ill he was. In 1967 Prim fell pregnant with her third child. She could not run any more so she had to return home to Pepe who gladly took her back as his health was fading and he needed her help with Carl and me. She gave birth in April 1968 to another son she named Christopher. He was Prince's only child and the father was proud of his son. Whenever he got the opportunity he took the baby out with him. One day Prince was out walking baby Christopher who was about three months old at the time when a police car closed down on him. He put Christopher down in the middle of the road and made his escape through the old Bass cinema. He hid in a lady's house who had no problem hiding him from the coppers. She even went to get Christopher and took him to Prim. That day a stranger saved his life and she did it because she liked him. It was for that reason Prince could not bring himself to bully people to vote for politicians. Peaches had a son and a daughter by Jim Bob. The boy went to live with Jim Bob's relatives and once again Lily was left holding another of Peaches' daughters.

After Steve died and some other members of the Vikings gang went to prison, Prince went to East Kingston and brought back some friends to Trench Town. They were Manny, Garry and Silver all of whom made it on Jamaica's most wanted list. They were linked to the PNP but were marked for death, as they would not co-operate in tribal politics. They were more interested in stealing to survive. The trio like all other OGs were fearless but well liked thieves. They would hit post offices, banks and supermarkets. They became the topic of many dinner discussions and could have been prime tools for politicians but they would not conform. When politicians gave them free money and expected favours in return, they ignored the orders made on them and that did not go down well the bosses.

Prince and his friends went to a dance in a JLP area one night and some Tivoli men saw their presence as a disrespect. The don of a group of men told them to get off their turf and Silver told him where to go and that he could walk anywhere in Jamaica if it pleases him. Silver did not know that the don known as Mackie had a gun so he was talking tough but when Mackie pulled up his shirt to reveal his revolver Silver ran for cover. Prince who was also armed went in to defend the argument and pulled out his gun. Mackie went for his gun but lost the draw and his body was taken away by an undertaker and Prince went home. When the news hit the road that Prince eliminated such a top notch JLP don, PNP politicians were hopeful that he would finally give in to them but they were kept waiting.

Prince and his friends went on a robbery in 1968 and he was caught in the area where the robbery was committed. Manny and Silver were picked up at a yard in Trench Town where they were camping out. The police had wanted them for questioning about a murder and charged them for it. There was no evidence to tie Prince to the murder charge so he was given a year prison sentence for the robbery. Manny and Silver were given life. Garry was later caught and given a life sentence also. It was not long before all three lifers escaped from GP with the help of greedy prison officers who were promised money from the stash they had hidden away. Prince did nine months of the year sentence he got and returned to the fold to join his outlaw friends. Manny, Garry, and Silver were often caught and sent back to prison only to escape again with a little help from the screws who were well paid.

One of Prince's friends from the Vikings gang killed a Chinese man in a robbery not very long after he was released from prison and the police went after Prince for the murder. They offered the murderer and his girlfriend protection if they would testify that Prince pulled the trigger. Prince was later chased by a police officer who pumped seven gunshots in his body. That was done during broad daylight in front of women and children. The police thought he was dead and took him to hospital as a formality but Prince was still alive when he got there. He was placed under police guard until he recovered to face trial. The real murderer and his girlfriend were the chief witnesses at the murder trial. Prince was found guilty and sentenced to death. He spent four years on death row, no one intervened on his behalf. His mother was poor and could not afford legal fees so it was inevitable he was going to be hanged. Baby Christopher went to live with his father's mother in Jungle where he was brought up. He was never allowed to visit his father in prison. Prince converted to Rastafarianism whilst waiting on death row. He wrote a song and gave it to a friend he knew from Trench Town. The friend became famous and that particular song reached number one on the music chart and millions of people all over the world have heard him testifying his innocence in that song.

Pepe invested a lot of money in shares in the Jamaica Flour Mill and became the biggest shareholder owning three hundred and sixty five shares. He used to tell us stories about when he attended the shareholders' meetings, how he was the poorest man there but owned the most shares. Most people owned twenty or fifteen shares but he owned a massive three hundred and sixty-five. Other shareholders in their suits looked on him in his simple shirt and pants with envy at meetings. Some asked him to sell them some of his shares but he would not budge, as he wanted them for our future.

Pepe knew his time was drawing nigh so he asked Lily to marry him but she declined. She was in a new relationship and was not about to give up her man for Pepe. Not knowing what to do Pepe changed over the names of the shares from his to Lily's as most of us were young and he did not trust his older children to be responsible with them. By putting them in Lily's name he had hoped she would be responsible as a mother and grandmother to take care of his loved ones when he passed on.

In 1970 Pepe died in his sleep (at least that was what people said) I think he was awake when he slipped away. I was in bed lying on my grandfather's stomach when I felt him hugging me tightly as if he never wanted to let go of me but suddenly his grip became loose. I looked at him and he was smiling at me (at least so I thought) so I smiled back. In the morning Prim got out of bed and told Carl and I to get dressed as we were going to visit Lily who was still living in Jungle. We showered and dressed but all the noise and activities that were happening did not disturb Pepe, which was out of character for him. It was when we were finally ready to leave we found out that our beloved Pepe was permanently sleeping. Prim tried in vain for over half an hour to wake her father but could not do so, she looked afraid so did Carl. As for me I did not feel anything. Prim sent Carl to get a neighbour who came in and confirmed that Pepe was no longer with us. His dreams of rescuing Carl and me from cruel Trench Town, seemed to have died with him.

Prim and Carl wept for Pepe, Carl shouted as loud as he could and said, 'mi grandfather dead oh'. I for some reason could not feel anything. I felt no pain, no joy and my tears were far away. I just went into a world of my own where no one could reach me. I heard Prim and others making comments about how I was behaving but I could not help it, I went about business as usual without a care in the world. I lost the person who meant everything in the world to me and I felt nothing. Everybody said Carl was Pepe's favourite but I was the last one to hold him alive so I got his blessings not Carl. I started taking notice of Prim for the first time when Pepe died. While my grandfather was alive I did not really know my mother. I realised then even when she was around I saw her but I never used to look at her but suddenly I needed my mother for the first time in my young life.

At Pepe's funeral I was still numb but I became aware of death for the first time, what I saw was frightening. My Pepe was placed in a hole and covered with dirt and cement I knew then the dead never came back. I became afraid of dying and everything associated with it including Pepe. I hated him for leaving me, why did he die I could not work it out, but it seemed it was my destiny to go through life without him. Pepe's children all wept for their father, Lily too wept for him, life was never going to be the same without him.

In 1972, two years after Pepe passed away, Prince was beaten to death by prison officers as he refused to walk to the gallows. His arms and legs were broken during the fracas. His neck was then broken as formality as he was long dead. The hangman was never used and he resigned after that incident. Prince was twenty-one years old. His mother suffered a nervous breakdown when the news reached her and has never been the same since her son's death. Christopher never knew his father another legacy of careless teenage pregnancy.

Manny and Garry were executed by the police on separate occasions and Silver went back to prison. Other Vikings members ran away and some were killed, Trench Town then became vulnerable. Prince was a thief but did not deserve to die the way he did. Yes, there is no excuse, he committed murder and that should not be condoned or excused, not even his only son (my brother) has ever made any excuses for his father. He acknowledges that his father was a murderer who deserved to be jailed, but none of his victims were exactly altar boys. He stood between tribal politics and freedom. He was killed because he would not conform no matter the price. Prince and Steve were truly original gangsters.

Chapter Three

Pepe's death devastated us in more ways than one. All the dreams he had for Carl and me died with him, our journey to adulthood was going to be rocky and rough and only the stronger of us would survive. Before Prince died Prim went to see him in prison a few times when he first went in, but as always she needed a man on the outside to take care of her. A man in prison was no help to her in any way. Her father's death was the turning point in her life. She no longer had anyone to look after her children while she roamed the streets. Besides, she was not sixteen again with no children and not as hot as she used to be. Peaches had settled down also but continued to have more children for her new partner. Prim got pregnant while Prince was still on death row I do not know how he took the news but someone must have told him. What a bitter way for him to die knowing that he was abandoned by his woman when the going got tough. She had a baby girl the same year Pepe died. The baby's father moved in with us shortly after Pepe was buried.

Prim had the instinct of a mother in the wild but no parenting skills. She was not able to correct us appropriately because she was not taught discipline herself. She would try her utmost best to feed and clothe us, but like an animal mother once you leave the nest she forgets about you and concentrates on those around her. She was not too concerned about Christopher who was only living ten minutes away from us, in fact her involvement with him was very limited. Christopher craved the attention of his mother and cried endlessly whenever she passed his home to visit Lily but most of the time he was shunned by her. She did not know all that her son wanted from her was her love.

Prim could not bond with her children there was always something lacking. I could see Christopher reaching out to her and she running away from him. His father was not around so he wanted the affection of his mother but she was too emotionally disturbed by her childhood to understand and give him what he wanted. He transferred his feelings to Carl and me, as we were the next close relatives he had. Christopher was proud to have a big brother and sister. We visited him on our own, sometimes Christopher saw us coming from a far distance and ran down to meet us. He hugged us so tight as if every moment with us was so special. He expected us to lift him in our arms not realising he was too heavy for me to manage. After all I was almost a toddler myself. Sometimes we fell over together but Christopher did not mind about the fall as long as he landed on Carl or me as he thought this was a game.

It was always traumatic when we had to leave Christopher who could not understand why he could not come with us. He cried until we were out of sight. He never spent holidays or weekends with us and I cannot even remember him visiting us for a day at our home.

Christopher's uncle Gramps, Prince's younger brother, recognised some of what was going on between the three of us and encouraged contact when he could. I remember one day Carl and I were hurrying to get home after visiting grandma Lily. We had to pass where Christopher lived so both of us were running fast, hoping that he would not see us. Carl and I were relieved not to see any sign of Christopher but just when we thought the course was clear, Gramps grabbed us by the collar of our clothes and took us back to his house to see our brother Christopher. He told us never to hide from our brother again. Christopher saw us and immediately ran in our direction, I opened my arms to receive him but with the speed in which he came forced me to lose balance. Gramps' sister was shouting telling me not to lift up Christopher because we would fall, but I ignored her. Gramps was telling her to leave us alone and Christopher was determined to get in my arms and I wanted to please him. With Christopher halfway on the ground and half in my hands Gramps sister came over to take Christopher out of my hands as we were off balance. She just managed to hold onto him when I fell to the ground and started to cry, Christopher began crying as well. Gramps got upset that he took a dry coconut still in its shell and hit his sister with it. She fell to the floor and passed out. Gramps was unrepentant and insisted that she should not have interfered.

Shortly after Pepe died I heard Prim telling her sisters and Lily that she was frightened to go home for someone was coming into our apartment late at night. I too became afraid but had never seen this person she was talking about. We were visiting Lily when Prim broke the news and for the first time I felt like sleeping at my grandmother's. When we got home late that night, Carl and I got in the same bed with Prim and baby Sue. I was frightened out of my mind I could not sleep neither could Carl. I kept whispering Carl and Prim names in case they fell asleep with me alone awake to face our nocturnal visitor. I made sure I was tucked between my bigger brother and mother and even though I was afraid I wanted to see who the person was. We waited until after twelve midnight and our visitor never disappointed us. He showed up and I heard Prim whispering to us there he is. It was dark so I could only make out the image. The face was pitch dark but the person was looking straight at us and he knew we saw him. He was sitting on a chair between the kitchen and the front door but where he could see us and we could see him. When our stares got too much for him he got up and went into the kitchen, we waited but he never came out. I never heard when he came in or when he went out but we never saw him again. I asked Prim many years after if she remembered our mysterious visitor and she said no. I wondered how something like that could have happened and she forgot about it, she even said to me that I remembered too many things for that young age. Maybe she was hoping I would forget and was uncomfortable about what else I might remember.

Prim's new man was resentful of Carl and me and openly talked about supporting other men's children. Most of his anger was directed at me because my father was in prison and never contributed to my upkeep. I did not really need to hear his complaint to know he did not give a damn for his actions spoke volumes. I could pick up his negative vibes and for the first time I felt like a stranger in my own home. Carl used to get a little pittance from his father so he was treated with a bit more dignity. Prim's new man beat her in front of us often banging her head on the wall. One day he banged her head so hard that the noise woke me up, I saw her sitting on the bed with tears rolling down her cheeks. She did not cry out and my body shivered. I just wanted to hold her but we did not have such a touching mother and daughter relationship, besides she had replaced me with the daughter she had by her new lover. I hated their new daughter with every cell in my body. I loved Christopher and Carl with all my heart but I hated their child I did not care for the father either because he hit my mother. I was going to get even with him and kill his daughter. I knew I could not manage that big strong man (my mother told me he was a boxer) so I decided to get his daughter instead. I hatched a plan with Carl to flush Sue down the toilet and then tell Prim the neighbour's dog ate her. The plan should not have been too hard to carry out as Prim often left Sue with us when she visited her friends and she was not aware of our plot to get rid of her precious new baby. Carl went along with my scheme until the last minute then he told me that he could not do it, because he would like to see God's face when he comes. I asked him what God had to do with Sue. While we were arguing about Sue's fate a policeman came up to our front door to ask something, I ran like a witch possessed by demons past the bewildered policeman. I thought he had found out about my plan and had come to arrest me.

When Carl found me some hours later in my hideout he told me that the copper came to the wrong door. He wanted our neighbour who lived next door. Carl said the cop wanted to know why I ran off like that and he told him I stole some milk. We never spoke about our failed scheme but I continued to resent Sue, I do not think Carl ever shared my views but he was always loyal to me. Carl was the boy but I was the dangerous one I believe I took after my grandfather. Christopher and I resembled Pepe but Carl looked like his father.

Prim had another son a few years later. I took to him but I could not come round to Sue. I started ill-treating her and like a faithful lamb she was always walking behind me for her next beating. I put her hands on a live electric wire that was undone in our apartment but left unattended. I first came upon it when it shocked me and I started placing Sue's fingers on it. I wanted her to disappear but she continued to be a thorn in my side and not going anywhere. I heard neighbours telling Prim to stop having children and to make sure Jim was the last one. She said yes but she said that when Sue was born.

Jim became very ill with pneumonia and was admitted to Bustamante Children's Hospital for a long time. On many occasions Prim could not find food to feed us, or bus fare to visit Jim. When she raised a few dollars it was a matter of what was priority, food for us at home or bus fare to see Jim? One day she used the money to visit Jim at the hospital and took us with her, as it was a long time since we had seen Jim. A nurse gave Prim a bowl of creamed potato to feed the baby and we all had to share his meal. Jim was clearly still hungry after the meal so he started crying. One of the nurses saw when Prim gave us some of the food and gave us a dirty look. I felt like an outcast. I wondered why she was so mean to us was it because we were needy? Jim was reduced to skin and bones and was wasting away before our eyes. When he was discharged from hospital he was still too skinny and we had to hide him away from the prying eyes of neighbours. Trench Town was not the place to be sick as everyone played doctor diagnosing the cause of your illness in a bitchy and vindictive way. Some people said that a duppy (ghost) was haunting Jim, others said he was suffering from malnutrition. It made no point telling them what the illness was because they just would not have believed us anyway.

The hardship for us continued and many nights we had to go to our bed without food. Our mother told us to drink water and go to bed. Sometimes we could not go to school as we had no food to eat. Prim's man gave her a little money but it could not go far. If it was not for an aunt of mine (Pepe's eldest daughter, not Lily's child) Carl and I would have stayed hungry many times. We were merely existing on the mercy of God and the little Prim could scrape to give us. Lily did not pay us any attention she only helped out Peaches' children. In our house Carl and I were like outcasts because we had outside fathers, so we had to rely on each other for support. Prim was in love with her man and could not see what we were going through. Whenever we voiced our opinion she would say we were lying or misunderstanding what was going on. She told us we were children so we should be seen and not heard. Our feelings were never taken into consideration and our views were not valued. We believed everything Prim said so if she had told me that a man could fly we would have believed her. We were so innocent and vulnerable.

I was about six years old when I was struck down with mumps, I remember feeling poorly and spending a lot of time in bed. I was often left at home alone. Carl went to school and Prim went out to talk to her friends but would leave the front door open so anyone could gain access. Prim went out one day and left me alone indoors where I was too weak to move. One of Prim's brothers came through the door, when I recognised him I was glad to see a familiar face but I was left to regret that moment forever. He started to touch me on my private parts and put his bearded face on mine in an attempt to kiss me. I can still feel his breath and facial hair on my face. He sexually abused me while I was crying but he would not stop until he was satisfied. When Prim returned home I told her what happened and she examined me. She went over to confront her brother and he told her I was lying. I only knew this because I heard her talking to someone about it. My innocence was taken away from me by my own uncle who I trusted. The incident was never mentioned again. Everyone was too embarrassed to speak about it as if they were the victims. I believe Prim was hoping that in time I would forget but the shame and mental pain live with me to this day.

A male neighbour who I knew for as long I could remember came home one day after a long absence, dressed in army gear and boasting to all of us that his shoes were made of leather and iron. He had joined the army and was proud of himself as not many young men in our community got that opportunity. I was standing behind him when he made some steps backward and landed on my left toes. If I was in any doubt that his shoes were indeed made of iron the pain I was in confirmed they were. I saw stars and all the colours that made up Joseph's coat. We did not know how bad the injury was until a nail fell out, and the wound became infected and smelly that was when I knew I had to seek medical attention quickly.

Our local clinic was situated at the corner of Eighth Street opposite the clock tower and not far from Trench Town School. It looked like a bungalow house specially adapted to use as a clinic. It offered a range of services from dental care to sexually transmitted diseases.

Prim told Carl to accompany me to the local clinic, as she was busy looking after her other children. I was six and Carl eight but we were left to deal with everything including the registration, I do nct think all the information we gave was correct. A nurse told Carl to sit down outside a room and took me inside where another nurse was sitting. One of the nurses held me while the other one squeezed the inflammation from the wound and I thought I would die. My scream could be heard all over the small clinic. Carl pushed the door open and begged the two nurses holding me to stop but they told him to go back outside. He went out helplessly I cried for Carl to come back but he stayed out of the room. One of the nurses picked up a pair of scissors and I thought she was going to cut off my smelly toe because it had decayed. I closed my eyes and waited for the worst to happen, but I felt something moving over my sore toe and when I opened my eyes it was cotton buds between the scissors. That was just as painful. After the nurses cleaned up the wound they dressed it and told me to go. When I went outside I saw Carl with tears in his eyes. He held my hand and we walked home. Carl followed me to the clinic for dressing every other morning until my toe was better. We both missed school for weeks.

We were feeling the brunt of poverty but the worst was yet to come. Prim was struck down with a mystery illness and became bed-bound. She was reduced from fourteen stones to merely seven stones I thought she was going to die. During that time her man was hardly around, we heard rumours he was seeing someone else. Prim had four children to feed but was totally bed-bound. Friends and relatives gave what they could but we had to make do with bread and water many days and that was when I found God. My mother asked Carl and I to pray for her. Carl shied away but me I prayed as if my life depended on it and it did. I asked God as loud as I could that night and many nights to follow to heal my mother. Some of the things I was saying must have been stupid to the point of being funny as people who were present laughed at me but God understood. Carl did most of the cooking and washing. He even washed our under-wear. I did the praying and then one day Prim got out of bed on her own and she was healed.

Tom, my biological father, came out of prison and came to see me. Prim was out and one of my aunts saw him and hid me in the house. Prim was not happy when she was told about this because she thought now that he was out of prison she would get some financial help with me. How wrong she was for Tom wanted to show off to his friends that he had children but did not want the responsibilities that came with being a father. Prison did not reform him in any way. He continued stealing but refused to support any of his children.

Prim recovered from her illness and got busy finding a primary school for Carl and me as I was turning seven and Carl nine. A new school was opening for the new academic year and she wanted us to go there. The name would be Denham Town Primary and it was situated off Spanish Town Road. Prim registered us during the summer break and was given a sample of the required uniform for the school. I was to wear a blue pleated skirt and orange blouse and Carl to wear a khaki suit. I got the full uniform but Carl had to wear khaki shorts and shirt, because Prim did not have enough money to buy enough material to make a pair of trousers.

Prim took us to school on the first day and came back for us but Carl and I had to find our way on the second day. The school had concrete walls around it and was adjoined to Denham Town Secondary. It had just one block with two floors, but for my tiny size it looked huge. The main entrance was on Spanish Town Road but we used the side entrance on Law Street. The school was ten to fifteen minutes walk away from our home. On our way to school on the second day we were nervous about the journey, as we were afraid of getting lost. We saw some children in the same uniform as us so we followed behind them. Carl found a piece of fire coal and drew lines on people's gates and walls so that we could trace our way back home after school. He was placed one class ahead of me so we were separated for the first time. This was upsetting for me because we were always together at basic school.

Primary school was a real eye opener, we seemed to be seated according to our colour and class. Our appearance revealed those of us who were poor and those who could afford a few more things. I was placed at the back to sit down with another child who had very short hair that looked as if her mother could not even bother to plait it. Her name was Melanie and we became best friends. Melanie was dark in complexion not very good looking but had a personality of a star. The problem was Melanie very rarely showed the star quality she had as we were always muzzled by the adults around us. Our teacher used to look at us with contempt. We started to believe something was wrong with us and made sure we stayed quiet in class. There was this brown skinned, long hair girl in our class who our teacher liked so we thought she was better than us. We were called ugly so many times I felt ugly.

Teacher's favourites were Diana and Lavern who sat next to each other in class. I fancied Headley a classmate who did not live far from me but he had eyes only for Lavern. I knew Lavern from Miss Kelly's school and she was always neat and tidy. Also she always seemed to have money to buy snacks. On television most of the people were white and at our local church the picture of God's son was white so I accepted my low status in society. The advertisements on television had brown skin or white people and the story books we read were snow white and Cinderella who were white pale and seen as beautiful. We did not see anyone in the story books looking like us, described as beautiful and no positive black history was taught in school so my self esteem was very low. Melanie and I used to try and defend ourselves when we got into arguments with our classmates but the truth was the words we were called hurt like hell. They called us low life and black tar. We replied that we were black and proud but they were just words to use for I was not proud and I do not think Melanie was either. It did not do my confidence any good either when my mother made comments like, 'is because her child is brown why she thinks her child is better than mine'. I also heard older people both black and brown commenting that if a black skinned person committed a crime the person's heart was black like them. Those comments helped to damage young people like me.

Some of the children would boast about the furniture and appliances they had at home and of course Melanie and I told them we had refrigerators, televisions and stereos. The truth of the matter was Prim did not even own an icebox. We used to beg ice from our neighbours and did our shopping on a daily basis as we did not have anywhere to store them. We were so poor I used to daydream that I was pretty and had nice clothes to wear, the food I wanted to eat and not what Prim could afford to buy. Our diet was mostly carbohydrates with protein and very little fruits and vegetables. Prim had to make sure whatever she bought could be shared for all of us and what was important was a full stomach not a balanced diet. So I would dream to take me away from my reality. That was one thing I had control over and no one could hurt me in my dreams where I was a star.

The first time I saw a gun was when someone tried to murder my uncle Moses in broad daylight - in front of me and other children playing downstairs from where we lived. Moses was hanging out with some local boys and his best friend Solomon. He and his friends were sitting in the compound downstairs from our apartment and I was playing with my friends not far from where he was. The loud voice of someone broke my concentration from my play and when I looked up, Moses was moving like an athlete on anabolic steroid with another man not far behind with a gun in his hand aiming it straight at him. Moses ran out of his shoes to save his life I got up and ran behind them to get my uncle's shoes not aware of the danger. I heard the gun clicking and clicking in the man's hand but it did not go off. I looked in the man's face but he ignored my stare and walked away, he did not give a damn about the children who were playing in the area. Someone said, 'is de bway Danny from Jungle' and I would remember that name for the rest of my life. He was very angry that his gun stuck but Moses was very lucky and one of our neighbours commented that it was Pepe at work from the grave that saved Moses' life. This experience was a sign of what was in store for the future of Trench Town.

One evening on our way home from school Carl got into a fight with a much older girl who flogged him properly. After that incident he was constantly bullied by the girl and her brother. Carl had a friend in his class but he was too afraid of the over-grown brother and sister to help. Carl was afraid and would grab my hand and dash home after school in the evenings, but sometimes they caught up with him and beat him up. I was too afraid to get involved and Melanie said she was not going to defend Carl as her bones were too fragile to take on Big Girl and her brother. Melanie kept asking me where those people came from and if it was from the 'Land of the Giants'. Carl's friend said he knew the entire family and they were all big. Melanie started swearing in the streets at the top of her voice, asking what possessed Carl to get involved with those people in the first place.

One evening after school we were running home when Big Girl and her brother jumped Carl from behind and started beating him. They had him on the ground and were punching and kicking him. Carl fought like a tiger but he was no match for them. I just stood by and watched my brother get the beating of his life as I was afraid and it tore me apart. They only stopped because a man intervened. Big Boy looked at me and asked if I was Carl's sister. Apparently some informer told him I was. I quickly said no and felt like a traitor. I understood then why Peter denied Christ, he was afraid for his life. When Carl got up off the ground his school shirt was torn and he had scratches on his face. The first thing he did was to look for me, my guilt felt like a knife pushed through my heart. We walked home in silence. Prim was very upset when she saw the state of her son. She had a few angry words with me. She asked me, 'how could you stand and watch yu brother get beaten and do nothing ? yu damn coward'. I felt even worse then. Carl stayed at home that evening and from the look on his face I knew he was worried about going to school the next day. It was obvious that Prim had no intentions of coming with us to school to sort out the bullying, so we had no choice but to defend ourselves. One thing I knew for certain I was not going to stand by and let Carl get another beating on his own, the next time they would have to beat both of us.

The next morning on our way to school I told Carl that we were going to fight Big Girl and her brother that evening. I explained to him that we would not wait for them to come to us but we would jump them instead. He thought I was losing my mind. He said Big Girl alone would crush me to death (that might be the reason why he was not upset with me for not helping him before). He preferred to take the beatings alone. I knew we stood a better chance if both of us fought. Carl handled himself well, but needed some help to take the pressure off him and I knew I could do that. He did not think I was qualified for that job but I knew I was, for Carl and I fought at home and I held my own reasonably well against him. No matter what he had to say, today would be judgement day.

At break I went into a few nearby classrooms and stole some pencils and a sharpener from children who had left their belongings carelessly on their desks. Melanie was on the lookout but swore she would not get involved in the fight, as she was too petite for such roughness. I sharpened the pencils and bound them up three at a time with elastic bands. Carl and I went to our aunt who had a bar near our school for lunch that afternoon to make sure we had some energy to fight. When I got back to class Melanie told me that she was going to play sick so that teacher would send her home early, because Big Girl knew she was my friend and would start on her as well.

That evening I went out the side gate to wait for Carl. Melanie was walking slowly in front of me she wanted to leave but curiosity got he better of her. I knew she was too nosey to go home, as she wanted to see the fight. Carl and his friend came running towards me with some tamarind whips in their hands. We all headed in the direction of our home with Melanie in front and kept looking back all the time. Suddenly, I heard Big Girl commenting behind us on how brave Carl got because he was walking and not running home as usual. We continued walking ignoring the cheap talk behind us. I saw Melanie taking something from her bag but I was more interested in what was happening behind me. Big Girl first came forward and poked Carl in the face and then her brother moved to massacre my brother. The whip Carl had fell from from his hand as they both jumped on him. I threw away my books and rushed in on them with my pencils. When Big Girl got the first stab in her back with a set of pencils I had she moved away from Carl and screamed out. Her brother turned around to see what was happening and I stabbed him straight in the face with the pencils I went for his eyes but missed by a mile. With my intervention Carl got time to recover and pick up his whip. He and his friend started to beat the hell out of Big Boy. I turned around to find Big Girl but I saw her on the floor crying with Melanie down on her with her teeth in Big Girl's head. I was on my way to join Melanie when I heard shouting coming nearer and nearer to us. I looked to see what was happening and what I saw were three big boys who looked just like Big Girl coming towards us. Carl, his friend, Melanie and me ran with all our might until we came upon an empty lot with bricks and broken bottles. We stopped there and waited for Big Girl and her posse.

I asked Melanie how she managed to overpower Big Girl to get her on the ground to be biting her. She said she had some salt in her bag in case she had to defend herself and she threw the salt in Big Girl's eyes. It was the salt that was burning Big Girl why she was crying and laid on the ground and not Melanie's bites. I knew Prim could not afford to buy new uniform for us so I took off my clothes to the bare essentials. Melanie also stripped to just her panties. Carl and his friend took off their shirts and quietly waited for the enemies as the war had only just began.

Melanie and I could not keep our cool like the boys. We drew a crowd with our bad language and almost nude appearance. We looked so funny people were laughing rather than rebuking us. I was ranting and raving, I spoke some unspeakable words no little girl my age should know much more utter, but the women in Trench Town were good teachers at cursing and I was a good student. Melanie's panties had a tear in them and mine were not that wonderful either. A young man made a grave error by commenting about them and Melanie asked him if he came to admire us and said that he looked as if he liked little girls. He was so embarrassed he did not bother to wait for the mother of all wars that was about to take place. Anyone else who wanted to comment about our panties had better sense and kept quiet.

Big Girl and her posse came into a barrage of stones and broken bottles. They too picked up stones and started throwing them at us, so they were well up to the task. Trench Town's wild children decided to do battle and all hell broke loose. We stoned each other with bottles and bricks and something had to give. I saw blood and was really angry for the first time in my life, I felt a sudden surge of blood running through my veins and my stomach got tight. I let the anger flow and move me in its direction. I had no control over my emotions I just wanted to do harm to the children I called my enemies. I picked up a broken bottle and ran straight up to Big Girl. She hit me with the one stone she had in her hand but I had made my mind to take one lick and then cut her out of her clothes. She looked me in the eyes, saw the look of death and started running and so did her brothers. We ran after them but they were too quick for us their size did not slow them down one bit. We stopped and got dressed I had a feeling the war was won, but Melanie said those who run today live to fight another day so I was not going to take any chances. I kept the pencils in case we had to fight again. The next day I saw Big Girl at school with stab wounds from the pencils on her neck and arm but she held her head straight as if she did not recognise Melanie or me. Her brother had cuts in his face and marks from the whipping Carl and his friend gave him but he too was calm. I had salt and sharpened pencils in a bag in case I needed them but nothing was brewing. The mighty lion and his sister were finally tamed. No parents came to school to sort out the problem even though their children had obviously been injured. In Trench Town we just had to do what we had to do. Bullying was rampant in school and some children stopped attending because of it but my friends and I would not have any of it. We were not exactly big in size but what we lacked in size we made up for with our voices. If people ever heard Melanie and me they would have thought we could move mountains with our mouths.

Big Girl's behaviour could not prepare me for what I saw that evening. Carl and Big Boy were laughing and talking to each other. I felt betrayed but Carl was always the forgiving one of the two of us. Melanie swore to heaven and earth that if Big Girl and her brother turned on Carl again all she would do was watch. Melanie said, 'Patsy yu brother evil, him mek wi sin wi self and den him tun friends with people who used to beat him. But de next time wi a go mek dem kill him'. I said yes to her but I knew I could not allow Carl to die alone if I could help it. After that I became more semi-independent of Carl and started spending more of my time with Melanie. Carl too let go and no longer waited for me after school. He walked home with his friends and I with mine.

The bullying at school stopped but the disrespect by our classroom teacher continued and we could not do anything about that. She clearly showed preference to those students who were of brown complexion or smartly dressed. I saw her looking at Melanie with disgust on one occasion for no apparent reason. Melanie was never rude in class in fact she only spoke to me during the break. I think she knew our teacher did not like her but we never spoke about it. One morning Melanie and I went to school late as we were waiting on each other. When we got to class our teacher used a thick leather belt and gave us a beating to remember. I cried so much but she only stopped when she was satisfied. When she finished beating us we were told to sit down and were given a look of death. At no time were we asked why we were late. The next day one of her favourites came late but she only slapped her with her hand, then gave her a smile and told her to sit down. She never smiled at Melanie or me we only got dirty looks. Our parents did not attend parents and teachers meeting so we were at a disadvantage. We supported each other and became soul mates.

At mid morning breaks before the lunch period the school would deliver ice cream in each class for sale. What usually happened was that those who could afford to buy, ate the ice cream in front of those who could not afford to do so. All we could do was watch them eat. It did not occur to the teachers that this practice was wrong, classist and downright humiliating to those of us who could not afford to buy ice cream, especially when it was more or less the same students buying ice cream all the time. The have nots were clearly separated from those who had.

Melanie and I played baseball and dandy-shandy during the breaks at school with some other children from different classes. We quickly learnt the skills of the games and always ended up on the same team. Ann-Marie another little girl who used to play with us during the lunch break was cruelly killed on Spanish Town Road just outside our school gate by a hit-and-run driver. He did not even have courage or conscience to assist his young victim. She was trying to cross the road when the driver from hell came speeding in the direction of Maxfield Avenue. Ann-Marie tried to get out of his way but it was too late, the car dragged her small body about two yards from where she was first hit. She did not stand a chance. The entire school went to the funeral. We all mourned the passing of our schoolmate who was taken away from us at such a tender age. I do not know if the man who killed our beloved schoolmate was ever punished neither do I care if he was, because not even the death penalty would be a justifiable sentence for the loss of one so young.

Prim sent me and Carl to our fathers in Jungle for money but most of the time we got none I do not know why she bothered sending us to be humiliated but she did. Sometimes Carl's father gave him two dollars and I might get one if I was lucky. Dan was in a new relationship and had lost interest in Carl. Tom always badmouthed Prim in my presence, he said the most horrible things about her and did not take my feelings into consideration. He thought he could turn up out of the blue after so many years and take Prim's place in my heart but that could not happen because she was by far the better person and parent. She never spoke one bad word against him in my presence.

Christmas and Easter were always big occasions in Trench Town even though most of us were not religious. It was only the commercial aspects many of us were interested in. During the festive seasons the thieves went on a rampage in the capital city because they wanted to get money to buy new clothes and they knew a lot of cash would be in circulation at this time. With the hustle and bustle it was easy for people to lose their money. Young women went in shops and crutch (steal) anything from clothing to food items. Some women made crutching their trade and could easily move a large cold chicken between their legs without losing it. Prim liked men who were thieves but I never knew her to steal a sweet.

One Easter Prim's man who was a fisherman had problems with his boat so he could not go to sea. There was no money in the house and everybody was sad as the holiday was upon us. Easter and Christmas were not the time to go without a good dinner and Prim's man started complaining about carrying other men's burden. He would always take out his problems on us including Prim. Prim told Carl and I to go to our fathers for money to help out. Both our deadbeat fathers lived close to each other so we went together. I stopped off at Tom's and Carl went up to his father. We planned to meet in five minutes, as we knew it would not take longer. I asked Tom for money but I could hardly get the words out of my mouth when the man told me to go away. I heard him calling my mother a dirty bitch while I was running out the gate. I saw Carl coming towards me and by the look on his face I knew he did not get any money either. His father was much kinder to him than mine. He had only told him that he did not have any money but Carl was still disappointed because he knew Prim did not have any food to feed us. We headed home in tears and I in particular was humiliated and embarrassed. We stopped and cried for a while then we went home to give Prim the bad news. The look on her face told me what she was thinking. Her man was not home when we got there but I heard her telling him what happened later when he returned home. He had to borrow money from someone to feed us while our fathers were sitting in their homes enjoying themselves.

I tried hard in school. I wanted to learn but there were too many distractions around. I could not concentrate for long on what the teacher was saying, as I was hungry. Also I came from a dysfunctional home and was too preoccupied with was happening there to keep up at school. We took exams every June to assess our ability and where best to grade us the following academic year. We were placed according to our academic ability. I wanted to go to a prominent high school when I turned twelve but I knew Prim would not be able to afford the fee as only the rich could send their children to high schools. I took the first grade test and came seventh in a class of fifteen. Carl came second to last and his friend came last in their class. Prim was not pleased with him but was proud of me and said so. I felt special at the expense of my brother.

Carl and I attended church with some neighbours of ours. Every Sunday we dressed in our best clothes and went to Sunday school. Due to this I was very good at religious knowledge at school. I always looked forward to going but Carl went by force, as he was more interested in the Rasta doctrine. We knew some Rastas who were always preaching to us but my mother did not think much of them and used to ridicule them behind their backs. I joined in the ridicule and ignored what they had to say even though it would have raised my self esteem for they were teaching us to love ourselves and not listen to the white bias in society. I already accepted that I was a second class citizen and so did my mother and for the time we were comfortable where we were.

One Sunday Carl and I went to church as usual with me in my very best dress and two ribbons in my hair that was combed in ponytail and Carl had on his best shorts suit. Our mother was so proud of the way we looked she beamed. Carl was on edge during the service. It was obvious that he did not want to be in church but was killing time. The pastor started preaching to us about turning the other cheek in fights, Carl could not put up with the pretence anymore so he got up and walked out of church. On his way out he commented loudly that Rasta should not mix in a Babylon. Carl clearly had an appetite for the Rasta preaching but this was fiercely undermined by my mother who thought the Christian way was the only way. As for me the holy one I could not wait for church to finish to go home and inform on Carl. When I did Prim gave him a piece of her mind. Carl was so angry with me he slapped me across the face with his hand and we started one almighty fistfight. I was on my way to get a weapon but he knew what I was up to and did not take the gesture lightly from past experience. He rushed over to me before I could reach a big knife in the kitchen and gave me one Bruce Lee flying kick. Two of my front teeth went flying with the kick. I forgot about the knife and went for my most dangerous weapon by the name of Prim. She gave him such a beating even I felt sorry for him.

Carl continued to quote Rasta phrases and exhibited a liking for their way of life but due to the lack of direction from positive believers he lost interest. Carl was looked upon as a little boy who was going through a phase and not to be taken seriously. And even though he made a big statement by walking out of church at the tender age of eight, because the church message at the time could not feed the hunger of a young black boy searching for answers and to find out who he was. Carl did not convert to Rastafarianism but he did not conform to the norm of Christianity either.

Many of us who attended our church were poor and could not afford to buy food to eat but pastor would still expect collection from us. If Prim could afford to give us two cents each for collection I would gladly give mine to pastor but Carl used his money to buy sweets. The church was never interested in its poor members, only what was in our pockets and no matter how poor the members were they tried to give. Sometimes some people begged money for collection rather than to buy food as pastor told them God would provide. One Sunday afternoon on our way to church an old passenger mini bus stopped at a bus stop near us to let out some churchgoers. One of the women who came off the bus was walking with her head held high. The conductor called out to her, to remind her that she had not paid her fare, but instead of apologising the lady asked him if he could give her fifty cents for church collection. The conductor was so angry he told her about her mother and father. He was clearly a non-believer who did not care where his soul would go when he died, so he told the woman pastor would soon rape her. Another church sister heard the argument and was so annoyed and offended by his comments she told the man he was blaspheming not knowing pastor was just a man and not God. He did not care much about blaspheming either, as he ignored her comment and continued to talk some wrong things about pastor and the fare dodger to the amusement of us young ones. Carl was glad he bothered to waste another Sunday to attend church for he found the whole thing amusing.

Our church, like many others had a large picture of the false painting of Jesus, which everyone who attended our church including pastor thought was a true likeness of the messiah. Every time I prayed I visualised the image of the white Jesus in my mind. I truly thought that the picture in our church was that of Jesus. I was ignorantly deceived by someone I trusted so much. Our pastor was ignorant of the fact of who the person in the picture was and what it represented and we his parishioners were too ignorant to know that he did not know. We followed our pastor blindly and from where I am standing now it looks as if we were heading straight for hell.

The Jamaica Omnibus Service (JOS) was the name of the national transport system and we had several buses running in Trench Town. My mother along with other women took the buses every Saturday to go to the Coronation Market downtown. Sometimes they walked as the bus would be packed like sardines. Pickpockets loved packed buses because they could carry out their theft in the hustle and bustle without being noticed. Some of their victims only found out after they left the bus that they had been robbed. Pinky was another schoolmate who lived only a few blocks from me. Her mother got picked on a bus on her way home from work on a Friday evening. She had thirty dollars in her purse from her employer for a week's work as a domestic helper. She was devastated because she was a single parent with five children and the fathers were not contributing to their keep. Pinky, her one brother and three sisters had to stay off school the following week because their mother could not afford to send them. They had to survive on very little until she was paid the following Friday. Pinky waited for Melanie and I near our school every evening that week just to find out what happened in her absence. By the end of the third day we could not wait to go out the gate to find Pinky. She was a laugh and we missed having her in the playground at break time.

Animals were despised in Trench Town and many of us could not afford to feed ourselves much more to feed four legged creatures. I could tolerate dogs but not cats and hated them with a passion. One of my aunts found a stray kitten and felt sorry for it. To my dismay she brought it to stay in our home but just the look of him upset me. With other people around I was all right around him but not on my own. One day the rest of the family went out and left me on my own with the cat. The kitten was terrified and looking for comfort so he ran up to me but I was frightened of it, I ran to the door but we were locked in. I was petrified and so was the kitten. The more agitated I got the more the kitten became troubled. I ran over to the closet and picked up one of Prim's shoes. The kitten smelt danger and was running around the small apartment like the caged animal he was and we did not have anywhere to go as the door was locked with the key. He tried to jump onto a chair but did not make it and landed on the ground. He was a bit disoriented from his fall and the confusion so I seized that moment to attack. I threw Prim's shoes so hard at the kitten it caught him in the head. I was told cats had nine lives but by the still look of the kittens body I knew he barely had one. I was disturbed by the dead kitten in the apartment with me but at least it was not moving, I stayed in one place on the bed until Prim returned home. When Prim and my aunt saw the kitten's dead body they were shocked. They looked at my guilty face and at the dead cat. My aunt asked me what happened and I told her I did not know and that the kitten just dropped dead in front of me. Of course they knew I was lying but they had no proof I killed it. Prim was laughing but my aunt cried for her cat. I wondered to myself why the hell she was crying for a dead puss (pussy cat).

I became terrified of cats from that day onwards so I knew visiting Lily was not something I would do too often, because she used to have a lot of stray cats in her back yard. They had kittens under the cellar of her house and it was then that cats and I became worst of enemies. I hated going to my grandmother's house and what made matters worse was that her toilet and bathroom were outside the back yard. That meant, for me to relieve myself I had to face my enemies. The cats were just as frightened as I was but try telling young Patsy that. My relatives did not take my fear seriously so another incident was just waiting to happen. Sometimes I wanted to use the toilet while I was there but I had to hold whatever it was until it hurt. I would hope and pray for Prim to get up and say her farewell but when I could not wait any more I relieved myself in the front of the yard.

One day Prim left us at our grandmother's and went out with her sisters. We had to stay with our cousins who were playing outside the gate. I wanted to do a number two and I knew there was no way on earth Lily would tolerate me doing that in her front yard, so I had to gather courage and went round the back of the yard to the toilet. I do not know which was more frightening the cockroaches in the pit toilet or the posse of cats under the bottom of the house. I was getting desperate as I had waited a long time before I made a move to go hoping the feeling would go away but it was coming with a vengeance instead. What was annoying was that no one was willing to follow me because they thought it was an inappropriate and daring request. I was hurrying to the toilet due to urgency when a little kitten came out in the open running up to me. I was so angry and in no mood to play hide and seek with the kitten so I picked up a piece of stick and hit the kitten and then ran to the loo. I was frightened but did not have time to think about much. My panties were barely down and I was letting off down the toilet. I left the toilet door open as inside was dark. As soon as I was relaxing a cat came at the door and was staring at me I quickly moved in reaction and almost ended up in the toilet with its inhabitants. If I had dropped in the toilet my little body would have disappeared in the liquid and solids, my family would have accused the first Rasta man they saw of kidnapping me. I cut my movement short and got down from the peculiar position I was in trying to use the toilet, which was too high for me.

I quickly washed my hands and vacated the area. When I returned to the others no questions were asked no answers were given. No-one ever mentioned a dead kitten to my relief so maybe that one had nine lives.

We had an old custom we used to practice when someone stole from us. We would use Bible and key to find out who the guilty person was. I did not fully understand it but the gist was if someone stole from you, you would get a Bible and turn to the twenty third psalm, then you would get a key that was on a ring, place it in the Bible and call the names of the people you suspected to be the thief. If the key rings on a name then you would be sure that was the guilty person. This was not proof and many people swore they did not steal anything after the key rang on their names but that was not the case with Pinky and her family.

I went round to Pinky's house on a Saturday afternoon to see her as I was hoping we could play some games of jacks. When I got to her gate I heard Pinky and her mother shouting at the same time. Instead of giving them their privacy I went straight in the house because by the tone of their voices it was clear they did not care too much for privacy. Trench Townians were notorious for invading other people's privacy and one person's business was everybody's. When I got in I heard Pinky's mother shouting 'is which one a uno so rass claat wicked, dat onu tief from unu own mada'. The tone of her voice and the bad language did not bother my young soul as I was used to it.

Indecent language was the order of the day in our community by both old and young. When she saw me she said, 'Patsy one a mi wicked pickney tief mi two dollar mi di a save fi buy a pair a shoes'. When I heard what she said I was glad I got there after she found out that her money was stolen for I would not have put it past her of accusing me as well. 'Dem ya pickney rada si mi walk barefoot dan han over back mi money', she said. Pinky first jumped in shouting and bobbing her head at the same time, 'mama try Bible an key, den yu wi find out a who tief yu money'. Her mother called her bluff and said, 'Pinky yu go get di Bible and mi wi get di front door key'. Pinky was taking her time to get back with the Bible and when she returned to the living room I knew there and then why she took so long. She had in her hand an old suitcase but could not find anything due to the mess it was in. By the state of its contents the word neglect would be an understatement. Rats were feasting on its belongings including the Bible, which only had some parts of the New Testament left in it, the rats obviously did not recognise the holy words. When Pinky's mother saw the Bible she went quiet and opened her mouth. When she recovered she commented loudly to herself, 'look wha di fucking rats done to God book'. I do not know why she was bothered for it was very clear that no one in that house was using the Bible so they would not be missing it unless they had another theft. They had to borrow their next-door neighbour's Bible and that was also another joke. When the neighbour's son came in with the Bible in his hand it had dust building up like the pyramids. Pinky's mother had the cheek to ask him where he found it and said that it looked as if it was used to work obeah (witch craft) rather than to worship with. She took it from the boy and started to perform the ritual of the Bible and key, by then a group of us had gathered around to see what was going to happen.

We the nosey parkers gathered around to be entertained by Pinky and her mother and we were not disappointed. Pinky's mother was shouting out the names so loud her antics had us in fits of laughter. Pinky was showing signs of nerves as her mother was about to call her name, the letter P was barely out of her mouth when Pinky ran out of the yard like a thief, down the road in guilt. Her mother said, 'mi a go pepper her backside when she come back ya tonight, imagine di tiefing gal know all along dat is she tief mi money an encouraged mi fi do Bible and key an a she who tief mi money'. I could not wait for Monday morning to come to give this drama to Melanie who was so much like Pinky.

Pinky told me the next day that she gave one dollar and fifty cents of the money back to her mother. She had used fifty cents to buy a bottle of cuss-cuss perfume for a child in her class, because they were going to exchange presents at their class Christmas do. She said she knew her mother would not have given her the money so she took it because she did not want to be the only one not to have a present to give. As it turned out all Pinky's troubles were for nothing because half her classmates did not bring anything and the person who pulled her name out of the bag did not buy her a present. Pinky then refused to hand over her cuss-cuss perfume because she was not getting anything in return. Every lunch break we sprayed Pinky's overpowering scent over us before we returned to our classes so everyone knew when we were around. Mr Coke, our school principal smelt the perfume on us one day and paid us a compliment and even though he was teasing us we were flattered. He became our friend after that. He always recognised us anywhere in the school and hailed us and I felt a bit special for the first time at school. Mr Coke had years of experience with children and knew how to get the best out of them and he surely did with the three misfits Pinky, Patsy and Melanie.

In our community we did not visit the doctor very much as our older folks would have some effective home remedies for any form of casualties. One well-known remedy for concussion was sugar and water mixed together. The mixture had to be very sweet to be effective. Big Girl, who was always calling her brother craven (which meant he was greedy), said that one day he would eat her mother out of house and land. Well, I was not surprise to hear he was craven for a boy his size needed two helpings of everything to survive. One afternoon at school in the playing field I heard Carl and his friends calling Big Boy bulla. Bulla was a round flat sweet cake; some were big and some small depending on who made them. Big Boy was embarrassed by his new name and ran upstairs to his classroom to hide. Big Girl was laughing so we knew she was the one who introduced the name to the school. Pinky could not let such a juicy piece of gossip pass her and went to ask Big Girl the story behind the name. Big Girl said her brother fell out of a mango tree at home over the weekend, her grandmother shouted from the house to their mother to make a cup of sweet sugar and water quickly and give to Big Boy. He was still on the ground in pain but had time and energy to say and a bulla too. From that day we changed his name to Bulla and he swore he was going to kill his sister for exposing him.

I used to play with some of the children living in our apartment block. We played on an old train that stood in front of the apartment block as far back as I can remember. Some people said it was haunted by a ghost so we did not venture too far inside. A new family moved on the third floor, there was a mother, two daughters and a son who was the youngest. The eldest daughter, Sonia, organised a group of us younger girls into an entertainment group. She arranged concerts and organised us to perform in our apartment block for our families, friends and neighbours. There I lived out my fantasies. I danced in a group and some of us recited poems and sang. I enjoyed my new friends but the friendship did not last very long. I was off school one day because Prim did not have any money. My mother had gone out somewhere and Carl went off to play with his friends. Moses had moved in with his girlfriend so he was not around very often. Sonia's brother was off school as well but his mother was at work and his sisters were not home. He and I got into a fight and our neighbour who lived next door held onto him trying to separate us and while she was holding him I got the better of him. I scratched him in the face with my nails before we were finally pulled apart. Prim was away for the entire day and Carl and I were left without food. I saw one of my aunts and two of her friends sitting on the ground a block away from where I was and I went up to them. One of the two women she was with was the girlfriend of one of my uncles, her name was Meg. They heard about me fighting and asked me what happened and as I was telling them they were laughing.

In the evening when Sonia's mother came home we saw her as she walked into the apartment to go up to where she lived. Within five minutes of her going in she reappeared and was coming straight at us shouting expletives as she hurried towards us. Meg told me if she asked me if I was the one who beat her son I should say yes, so I was waiting for her. She shouted in my face, 'a yu beat up mi son so'. Just the words I was waiting for so I shouted, 'yes', back at her. She was almost up in my face when Meg intervened and they started fighting. Everyone ran out of their homes to be entertained by the fight. They got so much gratification seeing the fight, they would not have it any other way. After the fight everyone who lived on the fourth floor refused to speak to me, even those who had known me before the new family arrived. I was rude to an adult and for that I was wrong but what the hell was that woman doing coming up in my face. She did not even bother to wait for Prim to get home to sort it out with her. I had Pinky and Melanie so I did not need those friends anyway.

In 1972 there was a general election to be held and the young Michael Joshua Manley had taken over the leadership from his father. He was to rival Hugh Shearer for the hot seat of Jamaica's premiere. The younger Manley was handsome, charismatic, classy and had an aura about him. He was someone who everyone wanted to know and was particularly popular with the younger generation. The Jamaica Labour Party was getting stale with their free corn meal and flour. The people wanted something new and longer lasting. So far both the PNP and JLP only over-promised but under-performed. The younger Manley had new ideas and looked genuine while his rivals were only giving lip service about their love for black people. Michael talked the talk and walked the walk when he married his black lover Beverley Anderson, a television personality. You do not get closer than that! The other white and mixed race leaders were happy to have black lovers but not black wives, that line they did not cross.

The PNP's popularity was growing mainly because of Michael Joshua and the JLP were getting nervous. One JLP MP called Manley's young supporters 'a generation of vipers' due to their open support for Joshua's PNP but with all the cheap talk, corn meal and flour there was no stopping the new Prime Minister to be.

You could not help getting caught up in the frenzy of politics in Trench Town. The first time I saw Joshua's picture on our neighbour's television I was smitten. It was love at first sight. I knew Prim was going to vote for the JLP but was silently hoping Joshua would win. I followed Prim to the polling station to cast her vote. A picture of Michael and his wife was on display as was Hugh Shearer but no one defaced any of the pictures; those were the good old days. Even the JLP faithfuls ignored Shearer's picture to get a good look at Mr wonderful himself (Michael). I heard Prim openly admiring the photograph. After the votes were counted on election day, Hugh Shearer threw in the towel and Michael Joshua addressed the nation for the first time as Prime Minister elect and he also became MP for Central Kingston.

JLP supporters blamed Shearer for their loss and showed their contempt by using pins and needles to pierce his two eyes on the souvenirs photos and posters. PNP supporters danced in the streets and taunted their political rivals. Some idiots took it very personally and started throwing stones at each other. Seaga's loyal supporters in Tivoli were not happy but had to keep calm as the PNP were becoming powerful. Political fever was also spreading outside Trench Town as Jamaica Broadcasting Corporation (JBC) was reporting politically related violence across the capital. One name that was popping up frequently was that of Bunny Boy, a PNP supporter.

Michael thought he joined the political arena to make change but he had a job on his hands and the JLP was only too ready to make his work so much harder. As he was to find out the hard way. Michael was speaking at a PNP rally when JLP gunmen came and opened fire in the crowd and also aimed at Michael. It was the infamous Bunny Boy who shielded and defended him that day. Bunny Boy was always in trouble with the law but managed to get out of trouble. There were strong rumours that he was on Joshua's payroll. The Prime Minister did himself no favour by attending Bunny Boy, the gunslinger's funeral when he died. Michael was treading dangerous water. A good man was being sucked into corruption.

Christmas was fast approaching and Prim had her hands on her cheeks wondering where she was going to get money for Christmas dinner and clothes for us. My grandmother had a stall in downtown Kingston selling toys. One of my aunts bought me a doll and it became my pride and joy. It was a white doll because at the time there were not many black dolls on the market and I had never seen one in all my tiny life. Prim sent us to our fathers again, Carl's father gave him five dollars and Tom told me to come the next day, he was in a good mood and laughing so I was optimistic. He also told me he was going to St Mary to see his father. It was the first time I knew that he had a family because he never talked about them to me before. He then told me that his mother was living in America. It appeared from the way he talked he was from a good family so how did he turn out like that and how did he find his way in Trench Town a place where he had no ties. From the way he described his family I said to myself that they would never accept me, the child of their black sheep and a woman who had children by several men and hailed from Trench Town, as our community never had a good reputation. Of all the children Prim had, I was the only one with relatives from outside Trench Town for the other children's fathers were also from her community. I did not like Tom but I was intrigued with what he told me about his mother and father and I got a sense of pride knowing that I had roots somewhere else.

I went the next day to see Tom. Prim did not have to remind me, I even went alone without Carl towing behind me. When I arrived at his house he had two girls there, one about my age and an older one. He introduced them as my sisters but I did not like them because I had already bonded with Carl and Christopher and did not want any more siblings. I saw a smile on Tom's face as if to say these girls were your true siblings and I gave him a look of death behind his back. Just who he thought he was, trying to turn my emotions on and off as if I was mechanical. He did not know I was a real person with emotions and well advanced for my age. I too could play the game for I was not interested in him or his daughters. I made peace with Sue whom I was at least tolerating. All I wanted to do was to meet my grandmother and grandfather and get the money he promised me. When Tom gave me ten dollars I almost fell over in shock but could not let him see my reaction. The funny thing was he had a girlfriend who I took an instant liking to. When I saw her and Prim squaring off in the middle of Collysmith Drive one evening, I knew Prim was not exactly the innocent party in that argument.

When I took the ten dollars to Prim it was the talk of Trench Town for many days. Prim and I told everybody who knew how stingy Tom was. Some people did not believe us until Prim showed them the money. Carl never felt bad about me getting more money than he did because he too was amused and shocked. We laughed and cried many times because of our fathers, but this time we laughed even harder especially when I told him how one of Tom's daughter's gave me five cents and cried to have it back. Because I was so dramatic he thought I was exaggerating never the less he was laughing his head off. How many times Carl and I shared our money yet Tom introduced me to his daughters and wanted them to take Carl's place in my heart, but one of them could not even give me five cents with a good heart. Tom was so embarrassed he told me to keep the five cents and said that he would reimburse her. I told Carl what Tom was up to but he said I was making things up but I knew Tom wanted me to hate Carl and Prim but I did not understand why. Tom was calculating and I could see him coming from a mile away but I had my plans for I was indeed his child. Prim was not a schemer and neither was Carl.

On Christmas day I went to the market with Prim and most members of the Smith clan were there helping Lily sell her wares. I was dressed in red shorts, a red and white top and was looking very good if I may say so myself. Pinky who was not far behind joined up with me and we left our parents sides and went off together while Carl went with some boys from our area to do their own thing.

Pinky and I had eyes for a set of dolly plates but did not have any money so we thought we could take it courtesy of stealing. The stall owner must have seen the word thief marked on our foreheads because she never let us out of her sight. Pinky became mad with the woman for looking at us and asked her, 'wi look like tief to yu lady, mek yu a watch wi so'. Well, the lady was not put off by Pinky's bluff and must have been used to barefaced prospective thieves like us. She took out a knife and told us if we ever touch her goods she would chop off our ten fingers. That was enough deterrent for us so we quickly moved on. We heard her laughing and calling us ginnals behind us. Not long after I heard a familiar voice calling, 'tiefing Patsy, tiefing Pinky' I did not need to look around to know that it was Melanie. The name suited us that day for we were on the look out for any dolly plates that were laying careless but could not find any. Melanie came over to us in a short dress much too young for her and shoes which looked like they was two sizes smaller than her feet. Melanie said it was blinding her but she did not have anything else to wear. Her aunt in England sent clothes for her whole family every Christmas but as usual they were too small. Her aunt was still remembering her as the little child she left in Jamaica.

Pinky and I laughed at Melanie who kept complaining about the tight shoes but it was getting beyond a joke, because Melanie could not keep up with us and stopped walking all together. She looked embarrassed by her ordeal. Some boys visiting the Christmas market looked at Melanie and started laughing, Pinky told them to kiss Melanie's arse and all three of us told them about their mothers. Then to take the shame off Melanie, Pinky and I took off our shoes and walked around the market barefoot with Melanie and the look on her face told me how grateful she was. We came upon a sound system playing in the park, and put down some barefoot dancing and drew a crowd. All three of us were good dancers, at least that was what we thought and no one could convince us otherwise. At that time it was all about Jimmy Cliff for me, when I heard his song 'Wonderful World, Beautiful People' I got down to the ground with Pinky and Melanie jumping and prancing all over the place. Everyone around us was in a festive mood; no gunshots were heard just fun everywhere. All through the day at the market I kept thinking about the rice and peas and chicken Prim had prepared for our Christmas meal. Our festive drink would be Flavoraid Cool Aid but to me it was what champagne is to the rich. I liked Christmas and Prim always made sure we had a nice dinner then even if it meant fasting on Christmas Eve.

On our way back to Lily's stall we came upon the woman who promised to butcher Pinky and me. She called us over and gave us one plate and cup each. Before we left she reminded us that what we picked up was what she put down so we should not even try that with her again . I enjoyed my day at the market with my friends so I was rather sad when Prim announced that she was ready to leave and as usual we had to look for Carl who was nowhere in sight. When we found him he was not ready but Prim bullied us into going home so I said my goodbyes to my friends and left. I knew I would see Pinky later in the evening because she did not live far from me but Melanie lived in Jungle so we would have to wait until school reopened in January to see her.

I went to see Tom again and spent the night with him and his girlfriend. He was living in one room of a board house. The family who occupied the house consisted of a grandmother, grandfather, mother and three young daughters - Megan, Sally and Plum whom I became close to. I bonded with them as if we were sisters more than I could my own half-sisters.

When school reopened for the new term after Christmas Pinky and I waited for Melanie to join us. She was coming from Jungle so we had to give her time to get down. Big Girl and her brothers passed us (they also lived in Jungle) they greeted us and told us Melanie was not far behind. That was good news to us as time was going and it would not look too good if we were late for class on the first day of the new term and once you start getting beating at the beginning of the year it continued for the rest of it. Melanie greeted us with enthusiasm and wanted to know what we had been up to over the last two weeks.

When we arrived at school Pinky went to her class and Melanie and I went to ours. Melanie asked me what was wrong with Pinky, I told her nothing because I did not notice anything out of the ordinary.

During the lunch break Melanie's suspicion was confirmed when Pinky told us that she was moving to the parish of St Elizabeth with her family. She said her mother was sick with cancer and that she and her siblings were to be cared for by their grandparents. At that time I did not know what was in store for my friend because I did not know that cancer was a terminal illness, even though Pepe died of it. As soon as Pinky told us the unfortunate news she disappeared out of our lives forever. She and her family moved the same weekend and we never laid eyes on her again.

One weekend Carl and I went to our fathers for money it was a disappointment for both of us as neither of us got anything, but we went to see Christopher before going home. On the way we passed two women who were arguing over their lover. They were both seeing the same man and were fighting each other in the streets over him. We went in the direction of the argument to see if we could get a good view of the excitement. We went down to the gully banking with Christopher following behind us. Carl went in front and held my hand and I held Christopher's hand to prevent him from falling. He kept laughing for no apparent reason and jumping at the same time, the three of us almost ended up in the gully on Collysmith Drive. Carl shouted at me to stop the fidgeting but it was Christopher who was causing the problem. He stopped laughing when our journey on the gully bank started to look perilous. That day for the first time I felt a sense of bonding that no power on earth could break, as it turned out it was the last time the three of us would be together again.

It was a Saturday morning the day after we visited Christopher when destiny decided to pay me a visit. I was playing in bed with Sue and she fell to the floor. Her father who was in the room sleeping heard her cry and without asking what happened got out of bed and hit me on the head. I ran out of the house and made my way to Tom's house praying by some miracle that this selfish man I had for a father would suddenly take me in so I would not have to return to Prim and her man. I liked Tom's girlfriend and she always treated me kindly so I thought things could only get better. When I got to Tom's house early that morning I did not have the nerve to ask him to put me up so I chickened out and told him Prim sent me for money. He shouted at me as he always did but this time I stood my grounds until he spoke the magic words, 'go get yu clothes an come back'.

I went down to Rema to Prim and told her I had come for my clothes and to my surprise she did not scold me or try to stop me, she just packed the few little items I had and sent me on my journey without a hug or kiss. I did not know she wanted to get rid of me so badly. Everything was moving in slow motion I did not remember seeing Carl around and if he was there he kept out of the way so no goodbyes were said. I packed the doll my aunt gave me for Christmas to take with me but she saw me leaving with it and took it back. I cried so hard, how could she be so cruel to me? I turned around to look at Prim but she spoke no words so I turned around and went in the direction of Jungle where Tom lived. If I thought life with Prim's man was unbearable then I had something to learn with Tom.

I went to school the Monday after I left Prim's home. Melanie and I met up earlier as we were living closer to each other. Before I left home in the morning, Tom gave me fifty cents and told me if Carl asked me for money I should not give him any. He also warned me that I should not stop at my mother's or speak to her. My suspicion about Tom hating Carl and Prim was then confirmed. I met Carl on the way to school and he looked distressed and unhappy. He probably did not have any breakfast, as this was a regular occurrence in Prim's home. He called me over to where he was and asked me for ten cents I was reluctant to speak to him and decided to lie by telling him that I did not have any money. He knew I was lying but did not argue with me but held his head down and walked away.

At lunch break Melanie went home for lunch and I bought my lunch and went behind the school building to eat it out of sight. Carl must have seen me and followed behind because as soon as I was about to eat he appeared in front of me. The look on his face was one of betrayal, he did not speak nor did I; he then turned around and left. I lost my appetite and threw away the food but it was too late Carl was gone. That look on his face was to haunt me for the rest of my life. The relationship between us was strained thereafter and we barely spoke to each other.

Melanie and I were playing with some friends on our way from school one evening and because of this I arrived home late and I met Tom at the gate fuming. He asked me if I stopped at Prim, I told him no but he insisted that I did and gave me the beating of my life. He hit me with a piece of stick and when I fell on the ground he used his feet on me, I thought he was going to kill me. What did I do wrong? I did not stop at Prim and what if I had she gave birth to me, where was this man for six years of my life when I needed a father. Some people tried to stop him but due to his ranting and raving they left me to die. He kicked me in my head, abdomen, back and chest. After he finished with me his girlfriend took me out on the street and was cursing. She said she was taking me to the police station but changed her mind.

The next day after school I stopped at Prim and told her that I did not want to go back to Tom because I was frightened for my life. I thought he would end up killing me but when he came for me she opened the door and let him take me. I did not know what to do but to go with him. I could not believe my mother was not even concerned about what was going to happen to me. I was beaten in my head my stomach everywhere. After school every evening I had to run home in case I did not get home on time and had to face the wrath of Tom. I was unlucky another day and got another beating with a piece of rubber tire I was turning eight years old. I went to the Denham Town Police Station the next day to show them the bruises on my body. I wanted somewhere safe to go but the police asked me who hit me and when I told them it was my father they told me to go home. The teachers at school saw the bruises on my skin but they too turned a blind eye. I had nowhere to run and nowhere to hide. I was let down by my mother, my school, the police and my community- the entire system let me down and I had no choice but to suffer in silence. If I was beaten in the streets by a stranger the way I was beaten by Tom, people would be asking for the death penalty, but a deranged man was allowed to get away with criminality, because he carried a sacred title of a father that he did not deserve in the first place.

As a child I had no rights under the law my parents could harm me in any way and get away with it. A child was beaten to death in our community by his mother and without an inquiry the whole thing was dealt with as an accident. The police were not bothered as they thought no mother intended to kill her own child. The mother might not have had murder on her mind when she was beating her child, but the cruel way in which she was doing it caused her son to die. I spent most of the time making sure I did not do anything to upset Tom, but that was a tall order for anybody more so the young child I was. Everything and anything upset him, it could be the way I spoke or walked. I wanted out of my torment but had nowhere to go and no one to turn to. I cried night and day and prayed for deliverance. I was crying one evening outside my gate when our Rasta neighbour who lived opposite our house came over to me. He told me nothing last forever you are coming and your father is going things will get better. He asked me what do you want to be when you grow up? I told him I wanted to be a movie star I liked the fame and glamour of Hollywood that I saw on television but my future was looking hopeless at that moment. My neighbour asked me what month I was born, when I told him my birthday he said, 'yu're born leader, yu a go be strong and wise'. I thought to myself how could I be all those things he said when I was so helpless now.

Only one person could help me but he was in his grave. I felt alone and frightened and I wanted my grandfather to protect me but he was dead. If the dead could see my Pepe would have been rolling in his grave at the suffering his Patsy was going through. When I was a baby he found me crying alone in a dark house with only a kerosene lamp burning for company and he rescued me but since his death I had to face all my tribulations on my own. I prayed earnestly for deliverance but it was not coming too soon. Sometimes I felt like going to join Pepe and end my misery. Many evenings I was too frightened to go home and my only support was Melanie who did not ask any questions but she knew something was not right as I became withdrawn. She was satisfied just sitting with me and I appreciated the silent support. In a way Melanie was like that sometimes, but I was too caught up in myself to realise what was happening to her but she spotted my distress as soon as it started, as it was familiar territory to her. I lost my sparkle thereafter.

Tom got into a fight with a man he had an argument with on the street. The man must have been too much to handle and Tom's friends were not around to help him so he came home in a hurry. He was not one to give up easily but knew he could not go and get his friends to tackle one man because they would see him as a saps (which means a weakling). So Tom's pride would not allow him to seek help from his friends. He did the most unthinkable thing instead. I saw him entering the yard huffing and puffing. He took a knife from our kitchen and then ordered me to follow him. I was on my way out of the gate with him when we saw Sally playing with some neighbours' children and he told her to follow us. He told us that he was going to find a man to fight and that Sally and I should hit the man in his head if the man overpowered him and pinned him to the ground. I had no doubt that Sally was going to hit the man on his head, but I was not too sure about me. I was thinking what if the man proved too strong for the one and three quarter people, for Sally and me could not add up to one. I also did not really want to help Tom. How he could have asked two young children to help him fight a grown man was beyond me? I knew one thing for sure, if I did not help Tom and the man worked him over properly, I would have to run away. I had no choice but to defend Tom and that meant hitting the man as hard as I could, so that he could not get up to attack Sally and me. Tom even chose the stones we should use and made sure we could manage our weapons. When we got to the place the man was supposed to be he was nowhere to be seen. I saw it as God smiling on me and thanked him quietly but rather than giving up, Tom had the nerve to ask people if they had seen the man that day. The people said no so we went home.

Tom's girlfriend, Mel who was sixteen-years-old did not escape the battering from him either and he would beat her severely. I felt sorry for her but I could not help myself much more help her. Her parents did not approve of their relationship due to his reputation but like many young women in Trench Town, Tom's lawless attributes appealed to Mel. A soldier liked her and wanted to marry her but he was not dangerous enough for her. Whenever Tom beat her and she moved out it would not be long before she returned which baffled me, because there I was looking for somewhere to hide from the beatings and she was returning to it voluntarily. Any man who could use his feet on his own eight-year-old daughter could not be any good and did not deserve a second chance but maybe she saw something I did not.

Sometimes I stopped and talked to Prim without a care because I still got a beating whether I did or not. Why I bothered to cling to Prim when she turned me over to Tom when he came for me I did not know maybe I just wanted one of my parents to like me. One evening when I got home from school, Tom told me that he would be taking me to St Mary to stay with his father. The PNP was rebuilding Jungle and the house we lived in was going to be demolished. People were busy finding alternative housing, as the old board houses were soon to be history. I took the news with mixed feeling because I knew I would not be seeing Carl, Prim and Melanie again, but was glad to get away from Tom. I went away the same weekend without saying goodbye to my family and friends, I did not see Christopher either who was living only a few yards from me. When Gramps and his sisters saw that we stopped visiting Christopher they spoke about me and Carl to him regularly to remind him of the brother and sister he had.

In St Mary I was taken away from the distractions of Trench Town so I was more focused on my work at school and so I learnt to read and spell quite well. I was given special attention by my teacher Miss Stevenson who was an expert at teaching. She found out that I had learning difficulties and tried to help me. Reading made sense for the first time in my life even though I was not doing very badly before. My grandfather was the kindest person I ever came across so I had to wonder who Tom got his characteristics from. Pepe had a selfish kind of love but my new grandfather was a people's person. After Tom dropped me off there he only visited once, due to a complaint made to him about me and he came to warn me off. He did not contribute to my keep and the few items of clothing I had were getting worn. My grandfather was a poor farmer who could not afford to buy new things for me. I ended up going to school without shoes on my feet. I was neglected beyond belief and this could never have happened while Pepe was alive.

My hair was cut off because my grandfather's wife, who was a devoted Christian, said she could not manage to comb it. She was angry that I was left on them without any financial support. She always quoted the scriptures and told me that God said those who did not work should not eat either. I believed I was a wicked person. I was always tatty and the neighbours' children said I was ugly. My hair was cut so short they called me picky-picky head. I knew my natural length hair was longer than all of them put together but I had to be contented playing black Cinderella. It was clear for all to see that I was needy but with no one to help people used to ask me why my aunts and cousins were so neat and tidy and I was so shabby.

We walked about two miles to school in the mornings and back home. My young aunts and I had a long day because we got up at six in the morning left home at seven to get to school for eight-thirty. We walked back home from school and waited until Papa's wife got home from work to start dinner at six in the evening. We had lunch at twelve mid-day and dinner was usually at night. The time between lunch and dinner was too long so Papa's wife used to take food from work for her children so they would have a snack before dinner but she said that I had to wait until the meal my grandfather provided was ready. They ate in front of me and I waited for dinner to be prepared. I was told that I was lazy so I felt guilty and believed that I deserved to stay hungry until I was fed. I was also a beating stick for anyone who felt the urge to hit me.

When I was staying with Prim I was used to the Smith clan arguing amongst themselves constantly but what I was not use to was being a part of the feud. I was used to having a close extended family, however dysfunctional they were, they all looked out for me when they saw me on the streets. Taken out of that environment where family members were not as supportive was a culture shock and very disturbing. I was left to sort out my own problems and it was like I was thrown to the wolves. I was not an angel but being beaten for things others got a smile for was not very nice. Tom's mother visited Jamaica whilst I was living in the country. She came to see Papa and the first time we met we fell in love there and then. I knew it in my bones she was going to be my saviour. She was to take the place of Pepe. She too had a selfish kind of love and was not the giving person Papa was but I knew she would give to me. She was short and plump with dark skinned. She walked out of a dead end relationship with Papa who she had four sons by and went abroad to make a better life for herself. She wanted Papa to go abroad on farm work but he said that he would not leave his home. She was surprised about this given that they always lived on other people's property. She told him that he had no ambition and that hurt his ego. Papa was a poor simple man who was satisfied with very little and saw it as a blessing and that's okay for me. I loved him for who he was.

Grandma was possessive, aggressive, ambitious and self-assured. When she wanted something she went after it. She was the perfect specimen of a strong woman, she was to become my rock. Seeing her at work in another family one could easily dismiss her as hard and cold but as my grandmother she would stand by me until the last breath left her body. Single-handedly she worked abroad and made a comfortable life for herself, and was always there to offer help to her children. All that she achieved she did so without a man by her side. She made some new dresses for me,

I did not tell her what I was going through but I think she figured it out for herself. When she was preparing to leave I started to cry and told her that I wanted to go home. My grandfather's wife took offence to my plea but Papa did not condemn me so I believe he understood.

Chapter Four

I returned to Kingston in 1975, Tom was living in Rose Town a neighbouring community of Trench Town. He was renting a room of a house and his brother occupied the rest of it with his family. Tom was at work when Papa's wife took me to his home. I was left with his girlfriend until he returned home in the evening. It was apparent by his comment that he did not know that I was coming and was not happy to see me. He did not want the responsibility of taking care of another person, I was nothing but dead weight that he was trying to unload. How could he expect an elderly man like his father, who was well in his seventies to take on such a responsibility for the rest of his life? Tom only cared for Tom. I met some of my cousins for the first time and shared a room with them. I became close to the two older girls who were also living with their father and stepmother. The older daughter was not happy so at last I found someone who understood how I felt.

Tom made it clear that he did not want me to visit or speak to my mother. He was still on about that when he was a poor excuse for a father. Every day I thought about Carl, Christopher and Prim. I could not ask anyone about them it was mental torture. I visualised them many times being hungry and this used to turn me off my food. Mel, Tom's girlfriend, was kind to me most of the time but I did not like her making comments about Prim. One thing I made very clear to them was that even if they beat me to death I had one mother and no one could take her place no matter what happened in the past. Tom could sense this even though I did not speak the words for my action spoke louder than my words. He even went as far as telling me one day that Prim did not like me but I knew that this was his way of turning my mind against her.

Mel enrolled me in Trench Town Primary School, which was only ten minutes walk away from our home. Tom was too stingy to buy a pair of shoes for me so he told Mel to get me a cheap pair of sneakers that cost about five dollars. I was one of the few students in this footwear as the school had a dress code and my shoes surely did not match my uniform. I was embarrassed about this but had no choice but to wear them. The school principal was Mr Cole, my old dean from Denham Town and I was so happy to see a familiar face. To my surprise he remembered me and asked where I had been and welcomed me to Trench Town.

There was a comprehensive high school virtually on the other side of our school compound. There was a mere fence separating the two schools and the gate was left open most of the time so children from both school would venture freely to and from each school. The problem was the high school was situated in Jungle and the primary school in Rose Town bordering Rema. A lot of students in my class had older relatives attending the high school. Children from the primary division would have automatic right to go on to the high school but some chose to attend other institutions for personal reasons. The main entrance to the primary school was on Seventh Street and the entrance to the comprehensive high was on Eighth Street. The schools have been serving the community for many decades and have educated many students in and outside the community. Children from Rema, Jungle, downtown Kingston, Maxfield Avenue and all over Kingston would sit together in class and play outside in the playing field. When school finished for a day children could be seen taking all routes to their different communities. Children from both schools walked through each other schools to get home and it was a beauty to witness.

I followed Mel one day to visit her mother in Jungle and nothing had prepared me for what I saw. The area was completely transformed and cleaned. No more piled up garbage on the streets and the people were making the effort to keep their surroundings clean. I met up with Sally, Megan and Plum who I was happy to see. I hailed them up and went on my way. The people in Jungle were living in small apartments built by politicians and they were very proud. I knew something was not right because there was no one walking from Jungle to Rema and there were no signs of any JOS bus in the area. I asked Mel why that was and she said they closed the border on Seventh Street due to drive by shootings by both sides. Rema was now segregated from Jungle and became a JLP stronghold while Jungle became a PNP stronghold. The bus company stopped operating in the community to protect their staff. I knew then it was going to be very difficult for me to make any contact with Prim and Carl and I did not know where to find Christopher and Lily who were living in Jungle before I went to St Mary.

The years we spent apart did not mellow Tom one bit in fact he became worse. He beat me for every and anything, sometimes he just took out his anger on me because I was an easy target. I learnt how to numb my feelings and put on a bright face at school. I developed two characters, one for home and the other for school. He did not buy any clothes for me and I was not allowed to go anywhere except school. The only other place I went was Jungle when I followed Mel to visit her relatives. He did not encourage me to visit Sally and her sisters even though we used to live with them.

One morning I was on my way to school with two other students and nothing in Trench Town had prepared me for what we came upon in the entrance of a lane off Seventh Street. There was a naked body of a woman with her legs wide apart, they looked as if they had been broken. By the way the body looked distressed, it appeared that she was raped and killed by more than one person. We were grown to be mentally tough but I was slightly shaken, as this was the first time I had seen a dead body on the street. I went up to get a closer view of the body and saw she had scratches on her face and neck so I assumed she was fighting for her life before she died. We went to school and told some other students about what we saw but the teachers did not talk much about the incident. Someone must have seen or heard something but no one came forward to give the police any information.

This was a very dangerous territory that we were entering. By staying silent we were allowing the killer or possible killers to get away with murder and we were also giving them a licence to kill again. On our way back home that evening the body was not there as it had been taken away by the police.

Rose Town had some well to do residents who were getting nervous because of the murder. There were some lovely houses around there but the problem was the area was too close to Trench Town and the violence was spilling over to us. Young men from Rema were coming over and some youths from our area were joining up with them and robbing people. The Chinese residents were the main target and they started moving out en masse. Dead bodies were cropping up all over the place especially in empty lots. They would be killed somewhere else and dumped there for collection. People continued to stay silent and the police were not interested. Some of the murders did not even make the news as lives were becoming cheap. It was not long ago black people were fighting against the killings of their own people by colonial masters but now they were killing each other. When a white man killed a black Jamaican the young and the old cried out but when a black person killed another black person there is a wall of silence. The message this sent was that it was all right for black people to kill each other.

There was a young man in the area called 'Johnny Too Bad' by his friends who was going around breaking into people's houses and shops. Young girls were afraid of him because he was known to have raped girls travelling alone. I met him on the streets and witnessed him bullying women but had no dealings with him. The police were after him but he always escaped their clutches. Johnny and his friends raped a sixteen- year old girl and beat her so badly she spent several days in hospital. The news of the rape spread like wildfire in the community but no-one took any action. Johnny went about his business as usual with no shame or care in the world as he was untouchable. He knew he could do anything and get protection from our silence. The police were becoming frustrated by the wall of silence they were coming upon so they knew it made no sense arresting Johnny only for him to beat the case and walk the streets again. The only way to stop him would be to kill him on sight.

Johnny lived in a tenement yard on Seventh Street. His family of six shared a one room in a five-bedroom house that had five different families living in it. Johnny was the only son in the family. He had three sisters aged fifteen, twelve and nine. The mother was cohabiting with a man who was the father of the youngest daughter. The other residents in the yard suspected that Johnny and his stepfather were molesting the three girls but only gossiped about their suspicion. The stepfather was overprotective of the two older girls and they were not allowed to speak to boys. The big surprise came when the nine year old was admitted in hospital suffering from gonorrhoea. We only found out because the mother was afraid that the child was going to die as she was crying and passing out frequently. The child had a high temperature so her mother thought it was dengue fever and asked one of her neighbours to accompany her to hospital. The doctors were concerned about the odour coming from the child and tested her for a sexual transmitted disease. They found that the panties she was wearing were saturated with discharge. When the mother was told that her child had gonorrhoea she was more concerned about what people would say rather than the safety of her child. She begged her neighbour not to disclose what they were told by the doctor but it was passed around to us in Chinese whispers. The mother did not leave her man and Johnny continued to live with them. We did not know for sure who abused the child and the family members were tight-lipped about the whole thing. Whether the abuse stopped or not no one knew, no one cared and no one did anything.

A police officer who knew Johnny well was patrolling the area in a car one evening and saw him leaving a bar. The officer opened fire in a crowd of people but everyone escaped unhurt except the target. Johnny's dead body laid in the streets for all to see. His mother heard the noise and came out to see what the commotion was about. When she saw her son's lifeless body on the ground she put her hands on her head and cried out saying that her son was innocently killed by the police. She along with some residents blocked the roads in protest of the killing of 'Johnny Too Bad'. I even heard people saying what a decent young man he was. Black people on a whole have a short memory. How decent could a rapist, thief and child molester be? It was those same people who were told of the terrible ordeal he put the sixteen-year-old girl through. The residents had energy to fight police brutality but not terrorism by lawless men. Johnny lived like a dog and died like one.

I went to Jungle with Mel to see her parents and got caught up in a fight between Jungle residents and the security forces. Women, men and children were throwing stones and blocking the roads. Six fat mamas came out with a metal portable fence they acquired from an empty lot and blocked Ninth Street with it. The fence was about six feet in height and seven in width and probably weighed over two tons. The things they were using to block the roads were damaging the surface, which was not a good idea, as it would take another ten years to fix the streets again in Trench Town. This was very far from their minds though; the people were so self-destructive, they did not think beyond the minute they were in. Gunmen came out with submachine guns and were firing shots at the police and soldiers who were sent in to restore peace. The police let off tear gas, Mel and I ran into a woman's front garden to hide. My eyes burnt as if pepper was in them. Some women including Mel were telling me to stop rubbing them but I wanted them to stop hurting. One lady washed my eyes and face with cold water until the burning stopped.

I heard people in Jungle saying the police were fighting against them because they were fighting with Rema men on the border of Seventh Street. They were accusing the members of the security forces of being JLP supporters. For over two days the gunmen traded shot for shot with the police and soldiers. The security forces came in to calm down both sides but Jungle men must have had a lot of gunshots to spare, because they turned on the police and soldiers like wild beasts. Gunshot barked! Ninth Street was where most of the action was so innocent people were staying well clear of there. While Rema and Jungle became political foes, Tivoli men were kept busy by the Spanglers posse at Matthews Lane. The Spanglers did not have a big community like Jungle, Rema or Tivoli but they could hold their own against any of them. Spanglers were PNP supporters therefore they were allies of Jungle men.

Mel was a PNP supporter and was blaming the labourites (as they called JLP supporters) for the violence between the police and her comrades. The Wild Bunch posse from Jungle was in full swing and Rema Thirteen was ruling the roost in Rema. Some of the young men in the area were using their position to abuse young girls who were too afraid to report them to the police. Some were the scum of the earth who went around enticing the young poor schoolgirls with money and others were serial rapists. The self appointed area leaders in the communities were the ones who should have been upholding the integrity of their areas but many of them were rapists and child molesters themselves, some were friends with the rapists and they only disciplined weaklings who could not defend themselves.

The war between the Jungle men and the police caused our school to close for several days. Children who lived in Trench Town, but attended schools outside the area were afraid to leave their homes, because they did not want to be hit by a stray bullet. The war only stopped when the gunmen ran out of ammunition. The guns they were using were more sophisticated than those of the police and soldiers. The US declared war on the ganja trade, Air Jamaica (the national airline), and Jamaica's nationals were targeted as potential drugs couriers whenever travelling to the United States, but more than half the guns on the streets of Kingston came from the United States, how did they get there?.

One night I was fast asleep in bed when I heard Tom shouting at the top of his voice at someone. I thought I was dreaming until the yelling woke me. I heard the front gate outside rattling - I stayed in bed but was listening intently in case I needed to find a hiding place. Tom was talking loudly about seeing two young men coming through the gate who wanted to rob our house. I did not want to be killed at ten-years-old so I was looking even harder for a good hiding spot. Under the bed was not original and I knew my cousins had eyes on those places already, but I was always thinking of outsmarting the enemy and under the bed would be the first place they would look. I could not locate a good hiding place so it looked as if under the bed would have to do. If I got under first then the others would be hiding me. Tom wanted to outsmart the men before they get into our house to rob us. He did not know if they were armed with guns and if there were others hiding. Tom shouted loudly, 'hey uno bway mi know uno and mi know wey uno live. If uno try anyting, mi a go find uno tomorrow'. They took the bait and left, God heard my humble prayer. I could not wait for day light to come in case they were waiting for us to go to sleep and then try again, but they believed Tom really knew where they lived and thank God for that.

Dead bodies were cropping up more than I cared to see so when Mel and I came upon a crowd in an empty lot viewing another body for collection I was not surprised. Some people were even laughing over the body. The familiarity of death was hardening the meekest of us. One man said, 'mi sorry a him but mi glad a no mi'. Many people who were viewing the body knew who the victim was but as usual they did nothing. The gunmen were getting powerful. With our silence they knew they could do anything and no one would say anything to the police. Many people did not trust the police either, because some of them had friends who were gunmen. There was a time when young men wanted to be policemen but then it became cops who wanted to be illegal gunmen. Some openly supported their outlaw pals and were proud to be friends with area leaders. Those cops who were law abiding, had a hard job maintaining law and order due to interfering politicians and corrupt police officers who would give the gunmen inside information, so they were always one step ahead of the cops. Some gunmen knew when the police were going to make a raid in their area and some of the guns taken away in raids would soon find their way back onto the streets.

One Jungle area leader was killed on Collysmith Drive while riding his motorbike. The killers were said to have fired shots from a white car and drove in the direction of Rema. The dead man's friends and fellow residents blamed the brutal killing on Rema men and blocked the roads in protest. Jungle gunmen were planning revenge on their political rivals, some even fired shots in the direction of Rema, but with all the road blocking that was going on the killers could not be kept out, because they were right there helping to block the streets. The murdered man was killed by his own friends in a power struggle. His greedy best friend did not want to share the building contracts they were promised by their politician boss. The housing contract was given to them by the new MP for the community. The top dogs who controlled the money did no work except bossing the workers around, but pocketed most of the funds. They built tiny one and two bedroom houses and apartments. A family of ten would have no choice but to live in them.

Many young men spent more time on the streets with their friends during the day, as a means of reducing the overcrowding and would visit their homes for their meals, if there were any and to sleep which was a drama in itself. Teenage brothers and sisters shared the same room and in some case the same bed. One family would have up to four people sleeping in the same bed. No one spoke out against this as this was normal in Trench Town from the times when they lived in the board houses. People were grateful to the politicians for taking them out of the board shacks so why complain.

Jungle was renamed Arnett Gardens and each housing scheme was given an interesting name. There was Texas, Havana, Brooklyn, Pegasus, Mexico, Angola and Zimbabwe. One kept the old name Jungle in remembrance of the old days. That housing scheme was the first one to be built.

Mel and Tom had another of their many fights, which involved him beating her up so badly she went to stay with her family in Arnett Gardens. I was left with Tom who was also not on speaking terms with his brother.

Rose Town was getting very violent and the people were sitting ducks for both Jungle and Rema men. There were no strong fighters in our community so both sides did whatever they wanted there. Jungle men were not interested in us until they heard that Rema men were visiting regularly. That meant trouble for Jungle men because that could only mean that Rose Town was not far from becoming a JLP stronghold.

The Jungle warlords paid us a visit one day dressed in white shirts and black pants. I wondered why they all had on the same colour clothing; it was as if they were an organised militia group taking orders from a secret service. They were firing shots in the air mostly and a few in front of them. They were not firing at any anyone so it was just a warning to the residents to rethink if they were planning to accommodate Rema men. This instead angered a lot of young men in the area and brought them closer to the other side because they saw the visit by jungle men as disrespectful.

The gunmen started killing indiscriminately to the dismay of politicians, so in 1976 they introduced an anti-crime squad to deal with those criminals who were going too far, but the damage was already done. An illiterate man with a gun was proving to be a lethal combination. The Echo Squad was formed to deal with the criminals but as soon as they eliminated one murderer the politicians armed another one.

The residents of Rose Town did not need any more warning as one was enough so they started moving out en-masse. Some left behind some of the most beautiful houses they had saved up their hard earned cash to buy and then had to leave them because of tribal politics. Many people cried when they were leaving but knew it was the houses or their lives. The young men in the area were glad for their departure so they could sell the zinc roofs and other useful materials for a pittance. Many of them were not even living anywhere decent. One would have thought that they would set themselves up in the houses now they were there for anyone to take, but instead the no-hopers destroyed what they could not get a buck for. They would not know anything good even if it came and slapped them in the face.

I lived on Nathan Street and many people on our street were looking for places to move out of the area, but this was not easy, because they were in competition with people from other war-torn communities. My uncle was also looking for another place to go and I knew if that happened I would be on my own as Tom was never one to do anything until it was too late.

My school was becoming a battlefield for rival political gunmen who had no respect for education, because many of them could not read themselves. What politicians did to us was indescribably wicked. They did not bother to assess those they were arming to keep us in our place, because they wanted power and did not care how they got it or who paid the price. Some of the gunmen were in fact mentally disturbed, some had learning difficulties and a few had serious psychiatric disorders, but politicians did not care, because they and their families did not have to endure the tribulations. We were constantly running home from gunshots. Our school was closed many times because of the disturbances and the gunmen would not think twice to walk into the schools flaunting their guns like trophies. They thought it was all about them and their guns. For many this was power they never dreamt of. People were looking at them for the first time and even if it was not for the right reason they were looking anyway. Some of the young boys in the school thought this type of exhibition was exciting and they too wanted to experience that euphoria that made others quiver in fright. Trench Town School lost its appeal with parents who started removing their children to send them to other schools. A neighbour who sent her daughter to my school transferred her child to another school out of the area and told Tom to do the same. He said he would, but I knew that was just mouth talk. I continued to skip the gunshots and hoped that I would not get shot. On one occasion when we had two full days of gunshots our school had to close. Tom came home and told me that he saw my uncle Moses down on the battlefield defending his territory. I did not care what he was doing I was only too glad to hear about him and that he was seen alive. I started planning how I was going to find my family in Rema.

A lady living at the first house on our street used to sell vegetables and other ground food for a living. She had one daughter and two sons who were well known in the area. One day some soldiers who were patrolling the area looking for gunmen, stopped their Jeep and jumped out on a group of young men talking in the street. Our neighbour was inside her yard selling but could see the main road from where she was. One of her sons was with the group of young men the soldiers were questioning. There were shouting and people started gathering around. Our neighbour's son who was the most outspoken member of the group, was stabbed with the bayonet by one of the soldiers, because they said he had too much to say. The lady saw when her son was stabbed and broke down in tears, the soldiers went back in the jeep and drove away. No one was arrested, no complaint was made against the soldiers and that was the end of the matter. Poor people did not complain, who would listen to them anyway or take them seriously.

Three people from our street moved away and others were seeking to do the same. Tom came to the house one day and asked me to follow him up the road to one of his friends, I knew he wanted me to do him a favour, but what he asked me to do was low even for someone like him who was already touching the ground. He went on a robbery with two of his colleagues in crime, stopped at one of his friends who was involved in the robbery with the money, but was too frightened to take it home even though we were only living ten minutes away. Police and soldiers were patrolling the area on a regular basis, due to the violence and were doing regular stop and search, so he asked me to carry the money from his friend's to our home. I heard one of his friend commenting on how brave I was and him saying yes and laughing, but I was so scared, I just wanted to get home in case a cop stopped me. He and another friend who also took part in the robbery walked behind me to see to it that no one took their money away from me. I hated him with a passion for what he was doing to me. Knowing how cruel Jamaican cops could be, how would I have explained myself to them if one had stopped and searched me? Tom's friend bought a ball for me. He did not even buy me a needle to sew my torn clothes, all I ever got from the money was a little food. From the look on the other friend's face who was left back at his house I knew he did not approve of what Tom did. No way would he have got his ten-year-old daughter involved in something like that.

Tom's brother found a place off Waltham Park Road to live and moved away. Half of the house we lived in was empty and the youths from our community knew this, so they started removing the zinc from the roof of the empty part. It was very frightening to sit indoors listening to them removing parts of our house, while we were still living there. I made friends with a girl by the name of Des, she too had lost friends who moved away so we became close to each other. She had two older sisters. One became pregnant at seventeen. I saw Tom calling her and whispering in her ears in front of me; he was never one to show respect. I did not like it, but it was none of my business and it seemed as if she was well into what he was saying. It might be that one unwanted child was not enough for her.

Des and I would meet up on my front porch when we got home from our schools in the evenings. We played jacks and dandy-shandy with some other children from another street. One strange man was coming in our street frequently and asking for a fourteen-year-old girl who was living at one of the end houses in our street. She was an attractive child and had flesh on her body and this was a turn on for the men who liked young medium size girls. A lot of men were lusting after her and commenting how sexy she was. The strange man came up to my gate one evening and asked if I had seen Kemi, our well sought after neighbour and I told him no which was the truth. I asked him where he came from and he told me Rema, I was glad to hear this, so I asked him if he knew Prim, he said yes and named out my relatives. He told me that Moses' best friend Solomon, was killed by Jungle men and that was the main reason why the border was closed between Jungle and Rema. Everyone had their own version of why the border was closed.

The strange man visited our street again and came up to my gate to ask if Kemi had been seen that day. Des's older sister was plaiting my hair and recognised him from his previous visits. She bravely told him to leave Kemi alone, because she was still in school and not ready for a man. He was so ashamed and angry he picked up a stone and threw it towards us, I was trying to get out of the way when it hit me under my eyelid and the spot swelled instantly. He said sorry many times, but if he was not so big I would have hit him back. I cried all night in pain. Tom saw my face the next day and asked me what happened, but when I told him he blamed me for what had happened. He did not even bother to take me to the hospital. Two days after the incident someone told me that the strange man had been killed by a cop attached to the flying squad. Apparently, he was wanted by the police for a while and was on the run. He would not give himself up, so they killed him on sight.

One day Tom was calling me but I was washing my school uniform around the back yard and did not hear him. He came to see what I was doing and was in such a temper, he used the back of his hand and slapped me in the face, I fell to the ground and then as usual he kicked me while I was down. I screamed out and he told me to shut up. I was so frightened that he would kill me and there would be no witness, I quickly muffled my cry. I managed to get up from the ground and was slowly moving away from him when he picked up an empty jelly coconut and hit me with it. The impact sent me crashing to the ground where I cut my knee on some broken bricks. He did not even look at me to see if I was hurt. I washed my wound in salt water and cared for it until it was better. I seriously contemplated poisoning Tom but could not go through with it. I prayed for deliverance and I knew it would come one day and that he was going to be judged in a higher court for what he was doing to me. To the foundation he must go down.

The shops in Rose Town were closing down daily. The last straw came when a shopkeeper was robbed and killed in cold blood. We had to start travelling to Maxfield Avenue to get milk and bread. There were a few Chinese grocers who were operating there, but were planning their exit as well. Children in school uniform were allowed to walk through Rose Town so all was not lost.

Mel sent one of Tom's friends to call me. She did not come herself, because she was frightened of Rema men and also she did not know how Tom would react if he should see her. She was missing Tom and could no longer wait for him to find her so she decided to make the first move. Tom was preoccupied with his work as a mini bus operator and was always bringing home different women. I went to see Mel, she asked me what was happening and I told her Tom was still the same. She condemned his actions, but was clearly interested in having him back. I spoke to her and went home. When Tom came home I told him that I saw Mel, he did not say much but smiled, because he knew the real reason why she wanted to see me.

On a Saturday afternoon I went to visit Mel but returned home before Tom arrived home, as I did not know how he would react if he knew I was visiting Mel. I was half way home when I saw Tom's van driving in my direction, he jumped out when he saw me and started shouting. I did not run as I knew I did not have anywhere to go, so I decided to go to him as usual for the beating. He was not upset because I went to Mel, but was accusing me of stealing his money, I told him that I did not take his money and somehow he believed me and drove away leaving me to walk home. When I got home, I found out that the man was actually accusing me of stealing over two hundred dollars. I silently wished the thief the best of luck.

One afternoon Des broke the bad news to me that her mother was moving away and they had been to see their new home that day. Des did not like the place where they were going to live, but knew she had no choice but to go with her family. I knew I was going to miss her terribly as she was my only friend. The day Des and her family moved away was like a funeral to me. I watched them drive away in the removal van and I was left on my own. I had no friend to play with, no mother to care for me and no one to protect me from Tom. Only three houses on Nathan Street were occupied; the one Kemi lived in, another one from which the occupiers rarely ventured out and ours.

I did not see Kemi much because she was mostly inside her yard or away visiting her friends. I locked myself indoors reading most of the time, because we did not have a television. Tom came home from work at seven o'clock and on a Friday it would be later. He thought he was doing me a favour coming home that hour and commented that I should be glad, as not many men would be coming home to a child early on a Friday evening. Who did he think he was, leaving me in such an area when everyone was moving out and telling me that I should be honoured that he was coming home early to babysit me? It did not occur to him what he was doing was wrong? What type of man would leave a defenceless child on her own in an area like that for one minute much more five hours?. The hours I went to school were not counted. Weekends were the worst, as I was on my own from morning until night.

One Saturday I decided to go to Mel and stay for the day, because I was too afraid to be on my own. I had planned to return home before Tom got home. On my way to Mel, right at the corner of Trench Town Comprehensive School and Rose Town I saw a young man looking towards me. I recognised him as one of the old rogues in Rose Town who was terrorising people. He did not know who I was, I saw him bend down and picked up a piece of broken bottle, I did not run, but went straight up to him and asked for direction to Maxfield Avenue. He looked me in the eye and pointed to the direction of Maxfield as if he did not really believe me. I do not know if Jungle men had killed his father and raped his mother why he wanted to kill me an eleven-year old child in retaliation. I had to walk the long way round to Maxfield Avenue and then to Jungle.

When I got to Sunlight Street off Maxfield Avenue, I turned there to make my way to Jungle. At the other end of Sunlight Street, I looked down in the direction of Rose Town and saw the same young man standing exactly where I left him. He was looking straight at me so I ran in fright. I was running so hard when I met upon a known gunman in Jungle who stopped me and asked me what had happened why I was running so fast. I told him about the young man who almost sliced me up. He listened for a while and then walked off in the direction of Trench Town School I had no doubt he was going to pay my friend a visit.

I spent the day with Mel and returned home before Tom got home. On my way home I was on the look out for the man I saw earlier with the broken bottle but he was nowhere to be seen. I wondered if the gunman from Jungle found him and executed him, for I never saw him again. I went to Mel everyday without Tom knowing. I went there every weekend, but walked the long way around Maxfield Avenue. When I was tired I took the risk and walked the shorter route.

As more people deserted the area Rose Town was fast becoming a ghost town, even cars and buses stopped running in there. The school children had to walk to Spanish Town Road, Maxfield Avenue or Cross Roads to catch buses to get to their homes. Some children who moved out of the area were still attending Trench Town School and needed to get the bus to their respective homes; the teachers were also vulnerable as the majority of them lived out of the area.

One night I was too afraid to go home so I asked Mel if I could spend the night at her house. She said yes, but was hesitant as she did not know what Tom would say and she was right. The next morning early he came to Mel and called me out into the pathway. He angrily asked me why I did not come home and I told him I was afraid, he had the nerve to ask, afraid of what? It was then I was convinced that Prim got pregnant by a madman. She was so darn carefree something like that was bound to happen to her, but it was me who was paying for her mistake. Mel went out and talked to him, I do not know what was said, but she followed me half way home in the evening. We met one of Tom's friends on our way and he asked me if I was not afraid to travel on my own in such an area and I told him yes. He swore out aloud and asked what type of man would allow his young daughter to go through that type of torment. He said that he was going to tell Tom his mind. He must have done for the next morning Tom told me that I could stay at Mel's, but I would have to visit everyday to feed the dog whom he had watching the house. He could collect the dog's food and feed the dog, but he had to have some power over me. I prayed for the time when this would be no more. Tom thought I was going to be the same forever, because he could not see me beyond that young defenceless child he was abusing.

Mel gave me the dog's dinner everyday to take to Rose Town. The first few days I took it and fed the dog then one day I was on my way there when I saw some people viewing a dead body. I dumped the food in a pile of garbage waiting for collection and went back home. From there on I dumped the food on Maxfield Avenue until one day I bravely walked to my old home on Nathan Street and gave the dog the food. The sight of the dog frightened me as he had been reduced to skin and bones. It was also that evening Tom commented to me how I was not feeding the dog, which I denied, but I could not work out how it took him so long to see the signs of starvation on the dog. The dog died shortly afterwards but the only regrets I had was that I did not kill it sooner.

I stayed with Mel and her family in Arnett Gardens (Jungle) for a while before Tom came to join us. The fact that he was staying in Mel's relatives home did not stop him from abusing her, which was very uncomfortable for me, but Tom was not one to consider other people's feelings. Living in the new Concrete Jungle opened my eyes and things were making more sense as I was getting older.

We lived near to Jones Town, which was home to some of Jamaica's most well known stickmen. Those men made a career by picking pockets. Many of them came from Jones Town but quite a few lived in Jungle and were friends with the Jones Town stickmen because they were PNP allies. They used any means to get money from their victims and were proud of their way of life. Some went out on the road daily while others chose Fridays, Saturdays and during the festive seasons to work as they could always make a big hit then. They did not care who they stole from. They robbed rich, poor, young and old people. They skillfully opened people's bags or went inside their pockets and relieved their victims of valuables. Gold jewellery was also in demand by the stickmen as there were always buyers for them. People in the ghetto liked gold jewellery and would model in them at street dances, so they were happy for the stickmen who supplied them with cheap gold they stole from other people. Some thieves cruelly used knives to cut people's bags and make holes in the pockets of their unsuspecting victims clothes just to get to whatever was in there. They sat on their corners (which meant places they hang out) and talked about how their victims shuddered with fear when they realised that they were being robbed. They were openly proud of what they did for a living and their techniques.

One afternoon some of them were hanging out in the pathway where we lived exchanging techniques with each other. A middle aged woman heard them boasting about their work. She told them that what they sowed they would reap. One self appointed spokesman quickly got up from the ground and started shouting, 'is not our fault why wi tief, is the government fault'. The lady shook her head and left them. There was no way of getting through to the stickmen who thought they had the God given right to rob innocent people. Some of them were so illiterate it made no sense reasoning with them, because they would not understand and would end up killing a person for their opinion. Their minds were very small and due to this they had a tunnel vision. The same government they were blaming was the one they voted for and would kill to keep in power. One had to have some integrity no matter what the circumstances you find yourself in. If one has integrity then you are self governed by your conscience and if you have to steal to survive then you would choose your victims carefully. When a large amount of people in any one country have to resort to stealing as a means to survive then that is saying something about the system and those who govern it, but when people steal from elderly people, single mothers and children then the thieves also need to check themselves.

I was living in Arnette Gardens (Jungle) during the 1976 election campaign. I found out then that bottles and stones were redundant and guns were the main weapons used by political rivals. The old political guards were stepping aside making way for more younger, ambitious men. Anthony Spaulding became Member of Parliament for Trench Town allowing Dudley Thompson to continue the PNP work in another part of the island. The younger politicians who joined the two parties seemed to be more interested in power and keeping it rather than making any change. Whenever they visited their dysfunctional constituencies they could be seen in deep conversations with their henchmen. All the OGs were either killed, neutralised or forced to leave the community.

Rampage and the slaughtering of human lives were on the increase. Never before in the history of Trench Town did the community witness so many atrocities. Violence was getting out of control so the Prime Minister declared a 'State of Emergency'. Soldiers were deployed on the streets of the capital to keep the peace. The country was in a state of unrest and times were hard. The Jamaican dollar was almost on equal par with the US currency and was not doing too badly against sterling, but the money that was in circulation was only getting to people who were not willing to share it. The pangs of poverty were squeezing the life out of many of us and as human beings with the will to survive, men who could not change the system joined it. Good politicians became bad and young men went to them offering their services as hitmen.

During the 'State of Emergency' soldiers and police came in the community constantly. The security forces made their biggest number of arrests during this time, so the jails in the capital were over-crowded. People were held between a couple of days to a month, then released. Most were questioned but not charged. Area leaders were called top ranking (the highest in the pecking order of the gunmen) and were given the privilege to go to the notorious General Penitentiary (GP). Men who found themselves at the make shift jail known as ' No Man's land', were labelled as fryers. This means they were last down the pecking order. A neighbour was picked up in a routine search and taken to 'No Man's Land' and his friends teased him for weeks when he returned home, but those who went to GP came back to a heroes welcome. 'No Man's Land' jail was between the border of a JLP and PNP area which was dangerous for those who were taken there. Sometimes the police and soldiers mischievously put men from rival political groups in the same cell only to see them squaring off. At GP the top rankings showed more respect for each other. Area dons from the JLP and PNP shared living quarters, but all they did was give each other the eagle eye there were no hands-on-fights.

The political heat was so hot leading up to the election in 1976 someone had to throw some water on it just to cool things down a bit. This came in the form of a peace treaty between the JLP and PNP. Mel took me down to Rema to see Prim for the first time in three years. I saw Prim washing some clothes outside and ran up to her, but all I got was a nervous smile. She kept looking over her right shoulder as if she was expecting someone. She said nothing to me, I felt disappointed that my own mother could not give me a better welcome after not seeing me for so long. Mel saw the reaction and told me to follow her and we went back to her place. I heard her telling her sisters what happened but I pretended not to have heard. I did not see Carl or any other relative, but after all those years Prim could have at least asked me how I was doing. It seemed to me she had given up on me, but I had not given up on her so it was not too long before I was planning my next visit, but I knew I had go alone in future.

Manley made several pledges during his election campaign and promised to revamp the educational system to give every child equality. When the island went to the polls in 1976 the election was plagued with illegal votings. Seaga and Spaulding won their seats by landslides. The amount of votes they got was greater than the number of people that lived in those areas. One of my friends and her mother were taken off the streets to a polling station where they were forced to vote in other people's name. My friend was eleven-years-old. The gunmen were laughing, they thought it was funny forcing a child of eleven to vote at gunpoint. Our next-door neighbour went to vote, but had to return home without doing so as someone had voted in her name before she arrived at the polling station. Men with high-powered guns were on patrol so people were voting under intimidation. Some people did not have a problem with what was happening around them as they had long accepted the primitive way of living. Those who did not bother to vote, someone made sure an ex was made on their behalf. People like Pepe who were long in their graves had people still voting in their names.

The PNP won the 1976 election and true to his word Manley delivered on his pledge in the form of the common entrance system. Rich and poor would be given the opportunity to attend prominent high schools in Jamaica. The difference was the poor went on their academic ability, while rich children went by the bank balance of their parents. The fact was, rich children would go to a high school whether they passed the common entrance or not, they only sat the exam as a formality and some did not even bother. I was proud to see the state primary schools battling with the more prominent and exclusive prep schools when the common entrance results were featured in the newspapers. Black parents were openly proud of their children for the first time in the history of Jamaica. Before the common entrance only a few selected needy pupils would go on to higher education through scholarships.

Equal rights for women were introduced and for the first time women were paid the same wage as their male counterparts. Women became more aggressive in the workplace and started going for jobs in management, because they knew the long arm of the law was behind them. Black faces were taking over in the banks that were usually staffed by brown and white people. The common entrance system and rights for women were overthrowing the colour bar in Jamaica. Children in Trench Town were also making their claim through the common entrance system and this was going to make a way out of the ghetto for many of us. I too wanted a way out of Trench Town and away from Tom. I knew I could do it if I put my mind to it after all I was born in the slum, but the slum was not born in me.

The Jamal education program was also introduced, this was aimed at adults who did not finish their education or never received one for whatever reason. This program was free and the aim was to eliminate illiteracy out of Jamaican society, Manley believed that a lot of the crime in the country was caused by ignorance.

The Prime Minister declared the word bastard a thing of the past and never to be used to describe any child born out of wedlock in Jamaica. Slavery damaged our family structure as our men were used as breeders to ensure that slave masters would always have enough people to work the plantations. Our men left the plantations in body, but not in spirit for they still practised plantation activities as they received no counselling to counteract that anti-family behaviour. They continued to sow wild seeds without a sense of responsibility. Some married men thought they did not have to support children that they produced outside their marriages. All children born in our country became lawful whether the parents were married to each other or not.

Manley's other trump card was the minimum wage. This stopped unscrupulous entrepreneurs who made people work from dawn till dusk and had not used their discretion on how much they offered the overworked employees. Many businessmen did not like the idea of a minimum wage, but Manley wanted to create a more equal Jamaica. The businessmen in the country did not like where he was going and were waiting to make their move. He was taking them too far out of their comfort zone for their liking. Manley reformed his party and told the country he wanted a democratic socialist party. He knew Jamaica needed help and could not afford to be choosy, so he invited Cubans in and took aid from Libya. The US saw Manley's move to associate with their enemies as a direct disrespect from such a little island. Besides they did not know that Manley possessed the "Black Heart". They thought only people with dark skin and dreadlocks had it, so Manley crept through the back door on them. The US government declared war on our leader, so it was inevitable that we would feel the brunt of their wrath. They had one of their very own disguising himself as a Jamaican just waiting to act on their command.

Manley became very popular in Jamaica amongst the poor after his slaughter on the rich. The big businessmen saw his new look policy as a rip-off. He was a modern day Robin Hood robbing the rich to feed the poor. But there was no way they were going to lay down and accept it. Seaga was more popular than ever in Tivoli Gardens, also a poor community, but as long as he kept them happy they did not care for anyone else. Manley's slaughter on the rich to benefit the poor did not make any difference to them, but my fellow ghetto people were not ones to vote for someone according to their policies, but because they liked them. Neither did they see the plan by the US to use the leader of the opposition to teach the disobedient Manley a lesson. Manley however, did not need Tivoli's support, as he was also popular with rural Jamaicans. One popular song we heard over the radio stations clearly supporting Manley and his policies was given regular airplay by the then Jamaica Broadcasting Corporation (JBC). The words were:

> My leader born ya, my leader born ya,
> no I na lef ya, no I na lef ya.
> Hit dem wid Jamal, hit dem with Jamal
> and den yu hi dem with the free education,
> hit dem with the free education.
> Equal pay for women, equal pay for women;
> hit dem with de minimum wages, hit dem wid
> de minimum wages.
> No bastard no de ya again, no bastard no
> ya again, everyone lawful, oh yea, everyone lawful.

Manley's policies became a hit amongst many people so he felt he could go one step more and declared his party a democratic socialist government. PNP supporters started calling themselves comrades and socialists even though many of them did not know the real meaning of the words.

The US hatched a plan to make Manley's new popular policies look dysfunctional due to poor leadership. Jamaica (like many of their Caribbean neighbours) relied heavily on America for supplies such as medication, petrol and loans so they knew exactly where to hit us hard. As soon as the 1976 election was over the JLP was planning for the next one and this atmosphere destabilised the island. The US pumped money into Seaga's election campaign to ensure that the Manley government was overthrown. Guns were imported from America into the country everyday and found their way into Trench Town. The Americans were using every trick in the book to get rid of Manley and send a message to other would-be 'disobedient politicians' in the Caribbean. Urgently needed Cuban doctors were coming into the island to work, but were paid by their own government. The JLP started spreading propaganda that Manley and some members of his cabinet were planning to turn the country into a communist state and that there were undercover communist activities at the Cuban - built school, 'Jose` Marti', based in Spanish Town. The rich did not believe the propaganda as many of them were fairly educated and could assess the situation for themselves, but they too jumped on the communist bandwagon to get rid of their enemy. Manley was declared an enemy of the rich who wanted to see the back of him and would stop at nothing even if the poor had to pay the price.

PNP supporters could see that Washington favoured Seaga so they showed favour to Castro. Young men from PNP strongholds were sent to Cuba to get military training. They called themselves the Brigadistas. I knew some who went to Cuba and returned to Jungle to fight political warfare. They could take a gun apart clean it and put it back together quicker than any soldier in the army. They thought somehow that they were superior than their peers because of the military training they received in Cuba. After returning back from Cuba some of the Brigadistas reported that their ragamuffin, indisciplined attitude did not go down well with their Cubans comrades, who were used to taking orders and respected authority. The Cuban comrades look up to Castro as the ultimate commander while the Jamaican ragamuffins were a law unto themselves. The PNP wanted to make revolutionists out of their gunmen, but the men who went to Cuba were only interested in how to fire a gun. A revolutionist is a soldier who fights for a well-meaning cause and for the benefit of the people. The Jamaican gunmen were only interested in eliminating those they hated. The Cubans did not know what to do with the indisciplined behaviour of the Jamaicans and the final straw came when pork was served to a group of PNP Brigadistas in Cuba and rather than telling their hosts that they did not eat pork they thrashed their own living quarters instead.

They were swiftly given their marching orders by the Cubans. Why were PNP supporters sent to Cuba to train for combat by politicians? No one knows for sure unless you were part of the conspiracy. One thing that we do know is that the Brigadistas returned to the island ready for the PNP versus JLP combat. Some of them later took part in some of the most brutal and infamous massacres on the island.

The PNP managed to organise up to fifteen militia groups that were networking with each other all over the capital. They were a threat to national security and if the eyes of Jamaica were not on them they could have reduced Seaga's mighty Tivoli to mere rubble.

I did not particularly like staying with Mel and her relatives, but anywhere was better than Rose Town. What made matters worse was the cat and dog relationship between her and Tom. I knew it would not be long before I would have to find another home as they were always arguing and Tom would be the one to leave as he was living with her. One day they were arguing and one of Mel's sisters said something to him. I did not hear what it was, but Tom ran out of the house to where she was and kicked her in her stomach. Mel was sitting on the bed in her room and heard when her sister screamed out, but she did not move from where she was. I was angry with her, for it was one thing for the man she loved to abuse her, but when he turned on her family she should have put her foot down. If she did not leave him for any other reason that was the time she should have left, but she stayed with him.

I went to school from Jungle, which was getting dangerous, because I was still attending the primary school, which was located in Rose Town. In the evenings we ran through the gates to make our way quickly through the comprehensive school. We had to pass Angola housing scheme to get to both schools and some dangerous men used to hang out there. I was friendly with a girl who lived in Jungle, but she was not liked by the men who hanged out at Angola. One day one of the men called me and said, 'you do not remember me, but I remember you from you were almost a baby and let mi tell yu something, lose that friend fast'. He said to me, 'show mi yu friend and a tell yu who yu are'. I did as he said and lost the friend as it seemed he knew more about her than I did.

Some young men who had dropped out of school and were living in Rema would wait for us at the gate between the primary and the high school during the lunch break and in the evenings. They knew we went that way because we lived in Jungle. They used the buckles on their belts to hit the boys in their heads and touched the girls on their breasts. We put our bags up to our chests, but sometimes their hands got through and I got more touches on my breasts than I care to remember. I got used to it and figured as long as it did not go beyond that I was lucky.

Then one day I was leaving school early on my own as I was not well. As I reached the gate I saw four of the dropouts waiting for some unfortunate girl to pick on and by the look of things I was to be the one. I did not turn back as I should have done, because I was alone and a touch was not going to satisfy them that day. They let me pass them and then grabbed me from behind but I was expecting it. No way on earth was I going to let four young boys not much older than me rape me without a fight. The first one I turned around to I put my fingers in his eyes. He backed off and the other three sprang on me like hungry cats. My bag went flying as I fought them like a tigress and managed to pull them onto the Trench Town High School playground which was taking them out of their territory. They tried to get me on the ground, but they could not overpower me to do so. I screamed as loud as I could and a lady from a nearby nursery heard my scream and shouted at them, so the cowards laughed and ran off.

I was surprised that my uniform was still intact afterwards so I went to get my bag and went home. I did not tell anyone I was almost raped. I could have gotten their arses busted but no real harm was done so I chose to turn the other cheek. After that incident I always waited for other children. At school we prayed morning, afternoon and evening. Those of us who had to go up to Jungle had to cut the evening prayer short just to get an early start before the troublemakers came out. One evening a group of us ran to the gate only to find it locked with the key. The principal locked it to keep out unwanted visitors, but what he did could have cost those of us living in Jungle our lives. We could not take any other route so we had no choice but to climb over the fence. Children who could not get over by themselves were helped by others. I was half way over the fence when my tunic got caught on the prickly part of the fence and ripped in two. My schoolmates had to tack it with pins so that I could get home covered. One older boy from the high school saw when we were pinning my uniform and came over to ask what happened. We told him what happened and he and his friends went to the gate to see the other children safely over the fence. Their presence at the school border during the lunch break and evenings reduced the activity of the troublemakers. I was never interfered with again but some other girls reported that they were attacked.

Chapter Five

Tom and Mel had another of their many fights and as I had predicted Tom needed to find another place for me to live. He asked Aunty Charm if I could stay with her and she said yes, so I was back with Sally, Megan and Plum. I was more comfortable and at home with them. Aunty Charm did not treat me any differently to her own children and was a fair and honest woman but a little conceited. Megan too was conceited like her mother, but Sally and I were more on the same level maybe because we were the same age.

I was now living in Brooklyn housing scheme where I came in contact with the good, the bad and the indifferent. I met Pablo, a young man, who lived opposite to our house. Pablo was about eighteen-years-old and very handsome. I knew a lot of young women who fancied him, but my love for him was pure as a sister's love for a brother. He was always a conscientious young man, but the odds were against him in Trench Town. He became caught up in the politics and corruption which were getting to him. I watched him changed from being indifferent to being a very disciplined young man. I knew then all of us had it in us to be the best person we could possibly be, if we were strong and the strength we needed had to come from within us, as one could be easily led astray by others in our community.

Pablo had two brothers Tess who was an area leader and Andy a young boy of eleven. I met Shaft and 'Cool hand Luke' (two well known rough scouts in the area) for the first time. I heard of them previously, but had never had the opportunity of meeting them. The badmen chose the names from their favourite American detective and western films. People were always whispering about who they were and what they did, but were too frightened to speak out in case someone told them. People were always watching their backs and distrustful of each other and some had good reasons to do so. Luke was a short stocky man of brown complexion and pleasant personality. He did not come over as this dangerous person to be feared and did not intimidate me even when I got to know him better. Luke was a lady's man. Shaft in my opinion was the more handsome of the two. He was tall, dark and too good looking, but by far the most intimidating of the duo.

I was standing at my gate one day when I saw a group of men, Luke and Shaft included, inside the front yard of a neighbour's home. They were apparently cooking, a favourite pastime of young men in Trench Town. They had a comradeship about them and would go through bonding sessions. A group of men would do what we called running a boat. This was where everybody contributed money, grocery or whatever they could afford and the very best cook of the lot would prepare the food. No-one would be left out of the sharings because he gave too little. That was what Prince and Steve were doing when the police raided our house and my uncle ran into the toilet with the pot of boiling food. They would cook ital stew, cornmeal porridge, ackee, calaloo or any other food they fancied. They were not keen on red meat but very much into vegetables. Some also smoked marijuana but not cigarettes and the interesting thing was, some did not smoke at all.

There was one young boy about fifteen-years-old with the group who was obviously excited and proud that he could be in the presence of such idols. He was following Luke around. That could be due to Luke's compassion as he could be more sensitive than the others. I stood there and watched his mannerism and that of Shaft. Shaft had a cooler nature about him and it was that side of him that intimidated a lot of people. I sensed it, but was not one to cower that easily. I went out of the gate to speak to someone in my short dress. I had outgrown it, but Tom would not buy me new clothes so I had to wear what I had and all my clothes were short. Shaft was looking at me, but he did not comment. I caught his eyes, but pretended I did not see him watching me. I was a bit embarrassed because I knew he was looking at my short dress. I heard him commenting to Luke about how short my dress was and that I needed to put on something decent. Luke looked to see who he was talking about, but did not respond in fact he did not react in any way. I think he guessed the reason for himself why I was wearing an outgrown dress.

The young boy asked Luke for a puff off the draw he had smoking, Luke looked at him and laughed then he said to him, 'if yu eat three a dem dumpling wey dread (Rasta man) a mek den yu can have a puff'. The young man said he could and Dread dished out the three dumplings and calaloo. The dumplings were like car tires and very tight. The young man could only manage one then gave up, but still wanted a puff from the ganja spliff. Luke immediately told him ganja smoking was not for boys, especially those who could not eat three dumplings so the youngster gave up on the idea of smoking at least for that day.

I saw Shaft the next day in our pathway. Someone had told me that he was seeing Pablo's sister, Pam. When he saw me he said in a quiet voice but very serious expression, 'yu frock too short'. I did not respond out of embarrassment and thought that if I ignore him he would not say anything else about my appearance. The next day Pablo was sitting in our front yard mixing Guinness punch and asked me to get a spoon inside our house for him. Shaft saw him and came in to sit down, I said hello to him for the first time. I naively liked older people's company, as I was interested to learn new things and found some youngsters my own age group boring. Pablo and I talked to each other, while Shaft listened and he only commented a few times. Pablo was not very interested in speaking to him even though there was no animosity.

The next day Megan, Sally and I were in the house talking when Shaft came in our front room. Like a lot of people in the community we left our doors open. The moment he came in the two sisters went outside. I found it strange and impolite so I stayed with him until someone called him. The next day he returned to our home and Sally and Megan went outside again. I knew something was not right, but I did not ask them anything. They did not want me to know something so I'd rather hear it from someone else. I got used to observing and relying on myself so I was not offended by their actions. Their grandmother was in the back yard washing some clothes so I sat in a chair around the table facing Shaft. The first thing he asked me was why I wore clothes that were much too short for me. As we were alone, I told him the truth that I could not afford to buy new clothes. He asked me where my mother was and I told him innocently that she lived in Rema, not even taking into account that he was a PNP activist, but that did not bother him. I told him it was my father who was responsible for me. He asked me why my mother gave me to my father, but I did not know what answer to give him. I looked in his eyes and for the first time I saw compassion.

I excused myself and got up to use the toilet, as I wanted to go for a long time and it had started to hurt a bit. I went in the direction of the bathroom and I saw when he got up and followed behind me. A little voice inside told me to stop and wait for his next move. He came up to me and held onto my hand I knew there and then what he had in his mind. I looked him in his eyes and told him to let go of my hand. I was fearless and it would appear that I took him by surprise because he let go instantly. Megan's grandmother came in to get something just as he was thinking his next move. He turned around and went back to the front room. I went straight outside where I saw Sally and Megan. I did not say anything to them about what happened and they did not ask any questions. The next day we were all at our gate standing when a friend of Megan came up and whispered to us that Shaft allegedly raped a twelve-year-old girl the evening after he left our house. I was shocked everything then made sense to me. Sally and Megan knew what he was capable of and that was the reason why they left the house when he came in. He must have gone out looking for a victim when the attempt he made on me failed. I saw him a few days later and he said hello as if nothing had happened. For some reason I was not afraid of him and I thought after our little incident that we understood each other. He knew that I would not give in to him quietly and I was going to be more careful with him in future.

The PNP politicians gave a contract to the area leaders to build a new comprehensive high school in the community. I thought this was unnecessary as Trench Town was short of students due to the political violence. The two schools would eventually rival each other for resources, we could hardly get experienced teachers to teach at Trench Town which was only going to be five minutes walk from the new school. Children from Jones Town Primary School would have rights to the new school. Many children from Jungle were destined to go there.

Sally and Plum were attending Jones Town Primary, but got transferred to Trench Town. Megan was attending Trench Town Comprehensive. We went to school together in the mornings. Randy Luke's cousin and his friends were in Megan's year at school. They were handsome boys, but they had a bit of a reputation. Randy said I was wild because I used to run whenever he came near me. He used to run after me and no matter how hard he ran he could not catch up with me. One afternoon he ran after me, I was running flat out and could not control myself and I fell flat to the ground. He helped me off the ground and wiped the dirt from my tunic, but he could not keep the laughter from flowing. I went to school in embarrassment and vowed never to run from him again. The next day when I saw him I just smiled and walked on, he laughed and we became associates after that. I was also fond of his friends. They were talented football players and represented the school in both Pepsi and Manning Cup competitions. Nick and John were best friends with Randy. All three were popular with the girls but Nick was a womaniser. He was not bad to look at and used it to his advantage.

    I went to see Mel everyday because I had to go there for lunch. I had my breakfast and dinner where I lived. I was given shelter and food by Aunty Charm but Tom did not contribute to my keep, he expected it to be done for nothing.
    I bought a bun one Saturday afternoon for my lunch and was on my way back from the shop when Shaft came up to me and took away my bun. He looked at it and asked me where the cheese was and I told him that I did not have any money to buy any. He gave me money to buy a slice of cheese and he held onto the bun until I returned. I gave him the cheese and asked for my bun; he gave me the bun, but took the cheese from me and said, 'if yu want cheese yu a fi gi mi half a yu bun'. I told him no but that I wanted the cheese he laughed, I believed it was the feistiness in me he was attracted to. He asked me if I was mad, I gave him half my bun and he gave me half his cheese. He left me and went up Ninth Street. I liked him but was still conscious of what he did. He had a lot of girlfriends including a girl at my school I did not agree with the relationship, but I could see why she was attracted to him as he was a really likable person behind his fearful image. She was fifteen, he was in his mid-twenties.
    The mentality of adults towards children in our community was alien to other people but normal to Trench Townians. A man in his late twenties who lived in our pathway with his girlfriend was always staring at me. He wore his hair in dreadlocks and many young men congregated in his yard. I grew up fast so I could smell danger from a mile and knew when to tread carefully and he was danger with a capital D. Late one evening he came home from wherever he was half-drunk. He came up to me in front of about ten people and told me he was in love with me. The people who were mostly adults, thought what he said was funny and so they laughed. I was embarrassed and did not know what to do, I naively told him he was only joking around because he was drunk. The fool could not get the message and kept grovelling about how much he loved me and that he would feel the same way the next day much to the pleasure of our audience. I was eleven years old and a man who could be my father was telling me how much he was in love with me and no one came to my rescue. What could a young child do for a grown man like that? I am still trying to work that one out. The next day he saw me but had the common sense to look the other way.
    I was returning from the local shop one day when I heard a loud bang I recognised instantly that someone had fired a gunshot not far away. I did not know who it was aimed at nor if it hit its target so I started to run as hard as I could. I was making my way down

Ninth Street on the side of Pegasus housing scheme when Shaft came out and grabbed my hand. He asked me if my soul was possessed by demons why I was running so fast. I asked him if he had not heard the gunshot, he looked me straight in the eye and told me that he fired the shot at some people who were looking at him. That was when I started to get an idea of who he really was.

I saw a pregnant young lady talking to Luke in our pathway and someone told me that she was expecting his baby. She seemed to be very proud to be his baby-mother. Even though he had many other girlfriends but a child would give her some status. Baby-mothers were special as they would be the one to make many boys feels like men. Sometimes the man would love another woman and this would cause problems between the girlfriend and the baby-mother. A baby-mother was the nearest thing to being a wife so many women felt privileged just by having a man's child, even if he never asked her to be his wife. Pablo's sister got pregnant by Shaft and I could see that he loved her, but I could also see that he cared for Megan's classmate Edna as well. I asked him if he loved Edna and he just looked at me as if he could not work out why I was asking him the question. He was careful with what he would say to me because I lived next door to his baby-mother. He thought about it carefully and then told me to mind my own business, but I would not let it go and kept asking him the same question over and over. He looked at me and told me to leave him alone, I ignored what he said and continued to press for an answer and he said, 'Patsy yu hear me a tell yu fi leave mi alone'. I got frightened and was about to leave when he said, 'a joke mi a mek come back'. He then asked me if I had a boyfriend I did not want him to ask me anything personal, so I did not answer him. He laughed as he knew then he had got me to stop asking prying questions. He told me afterwards that I was nosey.

To my knowledge most of the area leaders and top rankings went to jail at least once in their offending lives but Shaft always managed to escape capture. Luke made Jamaica's most wanted list of criminals and even went to jail. Shaft's elusiveness might have had something to do with his withdrawn mysterious character. He had runnings with the police but always managed to fight his way out. He was a wanted man, but only a brave police would challenge him to make an arrest. He challenged one of Jamaica's fierce crime fighters in Jones Town one day and almost lost his life. He set the police officer's car on fire and was shot in the right hand, but managed to escape with only a small wound. He could not go to the hospital so he had it dressed at home quietly by trained medics. I saw him the next day after the incident and told him he deserved what he got. He looked me in the face and laughed openly in disbelief that I could be so daring, rebuking him for challenging a lawman. He looked so handsome with that laugh. He was sussing me up but would not tell me what he was thinking.

I fancied Pablo's younger brother Andy and he liked me but he was a naughty little boy who wanted to play 'dolly house' with me. I liked his antics but would not allow him to get his own way and very few boys my age could overpower me to get their own way. I went off Andy when I saw him with a girl who lived in our pathway and I knew he had eyes for a cute little girl who lived down the road from us. Pablo was conscious in terms of his blackness and used to preach to me. He expressed a liking for the Rasta faith, but was also involved with some of the negativity around us. I was talking about young girls and sex in his presence when he severely rebuked me. He was not happy with the things I was saying and unlike a lot of men in our community he would not support such language from me. I was glad when he corrected me even though he was harsh. I had become used to adults discussing sex in front of children so I thought what I was saying was normal until Pablo told me it was not.

Manley was popular with Rastamen in Jamaica, as many believed that more marijuana was exported out of the country during his administration. They believed that he allowed them to trade their only resource so they could survive.

In 1977 I was turning twelve the August of that year, so our teacher was busy preparing us for transfer to Trench Town Comprehensive. I did not have anyone at home to prepare me to sit the common entrance examination and Tom would not pay the sitting fee. My teacher did the work for the transfer from the primary school to the comprehensive high. We sat our annual examination as usual but this time the grades would be used by my new school to assess which class I would go in. I had not done too badly and knew I was going in seven-one, the top class in my year at the high school which made me proud. Sally was to go in seven-two. I could not share my excitement with them at home because I did not want to offend anyone, so I had to keep my achievement to myself.

Tom gave Mel money to buy material to make my new uniform but she bought a green colour material when it should have been cream. I did not care for it but as usual I did not have a say in the matter. I heard Tom asking her in a sarcastic way what she had bought and she explaining that she could not find the correct colour material. Tom would not fork out the money for proper shoes so I had to be content with a Batta crepe. Sally and Megan had the correct material for their uniform and decent shoes. I was excited for the new academic year as I was now a young adult. Many students who lived in Rema and Rose Town found other high and secondary schools to go to, because they would be basically in Jungle's back yard and this could mean trouble for them. Others who could not get into other schools turned up in September and reported for class.

On my way to Mel's home to collect my lunch money, I saw the man who asked me who I was running from the day the young man from Rose Town almost attacked me. I came to know my sympathiser quite well, as he was always hanging out at the clock circle end of Angola's housing scheme. Due to this I always saw him on my way to school, we even knew each other's name, he was called Bagga. When he saw me in my new high school uniform he smiled and I smiled back at him, he said, 'who is a big girl now, Patsy a hope yu tun lawyer and defend mi'. I asked him how he knew I was going to become a lawyer and he said, 'it might not be a lawyer 'but yu going to be something, a can see it in yu eyes'. I knew then someone believed in me.

Bagga had some friends he sparred with. They had a bad reputation and people were complaining that they were interfering with them. The leader for them was Tango but it seemed Hitler (one of the posse members) had more power than him. Most of the Angola Posse members had houses in the housing scheme and would hang out on the front, so we had to pass them on our way to school. Luke and Shaft also had homes in Angola, but were not members of that posse. Shaft was targeted for assassination by the Angola men but they knew the person to take his life would have to make sure that he was dead. They wanted the people on their side so they were using the rapes he was doing as an excuse, as they knew the people were fed up with Shaft and his behaviour. They did not care for Luke either but first needed to divide them and then rule. Tess was not in their good books but they could not take on so many rough scouts at the same time so they were planning to get rid of them one by one. That way they would not have to share the contracts with too many people and also they would be the law in Trench Town with no opposition. The reason why there was some form of stability in the area, was no one posse was in charge and some posses members had some integrity.

One morning a dead man was found sawn in two in the gully on Collysmith Drive. Two Angola posse members were seen leaving the area where the body was found early the morning, but they did not know that they had been seen.

Tess reared goats and would leave them to feed in an open lot opposite to Angola. One day some of the goats went missing. Tess and his friends went all over Trench Town, Rose Town and Jones Town looking for his goats. They even ventured into JLP territory looking for the goats but no one saw them. A lot of people were whispering that it was Angola men who took the goats, but there was no evidence to back up the rumours. When the goats could not be found anywhere the fingers were then pointed at the dogs in the community. Angola posse led a mob and rounded up all the dogs in the area and slaughtered them. If the dogs had killed the goats there would have been blood everywhere but there was no trace of blood or any other remains. They killed the dogs knowing very well that they were not responsible for the disappearance of the goats. They went into people's homes and used machetes to chop up the dogs and parts of dogs could be seen everywhere.

On another occasion a man from Texas went missing, people said that he had been in an argument with a member from the Angola posse earlier on in the day before he disappeared. For days his mother looked for him. There was a rumour about him being kidnapped by Rema men who killed him and threw him into a pit, but only someone with something to hide would come up with such story to keep people looking elsewhere. A Rema man would not have ventured out of his area risking getting himself killed to get one man and the missing man was not known to go out of his area. Angola men were under suspicion again, but with no real evidence no one could take action.

Our principal Mr B was very popular with Angola men and he would stop and talk with them from time to time. Bagga once told me that Mr B was a good man and they called him the red car man. Mr B was a white man but he knew how to reason with them on their level. While Mr B was at Trench Town School they never ventured over to our school and made trouble except for when the war between them and Rema men became out of control. I liked Mr B and felt that he was a fair and honest human being, but not everyone shared my opinion. Some teachers and students felt that he was allowing standards to slip at our school so they were planning a revolt against him.

One afternoon we were summoned to our school auditorium by a group of senior students to discuss Mr B's style of leadership. It was obvious that he had not expected such a move and was clearly upset by it. Some of the teachers who conspired with the students were in the background, as they did not want any come back in case the attempted coup went wrong, but we knew who they were. The majority of us were not consulted about the decision to remove our principal and if it had gone to a vote Mr B would have remained, but he was so angry at his foes he walked out of the school never to be seen again. I was hurt, confused and not sure what was going on. Our vice-principal moved up to act as principal and a senior teacher acted as vice-principal. It was rumoured that our new acting principal was gay. No one had any proof of this but the way he walked and swung his backside did not help the situation. I liked him and found him to be a fair and honest man who did not bear grudges against his students and was willing to give second chances. The acting vice principal on the other hand was not one of my favourites and judged me wrongly. She was not forgiving and could not look beyond her own prejudices to find out the real person behind the image. She either liked you or hated you and did not hide how she felt. I do not think she ever thought I could be anything other than the no-hoper she thought I was. A lot of other students were saying the same thing about her and we all could not be wrong.

When we let Mr B go we shot ourselves in the leg as he had a good relationship with Angola men and was keeping them away from our school. On my way to school one morning Bagga asked me where the red car man was, I told him that he had left, but did not explain the reason for his departure. Bagga was clearly bemused by what he had heard, but I was not prepared to clear up things for him. One thing was for sure, someone else would. In the evening I saw Bagga with some of his friends and they were not amused with what they had heard. Just as we passed them I heard one of them said, 'onu get rid a de red car man and ave batty man ova de tun principal', I knew then there was going to be trouble.

Threats were sent to the students at school who lived in Rose Town and Rema. Some students who lived in Jungle were telling Angola men who the children were who lived in JLP areas. There were five of them in my class alone, two boys and three girls. I was close to the boys, because we were in the same class from primary school. I was very upset about the threats but could do very little. One of the girls was not making it easy for herself and the rest of them, because she openly criticised the PNP and made political statements in support of the JLP at school. She had no business in politics as a child, but then again Jamaica was meant to be a free country. She knew what she was saying could put her at serious risk but that did not stop her. She was the first one to heed to the threats and stopped attending school. The threats continued to come and Jungle men came over the school one afternoon looking for the others, those who were there had to jump over fences to escape with their lives. I was angry that I had to lose my friends because of politics, I was damn angry. Some of the students who left, dropped out of school and fell by the way side. If Mr B was still around I am sure he would have stepped in, but the others who were courageous to lead a rebellion against him were not brave enough to face the real enemy of peace. I knew then that our heroes died in vain, for what I witnessed at school was grown men threatening to kill children in the name of politics and depriving them of an education.

In the end most of the students who lived in Rema and Rose Town stopped attending school, only one of the five who were in my class continued. Not a lot of people knew where she lived and those of us who knew did not disclose it to anyone. Some students were whispering that Angola men were planning to harm our acting principal, because they did not like his gay lifestyle. It was later announced that he was on sick leave and he never returned. Our school was left without a qualified head or deputy. The acting vice-principal then stepped up into the role of acting principal.

One night at home we had a power cut and all hell broke lose. Rema men tried to invade Jungle with a barrage of gunshots and Jungle men were returning fire. The elderly were vulnerable not because they were at risk more than anyone else of getting hit, but their hearts and brains could not take the chaos around them. Some died of heart failures while others became disorientated. Women were on the streets making fire and lighting everything that could burn just to get some light. Not only Rema men were using the dark to their advantage, the rapists in Jungle also welcomed the power cut. Angola men were busy fighting Rema men so they had no time to slice up any of their own men. The gunshots cooled the next morning when soldiers came in to quell the disturbance.

Tom came to the house upset one evening. He was complaining to Aunty Charm that her brother was a fool and blaming him for being robbed by gunmen. He said that the gunmen stopped them on Spanish Town Road while Tom was driving a passenger mini bus and Aunty Charm's brother was the conductor. They stopped for the robbers thinking that they were prospective passengers and one of the men pulled out a gun on them. When Tom realised what was happening he shouted to his conductor to close the door for him to drive off. The conductor did not respond to his command as he was in shock and afraid of what might have happened to him, because he was the one they were targeting. Tom who was not an understanding person told off Sammy so badly not even taking into account how he was feeling from the robbery. The thieves took all the cash they had made for the day.

He said that he wanted money to fix the bus because it was damaged during the robbery. Aunty Charm did not have any money so she borrowed some from a cousin and gave it to him as a loan, which he promised to return. Days and months passed and he would not repay the money. One day Aunty Charm asked him for it and he told her that he would not give it back to her, because it was her brother who caused the accident. When I heard him I could not believe my ears. The man did not contribute to my keep at the woman's house, she gave me her children's clothes to wear because he would not buy any for me and he had the nerve to say that to her. I felt bad and wanted to find a hole and crawl in. Tom stayed with that family when he arrived from St Mary, they treated him like a member of their family when his own did not want to know and that was the way he repaid them. I heard Aunty Charm saying to him how she was the one feeding his child and providing shelter for nothing. He told her that he did not ask her to feed me and that she should have sent me over to him for food. When she got in the house she told me what I already heard that I would have to go over to Mel for tea, lunch and dinner.

I went over to Mel for dinner that evening and Tom was there, he said, 'this is where you should have been eating in the first place'. I did not respond to him, but I hated him with every cell in my body. I could not believe someone could be so unreasonable. He did not give a damn about my feelings. I was the one who had to live with Aunty Charm so how did he expect me to feel. Things were not the same as it used to be. We never ate together anymore and this added to the distance between the family and me. I knew I was alone in the world, but I put on a brave face. I could relate to the song by Smokey Robinson and the Miracles 'Tracks of My Tears', 'for although I had been laughing loud, deep inside I was blue, if those around me had looked closer they could have traced the tracks of my tears'.

I had to get up early during school days, so that I could get to Mel in time for breakfast and make it to school on time. I resented it but again I could not do anything about it. Aunty Charm was polite to me, but that did not ease my discomfort around them. I remember one day they were talking in the living room and as soon as they saw me they stopped, I pretended as if I did not notice anything and got on with life.

We were growing up in such an aggressive environment so we thought violence would solve all our problems. We lived in Arnett Gardens (Jungle) where politics was an integral part of our lives. We were conscious of the fact that the time would come for us to cast our votes one day and as we lived in a PNP stronghold we would have no choice but to vote for them. We children - Megan, Sally and I referred to ourselves as comrades just as the adults did. Some of us were more into it than others but we all had to choose. We became territorial, segregated and had a superior attitude believing we were better than the other side, while they were thinking that they were better than us. I remember how tense the atmosphere in our community was. At anytime someone could die or a young girl could get raped. We knew that what was happening was wrong but accepted it as part of our lives. In Trench Town the atrocities we faced everyday at the hands of our neighbours were cruel beyond belief but no one intervened. It was as if we were cut off from the rest of the island. The problem was, political crime was like a plague that spread to other communities that were weak and without resources, it would not be contained to just our community.

Political fever managed to spread to other dysfunctional communities such as Water House, Riverton City, Olympic Gardens, Payne Avenue, Greenwich Farm and Central Kingston. Everyone wanted a piece of the pie that the politicians were giving out. Manley borrowed money from the International Monetary Fund (IMF) and when the deal went very wrong the JLP used this as part of their election campaign. Their party supporters painted the letters IMF on walls and said they stood for, 'Is Manley's Fault'. The wealthy businessmen seized the opportunity to sabotage the government and held back on imports so that they could not reach the consumers. The people started blaming Manley for scarcity of goods. It was useless telling impoverished illiterate people Manley was only a small part of the problem. They could not afford to lose the little they were getting and the unscrupulous educated rich entrepreneur knew that. One of Seaga's election campaign adverts on the television saw him telling the nation that he would let money jingle in their pockets, if they voted for him. A lot of them liked freebies and thought the money would be given to them without them having to work for it. Seaga on the other hand did not care how they took the message as long as they intended to vote him in power. Manley followers on the other hand did not care if the economy suffered as long as he remained in power.

During this volatile period I was buried in Jungle and never ventured out of the communities I had lived in since returning from St Mary. I only knew one way to Prim's house and I could not walk there because it was a battlefield. I did not know beyond Maxfield Avenue and Jones Town. Tom was not interested in taking me anywhere, because he wanted to keep me in ignorance, so that I would not be able to find my mother and brothers. I was not allowed to go on school outings or anywhere else, my life was a drag. Christmas was not the same as when I lived with Prim and I did not even enjoy the festive meals anymore.

A lot of the police were supporting the JLP but the soldiers were loyal to the government to the bitter end. One of Jamaica's top policemen was Seaga's bodyguard so the soldiers were dispatched onto the streets to protect their leader, the Prime Minister. The PNP had a garrison area in Central Kingston, but like Trench Town when the area was divided by politics part of it went to the JLP. JLP supporters resided at the Southside of Central Kingston. Because the border between the two political foes was so slim some of the men were double agents who worked for both the JLP and PNP, and that was to cost some of them their lives.

The Skull posse members from Southside were JLP supporters and knew some of the double agents well. The double agents were not weaklings so they had some respect in Central Kingston. The Nessan brothers were top dogs in the Skull posse so any deal with the crew had to involve them. The PNP knew they were losing ground in the polls so they wanted to rid Central Kingston of the double agents and the Skull crew, so they could take over the area. This would not be a job for just amateurs so army men were called in to help with the work. It was expected that they would clean up after themselves and would not leave any evidence. Hired gunmen were too messy and often left too many clues behind them.

News broke early January 1978 that five men were killed at Green Bay, Port Henderson, St Catherine. The soldiers and the PNP were both implicated in the killings. The widely publicised trial that started in June of the same year revealed some unbelievable stories about the events that led up to the killings. Five soldiers were indicted for the murder, but later walked free. Five men survived the death trap to the surprise and disgust of the assassins, so trained gunmen were not necessarily better than the street ones after all.

One of the survivors was the chief witness told the story like this at the trial. He said he and his friends were not political activists, but were respected in the area by their subordinates. He said they were free agents (meaning double agents) and worked with anyone. They would not allow anyone to dictate to them, but their mistake was they would take money from both PNP and JLP bosses (and those people did not give anything for free). He said that a new housing project was being built in the area and he and his friends were always on the look out for work. A man by the name of Briggie told them that his boss wanted some men to guard the housing project from thieves and in return they would get guns and money. The Christmas season was drawing near so they did not have time to think twice about their new job offer, besides they were so trusting of anyone as long as money and guns were mentioned. He also said that he trusted the soldiers and did not believe that the army would set them up, (but which law abiding soldier would give arms to civilians to guard a housing scheme, especially men who were known to be hustlers and law-breakers).

The deal started from November 1977 and came to an end in January 1978 when the men were killed. The Skull crew heard about the deal and wanted a piece of the action so they were roped in. The survivor said he was in bed the morning of the killings, when a friend came to call him. He went with the friend to Law Street and Fleet Street where he saw two strange men. While there other men who were in on the deal were turning up. Some looked as if they were called out of their beds. A man asked him if he had any guns on him and he said no. An ambulance, a van and a car were waiting for them. Briggie came and took them to the boss. Some of the men went in the ambulance but he went into the van. They were not told where they were going, only that they were going for work.

They were all taken to Green Bay where they were dropped off at the gate and a man with a flashlight let them in. They walked down a hill and saw a man in a house who called them in and told them not to let the fishermen see where they were going. The house they went in was old and had no door or roof. They were directed out of the house and taken to the level area in front of the beach; there they met a man that they had seen before at one of the meetings to discuss the deal.

The level area had thorn bushes, sticks and cardboard around. He said they sat down on the ground to discuss business with the man, but he got up and walked away'. They stood up and he heard gunshots firing. He said that he crawled on his hands and knees to find a safe place to hide. He did not see any of his friends with guns and he did not have one to defend himself. He tried to make his way to the hill, but came across two soldiers and went back to the sea. While there he saw one of the Nessan brothers and some others in the level area. There was a helicopter flying around and people in army uniforms rushing around to make sure no one escaped. He crawled through the thorn bushes until he came out at a sugar plantation. The cane field was high so he hid in it and kept running until he came upon a road. He walked for a while before taking a bus home. Four others managed to escape through different routes. Five were not so lucky, their bodies were found riddled with bullets

The PNP was embarrassed, everyone knew they were behind the Green Bay Killings. The five soldiers, who were implicated in the killings, were given the best lawyers in the land who saw to their acquittals. Dudley Thompson who was promoted to a cabinet minister in the PNP openly told the nation that no angels died at Green Bay.

The Green Bay Killings was an unforgivable deed especially, as it was committed by men who were supposed to be protecting the people not killing them. Those who were guilty should not have walked free as the message it sent was, lives were cheap and any government establishment that did not like a group of people could wipe them out of society with no repercussions. But the truth of the matter was if those men who were quick to accept guns from anyone who offered them had indeed received them, the question would now be what were they going to do with them? How many lives would they have taken with them?

The Green Bay Killings sent shivers through my body, but we were not allowed to speak about it in Arnett Gardens as it was the work of their party. There were whispers that some of the top notch from the area took part in the Massacre.

Cassius Maquade a don from Tivoli Gardens was having a reality check. He spent some time in England and was confronted with the realities of racism for the first time. Those memories stayed with him on his return to Jamaica and he wanted to make changes in his community. He had strong backing from the residents of Tivoli, which was not good news for Seaga. Politicians knew peace would open the people's eyes, they would vote for a leader on his policy and not out of intimidation. For that Maquade was signing his own death warrant. Trouble was brewing between Seaga and Maquade, and those people who were close to Maquade were calling him boss. The respect he was receiving from the youths in the area was undermining Seaga's authority as chief commander.

After the Green Bay Killings, Maquade joined forces with representatives from the PNP to organise a peace rally in the hope that it would put at end to the tribal wars. Some men who were their soldiers went with them, but had other things on their minds and peace was not one of them. The younger soldiers had ambitions to be dons one day and peace would only get in their way of fulfilling their dreams of leading their communities into battle (and what about the guns and housing contracts, they could not let those opportunities go by). Where else could they live with such status without an education? Who would give them easy jobs such as killing, that only took a few minutes and after the first one the others became easy?

And what about the dreaded Goldie Locks of Rema along with the Rema Thirteen, Ninja and the Ninety's Crew, they too would be celebrating the peace, but did they really want it? Goldie Locks, the self appointed Minister of Housing for Rema, told the elderly residents that they would have to pay him rent for their properties or they could not live in a peaceful community. If someone should tell me now that there is no devil I would have to differ, for I have met his son in Goldie Locks of Rema. He was evil to the core. He would not want peace, because that would have put an end to his reign of tyranny and the evil one was not going to let peace get in his way. He would dance to their songs and speak to the enemies, but come tomorrow it would be back to work at the house of evil.

The peace treaty was celebrated with dances all over the place. It was meant to be a joyous and peaceful affair but there were gun salutes, as it would appear that they knew no other way of enjoying themselves. The finale was at the National Heroes Circle where they had a stage show. Bob Marley performed along with Peter Tosh and other reggae greats. Why the gunmen who wanted to carry on with their lives of crime, chose the National Heroes Circle, the resting place of our beloved forefathers, for such a farce, was beyond me. Those fallen heroes were against everything they stood for. While many wanted peace some did not and only attended to save face. Bob Marley called up Manley and Seaga on stage to hold hands, but a lot of us were not holding our breath, for we in Jungle knew the real deal that was going down. Bob Marley should have changed the words of one of his song 'War' and sing:

> *Until the political system in Jamaica*
> *that divides the people is finally and*
> *permanently discredited and abandoned*
> *there will be no peace.*
> *Until the prejudice in our nation which*
> *favours brown and white people over*
> *blacks is no longer, until the*
> *exploitation of the weak and dispossessed ceased.*
> *Until the basic human rights are equally*
> *guaranteed to all without regards to class,*
> *then the dream of lasting peace will*
> *remain only an illusion.*

At the peace rally Manley and Seaga shook hands and laughed with each other for all to see. The people shouted their approval. Some danced while others took the opportunity to speak to friends and relatives they had not seen in many years when the borders were closed.

One week after returning back to their communities the rapes, the stealing and the killings started again and the borders were once again closed. Those who really wanted peace were left feeling hopeless and the politicians were digging their heels in. The fight for peace was not going to be as easy as they thought. Cassius Maquade thought he could work on his people in Tivoli and then they could shine their light for others to see and change from their wicked ways, but politicians were making it clear they were in charge. Maquade thought he could do a better job as he understood the pain and suffering of the people in his community, because he was one of them and lived amongst them. He was getting too powerful for his own good.

There were other young men waiting in the wings to take over the mantle, but Maquade would have to be dethroned before anyone could wear his crown. Only death could remove Maquade and the only question was who would kill him? The ambitious young men waiting in the wings would not take on such a task, as Maquade was well loved in the community and they might have had a rebellion on their hands. Also if the assassination went wrong and Maquade survived an attack on his life a lot of men would have to run away. That job was for the professionals and who would that be? If the soldiers could show their loyalty to the PNP by eliminating unwanted weeds, what was preventing the police from doing the same for the JLP, after all there would be no repercussion, life would go on as normal. Maquade was marked for death.

Cassius Maquade was also a saving grace for the people living in Rema. Tivoli men were Seaga's darlings, Arnett Gardens (Jungle) had the backing of their member of parliament, Anthony Spaulding but Rema men were left as the neglected god-children of the JLP. They were part of the Trench Town constituency, but did themselves no favour when they went over to the JLP. They always had to depend on Tivoli men for handouts, as they did not have a political boss to supply them with goodies. Rema was a smaller community than Jungle so they had no chance at the polling stations even with the bogus votings.

Tivoli men wanted respect from Rema men, but the evil Goldie Locks would not have any of it and he was always supplied with arms. Cassius Maquade saw Rema men as allies who needed not to be feared, so he in turn did not think he needed to make them fear him. Goldie Locks unlike Maquade was hated in Rema, but people were too afraid to challenge him. Even bad gunmen in Rema were afraid to confront him when he stepped out of line which he did daily. Goldie Locks was a rapist who did not care who, when and how he raped. He raped the women of other gunmen who knew about the rapes but turned a blind eye. He raped an older girl who I knew when I lived in Rema. She was so distressed by the ordeal she messed herself. The area leaders from both Rema and Tivoli heard about the incident, but were too afraid to take action. They told the residents not to report crimes to the police as they would deal with it, but when the perpetrator was someone like Goldie Locks the crime would go unpunished. The girl could not go to the police because she was frightened for her life so she had to suffer in silence. She had no support to deal with the trauma and the politicians who created the problem were uptown with their children.

Goldie Locks was a pervert who humiliated the young girls in the community by demanding three in a bed sex and anything else he desired. He told them to gyrate on or under him depending on the position he chose to rape them, as he would not accept them 'laying, like dead logs' as he called it. If they did not move he used pins to stick them on both sides of their thighs to get them moving.

He told three girls to visit his apartment one night. They received the order during the day and knew they had to go or face his wrath. Deloris was one of the three girls. I remembered her from when I lived in Rema. He called himself a Rasta; would not eat pork and said he had certain principles he lived by and one of them was never to have sex with any woman who was on her period. Well, thank God for periods for a lot of girls escaped his wrath because of it. The three girls went to his apartment as they were told to do, he had the audacity to leave them there for a while and went out to see to other matters. The girls knew they could not leave the apartment and stayed in Rema so they waited for him to return. While he was away the three girls were discussing their fate. One of them was on her period and was hopeful that he would let her go. One of the other two wore a sanitary towel and hoped that he would believe that she was on her period, but was not hopeful that this would work, so she asked the girl who was really having a period to put some blood on her pad to fool Goldie Locks. She was told that it would not have been fair on the third girl, so she had to hope he would believe her just by feeling the sanitary towel she was wearing. (Why she did not put some tomato ketchup or pigeon blood on the sanitary towel was beyond me).

When Goldie Locks returned to his apartment and was told that two girls were on their period and one was not. The so-called Rasta man demanded that they showed him their sanitary towels, which they did. The one who was indeed on her period was told to leave the apartment immediately and the rascal who called himself a Rasta took out his anger on the other one who tried to mislead him. He kept her in his home and raped her for several days before releasing her. She could not walk for days while the other girl got off lightly. A lot of people knew this took place and the girls had to suffer the indignity of seeing him everyday knowing that they would not get any justice.

Goldie Locks enjoyed inflicting pain on innocent people who submitted to his aggression, and he used the political corruption in Trench Town in his favour. Anywhere else and he would have been arrested for the crimes he committed, but in Trench town it was allowed. Whenever he was attending JLP rallies and conferences, he would be dressed in the best suits money could buy. People seeing him on the streets and not knowing who he was could have easily mistaken him for a sane person, but the truth was his mind was twisted beyond imagination. You would have to know him and see him at work to understand. He had many girlfriends whom he ordered to go out with him and they had no choice but to have a relationship with him. He had one from Tivoli he killed and then told her sister it was her turn to date him. He even told her that when her time was up then it would be their mother next.

He became bored on one occasion and decided he wanted the taste of blood. One victim would not be enough that day so he set up some young boys to break into his shop and pretend it was a robbery. When the news came out that Goldie Lock's shop was broken into, people were wondering who had received an invitation from Madden Funeral parlour and was in a hurry to get there before the other invited guests. Everyone was suspicious of someone and started ignoring each other. They were not sure who did it and if it was their best friend they would have to disassociate themselves from that person, as no one wanted to be at the mercy of Goldie Locks. They thought the best thing to do was stay at home until the guilty person was found. Goldie Locks, who knew this was just a scam to feed his insatiable lust for blood, went on a rampage and beat every young man under twenty years old. Their mothers' could only watch and cry. After that he beat one of his girlfriends with his gun, stick and feet. She had blood coming from all parts of her body. Many people thought she would not survive the ordeal. Her mother was the only one who went outside the apartment block to see what pain her child was enduring by the hands of that wicked man. Other people just looked through their windows. One man was holding them to ransom. He had the backing of the JLP, so the danger he posed to the people was great.

Goldie Locks beat the young boys in the area if they did not do chores for him and demanded rent from the elderly residents many of whom were ill. He opened a shop and told the people they could only buy from him and if he did not have what they wanted then they would have to get something else in the shop. The man was a one man band who had young boys as young as ten and eleven stealing for him. He was a rebel without a cause and a law unto himself. Whenever there was a peace treaty between Jungle and Rema residents Goldie Locks would look to see who from Rema had relatives in Jungle and beat them after the show was over.

Christopher saw Prim at one of the peace dances held on Seventh Street. He recognised her from afar even though they had not seen each other for some time. He rode his bicycle up to her and circled around her, but she did not recognise her own son.

She thought it was a young boy who fancied older women and was making a move on her. Her friend who was standing nearby asked her if she knew him and she said no. She gave him a dirty look and was about to tell him off when Sue saw Christopher and told Prim it was her own son. How Sue recognised Christopher and Prim did not? It just went to show how much she was thinking of us. Rather than giving her son a hug she said to him, 'yu political party in power so yu must have some money'. What a thing to say to a child, especially when it is your own. She knew Christopher was too young to vote and she was treating him like a political foe. The real message behind that statement was that if he had any intention of asking her for anything, he should get it out of his mind. She used the tribal politics as the reason why she did not see Christopher and me, but the truth was, it was just a convenient excuse. What made matters worse was that she was too busy looking out to check if Goldie Locks was seeing her talking to her son than to concentrate on their discussion.

Christopher even saw her in downtown Kingston during a Christmas period while she was out shopping for her family and he was helping his aunt sell toys to make some pocket money. She went over to him and gave him fifty cents to the disgust of everyone who was present. The people who saw could not believe how cold and heartless she was, to give her child fifty cents at Christmas after not seeing him for a long time. There was no tenderness, love or compassion, for the child she gave birth to. She just handed over the fifty cents piece and she was on her way. When they had the peace treaty in 1976, I went to visit Prim and found her washing her other children's clothes, in 1978 Christopher went to see her and yet again she was near her home. At no time did she take the initiative to visit us. Many relatives took the opportunity to see their families that they had not seen for a long time due to tribal politics. Some met each other half way, but not Prim she was not interested.

My paternal grandmother came to Jamaica on a visit in late 1978 and she was staying with one of her grandnieces in Olympic Way. She told Tom to bring me to see her and he took me there. For the first time in almost three years I was venturing out of Arnett Gardens. When she saw me she felt sorry for me and asked her niece if I could stay with her and she said yes. Tom told me to pack up my few belongings and I was on my way out of Trench Town.

Chapter Six

When I got to Olympic Gardens my grandmother was upset about the neglectful state I was in and told Tom about it. She asked him why I did not have any clothes. He was so embarrassed he told her that I had clothes and even had the cheek to ask me in front of her and his cousin Debbie if I had clothes. She told him off about buying worthless cheap footwear for me. Then she bought me a pair of shoes and for the first time since I left under Prim's roof I wore proper shoes. Prim was poor but she would have never sent me to school without proper clothing and if she did at anytime it was because she could not afford to do it and not because she was stingy.

My grandmother made some clothes for me and Debbie gave me some. I met a new friend by the name of Bess who lived near to my new home. She attended a local secondary school in the area but I continued attending Trench Town. My new community was fairly calm compared to Jungle but violence from Waterhouse, a PNP stronghold was spilling over to us. Olympic Way reminded me of Rose Town that was destroyed by political violence.

My grandmother stayed with us for three weeks then returned to the United States. She promised Debbie to send money for my keep and Tom was to continue giving me lunch money, that was nothing new as that was all he ever did. Debbie showed me the bus journey to school. I had to take the number eight bus to Spanish Town Road and my fare was five cents each way. I got off at the old Majestic Theatre and walked through Rose Town when the thugs would let us through, but sometimes they intimidated us so much we had to walk the longer way up Maxfield Avenue to get to school.

Debbie was living on her own in a two bedroom house her grandmother left her when she went to England. Her grandmother and my grandmother were sisters. I had a bedroom to myself for the first time in my life. Debbie was a Christian and attended church every Saturday. I went with her and enjoyed many aspects of it, but the people were prejudiced even in God's house. There were some people who never spoke to me and would pass others and me on their way in and out of church without as much as saying 'good morning'. My eyes were beginning to open to the culture of prejudice outside Trench Town and the church was not immune to this.

On my way home from school one evening taking the shorter route through Rose Town (which was a sight for sore eyes) I saw that the house I lived in was gone and the area was an empty lot. I had to look again to make sure I was at the right place. Because I lived in Jungle and did not leave my community very much I was not aware of what was happening elsewhere. The youths in the area demolished the empty houses and many of them were still living on the streets that just did not make sense to me. When I reached near the end of Rose Town I saw a man riding on a bike, I almost died in excitement as the man was my uncle Moses, I called him but he did not hear me and went on until he was out of sight.

I followed some friends downtown to walk about and buy kisko pops and Tastee Patties. This was a first for me. I stayed close to those who knew their way around because I did not want to get lost. We took the number eight bus on Spanish Town Road to downtown. I knew I would get it back home but had to make sure I found where the bus terminus was. On my way downtown the bus passed a familiar place - the other end of Collysmith Drive and May Pen Cemetery where Pepe was buried. I knew then that Prim was not living far, but what confirmed it for me was when the bus arrived at my old primary school, Denham Town, and the police station where I went for help when Tom beat me and they turned me away. When I saw the school and the police station I knew I could find my way to Prim and Carl.

The next day at school I asked the girl in my class who lived in Rema if she knew Prim, she said yes and that they lived in the same housing scheme. I asked her if it was safe for her to take me with her after school one evening. She came back the next day and told me that she told Prim that I was asking about her and Prim wanted to see me. I mustered up the courage and went with her one evening. My aunts and uncles were so glad to see me it was like the prodigal returned. I went to see my aunt who had the bar and gave Carl and me lunch when Prim could not afford to buy food for us. She was sick and the bar was closed. I found out that Lily and my aunts had moved down to Rema from Jungle when the trouble started to intensify between the two sides. Prim's features had not change much but she looked older. Also she never regained the weigh she lost when she became ill when I was living with her. I was told Christopher was still living in Jungle.

Rema was run down and in serious need of repair. The four-floor apartment block that I lived in with my family was filthy and worn. The old train I played on with my friends was still there. Prim had moved downstairs on the ground floor in one of the two bedroom apartments in that block. Only Goldie Locks and a few other men seemed to have been benefiting from politics in Rema. The residents were in a catch twenty-two situation, as they would become a beating stick for both sides if they denounced tribal politics so they had no choice but to play the game. The funny thing about them was that they were not concerned about the conditions that they were living in as they were so taken up with this whole political affair.

When I saw my old community tears came to my eyes. Most of all I was in shock at how my mother was living. There was no running water and the residents were using a standpipe, which was far from hygienic. Most people washed at the standpipe while others took water back to their homes to bathe. Politics was tearing the people apart and breeding a new group of underclass in the country many of whom could not get any jobs, because as soon as they said where they lived the interview came to an immediate end.

The Rema residents were living below the bread line but segregated politics was very evident. Almost all the walls the community had writings on them in favour of the JLP or criticising the PNP. The people lived for politics. One of my aunts was even saying that the residents in Jungle had a different complexion from those who lived in Rema. Of course this was not true, but she and her neighbours believed it because they were so blinded by politics. The people were stripped of their dignity and the suffering showed on the young and the old, but no one was around to ease the pain the people were feeling. I looked around and remembered the days I used to walk from Rema to Jungle without fear. I wondered when the gunmen would wake up and put an end to the madness. Leroy Smart wrote a song about the memories of the old days and I remembered it then:

> *'We used to lick chalice and cook ital*
> *stew together.*
> *Played football and cricket as one brother.*
> *No true yu rest a Jungle and me block a*
> *Rema, yu a fight gainst yu brother, and dat*
> *no right my sister. Let us all live as one yea.*
> *Throw wey yu gun, throw wey yu knife,*
> *Let us all unite , everyone is livi ng in fear*
> *Jus, true dis ballistic affair.*

In the excitement of everything I realised only when I got home that I did not see Carl, but I knew I would be going back, so I had all the time in the world to see him and salvage my guilty conscience. I was determined to make it up to him one way or another. When I went to Tom the next day he hit me and told me that someone saw me leaving Rema and how it was because of him why I could still attend Trench Town School. I knew someone must have seen me and told him that I went to Rema, but him protecting me could not be true for I knew and talked to some dangerous men in Jungle that he did not know. Also a lot of people knew I was from the Smith clan and even though my uncle Steve was long in the grave, he was still highly respected. And people who knew that I was related to him wanted to protect me for his sake.

I ignored Tom and continued to visit Prim and I saw Carl the second time I visited. At fifteen Carl was over six feet tall, dark and handsome. Prim was more accepting to me than Christopher and I thought she preferred me. I felt guilty about that, but I worked it out later that it was not a matter of liking me over Christopher it was just that she felt I was more financially better off than my brother and would not need anything from her. On one of my visits I heard them talking about Goldie Locks and what he used to do. The reason for their reminiscing was, Goldie Locks was no longer with us, having been sent home to 'shut eye country' (dead) by a young man who was fed up with his bullying. The boy was from Tivoli and as Goldie Locks was not one to show respect to anyone irrespective of where they lived, he beat the young man because he did not obey an order. The youth threatened that day that he would be the one to kill Goldie Locks and it was not an idle threat it was a promise. Goldie Locks heard what he had said, but felt he was invincible. He did not feel the need to watch his back as he always did his dirty work and no one ever challenged him. Well, his luck was about to run out. He was riding a bike in Denham Town, neighbouring Tivoli Gardens, he stopped to talk to someone when the young man who wanted to take his life spotted him and ran into nearby Tivoli to get a gun. Goldie Locks had recently killed a woman after accusing her of being an obeah woman (witch) and had threatened to kill another one when he return from his ride out but it was never to be. The youth crept up behind him and shot him off the bike splattering his brain all over the concrete pavement. He died with his gun in his waist.

Some of the girls he raped spat on his body as it laid on the ground and his killer was respected from then on, as he rid the area of the menace. Goldie Locks girlfriend made the arrangements for the funeral. Some people said that his mother who lived in the United States sent the money to meet the cost. Ten people turned up at the funeral including Prim. They said that they wanted to make sure he was dead and going into the ground forever. They did not even bother to dress in their pretty clothes and jewellery as was usually done when a high profile person from their community dies, instead they turned up in their house clothes.

One young man went without shoes. He used to walk and swing his waist so people used to tease him about being gay. Goldie Locks hated him when he was alive, but as it turned out it was that young man without shoes who had to help carry his coffin from the funeral parlour to May Pen Cemetery. Prim who went there to nose also had to help carry the coffin. She was not very happy about it but was talked into it. When I heard about this I had to laugh. I do not know what she was doing at Goldie Locks funeral until she had to carry his coffin, for many times Lily and Carl considered running away from Rema because of Goldie Locks hatred of young boys and older people. I wondered what he would have done if he could see that it was the young man who he used to call 'batty man' who had to carry him to his final resting place. Not one badman attended his funeral. The custom was when one political gunman died then he would get the gun salute, but Goldie Locks did not even get the luxury of having firecrackers. And no Rastaman turned up to beat the Kete drum for their fellow Rasta who passed away. The funeral was rushed and the priest did not bother to waste good prayer over him.

Goldie Locks' murder was a blessing to Rema residents but they later realised he was saving them from the wrath of Tivoli men. With one tyrant out of the way another was about to surface. Tivoli men wanted to be the big daddy to Rema men, as they were giving them arms to fight Jungle men. They wanted to give them orders too and if they did not obey, it would be hell to pay. Nothing was for free so if Rema men wanted ammunition from Tivoli gunmen then they would have to take orders. Maquade was mellowing in his older years and as he was the don for Tivoli, Rema residents were safe for a while but time was running out for all concerned. Mr Death was around the corner looking for Maquade and it would only be a matter of time before he caught up with him.

One evening in February 1979 Cassius Maquade was on his way home to Tivoli, from a football match when he was gunned down by police officers. The car he and his friends were in was stopped by the cops who must have known who he was. The officers told him to get out of the car, which he did. He tried to reason with one of the police officers, but another gave the order to shoot. They did not wait for anything else and pumped up to fifty bullets in his body. The other two passengers were also killed. The driver was the only survivor, he ran like a man possessed to save his life as the police came to terminate on the order of a higher authority. People who saw the body said it was like a sieve. The police officers involved did not face any charges as their explanation was, Maquade was a wanted gunman. An old timer who was a good friend of Maquade, died of a heart attack the same day the news broke. He had been planning to write a book to expose the politicians. Maquade's death sent a message to all area dons, as they knew then that they were dispensable. Some took their time to take their hands out of the lion's mouth, but for many it was too late. They were known wanted men so they had no choice, but to carry on with their lives of crime until the long arm of the law caught up with them. Many outlaws were outraged even those of the PNP. They saw Maquade's death as the work of politicians.

Some out of fear for their own lives left the island for the USA but rather than turning over a new page they became more ruthless than when they were in Jamaica. They got involved in kidnapping and other deviant lifestyles they picked up from the mob. They wanted a slice of the drugs market and were hell bent on showing the Colombians that they too could be ruthless. They started to recruit young men from their communities to join them in the land of opportunities. The Jamaican drugs lords took the same JLP versus PNP lifestyle with them to the United States and were still killing each other in the name of politics. Some were carrying old grudges but the irony was PNP supporters turned against each other due to the almighty dollar they got from drugs. They killed people and posted their bodies home in barrels to their families back in Jamaica.

Paul, an older student from my school, had a friend from Maxfield Avenue who went to America and became rich. He wanted more soldiers from Jamaica to help him with his trade so he recruited some young men he knew from Jamaica including Paul to join him in New York. Paul was a very polite young man who was an average student. His mother was a single mother with five children who thought it was a blessing that a stranger would want to help her son. Without hesitation she allowed her son to travel to the Big Apple on a green card, which belonged to a much older boy. She thought her sixteen-year-old son, the eldest of all her children, would be able to help her and the other children. I was told by another student who knew Paul well that he had migrated to the United States. I thought a relative had sent for him and I wished it was me. I really wanted my luck to change.

Shaft and Luke were thorns in the Angola men's side and they wanted to get rid of them. The funny thing was that despite all the killings that they were doing they had police friends who they could rely on to do their dirty jobs. If they knew of any robbery going down by another man, and knew they would not get a share from the take, they would inform on the person and get the police to ambush them. If the thief was a small fry then they would just allow it to go through then take everything from the steal. Shaft and 'Cool hand Luke' as a team were formidable together and the Angola men knew they could not challenge them without high casualties so they had to divide them.

Their chance came when Shaft fell prey to his own weaknesses and raped again. The Angola men and their leader, Tango, got the excuse they were waiting for to act. Hitler who was also a serial rapist was lining up to discipline Shaft. They got the breakthrough when Luke condemned Shaft and made it clear he would not support a rapist. In spite of all the rapings Shaft was doing his women remained loyal to him, but they were alone because other people were showing their contempt as well. I was at school when a girl who I knew came up and told me that Shaft and Angola men had a fight and because he was on his own he had to retreat to Tiger Valley. She said Luke did not get involved and said he did not have any rapist friend. Well, he would live to regret those words.

Shaft was banished from Jungle, but was still a force to be reckoned with in Tiger Valley, below Jones Town. Many Angola men would avoid Jones Town as they knew Shaft was waiting for revenge. I saw Shafts girlfriend who attended my school wearing a black patch on her uniform as a sign of mourning. I asked her who died and she told me Shaft. There was a surprise look on her face, as if to say how come you did not know this. He was killed by a cop who was patrolling the area. I was saddened by his death, but could not cry because he did not deserve my tears, besides I knew he was going to die as the writing was on the wall. What if he had been born somewhere else, would he have been a rapist? Or maybe he was a rapist because Trench Town encouraged deviancy. With his good looks he could have rivalled any Hollywood leading man, but instead he was born in Trench Town where he held centre stage, and even though he brought pain to a lot of women he was still admired by many others.

Angola men rejoiced when Shaft died as there was one less opposition to deal with and they wanted to rid Jungle of other gunmen who would not play ball their way. Hitler was molesting young girls, but no one complained about this. Students from Charlie Smith High School had to visit him after class at his request. He was doing exactly what Shaft was sent into exile for. So it was obvious that Shaft was banished from Jungle because he was seen as a rival and not an ally. Angola men were trying to run Jungle as a one-community order and to go against them would be signing your death warrant, but Tess was silently watching them. Love him or hate him, it was his ability to challenge other gunmen that had Angola men looking over their shoulders and kept the one-man army out of Jungle.

An Angola posse member was walking through Jones Town one day when he was held up down at gunpoint by Shaft's brother and relieved of his gun. The man was disarmed without much resistance, as he knew he had no chance against another armed man who attacked him by surprise. He went on his way with his life, but when he returned to Jungle he went over to Pegasus where Shaft's relatives lived and killed them all in their beds. Their bodies were found early the next morning. He only spared Pablo's two sons but killed their mother. He left the two toddlers in a blooded bed beside their mother dead body. The entire community was horrified by the killings but did nothing. Tango the leader of the crew, turned a blind eye to what took place. He was leader in name only as it was Hitler who was in charge.

One Monday morning I went to school and was greeted by some students outside the gate who looked troubled about something. I recognised one of my classmates in the crowd and asked her what was the matter. She told me that Marlon, an older student was shot to death by some men from Rose Town. We were all in shock for the rest of the day. Our schoolmate was murdered a few yards from our school and no one offered us any counselling. Not the police or our teachers. We never walked through Rose Town again. Marlon got one shot and was running for his life but was chased and shot again until he was dead. It was a meaningless killing of a young man in the prime of his life. He had everything to live for and in one moment of madness it was all taken away. He was not a member of a gang or belonged to any political party, he was just a schoolboy trying to make his way home and the killer probably did not even know his first name. No politician visited our school and the media did not broadcast the murder.

The women in Trench Town were not to be outdone by the men, they walked in groups and called them themselves crews or posses. They walked with ice picks and monkey lotion (acid) to maim and burn each other. The young women from the posses would dress up in the latest fashions to impress each other and the men they went out with. One man could have girlfriends from three or more of the women's groups and the girlfriends would war with each other for his affection. They thought having his baby would give them status so if one got pregnant the others would follow soon after. Woe be unto those who could not conceive as the other rivals would call them mules and tell them that their wombs were dumb. Some of the men could not even find money to buy themselves a pair of shoes but were having multiple baby mothers. The women themselves could not afford to care for a baby, but that did not stop them from getting pregnant. Many grandmothers were the ones who were left to support the babies and their parents. Mothers in Trench Town did not know when to rid themselves of the responsibilities of their children as they were still supporting them financially when they were well in their twenties and thirties.

The fighting by women and the killing by the men were glamorised by some singers and DJs in their music. At dances gunmen were being glorified with songs and were respected more than the police. Even some cops joined in the glorification by gun-saluting lewd songs.

The first time I knew cocaine was on sale in Jamaica was when I heard a man telling one of his friends that he got the drug from Tivoli, and I was in shock. Then rumours started that several entertainers were dabbling in hard drugs so it was not surprising when one well-known singer was arrested by police and charged with being in possession of a class A drug. That incident was a sign of things to come. An entertainer doing drugs was not a good sign in Jamaica as they were held in high regards and the young would see drug taking as cool.

Some police officers were on patrol in Matthews Lane one afternoon and picked up one of the area leaders, they took him to Denham Town Police Station for processing. Tivoli men found out that one of their arch rivals was in the station which was almost in their backyard and decided to go to get his head on a platter. They were armed with all sorts of sub-machine guns and were making their way to the police station to get their enemy; a member from the Spanglers posse who was on a roof watching to see what would happen saw Tivoli men marching in the direction of the station and alerted his friends. The Spanglers massive decided to go and meet their enemies head on at the police station to protect one of their leaders. Boys as young as fifteen-years-old, went marching into enemy territory with guns of all makes and sizes. They were like wolves in a pack going to the aid of their leader who was about to be slaughtered by some hostile butchers. The police at Denham Town Police Station were no match for Tivoli men who were moving in on them fast to take out the prisoner whom they knew the police could not protect.

Gunshots barked when the Spanglers crew arrived in sight of the police station. If Tivoli men were in doubt of the police's ability to protect their prisoner, they had none about the brat pack from Matthews Lane who were facing them with high tech rifles. They retreated back into Tivoli - with the police shooting from one end and Spanglers from the other. The police found some space to move their prisoner to another lockup. That incident, like many others, showed the weakness in Jamaica's security force and their inability to protect its citizens. It was also clear that the gunmen had no respect for the law. Police stations were under-equipped and under-staffed, and those which were based in violent communities were not able to respond to the type of trouble that was likely to erupt and they had to wait for a long for backup to get to them. There were no bullet-proof doors or windows and no proper communication systems in place for them to call for help. The officers posted at those stations knowing that they could not beat the gunmen did the next best thing and befriended them to get protection.

The gunmen exploited the weakness in the security system and knew very well by the time backup arrived they would have done enough damage and gone into hiding. If they were later caught by the police their politician bosses would get them the best lawyer in the country and no witness would be brave enough to go forward so they were untouchable.

People were dying everyday and food was becoming scarcer by the minute. Businessmen stepped up their campaign to get rid of Manley so they were holding onto the food at the wharves. Also many stopped importing necessary items needed by the people so there could be a rebellion against the government. Many of those businessmen cared nothing about the people and knew they could still keep their businesses alive for a little while longer. Some were also tax evaders and were only on the island for what they could get. Manley could see through them and taxed them heavily, but they would not give in without a fight. They knew the country relied heavily on them so they had the power to hit hard. Several of them owned banks and hotels and employed staff who were disrespectful to black people who used their facilities. They were aware of what was happening, but did nothing as black people did not have a loud voice in the country and their complaints went nowhere.

The poor man stayed in the ghetto with no food and medical supplies while the rich could afford to import their goods from the United States. Rice became a luxury. If you did get it in some shops they married it with something else, which meant you could not get it unless you bought something else that was not popular and you did not need. The very poor were hit hardest as they could not afford to buy the rice much more the other something they did not need.

Manley was losing ground in the polls and needed help fast and Seaga was threatening more violence if a change of government did not come soon. He wanted a taste of power and did not really care how it came. The businessmen were also calling for an early election, as they could not afford to hold out the sabotage for too long as their businesses were suffering. People were calling for Manley's head on a plate, they no longer cared about the minimum wage and women who could not get soap to wash did not give a damn about the equal pay law. The people in the rural parishes were also feeling the pinch and wanted a change. They were fed up with the violence in the city as it was preventing some of them from making a living; many of them were farmers and sold their food in Kingston. They were terrorised by gunmen at the Coronation Street market and had to pay Tivoli and Matthew's Lane area dons protection money. Those who could not afford to pay or would not pay on principle had to go elsewhere to sell their goods.

I spent a lot of time at my friend's house, which was not to my cousin's liking, so she packed my bags and sent me back to Tom who had moved to another housing scheme in Jungle. He was living in Mexico with Mel. I spent most of the time inside the house as I hated being there. Tom hit me in the head one day and I prayed for him to go back to jail. I knew he had trouble with his fingers so I hoped the devil would lead him back into temptation. My wish was granted when he called me one day and explained that he was going to court that morning. He told me if he did not return home, I was to go to his brother's house at Waltham Park Road and ask him if I could stay with him. I did not want to go as I knew Tom and his brother had not spoken for years, and it was his responsibility to ask his brother not mine. But I gathered up the courage and went, as I was the one who would be homeless and not Tom.

Tom was going to be housed and fed at the expense of taxpayers for nine months. Also he must have enjoyed some aspects of prison life as he was always doing something criminal to get there. I found where Tom's brother lived and went to ask him for refuge and he said no. I was on my way to Mel when his common-law wife told me to get my clothes and come back because she felt sorry for me. I did not want to stay there as my own uncle was willing to see me on the streets rather than offer me a home, but I decided to go with destiny. If I had gone to Prim and asked her to put me up she would have refused, so she did not come into my thoughts.

I was back out of Trench Town again. This time I only spent four months there thanks to Tom. My grandmother found out I was staying at one of her other son's home and sent me money on a monthly basis for my lunch and bus fare to get to school. Whenever the money was late I had to walk to school and walk back home and go without lunch as I had no one else to ask for money.

My new community was fairly quiet. Some young men were taking money from a politician, but it was difficult for them to colonise the area as it was too open for all to see what was happening. Some had guns and were using them to rob but they were not in the big league like the Trench Townians. One name that was cropping up all the time was Desmond who was constantly in trouble with the police. He was handsome and smartly dressed. He was seeing a young lady who was living at the end of my road. He dropped out of school but she was still attending a secondary school. He used to stare at me but I was not interested in him and used to pretend as if I did not see him staring at me.

I fell in love for the first time with an older boy (Pete) at school, he was three years older than me. I did not tell him how I felt but he guessed for himself. He never said anything to me, but would greet me with a kiss on my lips whenever we met. I was a coward so if he did not make the first move neither would I. He came up to me one day and hugged me from behind I was taken by surprise and did not know how to handle the situation, he sensed my fear and let go of me. I was fourteen and never felt that way about anyone before and it was nerve-racking. He looked at me and went away. After school one evening I went to Half Way Tree to see a friend and saw Pete with my friend's sister who was one year younger than me. I was shocked and he could see the look on my face but said nothing. At school the next day he told me he knew how I felt about him, but I was too young for him and that I should wait until I was sure of what I wanted. I wanted to shout at him and tell him that I wanted him, but my pride would not allow me, and the hypocrite called me young. How old did he think my friend's sister was or did he mean too young for what he wanted?

He graduated from school that same year and went to the United States shortly afterwards. I saw him at the graduation ceremony where he kissed me on the lips for the last time. I was left with a broken heart, but I was young and life would go on.

I often went to the afternoon matinee at the cinema in Cross Roads with friends. The cinema was frequently packed, as children from many different schools would attend. One of my favourite films was 'Cornbread, Earl and Me'. Jungle men liked the movies as well and would attend afternoon movies when school children were attending. The lines were so long if we turned up late we had to find someone we knew who was near to the front and ask them to give us a cut (which meant standing in front of them). I asked anyone I knew, even Jungle men who would always find themselves in front no matter how late they arrived and they would also make sure I got a seat inside by telling a sucker to give up his seat.

One afternoon I was on my way to catch a bus home from Cross Road after I attended a school show. I said goodbye to my friends and Bagga who I saw with some of his Angola friends standing outside the cinema. I assumed they saw the film as they were still talking about it outside. I walked around to the number fifteen bus stop, as I wanted to go to Waltham Park Road. I was not far from the bus stop when I was stopped by a man in his twenties asking me if I knew who Tango was. I told him no as I suspected what he was up to. He said he recognised me as one of the schoolgirls who were always laughing at him and his friend Tango. He thought he was being clever, but firstly, I had not seen anyone as ugly as him before in my life and secondly, this man could not have been in his right mind accusing me of laughing at Tango and his friends in their face. I knew he was a JLP supporter who was looking for easy targets to kill. He had a knife in his hand and was telling me to follow him where he was going. I was afraid but I had to keep a clear head. I was in two minds should I lead him into an ambush and take him to Tango's real friends who I had left standing at Carib Cinema or should I make a quick escape. I decided to escape instead. I could not live with myself if someone was killed because of me even though they were trying to hurt me. I walked in the direction of the bus stop to the man's annoyance. He could not do anything without drawing attention to himself and he was well out of his territory. I got on a bus that was waiting for passengers and he could only look and walk away to seek out another victim.

The little fool wanted to kill me because I was wearing Trench Town School uniform. He was making the assumption that I lived in Jungle or I was a PNP supporter, even though I was attending school. The idiot wanted to be a don yet still he was picking on easy targets, children. He could not even talk his way out of a paper bag and wanted to pick up badness. He did not even know what could have happened to him there in Cross Roads. He must have been really bloodthirsty that day. He had one long cut in his face from the days when it was fashionable for badmen to have telephone cuts. For many it was a sign of badness but Mr Chin put an end to that slogan. Many businessmen operating in the ghetto got young men to protect their properties, and scar face men were very popular with the businessmen, but not Mr Chin. One scar faced young man went to Mr Chin offering his services as a security guard and was chatting tough with the badman attitude to back it up. He said to Mr Chin, 'mi caan be de security fi yu place yu no, cause yu si from when a tief si my cut, dem na, even bada fi stop ya so', Mr Chin replied, 'mi no wan yu, mi waan di man wey scar yu'. From that day badmen knew that it was more in their favour to avoid being cut in the face.

    I was on my way to the auditorium at school one afternoon when I saw a young boy staring at me, I did not recognise the person straight away but I heard him telling his friend that someone was his sister. I knew the boy was referring to me as he was staring at me. I looked at him again and recognised that it was Christopher. I could not believe the little boy who last saw me when he was four years old could still remember me seven years later. I heard his friend saying, 'is good people yu want to be yu family', but I told his friend that he was telling the truth. Christopher was attending Trench Town Primary School and was living only a few minutes walk from where I used to live. After that we saw each other from time to time but I never visited his home as I used to do when we were younger. Most of the time when we saw each other it was when we met at school or on the streets.

    I was on my way home from school one evening when I saw another familiar face, but I could not work out in my mind who it was. The young woman was walking with a toddler beside her and a baby in her hand. The person was looking at me as if she knew me from somewhere, but looked away as if she was ashamed of something. A lady who I knew was coming down towards us but she had to pass the young lady with children first and then me. She waved to the young lady with the children and then came up to me and smiled. I asked her who the lady with the children was and she said it was her friend's daughter Melanie. I almost fell over in shock. I could not believe my dear friend Melanie could look so aged and distressed. The lady told me that Melanie became pregnant by a man old enough to be her father and the two children she was walking with belonged to her. Melanie was the same age as me so I wondered which paedophile raped her and got her pregnant. My heart bled for my childhood friend but I had to go on my journey and seek and find my own destiny.

    Melanie was one of the children who played the Russian roulette game that was compulsory for those of us who were born in Trench Town. She lost but I had to go on as I still had a life left. I did not see her again. The age of sexual consent for a woman was sixteen, yet here was this young girl with not one but two children and no one intervened. Not the police, teachers and not the area leaders. The man should have been charged with statutory rape, but as I said before, we young people had no rights under the law and whatever laws they had written down were just writings on papers.

    I was shocked by Melanie's predicament, but it was Diana, our teacher's pet at Denham

Town Primary who really knocked me for six. Someone who lived in Tivoli and knew her, told me that Diana got pregnant at thirteen and dropped out of school, I was sad for her. How could such a promising student like her lose her way so much? Yet again, another older man was to be blamed. Life was truly like one big road with a lot of signs. All it took was for someone to read a sign wrongly and end up, down a dead end road. Well, this one will not be much of a surprise to you as it was not for me, I saw Big Girl and she called to me. I was even glad to see her. She was still attending school, but had got even bigger and the uniform she had on was having a very hard time.

Mel asked me one day to accompany her on a visit to see Tom in prison. I told her that I would not visit him in such a place, also I never benefited from what he had acquired. She was not very pleased with what I said and commented that she would tell Tom. I never thought she would, given how she used to talk about him but she did. When he came out of prison I asked him for some money to get a pair of shoes and he told me no, because he was the one who took the risk for his money, and there was no guarantee that I would visit him in prison if he was caught. I was not too disappointed because that was his usual response. At least he found out that he was nothing but an embarrassment to me. I survived without his assistance in the past and would continue to survive without it. I was envious of children at school who seemed to come from stable homes.

With gross mismanagement of the public funds by government members and the sabotage by the elite class the poor people were being crippled with poverty. Tinned milk and common salt fish became rare commodities. For many of us they were luxuries as the supermarket and shop shelves were almost empty. Medication was in short supply and if there was any many of us could not afford to buy it and many people with infections would have to use homemade remedies or die.

Our money was fast losing its value and people losing respect for it. We were not taught that if you count the cents they add up to dollars and the dollars add up to thousands so many of us threw the coins in the streets because they were not worth much. We who were passing the money in the streets were poor, but did not bother to pick them up. We did not respect it, neither did we have any real sense of responsibility to it as we were more interested in thousand of dollars and not small change. The banks and the shops were all short of change because most of coins were lying in the streets. When we purchased anything from the shops or supermarket we were given sweets or matches in return for our small change. This practice was open to corruption as some of them had the money to give us, but forced unwanted sweets on us to keep our money. After accumulating several boxes of matches and having lost the taste for sweets, I challenged a cashier at a supermarket in Half Way Tree for my change and was told in no uncertain terms how I was cheap and that I was the only person who complained. Then I was told to get lost.

We, the poor, were getting a raw deal but did not bother to complain. We were forced to buy things we could not afford but what could we do? Everyone was blaming the government who had a lot to answer to, but never had anyone challenged the elite class about their sabotage. I prayed to God not to fall seriously ill as I knew I would die. with no one around who really cared and the lack of funds I could not afford to be ill.

Chapter Seven

The year 1980 was a nightmare for me in more ways than one, I was not happy at my uncle's and was waiting anxiously for the year to finish as my grandmother was returning to Jamaica the following year for good. We knew the election was going to be held that year, but did not know which month and the suspense had everyone on edge. Tom came to see me one day to let me know that he saw me making my way to visit Prim. He told my uncle that I was not allowed to visit my mother. My uncle laughed and said he did not know this but never mentioned it again. I did not need anyone's permission to visit my mother and I was not going to ask Tom or anyone else if I could. They could kill me when they found out for all I cared.

I went to see my mother the next week after school and I saw Carl sitting on a metal bar outside the apartment block where Prim lived. He did not look very happy because Prim was upset with him for gambling with the money my uncle gave him at Christmas to buy a pair of shoes. My uncle Moses was not happy with Carl either and had beaten him when he returned home from his gambling spree, as he had lost all the money. Carl borrowed some money from a friend, went back to the gambling house after the beating and won back his money which he used to buy a pair of shoes and trousers.

I sat opposite to Carl, but we did not speak we just looked at each other, eventually he looked away, but I continued to look at him. One of my aunts saw me staring at him and asked me if I loved him and he looked a bit shy as if he thought I was going to say no, but I said yes and surprised him. Jamaicans very rarely tell their loved ones that they love them so he was not expecting it. That was the first time I told my brother I loved him. My mother gave me dinner and told me to go home before it became dark. She came out of the house to walk me to the bus stop while Carl said goodbye to me and went over to talk to some of his friends. As I was passing the group Carl was with I heard him telling them that I was his sister, I smiled and went on my way home. I thought to myself the time would come when we could speak about the past and ease the tension between us. Prim did not know the relationship was strained and that I was carrying the guilt for so many years.

The violence in the country became really bad. I was too afraid to visit Prim in Rema so I decided to stop going there for a while. Jim Bob, Prince's friend who had two children with Peaches my aunt, was living in Jungle but had to run away to Tivoli because

Angola men were after him. Peaches was the only one of the Smith clan who did not move to Rema. When the border was closed she went to live in Jones Town with her new man.

Silver, another of Prince's old friend, escaped from General Penitentiary and was staying at Christopher's house in Jungle. His problem was that he was never going to give up stealing which was going to lead him to his death. Some dons in Jungle did not welcome his presence as they saw it as a threat. Whenever an original gangster surfaced the new guards started looking over their shoulders. People in the area were also whispering about Silver being in the area. He sent fear in many as he had made Jamaica's most dangerous wanted list. He was never a danger to women and children, but people were just afraid of his reputation. When I heard he was in Jungle I was curious to see if he looked the same as I remembered him, but he stayed indoors during the day time. I saw Christopher but he did not tell me Silver was staying at his house. Someone told Silver that some men in Jungle were planning to kill him so he went to Tivoli where he had some friends he had met in prison.

Silver was a victim of his own reputation and because of that he was never going to be welcomed anywhere in the capital. People became nervous just by the mention of his name. He thought going to Tivoli would be different but he was wrong. Tivoli men did not feel comfortable with the old guard around either and were soon planning his departure. Silver liked to steal and they knew it so it was just a matter of setting a bait for him. Silver was a thief, but had principles and he trusted those around him, but people did not feel comfortable around him. He met many dons in prison and got on well with them so he thought things would be the same on the outside. What he did not know was, he was not a threat to them in prison, nor were they to him.

Silver was set up to rob the Caymanas Park Race Track by some men he thought were his friends. He was told that there was someone inside who was going to lead him to the money, but he should make it look as if he did not know the person. Silver went on his own to carry out the robbery, but when he got to Caymanas Park instead of meeting a man who was to lead him to the money he was met by a battalion of police. He was executed on the spot. He must have known before he died that he was set up.

The gunmen were killing their rivals as well as anyone else even the police. Men from Eastern Kingston and Wareika Hill (the original home of the late Silver) were making a reputation as being the most dangerous criminals on the island which they were proud of. They took pride in their fearlessness and often challenged the police in street fights to show how deadly they were. Some of them would boast about how cold they were and that it took very little to kill babies and women and when they were killing they laughed just to show how cold they were. Many copied the attitudes of serial killers they had seen on television when they were carrying out their murders.

The Jamaica Council of Churches was calling for peace but no one was listening, they held several meetings and invited representatives from the political parties but that did not ease the violence (the JLP did not even bother to send anyone to some of the meetings, but sent apologies instead). Maybe they did the right thing as the PNP would only attend to save face. The JLP however had other things on their minds that prayer could not help with. They wanted to win the election and the gun would make sure of it.

In April 1980 some men with machine guns were walking on Drakes Road off Mountain View Avenue in South Eastern St. Andrew, when they came upon police patrolling the area and opened fire on them. The police returned the shots but were outgunned by the men who were brandishing high-powered rifles compared to the handguns they had. The men kept the police at bay and were spraying bullets everywhere, people were running into shops and other people's places to avoid being hit. The police called for backup but the men escaped in Back Bush and were last seen making their way to Wareika Hill. Two men were found with gunshot wounds in the search for the gunmen, but they were innocent people going about their business and got caught in the cross fire. A Jamaica Defence force helicopter came to assist with the search, but the police were too chicken to go into the hills to find the men. Wareika Hill men ruled supreme because the police and soldiers always avoided going into the hills after them as they did not want to be ambushed up there. The men would come out make trouble and go back to their safe haven. Wareika Hill men were loyal to the PNP. Some of Jamaica's most feared criminals lived there. They were the dons of dons and even their enemies admired them for their ruthlessness. I heard young men and women singing their praises. What made matters worse was that they made our police force look inadequate (maybe we were training the wrong men to be police and soldiers)

One Saturday night in April 1980, gunmen dressed in military uniforms shot up a dance in Gold Street in Central Kingston and killed several people. Prime Minister Manley was Member of Parliament for the area and it was that same area the men in the Green Bay Killings came from. The election was drawing near and it looked as if the Prime Minister was at risk of losing his seat. A dance sponsored by the JLP as part of their election campaign was invaded by PNP hitmen who had planned the assault a couple of weeks before it happened. They recruited the best of men from every PNP stronghold. Angola men approached Joe Bloggs who lived next door to Christopher my brother for his services but he turned them down. Joe Bloggs was from the old Trench Town and was known to be dangerous in his own right but he chose to flex with his own kind. PNP men in Central Kingston were networking by giving information to the hit squad about the place and how to make their get away as they wanted to rid the area of all JLP supporters.

Manley had visited his constituency the Sunday before the killing and was greeted by boos from some people who had switched from PNP to JLP after the Green Bay Killings. Some of the men who marched with him did not like what they saw at Southside as the people were stronger than ever and were hell bent on making Central Kingston a JLP stronghold. Seaga could see what was happening so he started dangling the carrots before their eyes and decided to sponsor a dance in the area.

Shortly before the massacre took place, a police patrol car came on the scene and ordered everyone off the streets. The partygoers were told to go to their homes but many were upset and were cursing the police saying they were working with the PNP. A few went home but some went on to the dance at Nine Gold Street.

The gunmen arrived not long after the police left. They might have seen the cops and waited for them to leave. The gunmen drove on Gold Street and sprayed the entire dance with bullets. People were falling over en-masse. Some were shot others were trampled on and one man's body was riddled with bullets. The gunmen got out of their vehicles and walked into the hall firing shots on people who were already on the ground just to make sure the job was done properly. The men also had home made bottle bombs and threw one in a bar, and robbed the owner of three hundred dollars. Eyewitnesses said over a hundred gunshots were fired and several homemade bombs were thrown at them. The terrorism went on for over half an hour and when the gunmen were leaving they fired several shots at Central Police station to let the cops know they were in town. It was only when the murderers left that the police came on the scene. Five people died and many others were injured. All around Southside had the signs that Mr Death had visited. Windows, doors and walls were shattered or pierced by bullets, spent shells were all around. A bloody sponge on which a young man died was still on the sidewalk.

Everyone came out and condemned the killings - the PNP, JLP, church leaders as well as the murderers themselves - but the fact was we were all responsible. If we were together as a people no man or woman could walk into a dance anywhere on our tiny island and kill our fellow citizens and then walk away as free as a bird. We had no law and we had no love. A nation without law will only reap anarchy and a nation without love shall perish. Central Police station was not far from the incident but yet again the gunmen got away. After the initial investigation the incident was forgotten and no one was punished for it.

Our school became a fighting hot spot for Rema and Jungle men. The war got so bad that on one occasion soldiers were called in to protect us. This was not the Middle East or some other known terrorist country it was Jamaica the place that prided itself as the number one tourist destination. Soldiers had to be sent to our school to escort us out of the building while Rema men were on the roof of the primary school firing gunshots at our school. Our principal called us to assemble in the auditorium, but many children felt frightened, braved the bullets and ran home. Those of us who were left behind were waiting for the soldiers to calm down the situation so we could go home. Some of the soldiers went on the roof of our school to trade gunshots with the men, but the gunmen were not in any playing mood as they belted out rounds after rounds. I saw one of the soldier's body jerked by the impact of a bullet that hit close to where he was. He got off the roof as fast as he could and I realised then taxpayers money was being wasted training soldiers. If they could not defend us against street fighters how could they if the country was attacked by outsiders. The street fighters would have to be the ones to do the fighting, God help us. We had to meet in a church for the rest of the week as our school was being used as a battlefield. Not once were we visited by any politicians to acknowledge our plight. Our school was not recognised as a prominent high school as no rich people children attended so who really cared?.

We had to face rapists and murderers everyday, the behaviour seemed so much a part of everyday life that even the men who were committing the crimes thought they had the right to do so. In March 1980 another anti-crime team by the name of the Ranger squad was introduced to deal with the growing crime rate, yet the atrocities continued.

In May 1980 what was to take place made 'Green Bay Killings' and 'Gold Street Massacre' looked like child's play. The Evening Tide Home was sanctuary to some of Jamaica's poorest and vulnerable people. It was situated on Slipe Pen Road and there was an entrance through Jungle. Many residents from Jungle including me walked through the home to get to Cross Roads and Heroes Circle. The home was a wooden structured two-storey building dating back to 1870. It was understaffed, old and a real fire hazard. There were seven hundred and eight residents who were either mentally or physically disabled living there.

The home took in many elderly people who could no longer care for themselves and had no relatives, and they also gave home to boys and girls who were abandoned by their parents because they were born with some form of disability. Whenever I walked through the Evening Tide Home grounds I could see the caring staff looking after their charges and the children looking at us as if all they ever wanted was for us to stop and talk to them, but none of us did and many people laughed at them.

It was almost the middle of the year so we knew it was a matter of when rather than if we would have an election. The PNP was way behind in the poll and Jungle residents were getting nervous. It was rumoured that in the previous election over one hundred people in the area voted for the JLP and people were saying it was the elderly people at the Evening Tide Home who had voted for them. PNP hitmen tried to eliminate the labourites at Southside so nothing could stop them from getting rid of some old ladies who were virtually living in their backyard. If the PNP was to lose the election one hundred votes would not have made a difference as they were well behind in the polls, but the hitmen could not see that as they were blinded by hate.

I was on my way to school on Tuesday morning the twentieth of May 1980 when I arrived upon groups of people all over the place. I caught on quickly to what had taken place in the early hours of the morning. The Evening Tide Home was burnt down and one hundred and forty four bodies were found with another nine missing. Myers ward had two hundred and five elderly women many of who were bed-bound. It was there that the fire started and ran through the rest of the building like a tornado. The fire chief said he used forty-five men to fight the flame, but the building was already enveloped by the time the fire station received the call at half-past-one in the morning. The police said four men were seen running from the compound shortly after the fire started, but offered no evidence to link them with setting the fire. The staff worked hard to evacuate the residents without help as the fire was moving fast through the building and many of those who died could not help themselves in any way so they had to perish in the fire.

The phone wires were said to have been cut before the fire started, but the police could not confirm this as the building was completely destroyed and the evidence went with it. I went to the scene of the crime and nothing could prepare me for what I saw. There were parts of burnt bodies everywhere, the smell of burnt flesh will stay with me forever, I could not eat meat for many days. I left the scene and went on my way to school with tears in my eyes. I met Bagga who was standing at his usual spot at Angola. He asked me if I was crying because of the fire and he smiled when I told him yes. He said to me, 'what a wicked act'. The look on his face was one of guilt. Guilt that he set the fire or knew who did but he was not at all sorry.

For the first time I saw him for what he was a scum of the earth. I could not believe that someone could set fire to a building with so many helpless people and cut off the only source of help. Imagine you were a member of staff at the Evening Tide Home and the fire started. Most of the people you were caring for needed some form of help getting out of the building and you did not know who to help first. The fire was moving so fast all you could do was to help those who could walk and just watch the others die. Imagine again that you were one of those people who could not walk and you saw the fire coming at you, the smoke stifling you by the minute and you were calling out for help but no one came. The only thing that was left for you to do was to surrender to death.

All of us Jamaicans have the blood of the one hundred and fifty-three elderly women who died in that blaze at the Evening Tide Home on our hands as we allowed the murderers to go unpunished. We were not part of the solution to the problems that were occurring in our country. We spoke about what happened for a few days and then conveniently forgot about it, but we should never forget those women who died because politicians gave madmen guns to ensure that people voted for them at any cost. Those women died because they wanted to exercise their right to choose. We as a nation took one step forward and ten backwards. In August 1962 the country gained its independence from Britain, after fighting earnestly for the right to choose and to be our own masters, so why did black people kill some old ladies because they wanted to exercise that right?

The murderers were never caught as the police said they did not have any evidence to link anyone to the arson attack so we had another unsolved crime. Most people in Arnett Gardens said that Angola men were responsible for the fire at the Evening Tide Home but no one went to the police. Those who were responsible can hide from man but they will never escape the Judgement. As long as there is a God they will never escape the wrath. I do not believe the same God that made me could make such people they must be children of a lesser god. The politicians who should have been looking for holes to crawl inside to hide came out again as usual pointing fingers at each other and expressing sadness at what happened. Some were only too happy when the police said they had no evidence that the fire was deliberately started. After the funeral we went about our business as if nothing happened.

The church leaders in the country were on edge due to the rumour that Manley was planning secret deals with the Communists. Manley made a mistake when he did not clarify the situation with them, as they too were a force to be reckoned with. For a country that is so violent there was a church in every corner of the island. The problem was the church was too quiet where politics was concerned and they were more a brainwashing tool to the young rather than an empowerment to their flock. Many of us who were forced to go to church as children could not wait for the day to come when we would not have to go because the only thing that was getting some of us there was the broomstick. Not even the church could give me refuge from the wrath of Tom and it did not help my self esteem either so what was the point. Our churches continued to be trapped in the past of slavery and that was the reason why they lost their young people to the world. We wanted somewhere to belong and the people in our church were classist and racists. Christianity was seen through a white perspective and how could black children fit into such an establishment, so it was not surprising when many young men converted to Rastafarianism. For many of them this gave them an identity that the church could not provide.

Our pastor told us on one occasion that when it comes to God colour does not matter. But if this is true why did he have a picture of a white Jesus in his church and a picture of the Passover with twelve white disciples? That picture was saying two things to us, that either there were no black people around when Jesus walked the earth or he was prejudiced. If Jesus only associated with white people when he was on earth why should black people now take up the cross and follow him? I do not mean to be sacrilegious but if the church wants to be more effective and appealing to young black people they need to change their image.

When I went to live with my uncle I started to attend two Pentecostal Church of God Churches situated off Waltham Park Road. I attended one first and then changed to the other. They were popular and had a lot of members. They rivalled each other for parishioners but one lost out as the pastor was mostly living in Canada and was not around to keep his flock together. They both invited white guests from abroad to visit their churches just to encourage more of us to attend, as they knew we were brainwashed and would come out in our hundreds just to see a white person and the more people in church the more collection for them. The visitors were dressed in clothing and jewellery church members were told not to wear. One of the pastor's explanations was foreign people dressed and worshipped differently from Jamaicans. If that was the case why did they invite people to their church that did not share their principles and why discourage their parishioners from wearing jewellery if that was not going to hinder them getting to the promised land? A boy I knew at church decided to teach pastor a lesson in real hypocrisy, and stole the collection money and used it to buy sweets. If he had been caught he would have known then if pastor was a saint or a sinner.

I was in church one Sunday night ready to hear the holy word from pastor. But what we heard instead was a stern direction for half-an-hour about who to vote for in the upcoming general election. Our pastor talked about the government's association with communists and how those of us who could vote should make sure no enemy of the church got into power. The faithful flock knew exactly who they would be voting for after the service. Many of them were talking about communism and the mark of the beast on their way home. I was so frightened that if I could have voted I would have made sure Manley did his last term in office.

I went to bed that night and was restless - I was half asleep when I had a vision about Carl and Prim. I saw some men leading my brother in the gully on Collysmith Drive at gunpoint and he was crying and calling my mother by her name. Prim was following behind but I could not make out what she was doing as my attention was on Carl. They took him in the gully and I woke up. I was glad when I realised it was only a dream, and Carl was all right.

I had not seen my brother since the last time he was in trouble with Prim and Moses. He and I had not spoken much about the past or present. It was as if he was not happy with me because I left him on his own at Prim's; I thought I would have time to make it up to him so I did not push anything. What a mistake I made. One week after the dream I went to see Tom and he casually told me that Carl died and that I could go to the funeral. A piece of me died that day. I did not react and once again my body was numb like the day Pepe died. When I returned home I mentioned it to my relatives and they did not even comment much more sympathise. Who could I share my grief with. No one cared about my feelings (or my brother). I kept seeing the look on his face that day I told him I did not have any money and he caught me eating my lunch behind the school building. How was I going to live with the guilt now that he was gone? I would never get the opportunity again to say sorry.

I went to see my mother the next day and she was grieving dearly for her firstborn child. Her dead son was only seventeen-years-old. He was the only one of her first three children who stayed with her. She was washing some clothes by hand and had one of Carl's shirts tied around her head and banded her tummy with one of his belts. She was indifferent to me, not happy to see me but not sad. She asked me how I found out about the death and I told her Tom told me. I asked her what had happened but she was not ready to explain so I had to ask other people and all I could hear was, Matthews Lane men killed Carl. With all the grieving that was going on I still could not get in touch with my emotions. My mind was numb and my personality was split in two. One was caught in the body of young Patsy who was close to Carl and the other in the older Patsy who did not know who Carl was before he died. I tried to unite the personalities but had no control over what was happening to me. I could not get support from my mother or her relatives as they thought their loss was greater than mine. I was no longer close to Carl but I was going through hell. I was only ever close to Prim, Carl and Pepe and now that she had other children, she had them and her relatives to support her. I always had to depend on myself so I knew this time would not be any different. I had to deal with my feelings the only way I knew how to and block out unwanted thoughts. Prim was worrying about the cost of the funeral but Moses and her sisters gave her what they could. I was poor and could not help to bury my brother so he was going to get a simple funeral at May Pen Cemetery near to his grandfather's grave. Carl's punky ass father had the nerve to tell Prim that his mother gave him some money towards the funeral but because he did not have any money for his house he gave it to his wife. I hope he remembers those words because I will.

I did not go back to my mother's until the day of the funeral. I arrived there early that morning and got dressed there. The service was held on the compound of Prim's home. To my surprise there were two coffins present. When I asked whose body was in the other coffin, they told me it was uncle John's son. His sister was playing with her boyfriend in their house. The boyfriend had a gun that went off and hit her brother in the head. He died before getting to hospital. Two cousins were to be buried that day both died by the gun, still no one was ready to explain to me how my brother died. I went in my uncle's van to the cemetery while a lot of people walked down to May Pen to see Carl enter the grave.

When we reached the burial spot I heard one young woman cursing so I moved closer to her to find out what was going on. I saw her spitting on a grave and wondered who it was and then I heard someone saying it was Goldie Locks who was buried there. Tears came to my eyes. I could not understand how Prim could buy a burying spot for Carl near Goldie Locks grave. If the man was so dreadful in life can you imagine what he would be like in death. Goldie Locks' spirit is either wandering the wilderness or he is a rolling-calf (mythical, a dead human come back as a tormented animal) but his body could not be resting in peace. I was getting tearful but it was when I saw my brother going down in the ground that made me break down and my wailing started off the others. A lady who I knew from childhood comforted me through my grief. When one of my aunts showed me how near Pepe was, I took comfort that between Steve, Pepe and Carl, they must be able to manage Goldie Locks.

If he should make any trouble Pepe was never one to back down from a fight no matter who the person was.

When we arrived back to Prim's we ate the little our stomach could allow us in solemn moods. I asked no more questions about the events that led up to Carl's death but I knew one day I would have to face up to it. That night when I got home I cried all through the night but I made sure I was quiet so I did not disturb anyone. After that I made sure I had a quiet moment to cry on my own when the pain got too much for me to bear.

Prim and I became closer after Carl died. If I did not visit her for a while she would ask what happened and why I kept away. This was the first time she showed any real interest in me. I heard her man and her arguing one day and was alarmed by what they were both saying. I knew things were not very good between them but did not know it was that bad. It was as if she hated him but she would not talk to me about what was happening. I heard him saying that she blamed him for me going away and Carl's death but she would not add to anything, as she knew I was listening. I knew for the first time she reacted to me leaving her. Sue also told me in front of her that she cried when I was out of sight but what was interesting to me was the mention that he had something to do with Carl's death. He did not care for us much as we reminded him of Prim's past life but what part did he play in my brother's death I wanted to know. Prim was not forthcoming with any information because she was embarrassed that I would also blame her and she was right.

Several years after Carl's death I asked her what happened and she told me that she did not like to talk about it. I told her that she would have to face up to what happened and it might as well be sooner than later. The story is a familiar one but nevertheless important. Soldiers and police raided Rema one afternoon. They were searching building to building looking for guns and ammunitions. Carl was inside his room sleeping but the others, including Prim's man, were outside watching what was happening. The soldiers searched all the men who were out on the landing but Carl was not included because he was inside sleeping. The soldiers missed him when they searched Prim's apartment and did not go back inside any of the houses for a second time. Prim's partner went inside the house to wake Carl and told him to get out of bed. He said that nothing was going to happen to him and if the soldiers were going to do anything they would have acted already.

Carl got up out of bed as he was told and went outside to join the others, the soldiers then did what they intended to do all along and detained all the men even though no weapons were found. Carl was seventeen years old but was ordered to get into a jeep with some men including Prim's man. He was crying and calling Prim's name as I saw him in my dream. Prim said he was begging her to protect him and not to let the soldiers take him but she had to just watch them take her son away.

The soldiers took them to a lockup at Fletchers Land over by Central Kingston. They were way out of their territory, which was dangerous for them. They were not charged but were shouted at and accused of being criminals for several hours. The soldiers and police did not care about the danger they were putting the young men in, and released them late at night to make their own journey through no go areas. A good kind-hearted woman saw them on the street contemplating what to do and put them up for the night. That woman must have been a saint to offer so many strange men refuge at night in such a turbulent period. They left the lady's house early the next morning and walked through downtown Kingston making their way through Denham Town when a gunman came out of a yard nearby and opened fire on them. Carl who was the tallest one in the group was hit in the head. The man who fired the shot disappeared. He shot my brother with one bullet for no reason and then disappeared. Carl was taken to the Kingston Public Hospital by his friends. Blood from his head leaked onto their clothes, he was taken to theatre as soon as he arrived the Friday morning and was operated on. Even though he was in a critical state and only just came out of surgery he was placed on a normal ward with other patients.

Prim said when she was told of the incident she was too weak to visit the hospital so she asked a friend to go in her place. The friend visited along with Prim's sisters. When they got to the hospital Carl was alive but his condition was serious, they reported back to Prim that Carl was still alive so she went to see him for herself. She went to the hospital on the Saturday and he was on a drip and being given oxygen. The doctor in charge told her that if he was to pull through it was possible that he would be brain damaged. Prim's youngest sister held his left hand and told him to blink if he could hear her but he squeezed her hand with his. Prim was optimistic about the whole situation but next day when she visited the hospital Carl was not in his bed, when she asked the nurse where he was she was told he died the previous night. The only explanation she was given was, 'you should have expected it as you saw the condition he was in'. If the condition was so bad why was he not in intensive care, why was he not on a life support machine, and if he was on one by whose authority was it switched off? The doctor in charge did not even speak to Prim. I was left with more questions than answers. My brother was dead within three days of being shot. No one had the opportunity to say goodbye. I did not say sorry, so all that happened in the past remain unresolved. The truth was Carl was not worth the money he was costing the hospital so they did not bother trying to save his life. Prim was naive and grief-stricken she did what many others like her have done. She just accepted what she was told without any fuss. Who was she a working class woman to question a doctor?

My concentration span at school was short before Carl's death but it got worst afterwards. I could not concentrate for long in classes and my mind would always wander to other things. I was trying hard in lessons but was not aware that my problem was that I was not able to take in one subject for a long period of time and my tutor did not recognise the reason either. My learning difficulty was not spotted because I was not exactly what they would call a dunce or it could be that they did not think I had the ability to excel beyond the level I was then achieving.

Tom never asked me how Carl's funeral went or how I was feeling. He was mean to my brother in life and his feelings were not going to change because Carl had died. My feelings did not matter to him either. I saw Carl's father one day after school and he said to me, 'dem killed Carl' and he looked hurt. I said yes and smiled but was too angry with him to keep up any friendly discussion, because he failed my brother when he was alive and sorry was not going to bring him back. He had a wife and children and my brother was dead. Life would go on as normal as he was not in touch with Carl for many years before his death. I want him to feel at least some of the hurt Carl felt when he was hungry and when he got the bullet in his head. I want him to remember his firstborn child he neglected and if he is tormented by guilt, he should be. Carl died because our mother was young, naive and was not ready to be a parent. She bit off more than she could chew when she became pregnant at fifteen with no parental guidance. She was a victim of circumstances but because of her carefree lifestyle her son died. She was ignorant to a lot of things but her actions should not be excused for it caused untold pain to her children who did not deserve it.

Carl's death should also be blamed on his father who did not care about the life he helped to bring into the world. Instead he left his responsibility for another man to take on and that led to death. All the men in Prim's life let her down. She stayed with Sue's father because she realised that she needed help and stability for her children. She was trying to find a father for us as the men who donated their sperm to her were all losers but what she got instead was a son taken away from her as a toddler, a daughter who left home at seven and a dead son at seventeen. What a price for any mother to pay! My mother went from relationship to relationship looking for assistance for us when her father died. People would say she did her best for us but perhaps the greatest sacrifice she could have made for us was to go and find herself a job. In those relationships she lost her pride, dignity, independence and her children.

My brother died in body but he lives on in my heart, not one day passes that I do not remember him and his pain. Every time I see a young boy on the street with pain in his eyes I remember Carl. The man who killed my brother did not just kill him he destroyed part of me. Carl has gone home where no man on earth can hurt him and where he will never go hungry again.

Prim had four children from her last relationship two boys and two girls. At last her man had what he wanted a home with her and his children but trouble was brewing in their home. The children were close to Prim because she was bearing most of the responsibility. The children were speaking out loud about their contempt for him and some blamed him for Carl's death. I could see that Prim was not interested in the relationship anymore and her man had another woman with children living not far from their home. Prim's younger sisters were following in her footsteps and having children in one dead end relationship after another and no one intended to break the cycle of deprivation.

Carl's death gave me a new found strength and I was determined to beat the odds for both of us. My brother will live through me and because of that I have to stay strong, as long as I have life I will stay strong, I will never surrender.

The Prime Minister finally declared October 30th the day the national election was to be held and 990,367 people were on the voters list. Bodies were popping up all over the place and we were becoming desensitised to the killings. Some of us were losing the ability to differentiate right from wrong and others were too afraid to speak out against the leadership of both PNP and the JLP in case their supporters heard and killed them. The election campaign cost more than nine hundred lives including that of Roy McGann, a leading government candidate and parliamentary secretary in the Ministry of National Security. The PNP blamed the killing on JLP supporters saying that Mr McGann was taking party members home after a public meeting when he was stopped at a roadblock, manned by JLP supporters and police, and was killed. The JLP explanation was that a car roared past a labour rally and opened fire, when the police fired back McGann was killed.

Wherever the truth rested charges and counter charges continued to empower the armed gang members that carried the banner of each party. The two party leaders gave joint statements about putting an end to the bloodshed and that anyone in their party found guilty of any wrongdoing would be expelled and reported to the police, but the words were just lip service, as it was clear that neither men wanted peace or had any control over their party members. The entire country was out of control. There was no law and order and when the Prime Minister-elect was not safe in a democratic country who would be. Manley attempted to hold a rally the week before the election in the main square of Spanish Town, the oldest city. Before he arrived the rally had already been broken up by some police officers who opened fire on a group of people who were throwing bottles and stones at them. A soldier and three civilians were wounded, one man was stabbed and one woman trampled to death. When Manley arrived he tried to assemble the massive but the people were too disheartened by then and he was stoned out of the square.

Not only the security forces and politicians were victims. Three elderly women were shot dead in their beds in downtown Kingston a week before the election and two children aged between two and five were shot while playing in their yard. Jamaica went to the polls on the 30th day of October 1980 for the fifth time since independence to elect a government for a five-year term. It was the longest, most violent and bloodiest election campaign in the history of the country. The reality was reflected in the almost complete close down of commercial and productive activity throughout the island.

The media reported that schools and business operations were suspended for the day, some schools would be closed for the entire week. Government offices would be closed for the morning of the election to allow employees to vote. The polling stations opened 8am. to 5pm. Tight security was arranged for the entire island especially in the vicinity of the 6,477 polling stations. The military and the police voted the Saturday before in what the media said was a heavy turnout.

My school was closed on election day as it was situated in the heart of the trouble. You could say Trench Town was where it all started. I had a feeling Manley would lose the election. I did not want the other tyrant to win but what alternative did we have. My uncle wanted Manley to lose as he said it was time for a change. The people were anxious to get this money Seaga told them would jingle in their pockets if they voted for him.

Trouble had been brewing on Waltham Park Road for some time but I saw men with guns there for the first time on the day of the election. I saw Desmond on election day with a gun. Desmond was a little under six feet, dark in complexion and neatly dressed. He was not bad to look at either but I did not particularly like him. I did not rate him as a gangster as I was from Trench Town and knew infamous dons like Silver, Shaft and Prince so Desmond to me was a wannabe and that could be dangerous as he would have to earn his respect. He was a young man not more than eighteen when I saw him for the first time. My cousin Pedro was impressed by his reputation and would talk about him all the time and it was him who first mentioned Desmond in my presence.

On election morning Desmond who was dating a young girl who lived in my road, openly brandished his gun for all to see. She came out to support her man and shouted to him to lick a shot. I did not hear her but a neighbour told me. The men who lived up my end of Waltham Park Road were JLP supporters and were fighting Mall Road men who were PNP supporters. Mall Road men were strong and had allies from all over the bottom half of Waltham Park Road and knew they could overrun Desmond and his colleagues if they really wanted to. What saved us was Waltham Park Road was not a close up community like Trench Town that was cut off from main roads. In the afternoon on election day some PNP supporters came up and fired shots in a crowd. A mentally ill man was shot in the leg but he died of shock on the spot. The JLP gunmen were nowhere to be seen when the man was gunned down. I knew then that they were way out of their league and they should not have taken up what they could not handle. What they were doing was putting innocent people's lives at risk because when the real trouble started they would not be around. It was well known that Desmond did not even live on Waltham Park Road. At the time he lived in a PNP stronghold but hung out on the Waltham during the day time.

We went inside the house to get out of harms way and to follow the election reports on the television. Everything we got came courtesy of Jamaica Broadcasting Corporation (JBC) the only television station on the island. When the ballot started counting it was clear that the PNP was in trouble and even the Prime Minister was losing his seat at one stage. Seaga and Anthony Spaulding, the MPs for Trench Town and Western Kingston, were obviously winning their seats.

Ken Maxwell who was one of the election analysts for the television station and a staunch PNP supporter was sweating under the air conditioner. He kept commenting how it was not possible for the Prime Minister to lose his seat but the writing was on the wall. In the end Manley scraped through and won his seat but people said it was fixed as had he lost it. What was certain at the end of the day was that he lost the election by a landslide. The new Prime Minister elect made his speech for the first time. It was sadness in one sense for Manley and in the other relief that it was over. Seaga said he was the better of the two so let him prove it. We were now waiting for money to jingle in our pockets. After the election tons of spoiled food were thrown out by the businessmen while people were starving.

Manley left the economy in a mess. We were basically cut off from the outside world and people were looking forward to better things. The expectation from the new government was so high they would need a miracle to change things and Seaga himself promised he could do better so it was time for him to deliver. Manley's dream of a democratic socialist society became a nightmare to us all and even his other well-intended policies did not seem to matter anymore. What's the point of getting a scholarship to a prominent high school if parents could not the afford bus fare to get the students there.

Under the Manley administration foreign exchange was hard to come by and the little we had was being sold on the black market without passing through the system. We were not patriotic when it came to the good of our country as everybody was looking out for themselves. We expected so much from the government but were not prepared to help solve the problem. The US dollar was trading at two to one Jamaican dollar and we got four dollars to the pound.

Everyone was looking to the government to make their lives better but we expected to make no sacrifices to reap good. Seaga was going to get a taste of the bitter pill Manley had to swallow. Seaga did not stand a chance of lifting the country out of poverty and was self-destructive. He won the election on deceit. He promised us something he knew he could not deliver and encouraged our ignorance because he wanted to be Prime Minister of Jamaica to ensure his ambition. How did he propose to get money into our pocket for it to jingle when he knew many people on the island prefer handouts rather than to work for a living. Maybe if he had promised to create more jobs at decent wages people would not have been so disappointed.

Chapter Eight

After Manley lost the election there was a big exodus of gang members to the United States. Those who could go the legal way did so, others went in other people's names. Some were stow-aways on boats while others called upon their politician bosses to assist them to get out by helping them in obtaining visitor's visas. Immigration officers in Jamaica at the airports and at the US embassy all took part in the great escape. No matter how prestigious their posts were they could be bought as they all had a price. The United States officials would want the people to believe it was just the Jamaican officials who were letting in illegal immigrants, but this was contrary to the truth. If this was a one way affair so many people would not have beaten the system that we had no control over.

The Rema posse, Dunkirk Boys, Junglists and Spanglers were all leaving the island for the Big Apple. News got back to Jamaica by those who left earlier that there was a new cocktail drug on the market that was blowing up the place. Those who were there were making quick money but the snag was the Colombians controlled a big piece of the pie. The Yankees had the street market and it was that piece the Jamaicans wanted. They knew they could not compete with the Italians or the other drug lords because they did not have the finance or the organisation so they targeted the easier prey. The plan was to recruit men from Jamaica to pull off their plan as they would need workers as well as fighters to take over territory and defend them.

In 1981 'Cool Hand Luke' was stabbed with a bayonet by a soldier whilst asleep in bed. He was killed with one of his girlfriends, a brother and a friend. The cops even killed the dog in the yard. The lawmen went in to kill not to take anyone alive. Those who escaped had to hide under the cellar of the house while others fled for their lives. Luke was a marked man but rumour had it he was set up by Angola men who had police friends. One man who was accused of giving the police information left the area in haste either in guilt or frightened for his life. Luke was killed not long after returning home from a peace dance at Love Street. The dance was meant to be a truce between him and the Angola crew. Luke's death was the turning point in the lives of Angola men as the one man who opposed them the most, was finally out of the way.

That same year Randy, Luke's cousin, who attended Trench Town Comprehensive was also killed. He and other friends asked the principal for a year over at school so they could play in the Manning Cup football competition but they were refused. Disillusioned and with nothing to do, they left school and joined up with a local gang. Randy went on a robbery with some gang members and did not return home as he was killed by police. Who knows what would have happened if he was allowed to stay back at school and play his beloved football. Maybe it would have been a matter of delaying the inevitable or he would have had time to choose another career path from the one he chose. That we will never know. Everyone deserves a second chance no matter what their class is or how we view them because you might just save a life.

News was coming to Jamaica frequently about the riches and splendour of the gangs in the United States. They sent photographs of themselves with guns and money around them. Those back in Jamaica were envious and wanted to move to the Big Apple and many were saying they could be rich in a year or two. No matter what it took they were prepared to do it. A lot of young men from Trench Town were just waiting for a drugs don to send for them. Some as young as ten were leaving to be skivvies for drugs dealers. What was surprising was that mothers were allowing their children to go to the US not knowing where their children were going and to whom. All they could see was dollar signs. A lot of us who did not know the extent of the criminal activities by the drug dealers developed (foreign minds) and dreamt of the day when we would get the break to leave Yard. We thought that we could leave Jamaica for a year go to America and do minimal amount of work for a lot of money so we were could buy a house back home. The poverty were were enduring blinded us to reality.

I had my first reality check about the drugs gang in the United States when they killed a young boy and posted back his body to Jamaica in a barrel. The reason given was that he stole from his drugs boss. That did not deter many people as they were still leaving by the plane load. England was seen to be too slow where the market was concerned, so many people were not interested in going there. Those who went there were either finding it difficult to go to America or were on the run and needed somewhere to cool off.

February 1981 the Eradication Squad, another anti-crime task force, was introduced but the killings continued.

My grandmother returned to Jamaica in 1981 for good. I left Waltham Park Road and went to live with her off Hagley Park Road. That area was fairly quiet with a middle class atmosphere to it. Most of us children did not speak to each other. We would just walk past each other without saying anything. My lifestyle changed for the first time since Pepe died. My grandmother bought me lots of clothes and I was well fed and not in need of anything. I continued to attend Trench Town School so I continued to be in touch with the criminality there.

Angola posse members were leaving the island as well to go to the US and those who were left behind went on a rampage in Jungle. They were raping young girls and eliminating those they had no use for. Some youths in the area went to Westmoreland and stole some marijuana from men who had cultivated it to export abroad. When they returned to Jungle with their loot the news spread quickly that they had a large quantity of weed from a hit. One of the Angola bosses contacted the youths demanding the goods and even told them the ganja belonged to him. They did not even know which parish it came from but they wanted to make claim to it. The youths were frightened so they had to leave the area with their stash.

One of the Angola rapists went over to the housing scheme where Joe Bloggs lived, the man who refused the job as a hitman in the Gold Street Massacre. He was never forgiven for that and he did not care for them either after the arson attack on the Evening Tide Home. The rapist saw a young girl and held onto her. The girl screamed out and her cry alerted a group of men who were hanging out closeby. Joe Bloggs was amongst them and he went in the direction of the noise. He saw the girl struggling with the would-be rapist, who by that time had stabbed her in the back. Joe Bloggs told the thug to let go of the girl but he pulled out a gun on him instead. Bloggs who was also armed went for his gun and the coward ran away shouting threats of vengeance and that he would be returning with backup. 'Wait til me bloodclaat come back wid mi crew, yu a go dead bway'.

The house Bloggs lived in adjoined my brother Christopher's. They were all worried because they knew what Angola men were capable of. Bloggs had a friend by the name of Dukie who was also targeted by the evil force so he went to lie low. Bloggs knew something was going to happen so he was on edge. He had been faced with adversity before but this time was different, it was like he was waiting for what was to come. He sent his children to their mother and went inside his house by himself.

Ten Angola men arrived on his doorstep about two thirty in the morning. They called his name and told him to come out to them but he refused. A barrage of gunshots started not long after but he was managing to hold them off with the little ammunition he had. They were cowards so they would not break their way into his house even though he was outnumbered, instead they would wait for him to run out of bullets.

Bloggs traded shot for shot with the death squad for a long time so they decided to go to plan B and started pouring petrol on the house as they did in the Evening Tide Home tragedy. They told Bloggs to open his door or they would set the house alight, being the person he was, he did not want women and children to suffer because of him so he opened the door and they riddled his body with gunshots. He wrote one of his killers name with his blood on the bathroom wall before he died. People who were living close to the murder scene said Joe Bloggs held off the men for about three hours. Gunshots were barking like mad and even though there was one police station in the area that should have heard the commotion no patrol was sent out to investigate. Joe Bloggs was protecting a girl from criminals but the police did not think his life was worth saving.

Dukie, Bloggs' friend was killed several months later by Angola posse. They stabbed him in the face and shot him in the head and his chest. One of the murderers shouted, 'ah long time yu fi dead bway'. Bangles a disabled gunman was also exterminated by Angola crew for not obeying orders. I used to see Bangles frequently when I visited Tom at his house in Mexico (Arnett Gardens). He walked with a limp and could not have been more than four feet tall but that did not prevent him from picking up the gun. The day he was shot I did not hear or see who shot him but I heard him in a garden not far from Tom's home wailing like a badly injured animal. I quietly asked one of Tom's neighbours who it was crying and was told it was Bangles. I sat for an agonising hour listening to him crying in pain and even though other people must have heard it we just waited for the pain of anguish to cease for our guilt to die with the young man. The cry turned to whimpering and then there was silence. I knew he was dead. People were going missing in Trench Town, some without a trace, others would surface in the open lots weeks after they went missing. People were whispering that there was a pit in Rema that was being used to dump dead bodies. The residents were so afraid to speak out in case they ended up in the pit or in an empty lot for collection. Corruption, murders and rapes became the order of the day.

The corruption in our society was everywhere even in our schools. So it was not surprising our young men were graduating without a sense of responsibility. During the 1981 Manning Cup school football competition; a young high school girl was raped by several members of the Kingston College football team and the school covered up the crime.

I was in my final academic year and would have the last chance of supporting my school at the biggest football league competition. Trench Town had some talented players but we did not excel much in the sport. Kingston College, Calabar and St George's College were the favourites to win the trophy as they were on top most of the time. They were all prominent high schools for boys and most people wanted their sons to go to one of them. Before the common entrance system a lot of students could only dream of attending those schools. The boys attending those schools had naive high school girls throwing themselves at them and this went to their heads.

A young girl who attended a prominent high school for girls had a big crush on a member of the Kingston College football team. She was young, trusting and foolishly in love. He asked her for sex which she agreed to as she wanted to please him. The agreement was she would visit him at his school in the evening before their football training. When the girl arrived he had sex with her and so did his teammates. The creep just watched while the girl who was in love with him was raped. To be fair not all the players took part but most of them did. Their excuse for the crime they committed was that she came for sex and that was what she got. Yes she might have gone there for sex but she had the right to choose who she wanted to have sex with and if she agreed to have sex with one or two of them and not the rest then that was her choice.

I did not approve of what she did but no one had the right to touch her body without her consent. What made matters worse was that none of the boys were punished and the crime was not reported to the police. Everyone was worried about ruining the boys lives but what about the young lady who would have to live with her ordeal for the rest of her life. She made a mistake and paid the price, and would have to suffer mental pain for many years, but she did not break the law, the young men did, so why were they not punished? Instead the schools swept the whole thing under the carpet and the young men went about their business as usual. They went on playing football for their school and no one was bothered that they raped a girl who was probably under the age of consent. The young men learnt a valuable lesson from that incident that it was okay to rape.

I graduated from school in June 1982 I was to turn seventeen in August. Tom gladly relinquished all financial responsibility to his mother where I was concerned. Since the day she returned to Jamaica my grandmother took full responsibility for my well being without any help from anyone and did so to the best of her ability. She never one day allowed me to suffer the indignity of asking Tom for anything and he never offered.

I started attending evening classes to further my studies, I was lacking in confidence and was not quite sure what I wanted to do as a career. Tom came to live with us on Hagley Park Road. He told his mother he wanted to move in with us as he was not getting on with his neighbours 'surprise surprise'. A lot of people told Aunt (as we called his mother) not to take him in but she gave in to his pleas and what a mistake that was. He lived free expecting food and shelter from his elderly mother without any consideration that she was already caring for his daughter without any assistance from him. If she ever asked him for anything towards his keeps all hell would break loose.

Not only was he a burden, he brought his woman along with him to stay at their convenience. Whenever his mother voiced her objection to his woman staying at her place he vowed that he was going to kill me for taking news to his mother about his woman. He needed an easy target and I was just that. He even threatened to chop off my neck and I would not have put it past him. It was convenient for him to blame someone for the problem between him and his mother rather than recognising that his whole attitude was wrong. I tried to report him to the police at Half Way Tree Police Station but when I got there the policeman at the desk was not interested in what I had to say but more what were in my bra. The policeman was insensitive to my plight and was making it clear he wanted to have sex with me and I left the station in a helpless state.

Paul the boy who attended Trench Town School and went to the United States was said to be doing very well running a drugs corner. The story that was going around was that it was a drugs don who sent for Paul to work as one of his boys. The drugs don sent for many young men from Maxfield Avenue where he came from. The young men were supposed to work and build themselves up but it was a different story when they got there. The drugs don was the one who had the contact with the Colombians and the other drugs lords. The don would buy from them and then sell it to his boys for more, so he would be the one to make the most money. The boys were told they could not have any dealings with the drugs lords as that would be disrespectful to the don. Anyone who did not obey the rule would be killed. The boys were also the ones who would have to do the killing, ordered by the don, as he did not want to get his hands dirty and the police would not have anything on him.

Paul became the don's main hitman and carried out many murders at his boss's request but Paul was not making big money and hated this. The don sent for his brother and nephews and they started to make big money and were allowed to make contact with the main suppliers. The other thing that was a problem to Paul was that the don's relatives were never called upon to do a hit, so Paul was planning his next move. Paul was a likable boy when he was at school and was never one to harm anyone without a reason but that changed when he got to the Big Apple.

Spade, a friend of Paul's who was deported back to Jamaica, told me that he got caught in a house with a lot of money and crack cocaine. He served two years in prison and was deported back to Jamaica. He said he arrived in America two weeks after Paul. He left Jamaica because he was caught with a gun by the police. He was given bail to return to court but was planning to jump bail. He did not have any money to get a good lawyer so when one of the area leaders approached him with the news that the don would be sending a lady down with some documents to bring back some youths from the area to the United States, he gladly took up the offer. He could kill two birds with one stone. By leaving the island he did not have to go to prison and he would become rich in the process. The two cops dealing with his case were approached by the area leader who offered them money to drop the case. The money was to be sent down by the drugs don living in America. The police officers accepted the offer and were greatly rewarded.

Spade said when he arrived in the United States he was taken to a house, which he was to share with five other youths including Paul. All the newcomers were summoned before the don who had some parcels to hand out and to inform them of the rules. Rule number one was, they could be called upon anytime to kill someone so be prepared; rule number two, anyone who did not work, meaning sell drugs, could not stick around; rule number three, they were not allowed to buy work from other suppliers only the don and his relatives. He then handed them each one of the parcels he had which contained small crystallised looking stones. They were told the stones were crack cocaine other wise known as rocks. Marijuana was hard to smuggle in the country because of its distinctive smell and it did not sell as quickly as the rocks.

Spade was told he had to repay the money that was given to the two policemen back in Jamaica to drop his gun case, plus pay back for the work he was given as a start. He realised then for the first time nothing was for free. He did not know the don very well as he was still a youngster when the don rose to prominence in Jamaica but they were proud of him when news of his success got back to Yard (Jamaica). He thought that he was very lucky when he was told the don wanted to assist him to leave Jamaica, and as he always idolised the don he did not know very well, he thought all his dreams were coming through at last.

They were fighting all the time to keep control of the corner and were selling drugs constantly as the high life was addictive. Their enemies were anyone who was selling drugs so they were not only fighting the Yankees but their own countrymen as well as political allies. In the Big Apple they did not have any allies. This time they were fighting for the almighty dollar. Two newcomers were killed in the same week they arrived from Jamaica in a gang war with rival Jamaican gunmen who also wanted the corner that was very good for business. The youths who died were in their teens. When the don heard the news he laughed and told Spade and the other new recruits that death was part of the trade they were in so they should get use it.

Young girls and women, Jamaicans and Yankees, flocked them. One man could have up to ten girlfriends. Women, who they could not get freely, they bought. Women who were on drugs did any and everything to them for a fix. Many of them called their friends back in Jamaica and boasted of the sexual acts they were having done to them by Yankee women. One said he was half way through getting a head from a prostitute when he found out it was a man who was servicing him. He was embarrassed because his friends were there so he pumped a shot in the transvestite's head.

Spade said the first time he was called upon to kill someone he had the jitters. He was to kill a woman who double-crossed the don. She was working as a mule for the don. She came from her pickup point with goods but the stash was short. She had to die for that. He said he was given his first gun in Jamaica at the tender age of ten by an older man.

He fired shots during election time but had never targeted anyone before. His mother died when he was six and he never knew his father. He was cared for by an older brother who was only two years older than him. His brother became a thief to support them both and stopped attending school so that Spade could continue with his education. His life of crime started when his brother was gunned down by his own friends, who were angry with him because the police got hold of a gun he was using on a robbery. The police surrounded him whilst he was carrying out a hit so he had to throw away the M16 rifle he had and escape with his life. The gun was more important to them than their friend so they executed him for it. Spade was a witness to the murder.

Spade said he never smoked or drank in Jamaica but started the day when he was told to kill. It was especially hard for him as his first hit was to be a woman. The don realised he was nervous and told him that if he did not do it he would have to run away. Paul took him to one side and told him the boss was planning to use him as a human sacrifice as he was involved in witchcraft. The boss apparently sold his soul to the devil and on special occasions he had to sacrifice a young man to show his loyalty, this in turn would give him protection from the police and his enemies. Young men were chosen as they said the evil spirit wanted the blood of the strong and the young. Most of his victims were disobedient workers. Spade said he told Paul he did not believe him, as what he was hearing was unreal, but Paul told him that the boss did it in front of him once because he needed a backup in case the young man who was to be sacrificed put up a fight. As it went the young man succumbed to his fate. The boss used a knife to slit the boy's throat. He held up the youth to face him just to make sure the blood spurted all over him. They sent back news to Jamaica to tell the boy's mother that her son was killed by a gunman from a rival gang. The boss even sent some money to give her to show how generous he was. They loved him so much for his kindness.

Spade said he still could not believe what he was told but had to make a choice between his life and that of the woman. He decided it was her life but had to smoke one of his rocks for the first time, as he could not do it without getting high. He shot the woman in the stomach twice and left her to bleed to death. They all took turns to check if she was dead. The boss commented afterwards that the hit was more like a pussy who did it rather than the soldier he thought Spade was, because the woman was given two shots and left to die. Spade started to kill and taking more rocks to take him away from the reality of his disillusion with life. He was fast becoming an addict. Two of the youths who were brought to America the same time as himself were told to kill some people but they did not have the killer instinct in them no matter how much crack they smoked. Spade was told to kill them instead as they were a waste of space. He called them both and told them that he was given orders to kill them but he wanted them to leave the area instead. One of the youths broke down in tears, he said to sell drugs was one thing but to kill was another. He cried for his mother who was back in Jamaica not knowing what he was going through. Spade gave them some money and told them to leave the same night. The next morning he got up early to check if the youths had left. When he got outside he saw the body of the youth who had broken down with his throat cut. He did not have much hope that the other one had escaped, he believed there and then what Paul had told him.

123

Spade said Paul wanted the boss dead, as he did not agree with his style of leadership. He told Spade to join him but Spade said he became too paranoid to trust anyone. He was afraid the boss was using Paul to test his loyalty. Paul was one of the boss's most trusted soldiers, so how could he be planning his demise? Paul, on the other hand was not waiting for help as he knew the boss's weaknesses. Paul was more or less running the business but only the boss and his family were reaping the reward. What made matters worse was that the boss had all the money he had earned and he was too afraid to ask him for it. It was him who had killed the last boy who dared to ask the boss for his own money.

One morning Paul was on duty as bodyguard. He pumped two shots in the boss's head while he was showering. Not even the boss's obeah man could see that one coming. Paul paid for the funeral and gave his boss a good send off. He quickly took over from where the boss left off. The only thing he did not get involved with was the witchcraft and the reason for that was that he was too frightened of it. He married a white woman who used to work for the boss as a mule. He said he did not want any more black women, as they no longer served any purpose in his life. The Jamaican girl whom he was seeing and had a child by him was dropped like hot cake without an explanation, he did not even support his only son. Paul was tall, dark with a cool complexion so how could he be disrespecting his own colour that was so beautiful? Spade was caught in their drugs den with Paul's money and drugs, he was sent to prison. Paul relinquished all contact with him. Paul bought houses in Washington, Miami and Connecticut, he had expensive cars and his wife was living in style. He cut off contact with his mother in Jamaica and his family was his white wife.

Spade said he spent two years behind bars in America and his only visitor was one of the youths who he gave the money to run away. The youth told Paul that he went to another state where he met a girl from Jamaica and got married. He was waiting to hear about his green card. He explained to Spade that he had changed his life and was training to be a computer engineer. He worked part-time as a printer. He told Spade what had happened the night when he and his friend tried to escape from Paul and the boss.

He said that they had gone to the house where they were staying to get some clothes. While they were in the house the phone rang and it was the boss who told them to come over to his crack den. They told him they were on their way over and hung up the phone. They grabbed only a few items of clothing and were about to go through the door when the boss appeared with another young man and Paul. The trio attacked them but they fought for their lives. The other youth was being overpowered but he was fighting like a man possessed. He managed to hold off boss, Paul and the other man so his friend could escape. The last words he heard from his childhood friend's lips were 'run, John, run'. If he did not give up his life they would have both been killed. When Spade told him how his friend was killed he cried like a baby. He told Spade as soon as he started working full-time he would send money back home to Jamaica which he did, but Spade was using it to feed his drug addiction. He never heard from Paul except for once when he sent him a hundred US dollars with some pictures of himself with two guns in his hands and money all over the bed he was laying on.

Spade was found dead in an abandoned building off Maxfield Avenue. Some people said he gave up on life, others said that he was strangled. John got his green card and visits Jamaica frequently with his wife and children. The police finally caught up with Paul. He was given fifteen years imprisonment but was released after doing nine. His white wife sold all his houses and cars and moved to another State she never visited him in prison. Paul was deported back to Jamaica and was diagnosed with schizophrenia and his mother became his main support. His mother's love never ceased towards him despite him neglecting her when he was abroad. There were too many absent fathers from our household so many young men went out on the streets seeking role models but what they found instead were deviant characters just waiting to exploit them. Once you get involved it's so hard to get out especially when you live in the ghetto.

Many people hold those men who led children astray in high regards. The first thing they will remind you of is that those men made it possible for many children to go to school and eat food. Yes, that might be true, but what was the point of feeding ten and killing twenty? Also if the dons truly cared, wouldn't they have wanted a better life for the young boys. They would have wanted them to be lawyers, doctors and teachers and not the drugs dealers and gunmen they were encouraged to be. The drugs dons had the resources to do good and make change in the poor communities they came from, but chose to do evil. As long as we stay silent and do not show kindness to a child in need then we will always have the evildoers leading our young astray. The hard-hitting truth was the drug dealers were in fact supporting many hungry innocent children who looked up to them as if they were super-humans. No lawyer or doctor from Trench Town returned to help only the drugs dealer so they will always be seen as gods. You and I must change that.

On my way to Waltham Park Road to visit my uncle one evening I saw Desmond the area don. He was smartly dressed and looked handsome in his dark coloured shirt and black trousers. He called out to me and I ignored him at first but then he caught up with me and started to walk along side me. I looked at him and became attracted to him for the first time. So when he started talking too much I told him not to try too hard as he was winning. He was pleasantly surprised and smiled at me. My heart melted. I started a relationship with him but had a reality check when his girlfriend threatened to kill me.

I was thinking twice about our relationship but he was getting more attached and that meant trouble for me. A friend I went to high school with told me that Sally was in hospital with acid burns. She said Sally's baby-father was seeing another young woman who lived in Jones Town. Sally and her rival had frequent fights in the streets over their man. Sally who always had the upper hand over the woman was unaware of what was in store for her. The woman got a visa to go the United States, and decided to use the monkey lotion (acid) on Sally and was encouraged to do so by her friends. Sally saw her rival the day of the incident but chose to ignore her. They passed each other and Sally had her back to her rival. Someone called her by name and as soon as she turned around to see who it was a container of acid was thrown in her face. Sally tried to run after her rival but the acid was burning her eyes. The girl ran away and waited for the day to come when she would leave the island.

Sally's baby-father went to look for his other woman but she was long gone. Megan fainted when she heard the news and I just cried. Desmond's baby-mother threatened to use the monkey lotion on me but seeing Sally in hospital with the burns

125

made me realise this was no joking matter. I saw Desmond one evening and told him that we were no longer a couple. He was not having any of it and started out being nice just to soften me up but when that was not working he started using threatening words. I knew he was not afraid to carry out his threats on me a woman so I played his game until I got to my gate then I walked away leaving him standing outside. I was on my way home one evening when I saw Desmond waiting at the top of my road. He came up to me and told me to follow him to his friend's house. I said no. He pushed me against the wall of a house, pulled out a knife on me and then told me to follow him. I was frightened for my life so I decided to follow him. What a mess I put myself in! I thought of many things and said to myself just play his game and get out with my life.

I followed him to his friend's house when we got inside I looked in his face and I hated him for the first time. He appeared desperate and looked evil he told me to take off my clothes. I asked him if he was going to rape me he said not rape take. I was screaming at him so loud he looked nervous but would not let me go. It was as if his life depended on him being with me there and then. He was telling me it was all my fault why he was resorting to force. He kept telling me how much he loved me and wanted us to be together forever but I just wanted him to take what he wanted and let me go. He raped me and had the nerve to say we made love. When he finished which did not take very long I put on my clothes held my head high and walked out of the house. I heard him calling my name as I was going through the gate but I did not look behind me. I went home locked myself in the bathroom showered and cried.

I was not going to hide from Desmond anymore so I went to visit my cousins on Waltham Park Road as usual. A week after the incident I saw him standing on his own on a street corner and walked passed him. He looked at me and I at him with contempt. The look on his face was of a man who threw in the towel for he knew I was never going to let him conquer me. I never saw him again for many years.

In America the Bureau of Alcohol, Tobacco and Firearms ATF went after the Jamaican posses with a vengeance as they were getting out of control with the killings and drugs selling. In 1984, in Florida ATF agent J.J. Watterson started an investigation into the origin of a batch of guns sent to Jamaica by the Shower posse. Interpol had contacted the bureau for their assistance to trace the supplier of the twenty-two guns that had found their way on the streets of Kingston.

Special Agent Watterson reported that he started out checking gun stores in Miami and found out that the guns were part of a larger purchase of weapons which had been bought by Jamaicans in the States. Most of the buyers had given false names but the ones he could trace all seemed to live in apartments and houses that were protected like fortresses. He said within a year those same guns were turning up in murder cases all over the States.

In November 1984 in Miami, home of ATF agent Watterson, the Shower posse brazenly carried out a massacre of five people in broad daylight that sent a message to all security forces in America that the posse members were cold, evil and had no respect for life. The police report stated John Jones, Stan Baker and Wrongmove all of whom originated from Tivoli Gardens were visiting some people in an apartment where they stayed for a couple of hours then they left the building. They were on their way to their cars when they were robbed at gunpoint of their cash and valuables. The police report stated that the men believed that they were robbed by the occupants of the house they had visited. They returned later and killed five of the six people who were present. They were all shot in the head. The sixth person was a twenty- three-year-old white junkie who was shot seven times but survived the massacre. She committed suicide several years later.

The law enforcement agencies joined together thereon to fight the evil that was taking over their country. The thugs were not only killing men but they were killing women and children. The US authorities were seeking the maximum penalty for the scumbags. Some Special Agents infiltrated the gangs by posing as drugs lords with big shipments to supply while others posed as junkies. They even paid some posse members well to grass on the top dogs.

A friend of mine came to Jamaica from New York in December 1984 and told me the killings there were so out of control she was embarrassed to tell people she was from Jamaica. She said one of her cousins went to New York on a visitor's visa. She did not want to go back home to the poverty in Water House so they introduced her to a nice Jamaican man who was legal in the country and had a decent job. The man married her and they lived together for a while but when she visited an old school friend in Miami there she met up with a drugs dealer she knew from Jamaica. He enticed her with his BMW car and plenty of cash so she forgot about her husband back in New York. Everyone was telling her to leave her new man and return to her husband but the words fell on thorny grounds. The drugs dealer left her in a house where he kept his money and drugs supply but he mostly stayed with his wife in another part of Florida.

The police had been watching the house for a while and were contemplating to raid it. They got their opportunity one afternoon when she was taking shopping from her car to the house and they just walked in behind her. When she saw them she fell in a nearby chair as she knew drugs were in the house. They told her to stay put while they looked around. She was told to phone her man and tell him to come to the house for something she had to give him but he suspected foul play and fled to Jamaica. The police did not have enough evidence to press charges so they were using his girlfriend as bait. They were offering him, his girlfriend's freedom if he gave himself up. She stupidly thought he would go to prison and give her freedom but she was not worth one night behind bars. Pretty young girls like her were a penny a dozen in his eyes. The police also thought highly of him believing he would have turned himself in like a man, own up and let his baby doll walk free. No real man sells drugs to children and kills without a reason. He went home to Jamaica with his wife and children to cool off, while his baby doll was sent to prison for twenty-five years. She was nineteen-years-old. She will be deported back to Jamaica after she completes her time behind bars by then her husband would have moved on with his life.

The law enforcement officers in America were after posse members but they continued with the killing spree and many thought they were invincible. If they could survive the Jamaican police aggression and brutality then they could take on wimps who called themselves police in America but they were to learn that they underestimated the US Feds at their own peril.

On the 4th August 1985 thousands of Jamaicans from all over the United States assembled at a sports complex in Oakland, New Jersey. They travelled by buses, cars, trains and planes. Men, women and children, the young and the old all went to celebrate Jamaica's independence. Some men were there carrying guns and due to this the atmosphere was tense. A Spangler was killed the night before by a member of the Shower crew their old political foes. Spanglers, Showers and Renkers were all there wrenching at each other. A fierce battle started with a blaze of gunfire. Men with magnums, M16s and A-K47s were spraying bullets all over the place and people were running to find somewhere to hide from the onslaught. Three people were killed and several injured. Many people who attended the function knew who the gunmen were but refused to supply police with information including those who were injured in the gun spree. One woman whose relative was killed in the incident ran away to another state to avoid giving evidence against the murderers, as she was afraid for her own life. Spanglers were said to be killing from women to children - the Jungle massive were still killing each other in America. Every week news would come back to us of who killed who. Natty Dread, a Jungle man from Angola, was one of the first to rise and fall at the hands of his own. I could not believe it when I heard of his demise. It was so hard not to feel sad for them as they were people we knew.

    Jamaicans who own small businesses in America like restaurants, bars and grocery stores were in fear of the drugs dealers who used their places to sell drugs. Not only were they frightened of the drugs dealer but also of the police who were targeting their businesses to shut them down. Many Jamaicans believed that because they came from the same island as you they were entitled to use your place however they saw fit. When black people arrived in cities like New York and London there were not many places for them to go to socialise. Due to this many of them ended up in mental institutions, as they had to deal with broken dreams, racism, limited resources and poor social infrastructures such as housing and jobs. As the resilient people we are, many decided to take matters in their own hands and organised parties in their own humble homes until they could expand to open a club or a pub only to see it destroyed by drugs dealers.

Chapter Nine

The new Prime Minister of Jamaica had been in government for more than three years and the change he promised was not coming as fast as many of us thought it should. Downtown, Kingston was taken over by traders many of whom were going to the United States to purchase their goods and selling them locally. They were selling clothing and footwear but some expanded their business and started to trade other wares. By the mid-eighties the cost of living was so high there were more sellers than buyers. The trade helped a lot of poor people who had no other means of making a living but the downside was, it ran the local manufacturers like tailors and dressmakers out of business. The traders were also buying the US dollar on the black market. The well needed foreign exchange was not passing through the system as it was going straight back to United States to buy goods, so the only beneficiary was America. Jamaicans abroad including the drugs dealers contributed more than half the foreign exchange brought into the country but a lot of it was sold on the black market and the government only showed interest in white tourists' money.

Guns were being brought into the country at an alarming rate so somebody at the main ports must have been conveniently closing their eyes to the problem. Drugs importation became big business. The United States was no longer interested in our affairs as they got what they wanted when Manley lost the general election. Seaga was left high and dry by Washington. Our currency was losing its value day by day and the economy was in as much mess, if not more than when Manley was running the country. What we needed was both parties working together for the betterment of the country but what we had was a division. Jamaicans were leaving the island and becoming successful elsewhere but could not do so in their own country as there was no encouragement or faith shown in them. Young people were leaving universities and could not get jobs in the country but once they left the island many became expert in their field of work.

The country was also importing workers while their own people were forced to seek jobs elsewhere and young people were walking the streets without a skill. Why were they not setting up training centres all over the country to teach young boys a skill in computers rather than in political warfare? This I suppose would not benefit politicians in the long run but it would indeed greatly benefit the country.

In Jungle Angola men were stamping their authority and undermining other area dons like Tess. They had the biggest and most feared crew. A gunman opposed them and they killed his mother to teach him a lesson. They killed, robbed and raped. Tess came out of prison and was telling the girls to report the rapes to the police but it was easier said than done. The breaking point came when they kidnapped two schoolgirls and locked them in a house in Angola and every posse member took turns in raping them. Their torment went on for days until they were rescued by the Member of Parliament for Jungle who was called in by concerned residents. And even though he rescued the girls the crime was never reported to the police. Tess led an army of PNP men in Trench Town to rid the area of the thugs who were out of control. Men from Payne Avenue, Wareika Hill, Matthews Lane and other PNP garrison areas in Kingston were called in to take on the Angola crew. This was what it took to rid Jungle of the Angola posse. This group came about shortly after the demise of the Vikings crew so they were created and armed by politicians but no one, not even their greedy bosses (politicians) had anticipated the atrocities they would bring. The police were not equipped to deal with them so men of their own kind had to be brought in to fight them and it took the best of PNP Brigadistas to overthrow the mighty Angola Posse. The arson attack on the Evening Tide Home was the last straw for many people, but it was Tess who instigated the attack on Tango's men after applying pressure on PNP politicians for their support. One of the main terrorists knew they were after him so he was planning to get Tess before the Brigadistas could get to him. He went over to the house where Tess's mother lived to look for him with a gun but Tess was not there. A newcomer to the area by the name of Natty Pete saw when the thug went into Tess's pathway and went after him with some other men and he ran into Aunty Charm's house and grabbed up Sally's baby. He held the baby in front of him as a shield. For the baby's sake the men allowed him to leave with his life.

 Tess's mother was evacuated by Natty Pete and some of her children as she lived close to Angola and they were targeting the house because of Tess. If they could kill one older woman, what was stopping them from killing another ? Pablo, Tess's brother who had converted to Rastafarianism heard about Angola men going into his mother's house and decided to go and assist with the evacuation. To this day it breaks my heart whenever I remember his words before he went to move his mother. He said, 'mi no wan fi pick up gun again, but de man dem a force mi to', with tears rolling down his cheeks he armed himself and went to defend his family.

 When Tess and the rest of PNP Brigadistas moved in on Angola men in full force some of them ran away like cowards, but the main men fought back, it was like Armageddon. Women and children locked themselves indoors to hide from the bullets from both sides. The men traded bullet for bullet. Tango's men fought ferociously as they knew their livelihood depended on them winning the battle but they ran out of ammunition and retreated out of Jungle. They made several attempts to attack Jungle but they were outnumbered every time. The people rejoiced when they left, no one missed them and they never returned. Pablo left Trench Town and moved to be with people of his own kind. Sally said she saw him not long after he left his old community and he was a new person. His last words to her were, 'Jungle, that wicked place I'll never go back there'. I never saw Pablo again but I will always have him in my heart.

 Natty Pete stayed in Jungle after Angola posse left and took one of the houses left by them. He started dating Tess's sister but trouble was brewing between the two men.

Tess's crew had frequent gunfights with Natty Pete and his boys. There were several rumours about what started the feud between the two men but my opinion is Jungle was not big enough for the both of them. Tess's sister had an argument with one of Natty Pete's soldiers and she stabbed him with a knife, he vowed revenge but she underestimated him. Late one evening she went to see two friends in a pathway. They were all walking and talking when the man she stabbed rushed out of another pathway, on them and shouted, 'yu tink de stab a go so' she bravely held on to the M16 he had in his hand and they were fighting for the gun, but he got the better of her and let off the gun into her side. The other two girls were hysterical and ran home crying. The man and his friends sent threats to deter them from going to the police, they were frightened so they stayed silent. The dead woman was no angel but she did not deserve to die the way she did. The punishment she got did not fit the crime she committed. The man who killed her did not go to prison for her death but he is doing time for another crime, while Natty Pete was killed by a young cop in the Flying Squad.

I visited Jungle after Natty Pete died to see Aunty Charm. When I entered her pathway there was a young man there who appointed himself as the new area leader. I used to see him when I lived there but we never spoke. As I passed him he came up behind me and pulled my dress and slapped me on the backside. I asked him what was the matter and he said that he could do anything he liked as he was the new area don. I looked at him and tears came to my eyes just to see an asshole assaulting me and there was nothing I could do about it. If I had gone to the police they would have harmed my relatives, I walked into the house and closed the door on him. The young man was quick to take up where the other tyrants left off. He was proud to be the new king of the Jungle but I saw many kings there and all lost their thrones. Several months later the new don was killed by police with his gun in his hand.

Trouble was also brewing between Rema and Tivoli residents. Seaga was the Member of Parliament for Tivoli and he was also Prime Minister. He was spending a lot of money transforming his constituency but Rema was left begging the crumbs left over from their more well off political ally. Some Rema residents were not happy and voiced their opinions. They did not think it had been worth their while voting for the JLP, and to think they turned against their neighbours in Jungle for nothing. News was being taken back to Tivoli by spies living in Rema who were happy to live in the slum and could not see what all the fuss was about.

Tivoli men did not like what they were hearing and decided to pay their political ally a visit in case the rumour of them not voting for their party at the next election was true. They knew most of the so called gunmen in Rema had left the island for shut eye country (dead) or the United States so they would not have much to deal with besides, they had the artillery to back them up.

In 1984 Tivoli men visited Rema to teach the people a lesson, whoever told Rema residents Jamaica elections were democratic? The men did not go there to mess about, they set homes on fire and executed men and women. A middle age man who I knew as a child was burnt to death in his house. Tivoli men set his house on fire and when he tried to escape they fired gunshots at the house. It was a case of choosing death by the gun or fire and he chose the latter.

The shooting went on for a long time. No police went to the battleground even though Denham Town and Trench Town Police Stations were within close proximity of the onslaught. There were children crying, old folks getting nervous breakdowns and women crying to the almighty for the destruction to stop but it went on and on. Rema residents were trapped between the death squad and their political foes the Jungle massive. Some Jungle residents went down to the border on Seventh Street to get a glimpse of what was going on. Many were calling the frightened people down in Rema who had gathered below the old Bass cinema contemplating their next move. They did not trust the people who were calling them as they had been at each others throats for many years. Prim and her children were there with the crowd not knowing what to do.

Tivoli men were moving in fast on them shooting anyone in sight. Eight young men decided to defend themselves to halt the onslaught as the alternative was to perish with those who were already killed. They were the Rats. I do not know how they came by the name but I'm glad they decided to fight that day as Prim would have been killed. They went to face the might of John Jones and his massive. They fought a good fight as Jones and his men were retreating backwards but the trouble was the Rats did not have the ammunition to stay with the fight. When their rounds ran out the death squad knew because the shots were no longer returning. They moved in for the final kill but a miracle took place that day. Little Joe, one of the Rats, ran up to where the crowd had gathered below the old Bass cinema and the Tivoli men were closing in on them. He looked up and saw the Jungle men calling them and looked down and saw Tivoli men advancing in on them and he decided to go to his old political enemies for sanctuary. He took off his white vest, tied it on a stick and held it high in the air and walked straight to Jungle. The Jungle men waiting shook his hand and the other Rema residents went up to join him. The death squad saw what happened and retreated back to Tivoli as they were not prepared to take on the might of the Jungle massive.

When I visited Jungle the following week people were still talking about the brutal attack on innocent women and children. Some of the Jungle men were saying they wanted to assist the Rema men from the start but had mixed feelings about the whole thing because they had been enemies for so long. Some of them were worried for they still had relatives down in Rema. There was weeping and wailing in Rema many days after the death squad visited them. Seaga visited the area and gave a well rehearsed speech but we all knew the hit was ordered by someone higher than John Jones. You can fool some of the people some of the time but you cannot fool all the people all of the time. As usual another peace treaty was signed and the people attended another peace dance but the old grudges were still festering. No love has lasted between the two sides since.

Street dances were a hit in the inner cities. There was one every night of the week and each sound system would have a venue they played. The music gave a lot of poor people an outlet to let off steam and to get away from the day-to-day violence. Most upcoming artists would get their break chatting for a sound system and then would find their way onto the radio with a hit song.

I went to one of the street dances at Cross Roads one night and met Sally there. She and her sisters were regulars at dances so from time to time we would bump into each other. We were deeply conversing when suddenly I heard noises and movements all around me. A man jumped out of a van and shouted, 'police, police, no body move, no body get hurt'. We knew then the special crime fighting team 'The Eradication Squad' was making their presence known at the dance. All the finest cops were part of the team. The problem was some of them had more dirt in their closet than the ground they walked on. Two cops in that squad were caught in America and questioned about their involvement in narcotics and many others had been accused by members of the public of taking bribes. A helicopter was in the air circling the area where the dance was being held and women, men and dogs were jumping out of vehicles. We tried to escape through a back road but the entire place was blocked off. One dog followed in every direction I went. Everywhere I went the dog was behind me with his damn mistress.

Women were told to go in one line and the men in another. One male officer was calling the men who were wearing imported or expensive footwear to get into an army truck. Some men took off their shoes and threw them away. When the cops saw how many men there were without shoes and well dressed they told them to get into the truck. I was searched by a woman in plain clothes, I was not even sure if she was a cop or a civilian but was glad when she told me I could go. I heard one girl shouting behind me to a woman who was carrying out a search on her, 'hi, ah mi front yu a touch, yu a lesbian'. After Sally was searched she went straight in the direction of Jungle and I headed towards Hagley Park Road. The next day I heard that the people who were arrested were released as the police did not find anything illegal. People were only there to enjoy themselves.

The cinema was one of my regular enjoyment spots. My favourite was Saturday matinee and occasionally I went to the midnight movie on a Saturday night. Mostly I went alone, but sometimes I was accompanied by friends. My favourite films were love stories and karate but the cinema showed many American action films as they were in demand by the general public. As soon as a new film was released I would be one of the first people to see it. I enjoyed the music that was played at the intermission, which would be a mixture of soul and reggae. Married men would bring their sweethearts there and leave their wives at home with the children, which could also end up to be a form of entertainment for us when the wife found out where they were and paid them a visit at the cinema.

One afternoon at a one o'clock show a couple came in and were sitting a couple of rows in front of me. They were hugging, kissing and laughing with each other obviously enjoying their time together. At the intermission the lights came on and I went to get a drink. As I was going back in the hall I saw a woman in front of me looking curious in front of her. She then said, 'is not Freddy dat with a woman', I followed her stare to see where it would lead and to my surprise it was the couple who were enjoying each other in front of me. The woman went up to the couple and hit the man in his head, he stayed in his seat but told her to go away. The woman did as she was told and went back to the seat but she was yelling at them. I was flabbergasted when the woman blurted out, 'mi waan fi know if ah mi or she yu carry in front a pastor'. I could not believe the jerk was married and his wife caught him with his mistress and he told her to go away. The wife said she would wait for them outside when the film finish so I could not wait for the end of the film

133

to go outside to see better things and the film I was watching suddenly became boring. I heard one lady making the same statement to her friend. I made sure the wife was in my sight so I would not lose her in the crowd.

As I was following the wife to one exit I saw the happy couple going through another but as we were in Jamaica where people liked excitement someone came to the wife and told her where her husband went. She moved in that direction and so did the crowd including me. We caught up with the couple but the mistress was getting in a taxi, which drove off full speed. The husband was left to face his wife on his own, they were arguing in the street until he got embarrassed and called a taxi. He told his wife to get inside the car but she refused so he pushed her in. One man who was present said, 'why yu neva bloodclaat do dat long time, yu likle cratches, fi yu sweetheart musy can caan wuk more dan yu wife why yu mek sure she go home safe before yu wife'? Wife and husband were driven away in the taxi but by his action we all assumed his affair with the other woman continued.

My friend Bess who I was close to when I lived in Olympic Gardens went to America to live. Her father who was residing there filed for her and her sister. We kept in contact and when she visited Jamaica we linked up. On one of her visits I went with her to sort out some business and because we were going several places we hired a taxi from downtown Kingston to take us to our destinations. As we were getting into the taxi a young man from nowhere came up and asked the driver if he could drop him off somewhere I did not recognise. I took one look at the gold jewellery glistening around Bess's neck and knew straight away why he wanted to drive with us. The taxi driver who wanted the double fare told him it was up to us and we both shouted, 'no' at the same time. The young man knew that we had caught onto his game so he went away to find another innocent victim.

The taxi driver turned around and looked at us in the back seat as if he was aware of our presence for the first time. We looked smart and lady-like but the way we dealt with the stickman on the prowl for victims made the driver realise we were not exactly nuns. He cheekily asked us, 'ah wey mi know uno from'? Bess and I both looked at each other questioningly for neither of us recognised him from anywhere. He did not wait for an answer from us and we were even more stunned when he said, 'uno fava two gal wey rob mi last week'. Bess only arrived in the country two days ago and I was very sure I only took the bus in the last year. Bess gave him a dirty look and I told him not to take any rassclaat liberty but as it turned out we had to end up robbing the asshole.

We were on our way up Hagley Park Road making our way to one of our destinations in Half Way Tree when the driver turned off on Waltham Park Road. At first we thought he was cutting out the traffic that was on Hagley Park Road but then he pulled up and got out of the car at a rum bar. He went over to join some of his drunk and ready friends who all had glasses in their hands. He shouted to us that he was going in the bar to have a drink and chat with his friends. We objected and reminded him that he was working but he kissed his teeth and went inside the bar. That was the disrespect we got from some people in the service industry on the island and they expected us to accept it. We could see him standing at the bar door chatting away with his friends. He had a glass with liquid in one hand that I assumed was white rum. He had taken us several places already so we were wondering if we should just pay him and get another taxi. As we were talking to each other in the car we saw another taxi coming our way, I got out, waved it down and we both crept away hastily towards the other car. Some young men nearby caught on to what was happening and were laughing out loudly. I looked over to the bar and saw the drink-driver all taken up in his conversation, he did not even look to see what the joke was about. He said that he was robbed by two girls but he set himself up to be robbed. Needless to say none of us felt guilty for running off and not paying him as far as I was concerned he got what he deserved.

Bess rented a car to get around for a few days as it was easier than depending on unreliable taxi men who were not always courteous, because they were only in the business for the money. We were driving on the Boulevard late one evening when a police patrol car drove up behind us and indicated for us to stop. Bess stopped the car and two male police officers came up to each of the front windows where we were sitting. The one on my side asked me to get out which I did and Bess got out as well. The one close to me asked, 'yu have any gun ina de car'. I told him no but that he was welcome to search it for himself. He replied, 'mi tink yu did a go scy woman no carry guns'. With those preconceived ideas from police I could just imagine what he thought of people living in the ghetto and how he treated them. They did not search the car only told us we could go. Ten minutes down the road another patrol car signalled us to stop, as if we had the same brainstorm Bess and I started pulling our skirts up to our waist. I lifted one of my legs onto the seat until part of my crutch could be seen while Bess opened her legs as far as room could allow. One male police officer came up to Bess's side of the car and was about to say something when his eyes caught us. His face broke out in a smile and he called his colleague over to help him out. His colleague who was the more forward of the two came over to my window and I made sure he had a good view of me. He was talking but his eyes were between my legs and most of his words were slurred and broken so it was difficult to understand what he was saying. He managed to ask us if we were going to Rae Town street dance later that evening and we said yes just to get rid of them and drove off.

I enjoyed going to dances and clubs and so did my friend Donnet. She was a party animal and used to rave most nights. She was a regular at most bashment dances and associated with some devious characters she called boyfriends. She introduced me to her latest beau at a dance one night and I recognised him as a known pickpocket. I asked her what she was doing with a thief and she told me as long as he was not stealing from her and her relatives, she did not care much about his chosen career. I asked to be excused and promised not to interfere again.

One night we went to a club together and Mr pickpocket himself appeared. They both went on the dancing floor to do a close up dance. Donnet had on a gold chain that was given as a present, when she returned from the dance floor I noticed her chain was missing. I asked her for her chain and that was when she realised it was missing. She was suspicious that her shady character of a boyfriend might have taken it and she was clearly embarrassed. We went to look for him but he had disappeared and could not be found for the rest of the night. She went on about how she did not expect that from him and I had to break my promise and ask her what she expected from a thief. The little creep never showed his face again but Donnet was too angry to miss him. She went on to the next relationship with another unscrupulous boyfriend from the ghetto as she was not into any weaklings. She said dangerous men were more exciting and that ghetto men made the best lovers.

I loved Donnet and accepted her despite her stupidity where men were concerned and we always came good for each other when it was needed. Her new boyfriend was an area don who had two baby-mothers - one he was still with and another he ignored along with their child. I begged Donnet not to go out with him but she said I was jealous because she had a don for a boyfriend. She felt on top of the world when he beat up his baby-mother for her. The baby-mother was a few years older than Donnet and was jealous of her younger rival. It was a vicious circle because the same thing happened to the other baby-mother who lost her position to the younger baby-mother who was now losing out to Donnet. She met Donnet at a dance and told her off, the two women squared off for their don man. They disrespected each other in the worst possible way in front of all the patrons at the dance and felt no way about it. When their man heard about the fracas he hand flogged his baby-mother throwing in some kicks as well. Donnet laughed when she heard and she said to me, 'Patsy, mi tell yu im love mi'. One older lady saw the baby-mother crying and said to her, 'don't worry too much bout im an his new girlfriend, fi yu trouble a over an fi har own just a start'. Donnet laughed off the words and whined to Little John's hit song, 'hold yu hand when yu si yu mate, whine yu body cause she no ready, and dem ya girls caan knock yu body, knock yu body, knock yu body dem caan knock yu body'. The baby-mother did not leave her man but she had to stay on the side and watch him with Donnet going about their business.

We were young and feeling on top of the world, Donnet was not fat but the chubbier of the two of us. She liked the latest wear and could afford to buy some of them as her man gave her money from his illegal doings. I got a lot of my clothes from America from my relatives but some I bought locally. I bought a pair of shorts at a store uptown. The size made it look more like knickers rather than shorts but I was hell bent on causing a stir in Half Way Tree Square. I bought it two months before wearing it as I was waiting for the right time to do so. I had not seen anyone in Jamaica in anything as small as what I had calling shorts so I knew some people would not appreciate seeing me in it, but I was out to shock them more than anything else. I had to make a trip to St Mary so I decided it was time to get out my little number. It was so short and tight I could hardly pull it up much more get a knickers on under it, I put on a tube top for good measures. I looked like one of the girls in the playboy magazine and a young girl asking for trouble. Making my appearance on the street was nerve racking, but I held out and headed out onto Hagley Park Road where things were fairly quiet. I got some stares and whistles but the men controlled themselves.

When I got to Half Way Tree bus terminus I went up to check which ones were going to St Mary and all the drivers who were men happened to be going to my destination. I even saw one man taking off the Montego Bay sign from his van. The women were cruelly critical but the men thought I was the best thing since slice bread. One man of God was out in the hot sun preaching the second coming of the Lord turned around and saw me. He pointed at me and said, 'there are signs around us that the Lord is near, the time is upon us, when young women start walking the streets almost naked we know he is not far'. I was condemned to hell and blamed for polluting the place and called evil. For me, all I was doing was wearing some clothes I liked. I chose a white Toyota van and the driver opened the front door for me to get in. Two passengers travelled in the front seat so a man who was in front of me was making his way to the seat next to the driver and was told to move him claat out of the way and allow me to get in first. It was a tight squeeze in the front so I had to open my legs a bit to allow the driver to use the gear stick and this he used every second. The man beside me asked, 'driver why yu a change gear so regular?' The driver told him to mind his own business and that he was upset because he was not sitting where I was. When I arrived in St Mary the women were less intimidated by me and many told me that I looked nice and the men were great. None touched me they just wanted to have a look. I saw a young man who I knew from my grandfather's district, he ran up to me and said, 'yu look good gal'. I never wore my shorts on the streets again but anytime I looked at it I remembered the different comments made about me by people who did not know me. I was called a sinner, evil, princess, angel and slut depending on who were making them. When I told Donnet she thought I was too brave but it was the words of the preacher that made her laugh till tears came to her eyes.

When Bob Marley the king of reggae music died in 1981 we were all sad, but took comfort from the fact that he would not have to suffer the pain from the illness that took his short but memorable life. But the murder of Free I, a famous radio personality and Peter Tosh went through the nation like a shock wave. They were both murdered in 1987 in Tosh's home. Apparently Free I was in the wrong place at the wrong time. Murder was becoming such part of our everyday life that many of us were not bothered anymore. Not even the famous were immune to the killing fever that took over the island.

I was visiting some friends in Jones Town one evening. We walked out to the bus stop at Torrington Bridge for me to catch a bus home when we heard some gunshots and knew they were coming from Jones Town. We went back in the direction the gunshots were coming from to find out what was going on. When we got to the Admiral Town Police Station, the area was completely sealed off by police officers who were crawling all over the place. We knew then someone important was shot or killed as police woul not bother to use up so much manpower for a local resident but we were wondering who that person could be.

One young lady came up to us and asked if we knew who had been killed. We said no, as it was only then we realised someone had died. She said it was Blair. He was a popular police officer who lived in Jones Town and was based at the Admiral Town Police station. We were all in shock, who could be so cold hearted and daring to carry out such a killing in daylight on a cop. Another officer who was present at the murder scene had to lie on the ground and play dead until the shots stopped firing. That was what would lead to the destruction of the brutal assassins. When the cop who survived the carnage got up from the ground he said, 'I know who they are'. They thought they were invincible and brave to kill a policeman in broad daylight but they were only kidding themselves and the other brainless boys who admired their artificial bravery.

One of the young men who carried out the assassination went to brag to his friends about the hit he did. We found out the same evening who they were. They originated from Jungle and Jones Town but some had ties in other dysfunctional areas. The one who actually killed Blair was a young man no more than twenty-years old. He had a baby face and could have easily been mistaken for a saint. He bragged about killing a Christian woman who was on her way home from church on a Sunday afternoon with her children. She put the Bible over her face as a shield before he opened the gun on her. He said she begged for her life but he showed no mercy, as she was a police informer. His audience was impressed with his so-called bravery and cold-heartedness, some held him in high regards as a soldier.

He told his friends that he had been planning to kill the cop for some time and watched his movements for a couple of days before he moved in for the kill. He had some friends living in the same area as Blair who were giving him information about the police officer's daily routine and the various getaway routes. Blair was a man of habit and was close to the people in the community he came from but some outlaws thought he should not have been there. He played dominoes out on the streets with his friends when he was off duty. This helped to keep down criminal activities, as his presence would deter the criminal minded and believe me there were many in the area as it was more acceptable to do bad than good.

The thug said Blair was busy concentrating on the hand of dominoes he was playing when he crept up behind him. He clicked the gun in one of Blair's ears, he thought it was a colleague and told him to stop messing about, but when he heard the click a second time he knew whoever it was had different things on his mind. He turned around to see who it was and met a bullet in his face. The creep started firing shots at everyone around the domino table but some fled others played dead and the assassin was not very good. Blair was pronounced dead the same evening and his colleagues were soon planning their revenge. They wanted to eliminate the murderers quickly before some of them could manage to leave the country. The dead cop's mother vowed that her son's death would not be in vain. No one took to the street to demonstrate about the brutal killing of a policeman but if it had been a criminal, women, men and children in the community would have been out blocking the roads.

Within a year the police caught up and killed all the culprits including those who provided information about the dead cop. Many people said Blair's mother used obeah to get all her son's killers executed. If it was indeed obeah then more power to her. Two of the youths who killed Blair were to leave the island soon but they did not make it, as they were tracked down by police and exterminated one by one. Their girlfriends cried and their mothers wailed. Many wanted to protest about police brutality but forgot about the cop who was gunned down by their sons in cold blood. No mother would like to see her son get killed but we should not accept their wrongdoings especially when it's murder.

When we heard that the United States authority was waging war against Jamaican criminals that did not deter many people from smuggling drugs. It was as if it was an invitation to step up the courier service. Many women and even children were being recruited for the job. I could not believe my ears when a woman told me that she put the drugs on her child's body to go through customs. I would not even do that to my dog Rover. The first man to feel a touch of the American new custom-built prison sentence for Jamaican criminals was a don from Water House who was given fifty years for various criminal activities. He was wanted for rape and murder in Jamaica but escaped to the United States to deal in drugs. He had no intention of turning over a new leaf and ran out of luck. He should count himself lucky as he got off lightly with the lawmen in the United States, for if he had remained in Jamaica the cops would not have taken him in alive and he knew it.

My uncle Moses had a friend we called Phil who was always polite and nice to me, he was not very good-looking but I liked him. When he left Jamaica and went to England I knew he had one thing on his mind and that was to get rich fast and the only means of doing so was to sell drugs. Jamaicans were not original, all it took was one person to come up with something and everyone would be lining up to do the same thing. The drugs market was saturated but people were still flocking it. Something would have to give way sooner rather than later so they started robbing and killing each other to get rid of the competition and to get their hands on fast money. The American authorities were hunting down the drug dealers and the market was slowing down, so Britain was looking good for the predators. The pound was strong and business was bright. Some of the drugs dealers from America were creeping over to the UK, others were returning home to Jamaica to hide. The Feds were after the Spanglers and Shower posses so many members were looking for hiding places. They could not remain in one place as their big time but creepy lawyers could no longer make deals to keep them out of prison. The posses tried to fight back to protect their growing empire by killing people who they suspected of being informers but the law enforcement agencies had invested heavily in destroying them and dug their heels in. A police report stated that the Shower Posse membership had grown to over five thousand in a dozen American cities including New York, Connecticut and the capital Washington and spilling over to Toronto. Both Spanglers and Showers were a force to be reckoned with and even the mighty Wareika Hill and Jungle massive had to take back seats to them in the United States.

Women and men with American visas were being recruited to work as mules to take drugs back to the US. Some who did not want to do it changed their minds when they saw the guns in their face. They were told if they had intentions of remaining in the US to double cross their new self-appointed boss, their family back in Jamaica would be killed. Some higglers who did well out of the buying and selling, got used to the high life and decided that they too would move up to bigger and better things and started smuggling drugs. They would leave the country every week to take their illegal wares to the US and returned with clothing to sell back in Jamaica, it did not take custom officers long to catch on and start searching them inside out.

A visa was not needed to get to England so all a mule needed was a ticket to travel and someone to clear them at the airport. The problem was they were drilled intensely by immigration officers, which made many of them crumble under the pressure and show signs of guilt. Two in five smugglers were being caught. The loss was costly for the dealers but they could afford to make a profit with the others who were getting through but not enough to take the British market by the throat. Some of the mules were

139

swallowing up to twenty parcels of cocaine, others plugged it in their backsides and some women pushed it up their vaginas. Some had hysterectomies just to make extra space for their consignments. One woman said her man had a big dick so anytime she was going to work, she would have sex with him the night before so that the next day she would be set for her journey.

The lawmen in America stepped up their attack on the Jamaican gangs and made numerous raids in 1987. The mass media in the country was influencing the actions that were being taken by the police. The Jamaicans were labelled the worst type of criminals the country had ever seen. They reported that the Italian Mafia did not enjoy killing women and children the way the Jamaican gangs did. Over one hundred arrests were made and many escaped. The ATF were hell bent on bringing the Shower Posse members to justice for their alleged crimes but especially for the murder of the people they killed in Miami. They crossed the line when they started killing white people. It was accepted to the whites in power for black to kill black but when they turned the gun on whites they were getting too big for their boots. No white authority would allow black men to kill white people and walk free even if the victims were junkies. The Shower posse sealed their own fate when they killed the white junkies who they believed robbed them. Not only did they set fire under their own tail but that of the other posse members, as they were all tarnished with the same brush. The heat was on for the Jamaican posse members and some quietly crept back to Jamaica to cool off.

Many youths back in Jamaica who could not get the break to reach a foreign country to try hustling on the front line were trying to get into music. Those who could not sing tried to toast (DJ). That field was also saturated but one did not need to have any qualification to pursue that career path. Those who could not get the break in the music could not wait to leave the island and for this they would beg, borrow, steal or murder. The same attitude they had with the drugs was the same with the music. Everyone wanted a number one hit song overnight and to get rich quick even if their music stinks. If they could have put a gun to our heads to force us to buy their filth they called music they would have.

I was getting older and things were making more sense to me but I was having problems exploring different pastures. I remember my late grandfather telling me that I could be anything I wanted to be, but how could I when my surroundings were so oppressive to me, a young black woman. My older relatives meant well but they accepted their position in the status quo as second-class citizens and wanted us younger ones to join the ranks and accept our position in the lower class. I was never going to accept that I was inferior and rebelled against the passive indoctrination by my well meaning relatives. I was told off on many occasions but I knew there was something great waiting for me if only I could reach out to it. We love our older folks and learnt a lot from them but when they die their legacy of colonialism must die with them.

My paternal grandfather passed away in 1985, he was ill for a while and then he slowly slipped away I am so proud to have known him. He was a simple man who wanted a simple life and never begrudged anyone for what they had and what he did not have he did without. I tried to live by that and never put my basket where I could not reach it.

In late 1987 I was assessing my life. I had left school five years earlier but was not sure where I was going and what I wanted to do. My grandmother saw me through school and went back to the United States. I had some jobs but none that I got satisfaction from. I had nice clothes, food on the table everyday, but I wanted to do something challenging and not just routine.

Tom told me to leave his mother's house shortly after she left. When I refused he went in the kitchen for a knife to slice me up, thankfully my cousins who were at the house held on to him so I could get out with my life. A few months later he was sent to prison for theft. He never gave up his trade of breaking and entering and I could always depend on him to break the law and end up back in prison to give me some respite from his ill-treatment.

The relationship between Tom and Mel finally phased itself out. They had been seeing each other secretly from his new lover. I could not work out why she brought herself down to that level but one day we were talking and she said to me, 'mi waste all mi youth pon Tom and now mi no ave notting fi sho fi it except di three pickney im give mi and na support'. She felt that she would not meet anyone new as she was overweight with three children. She accepted Tom visiting her occasionally for the intimacy of a male companion and most of all she did not want to be single. She had been with men from her early teens and had never been single since she first started dating, so most of her time was spent knowing someone else and not herself. This scenario was not unique to Mel as many young women in Trench Town have been through that passage. It was as if they were some inferior being to the male of the species. When the women cooked they made sure their men had the best of everything and the food presented neatly fit for kings but they and the children were not party to the royal treatment. Tom never appreciated what Mel did for him at home. Many times she could not even buy herself a pair of shoes and her man was dressed well everyday.

I could not help feeling sorry for Mel because I remembered when she was young and full of energy. She had her whole life in front of her and threw everything away for the love of a man who did not deserve her. The women in Trench Town did not give me worldly riches but what I learnt from them was a wealth of knowledge. No way was I going to spend my life with one man giving him my all and depending on him for my daily bread. If I want a pair of knickers or sanitary towels, I would not want to suffer the indignity of asking him for the money and when he becomes tired of me he moves on the next available woman, leaving me helpless and disillusioned. I was never going to be afraid to be single. The children Mel had by Tom were several years younger than me and because I hated Tom so much I could not bond with his children. I remembered when Mel was good to me, but I also remember when she was not. Her daughters and I never had any sisterly relationships and I had passed the bonding stage with siblings after what happened to Carl and me. Tom's new lover was also a victim of his wrath. She was one year older than me. He beat her so badly one time, she was swollen all over. She came to our house one day to visit Tom and said to me that the evil he was doing to other people's children would follow his children. I was taken aback by her comment given she came to our house on her own accord to visit him and no one was forcing her to be with him.

The statement was also directed at me, which was not a fair comment as I too was victim of his wrath and in many cases because of her. She knew what he was like and heard about what he did to Mel but thought it would not happen to her.

I never bothered to tell Prim of my problems for she was only interested in my successes and not my disappointments. Tom thought I would not have grown up and that he would have control over me forever but I was rising and he was falling.

The wealth in our country was moving around in a small circle and very little was trickling down to the poor. Prim and her relatives were still trapped in poverty and none were making any headway at getting out. The shares Pepe bought at the Jamaica Flour Mill were sold by Moses a couple of years after Pepe died. Lily said she had not given him permission to sell them. He did not bother to seek financial advice because he wanted quick money and did not respect the value or sacrifice the man who bought them had made. For him it was easy to give away what meant so much to Pepe and some of the children were not even told of the transaction. Fred moved his family out of Trench Town never to be seen again. Three hundred and sixty five shares were basically taken away from Moses for nothing. Lily was taken to Flour Mill by a good friend of the family to find out what happened to all the shares. The lady at the reception told her that they were all sold by her son, Lily passed out cold in the reception area. When she was revived the lady told her to have Moses arrested, but what about the people at the flour mill who bought the shares illegally? Moses was a young man who acted in greed and haste but was exploited by some cruel and devious businessmen who had been after Pepe's shares for a long time. Moses was way out of his league from the first time he walked into their office without a legal representative to enquire about the value of the shares. The vultures seized the opportunity to steal them off him and no one in the company questioned the illegal transaction because he was naive. How could Moses sell all the shares that were also in Lily's name? The dealers at the Flour Mill must have had a laugh when he left with his little bag of money thinking he was rich. Someone out there was living off our birthright while we suffer in poverty but one day their past will catch up with them.

Lily never recovered from the shock of the stolen shares. She was later diagnosed with cervical cancer but was never told of her diagnosis, the doctors told the family she would not have a long time to live but she outlasted their prediction. Her life in Trench Town had proven to be a rough one. What if she had remained in Clarendon?

In Trench Town the people continued to support politicians and still yet they had to dwell in squalor and any little handouts were greatly appreciated. Tivoli residents believed that their member of parliament was looking after them and because their community was cleaner than others they would follow him to hell. It was the same divide-and-rule tactics that the slave master used on the plantations to keep slaves in their place that was being copied to ensure politicians power. If Tivoli was so great and he loved the people so much why did he not move down there and live with them as one big happy family? No, he would not, because that would mean he would be lowering his standards, as Tivoli was not the place to raise his well-balanced children. What he built was a five star ghetto to keep the masses happy but made sure they stayed there to support him. The appearance of Jungle was much better than Rema but not in the class of Tivoli. When PNP lost the 1980 election the building work there slowed down and the problem with that area was, there were too many chiefs and very few Indians. Yet still it was the least oppressive regime of all war torn areas, that might be the reason why it had so many problems. In places like Matthews Lane and Tivoli there were three or four dons who gave the orders and their subjects had to obey. In Jungle there were at least ten or more top notches, sometimes you had to wonder who was giving the orders. Rema men seemed to be chaotic and somewhat confused. They were not exactly getting much for supporting the JLP but felt that they had to carry on fighting.

The houses in Rema continued to be without running water and the rubbish piled up day by day. They were their worst enemies as they would rob the men who went to collect their rubbish. I do not know what they thought a man collecting garbage could have in the truck other than garbage. In the hills the homes of the rich and the famous were grand, their dogs were fed food that was luxury to Trench Town residents. When we had a power failure (which was frequent) the island would be left in pitch darkness then we would look to the hills where our rich compatriots lived to see their emergency supplies coming on and lighting up the hills. They were so detached from our struggle they looked down on us with scorn.

Poor people went to street dances to listen to reggae music as a means to escape the harsh reality of life. That was all they could afford to do. The music was a source of strength for many of us. There were singers who were conscious of our plight and they mesmerised us with their redeeming lyrics and soothing voices. Some of the songs were about the injustice in society and the cruelty of ghetto life. We loved them and depended on their words to survive Trench Town.

Donnet's big time boyfriend went to America and instead of sending for his baby-mother and children he sent for Donnet. When she came to tell me the good news she was bragging about how life would be grand and that her man was rich beyond words could describe. I must admit for the first time I felt a pang of jealousy. She told me that she would always remember me no matter what, I believed her as we were good friends. She went away to America on a single entry visitor's visa, to her don man who she could not wait to see. I missed her and was getting lonely as most of my friends were leaving Jamaica to find a better life somewhere else. I did not hear from Donnet when she left Jamaica so I thought life was not working out for her as she thought it would.

I returned to my grandmother's house when Tom was in prison. He came out and beat me up so badly and told me to get out of his mother's house, I cried and went to Prim's. I told her he beat me up and she ignored what I said. Lily tried to comfort me when she saw me sitting on my own crying, but my own mother did not even as much as ask why he hit me. She came up to me before I left and said, 'is your father'. How many times have I heard that but it was even harder when it came from her. She was detached from the whole thing she just did not want me as an extra burden on her. I was still going to see her despite the way she treated me I just wanted her to love me as she loved her other children. I lived off Hagley Park Road for quite some time and she never visited me there once. Her reason for not visiting Christopher was that she was afraid for her life, I wondered what her excuse was for not visiting me. Every time I saw her I initiated the visit, except for once when she sent Sue to check if I was okay. She never bought me a present or gave me a dollar in all the time I had been visiting her.

Christopher gave up trying to get close to her as he was not getting anywhere. He reached out his hand to Prim on many occasions and all he received was rejection, so he licked his wounds and went away quietly. Me, I was a glutton for punishment I kept going for more rejections, when I lived with her I made a decision in my young life to leave home as I felt like an outsider living with her and her new family. Carl, Christopher and I were evidence of Prim's wild days and represented nothing positive to her, we were not wanted. We came about by pure accident to people who were just enjoying themselves sexually. We did not really belong to anyone - we were nobody's children. I cannot help feeling that if Carl had somewhere to go like Christopher and me, he would still be alive and would have been treated like an outcast by Prim, the same way she treated Christopher and me who were not brought up by her.

In November 1987 I made up my mind to visit a foreign country to see other people and experience a different culture. I did not know what the future held for me but I was responding to the voice inside me. I asked my grandmother's brother who was living in the United Kingdom if I could visit him there and he said yes. I left Jamaica on 1st December 1987 for London, England. A male friend asked me to look up his father when I arrived in England. He was upset and swearing about how his father left Jamaica in the sixties and could not afford to send them money. It did not matter to him that he was now a grown man and should be supporting himself and not relying on what would be by then an elderly man. He gave me his father's address and I promised I would try and find him. I thought it would not be too difficult to find his father as the address was in London where I was to stay.

Before I left Jamaica another anti-crime team by the name of The Area 4 Task Force was introduced. What would they achieve where the others before them had failed, we would have to wait and see.

Chapter Ten

On the British Airways flight to England the stewardesses were so cold and rude I wondered if my presence on the plane was offending them, but the man next to me said to me they were racist. I had to ask him what he meant by that and he said they hate black people. I realised then nowhere was perfect, everywhere had its own faults, there is no perfect place on earth. I was also taken aback by the appearance of London. I saw the houses and flats made of bricks and thought they were factories and bakeries. I was surprised when I arrived at my uncle's home and realised what I believed to be a bakery was going to be my home for a while. I also realised that people living in England were not all rich and most of them were just trying to make ends meet.

The first person I met up with from Jamaica in London was Phil, my uncle's friend. He was sharing a flat with some friends and the living condition that was less than ideal. He told me he did not really like it but what was there to return to as he would have to go back to Rema. We became good friends and he had a lot of respect for me but I felt sorry for him, as I knew he did not have his right of stay in Britain and unless he walked the straight and narrow he would be deported back to Jamaica. He would keep me informed about the violence back in Jamaica and America involving gangs. We could not work out why Jamaicans living in America took their gang war there with them. Phil told me not to associate with too many Jamaicans from Trench Town who were living in the UK. It was a pity he did not take his own advice.

I tried to find my friend's father but found out that the address was far away from mine so I gave up. I met a man and got married and decided to stay in the UK at least for a while longer. The marriage was one of the worst times of my life but I was growing up and learning more about myself. I realised I married a man who reflected the men with whom I grew up around in Trench Town, especially Tom.

It was always upsetting for me reading the Jamaican Gleaner and seeing the news of the killings in Trench Town. I heard more and more news about gang members leaving America and coming over to England, as the ATF agents were after them and some had been placed on America's 'most wanted list'. One young man I knew by the name of Freddy crept into Britain to hide out. He was a saint in Jamaica but went to America and became a cold-blooded murderer and he even got involved in kidnapping. He killed a young girl because she had problems with her drug boss who he wanted to impress.

I first realised he was in the UK via a television programme about 'Yardie' gangs. The British police had information that he was hiding somewhere in London. The name Yardie which was patois for Jamaican, was being criminalised in the UK by the media and the police who did not understand what it meant. I was angry about that but I was never ashamed of the police trying to bring Jamaican gang members to justice. The police caught up with Freddy who was staying on the North Peckham Estate. They gave him so much respect he did not deserve by going for him in a helicopter, vans and with dogs. If only they knew the thug was nothing without his gun. They were not sure it was him so they waited for him to smile as he wore a gold tooth, when he did about ten of them pounced on him. He surprised them by walking calmly with them to a van. They took him away and he went without a fight - that was the Freddy I knew, not the murderer he became. He was sent back to America to face charges of murder and was given twenty-five years in a state prison. He should have thanked Scotland Yard for getting to him when they did, because his drugs boss landed in Heathrow Airport the very day he was apprehended by the police in Britain. Rumour had it that he came to kill him. Freddy was also seen on a video tape raping a woman with two of his friends. They said they were gangsters but had all sorts of incriminating evidence against themselves.

Manley won the general election in 1988 because people were not impressed with Seaga's leadership and it was back to the other problem. Seaga called a snap election a few years after the 1980 election as a tactical ploy so that he would be in power for a longer time. Manley who did not have time to regroup his party after the landslide victory against them the last time, decided not to contest the snap election as he knew he stood no chance in hell. Since the first general election the people have been voting in and out the same politicians with the same problems. When I arrived back on the island after being away for a couple of years the people had the same old mentality but they appeared worse off than when I lived there. Some of them were telling me that I had changed but I thought they had changed and for the worse. A friend who was visiting from America told me it was me who had changed and was seeing the people I grew up with in another light. The people who were below the poverty line were grateful for whatever they got but those who had a little were greedy and that was the general attitude of most. One girl asked me to give her my wedding band, when I told her that I could not do that because my husband would be angry, she could not understand why he would deprive her by being angry. She said he could always buy another one in England because things were cheap there and that he could buy me many wedding bands. It was pointless trying to explain sentimental value to her as she was too narrow minded and self-centred.

My genuine friends were just happy to see me but the so-called ones wanted what I did not have. The things they were asking for I would have to be managing ten jobs and something illegal to get the money to buy them. Family members were the same. Some I knew when I was living in Jamaica, others I did not, but they wanted me to give what I did not have and could never afford to give. One asked me to buy her a house when I told her that I was living in a rented property she stopped short from telling me I was lying. I became stressed out due to the begging. Everybody I met wanted something. They all wanted over five hundred dollars. Some had the audacity to ask for more than what they received.

146

I was getting to hate their greed so much I did not even want to see them. There was this expectation that money grew on trees in America and England and anyone who visited Jamaica would have their suitcases full of it. It was easier convincing them that monkeys could fly rather than them understanding that people visiting Jamaica from foreign lands did not have money.

My friend who asked me to visit his father in England was upset that I did not find the son of a bitch for him and said I was 'fuckery'. The shoes I gave him softened his attitude towards me and I promised him that I would try and visit his father when I returned to England. I went to the Victoria Mutual Bank in Half Way Tree to collect some money a friend sent me, to rescue me from poverty as people begged all the spending money I had. They were begging me and I had to beg from someone else. I got to the bank around ten o'clock in the morning. I went up to this customer service clerk to ask if my money had arrived. She told me that she had to ask the head office in downtown Kingston to send it up to them. I was then told to have a seat until I was called. I sat waiting for over an hour and no one called me so I went back to the lady to ask her what was happening. I thought she would have some sympathy as I was patient for so long but when I asked her if the money had arrived, she told me to get out of her way and sit down until I was called. I was so angry I asked to speak to her supervisor who was helpful but the alarming thing was some people found her disrespect amusing. I had to have strong words with her, she ignored me and pretended as if she knew nothing of what I was saying to her. The entire transaction took well over four hours.

A few days later I went to Workers Bank at Half Way Tree, except for two people the entire work force there needed intensive training in customer service and equal opportunities. I had a bank account when I was there but as I was not using it for a while, the teller told me that it was inactive and that I needed to make a lodgement to activate it again. I asked her to tell me how much was in the account before I put anything in it and she rudely exclaimed, 'de same old thousand dollar yu put in de, yu ting any body wan tief dat, thousand dollar an no noting'. I could not believe what she said to me for I was a poor woman and my thousand dollars had the same value to me as what a million dollars meant to a rich man. Besides I thought because it was a savers account I would at least have gained some interest on it. My uncle said I should have been grateful they did not use the money to cover running costs.

The lady told me to fill in a form which I did but I had to wait while she attended to some people she obviously knew. A man came in with a cheque, which he did not sign and handed it to her. She gave it back to him and told him to sign it, he whispered something to her and looked embarrassed about what he was telling her. I was standing not far from him but did not hear what he said. But when he finished she blurted out, 'what yu sey, yu caan read or write'. The man bowed his head in shame it broke my heart, as I could not believe someone in her position could be so unkind and ignorant regarding customer care.

She then decided to grace me with her presence and took the form I had completed and told me to stand aside. I did as I was told trying hard not to get into an argument with Mrs Brutus. She told the man with the cheque to wait as well without an explanation. We were both waiting for well over an hour, she told me what was happening only because I asked her. The man who was waiting, still had on his working clothes. He looked tired from the day's work and even more so as it was the end of the week. It was coming up to the Easter holiday and he looked concerned as he was being paid his last wage before the holiday and probably wanted to take the money home to his wife and children. He went up to the teller and asked her, 'mi boss no ave no money in a im account why mi wait so long', but the woman did not even bother to answer him. He was humble as ever and went back to stand up in the corner where he was. Her colleague heard when the man asked the question and told her to explain to him why he was waiting but she told the colleague, 'me caan badder'. I was so angry I had to intervene and told her off, she did not say a word to defend herself. The longer I was there watching her performing her duty the more I realised she had no reasoning ability. Whoever interviewed her for ther job could not be suitable for their post either. She would not know how to talk her way out of a paper bag much more to the people she was serving.

    She was not the problem, the fault was with those who interviewed and offered her the job as a bank clerk. It took more than checking money to be a teller as they have to know how to deal with people and that was what was lacking, the ability to deal with the public politely irrespective of race, class or creed. Her attitude towards the people she was offering a service to was not acceptable but many of them who came in the bank allowed her to insult them without reporting her to her superiors. A white woman joined the queue and she was treated like royalty by the bank staff who were all black, I was angry but not surprised as this was always the case. The owners of the banks had been aware of the overt white bias in their institutions but made no major step to solve the problems as most of them were white and the black people in Jamaica would not boycott their businesses. Despite their open contempt for us we would continue to support their establishments.

    The white bias and general disrespect were evident in most establishments in Jamaica and it appeared that the staff were given very little or no training in customer service, only how to take our money. The customers were so used to the bad treatment they accepted it as part of the service provided. By not addressing the problem the entrepreneurs encouraged their staff to ill-treat customers who were the lifeline of their businesses. The politicians who did not want to rock the boat, turned a blind eye to the problem as they knew the men with the money could make or break them as Manley found out.

    The car rental establishment in Jamaica was a big rip-off. It cost a fortune to rent a basic car there and was more expensive than anywhere in the region. The plate of the cars had the letters RR on them, which would differentiate a rental from a private car. This left visitors to the island as sitting ducks for touts and robbers. People who drove them were classed as being rich and the locals defined the RR as 'rotten rich'. Anyone who drove a rental was viewed as very rich and would be targeted by thieves even if they borrowed the money that paid for the car. The danger about the robberies was people got killed in the process and some of the victims did not even have money on them. Most petty thieves in Jamaica were not very bright and thought everyone who visited Jamaica was a millionaire and would draw all the money from their bank accounts to take on holiday with them.

    I went to downtown Kingston with a friend to buy our weekly shopping. There was the usual hustle and bustle with everybody busy doing their Saturday shopping. One lady who was selling near the Coronation Street market was being bullied by some young men. They were telling her that she could not continue to sell at her usual spot anymore if she did not give them money. They said anyone who wanted to sell at the market had to pay them protection money. The lady was obviously frightened but said nothing only shivered with fear. Several young women joined in the intimidation and told her she had to leave the area if she did not pay up weekly. They made it clear that they were from Tivoli and that they controlled that particular area. One market trader told us that many of them were paying Tivoli men protection money so that they could continue to earn their bread and butter. Others over the other side were believed to be paying Matthews Lane men protection money as well. I wondered to myself who would protect them from the villains collecting the money.

Most of the people who traded downtown Kingston were women with children who came from rural Jamaica with their ground provisions to sell. The selling was their only means of making a living so they had no choice but to pay or suffer. It reached to the point where it was pointless reporting the matter to the police as the gunmen took over the streets completely and were not afraid to challenge the police who carried hand guns compared to the high powered rifle of the outlaws. Also the police did not view intimidation as a serious offence when they had so many murders to deal with. They would only investigate when the intimidation ended in murder but by then it was too late for those concerned so the traders had to deal with the matter themselves. A few tried to pay but when the men became too greedy and started demanding more money some had no choice but to stay home and suffer in poverty. The alternative was to sell their goods and hand over their money to men who never worked in their lives. People including me tried to justify the crimes the gunmen from poor communities did by saying they were victims themselves. Yes, that was true but how can we justify them depriving women and innocent children of their daily bread.

When I returned to England I went to look for my friends father in Wembley, as I would have no more excuses to give him when I return to Jamaica. A woman answered the door and told me that my friend's father had rented a room from her for many years but died six months before my visit. He was living in the room by himself but was like part of the family as he did not have any relatives in Britain. She said he did not come to terms with his new country and lost some of himself. Many people who did not know him thought he was mad but she knew better. He could not help his children back in Jamaica as he needed help himself. He had a woman for a long time but she disappeared just before he died. He told the lady he had children back in Jamaica but lost contact with them. I told her the children in Jamaica did not know anything about his life in Britain and that as far as they were concerned he was alive and wealthy. She laughed and said he was neither of the two. I decided to wait until I visited Jamaica the next time to break the news to my friend if he waited that long without hearing anything he could wait a bit longer. What he did not know would not bother him.

The ATF was still pressing their case for John Jones, Wrongmove, and Stan Baker who they wanted for several crimes including murder, cocaine distribution and extortion. It was not until 1988 that the ATF had enough hard evidence to take before a federal grand jury. They wanted thirty-four members of the Shower Posse, including the trio, to stand trial for crimes against humanity.

The irony was the Shower posse had been linked to a lot of crimes before the killings took place in Miami where a white woman was shot yet it was not until that incident the ATF stepped up their search for the trio. What that told us was black lives meant nothing. Only when a white junkie got killed did the authorities take the whole thing serious. All three men felt the heat and ran home to Jamaica where they hoped to be protected by their political bosses but they were up against the odds. The JLP had lost the previous election to the PNP and could do very little to assist their hitmen and the Americans were hell bent on bringing them to justice. The ATF did not think much of our corrupt legal system in Jamaica either as they wanted to remain top dog in that department, so they were trying every trick known to man to get the trio back to the US.

They became hopeful when John Jones and Wrongmove were arrested by the police back in Jamaica and sent to the General Penitentiary. The Americans went in for the kill and used every means at their disposal to extradite the men back to the United States. The two men fought back with venom as they knew they were looking at multiple years behind bars, that would not kill their bodies but it would surely destroy their minds. They exhausted every legal means in Jamaica to fight the extradition warrant and when that failed they turned to the Privy Council in London. Even today Britain still has some say in Jamaica's affairs by the way of the Privy Council. If their problems had not clouded their judgement they would not even have bothered to go there as not even prayer could save them from their predators.

I returned to Jamaica in 1992 but did not see the young man to tell him about his father. Another friend told me he was away on holiday in the United States. I spent almost six weeks in Jamaica as I was going through a lot of stress in Britain in my personal life and wanted to get away badly. Some things I had to accept and move on. Some people I knew for a long time decided to spread a rumour that I was in the country that long because I could not go back to England as I was deported That told me I had outstayed my welcome. They were happy to see me when I first arrived but as soon as they got what they wanted they were no longer interested in me. Some of them changed so much towards me I could not believe it but it was then I started to grow up. The other problem was everyone thought I lost my sense of direction just by living in the cold, they did not trust me to direct them anywhere. I was directing a friend to my home and he took a different turning from the one I told him to. He took us up a dead end road, when I asked him why he did not turn on the road I told him to, he said he did not think I remembered my way home. He then went on to tell me that I might have a bit of madness in me as most black people who go to England, return home mad or kinky.

I was in Jamaica at the time when the Wrongmove case was in utter confusion. Some people were not pleased because he was sent back to the United States to face criminal charges. Many people saw the illegal extradition order as a trick played by the ruling PNP against an old political foe. The ATF was digging their heels in to get John Jones, Wrongmove and Stan Baker back to the US to face criminal charges, so the Jamaican authorities had to do something quickly and that meant handing over the man who posed the least threat to start a riot on the island. The appeal in Britain was still pending when the Jamaican authorities passed an order to send Wrongmove back to the United States. Wrongmove was sent to a prison in Miami where he was charged for murder, conspiracy and drug dealings. The Jamaican authorities tried to save face by getting him returned to the island through diplomatic means but failed miserably. Now that the ATF had him where they wanted there was no way they would have let him walk free. He stood trial and was convicted on drugs charges for which he got twenty-four years without parole and still had the other conspiracy and murder charges to follow after his first conviction. He would have a lot of time on his hands to sit and think about all the crimes he committed. If he could not forgive himself he should pray that the almighty does.

The Lords back in England had ruled that John Jones should face charges in the United States for the crimes they alleged he had committed. So he was left to rely on his political bosses to bail him out of trouble but even he should have known he was a drowning man. Rumour was rife that John Jones was planning to tell everything if he went down and that he would not go down alone. Many high profile public figures were getting nervous as such a threat should not be taken lightly. If the rumour was true he was signing his own death warrant, he should not have taken the men who gave him orders lightly either. Politicians knew Jones was dispensable as men like him came a penny a dozen and there were always more of him where he came from. There were many foolish young men waiting in the wings to take his place and none of them remembered or cared about how Maquade died. Everybody wanted a touch of glory and the politicians were only too happy to oblige.

As a 'don dadda' John Jones enjoyed certain perks in prison that other prisoners could only dream of but time was running out for him. A fire which started in the cell Jones occupied took his life and that of another prisoner. The media report stated he was burnt beyond recognition. Some people were saying it was not Jones's body and that he had escaped to another country but a picture of his charred body shown in the local newspapers soon gagged those who were hoping it was not him. No one knew how the fire started and no proper investigation was made into the case. Everything was quietly done. The fire was said to be blazing like mad but only spread to two cells and it took wardens several minutes to respond to the crisis even though they were aware of the fire.

Some people said Jones was planning to escape and the plot went wrong which was what led to the fire in the first place. The PNP blamed the JLP and the JLP blamed them. John Jones rose to prominence through politics and that was what led to his demise. He was a legend in most people's eyes and exceeded even the likes of Maquade. He became too big for his own good. The PNP were facing a rebellion if they had surrendered John Jones to the United States authorities as they had tested the water with Wrongmove who they used as a sacrificial lamb for Jones. He was sent to the US to see how the people would react and that did not go down too well so they knew they would have had bigger trouble if they handed over Jones. On the other hand the JLP was in a tighter spot as John Jones knew all their secrets. The JLP knew if they did not keep him away from America he could single-handedly bring down the party.

Could the PNP refuse to send John Jones back to the United States and face the wrath of Washington as they did in 1980 or could the JLP risk him going to the United States, and see the end of their reign in the political arena? The price was too high for both parties. Whoever was to blame in my opinion Jones was assassinated by people in high places. Whichever side was guilty the other one should have been grateful. We should never exclude the work of the CIA either as to do so would be foolish. Jones' funeral was attended by Seaga and almost everyone who lived in Tivoli. People from other nearby communities went out on the streets to catch a look at the mourners.

In an interview a reporter asked Seaga about his links with John Jones and he replied, 'as long as you and other people keep looking at the man's background rather than where he stands in the community, you will always ask a question like that'. He went on to say, 'ask the lawyer if he looks at the background, ask the clergyman who takes a confession if he looks at the background. Look at the man in terms of how his community respects and treats him as a protector'.

Was Seaga telling us we should respect and hold murderers in high regard because of who they are. If that was the case why do we have such a man on our governing body. I have never heard such bullshit in any other so-called civilised society. Only in Jamaica could a public figure say something like that and go back to work the next day without everyone calling for his resignation. The so-called area leaders he mentioned and showed so much respect for were men who committed some atrocious crimes and did not deserve our respect. May I remind Seaga that some of the people who idolised the murderers called area leaders did so out of fear rather than admiration while others did so out of ignorance. So this so-called 'respect' Seaga spoke about is all superficial. What are we teaching our children, that it is okay to kill as long as you have certain credibility? Seaga could say what he did because he helped to create the type of community he was talking about, where a man could rape, kill, rob and still be respected. As a former Trench Townian I came from the heartbeat of the ghetto and want people to know when Seaga made that statement, he spoke for himself and for those who hold him in high regards. My words are: 'To no murderer respect due'.

The young men from the ghetto had a short memory. Some were downright stupid and others greedy for as no sooner had John Jones died many were lining up to take his place. The thrill of being a don was worth the short life-span and some just thought death could not happen to them. I heard many of them both PNP and JLP men, making comments in my presence saying if Cool Hand Luke and Jones had done this or done that differently they would still be alive but that was just a way of comforting themselves for what was to come. John Jones did not get a chance to tell his story and I could never do justice to whatever he would have said but I hope this book will give him some peace in the grave. Men on both sides told me how they were used by politicians to kill each other but if they knew that was what was happening why did they do it? Some of the things I was told were just too sickening to put on paper.

Pepper who had taken over the leadership of Tivoli Gardens while his father John Jones was in prison was gunned down on Maxfield Avenue with an M16 rifle. One of the rumours that came out of Tivoli about the killing was that Pepper was killed because a crew in Jungle found out he was trying to lure their leader in a death trap.

A new set of murderers went on the loose in Trench Town who called themselves 'Papaless'. They were the sons of the gunmen who were killed by police or by rival gangs. One who stood out for me was Greg's the son of the late 'Cool Hand Luke' who was killed in almost the same manner as his father. I could not help shedding a tear for him when I was told he took up the gun like his father and was killed likewise. Greg and other papaless boys got into gang warfare and were forced to run away to other areas such as Tivoli and Maxfiled Avenue. One of the dissidents who ran away from Jungle to Tivoli wanted the head of the Jungle leader on a platter so he hatched a plan to lure him to the slaughterhouse. One source said Pepper was sent with the offer of an invitation to a peace dance in memory of the late Cassius Maquade where the leader would be killed. On his way to visit his mother in Barbican, Pepper stopped and paid the Jungle don a visit at his usual hang spot and invited him to the fake peace dance. The man and other crew members who were hanging out together accepted the invitation in good faith and promised to attend. Minutes after Pepper left, Spencer, another Tivoli man, rode up on his bike to where the Jungle crew were and shouted that they would soon be sorted out. No-one knew for sure if he was getting mad or what, but if that was what he said he must have been having some mental health problems for by doing so he was baiting up his leader and his own life. The Jungle crew got suspicious by what Spencer said and put two and two together and worked out that the invitation to the peace dance was a trick to lure them to their death so they decided to teach Pepper a lesson instead. They waited for him to return from his journey so they could pounce on him. Not knowing what was in store. Pepper made his way back to Tivoli in good spirits. When he and his followers got to Maxfield Avenue a gunman came out of a side street and sprayed them with bullets from an M16 rifle. Pepper was hit in the stomach and two of his soldiers were slaughtered.

The bodies were taken to Kingston Public Hospital where hundreds of Tivoli residents lined the streets outside and in the hospital. Many were said to be interfering with the work of the medical team. They were demanding justice and asking for the head of anyone who supported the PNP. Pepper died while doctors were trying to save his life. When the Tivoli masses were told of the death they cried and wailed for their leader. Some of them even assaulted the doctors and nurses who were trying to save his life. The hospital staff were called names like dogs, John crow (vulture) and PNP supporters and many of them were threatened. Police had to be called in to maintain peace and order.

Whichever of the rumours that came out of Tivoli was true no one knew for sure but one thing was certain Spencer, the person who they said alerted the Jungle crew about the plot to kill their leader, was killed by Tivoli men and tagged as an informer. Pepper's funeral was attended by almost the entire Tivoli community. Seaga was also seen amongst the mourners. It was the same evening of Pepper's funeral that John Jones, his father, was burnt to death in his cell. PNP and JLP supporters fought each other over the death of Pepper for many days but at the end of it all there were no winners they were all losers. Each side suffered tremendous losses that they could have both done without.

With John Jones dead and Wrongmove behind bars, it was two down and one to go for the ATF. Before they wrote Jones off their list, they visited Jamaica to make sure it was their fugitive who died. Stan Baker who was said to be the most sophisticated of the trio was managing to avoid arrest in Jamaica.

In Britain the police wanted to stop the flow of Jamaican gangs on their turf and had been bracing themselves for some time for the influx of criminals. They were told by their US counterparts that the Jamaican criminals would be running to hide in Britain and start up their evil drug trade there. Late in the year of 1992 several raids were made in South London and over a hundred people were charged with crimes. The police officers who were in charge of the operation were quietly recruiting Jamaican criminals as informers to catch other outlaws. Some police officers were in it for their own reasons and so were the informers who used police connections to get their criminal friends from Jamaica into the UK. The police in Britain who were always suspicious of their Jamaican counterparts when it came to corruption were not lily clean themselves as they recruited men who were running away from the authorities in Jamaica for crimes they committed there. When they made an arrest of a drugs don that meant promotion for them and that was what they wanted anyway, anyhow.

One of the most prominent cases was when British police used their connection to get criminals on the run in Jamaica into Britain. This was done on the request of one of their paid informers who wanted to get his friends away from the long arm of the law in Jamaica. When the men arrived in Britain they went on a robbing spree courtesy of Scotland Yard. Some of their informers even took the opportunity to kill as they knew their bosses would soon get them back on the streets to commit more crimes. Whenever they were picked up by innocent police officers they would be back on the streets in no time on the request of their influential employers. Some of them were arrested and released so many times the special crime unit set up to quell the activities of the gangs became a mockery.

Most of the people who were arrested in the operation to rid Britain of the drugs gangs were illegal immigrants from Jamaica while a few were from other countries. Many young men who I grew up with were caught in the raids. Some I felt sorry for others I did not. If they were prepared to do the crime they should have been just as ready to do the time. Many talked about the poverty they had endured in Jamaica but when they got the opportunity to change their lives after leaving the island they chose to do evil.

Also the crime wave in Jamaica was like a contagious disease and found its way to Britain in the black community. When someone was murdered in Jamaica people here would take revenge on friends and relatives of the perpetrators. Others just brought their gang warfare here. Many leaders in the community said black people did not trust the police and that was the reason why we did not report crimes to them but that was only part of the problem. Historically black people do not report crimes. In Jamaica most of the police are black but we still do not trust them. When it comes down to the nitty-gritty, the real problem is fear and nothing to do with race because we will not trust anyone, black or white who we think will put our lives at risk. Once we overcome our fears we will then start to trust.

Many young men in England are buying guns and think it is fashionable to be seen with a gun. No one is safe around them as the fools brandish their guns in public for all to see. The sad part is some of them have children who witness this. I went to a dance in North London at a night club that was a famous hangout for Trench Townians living in Britain legally and illegally. One asshole took out a gun and fired it in the air, I wondered how he got past the security with a pistol. But I should not have been surprised as it was the men who were searched and not the women and careless men have careless women who would be only too pleased to assist their men by taking in guns. One man came in the club with his entourage walking with the confidence of a king. He was immaculately attired in designer clothes as were his followers who all looked privileged to be around him. They looked like well trained puppies being territorial of their master following in every direction he went.

Someone whispered to me that he was a rich kid and had a contract on his head. I wondered then if I should be in the same place with a man who was marked for death, for the men who wanted him dead would not give a damn about my life if I was accidentally killed when they came to get him.

The young men were moving around him so closely it was as if they were being paid well to take a bullet for him. The eldest one in the group could not have been more than twenty-five. They were so young and had everything to live for if only they knew it. Why were they prepared to die for someone else, only they knew. Maybe it was the money he was supposed to have that made them think their lives were no longer worth living. The rich kid bought several bottles of champagne and his flock drew even closer to him. He handed out some plastic cups he got from the bar to his lap dogs and some star struck girls who recognised him. He was their ghetto celebrity. When he poured the champagne in the girls cups they purred like satisfied kittens in their best dancehall dresses. Some of them dressed so x-rated they looked like they were more ready for the streets rather than a club. The more x-rated the girls were the more popular they were with the young men. I was overdressed in my mini skirt and tube top. I did not get a glance from any of the male attendants as they were more interested in the nearly naked women. The rich kid and his followers took some of the most expensive bottles of champagne and as if they did not know what to do with them sprayed each other with about five bottles. That was meant to show rival gangs that they were so rich they could afford to waste expensive drinks. The other groups were not to be outdone so they too bought champagne and sprayed us all. If I had no intention of cleaning my clothes they made sure I changed my mind. No one apologised for wetting me it was just 'tough luck'. The other people who got wet were laughing as if it was all part of their childish joke.

When the rich kid saw that the other groups were outdoing him with the champagne he took out some twenty and fifty pound notes and lit them with his lighter. I closed my eyes in shame and anger. The other groups joined in and everything became silly, those people were not children they were grown men. I did not wait for anything else and went home. I heard from an associate the next day that the dance finished early as two girls got into a fight over their man who was in prison.

Imagine many of those who attended the dance came from poor communities back in Jamaica. Some of them went to bed without food many nights in Trench Town, Water House and Tivoli. They escaped the poverty something that many others have not managed to do and they were burning money to prove success. One rich man said long ago that not everyone could deal with success. At the time I was angry at the remark but now I'm inclined to believe that he was right. Many of them still have poor relatives back in Jamaica who would welcome the money that they were burning. They deserved to be deported back to Jamaica into poverty to look into the eyes of those whom they could have helped and did not. Many of them would say that they took their own risk to make the money so they have the right to use it however they like, but when you burn money when people you once lived with are going without food you deserve everything that is coming to you. Some of them have a front displaying themselves on videos in

155

the most degrading way when they know damn well they did not have their proper stay in England. If I was in their shoes I would have stayed home and hide.

I returned to Jamaica in December 1993 with family members. I always enjoy Christmas there so I was looking forward to the holiday. My grandmother had returned home from the United States and was back at her house and Pamela, one of Tom's twin daughters was staying with her. I met Pamela for the first time. She, her twin and another of Tom's daughter were born in the same year as me. I made a mistake and travelled on a chartered flight. They would not accept my hand luggage saying it was too heavy so I had to pay to send it down on another flight. I went the next day to collect my luggage at the airport and was told by an Air Jamaica staff that it had not arrived. I went home and phoned the airport, a lady came on the phone, asked for my number and promised to ring me back. She called me back in fifteen minutes, told me that my goods were at the airport and that I should come and get them. When I arrived at the airport the second time I had to go through a lot of palaver just to get in the office where the custom officers were. When I first asked for my luggage I was told it had not arrived but when I told them it was there, a woman made it quite clear I had to wet her palm (give her money) with a hundred dollars before she would go for it. When she came out with the bag it was half the size when I checked it in back at Gatwick Airport. By the time I finished with the whole process I must have wet ten different palms just to get my own goods. I did not need to look through the bag to know some of the things were missing, but only to find out what they were. They took my shoes, make up kit, knickers and a pair of sandals.

One day a middle-aged man approached me while I was visiting some friends off Waltham Park Road and said he was told that I was visiting from England. When I confirmed that he was informed correctly by his source who he would not disclose, he asked if I wanted to make some money. I asked him what I would have to do to make the money and without a care in the world he told me by taking drugs back with me. He did not know who I was and what I did but he was asking me to be a drugs mule. He kept telling me how many people would love to get the opportunity he was giving me. He said I was perfect as I already lived in the United Kingdom and the officials would not be too suspicious of me. I mentioned to him that I was perfect to him to be a mule and the United Kingdom authority would love to give me some perfect time behind bars for drugs smuggling. He looked offended that I should be so negative. He showed me his expensive BMW car and said he lived in the hills all because of his drugs. I asked him why he did not take the drugs to the UK himself and who he had there to distribute the drugs for him. That was when he came to his senses and asked me if I worked for the police why I was asking him inquisitive questions. He told me by the look of me I was a broke foreigner who could do well with some other means of living on the side. I responded that I did not put my basket where I could not reach it and any room I go in I must always have the key to let myself out. I knew I was leaving Jamaica soon so he did not intimidate me and he could not hold my family to ransom for me to do his dirty work as many of my relatives were hard-core villains themselves and would welcome the opportunity to relieve him of his BMW.

On that visit to Jamaica I attended the annual entertainment ghetto bash in Craig Town. It was a charity event and the aim was to give people who could not afford to pay to see their idols perform the opportunity to be entertained free of charge. I was keen to attend ghetto bash and so was my partner who was with me in Jamaica, only Pamela was hesitant about the idea but she gave in under pressure from us. The man who was with me was naive about Jamaican life and had a false nostalgic feeling of the country which was the birthplace of his parents.

He and other visitors tend to want to venture through dangerous places without understanding the risk they were putting themselves at. But this day we both wanted to go to Craig Town so it was up to me to make sure we took precautions. We were in a rental car with the RR sign on it. When we got to Jones Town which was an adjoining area to Craig Town, I told the man to park the car in front of Admiral Town Police Station but he drove past the station and took us on to Pen Street, which was so narrow we could only drive in straight or reverse out. We ended up parking the car about a hundred yards from the police station. We got out of the car and walked down to Craig Town where the action was. I had a camera on a string around my neck and a gold bracelet on my right hand. We got to the middle of the action around eleven at night and stayed for about three hours then we started to make our way back to the car. There were other people moving in the direction we were going so we felt comfortable as we were not alone. A lot of people were still on the street some gambling others selling soup, boiled corn and jerk chicken. When we were near to where our car was parked, a young man who we left on Pen Street on our way to the bash ran up to us and asked us to give him payment for watching the car. We gave him one hundred dollars, he was not happy but did not bother to protest as he was in a hurry to collect from the other people who were also driving rental cars. He was in an unnecessary hurry, I thought he wanted to get to all of us before we drove away, but I was so wrong. He wanted to get money from us before what was going to happen took place. Some men were sitting waiting for all rental car drivers to return.

Because of the hustle and bustle going on around us we did not see anything suspicious so we went to our car. I got in the front passenger seat beside the driver and Pamela went into the back. The driver moved the car forward but he would have to reverse to get onto another street to turn the car around. We did not want to drive the car too far from the police station as this could be dangerous for us. As the driver was about to put the car in reverse a young man came up to the car door and told him to get out. Our windows were down and the safety locks were undone. The driver was taking his time to get out of the car and was hastily helped out by the gunman who told him in no uncertain terms that he was not messing about. As our driver was panicking he was led away into a yard with an old dilapidated board house that he, a visitor to Jamaica would not have seen in all his life on earth. When I saw where they were taking him I got out of the car and so did Pamela. We were told to get back in the car, which Pamela did as quick as she could but I was disorientated by the fact our driver was taken into a yard out of sight. One of the men with a handgun came up to me and said, 'yu no ere mi sey yu fi go back ina de car'. He came up and held on my hand and I went up to face him. I had to be thinking fast as things were moving so quickly around me. I decided to flirt with him as I had disobeyed his order and he might have been angry. I held on to his hand and looked him in the eye but the creep could not keep eye contact and nervously looked away until his eye came to the camera around my neck.

157

He pulled the camera string from my neck and it snapped in his hand. He looked me over and then commented on how fat and round I was. I started to pray that he would not get the idea of raping me and as if my prayer was answered his eyes caught my bracelet and he turned his attention to it. But before he could take hold of it a soldier patrol vehicle approached which made him move away from me. The soldiers were not aware of the robbery and drove on. I ran into an open lot and came upon another gunman with a rifle and I became aware of my surroundings for the first time. I looked in the direction of the police station and saw the officers looking on at us being robbed. I was flabbergasted.

The gunman in the open lot was more approachable than the one who took my camera. I asked him what happened to the man who was taken into the old yard and he said he was okay and that he would be searched and released. We were in the middle of the conversation when the son of a bitch who took my camera decided to prove to us that his gun was loaded and fired a shot in the air. That was it for me I ran as hard as I could to the police station, I heard one of the men behind me saying, 'run fatty run'. I wanted to stop and tell him exactly where fatty was but I was not brave to take him on with his gun.

When I got to the police station, I tried to tell the officers what happened but they were not interested. One even had the nerve to ask me what I was doing down in Jones Town. I realised it was foolish trying to report to the police something they had witnessed themselves so I waited to see what would happen next. While standing at the police station I counted about ten men who were robbing people. I saw our car moving in the direction of the police station, at first I thought it was some of the culprits who were in it, but when I saw it coming closer to the station I knew then it was not them. I had to go out in the street to get the driver to stop for me, I heard him and Pamela arguing about something but could not make out what it was. When I got into the car I asked what the argument was about, Pamela said she did not see which direction I went in so she asked the driver to follow her to find me but he said that he was going home. He told her there was no point looking for me because he saw one of the men taking me into a gully to rape me. It was funny he did not think they had taken me down to the gully to kill me, but to rape me. I could not believe I got out of the car to face the gunmen and plead for his life and he was on his way home to leave me in their hands. Just as well I was not taken in the gully to be raped or I would have been left to die. He must have been seeing things when one of the gunmen butted him in his rass head. That relationship is now history.

The country was so riddled with crime one did not have to be disaster prone to be robbed many times in a week. It was always painstaking just listening to the news or reading the local newspapers. While I was living in Jamaica I had become desensitised to the familiarity of death but my spell in England cured me of that psychological illness. A young man who was on the island at the same time as I, travelled down to attend the funeral of a relative. He was born in Jamaica but went to live in England with his parents. Both his parents returned home to retire and he visited them from time to time. Gunmen followed him to his parents' home whilst he was driving his rental car from a shop. He was not aware of their presence and went into his house. The armed robbers forced their way into the house and robbed everyone. The young man's mother who was blind kept asking what's going on but then a shot was fired. She said she thought it was her husband but she heard her son groaning and knew it was a cry of death. He died on his way to the hospital. The family ended up burying two dead relatives.

When returning residents go on holiday to Jamaica especially those of us who stay in Kingston we have to be careful where we go as danger could be lurking just outside our gate. We complain to the authorities about the problems we face but get ignored all the time. Only the specialist tourist resorts were protected twenty-four hours a day. Some people would get upset and said crime was everywhere so we should not single out Jamaica but for the size of the island and the frequency in which the brutal crimes are committed we have to speak out. The main victims of the crimes were poor people but it would not be long before they turned their attention to the rich.

An elderly man who lived in Birmingham, Britain for over thirty years left Jamaica in search of a better life in the sixties. What he experienced instead was racism at its worst. He and his family had a hard time locating suitable housing as many whites would not rent black people accommodation. They had signs on their door 'no dogs, no blacks and no Irish'. He, like many Jamaicans, ran what we call a pardner to save up money to buy their own home while they stayed in places not fit for animals much more human beings. He was one of the first black people to open a shop in Birmingham, which was a big achievement considering where they were coming from. Jealous white people who could not afford to own a pepper stall much more a shop burnt down his place several times but each time he managed to reopen and do business as usual. He had his dream that one day he would return to his beautiful island of Jamaica where he would not have to deal with racism. Many of the people who left Jamaica in the sixties held on to their roots due to the severe level of racism they were experiencing in England. They raised their children as Jamaicans and to be proud of the island, so Jamaicans and their offspring come across as the most patriotic of the immigrants living in Britain.

After years of abuse the man decided to return home to his beautiful island. He sold his house in Birmingham and bought a nice pad in rural Jamaica. As soon as he arrived on the island the locals were looking on with envy. Not knowing about his struggle all they could see were pound signs. It was not long before they were planning his destruction. He was robbed and killed inside his house. All the dreams he had of returning home to rest in peace and tranquillity died with him. How could we make excuses and blame poverty for the killings. Are we saying poor people are not responsible for their actions? Is poverty a reason to kill?

One day I went to downtown to get some fresh fish, a friend took me in her car. When we got there I saw a young man selling snapper fish (my favourite with parrot running a very close second). I asked him how much per pound for the fish. I was trying hard to conceal any accent that I might have picked up living in England. I knew if he detected just a faint foreign accent he would have overpriced the fish. He told me forty dollars so I ordered four pounds in weight. He wrapped up the fish and gave it to me. I gave him a five hundred dollar note because I did not have anything smaller. When he saw the money he turned into a monster it was as if he had never seen so much money in his life. He took up a knife and told me to get the fuck away from him and that if I asked him for my change he would cut me up. I took him seriously and walked away in tears. I did not cry because he took my money but the way in which he did it. Things had become so bad in Jamaica that a man was willing to butcher me for my own money. Those who saw just looked at me as if I had done something wrong. A man whom I told about the incident said I should have reported it to the police but I knew that would do no good. Besides I did not want someone to go to prison for five pounds but he was so damn intimidating. Some people said to go to the area leader to have him dealt with but the area leaders themselves were nothing but common criminals so why would I want a thief to beat a thief.

The country was in chaos criminality was the order of the day. Some Jamaicans who left the island many moons ago and visited once or twice every ten years were so detached from the violence in their home country they could not see what the fuss was about. They became protective and angry whenever foreign newspapers reported any issue of violence in their country. They did not know the people who were being killed or affected by the killings so the acts of crime were nothing more than words on pieces of papers to them. Rather than helping to address the problems in their beloved country they pointed fingers at other places where crimes are being committed just to say we are not the only ones doing it.

In 1992 Michael Manley handed over the leadership of the PNP to the younger PJ Patterson and it was the end of an era. He made sure he went out on a high. Like him or hate him he gained the respect of many world leaders even those in Washington whom he dared to challenge. As a Jamaican living in a foreign country people were always asking me about the dynamic man Michael Manley who was one of the country's most outstanding Prime Ministers. For me he was a good man turned bad by the corrupt system of our politics. He had good intentions but once he joined politics he found out the hard way that he would have to fight fire with fire and that he did. Before he knew it he was being drawn into something deep and nasty and there was no way of cleansing himself of the blood of the many people who died in the name of politics he was a part of. As much as I liked Manley, my beloved brother was killed by the hands of PNP gunmen who were fighting to keep him in power.

PJ Patterson ran as leader in his own right for the first time in a general election in 1993. For the first time Jamaicans had the opportunity to vote for a black man. He was not necessarily the best man for the job but the black people wanted to see a Prime Minister who looked like them for a change. At a JLP rally Seaga sealed his fate in the election by holding up a black scandal bag and made jibes at Patterson. The people become angry and said he was not only disrespecting Patterson but all black people in the country. That behaviour would not go unpunished at the polling stations but they should have called for his resignation. The people hailed PJ Patterson as the 'Fresh Prince for us and looked like us'. Seaga knew he was walking on thin ice and shut his mouth where the racist jibes were concerned and allowed his puppet Hugh Shearer a black man to come out to defend the cause. Hugh Shearer made a speech on television saying more or less black people were ungrateful because they were supporting Patterson only because he was black and that they should remember

Jamaica was built by white people. How could he forget the sacrifices and hard work of our ancestors who came to the island as slaves and worked for many years without pay to build Jamaica and other places. The brother had truly lost the plot and the election for the JLP.

The people had high hopes when they elected their first black Prime Minister that someone who looked like them would make a change. Then reality hit them that nothing was changing. The cost of living was getting higher and the crime rate continued to soar. It would appear that he was even more harsh on the poor than his predecessors were. It showed that a black man who has not been debrainwashed could be just as lethal (if not worse) than a white oppressor. He would not think twice to put up taxes or increase prices on certain goods but was reluctant to increase wages and formulate a fair (and well needed) welfare system to help the poor. His argument was that we could not afford a welfare system to take the pressure off the poor like a developed nation such as the USA has done. So let me ask this question why did he introduce the Government Consumer Tax (GCT)? (copying those countries who have welfare systems). If you do not give how can you expect to receive. Introducing the GCT was like drawing blood out of a stone. Some people have no income while others are just trying to survive on very little. The elderly are made even poorer trying to survive on a meagre pension. The price of medication is well out of the reach of the average pensioner and the utility charges are extortionate. In the developed nations the rich want to stay rich at any cost but they know no system survives without peace. They know very well that some of the riches must be trickling down to the poor to keep them happy or there will be no peace and if there is no peace society will cease to exist.

It was even rumoured that Prime Minister Patterson came to the UK to ask the British government to pay him the pension of those who retired back home in Jamaica. He was refused of course but it was very out of order to ask in the first place. Did the Prime Minister stop and think for one moment that he should have consulted the people concerned before asking? No that was not the style of the average Jamaican. Who knows maybe if he had informed the people concerned of his intentions and the reasons behind his plan they might have considered his proposal but the dictatorship did not go down well with the people had who slaved in freezing cold conditions to secure the pension he wanted to control. His action mirrors society at large - do not ask for anything just take it.

In July 1993 another anti-crime team was born by the name of (ACID) Anti-Crime Investigative Detachment. This came about to quell the violence leading up to the general election. During this time many lives were lost.

One day my grandmother phoned to tell me that Tom was held up on the street by some men with knives who tried to relieve him of his possessions. He refused to hand them over and put up a fight (well that did not surprise me). He was beaten up and had to go to the hospital. By the sound of my grandmother she was concerned about his welfare but I said to myself maybe he had some idea for the first time how his victims felt when he was robbing them. She said he had told her to ask me for some money to assist with the medical bill. When I hesitated she begged me to send the money saying to let him eat his condemnation. I still was not convinced for only I alone bore my pain but for her sake I sent him fifty pounds. When I phoned her to find out if the money was collected she told me yes and that Tom said he thought I would be sending two hundred and fifty pounds rather than the amount I had sent. That man had never given me fifty dollars in my life and when I was ill he never took me to a doctor for him to pay medical bills and yet he was expecting me to give him a weeks pay. I had to wonder if every human being has a conscience. He even had the nerve to tell friends of the family that if it was not for him I would not be where I am. That comment should be treated with the contempt it deserves; ignore it.

I went to visit my uncle in Clapham, England and I went in the corner store on his street to pay a courtesy call to the lady who ran it. I was conversing with her when Christopher's aunt came into the shop. I was taken by surprise. She told me that my brother was also in England and I could not wait to see him. She took me to visit his place of work the same day. When we walked into the shop he recognised his aunt first and was about to smile, but when our eyes met the smile on his face dried up and it was like he was looking at a ghost. I broke the silence first and jumped on him, he just stood there speechless. He came round but I was the one doing most of the talking. Now we are closer than we were, and sometimes I wish Carl was here with us. Sally went to live in Canada where she is now living with her new husband and sons; her childhood lover is with another woman. She must be reflecting that there was no need for her to be fighting over him for there was no guarantee that they would be together forever. If many of us young girls knew then what we know now we would have saved ourselves a lot of pain.

On one of my visits to Jamaica I went over to Jungle to see Megan and the rest of the family. When I went into the yard I saw Tommy, Megan's younger brother who obviously did not remember who I was. He looked like a very angry young man. I could not believe the sweet little boy I knew could look so desperate. I asked him for his sisters and he rudely told me they were out. I wanted to ask him if he remembered who I was but the look on his face was saying get the hell out of here. I quickly made my way out of the yard without another word. I saw Megan and Plum and they took me to see Aunty Charm who was not well and looked drawn. I promised them I would visit them the following Sunday but changed my mind when the news reported that there were gunshots firing over in Trench Town. In my younger days I would have chanced it but I lost the appetite for violence so I stayed away. Some people told me that Tommy was getting out of control and that his mother was being stressed out because of it. Not long after that she suffered a nervous breakdown and was walking the streets aimlessly. She later died. I felt a slightly guilty for not keeping in contact with her more as she was always glad to see me when I visited. I was told of her death long after she was buried.

Lily, Prim's mother, was suffering from senile dementia and was cared for by Prim. I used to speak to her on my early visits back to Jamaica but as time went by she drifted away in her own world. She recognised my name but not my voice and because she was blind it made matters worse. On one of my many phone calls to Prim she told me that Sue and Gus, her children, were shot by gunmen and were in hospital. Her version of the story was that Gus was sitting with some of his friends outside their compound when some men dressed in women's clothing with guns came up to them and opened fire. Gus ran but fell to the ground, the gunman stood over him and opened fire but they all missed except for one shot that he received in the lower part of his abdomen. Sue heard the shots and went outside to see what was going on and saw the gunman over her brother. She ran up to the man and shouted and he turned the gun on her hitting her in the stomach. The shot went straight through her body. Gus came off the worst as his shot remained in his body. The doctor at the Kingston Public Hospital said it would be too dangerous to remove it. One young man was not so lucky as he was killed on the spot.

The men who shot them were from the same political party but from rival gangs. They started fighting each other as the cold war between them and Jungle residents ended after the Rats sought refuge in Jungle from the Tivoli hit squad. The gunmen were sitting idly with guns so they had to find new use for their artillery so it was not a surprise they turned them on each other. They were getting ammunition from their drugs dons in America who did not care if they killed themselves or not. Many of those who beat the poverty of Trench Town and went to America rather than send necessary items like clothing, books and food back to their poor communities sent guns instead and the fools back in Trench Town thought they were being helped in a big way.

The security forces had their hands so full with crime they did not know how to deal with the general public. Everybody was treated like criminals until proven otherwise. When they go to Trench Town the good suffer for the bad. Police and soldiers alike would unleash their frustration on innocent people it was almost a crime to be poor and living in Trench Town.

Jim, one of Prim's sons who grew up in the area, is seen as cowardly if anyone is innocent of crime he is the one. He is a man of very few words and doesn't speak unless spoken to. If Prim is being beaten by someone I think he would have to be pretty sure she was close to death before he would intervene. My other brothers who are quick to act view Jim's behaviour as cowardice but I think he has a good attitude for someone living in Trench Town. He is the brave one because where he comes from it is easier to turn to crime than abstain.

One day, soldiers dropped curfew in Rema because of the criminal activities in the area. The people who were in the know were alerted of the curfew before it happened, courtesy of some bent cops and only the innocent were left behind to face the music. Unaware of the curfew Prim asked Jim to go to a local shop to get some rice for her. While Jim was at the shop the soldiers corralled his housing scheme looking for bandits and Jim returning from the shop walked right into their ambush. Prim and the others saw the soldiers coming and ran into their houses for protection but she was watching from the window for Jim to return.

Prim saw when a group of soldiers jumped on her son and started beating the hell out of him. She ran to where they had him and started pleading for his life but she was ignored and the beating continued. Jim fell on the ground and one of the soldiers stamped on his head. They only stopped beating him when they were satisfied.

The security force had a hard job, we all recognised that. A lot of men from Rema were murderers and needed to be rounded up and face justice but was it fair for police and soldiers to brutalise innocent people? The other question would be how would they know who was innocent from those who were guilty when no one was willing to talk? Their job was very difficult. For the innocent people in Trench Town as long as you keep quiet about wrongdoings you and your children will always be targets for frustrated and incompetent police and soldiers.

As time goes on the police and the criminals were becoming cold and heartless. Some police who were kicked out of the force came out of the closet and started to deal in drugs openly. Many went to live in the US, Canada and the UK while those with nowhere to go stayed on in Jamaica and carried on with their illegal doings. Many of them still had friends in the force so they could call upon them for favours anytime.

The troublemakers who remained in the force stayed on as they could do their dirty work and hide behind the job and businessmen knew who to call upon to do their dirty work when they wanted it done.

Montego Bay, the main tourist city, did not like to see undesirables on the streets as it could be bad for business. The businessmen lobbied the government on numerous occasions to get the street people and small traders moved from the area and made subtle threats that they would go elsewhere with their trades if the tourist industries were not protected from nuisance harassing the tourists. As the country needed the foreign exchange the government had no choice but to take action. The larger businessmen accused the small traders of hassling the tourists and said that the harassment would put people off from visiting the island but what they really wanted was to get rid of their competitors.

A lot of the small traders were desperate people trying to sell their wares to make a living. Many of them went too far by following behind tourists just to get a sale but with the appropriate training that could have been remedied. If they refused training then they could then be asked to leave. No one should expect people with no social skills to act or behave like the imported university graduate hoteliers. The small traders were taken off the streets by police and specially trained security guards were hired to keep them away. The street people were still present on the streets of Montego Bay, which did not go down well with the industry but they did not have an acceptable excuse to give for the government to get rid of them. Their appearance alone would not go down well with many touchy Jamaicans so they were biding their time as they wanted Montego Bay to themselves and the respectable and only the 'good' were good enough.

The police were once again called in to do some dirty work for the tourist industry to rid the city of some undesirables that no-one would miss, however, their plan backfired when St Elizabeth Parish Council learnt of the happenings and called for an investigation into some street people who were taken from Montego Bay and dumped in a mud gully in that parish and left to die.

A survivor of the attempted massacre described how he and thirty-eight other people were taken from the city of Montego Bay and transported to the parish of St Elizabeth and dumped. The survivor who was reported to be fifty years of age said he was sitting beside a furniture store eating some food when a St James Parish Council truck drove up. A cop came out and told him he was taking him to the hospital assuming that he was mentally ill because he was living rough on the streets. He was forced into the truck by men who used brute force. The men tied his hands with ropes they had in the truck and he cried out. A police officer who was wearing a blue seam uniform sprayed tear gas in his eyes and ordered him to sit. The men drove around the city and rounded up all the other street people in sight to a total of thirty-eight. They were all sprayed continuously to make sure they could not see where they were going. The man said he realised something was wrong when the journey to the hospital was taking too long. When they reached their destination it was almost daybreak but the place was still dark. Their abductors cut the rope and told them to get out of the truck. One of their jailers explained to them that the first one to run down the hill would get the best room. He said he did not move and decided to wait until it was brighter. When they could see where they were he realised that they were at the edge of a mud lake and only thirty-two men were left standing. He said the other six probably ran down the hill as they were told to do. All six had mental health problems. Some residents reported that they heard cries coming from the area. The man said since he spoke out against the incident he has been shot at and wanted people to know that he was not mad only poor and that he had been in the US army and served in Vietnam for two and half years. When will the time come for upper class Jamaican to stop fucking the lower class?

Under pressure from certain sections of Jamaica the Prime Minister reluctantly called for an inquiry. The outcome of this gives me hope for the future but the attitude of the high-ranking people who were involved shamed us all. This was the first time poor people's rights were violated and they were empowered to fight and won. During the year long inquiry members from the Jamaica For Justice team who supported the victims were threatened. Members from the parish council of St James and the police officials who ordered the removal lied on the witness stand. There were conflicting statements and the list goes on. The commissioners - a retired judge, a minister of religion and an Attorney-at-law - were critical of the dumping and of those who were involved. They described the whole thing as 'a grim picture in national life'. They accused the witnesses of using 'privilege as a shield against full and frank admission and in a conspiracy to conceal the truth'. The commissioners report stated that police officers and members of the parish council refused to answer questions and tried to blame other people. Not one person admitted to a single thing in the whole sordid affair. The commissioners made some recommendations, which the government said they would accept. They agreed to set up a national Homeless Taskforce, which would conduct an in-depth study of the homeless nation wide, assess their needs and determine how best to meet them. The victims were awarded twenty thousand dollars a month for the rest of their lives. Power to the people.

I was in Jamaica in mid-1999 and happened to visit another tourist spot in Ocho Rios in the parish of St. Anns what was there was the open display of prostitution that the tourist industry turned a blind eye to in order to keep the visitors happy. Young girls and boys as young as fifteen were out on the streets looking for punters. Many were introducing themselves to the willing tourists but no reports of harassment were reported to the police. The tourists' spots in Jamaica are fast becoming a safe haven for paedophiles who prey on young boys and girls. Right before our eyes young men and women, boys and girls go away with the punters and no one intervenes. A visitor to the island could be excused for thinking paedophilia was legal in Jamaica.

To bring those visitors who have sex with children to justice would mean to lose some of the well-needed foreign exchange and the industry could not afford that. I was also of the opinion that prostitution was illegal in Jamaica so why was it allowed in the name of tourism. Every action has a reaction and the tourists' prostitution brings nothing but imported diseases like AIDS and herpes and unhealthy sexual habits like anal sex, which was like the plague to most people when I lived there. Young innocent girls and boys exposed themselves to all sorts of danger in the name of poverty and in some cases greed. Some of them participated in sexual acts for money that even animals in the wilds would look on with disgust.

Reports coming from the National AIDS Committee (NAC) in Jamaica disclosed that every eight hours someone on the island is infected with the HIV/AIDS virus and every week a child is born with the virus. The cost of a lifetime treatment for an infected person is between three and four hundred thousand Jamaican dollars and a lifetime is said to be seven to ten years. With these statistics the question to be asked is the foreign exchange worth the lives of our young? One newspaper columnist reported that Jamaica was fast becoming the whorehouse of the Caribbean.

What was also interesting to see in Ocho Rios was the poor condition of the roads. Tourism was booming but the town was in a bad way. Not far from the hotel Jamaica Grand, an all-inclusive resort, the locals lived in shacks. The hoteliers spend millions on building first class resorts to make sure the tourists do not have to venture out to the unsightly reality of Jamaica. They do not think that they should help improve the place as they believe they are already doing the country a favour by investing in it. One part of the road was so dark I had to go back to my hotel as I was afraid to become a target for thieves and rapists. Maybe the darkness was part of the attraction as many of the prostitutes and tourists were seen heading in that direction and getting lost in the dark without a care in the world.

The ignorance coupled with greed and poverty is a deadly cocktail in Jamaica as corruption and lawlessness take over. When I returned to Kingston from Ocho Rios I went to see some friends in Trench Town to have a chat. One woman I did not even know when I was living there asked me to lend her my passport to travel to America. She said her boyfriend was there and she could not wait any longer to see him. I told her she would have to wait a little longer because she could not pass for me not even if she travelled at twelve midnight when immigration officers were tired out of their minds. She said she would make sure she got through on the false passport even if she had to sleep with the pilot, immigration or custom's officer. I asked her if she was that desperate that she would play Russian roulette with her life by sleeping with complete strangers she did not know anything about. She looked me in the eye as if I was from another planet. I got angry with her when she told me I could say what I wanted because I did not know what poverty was. I asked her if she was not afraid of AIDS. With just as much ignorance as when she said she would sleep with anybody to get to America, she told me if she caught AIDS she would go to a doctor and get it cured. Well, well! Trench Townians were not able to solve all their other social problems, but managed to find a cure for AIDS and selfishly kept it a secret from everybody else. Imagine Jamaica in the 1990s and an adult over eighteen did not know there was a disease called AIDS and that there was no cure for it. The dangerous part was that she was not one to shy away from sexual contacts with strangers and not once did she ever mention safe sex in her conversation. What was equally alarming was that there were many others who had the same mentality. Not far from where she lived, two young ladies were suffering from AIDS through ignorance as well. They used to make it a regular habit to sleep with visitors to the island for money. They were naive and had unsafe sex to their peril. AIDS is leaving a lot of children parentless and is now a serious issue that will have to be addressed.

AIDS in prisons was also a cause for concern. A medical officer for the Correctional Services told one of the local papers on the island that AIDS in the prison population was six to ten times greater than in the general public. Overpopulation was said to be the primary reason for the problem. The St Catherine District Prison was built to accommodate 671 inmates but had well over a thousand inmates at any one time. The General Penitentiary was built for 895 but was holding 1,232 up to April 1999. According to the officer more than fifty per cent of the inmates with the disease entered the institutions infected and pass it on to other inmates. They were not sure how many inmates had the virus as screening was done on a voluntary basis but said about seventy five per cent of them came from dysfunctional communities including Trench Town. Many of them were serving short terms and were going back to their homes and partners, to spread the virus as many were reluctant to tell their partners due to selfishness on their part and stigma and victimisation from friends and families. No one wanted to be alone so by keeping their illness a secret they were guaranteed a partner.

Everybody wants to go to a foreign country by hook or by crook. What those who left on the island do not know and do not want to know is that it would be better if they remained there and put in the same work there as they would if they went abroad. Many of us are doing well for ourselves but many more are suffering in foreign countries and the places where some Jamaicans live are worse than when they were back home in Jamaica. Emigration is the number one breaker of the family in Jamaica. Many of us leave the island with good intentions but what it has done is weaken the family structure and brain drain the island. Single mothers left their children with friends and relatives and have not seen them in many years - as they are illegal in a strange land where some have to be working three jobs to make ends meet. Children left back in Jamaica have grown not knowing what their parents look like or if they will ever see them again. They receive goodies in barrels but some will never see their daddies and mummies again as they are either dead or behind bars. Others are stoned out of their minds on coke and cannot afford to look after themselves much more their children back home.

I met up with some old associates at a night club which was my regular hang out spot when I'm home in Jamaica. I used to love the street dances when I lived there but with the frequent crimes I resort to indoor activities. The combination of reggae and soul keeps me moving all night long. The old chums I met up with told me that my friend Donnet was not doing very well in the Big Apple. Her man found a younger girlfriend and was treating Donnet the same way he treated his baby-mother in Jamaica. I had told Donnet if he did it to one woman he would do it to another but she said no it was his baby-mother's fault why he treated her badly. I was given Donnet's number as they said she had been writing and asking after me. She was told that I no longer lived on the island but heard

I visited frequently. I took the number there and then in case the woman forgot to give it to me before we left as it happened before when I wanted another friend's number and our mutual friend left without giving her details. I danced the night away with a young man not older than twenty. He followed behind me for a long time telling me how nice I looked. When I asked him how old he thought I was he said seventeen. I thought he was rather sweet but did not want any one I knew to see me with him and accuse me of robbing the cradle. He had style as well as he bought me drinks unlike some of those older cheap men who were asking me to buy them drinks. One I met on holiday there invited me out a few times and every time we went out, whenever we had to pay for anything he always happened to be bending down tying his shoes lace. But as soon as the bill was paid he got up. I had to lose him quickly. When I was leaving the club I had to break the sad news to my young admirer that he was much too young for me. If only he was a few years older... My heart bled a little as I walked to my taxi.

When I lived in Jamaica, Trench Townians did not bother to pay rent but lived free in the one and two bedroom, match boxes politician built for them. There were some people who genuinely could not afford to pay, but there were others who thought their bills should be paid by other people. Utility companies were too afraid to visit the community to disconnect their supplies for arrears. On this visit not only did they have telephone installed but also cable television, which they have to pay for or they will get disconnected. It would appear that the telecommunications and cable company both found sensible and safe ways to deal with the aggression of those who expect to use their services but refuse to pay for them. Some cable packages boast the most notorious porn films that even hard-core blue movie lovers would blush at. Needless to say the dysfunctional Trench Town with the dysfunctional families now have porn of the worst kind right in their living room courtesy of cable television and all it takes to view it is a remote control. So it was not surprising to know that many children are watching the porn films being entertained by oral, anal and other depraved sexual acts. Thank God cable television was not around when I was growing up there, because I would hate to think what sort of things would have taken place. As children, the sex that most of us witnessed between our parents in the one room we all shared, seemed like child's play compared to the blue movies on cable television.

I went to a relative's home and saw one of her sons aged nine viewing a hard-core porn movie. He was so mesmerised with what he was watching he did not hear me entering the room. I looked at him and the first thing that was evident was the tent like image of his trouser front that was projecting. In the film two lesbians were performing an act on each other and he got excited and shouted 'Pussy, pussy to bloodclaat'. I then made my presence known he blushed and turned over the station to cartoons. I went outside to ask his mother why she allowed him to watch such filth and she said it was hard to stop him from watching it when she was not around. I wondered to myself who was the parent in the house. With all of its problems Trench Town does not need to add pornography to the list.

Chapter Eleven

The United States law enforcement agencies were getting fed up with the high crime rate and passed a law to deport anyone living in their country legally or illegally who had been to prison for what they deemed as a serious offence. Many people who migrated to the US as children and learnt all the tricks of the criminal trade were deported back to Jamaica. The island that was struggling with the chaos of local crimes suddenly had to deal with the imported American nightmare. Many of the deportees were strung out on drugs and had no sympathy for their mother much less strangers. Many sold drugs in America and continued their evil trade in Jamaica. According to police statistics disclosed in 1999 criminal deportees were a serious threat to security and they were out of control. During the period June 1997 and January 1999, deportees were responsible for 600 murders, 1700 armed robberies, 900 rapes, 150 shoot-outs with police, 200 cases of extortion, 30 cases of murdering witnesses and 10 cases of arson in Jamaica.

The country was at its wits end trying to work out a way to deal with those new type of criminals plus the ones they already had. The Attorney General applied to the Supreme Court asking for authorisation for the police to monitor deportees who have committed crimes in the US. People were saying it was an infringement of their civil liberty and that the criminals should contest such an order. What a load of shit if ever I heard. Those types of murderers should not have the liberty in the first place to be contesting anything. In 1998 alone 2,161 criminal deportees were sent back to tiny Jamaica. Many found their way back to Trench Town from where they came and continued in their criminal ways. Even the suckling on the breast they killed.

We are now in the 21st century and it is fair to say that we are a nation in trouble but now the disturbances are no longer confined to the dysfunctional communities, but cover the entire country. In April 1999 the island had a period of social unrest, which was in evidence over the entire island. The rebellion was triggered by a Government's proposal to increase petrol tax. People from all social classes and religions took part in the uprising, expressing their problems with the Government about the proposal to increase petrol tax. The church leaders said their actions were not political but more humanitarian and that they had to take a stand for the poor. The country was at a complete standstill and the news of the riot spread to the outside world thanks to modern day technology, and some countries were even contemplating cancelling flights to Jamaica. I was staying in America when the riot started and was wondering if it was worth going home to Jamaica as planned.

Many criminals seized the opportunity to go to work. They looted and burned business places to the ground. For them it was not about the government proposal it was about a perfect opportunity to carry out their dirty dealing while no one was looking. A police officer from the Special Anti-Crime Task Force was apprehended with seven other people looting mackerel from a pickle factory in Kingston. He was caught with six kegs of the mackerel in the trunk of his car and three on the back seat. The death and destruction round up after the rioting scored nine people killed and fourteen members of security forces shot and injured by gunmen. The Police Information Centre said four police stations - Gold Street, Seaview Gardens and Olympic Gardens in Kingston and Yallahs in St Thomas - were all attacked either with gunshots or home made bombs and sixteen police vehicles were damaged. There were eighty-eight cases of looting and twenty-six cases of arson. Over one hundred and fifty-two people were arrested for various offences.

It seemed as if the criminals had stepped up their campaign of tyranny and everyday they killed someone. I went to Trench Town to see some friends on my visit to the island and you could feel the tension in the air. How the people lived in it I do not know. One lady told me conditions were worse than ever. She asked me to remember ten bad experiences living in Trench Town and my God, I could think of many horrific times. She told me to multiply them by a hundred and it still could not measure up to what they were enduring. One of her daughters had to leave her home as she was given twenty-four hours notice to leave the area and she had to go. There was no one to go to for help and it was pointless pleading for your life.

She remembered on Mother's Day 1998 she had bought a present for her mother but could not take it to her even though her mother was living only ten minutes away. The gunmen invaded their pathway from one end to the other searching for rival gunmen and firing rounds and rounds of shots. All the residents could do was pray to God and wait. She thought her time had come when one of the gunmen outside said, 'kick down the doors and kill them all', but his friend talked him out of it. Most of the guns and ammunitions were coming from America sent down by drugs baron to make sure the young men killed themselves. If they really wanted to help the boys from their old communities why were they spending so much money on guns to take lives and not on things to improve the quality of life for the ones they left behind? And why were those guns and ammunitions passing through customs at the American and Jamaican ports undetected?

One young man, who was deported from America, returned to Jungle where he used to live. From what I have heard he built a swimming pool in his yard. He had money from his drugs dealing days in America and even imported guns into the island. He hired out his guns to young men and could make over a thousand pounds in one day just on gun hiring. There are regular gun wars in the area, business is booming for those who own guns. Many of them who left the island and accumulated wealth abroad, when they return home to Trench Town they cannot let go of the life that was left behind. What's so sad is that many of them can avoid going back to their old way of life but it seems they are destined to die that way. It is not a matter of if they will die, it is a matter of when, but ten minutes of glory seems to be worth the visit to the undertaker. They do not respect their lives and they respect no one else's.

The Colombians have found an ally in Jamaicans with the drugs and are using Jamaica as a drop off point for drugs destined for America. Some fishermen found a cargo of cocaine at sea apparently thrown over board by the couriers taking it to its drop-off point, they must have seen some coast-guards and got rid of the consignment. When the news spread of the finding, fishermen from all part of the island were out looking for drugs as a means of getting rich quick. Nobody believes in climbing the ladder of success legitimately. Drugs are devastating the country in as much as most of the crimes hitting the country are drugs related. Many of those who were deported from abroad not only sell drugs in Jamaica but they are addicted themselves. The Barbican base, which was one of the first drug dens on the island is said to be doing good business. The people who sell the drugs do not care who it affects or how it affects, all they can see is the almighty dollar. Young men who did not even smoke cigarettes are now addicted to crack cocaine. They will do anything for the stuff, even sell their mothers. Drug dealers are calling themselves area leaders and are flooding the island with crack. It is really painful to watch the addicts destroying their lives with drugs. Some argue that if they do not sell it someone else will, but why can't they be the one to do the right thing? Ghetto people only know crime they do not know any other way and to talk them out of it is like hitting your head against a brick wall.

Another crippler in the society is the designer clothes. They are just as deadly as the crack cocaine to Trench Townians as they use clothes to show their class. Young women sell their bodies to buy them and young men steal to get them. A dance in Kingston was held up by gunmen who ordered some patrons to take off their designer wear and hand them over, expensive footwear and all.

In July 1999 alone there were almost one hundred murders. Sixty-six people died over seventeen days, including twenty-two who died in the space of six days. Even though the war was no longer confined to Trench Town, the killings there and in nearby Jones Town accounted for more than half the death toll. When the news broke in England, I phoned Jamaica to find out more about the killings, many people I asked did not know anything about what was taking place in their own country, thanks to cable television. The locals pride themselves on watching only American programmes, which do not always include local news. If a storm was aiming for Jamaica they would have to be told as they did not listen to their local news to know what was taking place. On many occasions I was the one to inform relatives on events in Jamaica because they did not know. The view they took was, if it was not happening to me it was none of my business.

One source said a young man was out on the street minding his own business when two young children came up to him and started interfering with what he was doing. He told them to bugger off, but as they had a gunman brother that would not be the end of it. They went for their mother who came out firing on all cylinders with her tongue, she told the young man some filthy words right in front of her own children she was meant to be protecting. She had her gunman son, so she could do or say anything or so she thought. The man would not put up with her foul mouth and slapped her in the face so she went and called her gun-toting son. He went up to the young man he grew up with and gunned him down in bright daylight. Another young man who was close by and witnessed the murder told the gunman exactly what he thought of his actions and he too was terminated by the son of a bitch (and I mean that in every sense of the word). Some other men decided to revenge the double murder and all hell broke loose. People who were relatives or friends with the enemy were given twenty-four hours to leave the area. They gathered their few pieces of belongings and fled for their lives. Those who had nowhere to go took refuge in Admiral Town Police station with their infants. Mothers who sort refuge at the police station complained that they had not been able to cook meals for their children for days and they were living on bread and tinned food.

Residents uptown were also feeling the pinch of the powerful gunmen who had taken over the country. Six people died in an incident in Red Hills including a sixty-seven year old woman who was shot in the head. The Daily Gleaner reported that the lady was killed because her relatives were said to be involved in a killing the week before. A popular entertainer was accused by residents of triggering a bloodbath in their area of upper St Andrew. It all started when a video camera he had was stolen by someone he knew. In his defence he said he went to the person he was told took the camera and the thief threatened him. A young woman who they said informed on the thief was critically shot. In an act of revenge other gunmen went and killed six people living off Red Hills Road. Police went to the area to assess the destruction but Mr death had visited and left. An elderly man saw the police when they arrived on the scene, he ran up to them and pleaded: 'Lawd, a caan tek it nuh more, beg some police escort fe move out me family.' I was touched. Because of ignorant gunmen elderly people were running for their lives leaving their homes behind not knowing where they would end up. They are not fighting for a cause, they are not fighting for justice, they are only fighting because they are armed with high-powered weapons.

Many businessmen became fed up with the crime culture in Jamaica and moved out. Some were frightened for their lives others were tired of paying protection money to criminals. The only people the businessmen needed protection from were the ones they were paying the money to and it was plain to see that the police were unable to control corruption that was so deep in society. One of the men who robbed me in Jones Town and fired the shot in the air was killed in the violence in Jones Town. 'Who said there was no God'. An elderly friend always reminded me be patient when you pray to God for something because he is slow to react but he is always sure. Desmond the young man who I used to date was also gunned down on Waltham Park Road in a shop. People said his murder was a paid job ordered by someone he robbed.

The murder spree in July triggered the government to deploy police and soldiers in war torn communities. A Cabinet session held in July was dominated by the violence that was taking over the country. The Prime Minister said the situation had now warranted the Jamaica Defence Force (JDF) to play more than a back-up role to the police. In his statement to the Cabinet he said, 'If we say that we are at war, then the Jamaica Defence Force will have to see itself in this fight not only as backing up the work of the Jamaican Constabulary Force (JCF), but as having a significant - indeed, a lead responsibility for the defence of the island against lawless elements.'

He also said the Government requested assistance from a number of international security agencies but he would not say who they were or what help was requested.

Fifteen communities were to be targeted with Trench Town included. The Prime Minister said that with the massive joint police/military initiative, criminals would not be allowed to migrate from their regular haunts to set up activities elsewhere. The security forces would only be recalled to barracks when all the weapons and ammunition within the targeted communities had been located and the criminals brought to justice. He also said businesses who have to pay protection money to operate in certain areas would be monitored under the new security arrangements. As a patriotic Jamaican rather than throwing scorn on what was said, I held my breath and hoped that the plan worked.

In the aftermath of the violence in July the church held a Spiritual Awakening Service in memory of the people who died as a result of violence. A woman who lost her son four years ago attended the service and told the gathering how much she welcomed that forum as she had to deal with the death of her son without support. Her son was killed while staying at his sister's house in Portmore, St Catherine. He was stabbed more than twenty times and his throat was slit. She could not look at his body but was told that his neck was almost cut off his body. My heart went out to her as I understood. I wish I was near to hold her. I do not know what it feels like to lose a child but I know what it is like to lose a loved one and have no one to talk to. I carried the burden of my brother's death for many years without talking about it and now that everything has been bottled up the pain is too much for me to bear on my own. I realised that my brother is in the ground but I never really laid him to rest in my heart. One day for both our sakes I will say goodbye and let him rest in peace.

The new security initiative introduced by the Prime Minister brought the arrest of fourteen wanted criminals in one week. Twenty-four illegal guns were found and one hundred and twenty-one ammunitions seized. The police commissioner said he was pleased with the new security measures as the number of violent killings were down from twenty-four the previous week to seven since the operation started. I was bewildered to learn that with police and soldiers on the streets seven people were killed by outlaws. The commissioner might think that this was a success compared to past happenings but as a Jamaican living abroad I was embarrassed and all other well meaning Jamaicans should feel the same. The criminals have shown that they have no respect for the law of the land. Up to that week (end of July 1999) the death to date since the beginning of the year stood at five hundred and two. When you think of the size of the island and the amount of people living there, we have to accept the sorry fact that our country is officially one of the most violent places in the world not at war.

The commissioner stated that they were willing to pay for any information leading to the recovery of any illegal firearms and ammunition or the arrest of people wanted for crimes. The Private Sector Organisation of Jamaica (PSOJ) and the Prime Minister were discussing increasing the reward through the Crime Stop Programme to recover illegal weapons. Those actions exposed a country in deep trouble and needing all our help to combat the germ that was infecting our people. All decent patriotic Jamaicans should not expect a reward to report criminality it should be our civil duty.

The US Attorney General was scheduled to meet with the Minister of National Security and senior officers of the police force to discuss measures to assist Jamaica to fight the spate of crimes. The US could start by apologising to us for the part Washington took in the 1980 blooded election and compensate the relatives who have lost loved ones by guns manufactured in their country. They could also do us a huge favour by monitoring their ports more carefully to stem the free flow of arms entering Jamaica. At least Castro knew when to withdraw from Jamaican politics when he saw it was neither in Cuba's or Jamaica's best interest to arm fools.

Cuba's withdrawal from the running made way for the big artillery from America to come in by the trailer load. Time and time again people reported that there was an underground secret place in Tivoli where they have all make of guns yet the police have never been able to locate and destroy the place. One hilarious story I heard out of Tivoli was of two girls arguing over the same young man who was residing in America. One went to one of the so-called area leaders and reported that she was being interfered with. I had to wonder in amazement when I was told that the man who the matter was reported to and was not much older than nineteen, used a broken broom-stick to beat the troublemaker. He flogged her as if she was his daughter and no one could tell him to stop.

In blooded July our great musical hero Dennis Emmanuel Brown died quietly in the University Hospital in Kingston. When the news of his death came over a black radio station in London I phoned Jamaica to confirm the story. As it was to be I was the one to inform my relatives there of Brown's departure. Some were too caught up in the war to hear of anything else and others only watched cable television that featured solely American news, and those stations did not even bother to mention the passing of the crown prince of reggae. Dennis Brown died at the age of forty-two but seemed older to me as I have been listening to his music for as long as I can remember. He started singing from the tender age of nine.

Reports out of Jamaica said Brown was ill for some time but when his condition got worse he was rushed to the hospital where doctors tried to save his life but he died. As usual the rumour mongers came out with their diagnosis of his illness and the cause of death. But to us who loved him dearly the cause of death is not important. What is important to us is the legacy of clean sweet reggae music he left behind. Dennis Brown made seventy albums during his career and numerous hits including 'Money In my Pocket', 'Revolution', 'Love And Hate', and my favourite his monster hit 'Sitting And Watching'. God called his servant and he returned without a fight but he will live in our hearts through his music.

In August 1999 police officers rescued a woman from near death in Tivoli after she was held against her wishes by some bandits who called themselves area leaders. The woman took money from some people under false pretences and would not return it when she was asked to. The self-appointed lawmen were told of her deception and decided to be her prosecutor, jury, judge and executioner. They had her in a room beating her for several days. The police were tipped off by concerned residents and they moved in on the thugs. The police said the woman who was being tortured was a forty-year-old higgler and was a resident of Tivoli. She had been badly beaten and her arms were broken.

On approaching the scene of the crime the police officers said they saw several men running from a room and a woman came out crying. The woman told the police if they had turned up five minutes later she would have been killed as one of her tormentors pointed a gun near her head and fired a shot. He promised to kill her in five minutes.

In 1997 the police had found a specimen of what they said was human blood, bone fragments and tissue on the wall of the same room where the woman was held. It would appear that was where Tivoli bandits killed their victims and then dumped them elsewhere. The police said they believe three people, a Trinidadian woman and two Jamaican men who went missing in August 1997, were killed in the room. Their bodies were never recovered. In the ghetto they always had their own justice system and were not afraid to dish out rough punishment but I am glad someone had the courage to inform the police before another person was killed. Matters of wrong-doing should be reported to the proper authority and not rapists and murderers.

In August three weeks into the Prime Ministers new crime-fighting strategies the guns started blazing again. The Police Information Centre (PIC) reported that three people, including a pregnant woman, were killed and a three-year-old child was injured when four men armed with high-powered rifles did a house-to-house search in Jones Town. The police believed that two of the men lived in the area but fled when the joint police/military curfew was imposed in the area in July but they returned threatening residents and demanding weapons they had left behind.

The opposition party, JLP, called for a review of the new crime strategies and said the police crime data showed that the number of killings had increased significantly and that the government should face the sad reality that the problem had not been brought under control. Apart from criticising I wonder what positive contribution they have to make? For the problem was not just that of the ruling party but all concerned Jamaicans.

After all the bloodshed and heartaches I saw a report in one of the Jamaican newspapers of my compatriots making fools of themselves at a JLP rally that took place in St Catherine. I could not believe the people who had gone through so many years of bitterness because of politics were so keen to support their oppressors. One has to wonder if they have any brains at all. There were no whites or Asians in sight only the faithful blacks who were always the ones left in the poverty trap and to be affected by the killings. Why black people believe they have to be in the thick of Jamaican politics is beyond me? Despite their support and jubilation after the election they would end up on the losing side no matter who they voted for. The other races who were invisible at the political rallies would come out winners.

In blooded July Stan Baker was extradited back to America to face charges from murder to drugs dealing. He was picked up in 1994 in a shop in Kingston. His luck had finally ran out. The United States filed for an extradition order as soon as they became aware of his arrest. He too fought tooth and nail to remain in prison in Jamaica, but the US authorities wanted to bring him to justice on their turf. When the order was passed for the extradition to go ahead many people including students from the University of the West Indies staged a demonstration against the extradition order. According to the demonstrators he should have been allowed to remain behind bars in Jamaica as he would face the death penalty in America. The only thing that surprised me was that they did not call for his release from custody all together.

When will black Jamaicans realise that they should not defend criminals who deserve to be punished? That we do not have to stone each other in the streets to show support for a political candidate. Why can't we vote on the policy of a political party and not because we are bribed or that we like the look of a candidate? When will we learn to vote for those who have our best interests at heart and not those who are in politics for themselves? If we are going to move positively into the new millennium we must change the way we conduct ourselves, period. We must make sure the government we intend to choose has education high on their agenda and if they do not, we must demand it, knowledge is the first step to freedom and only an oppressive regime keeps its people illiterate. If the majority of the people are illiterate then they are unable to make informed decisions and that includes choosing a suitable government.

In 1699 slave-masters kept their slaves illiterate to keep them on plantations. In 1999 politicians keep their supporters illiterate to keep them voting for them. I implore Trench Townians to rise up against politicians like your ancestors did against plantation owners, demand free education and not free guns that will lead to your destruction! With education you have everything to gain and the only thing you will lose are your chains of oppression. You will be free from politicians who depend on your confused minds to bring them votes. You will be free of the area leaders who are nothing more than modern day overseers. You will be free to choose a political party that represent your interest. An illiterate and armed black man is a danger to himself and those in his immediate surroundings.

We must stress the need for education to the black man as many of them are too quick to turn to crime as they do not see an alternative. Many sow wild seeds all over the place without a sense of responsibility. The problem will not go away if we wish it away but only by doing something about it. We must ask for change in the school curriculum. We must rewrite our history to include our great inventors, kings and queens. When I was at school the only black history we were taught was, us as slaves and fighting against slavery. Black children need to have positive role models past and present so that they too will feel the urge to aspire to greater things. We need to challenge what the future holds for us and turn the negative into positive.

I only became aware of the greatness of our race when I left Jamaica and it was because of this that I was able to shed some of my anti-social behaviour. Some of us who left Jamaica and went to live in Britain, the USA and Canada are doing well for ourselves in a way that would be impossible in our own country. Why is it we were able to excel in another country and not our own? What is the point of Jamaica importing workers when they have young men turning to crime and the best of their women and men leaving the island?

The 'crème de la crème' of our society were happy to use and abuse their poor compatriots and leave them to self destruct. They tried as hard as they could to keep the problem hidden from the outside world as it was bad for those in the tourist trade. But now the horse has jumped over the moon and our backsides are left bared for everyone to stare at, we are now hearing about a group from the elite class calling themselves 'Citizens For Civil Society'. What a big joke if ever I heard one. If I remember correctly one of the so-called member's father belonged to one of the political parties and he was not exactly free from corruption.

Also that member was caught with an illegal gun by the police. The whole thing was kept quiet and little was ever mentioned about it, so what civil society were they talking about. Crimes committed by the rich should not be excused, and I would like to remind some of them that they helped to create the problem they are now condemning. They can kiss me and my dead brother's arses. They do not speak for me but only for themselves. Even the name they give themselves should expose them for what they are. What are they trying to say, only murders ordered by some quarters of society should be tolerated and the others are unlawful. Black people in Jamaica should only join forces with those who genuinely support our cause and not make fools of ourselves for those who do not respect our lives. When I was in Jamaica I knew some white people who migrated to America only to return in less than a year. In the Big Apple they were nothing but ordinary people and they could not accept black people in power over them, so they had to return to Jamaica where they could return to the fold of their close knit group. They are the first to turn up their noses at other people but starve them of luxuries and they expose their frailty as human beings with faults just like their poor compatriots. Their privilege position only stands as a shield to their weaknesses.

A couple of years ago a boat from the USA docked at the downtown Kingston port for a few days and the crew members invited some influential Jamaicans on board. They were invited to dine with the crew and the other occupants. I remembered how one of the crew members expressed his amazement by the actions of their Jamaican guests. He said they laid out a buffet, which included American apples for their guests to show their appreciation for being allowed to dock in their water. He explained that as soon as the well to do Jamaicans were told to help themselves, they made one almighty rush for the apples that one would have thought gold was found under the sea. Some people were eating the fruit as if they had not eaten all day and at the same time putting away apples in their bags. He said what surprised him was the people aboard the ship were upper-class Jamaicans and he could not see what all the fuss was about given that Jamaica had some of the finest exotic fruits he had ever seen. That goes to show when people are starved of something they desire they will forget that they are civilised when it is dangled in front of them. It was illegal to import American apples in Jamaica so the islanders go mad for it not because it tastes better than our fruits but because it was foreign property and anything coming from abroad is considered superior.

The other example of their greed always surfaces for all to see when a disaster took place on the island. They always seized the opportunity to beg on behalf of the poor and those affected by the disaster but the truth was, once the goods arrived on the island they stayed in the hands of the rich and the greedy, and very little if any would reach the people who really needed them. One man who worked at the Jamaica Broadcasting Corporation (JBC) told me he had contact with people who helped to organise the goods coming into the country from abroad, and they would make sure they took their lot before issuing to the people they were meant for. They made sure they took the best of everything and passed on what they did not want. So there are no citizens for civil society in Jamaica. We were all on the game doing our own thing, it was a dog eat dog mentality.

The group said they would become a pressure group and lobby the government for change. They had several marches in the capital demanding the resignation of the National Security Minister who people said could not even secure his puppies at home. They also wanted the Finance Minister, who could not even balance his own private books much more the country's budget, to resign. It was reported by the local news agencies that they had good crowds at their rallies but were expecting more people. Even though many people agreed with some of the things they were saying their agendas did not necessarily represent all Jamaicans. For too long middle-class Jamaicans set agendas hoping that their poor compatriots will tuck in somewhere, but the poor turnout by the lower class spoke volumes. The ghetto people were expected to meet the Civil Society group on their turf but how many of their members were prepared to travel to Trench Town to witness the living conditions for themselves when many boast that they "don't go beyond Half-Way-Tree". And supposing people from Trench Town had gone on the marches, many would return home to empty cupboards and hungry children, while their richer compatriots would go home to feed their children in the comfort of their well-secured homes.

Chapter Twelve

At the 22nd annual awards banquet of the National Association of Jamaican and Supportive Organisations (NAJSO) held in Ocho Rios. The Prime Minister PJ Patterson urged representatives of the above groups to let their voices be heard and let the world know that Jamaicans were decent law-abiding citizens, who had achieved the highest level in various endeavours. He told them to use their influence in the political circles where they reside to protect Jamaica's image. He said crime and violence should be of paramount concern to every Jamaican especially when so many of us are affected and that the extent of domestic violence remained far too high. Patterson blamed the drugs market and the influx of deportees from the United States, Canada and the United Kingdom but not once did he blame himself or his political colleagues who have armed law-breakers to ensure them votes.

Jamaicans telling the outside world that we are law-abiding people who have achieved the highest levels in various areas of endeavour, would not be telling them something they did not already know. What concerns many people is the high level of crime on the island, especially when Jamaica promotes itself as a first class tourist destination. People want to know that they will be safe when they go on holiday and not who is a scientist or an astronaut in Jamaica. NASA might be interested in that but not tourists looking for fun and relaxation.

The same week that the Prime Minister made the speech, one of Jamaica's most prominent female retired politicians was slain in her home in St Andrew. The killing shocked the nation. No one expected it but by now they should have, as it came shortly after the country was recovering from blooded July. Local newspapers reported that the lady who was eighty-seven-years old was in her bedroom when she was killed. Her body was discovered lying on the floor near her bed with both hands and feet tied with wires. Her mouth was stuffed with a piece of cloth. A police report stated that she was strangled to death. They suspected that the killer or killers might have known their way around the house and were perhaps known to the deceased. The killers gained entry to the house by using a rope to lower themselves through one of the five skylights, which led them to a hallway near her bedroom. They forced the grill open and entered her bedroom. Her chauffeur who occupied another section of the house, said that he heard strange noises outside in the yard but stated he did nothing as the noise quietened down. Money was said to be on the premises but the police reported none was found when they searched the house for evidence so they suspected the motive was robbery.

An eighty-seven-year-old frail lady was tied and killed like an animal and the police were still searching for leads several weeks after the killing. Jamaica was my beloved country but I am now becoming frightened to even visit the place. If they could do that to an old lady what would they do to me? No one in Jamaica at this time is immune from the senseless killings and no amount of patriotism is going to mute me from speaking out because we must do something fast to stem the flow of death. It is quite clear that none of the main political parties are able to solve this problem and I certainly do not have any confidence in the third one so where do we go from here. What we need is fresh blood, honest men and women of integrity.

During another visit to Jamaica I had the unfortunate task of going to the bank again. This time I went to The National Commercial Bank in Half Way Tree. I waited for over an just hour to get to the teller and there were only six people in front of me.

I recognised the man who was immediately behind me from Brixton, London. He was complaining about the long wait when a dreadlocks man in front of us heard and started shouting at the top of his voice about how we were always critical of Jamaica and that we would have to wait wherever we were. He said he travelled to many different countries and that he had to wait just as long, sometimes longer than he does in Jamaica. I wanted to ask him where those places were so I would not visit them, but was afraid to risk his wrath. The brother went on such serious ranting and raving you would have thought someone had hit him.

Jamaicans do not accept criticism well and comments are usually taken personally to the point where some people want to fight. He said we were picking on Jamaica, but did he think we were doing so because we did not care or was it because we cared so much? The person who does not care would not give a damn if the island disappeared off the face of the globe. One young lady told me she does not want anything to do with her native Jamaica anymore as the people were too wicked. She said she would be destroying her Jamaican passport and applying for an American book, and if anyone called her a Jamaican she would be suing them. I am a born Jamaican and I will die one, but I will not stop criticising wrong,doings and I do not want to hear anyone telling me crimes happen everywhere for when I am ready to attack elsewhere I will.

Some representatives of the PNP passed a resolution in August 1999 aimed at countering the influence of talk shows on the public perception of the effectiveness of the party's policies and programmes. In other words they do not want any forum that opposes them publicly as this might open people's eyes and that may affect the way they vote, but isn't that what democracy is about? Informing people and letting them make up their own minds. To silence the media would be the same as silencing the man in the street and I would personally challenge any such move. Freedom of speech is not a privilege for us black people in Jamaica but a right purchased by the blood of our fore-parents and no politician black or white can take that from us.

The party delegates said in their defence that there is ample evidence of the public being misinformed about the purpose and state of their policy, the character of the PNP and the performance of the government. They are the ruling party, if the rumours about them are untrue then they should inform the public otherwise. They could also take their case through the courts but to muzzle the media would be a big mistake. Only a dictating government would consider such a move. The media do not need to spread lies about the performance of the government as we are all feeling the pinch of the performance. Instead of concentrating on putting in a good performance they are more concerned with how they can pull the hood over people's eyes so that they continue to vote for them blindly. The gunmen are making too much money from drugs so their little handouts at election time to secure votes are no guarantee so they now have to resort to other means of getting votes.

In the middle of 1999 at a PNP meeting in Montego Bay to elect a new chairperson for the North-West St. James constituency, a fight broke out amongst supporters. Four people, including the party councillor for that ward, were stabbed. Supporters of the losing candidate fought to gain entry to the election room, on the grounds of Cornwall College, as they were being prevented from entering so that the contest would be a one horse race. Knives were drawn, bottles and chairs were thrown across the room sending delegates running for cover. Neither the strong presence of the police nor that of the State Minister could quell the violence, which went on for over an hour. The Prime Minister should have called the election void and the candidates should have been expelled from their respected parties, to send a message to the louts but instead they called an investigation. If the candidates had any decency about them their supporters would not have acted the way they did. One candidate was determined to win and made sure her henchmen kept anyone who opposed her out, while the other candidate made damn sure he went out with a bang and that should not be allowed in any civilised society.

Even though public opinion of the police has never been good certain members of the force continue to carry on with their illegal ways of working without a care in the world. Every week another story of police brutality or corruption is uncovered. It would appear that the people who were recruiting the men and women to serve the country were not qualified to do so, as there are too many people, especially men, who join the force who do not have any integrity. This is not an attack on those hard-working cops but those who tarnish the good name of the security force.

Four policemen including an inspector were charged in August 1999 in connection with two recent jailbreaks where four people escaped. The prisoners were in jail for crimes such as rape, abduction and possession of illegal firearms. Needless to say those men are a danger to the public and should not have been allowed to escape from a secure lock-up. The police report stated that the prisoners cut their way out of their cells at the Gun Court Police lock-up on South Camp Road, Kingston. The grill bar from each cell and the main gate were all cut with hacksaw blades and no one saw or heard anything. As far as I was aware police search every inmate before they are taken to their cell so how the hell could a hacksaw get to the prisoners? The Police Commissioner said it was total carelessness on the part of the police but I smell something more sinister than that. There are too many unanswered questions like how did the men get the hacksaw in the first place? How could they manage to cut the main gate of the station without being noticed? Where were the on-duty police officers at the time? The police explanation to the public was that the men first cut their way out of the cells and then cut through a bar at the main gate leading outside. Thanks to our super-efficient police force for working that one out and letting us know.

One of the escapees was recaptured not long after the breakout, maybe he refused to hand over the money he promised to the police. He was tried in the courts and sentenced to fifty years imprisonment. His sentencing alone sent shivers through me. That alone explained that he was no petty thief and to think he was out running loose on the streets after committing some dreadful crimes. I have good faith in the judge that he did not give him so many years because he did not like how he looked, but because whatever he did warranted the sentence he received.

The police reported that since the start of 1999 forty-nine prisoners have escaped from police custody in ten jailbreaks. Over eleven cops were sent on leave pending investigations into some of the breakouts but the incident was dealt with as negligence rather than foul play. If the police continue to cover-up for their colleagues and not expose the rotten eggs amongst themselves they will always be tarnished with the same dirty brush. The wrongdoers continue their wrongs because they can depend on their colleagues' silence and poor investigation on the part of their superiors.

With the escalating violence that is crippling Jamaica the tourist industry is looking shaky. Thank God for that because it is only when the precious tourist trade gets bothered that the rich start to take notice and take action. The new monopoly to the Jamaican tourist trade, the boat cruises, were considering if it was worthwhile continuing their route to Jamaica because of its high crime rate when they could get the same if not a better deal in other Caribbean islands where their passengers would not be at risk of being killed, raped, tortured or kidnapped. Yes, kidnapping, anything goes now in the land of wood and water. Name the crime and they are capable of it. I even heard that there are some women in a gang calling themselves the Shottas Posse robbing and terrorising people just the same as their male counterparts. Two were even going around raping men. They must be really desperate. One man was so traumatised by his ordeal he stopped working as a taxi operator. He said he was too embarrassed to report the rape to the police as he knew he would be ridiculed. The women who raped him had guns and forced him to do sexual acts on them and took turns sitting on his face. He could not even confide in his partner as he thought she would blame him. When the story broke out some people said they did not believe him, some men thought he was weak while others wanted to be the next victims.

The Prime Minister again clutching at straws called a meeting with certain sections of the music industry highlighting the effects violence in the music has been having on society at large. Once again I hear the Prime Minister pointing his finger to every other place except the politicians. I agree with him that violence in the music is having a big impact on the youths who see many of the entertainers as role models and take what they say in their music literally, but when will we get an honest account from the Prime Minister about the part politicians played in crimes. After the account we also want an apology as many of them started the gun culture that is now destroying the country and we want them to acknowledge that fact. Why aren't the men who were the gun-slingers for politicians coming forward telling their side of the story?

This might be a big surprise to you as it was to me, Mr. Dudley Thompson apologised to the nation in August 1999 about the statement he made twenty-two-years earlier when he said 'No angels had died at Green Bay'. He said he regretted having made the comments even if the men were not angels they should have been given the benefit of a trial for their guilt or innocence relating to any criminal charges to be established.

He went on to say it was clear that the men were led to Green Bay as part of a planned operation by the security forces but that they, the politicians, had nothing to do with it. Mr. Dudley Thompson please do not insult our intelligence. None of the soldiers who were implicated in the massacre went to prison and why was there a major cover up by the ruling People's National Party? If you want us to accept your apology you have to come clean with all you know or just sit down and shut your mouth like the Prime Minister and the leader of the opposition.

What would be the motive of the soldier's to eliminate JLP supporters? If they had personal vendettas they would not need to take their victims to Green Bay to kill them they could have done that at Southside and do what they have always done and claimed the men attacked them first. The fact that they took the men so far to kill them shows they had something far more sinister to hide. They were clearly taking orders from someone in high places and I believe Dudley Thompson knows more than he is telling us.

Somebody out there must know something and some of the soldiers involved are still alive. It is time to bury the ghost that has been haunting you for so long and point the finger to those who gave the orders. I cannot understand those men who are now behind bars in Jamaica and the United States and will be there for a very long time. Why aren't they exposing the politicians for what they are? Many might feel guilty or embarrassed for the part they played but we already know who many of them are and what they have done, so it is full time to say who your bosses were. The politicians would certainly try to deny their involvement but I do not believe many people would trust them.

In the midst of Thompson's open apology many sections of Jamaica have been calling for a Parliamentary Truth Commission, which would see politicians confessing their wrongdoings. A former JLP minister who is now a radio talk show host promised to tell all he knew about the association of politicians and gunmen if provided immunity. But he went on to say that the Department of Public Prosecutions (DPP) would not have accepted the information he would give as some of it would be hearsay. Both the Prime Minister and the leader of opposition said they would not take part in the truth commission if one was set up. The Prime Minister said he had nothing to disclose and the leader of the opposition said that the time would be better spent looking towards the future rather than looking back. The Prime Minster must be having a laugh when he said he had nothing to disclose. How could he be a living person on the island and also part of a political party, which took part in the corruption and not know anything? To miss what was going on he had to be blind and deaf (maybe that is why he is not able to hear the cry of his oppressed people and to see the pain on their faces). No one was saying he was directly involved in any wrongdoing but to imply that he did not know anything is a joke. The leader of the opposition said we should concentrate on the future rather than dwell on the past. Well, Mr Seaga, did you lose anyone to political crime? I do not think so, but I have, and I can never forget the past.

When there is a miscarriage of justice or criminal atrocities and there is no justice or acknowledgement, there will always be a big infested wound in society that cannot be healed. A crime committed twenty or thirty years ago should not be dismissed for it is never too late to do the right thing. For nineteen years I have mourned my brother and the pain does not get any easier as time goes by. So, Mr Seaga, you can go on to think about your future but I will always remember my past when my brother was innocently gunned down by a political activist who was never brought to justice. I have to bear the pain of seeing politicians with their families intact doing business as usual as if my brother was a thing and not a real person. It is never too late to say sorry in the hope that a healthy society may emerge.

An advisor to the PNP said that the Prime Minister had been concerned for a long time about the contents of the songs and how they were promoted on radio and by sound systems. He felt the music industry was being affected and he gave examples of people in the industry who were killed by the gun. Reggae music needs a big clean-up but one thing that must be made clear is that those people in the music industry who were killed, were not done by the contents of songs but by the cold-heartedness of those who pulled the trigger.

What we cannot ignore however, is the lewd contents of the songs and music like the one titled, 'Bullets Like Rain' can only distort the minds of the already confused inner-city youths. They will think that it is okay for them to commit crimes because they are poor and if a famous singer thinks so then it is all good. Entertainers must be aware of the impact they have on ghetto youths and use their influence to do good. To be fair to the artist he did not write the song. The person who wrote it said he did not mean any harm and just wanted people to understand about the plight of the ghetto youths. Yes, we understand that and no one does so more than I who had to go to bed without dinner for days, but that still does not make the contents of the song right when there are so many disturbed minds around. He was looking at the bigger picture of poverty in the ghetto but we ignore the smaller one at our peril, for those same ghetto youths will hear the song 'Bullets Like Rain' and think they have a justifiable case to rampage just because they are poor and poverty is not an excuse to murder. I refuse to believe that, for many people are poor but they do not go out and kill. A killer will always find excuses for his wrongdoings. So it is up to all of us to make sure we do not give them one. We should not advocate murder no matter what our social standing is and we should not say the words idly either. What we must remember is that in most of the killings carried out by poverty-stricken young men the victims were poor themselves.

In October 1999 twenty-three prisoners escaped from the General Penitentiary Prison. The police confirmed that the men who escaped were serving time for crimes ranging from armed robbery and kidnapping to murder. Yes, another breakout! When the prison authorities became aware of the breakout and alerted the police most of the escapees were well away. The ones who plotted the escape had their vehicle ready to transport them to their hideouts but some who seized the opportunity had more difficulty getting away. Two escapees were caught within twenty-four hour of the breakout and returned to prison. Another two were killed several days later in the streets by police from a special task force who must have been looking for promotion as it would appear that the more people police kill the higher up they go in the force. They very rarely take outlaws in alive and use the fact that the men were escapees as a reason to kill them while pursuing their ambition. It is quite strange that in Jamaica more than anywhere else in the western world police bring in more dead criminals than live ones. No one question this practice so they use it to their advantage. Why is it that in Britain and America where the so-called Yardies have access to more high-powered weapons the police manage to apprehend the criminals without much bloodshed? Is it that Jamaican police are not capable of dealing with criminals or are they murderers themselves? As many gunmen know they do not stand a chance with the Jamaican police some have no choice but to shoot their way out as either way they are going to be killed. In foreign countries they tend to put up less fight when they are about to be arrested.

One of the escapees who was caught and sent back to prison said at an inquiry into the breakout that they climbed through a drainage pipe to their escape. When they were going over the high fence of the prison an inmate tried to alert a warder who was stationed not far from the escape route but he was behaving suspicious. I had to laugh when I read the report in the newspaper. This sounds like a story from one of Jamaica's comedy shows but that was not the end of the joke and shame. Prisoners reported that some of their cellmates had mobile phones, and there I was assuming that the screws plotted the whole thing. Well, I apologise to them as they were not responsible for everything, just some of it. The wardens must have played a part for things to run so smoothly and anyway how should I know caged criminals would have access to mobile phones to be making contact with the free world. I have my freedom and a job and can hardly afford to pay for my mobile bill so how do caged criminals manage to pay their bills? My mobile phone company disconnected me for non-payment of the bill and demanded their money as well. I said to myself that I would not pay them the arrears after the disconnection but when I saw a letter from them inviting me to court if the money was not paid within seven days I found the nearest bank and paid the arrears because 'mi fraid a prison more dan mi fraid a gunman' and any door I go beyond I must know where the key is to get out. The phone company was quite right to demand their money. People should not expect luxury if they cannot afford it. I have a house phone and it hardly rings so what was the point in having a mobile except to move with the crowd. The phone company put an end to all my palavar. They offered me weekends and evenings free but as a former Trench Townian I was hoping they would extend it to weekdays on peak-time as well so I would not have to pay. (People can't say I sold out completely as I still have a bit of a hand-me-everything-for-free mentality).

If people thought the story of prisoners having mobile phones at the General Penitentiary was funny, they had a lot more laughing to do when a warder took the stand at the hearing and told a bewildered Commission of Enquiry that some prisoners had padlocks and keys to various sections of the prison including their cells. 'Hey, hey', I laughed, is this for real. The prison officer said he did not know who authorised such a privilege but officers did not venture into certain parts of the prison, like cells where mentally ill inmates and toilets were situated so prisoners had to open and lock doors in those areas as the stench was too much for the wardens. No wonder prisoners had safe havens to plot escapes as they knew wardens had no-go areas and as they wanted their freedom they would put up with the stench if that meant freedom. At the end of the inquiry some people were suspended and then returned to work. The government could always depend on the people to create another scandal to ignore the others that happened before.

A young man was arrested in Clapham, England, a few weeks after the jailbreak and the police confirmed he was one of the men who escaped from GP. He apparently travelled to Britain on a false passport. To get a passport some reputable person has to sign the form. I find it very hard to believe that he left the island without the knowledge of someone in the know. Those officials must have been paid well. I would not be surprised if he was informed on by the same people he paid to leave Jamaica. News on the street was that he was recruited by a criminal from the black underworld in Britain to kill a man. The contractor did not have the guts to pull the trigger themselves or did not want to do time behind bars so he sent for one of the dog-heart Jamaican shottas (who had no God damn common sense and will do anything for a plane ticket) to do their dirty job. Well, he did not get to do what he was sent for as he was apprehended by the British police.

He should thank his lucky stars that he was arrested in England and not in Jamaica or else one of the local undertakers would be making space for one more guest. If I was the young man I would have taken the plane ticket and disappeared into thin air when I arrived in England, because no man or woman could pay me to kill another human being. If anyone wanted someone dead they would have to do their own dirty work themselves and pay for their crimes.

A street vendor in Jamaica living in Kingston was killed at her stall by gunmen in November 1999. Rumour on the streets was that it was a hit by one of the escapees who was still at large. The lady was said to be well liked and widely known in her community. She was killed at midday with people going to and from their business but no one reported anything to the police.

The breakout from the General Penitentiary had people talking for months after it happened. No one in authority lost their jobs and most of the men were still on the run three months later but we all know someone out there knows who they are and is even helping them to stay at large. I wonder how they would feel if one of their relatives had been killed by the men who escaped from prison, and other people were protecting the escapees who had caused them so much pain. The authorities in America and England were given information about the escapees and told that many could be making their way to those countries but the question would be how could they get past the Jamaican authorities in the first place? They should have had the fugitives' pictures in every newspaper on the island and all over the airports. But then I forgot that they would not want to frighten the tourists away by advertising that there were hardened criminals on the loose. But if they really want to bring back those men to justice they need to do the unthinkable.

The escaped prisoners on the other hand might feel the walls closing in on them and in becoming more desperate, may repeat their actions that originally resulted in their imprisonment. No one will employ them but man must eat so no doubt they will have to rob and plunder to survive and as this is no new avenue for them, there will be untold bloodshed and tears until they are caught. The chances of them giving themselves up is nil and who could blame them. They saw what happened to their fellow prison inmates when they came in contact with the police. The prisoners on the run are like cornered wild beasts with nowhere to run and nowhere to hide so their only option will be to terrorise the weak and vulnerable. How many elderly people and children will become their victims? We will watch and see.

Chapter Thirteen

I was resting in my living room on a Wednesday evening unwinding from another stressful day at work when my phone rang and I reluctantly answered it. The operator said it was a collect call from someone in Jamaica. I had to ask him several times to repeat the name to make any sense of what he was saying. He said Casey was calling. I realised he was saying Stacey, Prim's youngest daughter. I hung up my phone without saying whether I would accept the call or not but I decided to call Jamaica to find out if something was wrong with Lily who had not been well for some time. She had been suffering from senile dementia for several years and lost her sight due to glaucoma so I was worried about her. To my surprise it was not Lily Stacey phoned to tell me about but a nephew of Prim's who was gunned down by the police. I do not know why they thought I would be interested to accept a collect call to hear about the killing of someone who had no respect for me when I was in Jamaica on my last visit. I asked Stacey why was I called collect in the first place and she said because he was my cousin. That was true but did she ring his other relatives abroad collect to break the news to them? I was never close to that cousin she was talking about or most of Prim's family for that matter, so why were they ringing me urgently to break the sad news? I did not have long to wait to hear the reason. According to her Sue, Prim's other daughter, had been trying to ring me for over an hour (collect of course) to inform me of the tragedy. Do not get me wrong I was shocked to hear about his death but did not see why I had to pay to hear it. Stacey also wanted me to know that the family did not have any money so Prim was asking me to send some money to help with the funeral cost. I found out then the real reason for the phone call. I told her I did not have any money to assist but as usual they did not believe me as I was living in England where I am supposedly picking money from a tree planted inside my flat.

I tried to explain to her that even though I try to help them as much as I could they need to help themselves too and not depend on me. The collect calls were getting too frequent with them phoning me to help them sort out their financial problems. She said she did not want anything from me. Typical of Trench Townians they're begging and being rude at the same time. I told her that I had no help from any of them when I left Prim and it was unfair of them to expect too much from me now that I have past the worst. She said if Prim and her relatives could have afforded to support me they would have.

187

I wondered to myself what was the cost of emotional support. I told her that I would not put myself in debt to help finance the funeral especially as I promised Lily before she became demented that I would help finance her funeral cost. Lily came up to me one day like a child. She looked at me with a smile and asked me if I would help to finance her funeral cost when she died and I said yes. How could I look my grandmother in the face and say no. She had so many children and she could not depend on them to cover the cost of her funeral expense so she had to make sure she asked someone whom she thought she could trust. What was interesting as well, even if she had not ask you could bet your bottom dollar her children would approach me. A few months after my promise to her she started exhibiting signs consistent with dementia. Maybe she knew something was not right with her. I made her a promise that I would keep but what made me angry was to see how badly she was being treated by some of her own children and other grandchildren who she treated favourably over Carl and me. She was never there for us, only Pepe was and he died when I needed him most.

In my anger I told Stacey it was not my job to bury all her family members and that I would not use the money I had for Lily's funeral to bury anyone else. She quickly asked what about Prim who would bury her? As far as I was aware Prim had six children alive four of whom she brought up to the best of her ability, including Stacey, and two she did not even bother with. I asked Stacey whose responsibility it was to bury Prim and she said, 'if yu no bury har den de government caan bury har, because me na wuk fi bury nobody'. If I was in doubt about who was expected to foot Prim's funeral cost then I was assertively informed by her daughter. She said if Prim had aborted Christopher and me then we would not have had any life. In other words we owe Prim big-time for giving us life even if she did not do anything else. I wanted to know what about them. She gave them lives too, as well as taking care of them so did they not think they owed her? My family use poverty as an excuse as to why they are unable to assist their mother but they could always do what Christopher and I have done and go and find work. As far as I am aware Prim never gave birth to any handicapped children. I also had to inform Stacey that when Prim fell pregnant with Carl, Christopher and me, it was not because she wanted children, but for the enjoyment of sex between her and her men. Stacey was offended, she did not accept me talking about her mother the way I did, which I understood, but she could never have understood my pain as she never experienced my tribulations. She grew up with her mother and if they did not have much, at least they had each other. Christopher and I did not have that luxury. Giving birth to us and leaving us to the kindness of other people does not exactly give Prim the right to be in our lives now that we do not need her. If we allow her in our lives it should be a privilege and not a duty. The time she spends talking about us behind our backs, she could do the right thing and apologise to us if she cares to.

The young man who died was called Earl. He was disliked by many people in his community but liked by some depending on who you speak to. Whenever I visited Jamaica people who knew I was related to Earl reported back to me some disturbing news but made me promise not to say anything, as they were afraid of him. A man who I knew as a child growing up in Jungle, teased me about having a hitman cousin in Rema. They wanted to know how I managed to be related to people who were so different from the way I was in every possible way. Whenever I asked them where they heard their stories about Earl they said everybody knew about Earl and his antics.

I was about five years old when Earl was born and I remember seeing his mother, one of Prim's younger sisters, walking with him in her arms with a towel wrapped around his tiny body. I cannot remember her being pregnant but there was the baby one day. She was still living in Jungle at the time but met a young man who lived in Rema near to where I lived with Prim. When she arrived with baby Earl she was looking anxious about something, which I picked up even at that tender age. A family friend of ours took the baby from her and walked over to a young man who was sitting on a stool in the compound of our apartment. I became aware of his presence for the first time and I looked to see what Pinny, our family friend was going to do with the baby. She handed Earl to the young man and told him he was the father. The baby's mother who was looking on to see what would happen was being ignored by the young man who held onto Earl awkwardly. After more than five minutes he gave the baby back to Pinny and went about his business. He disowned Earl and never looked at him again to my knowledge. I never saw him again.

Earl was cared for by Lily as her daughter was busy getting on with her life as a teenager which did not include a baby whose father was not interested in him or her. He grew up around his mother but from what I could see it was a detached mother-and-son relationship. It was as if she blamed him for the break-up of her relationship with his father or he was a reminder of her past that she wanted to forget. She later had two daughters from two other relationships. As Earl was growing up he looked outside his family circle for acceptance because he wanted to belong and be valued. Rema with its sinking sand of criminality was only waiting for the right moment to swallow him up. Lily tried to offer assistance with minimal help from his mother but she was in no way capable of steering him out of trouble. Even when she was younger she could not manage to guide and provide adequately for her own children. She could only watch helplessly as her children turned to crime to survive the harshness of Trench Town.

Earl's mother treated him differently from her two daughters. It was as if he was forced on her without consent. In fact when he was growing up some people did not even know he was her son until they were told. He called her by her first name. The Smith clan watched him grow into a delinquent without much power to stop him as he ignored their passive pleas. In addition he was confused by their mixed messages when they took things from him they knew he had stolen and supported him when he was fighting. His violent aggression was looked upon as bravery and encouraged by his relatives who wanted a family member who could protect them in bad Rema. His good side was not supported so he mostly showed the side everyone was proud to see, the hard, cruel and awesome Earl. When Lily could not afford to feed him, he got a little food from his other relatives who thought food alone was sufficient for his well-being. When his family could not find food to give him, which was a frequent occurrence, he had to fend for himself as selfish Jamaica did not provide for its needy young. No one really cared if he died through starvation. He knew he was an unwanted child of his parents and was aware that Jamaicans in the wider society did not take too kindly to ghetto children so he built a barrier around him to protect himself from further pain of rejection. He cared for no one and no one cared for him. He was left to his own devices and to work out his own problems. He came and went from his home as he pleased and at various hours of the night he was on the streets. No one knew where he was and no one bothered to find out.

He did not like school as he was a misfit and education was the last thing on his mind. What he wanted to do in the future did not exactly require a diploma. At the age of sixteen he could barely spell his name. Like me, he had a learning difficulty induced by his home life but as usual it was ignored by uninterested teachers who were judgmental of children from dysfunctional families and communities. Ignorance was a way of life for him, his friends and his families, so he was more comfortable at home. There he would not be judged by teachers who were caught up in their own prejudices and children who made him feel inferior in their smart uniforms and well balanced lunch, compared to his scruffy looking khaki suit and dried bread (if any) for an afternoon snack.

I became aware of his delinquency for the first time on a visit to Jamaica when I visited the family in Rema. Some people did not like me visiting them as they said my mother and her relatives did not care about me until I had past the worst. On my visit Sue, Prim's daughter who followed in her relatives' footstep had an illegitimate child by a young man who lived in Tivoli. She was not speaking to Earl so I asked her what was the matter. She said Earl gave his friend a gun, which was used to shoot her child's father. I asked her who her baby's father was and when she showed him to me one day I could see that she was heading down the same dead end road her mother took, but she told me her man loved her and cared for their daughter. I heard that so many times from young ladies who fell in love and had children thinking the relationship would last and when the first one ended they go on to the next and the next having children by almost every man who lusted after them.

After Sue's man was shot he spent less time with her as he could not visit her in Rema but he still had enough time to get her pregnant a second time. He met another young woman in Tivoli and Sue thought she would teach him a lesson and play the game as well. Not long after she was pregnant by her new man and fell in love with him. Her children's father asked her to stay with him but she thought the grass was greener on the other side so she ditched him for her new lover with whom she went on to have two children. They are now married. Her first children's father has settled down in his new relationship, has a new family and basically ignores the children Sue had with him. Sometimes if they are lucky he gives them two hundred dollars. What bothers me is when they expect me to help out in hard times when all that happened to them could have been avoided. When her little sister Stacey got pregnant in her teens like her mother the writing was on the wall. No one was prepared to break the dreaded cycle of doom.

Since the war between the Rats from Rema and Tivoli men the two sides have never been reconciled. People from both communities hate each other and are maiming and killing one another in the most horrible way. People on the outside cannot even start to understand the psyche behind all the confusion. The animosity between both sides runs so deep that they would both kill innocent women and children just to hurt each other. Rema people who are living in a virtual dump and have nothing to celebrate or feel good about resort to internal tribal wars showing contempt for every and anyone. One does not have to be involved in any tribal war their only crime would be living on the other side. A young man, on his way from a church convention, was walking through Rema with his Bible in his hand when he was recognised as someone who lived in the vicinity of Tivoli. He was pointed out by a group of men, including Earl, who were hanging out on a compound in Rema. They jumped on the man like a pack of wolves and beat him senselessly. He begged for his life and told them he was a Christian and was not involved in any tribal war but his words were not heard by the men who were deaf with anger and revenge. They shot him with a pistol, poured kerosene oil on him and then set him on fire. His cries stopped as he surrendered to death and hoped to die soon to end his torture. Everyone present witnessed the horrific murder in broad daylight but no one was brave enough to call the police or save the young man's life. He was tortured until his body could bear no more and he gave up on life.

I did not let Prim and her family know I had heard about Earl's involvement in the man's death as I wanted to protect who told me but every time I remember it makes me sick to the stomach. I looked at him and wondered if the harshness of his young life had prepared him to be so brutal. The killing was mentioned to me by a relative but Earl's name was never called in the discussion. They were protecting his wrongdoings and for the first time he was getting their attention and support. It took him to turn to crime for them to know he existed and that was only because they wanted someone to protect them from other gunmen in Rema. Earl was being used by his own flesh and blood, including his mother, who appeared to be interested in him for the first time.

Earl wanted to be valued and knew only one way to get that in Trench Town, his luck came in one fine day courtesy of another raid on Rema residents by Tivoli men. The tyrants from Tivoli made their presence known with a barrage of gunshots. The occupants in Rema were taken by surprise and could only run for their lives again. Many found refuge in Jungle and waited for the vampires from Tivoli to get enough blood for the day and return to their castle behind May Pen Cemetery. But before they retreated back to whence they came, they went into homes and smashed televisions, refrigerators, radios and anything they thought were of value to their enemies. The police who came on the scene of the crime were either too helpless to act or on the side of the raiders. One lady shouted to a police officer, 'si dem a mash up me tings de' and he replied, 'so fucking what'?

The police could not or would not help them, so Rema men took matters in their own hands. Earl and his friends waited for the opportune time to take revenge. They were going to teach anybody they got hold of from Tivoli a lesson. A few days after the raid by Tivoli men on Rema residents one almighty rain came down on the island. When I was a child growing up I used to hear my elders associating rain with blessing from above, but Earl and his colleagues in crime chose to use the showers as an advantage to strike back at their enemies. They dressed in black raincoats like the Italian Mafia going on a hit and walked in the pouring rain heading straight for Tivoli. They walked through May Pen Cemetery and came out through the front entrance of Tivoli near to the high school. They came upon some people taking shelter under a shed including an old man who could not even walk steadily much more run for his life. They opened fire on the group and did not wait to see what damage they did, but hurriedly made their way back to Rema. It was later reported that an elderly man was killed in a shoot out by rival gunmen. When the story about the killing came to light, Earl was named as the main man. Tivoli men wanted him dead. Earl was given a hero's welcome back in Rema by the residents who were glad someone had achieved some justice but it was an eye for an eye which was leaving everyone blind.

His notoriety spread from there on and people labelled him as a hitman. His relatives beamed at his success as he had graduated to don status with honours. Not many men would have ventured into Tivoli and returned alive. The downside for Earl and his friends was that they did not have the amount of ammunition as the Tivolites who had the don daddas in America, Britain and Canada sending guns to kill and plunder. Earl's popularity spread all the way to the local police stations, which would make him a marked man for the rest of his life.

The police were after him and finally picked him up in a curfew with some of his friends. The overworked police officers were busy dealing with other people, left Earl on his own to sit on a bench in the reception area. They intended to interrogate him later but he crept out unnoticed in the confusion. He knew the cops would return for him so he went to Spanish Town to seek refuge from some of Lily's relatives. He spent a couple of years in Spanish Town but was soon pining for the attention he got when he was living in Rema. In Spanish Town he worked with a cousin but was less than pleased with living his life as an honest citizen. The police stopped searching for him and it was as if he had disappeared off the face of the earth, which he could have used to his advantage and made something better of his life, but it was not to be.

The men living in Rose Town were not very happy with Rema men and waged war against them. A self appointed don from Rose Town wanted to be kingpin in Rema as well, but some of the youths would not have it so they fought each other for ownership. A young girl who had two children by one of Prim's nephews and was a sister of a friend of mine, was riding a bike off Spanish Town Road, opposite Majestic Cinema when a group of men appeared from the direction of Rose Town, strolled up to her armed with iron pipes, knives, guns and sticks. They swarmed the poor woman like vultures eating away at her flesh. She was beaten with all the objects they had until blood poured from her nose, head, ears and everywhere. It was late evening but still quite light for passing motorists to see what was happening but everyone went about their business as if they were watching a movie that was not real and very soon the woman who was being beaten would get up and walk again. Only when her body laid lifeless on the ground were the beasts satisfied to leave her dead. People knew the act was barbaric but no action was taken to bring her murderers to justice.

On my last visit to Jamaica I went to Rema to visit my family and saw Earl there. I was not surprised to see him as I was told he had returned to the area. His mother pleaded with him to return to Spanish Town but he told her he was born and bred in Rema so she should leave him alone. What he did not know was, that was where he would die as well. He was standing with his back to me and did not bother to turn around when he heard my name called. He was gambling with some friends on the landing outside Prim's apartment and had on a pair of trousers that was two sizes larger than him, but that was how the young men were wearing it so he thought he was moving with the crowd. I noticed something in the waist of his boxer shorts around the back but I had to move a little closer to recognise that it was a gun. I looked in his face and he looked very angry, maybe he had not had a good laugh or cry for a very long time. I doubt if he was ever told that he was loved by anyone. What I saw was a misguided, ruthless, angry young man who thought he was invincible. He looked straight past me and I ignored him too. The fact was we were never close and if he did not think I deserved acknowledgement from him that was fine with me. I really did not have any hard feelings against him for that. We were only blood related but not bonded in any other way so I respected his wishes not to want to talk to me. When I queried why he walked with a gun in his waist I was told he even slept with it. I thought to myself not even that would save his life for I knew a lot of men in Trench Town who died with their guns in their hands and he was heading down the same road.

Earl was robbing for a living and was not afraid to use his gun to get what he wanted. To my surprise his relatives, who said they had converted to Christianity, were accepting stolen goods from him. I had no doubt that if they had refused to take things from him, that he would continue to steal, but the fact they accepted his stolen items was proof that they agreed with what he was doing. Some of them would say how mean he was when they did not get all they wanted or if they did not get anything.

When I got back to England I was speaking to Prim on the phone one day but she sounded upset about something. I asked her what it was and she said the cousin who Earl was staying with in Spanish Town took a picture of him to the police accusing him of being involved in the murder of a cop. Apparently, there was some reward money and the young man wanted it to purchase an American visa that was being sold by a contact at the US embassy. Earl was a known gunman so the police would not have difficulties believing the story and Prim wanted to protect her protector. She said that she could put her life on the line and swear that Earl did not kill the police officer as he was in her presence the whole time the murder took place. I told her that she might be telling the truth but the police would never rest until they killed him. No way would they let him go free without avenging their murdered colleague. I told her I would never condoned or support Earl in what he was doing as it was wrong. She went quiet and I knew she was not pleased with what I was saying but that did not stop me from continuing talking for I knew she was listening. I asked her to think about Carl, the son she bore, who was brutally gunned down by someone like Earl. Still she did not respond and I knew then she had totally detached herself from the whole thing and could not understand how the relatives of Earl's victims feel. She had totally blocked her mind to the process only her loss was painful and no one else's mattered. I told her that he might not have killed the policeman but the truth was he was no missionary. I clearly informed her then to be prepared to help bury him for it was not a matter of if he would die, but when. I also made it clear that I would not contribute to any funeral expenses so they should not ask for it when the time comes.

She was offended by my words but they had to be said. It was like their minds were retarded by ghetto life, which prevents them from differentiating right from wrong. They always said blood is thicker than water but for me emotional ties count for more and I think it was a pity they did not apply the ode to all their relatives rather than being selective with who they support.

According to Stacey, Earl was sitting on his mother's front door step dozing in the strong Jamaican midday sun. He was tired from the previous night as he used to go to his bed quite late, sometimes early mornings. While he was half-asleep someone shouted his name to alert him to police officers who were making their way in his direction. He got up disorientated by the sudden disturbance from his slumber and ran straight into the advancing coppers. When he realised where he was and who were facing him, he made a U-turn but a bullet was plugged into his back from the gun of one of the cops who were huffing and puffing like hungry lions. Earl knew he stood no chance so he put his hands up in a gesture of surrendering but more bullets pelted out at him from the legal armed assassins. He knew then he had to run or die so he made another attempt to escape but failed miserably due to the gunshot wound. He could only manage to make it to his mother's open arms and for the first time the mother and son embraced. She held onto him and begged the cops not to kill her son. He was crying and telling her not to let them kill him but the officers were not in any mood for sympathies. One of the cops jumped up and gave the mother a flying kick to get her out of the way and she and her son fell to the ground. They used the gun to hit him in the head and a cousin went in to shelter him from the blows and deliberately received the might of a gun in the back of her head, blood flowed instantly like a running tap. She was then tossed aside by the ruthless lawmen who did not care who they injured to get to Earl. Sue, Prim's daughter, went in to face the music and held onto Earl who was calling her name and begging her to take him away. Sue held him in her arms and cried helplessly knowing she could not take him to hospital as the cops would not let her, so she hugged him tight and wept. He cried and begged the police officers to arrest him, but lockup was not on their minds. He was taken away in a police vehicle and when he was later seen again he was in the Madden's Funeral Parlour with gunshot wounds all over his body including his head.

When the news got round that he was at the Madden's Funeral Home, enemies and foes went down to view his body. The informants made sure they passed on all the hiding places of the men to the police and all of them were searched for the first time in the raid. Earl's friends were hunted and rounded up one by one and put to lie face down in the streets as the cops looked for more gang members. A heavily pregnant young woman was foolishly advised by onlookers to lie on her baby's father to prevent him from being killed but she was grabbed and sent crashing to the ground by a deranged lawman. They wanted Earl's death to look as if he refused arrest so they took the other gang members in for questioning.

I was not surprised to hear the sad news but upset that a life could be ended in such a degrading manner. I still stand by my decision not to assist with the funeral cost in memory of my dead brother who had his life cut short because of someone like Earl who thought he could take a life because he walked with a gun in his waist. With all the money he was robbing neither mother or son saved any for his funeral cost even though they must have known his days were numbered. They should have learnt from other warlords who rose to prominence in Trench Town and then had to bite the dust as quick as they surfaced.

    I cannot help thinking that maybe if Earl had someone to care for him and tell him frankly it was wrong to steal, kill and rob people he would still be alive today. He messed up big time, but if there was a case where parents should be punished for their children's action this was one of them. By ignoring her son's emotional needs and accepting stolen goods from him, his mother encouraged his ruthlessness in every possible way. She taught him no values and showed him no love when he was a child, so he had no insight into what it was like to lose a loved one. He intimidated his victims without empathy and humanity and his mother's action helped to murder him like many young men who died in Trench Town. His father was man enough to have sex but not man enough to take on the responsibility of a parent and raise the son he helped to bring into the world. Like most young men in Trench Town, Earl suffered from a serious case of lack of fathering. His father should be tried in the court of law for accessory to the murder of his own son and flogged with the tamarind whip.

    The police officers who murdered Earl did not have justice on their minds when they went for him, only revenge. The police reported that Earl had a gun on him when he was killed while his relatives said he did not. I have to be honest and say I believed the police's version as I saw with my own eyes Earl wearing a gun as a fashion accessory when I last saw him, but I challenge the accuracy of their account into the killing. All the eyewitnesses said he did not fire a shot from his designer accessory pistol. Also when he was put in the police vehicle he only had one gunshot wound in his back. It must be known that he was first shot surrendering with his hands over his head. He had no one in high places to talk for him so they thought they would not be exposed. What they did not know was that he had a cousin writing a book while the killing was taking place, so his story will be known. The cops who killed him were no better than he was, cold-blooded, ruthless and brutal. At least Earl had an excuse, he was a gangster who lived by the gun and died by it, but what was the police's excuse?

    No inquiry was called into the killing of Earl, the unknown thug who was killed by the police. As far as wider Jamaica was concerned it was one less criminal on the streets to deal with but I knew the face behind the label. A needy, fatherless, angry young man who was my cousin. He had to grow up before his time due to the harsh environment in which he lived. He was exposed to criminality from the day he was born. In fact he was born into criminality due to his family ties and while his wrongdoings should not be condoned he was only a product of the place he came from. Trench Town was an institution for higher learning in crime and Earl was one of its brightest students. His immediate family did not possess the resources to raise him appropriately but it takes more than families to raise children or as our African cousins would say it takes a village to raise a child. In Jamaica it should be communities and if the community in which the child lives is dysfunctional then the government should intervene for the sake of the children.

    Many young men like Earl were treated like animals by the police, teachers and other prejudiced middle-class Jamaicans so they fulfilled their desires and acted to type. Earl did wrong and paid with his life but I pray that God will forgive him and redeem his soul for he was only living what he learnt. The song written by an American highlighting the problem of children living in the Chicago ghetto can also be related to Trench Townians only if a few words were to be changed as follows:

> On hot and sunny Jamaican morning a poor little baby boy was born in the ghetto, and his mama cried. For if there's one thing that she doesn't need is another little hungry mouth to feed in the ghetto. People don't you understand a child needs a helping hand or he's gonna be an angry young man some day. Take a look at you and me we're too blind to see or we simply turn our heads and look the other way, and so the world turns. And the angry little boy with his running nose plays down in the stream where the dirty water flows in the ghetto. He starts to roam the streets at nights, he learns how to steal and he learns how to fight in the ghetto. And then one day in desperation the angry man breaks away, buys a gun, steals a car tried to run but didn't get far and his mama cried. As the crowd gather round the angry young man face down in the street with the gun in his hand in the ghetto as the young man dies.
> On a hot and sunny Jamaican morning another little baby boy is born in the ghetto.

I misplaced Donnet's telephone number so I could not phone her and I did not have the number of the person who gave it to me. Then one day I was going through a handbag I used in Jamaica and found the number with three thousand Jamaican dollars. That showed how little value the money had for there was no way I could have three thousand pounds and forget about it. I gave the money to a friend who was going to Jamaica for the last time I kept Jamaican currency, when I returned to the island they were no longer using that money. I looked like Fitsue in the film 'Land of the Giants' with a bag of money that was of no use.

I phoned Donnet who was surprised to hear my voice but she was expecting me to call as our mutual friend told her she gave me her number. She asked me how I was and as I was still shaken by Earl's death I began to tell her the whole story. As I uttered the words, 'my mother' she stopped me to ask, 'yu ave mada'? I said 'what'? and she said she thought my mother was dead, as she never heard me talk about her much and did not see her around either. Those words from Donnet only reinforced what I was already thinking. I was feeling a little guilty about what I said to Stacey but after I heard what my friend said, I knew I did nothing wrong. She wanted to know like everyone else if I had any children and if I was married. I told her I was divorced, single with no children.

She was also single but had three children. Her man was killed by his own friends in a drugs deal that went wrong. I told her I was sorry and she asked, 'what for? I'm not'. She said she was glad he was dead, she prayed night and day for deliverance and had no regrets. She knew he stopped loving her a long time ago but he refused to let her go.

He told her that he was the one who made her leave the poverty in Jamaica and it would be 'til death do they part'. His new woman disrespected her and she was more of a housewife and a sex slave for him, and he had used his gun to beat her. One day Donnet went away for two days. When he found her he put a gun to her head. She was so frightened for her life she went home with him as he had killed before and she had no doubt he would kill her. She had no money or place to live and friends were too afraid to offer her any assistance. Because she did not have the right to stay in America she did not have the guts to go to the police. If she had returned to Jamaica he could have stayed same place in America and ordered her death. With nowhere to hide and no one to turn to she tried praying (after all she had nothing more to lose) but one day he was executed by his own friends. Donnet got work looking after an elderly lady and was contemplating what the future held for her and her children. She said she was proud of me and knew I was stronger than her as she always liked men to look after her and I liked to be independent. I thought we were two of a kind but she was too afraid to walk alone. Even when I was in Jamaica she would not go to the movies if I was not going but I went alone many times. From as far back as I can remember the only person I was ever dependent on was Carl and from the day I severed the string in our school ground I never looked back.

Donnet told me the problems of many of our friends who left Jamaica for the American dream and all they are experiencing is the nightmare, but what can they return back home to. Our community is a battlefield so why swap one harsh condition for another?

Chapter Fourteen

The fight against drugs and crimes by the US authority has resulted in many Jamaicans ending up behind bars and some deported back to the island still carrying on their lives of crimes. As the island has no positive system in place to counteract the state of lawlessness, crime will always be a way of life for many Jamaicans and even though many of us are making positive contributions wherever we are, the evil deeds of our countrymen cannot be camouflaged.

The Prime Minister made another of his glossy speeches in New York, December 1999 and said the death rate was going down. He announced to a gathering of Jamaicans living in the US, that serious crimes were on the decline and the island could end 1999 with the lowest crime rate since 1971. He also told the crowd that they should play a part in politics at home and should not feel less Jamaican because they were living abroad. Maybe he could start by encouraging Jamaicans living on the island to stop referring to us as foreigners when we visit and respect our money and not just the white tourists' money.

While he was giving his speech gun warfare was the order of the day in the streets of the capital back-a-yard. One such war was erupting in full view of Central Police Station in downtown Kingston. Three people were reported killed in the conflict and several others injured. It was reported that the war had been going on for over four weeks so the Prime Minister either did not know about it, or was trying to pull a fast one for the sake of money and that was so wrong. The island's newspapers reported that the disturbances were mainly happening in the downtown area but were spilling over to other communities. A curfew was imposed in the affected areas, but residents said they were too frightened for their lives, because the gunmen watched when the lawmen left the scene and then attacked them. One young man was chased into a yard and killed while another man was killed in front of his mother, who was then shot in one eye. Many residents were moving out. So many people on the tiny island were being displaced and dispossessed it was heart-rending to hear. The Prime Minister was inviting us to return to the island but exactly where does he expect us to live when many people on the island are finding it difficult to locate safe havens from ruthless gunmen?

I would have respected the Prime Minister more if he had held his hand up in the air and begged for help as we all know he alone cannot stem the flow of blood, but he needs to be honest and open. Massaging the truth will not protect the tourist industry in fact it will only be a matter of time before the gunmen move into those areas. The time to act is now. The crime rate on the island will never go down as long as outlaws who proudly call themselves shottas and cold-blooded murderers with high-powered rifles are roaming the streets. We need to get the guns from the thugs who have no respect for human lives.

We as a nation eat, sleep and dream of crime. At home we see our parents fight each other. When we do wrong they beat us. At school they beat us and the police kill criminals instead of arresting them so we grow up thinking the only way to solve problems is to fight. We need to change the trend.

I remember as a child growing up when the words on most people's lips were that they wanted to go abroad to make some money to return home to build a house. Now everyone wants to get out with no intention of returning to the island they once called paradise.

According to a report by the Association for the Resettlement of Returned Residents more than 80,000 Jamaicans returned home in the last twenty-five years but more than 12,000 then returned to the country from where they had come. Many people who left Jamaica in the 1950s and 60s are now pensioners who would like to return home but are confused about what decision to make. Their dilemma is staying in a cold country with resources that favours whites over blacks, or return to Jamaica where they could lose their life savings and in some cases their lives.

The high cost of living is having a strong hold on society and many vulnerable returnees are being ripped off by greedy lawyers and custom officers. The high tariff charges are only an indication of how the perception of Jamaicans is towards people living abroad. One telephone advert on the island was even encouraging people to phone their loved ones abroad collect which means the person receiving the call should foot the bill. The slogan reads, 'phone your loved ones abroad collect, they will love to hear your voice'. Oh yes! Not if I have to pay.

The amount of people living on the streets is just a sign of the state of the economy. Many of the street people are mentally ill and tormented everyday of their lives. Kingston alone is reported to have over five hundred people living rough but from what I could see from my visits the figure could be much more. There are a few charities that help out but not on a scale to make a difference. Children, the future of our nation, are said to be leading the statistics when it comes to poverty. A report by the United Nations Children Fund (UNICEF), titled, 'Changing the Future for Jamaica's Children' stated that almost one in every two of Jamaica's children aged eighteen and under live in poverty. Children from low-income family are more likely to be exposed to abuse and neglect due to poor childcare arrangements. Their parents are more likely to be concentrating on generating resources, which result in them paying little attention to their children.

Everyday the poor have to contend with the high cost of living, redundancy, low income, stress, poor housing and little or no welfare assistance. My experience in Trench Town taught me that lack of parenting skills, poor early education and anti-social behaviour lead to crime and violence which was reflected by the end of 1999 statistics of 848 reported cases of murder of which 224 were classified as a result of domestic violence. Poverty encourages inequalities in the education system, with the less fortunate (like Earl who died a violent death) attending school tired, hungry, uninterested in school activities and having less support at home. Children from well-off families tend to succeed more and are more balanced.

Jamaica's primary to secondary education system is said to be amongst the best in the world, yet many young people have left educational institutions illiterate. In 1955 - 1962 the late Norman Manley of the PNP introduced over a thousand free places to secondary schools. Promising young people who could not afford to attend resourced schools did so with the free scholarship. Other government leaders followed suit afterwards and offered more places to secondary schools and also to colleges and the University of the West Indies. But it was the younger Manley who revolutionised the education system from primary to university and if that system had been executed without bias, Jamaica would have been standing tall amongst the nations with the highest literacy level. The Jamal education programme was to eradicate illiteracy amongst adults who were not able to read or write. However, this programme has been reduced to a stigmatised failure no one wants to be associated with.

In 1986 the JLP introduced fees for university and colleges to the point where many students had to drop out. What was more shocking was when the PNP, under Patterson's leadership, announced in 1993 that only primary education would be free. This undid the work of his predecessor Manley Jr. Mr Patterson said parents who wear designer clothes should spend some of the money on their children's education but what about those who are not wearing designer clothes and have to be paying enormous fees they cannot afford. The common entrance system is still in place but they might as well abolish that as well, for there are a lot of children who have passed and are awarded places in prominent high schools only to give them up for less resourced schools due to high school fees. We are back to where we started in the 1950s when only the rich had access to further education.

Good education stimulates the minds of the young so that they will think to contribute effectively and not ineffectively. What the future holds for the children of Jamaica no one knows but it looks gloomy for the poorer ones. The Registrar General Department annual report to the end of 1999 states that almost 25,000 babies were born in 1999 many of which could be from low-income families due to the high level of unpaid hospital bills. Only time will tell whether those babies prove to be destructive or effective to the island of their birth.

An American bridal publication in its third annual review of the world's best honeymoon survey, rated Jamaica as the best destination for weddings and honeymoons. The island was also ranked high in other categories including number two for best beaches and best partying. Yes, we do know how to party. The all-inclusive hotels were also amongst the honours list with Sandals, Superclub and Couples given the top three spots respectively. Travel agents from around the United States took part in the survey, which appeared in the December to January 2000 issue of Modern Bride. Many Jamaicans beamed with pride when they read the survey, but I wonder what they would have said if the magazine had shown the other part of the island that they want to hide from visitors. Downtown Kingston is a sight for sore eyes. The potholes in the roads are so wide that they become ponds during the rainy season.

There are so many old abandoned buildings it is frightening walking past them in case someone jumps out on you. The government buildings including the prisons, police stations and other offices are so rundown that rats and other insects are also occupying them.

A report in the 'Gleaner' newspaper in a December 1999 issue said a police officer was shot twice in the line of duty. He was the father of five children aged from seven to twelve. He was first shot in the head during the riots in April, he luckily survived but had to pay for the medical bill himself. He said if he did not come up with the money himself he would have been suffering. He returned to work in November 1999 and was shot in the left foot two weeks later by gunmen while on patrol in the volatile Dunkirk area. When the Police Federation was contacted they said the government did not give money to police officers were got injured on the job but families of those who were killed in the line of duty could get a grant up to a million dollars. Police officers were not insured so it was up to individuals to take out private insurance. What an injustice. Young men and women who have joined the police force to uphold law and order were not insured or protected by government funds but when Jamaica's football team was gunning for glory in the World Cup the private sector was encouraged to dig deep in their pockets to finance a cause that was not life or death. Trust Jamaicans to get their priorities wrong. I too was proud of the football team but how can I accept the vast amount of money that was spent just to see them in France, when police officers who have been injured on the job were struggling to make ends meet. The Federation spokesman said injured officers should claim back medical expenses from the Justice Ministry but admitted that the money might take some time to be reimbursed. How can they expect officers to survive on the meagre salary, support their families and pay their own medical bills and to add insult they have to wait to be reimbursed? Corruption in the police force we now know is encouraged by the government as it would take a saint not to heed to temptation under those working conditions. The security force on the island is overworked, over-corrupt, under-resourced, understaffed, under-performing and over-stretched.

In June 2000 I visited Jamaica and travelled by British Airways. Well, I must be fair and mention that the service has improved since my previous trip in 1987. It seems the staff have been getting some training in race relations and customer service. I had no such luck with the Jamaican authorities. As I pride myself as a patriotic person I have never sought a British passport. I always hold my Jamaican blue book high no matter the cost, but I am rethinking that now. What is the incentive of having a Jamaican book I have to ask? For whenever we travel abroad the airport officials think we have ganja piled high in our luggage, but let's say they are prejudiced against us. Imagine, when we travel to Jamaica, we have to complete immigration forms which ask how long we are staying. I deliberately missed that question which was not picked up by the immigration officer but the custom officer who was supposed to be paying attention to goods arriving into the country asked me how long I would be staying. When I commented that only Jamaicans ask their nationals that question the man rudely replied, 'yu live ya'. I told him that since I was being treated as a foreigner then I would become one and apply for a British passport. He replied, 'do as yu like, nobody no miss yu'. Thanks very much.

The other factor that disgusted me was the vast amount of imported goods from the United States in the supermarkets - tourists could be forgiven thinking they were visiting the fifty third state of America. A small island like Jamaica struggling to balance its budget has no business importing mineral water from America. What made matters worse was that many had passed their sell by dates. Maybe that was the reason why they were passed on to us for a knock down price. There were second-rated American fruit juices on the shelves and I had to search for Jamaican fruit juices. The only Jamaican drinks that were plentiful on the supermarkets shelves were the coconut drinks and some of them tasted more like tap water. Jamaica boasts some of the world's best exotic fruits yet we are importing watered down apple juice.

I was hungry so I asked a relative to take me somewhere nice to eat and she drove straight into one of the Americans big fast food restaurants that seem to be doing very good business on the island. I asked her about Chelsea jerk chicken or fried fish and festival at Hellshire. She looked at me in surprise as if to say why would you want to eat those things. The old and the young are eating fast food and traditional meals are no longer considered appetising. The only time I witness patriotism amongst Jamaicans living in Jamaica is when some athletes from the island take part in sports and do well, at other times it's every man and woman for him or herself.

Even the way some of the girls dance in public is something for us to really look at ourselves as a nation. In public places they can be seen performing their acts, which would be more suited for the sex shops rather than the dance-floor. I do not know why they are not being arrested for performing indecent acts in public places. There is nothing entertaining about the new types of dancehall queens. Their moves are lewd, nasty and totally degrading. What was also evident was the poor esteem amongst young men and women alike. No one wants to be black anymore. Everyone wants to be brown. Bleaching creams are being used like drugs despite being illegal, and are being sold under the counter. Some creams have the dangerous components like mercury and a high content of hydroquinone, which is a very strong bleaching agent that will damage the outer layer of the skin but warnings are not heeded. People who cannot afford to buy bleaching creams make their own with things from hair perm to toilet bleaching agents like harpic and washing bleach. People might ask why mention this subject in a book, if people want to use bleaching cream then it is up to them, but the amount of young people that are using the bleaching creams and risking their health makes this a social problem. We do not want to add an outbreak of skin cancer to our problems.

In July 2000 police officers opened fire on passenger mini-bus injuring six people. It happened in the afternoon. According to the police they received information that a group of gunmen was on a bus, which was on its way to Spanish Town. They caught up with the bus in question and signalled to the driver to stop but he increased his speed. The cops gave chase and opened fire on the bus, even though it was clear to see women and school children were on board. Six people were shot including two students. After the shooting all the passengers were searched and nothing illegal was found. A passenger said the driver did not stop when he was told to because his documents were out of date. The cops were not privileged to this information so they decided to deal with the matter by shedding blood. The officers were removed from front line duty and that was the end of the matter.

In August 2000 a forty-eight-year-old businesswoman was abducted and killed. She was picked up on a Monday by gunmen along Red Hills Road, St Andrew and her body was found the next day in a cow's pasture. The body was buried in a shallow grave under piles of stones. Police information said that her partially nude body had gunshot wounds to the head. It appeared that she was strangled and then shot. The police also said that they thought the responsible parties were men who were deported from abroad and then escaped from prison. The deceased operated a petrol station at Waltham Park Road and it was believed that she was followed from her place of work to Redhills Road where she stopped at a shop. A few weeks after that two gunmen held up a petrol station on Half-Way-Tree Road, just walking distance from the local police station. The robbery took placed nine-thirty in the morning in full view of people who were going to work or going to do business. The police report said the robbers got away with $700,000 in cash, $120,000 in cheques, $74,000 worth of phone cards and $700 in US currency. Not a bad day's pay for a few minutes work. Before that robbery took place two other petrol stations were held up.

The business community, who have been silent for so long on the issue of crimes suddenly came face to face with the bogeyman who has been haunting the poorer islanders, and they became very afraid. They formed an alliance within weeks of the crimes against their colleagues being committed. They set up a group by the name of (PSOJ) Private Sector Of Jamaica and wrote an open letter to the Prime Minister demanding that he do something to stem the flow of blood. They said the time had come for us to ask for outside help but what shocked me was the part that read 'In our country crime has escalated to an alarming rate'. Where were they in 1980 when 900 people were reported killed? Where were they when Evening Tide Home was burnt down killing over one hundred and fifty-three elderly women? Where were they when school children were being killed by political gunmen? Where the hell were they when we needed them? Crime did not escalate in year two thousand, it happened long before then. One of the businessmen said that the government should act swiftly to counteract any crime that is visible. What does he mean by visible? Visible in whose eye, I would like to know. For it was the invisible crimes that started in ghettos like Trench Town that spilled over into the wider society.

The PSOJ have also asked the government to investigate the issue of the thriving extortion racket that is in operation in the capital which they say is slowly crippling the business sector. Most of the victims have refused to report anything to the police out of fear but a few have been whispering. One man said the gunmen asked for a donation for their communities, but if they refused to hand over anything they would be killed. Some people are said to be paying as much as $50,000 per month to men who have never worked in their lives. Business is said to be booming amongst the extortionists and that it has developed into a million dollar industry.

The Prime Minister in his reply to the PSOJ's letter introduced a new anti-crime unit. Mr Reneto Adams has been appointed to lead the new unit. He was a member of past anti-crime forces. In a speech the Prime Minister said that the security force would be targeting all criminals, including those who are involved in the extortion racket. Mr Seaga came out saying he hoped it was PNP supporters who are going to be targeted as they were the ones doing it. Typical, instead of seeing criminals at work he had to get politics involved. Who did he think he was fooling? It was a known fact that Spanglers (PNP supporters) control one side of downtown racketeering and Tivoli men (JLP men) control the other side. The Prime Minister made a similar statement when the previous anti-crime unit had formed but nothing much changed.

Trench Town remains a battlefield and politically motivated killings are on the increase. The roads in the community are un-usable and public transport has ceased to operate there. The residents are still keen on tribal politics and go out in large numbers to support their MPs but few mothers and fathers are seen at parents teachers meetings to discuss the welfare of their children. Times are hard and people have to be tightening their belts to make ends meet but politicians are still able to send their children to the best schools. They continue to over-promise and under-perform but they know from past experience no one will be calling for their resignation and if they do they can always call upon their henchmen to silence their critics forever. The few area leaders who are left in the community will always be skivvies for dirty politicians as they do not know any other way to make a living. In many ways they are the ones who corrupt the young men in the area by giving them guns rather than books. Young men look up to the so-called area leader because he might give them a pair of shoes and that means a lot to them as some have never seen their fathers never mind getting a sweet from them, but if a man really wanted to help you he would encourage independence and not dependence. Give a man a fish you feed him for a day give him a fishing line and he can feed himself for life.

It is now deep in the new millennium and nothing has changed. The death toll on the island at the end of December 2001 was well over one thousand civilians and one hundred and nineteen members of the security forces. Some of the prisoners who escaped from GP are still at large and Stan Baker is in prison in America. He was sentenced to twenty-eight years for racketeering, conspiracy and possessing cocaine with intent to distribute. He pleaded guilty and could be eligible for parole in eight years. In a press conference Baker told reporters that living in poverty in the US exposed him to a life of crime. He told the reporters, 'the end results were terrible, I lost. I separated myself from my two kids. I have some solid words for the kids out there, crimes does not pay.' I wonder how many of them will hear and heed those words.

Many people said that Stan Baker was the brain behind the Shower posse. Most of the posses that were operating in America have been decimated by the US authorities but young men still hope of leaving Jamaica to experience the American dream but what is waiting for them is the nightmare. The young men who were on the killing spree in England and killed two young women in front of their children have been given multiple life sentences. Were the few moments of glory worth all their youth behind bars? To think women like me were their lovers and nestled between sheets with them after they killed women in front of their children. The girlfriends of those men must have been very brave for there is no way on earth I would like to be in a dark alley with those men much less in bed in the dark.

Deloris, one of the young girls who was raped by Goldie Locks in Rema, was killed in January 2001. She barely made it to forty. Ever since she was twelve-years-old she was used like a prostitute by the men in her community, it was inevitable she would be killed by their hands. She was attractive from a very young age, she had dark complexion and was chubby but not overly fat. Trench Town men like a well rounded woman and coupled with her good looks she became a target for lusty men, who made their intentions for her known and I picked up on it when I lived there. She had no badman brother to defend her and her mother was helpless about what was to happen to her child. She was forcefully asked to have sex with many men who, when she refused beat her and took advantage of her. She was called a slut, but the truth was she was a helpless victim. People said that she did not have to go to every man who requested sex from her, but after being beaten and raped continuously with no one to intervene on her behalf how could she say no? The gunman who killed her put a gun to her head and pulled the trigger. According to him he was only trying to scare her. Trench Town had been very cruel to her.

Lily died in the summer of 2001. Soon after she had her breakfast she started gasping for breath. The family members called the hospital but no emergency service responded. The reason for this was, the entire city of Kingston had closed down due to a week of unrest. Lily never could deal with the sound of bullets when she was younger and alert and her heart finally gave in. She fought cancer and senile dementia but not the sound of gunshots. Her body had to remain in her small apartment in the hot Jamaican weather for two days until a private mortuary came to take it. It had started to decompose. What if she had remained in Clarendon - would life had been easier on her? I stood by my words and sent down most of the money to finance the funeral cost but as usual the family never cease to amaze me. One son said for all the good his mother had done for me I should have covered the entire expense. I had to ask him if he was getting me mixed up with someone else, because I can never remember Lily giving me a sweet. Greed will always get the better of some people for them to talk bullshit.

Stephen, a young man who lived in the same apartment as Prim was gunned down while using a payphone on Half-Way-Tree Road. Some men driving a car saw him and fired the shots. A young man was held for the murder but released because the witnesses were too afraid to give evidence. A few years later the accused was gunned down while leaving a fast food take-away in almost the same manner in which Stephen was killed. That is what you call divine retribution. His mother cried and said her son was too young to die. I want her to know Stephen was twenty-five-years-old when he was killed. She said that her son never did any wrong and did not deserve to die the way he did. The only thing that was left for her to say was that her child was a missionary. Lady, if you had wanted to save your son's life let me tell you some of the questions you should have asked him and just maybe he would still be alive today. You should have asked, son where do you get money to rent a car when you've never worked in your life? If you're such a good boy why are all of your friends murderers? Where were you on the day Stephen was killed and why do the police suspect that you're involved? When he brought home goodies that you did not give him money to buy, you should have refused to take them. No one is saying that you should not cry for your child but I hope you can understand that he was subjected to exactly the same punishment that he used to dish out.

July 2001 was twenty-one years since my beloved brother passed away. I do not know what he would have turned out to be as he was never given the opportunity to fail or succeed. I thank God we were brother and sister and even though our spell together was short, it was magic. I have memories I will cherish forever. Prim told me that she went to visit his grave at the May Pen Cemetery and she could not see it as it was covered with human remains that were dumped there after being executed. Those people were never recorded in the annual statistics. Unlike many young people who died violently in Jamaica and are forgotten, Carl's story will no longer be silent, I will shout it from the mountain top. Many families are afraid to speak out but I will not be muzzled in the name of my brother Carlton Tomlinson. Peace.

> *Just yesterday I was hoping for tomorrow*
> *and I trust and pray it would bring a*
> *brighter future.*
> *My life's been filled with ups and downs,*
> *sometimes I never knew which way to turn.*
> *When the goings gets rough, the tough gets*
> *going, cause I'll never give up my pride.*
> *Even though I'm broken up inside,*
> *I'll never give up my pride.*
> *Even though they've tried to push me aside*
> *I'll never give up my pride.*
> *(song Luciano)*

CONCLUSION

When I told people that I was writing a book several of them asked me what was the purpose of doing so. I told some it was to expose the corrupt political system in Jamaica and others that it was because I wanted to tell my story and yet others I told it was to keep my brother's memory alive. Now that I have time to reflect I realised what I really wanted to do was to tell them all.

Carlton Tomlinson, my beloved brother was killed in July 1980 by an unknown assassin loyal to the People's National Party (PNP). I do not know if the gunman is still alive but he was never brought to justice for my brother's death. Carl was killed because he was poor and in the wrong place at the wrong time. He was murdered over twenty-one years now and the place where he died remains a danger area and continues to be a wrong place to be. Children like Carl, Christopher and I are born everyday in Trench Town to parents who have sex just for fun, but have to contend with unwanted young ones they are not emotionally or financially able to support. The children are left to their own devices and only the stronger of them will survive, as the ambitious politician or the ruthless area don is just outside their door waiting to lead them to hell. Carl was a sacrificial lamb for politicians, as his death was a message to anyone who visited the Spanglers turf, 'if you do not vote for the PNP you will be murdered'. The medics at the Kingston Public Hospital did not think much about his young life either and had no respect for his relatives because they were poor. When he died a doctor did not even bother to explain what happened and it was left up to a nurse to make inappropriate comments - that was all we were worth.

The men who helped to bring my siblings and me into the world thought that their sperms were some divine blessings and once they passed them on to our mother's womb we should be forever in their debt. They did not take responsibility for us and believe we should be thankful for any little assistance they offered. Our mother believes we should be grateful as well just for having us in cruel Trench Town as it was such a sacrifice she could have done without. She feels she was a good mother for having us and did not even consider abortion and we were all born healthy, so we give her ten out of ten for being a perfect woman who had healthy babies, but nought for being a mother. Christopher and I are grateful for our lives and to be a part of the human race, however, cruel it has been to us. But what did we mean to Prim? for I cannot understand the psyche of a woman who could not abort a child, but could easily hand over two of her children to other people without keeping in contact.

Some mothers have children as old age pension and expect dividends from their off-springs when they have grown up. My opinion is that parents should not expect from their children what they did not give. If children are their old age pension then they must invest in them. You cannot plant corn if you want to grow peas for what you sow you will reap. The dependency mentality is in evidence in all aspects of Jamaica's life, everybody wants something from somebody. Young women getting pregnant knowing that they are not able to support the child so they go out begging and blaming society and men but not themselves. Young men stealing and begging and have no idea of what responsibility is. This mentality must be eliminated.

Twenty years ago the life span of a young man living in Trench Town was thirty today, it is as low as twenty. The average age for a young girl to get pregnant is fifteen and usually six in ten women have children by men who have been in trouble with the law. The ramification of this is most children will be born to men who are in prison or dead. The one parent family is a crippler, and in a lot of cases the mothers are usually more involved, in developing their new relationships than spending quality time with their children. There are no safety nets in place so many young people just fall by the wayside waiting to repeat the sins of their parents. It is a vicious circle which only a few have managed to break but for the majority the ball continues to move around.

The PNP and JLP are still exhibiting unhealthy competitiveness and their supporters continue to follow them blindly. Politicians in turn show their appreciation and attend funerals of known criminals from their constituencies. Some politicians claimed they attended area dons funerals because they were respected in their communities, and others stated that the dons helped them to make contact with people in their constituencies. What message is that sending to victims of those criminals? That it is okay for dons to hurt them because they are respected. What are young boys learning? That if they become gunmen they will be respected. A general election is due in the year 2002 and the blood is spilling fast and furious with the main players showing no mercy. But I want them to know that the voices of the one hundred and fifty-three elderly women who died in the fire at the Evening Tide Home are crying for justice from their graves and with this book those voices will be heard.

In Trench Town, men with behaviours consistent to some serious mental health and psychotic disorders were armed by politicians to keep us in our place. Some of those men should have been in prisons or secured mental health institutions and not amongst vulnerable people like children and the elderly who suffered dearly in Trench Town. The men robbed, raped and murdered, but used the depraved political system as a cover to carry out their lust for blood and got immunity from prison in return for securing votes for power hungry politicians.

Crime and violence is now on the agenda for most Jamaicans since it has spread out of Trench Town and into other well to do areas, but how did it get to this level? Everyone thinks crime is hustling and if a man is hustling to feed his family he should not be punished, so cops started taking bribes rather than making arrests, market traders taking over the streets to the point of hindering traffic and give the excuse that their children had to be fed, men from downtown, Kingston were demanding money from businessmen until it became a booming racketeering trade. Police are idolising drugs dons to the point where some even offer themselves as bodyguards, and the rich compatriots ignore the crimes committed in poorer communities. It was the little things that escalated into bigger things.

The government has introduced some ineffective crime task forces that have not made any impact on the core cause of the problem, as there are too many short-term fixes and too little long-term solutions. The political system is like a sink of iniquity and anyone who gets involved in it becomes contaminated. The warlords have taken over the streets of Kingston and only one brave cop (Reneto Adams) stands between them and anarchy.

I would like to look the politicians in their eyes and tell them you killed my brother. I want them to see the pain in my eyes and know that we the poor people in Jamaica are human beings with tears and blood. We are not toys for them to play with. We bleed when we get cut and cry when our loved ones are killed. Some of us never come to terms with the deaths and want answers. We are Trench Townians but we have ability to be more than killers and breeders. With the appropriate infrastructure we can be doctors, lawyers and inventors. Do not see us in one light and block the path to our success to ensure your ambition. We need to create a society where all children are given equal opportunities to reach their maximum potential, where we do not accept criminal behaviour because we like or fear someone, where the security forces will be free to carry out their duties and bring criminals before the courts and they are punished for what they have done.

I have survived Trench Town and I'm alive to tell my story. Carl is dead but through me Pepe's dream is still alive. Thank God for my grandparents through them I had hope. Many times I sit and think about the senseless killings and the ruthlessness of politicians whose only quest was to seek power at any means. As a child I witnessed many atrocious crimes and was also a victim. The Green Bay Killings, Gold Street Massacre and the arson attack on the Evening Tide Home. The rapings and murders by posse members. The neglect by my mother and the physical abuse by my father are just some of the bad memories that will stay with me forever. Writing about my past has helped me to move on with my life but I will never forgive the unforgivable.

Pauline Edwards now resides in London, she works as a Social Worker and writes part-time.

The Three Sodburys
An Introduction

Gordon Tily

Cover Photograph
A Murray Dowding photograph taken c.1912 showing Chipping Sodbury main street looking towards Little and Old Sodbury with the Cotswolds on the sky-line.

With grateful thanks to
my wife, Janet, and my son, Edward,
for their very practical help and moral support.

Copyright © **A.G. & E.G. Tily – 1994**
All rights reserved. No part of this publication may be reproduced or transmitted in any form or by any means, electronic or mechanical including photocopying, recording or in any information or retrieval system without prior permission from the author.

Typesetting in 10/11 New Century Schoolbook by
Tilset Services, 22 Prestbury, Yate, Bristol BS17 4LB.

Published 1994 by Tilset Services of 22 Prestbury, Yate, Bristol BS17 4LB
Printed by Potten Baber & Murray Ltd., Whitehouse Street, Bedminster, Bristol BS3 4AS

ISBN 0 9523542 0 9

Dedication

This book is dedicated to the memory of Percival Abel Couzens, Historian. He was born in Old Sodbury on the 7th April 1905 and died on the 25th April 1992. He is now back home again, buried in Old Sodbury Churchyard.

Percy attended the St. John's Church of England School at Chipping Sodbury from where he gained a Scholarship which took him to Chipping Sodbury Grammar School in 1915.

In 1921 he joined the Great Western railway as a clerk and served in various capacities, finally retiring from the Bristol Divisional Office in April 1963.

For many years he was active in the Baptist Chapel and Local Government at Parish level.

Percy was fascinated by the history of the area in which he had lived all his life – the Sodburys and Yate areas and was a disciple of the late Murray Dowding, whose photographs can be found in many collections. As a result Percy published his first book, *The Continuing Story of the Sodburys*, in 1972. This was followed by a number of other books, *A Companion into the Southwolds* in 1975, *The Sodburys,* an abridged version of his first book in 1976 and finally the books in his Annals series, *Annals of a Borough* (Summer 1989), *Annals of Two Manors* (Autumn 1989) and *Annals of a Parish* (Summer 1990).

The impact that Percy Couzens has made on this area in a historical sense has thus been considerable as has the contribution to our knowledge. He is already sadly missed and it is hoped that this book, dedicated to him, will help to keep his memory alive.

Percy Couzens

Foreword

I was responsible for doing the typesetting for Percy Couzens' Annals series for the Sodburys and Yate, which is when I came to know Percy well. By then, of course, he was in the autumn of his years but his physical infirmities by no means clouded his intellectual capabilities and I have always felt privileged to have known him and worked with him.

Unfortunately, all of his books are out of print and for those not fortunate enough to have bought one at the time, there is no book on the history of the Sodburys now available. This is why I have produced this book, to fill the gap. It is unashamedly taken from Percy's books and from his research but with the grammar brought into the modern age and the presentation the result of modern technology. If there are gaps in the history they are the ones which Percy himself left and, given time, no doubt they will be filled, if not by myself, by others who even as I write are going on with their own researches into the history of the area.

This is why I have called this book an Introduction. I am well aware that it is general in its content, barely brushing the surface on many of the topics covered. I hope that it will form a basic source of reference to all those interested in the history of the area without cramping the style of those dedicated people who want to make a more detailed study of certain aspects.

In deciding on the format of this book, it was suggested to me by my son Edward, that I should perhaps consider that if and when other authors wanted to publish their own work, they may well think it not a bad idea to use a similar format so that over a period of time a whole set of matching volumes on the history of our area could be generated, covering not just the Sodburys, or even Yate as well, but the whole of South Gloucestershire. This would apply to small publications of some twenty-four pages to ones larger than this one and cover every aspect of history from the specialist to the broad brush. It is, perhaps, a large ambition but the sort of ambition of which only the human animal is capable and which has taken us from the cave to the present day – history again. It would be very satisfying, though, to have a whole shelf of books on the history of the area which are companion volumes to this one as well.

Meanwhile, I hope that this book fills a need as I know Percy would want to happen. Enjoy.

Gordon Tily
May 1994

CONTENTS

Chapter One	– Pre-History	11
Chapter Two	– Saxon Times 577–1066 AD	22
Chapter Three	– The Arrival of the Normans	32
Chapter Four	– Medieval Times	57
Chapter Five	– The Tudors	84
Chapter Six	– The Stuarts	109
Chapter Seven	– The Eighteenth Century	139
Chapter Eight	– The Nineteenth Century	176
Chapter Nine	– The Last Hundred Years	221
Appendices		262

    A. The Laws of Breteuil ... 263
    B. Some Leading Inhabitants of Chipping Sodbury ... 270
    C. Poor Rate 1727 – Chipping Sodbury Borough ... 272
    D. Poor Rate 1727 – Old Sodbury ... 276
    E. Voters at Elections in 1776 and 1811 – Old Sodbury ... 279
    F. Trades and Professions in Chipping Sopdbury ... 281
    G. Some of the 687 People Living in Old Sodbury in 1805 ... 282
    H. Old Sodbury C of E School ... 284
    I. Manor of Old Sodbury – Jurors on the Court Leet, 1845 ... 287
    J. Descent of the Manor and Borough ... 288
    K. Descent of Little Sodbury Manor and Combined Manors ... 290
    L. Incumbents in the Parish Churches ... 292
    M. Benefactions and Charities ... 294
    N. Last Will & Testament of Isabella Tily (née Clarke) ... 296

Index ... 299

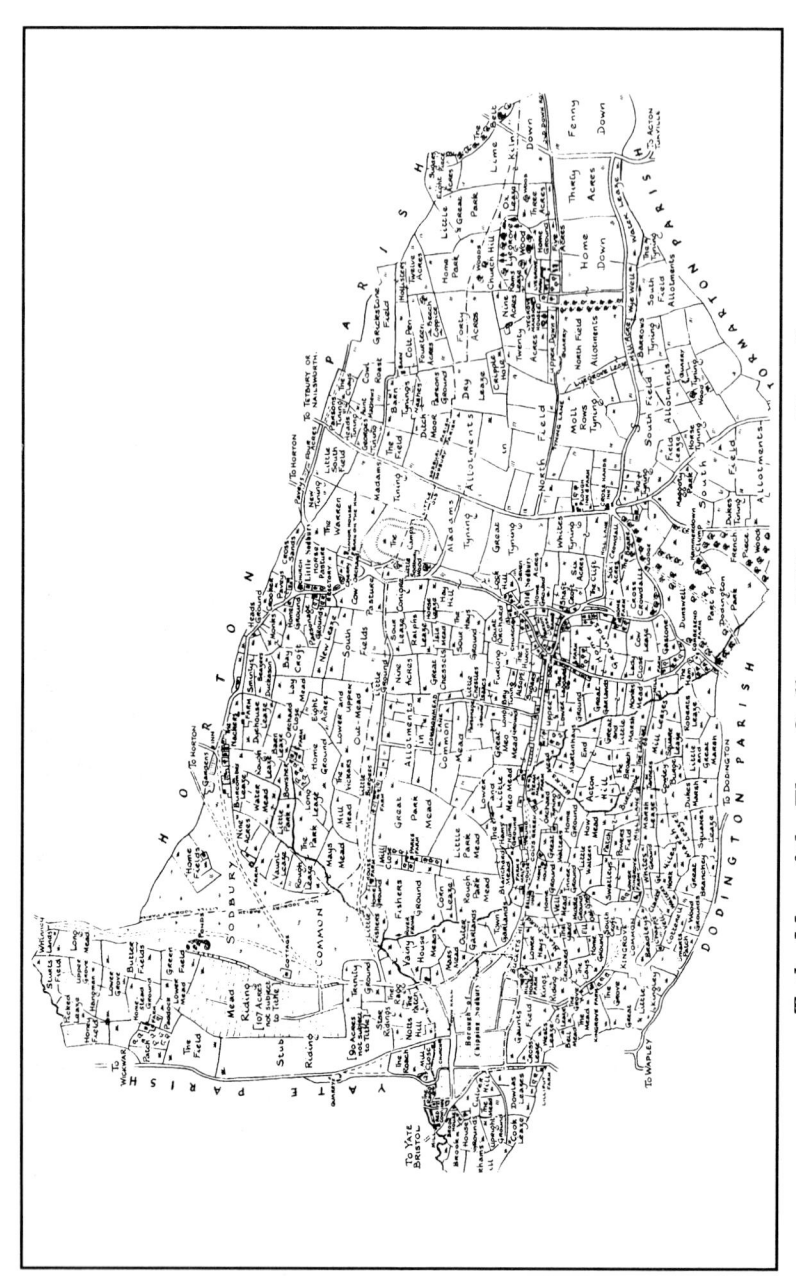

Tythe Map of the Three Sodburys, 1839 – courtesy Harry Lane

CHAPTER ONE

PRE-HISTORY

The map opposite shows the area of some 4,929 acres making up the three Sodburys which consist of Old Sodbury, Little Sodbury and Chipping Sodbury.

The illustration on the following page also shows how the area lies in relation to two parallel ridges of higher ground running roughly north to south about two miles apart. In the distant past the whole area was under water at least once. At other times it was swept by hurricane force winds and still others scoured by torrents of water from melting glaciers.

The western ridge whose highest point is at the top of the High Street in Chipping Sodbury, is made up of carboniferous limestone which has been greatly in demand for road making and for burning to produce lime and has resulted in the enormous hole in the ground to the north of Chipping Sodbury, once a series of quarries along the Wickwar Road. The rock strata in the face of the quarry shows very well how the layers of rock have been displaced by tremendous forces long ago.

The eastern side of this ridge is a much gentler slope of rock. It lies beneath a bed of clay which covers most of the area up to the steep slope of the higher ridge starting at the Dog Inn at Old Sodbury and falling off in a more gentle slope again to the east past the general line of the A46 Bath–Stroud road.

The main ridge is made up of Mesozoic rocks and parts of it are particularly rich in fossils. On the southern boundary of the middle section is a less conspicuous ridge of higher ground roughly at right angles to the other two which first drops towards the centre and then rises again as one looks towards the northern edge of the area so the topography of the three Sodburys is a basin of varying depths. Within the neighbouring areas deposits of Celestine, known locally as 'Spar', Coal, Fullers Earth, Millstone Grit and Brown Hematite have been found at different times. Finally, a stream, the River Frome, rises in the grounds of Dodington House on the main ridge and finds its way across

The Three Sodburys – An Introduction

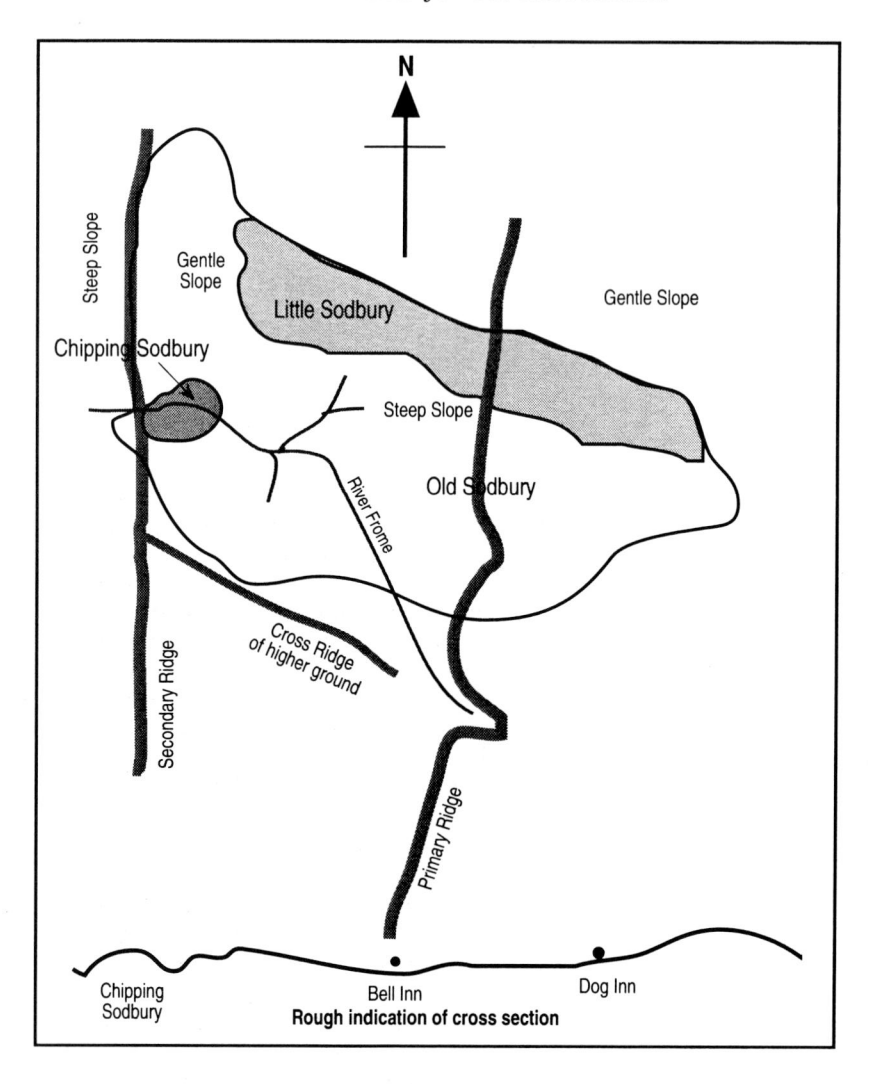

*[Map showing the three Sodburys with features labelled: N (north arrow); Steep Slope; Gentle Slope; Little Sodbury; Gentle Slope; Chipping Sodbury; Steep Slope; Old Sodbury; River Frome; Secondary Ridge; Cross Ridge of higher ground; Primary Ridge; Chipping Sodbury; Bell Inn; Dog Inn; **Rough indication of cross section**]*

the clay, collecting a few tributaries on its way, and passes behind the church in Chipping Sodbury and then through a gap in the secondary ridge at the bottom of Brook Street before making its way through Yate and on to the River Avon at Bristol.

The primary ridge is part of a rock formation extending north and south from the Midlands to the South West, known as the Cotswolds. It is exactly the type of terrain upon which signs of early man can usually be found. The lower parts of the country were taken up by forests and marshes and the soil was very heavy so making it less attractive to their primitive agriculture. Nevertheless, what they achieved with deer antlers for picks, oxen bones for shovels and other tools of stone and wood was tremendous. Among their accomplishments are the large elongated mounds they raised over the burial places of their dead. There is one of these at Grickstone Farm, just outside the parish boundary of Little Sodbury. The following story is taken from the Gentleman's Magazine 1844, Part 1, page 636:

A few weeks since, as some labourers employed on Grickstone Farm, in the parish of Horton, Gloucestershire, were ploughing over a mound on an elevated piece of ground, called Church Hill, the earth suddenly gave way under one of the horses, and it was found that an entrance had thus been effected into a rude chamber, measuring four feet in each direction, and containing the remains of six or eight human bodies, together with a vessel of very primitive shape, made from a blue sort of earth, and apparently baked in the sun, as it evidently had not been subjected to the action of fire. Some charred human bodies were also found, which had probably been the contents of the vessel in question, as they were found near the same spot. The falling in of the earth and stones, and the unscientific exploration of the workmen, however, render an accurate description impossible. The bodies appear to have been indiscriminately placed, and appeared as though they had been in a sitting posture. The size of the chamber would not allow of their being extended at length. The sides and top were formed of single flat stones, around and outside of which smaller stones had been loosely built up in the form of a wall. Connected with this, and lying at right angles on the eastern side, was another similar to the former. The dimensions were about six feet by 2 ½ feet; in this also were the remains of two bodies. Supposing that this was not a solitary vault, openings were made in several places in the mound, which was about 40 feet in diameter, and appeared throughout to be constructed of loosely built up stones of the same description as those dug from the neighbouring quarry; and afterwards another chamber similarly formed to the last of about 6 feet by 4, and lying about 12 feet distant to the west was discovered. In this were fourteen or fifteen human skeletons, all with heads to the east. The bodies must have been of all ages and sizes.

These remains were of the first people who can be identified with our area. The variation in age of the people found matches the discoveries made when more scientific excavations were carried out on a barrow at Lugbury, near Nettleton, a few miles away. There the remains ranged from 1 to 50 years old. Although modern technology would have allowed a more exact time to be estimated for when these people lived and died, it is generally accepted as being between 2,300 and 2,000 BC. At Lugbury the stones making up the barrow are still *in situ*. They are very large and it is reasonable to assume, because of other similarities, that similar ones existed at Grickstone but were used for other purposes later. The Ordnance Survey map shows one large stone on the parish boundary, near the farm, where it can still be seen.

Where these people actually lived is something of a mystery since no real settlement site has, so far, come to light on the Cotswolds. Grickstone is a reasonable spot with some shelter and a water supply and half a quern and a rubbing stone were found there. It has been suggested that their houses were bee-hive shaped huts of stone which, when they were abandoned became just heaps of stone, making a convenient source of supply for later builders, so removing any archaeological evidence of their existence.

The people living on the Cotswolds after about 1800 BC were similar to those who built Stonehenge. Opposite the spot where the Hillesley road leaves the A46, a mile beyond Starveal is a tumulus now surrounded by trees, marked on maps as "Nan Tow's" tump. A story used to be told that one of the earlier Dukes of Beaufort had had a witch buried alive in her house there but it is much more probable that curiosity led someone to dig into the mound where a skeleton was uncovered within a beehive shaped cist. Such burials were found a short distance away in the barrow at Leighterton.

Even in the Roman era the tumuli were 1,500 to 2,000 years old. Barrows and tumuli must have provoked as much interest then as they do now and signs of examinations in those days have been discovered. Also, as with the houses of the people, they made a ready source of stone and a number of them probably disappeared from this cause as well.

More recent discoveries show that there was more widespread trading and travelling than was thought originally. Just as in later centuries adventurers explored the New World and the Far East, so before them people came here from the Mediterranean area for similar reasons and the countryside became covered with their trails.

In July 1968 one sinister event from that period came to light when a trench was being dug across West Littleton Down for laying gas pipes. Just east of Wallsend Lane, the skeletons of two young men of about nineteen were discovered in the trench who appeared to have been thrown into a ditch or pit. Examination showed that one had been speared in the pelvis, while the second youth had a head wound and spear thrusts in the pelvis and spine with the bronze spear heads remaining embedded in the bones. Radio carbon dating showed that their deaths had occurred in about 977 BC. At the last visit these skeletons were on display in the Bristol City Museum & Art Gallery where the marks could be clearly seen.

The people in this area had reached the Iron Age by about 500 BC and were living in scattered farmsteads. For reasons best known to themselves, they built a rectangular area of earthworks covering about eleven acres on the hill between Little and Old Sodbury consisting of a series of mounds and ditches.

Iron Age 'Camp' at Little Sodbury. Photo taken looking from Chipping Sodbury towards Badminton.
Photo courtesy Westair Photography

Although there has never been any scientific exploration it is generally accepted to have been founded in this era so the popular name given it as the 'Roman Camps' is in fact wrong. In his book *Discovering Regional Archaeology. The Cotswolds and Upper Thames*, James Dyer describes the Camp as follows:

This is one of the finest multivallate hill forts on the edge of the Cotswold escarpment. Rectangular in shape it encloses about 11 acres. On the north east and south, are widely spaced double ramparts 100 feet apart. The inner rampart of glacis construction stands 5 feet above the interior of the camp, and 15 feet above the exterior. This bank curves around the north west corner and runs half way along the west side. The silted ditch outside and inner rampart is 26 feet wide and 7 feet deep. The main entrance is mid-way along the east side, where the rampart ends are slightly overlapped. The core of the rampart, composed of fire-reddened limestone, is clearly visible at this point. There are indications that the outer rampart is unfinished, since it is irregular in height, although in places reaching 12 feet high. A wide berm separates it from an equally irregular outer ditch which fades out on the north side. Although the south break, opposite the entrance in the inner rampart is the most logical for access to the camp, there is a possibility that the north break may also have been an entrance gap. The rampart at this point is turned out and there appears to have been a guard chamber on the north side.

It used to be popularly believed that the people of this time were savages who ran around clothed in animal skins and woad but a very different report is given by a Greek traveller of that period who, in talking of them said that vanity was one of their chief characteristics. He said that they smeared their fair hair with chalk wash to make it still brighter and then drew it back tightly from their foreheads so they looked like hobgoblins. He went on to say, "Their nobles let their moustaches grow so long that they hide their mouths and when they eat get entangled in their food. They use amazing colours, brightly dyed shirts with flowing patterns and trousers called breeches. Their appearance is colourful with voices deep sounding and very harsh. They are boastful and threatening but their intellects are keen and they are quick to acquire knowledge."

Evidence was found this century near Brook Street of these people living in the Sodbury area in the shape of an axe. It belonged at one time to the late Murray Dowding, a local resident and photographer with keen historical interest but where it is now is not known.

During the last century BC the greater part of what is now Gloucestershire belonged to a section of the Celts known as the Dobunni. They were highly civilised and had a settlement at Bagenden, near Cirencester. They minted coins of gold and silver, gold specimens of about the size of a penny, called 'Staters' bearing the name Corio having been found at Yatton Keynell and Kingswood, Bristol.

While the brief visits to England by Julius Caesar in 55 and 54 BC would not have caused much of a stir this side of the country, the full-scale invasion by the Romans in 43 AD most certainly did. Unfortunately, those parts of the history by Tacitus which covered the over-running of our area have not survived. It used to be said that the Roman army made use of Little Sodbury Camp and the rectangular shape lent support to this theory but more recently Professors Graham Webster and D.R. Dudley published a book, *The Roman Conquest of Britain*, in which they say that the Roman occupation of the site was only temporary if it happened at all. Local Celtic resistance soon ended and it was not long before the Romans had conquered the land as far as the southern reaches of the Severn.

The Roman legions consisted of many people from other areas than Italy so the number of newcomers who were actually Romans was relatively small. The majority of the native people remained Celtic despite some intermarrying but side by side with those who still insisted in living in the traditional way there were those, more prosperous, who copied the Roman life style.

The Roman occupation from 43 AD until 410 AD was one of the longest periods of peace enjoyed by our area. If they had come at the time of the Spanish Armada instead, they would only have finally left at about the time of the Second World War. During the centuries they were here, great advances were made in the methods of agriculture bringing into cultivation many previously untouched areas. Woods were cleared or much reduced in size, partly by the demand for fuel which was needed in large quantities for heating, and cooking required charcoal.

The locals learned Roman customs and on retirement Legion personnel were given grants of land which became small farmsteads, villages and large towns, examples of which are Bath (Aqua Sulis), Gloucester (Glevum), Cirencester (Corinium) with a port at Sea Mills (Abonae). There were other sites at Kingscote, Easton Grey and Hall End, Wickwar whose Roman names are not known. Many of the Roman officials and settlers lived in comfortable 'villas' which often included central heating, while acting as the headquarters of an estate, provided accommodation for slaves and animals as well. There were also smaller farmhouses which, together with houses in the new towns, provided homes for the Romanised Celts. How the people occupied their leisure time can be seen by visiting Bath and the ruins of the amphitheatre at Caerleon. A map published by the Ordnance Survey of Roman Britain contains a great deal of information in addition to the maps and is well worth buying.

Usually the first sign of a new site is the discovery of a beautiful pavement made up of thousands of small square stones called 'tesseri'. The Saxons called them 'Chessels' and the name often was preserved in the names of fields. When it was realised that two fields of that name existed at Old Sodbury investigations were carried out but unfortunately these failed to produce anything.

As today, all these places needed a road system and there must have been many roads criss-crossing the area. The main artery, the Fosse

The Three Sodburys – An Introduction

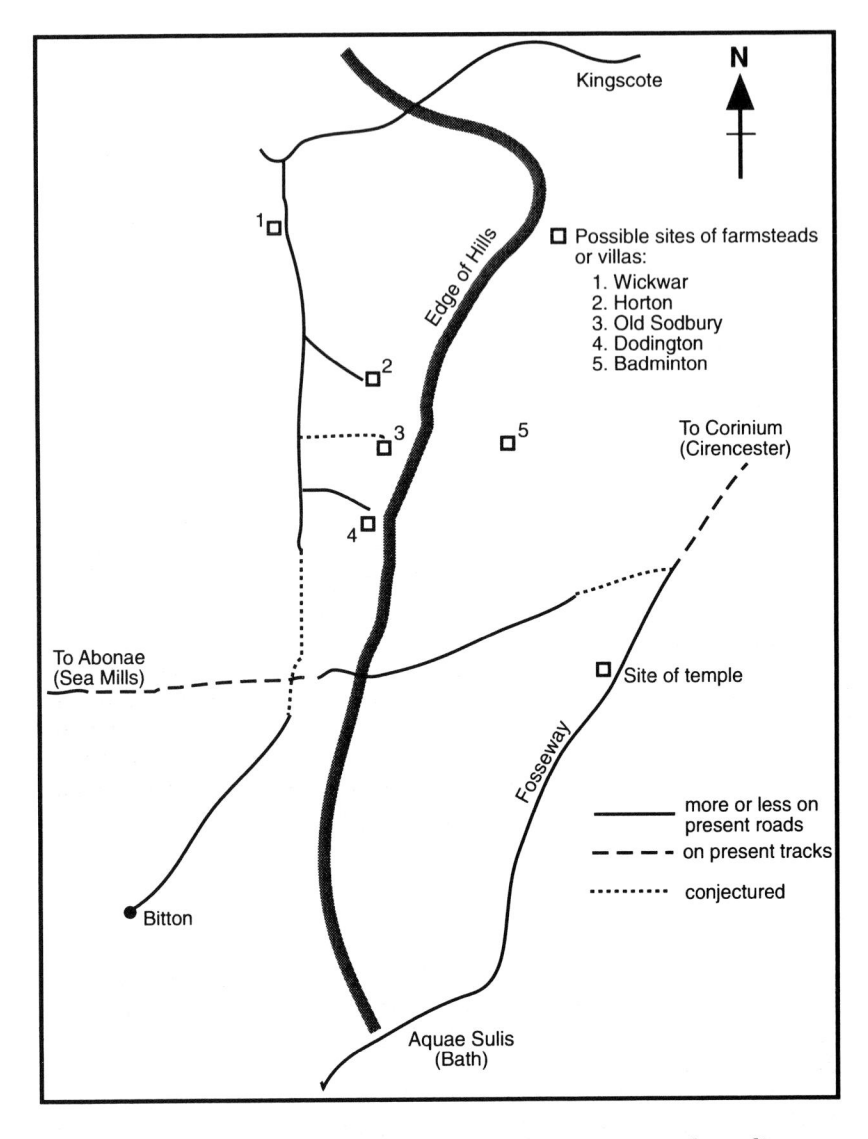

Map legend:
- Possible sites of farmsteads or villas:
  1. Wickwar
  2. Horton
  3. Old Sodbury
  4. Dodington
  5. Badminton

- To Corinium (Cirencester)
- To Abonae (Sea Mills)
- Site of temple
- Kingscote
- Edge of Hills
- Fosseway
- Bitton
- Aquae Sulis (Bath)

- ——— more or less on present roads
- – – – on present tracks
- .... conjectured

Way or Akerman Street ran from Bath to Cirencester a short distance to the east and there would have been another main road between Bath and Sea Mills with yet another from Bath across country to a ferry over the Severn leading to Caerwent and Caerleon. Possible remains of this can be seen between the top of the hill at Westerleigh and Hinton and traces are said to have been found at Hall End, Wickwar. There were almost certainly a number of minor roads which perhaps became some of our modern lanes. A sketch of the nearest sites together with the probable road system is shown on the previous page.

Once this area had been occupied and had settled down, it seems to have become a peaceful backwater with few traces left of their lives.

Leland, when writing in the 1540s, described how cremated remains of the period were found in a glass container at Dodington. A coin was found while renovation work was being carried out around 1820 on the site of what is now the Cross Hands Hotel. In his *Memoirs of Bristol*, the Rev. Samuel Sayer in 1821 described the coin as roughly one and a half inches in diameter. The official description is:

Billion (low grade metal covered with a silver wash) Antoninianus of Marius proclaimed Emperor in Gaul AD 267. Obverse IMP. C. MARIUS. P.F. AVG. with radiate draped bust. Reverse CONCORDIA MILITUM with two right hands clasped.

The building, which was now an Inn, was called the Cross Hands and the find was commemorated on the sign which showed a pair of clasped hands and the inscription CAUIS MARIUS IMPERATOR BC 102 CONCORDIA MILITUM. The date, of course was wrong as the official description above shows.

During ploughing operations early in the present century at Grickstone Farm, a large stone was dug up and thrown away into a local hole. A farmer retrieved it, however, and passed it to his nephew on Springfield Farm, Horton where it is now preserved. From its shape it could have been an altar. It is one foot eight inches wide, two feet five inches long and several inches thick. The surface is damaged but the remaining inscription can be read as:

SILVANIUS.
PAX ROM. IMP.
LEG. II AUG.

There have been some eight occasions in this country where it is known that after a particularly successful hunt an altar to the god Silvanius has been erected as a thanks offering. Probably Roman officers came sometimes to hunt in this area; the Legio II Augustus was stationed at Caerleon just across the Severn for a number of years.

Michael Toghill discovered some pottery shards in Wilson and Turner's quarry on the road to Wickwar in August 1953 which he showed to the late Murray Dowding. He in turn contacted the City of Bristol Museum and after examining them, the conclusion was reached that the remains were Samian ware of the Roman period and that there might have been a settlement or villa in the vicinity. Further research on the site was not possible due to the quarry being extended, so destroying it.

A large number of Roman coins and other remains were found at Hall End Farm between Yate and Wickwar whilst quarrying celestine. It is possible that the site was an inn on a road from Bath to the ferry at Aust and other settlements across the Severn.

Christianity finally came to Britain and like everywhere else in the Roman Empire, believers were at first persecuted and martyred. In 313 AD, however, Christianity was made the official religion. The underground organisation that must have existed must have been strong because one year later no fewer than three British bishops attended the Council of Arles.

Raids on Britain by the Saxons and Picts had been going on for a number of years until in 367 AD they attacked in strength and defeated the defending forces. They were driven out again but Rome itself was under attack. When, in 406 AD, a usurper named Constantine took an army from Britain to fight on the continent the defending forces left were very small. Only a few facts have survived from this troubled period of English history, known popularly and appropriately as the 'Dark Ages'. Over the next century the English inhabitants managed to retain some independence in some areas of the country but by about 500 AD the situation was grave. At about this time a leader named Ambrosius Aurelianus arose to rally the native population and under him, or some other competent leader, they won a number of battles which culminated in an overwhelming victory at Mount Baden in about 518 AD.

A gleam of light comes from the writings of a monk called Gildas, who wrote about 530–540 AD and to whom Bede, who wrote his *Ecclesiastical History* around 730 AD, refers. According to him the south of England was by now split down the centre, into two roughly equal parts. The eastern part had been conquered by the invaders, now called English, while the western part, including Wales, was still held by the original Celts, now called the British, who appear to have reverted to a pre-Roman way of life with scattered farmsteads and small settlements rather than cities and towns and our area, in 547 AD had become one of five petty kingdoms. Bede, in his history says of this period:

The Britons, being for a time delivered from foreign invasions, wasted themselves by civil wars, and then gave themselves up to more heinous crimes.

It was of the 'heinous crimes' and in particular of 'backsliding' that Gildas complained indicating that up to then Christianity had still survived.

Those responsible for spreading Christianity gave a new Christian look and meaning to some pagan festivals, simply superseding them rather than confronting them, as Christmas and Easter demonstrate. It is thought that previous British beliefs had been centred mainly on the Druids with their sacred groves and an emphasis on oak trees. It is possible that the Christians substituted a sacred area for these which was surrounded by a circular ditch and earth or stone boundary wall. This area then became the cemetery and there was probably a hut as well housing one or more of the priests who circulated among the farmsteads. The presence of the yew tree in so many churchyards to-day may have been yet another attempt to suppress the old beliefs by providing a substitute for the previously sacred oak.

It is reasonable to assume with no evidence to the contrary that this area was no different from anywhere else with a number of scattered farmsteads in an area perhaps as large as two or three present day parishes and a central sacred area.

Although the Christian faith as practised by these people was fundamentally the same as that practised on the Continent there had developed two differences which were to give rise to a great deal of controversy later. These related to the form of the tonsure and the date for the observance of Easter.

CHAPTER TWO

SAXON TIMES, 577 AD – 1066 AD.

In this country we are fortunate in having the Anglo-Saxon Chronicle which records events for many centuries starting with Advent. It should be remembered, however, that the existing copies date from the ninth century. Two entries read as follows:

    AD 571   Cuthwulf fought with the Brit-Welsh at Bedcanford and took four townships, Lygeanburg and Ægelesburg, Benesington and Egonesham and the same year he died.

    AD 577   Cuthwine and Ceawlin fought with Britons and slew three kings, Commail and Condidan and Farinmael at the place called Deorham, and they took three 'chesters', Gleawanceaster and Cirencester and Bathanceaster.

In 577, having consolidated their gains and replaced Cuthwulf, the Saxons began to drive a wedge between two of their opponents and the third at Bathanceaster by advancing along a road linking the former Roman town at Bitton to the Fosseway some twelve miles to the north. Realising what the Saxons were up to, the combined Britons made a stand at the point where the road ascends the hill at Dyrham. It is believed by many that the ensuing battle took place at the existing 'Bury' or camp at Hinton which is about three-quarters of a mile west of the Tolldown Inn where the road from Pucklechurch to Christian Malford crosses the A46. Strangely, there is no record of any skeletons or other remains being found as one might expect at such a site.

    In 1936 a Mr. B. Grundy wrote a book called *Saxon Charters and Field Names in Gloucestershire* and on page 95 he deals with the boundaries of a grant of five hides at Æsctum (Cold Ashton) to Bath Abbey by King Athelstan, in 931 AD. He describes as a ridgeway the minor road which now links the A46 with Tog Hill and Lansdown. For the sake of clarity he numbers certain points of which 18, 19 and 20 are of interest:

No.18 is 'the loam pit'.

No.19 is 'From the pit east to the Heathen Burial Places' (the position is given).

No.20 'Then from the Heathen Burial Places to the Salt Carriers Path' i.e. the Ridgeway.

Saxon Charters quite often use heathen burial places as landmarks which appear to imply a burial place distinct from barrows and lows. What the term means is uncertain as they are not associated with any surviving tumuli but it may apply to a Saxon cemetery from when they were still pagans. It is possible that the 'fallen' from the Battle of Dyrham were buried here as it lies roughly a mile or so north from what is now the picnic site at Tog Hill and with no further evidence currently available, this may be the only clue to the true site of the encounter.

Despite their foresight the Britons were very badly defeated and shortly afterwards the Severn became the new eastern boundary of the British (Welsh).

Although originally called West Saxons the conquerors soon became known as Hwicci with territory covering a large part of what is now Gloucestershire and Worcestershire. Perhaps locally their boundary was approximately that of the modern boundary between Gloucestershire and Wiltshire running near Rodmarton, Didmarton, Tormarton and Marshfield. The "mar" in each case comes from a Saxon word meaning a place on, or near, a boundary. The "ton" or "tan", sometimes ending in 'e'. was the name of a homestead or settlement.

It is the phonetic version of a place name that matters so before trying to guess at the origin it is essential to find the earliest example known and to try to pronounce it remembering that it could have been written down by someone not entirely familiar with the tongue in which it was spoken. So returning to Didmarton and Tormarton, these appear in records as follows:

972 Dydimeretun; 1086 Dedmertone; 1200 Dudemerton; 1220 Dodimarton; and 1086 Tormentone; 1183 Tormertona; 1209 Tormerton. It is reasonable to assume that both names are derived from the name of a person or a feature which has been applied to a settlement or farmstead with the extra information that it is on the boundary. Other "tons" in the locality are Codrington (1318 Cuderintuna), Dodington, Horton and maybe Gricks/ton.

There is a Welsh word similar in sound to 'Grick' which means a stone. If it is remembered that the upright stones at the Grickston barrow were still in place, perhaps, at that time then the name would be appropriate.

In his writings, Bede said that the Hwicci were very early converts to

Christianity and bearing in mind how close was Wales, the refuge of the British, and that there must have been Britons still living among them, it is reasonable to assume that the Hwicci would adopt the British version rather than the more orthodox version. Something such as that is needed to explain the following, related by Bede regarding St. Augustine in 603 AD.

> *In the meantime, Augustine, with the assistance of King Ethelbert, drew together to a conference the bishops, or doctors of the next province of the Britons, at a place which is to this day called Augustine's Ac, that is Augustine's Oak, on the borders of the Hwicci and West Saxons; and began by brotherly admonitions to persuade them, that preserving Catholic unity with him, they should undertake the common labour of preaching the gospel to the Gentiles. For they did not keep Easter Sunday at the proper time, but from the fourteenth to the twentieth moon; which computation is contained in a revolution of eighty-four years. Besides, they did several other things which were against the unity of the church.*

Both this meeting and a later one achieved nothing and the division continued. The meeting taking place on the boundary between the Hwicci and the West Saxons rather than on the boundary between the Hwicci and the Brit-Welsh supports the view that the Hwicci were already converted to Christianity.

Hwicci history is complicated, as is all our history of the seventh century. Although the differences between the British and Roman churches may seem minor to us now, at the time they caused a great deal of bitterness. It was finally sorted out by King Oswy who summoned a representative from each side to plead before him at Whitby in 664. The two contenders eventually appealed to their respective saints, the British to St. John and the Roman to St. Peter. The King in deciding in favour of the Roman beliefs quoted his reason for so doing, the story that St. Peter had been given the keys of the Kingdom of Heaven. The influence of the British church from then on faded rapidly until it was practised only in Wales.

In 680 Bishop Bosel was installed at Worcester with his See the territory of the Hwicci. One of his successors, Ecqwine (693–717), granted some land to a man called Eanulf to found a monastery at 'Geate'. Rather than an imposing stone building, the monastery was probably timber built and used to give accommodation for Eanulf and a small number of priests.

What is clearly on record is the name of a man holding an estate in our neighbourhood at least as early as 717, if not earlier. It is reasonable to

Saxon Times, 577 AD – 1066 AD

assume that the monastery would have had other people living nearby. Its foundation is of further interest having regard to the highlighted part of the following extract from Bede.

> The Picts also at this time are at peace with the English nation, and rejoice in being united in peace and truth with the whole Catholic church. The Scots that inhabit Britain, satisfied with their own territories, meditate no hostilities against the nation of the English. The Britons, though they, for the most part, through innate hatred, are adverse to the English nation, and wrongfully, and from wicked custom oppose the appointed Easter of the whole Catholic church; yet, from both the divine and human power withstanding them can in no way prevail as they desire; for though in part they are their own masters, yet elsewhere they are also brought under subjection to the English. Such being the peaceable and calm disposition of the times, many of the Northumbrians, as well as the nobility as private persons, laying aside their weapons, **rather incline to dedicate themselves and their children to the tonsure and monastic vows,** than to martial discipline. What will be the end thereof the next age will show. This is for the present state of all Britain in the year since the coming of the English into Britain about 285, but in the 731st year of the incarnation of our Lord, etc....

When Bede wrote the above in 731 AD, a considerable part of the Midlands and the South of Britain made up the kingdoms of Mercia and Wessex. King Ethelwald of Mercia overran Wessex in the same year and although he had some problems to start with he eventually stabilised the situation and was king of both when he died and was succeeded by Offa in 757.

During a part of both these reigns, from 743 to 775, Milred was Bishop of Worcester. and he granted some land to Eanbald at Sopanbyrg, or at least in the area that was to be known by that name a century later. There was a proviso that Eanbald and his successors must be in holy orders or the land would revert to the church. Eanbald subsequently granted the land to Eastmund on the same conditions but after Eastmund's death the conditions were ignored. This probably happened in the time of Bishop Heathwred (822–848) because Eastmund Presbyter signed the settlement of the dispute between Worcester and Berkeley relating to the monastery at Westbury in November 824. The Bishops had considerable tracts of land at their disposal because at that time it was the recognised system that a king gave thanks for a victory by giving lands to the church. Since Bishop Milred, who granted the lands, died in 775, it follows that by that date there appeared to be two estates in our immediate area, one at Geate (Yate) held by Eanulf and another at Sopanbyrg held initially by Eanbald.

At the beginning of the ninth century the countryside locally was divided into farmsteads owned and worked by the 'Ceorl', under whom every community took care of its own peace and justice. Some farmsteads were grouped together in a 'ton', while other separate ones were known as 'hams' which were attached to a 'ham/stead' or chief farm. It is believed that there were two Saxon words, 'ham' a settlement and 'hamm' a water meadow, so a modern name ending in 'ham' could refer to either. Perhaps Brins/ham and Ham/(p)stead next to the Sodbury to Wickwar road are survivors from then. The practice of combining a number of 'tons' and 'hamsteads' into a 'Hundred' is thought to have begun about then. How the size of a hundred was decided is still a matter of controversy.

As well as the farmsteads there were areas of waste land on which all free men held certain rights such as feeding their swine on the beech mast. The unit of land measurement was the hide, now generally accepted as 120 acres. Large ploughs were pulled by four or eight oxen to cultivate heavy land after the trees and scrub had been cleared. An example of the typical produce from a farm is shown in the following:

Two tuns of clear ale, one cumb of mild ale, one cumb full of British ale, seven oxen, six wethers, forty cheeses, thirty ambers of rye corn, four ambers of meal, and six lang pero (the meaning of the latter is unknown).

This represents the elementary form of annual taxation known as the "King's Feorm" which was due from a Westbury upon Trym farm of 60 hides and was supposed to represent sufficient supplies to keep the king and his retinue for twenty-four hours. Twenty-five years earlier King Ine of Wessex expected from a ten hide estate in his realm:

Ten vats of honey, three hundred loaves, twelve ambers of British ale, thirty ambers of clear ale, two full grown oxen or ten wethers, ten geese, twenty hens, ten cheeses, an amber full of butter, five salmon, twenty pounds weight of fodder and one hundred eels .

The English farmers who produced these contributions on top of their own necessary food worked hard and long, most of them in the places where they were born. Generally speaking villages were self-supporting with salt and iron being the only two main imports. The annual round of work was interrupted only when war or some other calamity affected the neighbourhood. Wheat and rye was sown in the autumn and oats and barley in the spring. The harvested grain, dried and then winnowed, was ground by the women or at the primitive water mill. Lean cattle fed on the common pasture and struggled to survive the winter. Beech mast

Saxon Times, 577 AD – 1066 AD

from the local large wooded areas helped to feed herds of pigs. Wood was needed for fires, buildings and tools, and the extra clearings so created increased the amount of land available for cultivating year by year.

These people lived simply in shacks of wattle and daub with earth floors. The same roof often covered the cow shed. The only artificial light was provided by the fire around which they slept, or perhaps a rushlight. Their clothes were made from rough wool or goat's hair and their food was vegetable broth and brown bread with bacon, beans, milk (sheep or goat), cabbage and onions as and when it was available. Honey was used for sweetening from which they also made mead to drink as a change from small ale brewed from barley. During the summer they ate a variety of boiled meat and game and salted down meat in the autumn ready for the winter.

The large land owners and others who were above the bare subsistence level, lived in wooden houses shaped like an inverted boat. These had a fire trench in the kitchen area, rough dining tables and partitions at each end giving a certain amount of privacy. Considering the building materials and construction used, it is not surprising that there are so few examples of Saxon houses or villages remaining.

Mercia, in which our area lay, and Wessex remained as separate kingdoms until in the 850s Mercia was ruled by Burgred, the son-in-law of Ethelwulf, who was King of Wessex. These and the other kingdoms that formed England were reasonably prosperous to the point that they attracted the attention of the Danes who began to raid the island each summer. Originally they plundered and then left again but later attacks lasted longer and they began then to stay for the winter. Mercia suffered as badly as the other kingdoms.

Although Mercia fought back, in 865 Burgred was forced to buy peace with the Danes. He abdicated in 875 and went on a pilgrimage to Rome. His successor was Ceolwulf II, a Danish puppet, who allowed the Danes to take over South Gloucestershire. The only trace of their occupation locally is the word 'Riding', used in a similar way to the Ridings of Yorkshire.

Within a few years King Alfred came to the Wessex throne. Wessex had managed to maintain some measure of independence and Alfred proved to be a good leader. He had varying success in battle and a few encounters ended in stalemate one of which was near Wareham. From this encounter the Danes retreated to Exeter and then came north to join the Danes in Mercia. These must have been dark and uncertain days for the people living at Geate and Sopanbyrg. Mothers had no need to invent bogie men with which to threaten their children; the real live Danes were always liable to be just around the corner!

In the mid-winter of 878, marching from Gloucester, it is said over snow, the invaders brought off a master stroke, catching Alfred by surprise at Chippenham. He was forced to fly for safety to Athelney in the middle of the Somerset wetlands where other Saxon leaders and their men joined him. There Alfred began to rebuild his forces and a landing party of Danes from Wales was wiped out. Eventually Alfred headed a considerable army which inflicted an outstanding defeat on the Danes at Edington from which they retreated first to Cirencester and then in 879 further eastward again.

In 886 Alfred was accepted as the overlord of Mercia which was now ruled on his behalf by Ethelred who married his daughter Ethelflaed. During the brief lull which now followed in his fight with the Danes, Alfred did all he could to encourage scholarship and learning in his kingdom. The respite also gave Bishop Waerfrith of Worcester the chance to sort out something which had been upsetting successive Bishops for half a century. Originally, it will be remembered, lands at Sopanbyrg had been granted to Eanbald who on his death passed them on to Eastmund. On Eastmund's death in 824, however, the condition that the occupier should be in Holy Orders had been ignored.

In 888 the Bishop brought his complaint that the land at Sopanbyrg was occupied by three laymen, Eadnoth, Aelfred and Aelstan, to a Witan at Droitwich and it was ruled that one of them, or one of their family, must take holy orders . Nobody suitable for ordination could be found, however, and a compromise was reached by which Eadnoth gave a large down payment to the Bishop and agreed to pay an annual rent for which his occupancy of the land was confirmed.

The Danes continued to be a menace and before Alfred died he established Garrison towns, of which Bath and Cricklade were local examples, with each settlement in the protected area providing men, weapons and armour according to its size.

In 899 Alfred was succeeded by his son Edward and Ethelred continued to rule the Mercians on his behalf until he died in 911 when his widow and daughter of Alfred, Ethelflaed, took on his duties. She carried them out for seven years so well that she is remembered in history as 'The Lady of the Mercians'. Traditionally she is said to have some connection with Sopanbyrg but nothing has so far come to light in support of this. She was responsible, however, for founding Pershore Abbey whose Abbot later in that century held some of the land that is now Hawkesbury.

When Ethelflaed died in 918, Edward absorbed Mercia into Wessex and his kingdom was extended still further at about this time when a number of Welsh princes submitted to his rule. Athelstan succeeded him in 924 and is commemorated in Malmesbury Abbey where he had a large number of connections.

Saxon Times, 577 AD – 1066 AD

Athelstan was succeeded by his son Edmund I in 940, who came to an untimely end in 946 when he was fatally wounded helping his steward during a brawl at a feast at Pucklechurch in a hunting lodge, popularly believed to have been at the rear of what is now the Star Inn.

Edmund I, was followed in turn by Edred 946; Edwy 955; Edgar the peaceable who was crowned as the first King of all England in 958; Edward (the Martyr) 975 and Ethelred (the Unready) 979.

They all had trouble with the Danes who by now were not content with simply raiding and were out to conquer England. The Danish King Sweyn succeeded in taking over the country in 1013, but died during the following year. His son Canute was elected as King by the Danes, but Ethelred re-asserted himself for two years preventing Canute from taking the English Crown. Ethelred was succeeded by his son Edmund Ironside who was forced eventually to divide the kingdom with Canute. This only lasted for seven months, however, because Edmund died in 1017 and Canute became sole ruler.

Gloucestershire first appears in records under that name in somewhere about 1008 to 1017. At some time in the previous century the old kingdom of Mercia had been divided into shires for taxation purposes on boundaries which were probably similar to those prior to the formation of Avon in 1974. Marshfield, Badminton and Didmarton were on the old boundary between Mercia and Wessex and this is now the dividing line between Avon (originally Somerset), Gloucestershire and Wiltshire.

The Shire Stones in Marshfield on the common three counties boundary. A Murray Dowding photograph showing Mrs. Dowding and Murray Dowding's motorcycle.

The Three Sodburys – An Introduction

Towards the end of Canute's reign a young man called Wulfstan came to Southstoke (now Hawkesbury) as rector. He was later to be canonised. He would thus have known Sopanbyrg and Bristol which by now was a prosperous port although not known by that name as yet.

In part, Bristol's prosperity was based on a diabolical trade in slaves who were shipped from there to Ireland to a supply depot operated by the Danes and covering most of Europe. In later life Wulfstan vigorously opposed this evil trade. It is thought that around this time 50,000 people lived in Gloucestershire and of these, one in four were slaves compared with one in ten elsewhere in the country. The slave population was made up from prisoners taken in the wars, law breakers and children sold into slavery by their parents. Parents had the right to sell their children once they had reached the age of seven. Anyone over thirteen could sell themselves and this happened frequently in times of famine. The laws regarding slaves were revised from time to time, one example being that no Christian could be sold to a pagan although ways were found to get around this. Punishments for misdemeanours against anyone other than their owners were very severe. If a male slave was convicted of theft a number of his fellow slaves were ordered to stone him to death, each of them having to hit him three times or get three whippings. Female offenders were burned to death with her fellow slaves having to provide three billets of wood each or get three whippings. Some of them did achieve their freedom, however, which was granted with appropriate ceremony.

At this time the English were among the most civilised people in Western Europe, famous for their scholarship and workmanship of various kinds. The whole country was well organised with villages grouped into 'Hundreds' in which the inhabitants were responsible for each other's behaviour. There were Hundred Courts, Shire Courts and over all the Witan in which bishops sat with the Earldormen.

Canute was followed by Harold I (1035–1040) and then Hardicanute (1040–1042). The old Saxon line then re-emerged in Edward the Confessor who had been brought up in Normandy and so both in speech and customs was a Norman. Not surprisingly, therefore, Edward felt that he wanted to have a representative in Normandy. One of these was Brictric, the son of Algar and grandson of Leofric, a young nobleman of high standing who at some time held a number of large estates totalling some 75 hides. While his home territory was Tewkesbury, his estates included Sopeberie in the hundred of Ederstan in the county of Gloucestershire. He was well known both in England and Normandy and it was there that he met a young lady called Matilda, the daughter of Count Baldwin, who, it is said, fell in love with him. Unfortunately Brictric did not fall for her in return and so he won the undying hatred of a lady who later was to become Queen as the consort of William I. She took her revenge after the Battle of Hastings by imprisoning him at Winchester and seizing his lands.

There was constant bickering between Edward during his reign and Earl Godwin, who was the father of several warlike sons, to the point where there was nearly a battle between them more than once. Eventually, when Edward died in 1066 Harold Godwin ascended the throne as Harold II. He was not allowed to enjoy his inheritance for long, however, as his banished brother Tostig arrived near York with an army of Norwegians and defeated the local Earls. Harold rushed to help them and won an overwhelming victory at the Battle of Stamford Bridge, only to receive terrible news a day or so later. William, Duke of Normandy, believed, rightly or wrongly, that it had been Edward the Confessor's intention that he should inherit the throne of England. On Edward's death, he immediately began gathering together an army of adventurers and then invaded the south coast. After a series of forced marches, Harold waited for him at Hastings, where Battle Abbey now stands but many of the Saxons did not support him which contributed to his defeat and death.

England was now in Norman hands and William divided the country up among his noblemen. William, Duke of Normandy, became William the Conqueror, the first English king of that name.

CHAPTER THREE

THE ARRIVAL OF THE NORMANS

Very little is known about the first twenty years of William's rule except that the adventurers who had joined him for the conquest received their rewards in lands taken over from the Saxons of whom few survived as rich men.

Brictric lost his lands in Sopeberie, the new owner being William's Queen, Matilda, daughter of Count Baldwin, the same lady Brictric had rejected some years before. Her revenge was complete. According to a Tewkesbury monk Brictric was dispossessed and thrown into prison where he died. Another version, however, says he survived his captivity to be released when Matilda died.

One Saxon who appeared to be unaffected by the changes was Wulfstan. He had been Rector of Hawkesbury and by 1066 was the Bishop of Worcester, a position he kept despite attempts to remove him. One such attempt was made by Lanfrac, the Archbishop of Canterbury, who regarded Wulfstan as a severe thorn in the flesh, one reason being because Wulfstan refused to speak the Norman tongue. The Archbishop persuaded the King to unfrock Wulfstan and he was summoned to Westminster Abbey. Realising what was afoot Wulfstan marched across Edward the Confessor's tomb, plunged his staff into a crack in the stonework and threw his discarded vestments on to it saying, "If I am to be stripped of my office I will return the honours to him who gave them to me."

A stunned silence followed while unsuccessful attempts were made to pull the staff out of the crack into which it had been jammed. The failure to release it so impressed William he allowed Wulfstan to continue in office. It was perhaps because Wulfstan remained in favour with William that slavery was abolished throughout the kingdom.

William re-organised how the country was run, keeping a fifth of the land for himself and his family and giving a quarter to the church. The

The Arrival of the Normans

remaining 11/20ths were shared out among his followers as 'fiefs' or 'honours' for which, in return, they had to provide a fixed number of mounted and armoured knights. They in turn, to meet these commitments, divided their land into manors 'enfeoffing' the holders as their vassals. They in their turn spread the load by sub-division until every substantial holding provided a fully trained and equipped knight.

William introduced one law which caused some confusion when it was enacted that four roads in the country were privileged. Anyone who assaulted or killed a person travelling on one of them was guilty of committing a breach of the King's peace. The four roads named were Watling Street, Ermine Street, Fosseway and Icknield Way and later, instead of amending the law when the cover was extended to other roads, their names were changed. It is believed that one such change locally was to the road from Bath to Cirencester, originally in Saxon times Ackerman Street and changed to Fosseway.

Queen Matilda died in 1080 and William gave her lands at Sopeberie to Odo, Count of Champagne and third husband of his sister, Adelaide, under the tenancy of a man called Hunfrid.

While spending Christmas at Gloucester in 1086, William decided to have an inventory made of his English kingdom. This was by no means a new idea as parts of a Saxon 'Tribal Hideage' have survived which, while not fully understood, was intended to achieve the same purpose. William's questionnaire was to be made on oath by the sheriff, all the barons and the whole hundred, the priest, the reeve and six villeins of each village. A record was then to be made showing the name of the manor, who had owned it in King Edward's time, in 1067 and in 1086, the number of hides, ploughs, mills, villeins, cottars, slaves, freemen and sokemen, the area of wood, meadow and pasture, and then an estimate was to be made of the value of the whole estate. The middle date was necessary because of the 'unofficial' movements of title since William's first awards. The record also had to show if the value of the estate could be increased.

The work of gathering and recording the data was carried out by church scribes and it is thanks to their efforts that the results have survived to the present day.

William did not live to see the results but a Saxon Chronicler testified to how thorough they were when he wrote:

> *He caused the survey to be made so narrowly that there was not a single hide or yardland, nor, shameful to relate, was there an ox or a cow or a swine left out, that was not set down in his writing.*

34   *The Three Sodburys – An Introduction*

The next two examples refer to this area:

Brictric, the son of Algar, held Sopeberie in Ederestan hundred. In the time of King Edward there were 10 hides and 4 plow tillages in demesne and 12 villeins with 5 plow tillages, and 4 bordars and 18 servi, and one park and a mill of 5s. rent. The steward hath lately added one mill of 40 den. There is a wood one mile long and one broad. Hunfrid pays for this manor £16. 10. One yard in Wiche belongs to it which paid 25 sextaries of salt. Ursus the sheriff has so oppressed the men that now they cannot pay the salt.

William's personal physician, the Bishop of Lisieux, Gilbert "Maminot", held lands at Rodmarton, Lasborough and Sopeberie which he let to Hugh Maminot, presumably his nephew. It is the item which refers to his holding at Sopeberie which is taken to refer to Little Sodbury. It is thought that before 1066 the lands had been held by a Saxon called Aluuard. The item reads:

5 hides taxed, and two plow tillages in demesne and four villeins and two bordars with two plow tillages. There were four servi and twenty acres of meadow and a little wood. It was worth £8, but is now worth £4.

The clerics doing the survey must have experienced enormous difficulties, not least being those of language and illiteracy. The people giving the information had to remember what conditions applied twenty very confused years before. This was bound to lead to discrepancies in the testimony given, both from honest mistakes and for personal reasons. Finally all the notes made in the field had to be written up into one record and clerical errors are not new.

A summary of the Gloucestershire entries shows there were 363 place names recorded (the modern names have been used) with, among other things:

Four boroughs: Bristol, Gloucester, Tewkesbury, Winchcombe.
Three Castles: Chepstow, Gloucester, Sharpness.
Four markets: Berkeley, Cirencester, Tewkesbury, Thornbury.

There were ten churches with one priest and one hundred and seventy eight mills. Three places, Alvington, Gloucester and Pucklechurch, made renders of kind in iron. Ten places, including Sopeberie, had connections with the Droitwich area from which they obtained supplies of salt.

An explanation of some of the terms used in the Domesday Book, as it came to be called, may help the understanding.

The Arrival of the Normans

Villein This was the villager who was the mainstay of the manor. How rich or poor they were seems to have varied and they had lands and tools leased to them which could not be taken away again without good reason. For rent they paid in kind with labour and produce.

Bordarii This was a lower order of villein, who dwelt, perhaps, on the fringes of the manor.

Servii These were no better than slaves which they probably had been before slavery was abolished.

Hide An area of about 120 acres.

Yardland A quarter of a hide, i.e. 30 acres.

Sextary A medium unit of both dry and wet measure. Thought to equal a Summa, or a Mitta, or two ambers, or a pack horse load which seems most appropriate with regard to the salt mentioned in the quotation for the Sopeberie lands.

It would have been Hunfrid's steward who added the mill which was probably a wooden building with a wheel projecting into a stream and turned by the current. Where the new mill and the park mentioned in the quotation was is not now known.

Ederestan(e) Hundred consisted of the modern parishes of Marshfield, Dodington, Tormarton, West Littleton and Sodbury and later became part of the larger Grumboldston or Grumbold's Ash Hundred which, in turn, was sub-divided into upper and lower sections.

Count Odo continued to hold Soperberie after William's death and the ascension of William Rufus, having also been made Earl of Holderness in Yorkshire, and Earl of Albermarle in Normandy.

He was succeeded by his son Stephen who married Hawise, daughter of Ralph de Mortimer. The marriage produced two sons, both called William, which for record purposes were called 'primogenitus' and 'junioris' and for the purposes of this book will be called 'I' and 'II'. Count Stephen was alive in 1127, so his son, William I, cannot have succeeded him until after that date.

At about this time the family took the name of Crassus, (the Latin for obesity) and this was later changed to the Norman 'le Gros' meaning the same thing. Some members of the family later changed this to 'le Gras' whom members of the Grace family claim as their ancestors.

In the 1130s either Stephen or William Crassus was Lord of the Manor of Sopeburie (Sobburia) with probably a number of people who held their lands of him.

It is not known who held what was to become Little Sodbury. Horton, which had been Todeni's reward for carrying William's banner at

Hastings, had passed through his daughter and son-in-law to the Salisbury Cathedral authorities and it is believed that the Court was being built.

A similar building probably already existed at Sobburi of which the remains could be seen in the 1540s south of Old Sodbury church; but whether the Crassus family actually lived there is not known. There were churches next to Horton Court and Sobburi Court, and there may have been a house and perhaps a church at Little Sobburi.

There must have been a village of some sort in the area but as the houses were probably made of wood or wattle and daub, it is unlikely that any site could be identified even if it had not been built on later.

When in 1100 William Rufus was accidentally killed by a stray arrow in the New Forest, his brother became Henry I. Henry's only son was drowned at sea leaving him only with a daughter, Matilda. During the King's lifetime, the great Barons swore to support her and to make her Queen eventually. When Henry died, however, some of the Barons changed their minds and looked around for an alternative. They chose Henry's nephew, Stephen, who was in fact crowned King. Naturally Matilda disagreed violently with this and some three years after the Coronation in 1135, supported by her half-brother Robert, Earl of Gloucester, began a Civil War. The next nineteen years of terrible strife was described by a chronicler at the time:

> *Every powerful man built his castles and held them against the King and they filled the land full of castles. They cruelly oppressed the wretched people by making them work at these castles, and this state of affairs lasted the nineteen years that Stephen was king, and ever grew worse and worse. They were continually levying an exaction from the towns, which they called 'tenserie' and when the miserable inhabitants had no more to give, then they plundered and burnt all the towns so that you could even walk a whole day's journey without finding a man seated in a town or its lands tilled. Then was corn dear, and flesh, and cheese, and butter, for there was none in the land. Wretched men died of hunger. Some sought alms who at one time had been rich; some fled out of the country. Never was there more misery. The earth bore no corn; you might as well have tilled the sea, for the land was all ruined by such deeds; and it was openly said that Christ and his saints slept.*

Contrary to the description above, some people appeared to find time for normal activities. In 1140 the church at Sobburi (Old Sodbury) was confirmed as belonging to the Abbey at Tewkesbury. Also, in 1142, the Priory at Bradenstoke, near Dauntsey was founded and the first

Cistercian abbey at Kingswood (Wotton) had just become established.

During these years there was some campaigning near to Bath and Bristol which must have had local repercussions as Matilda's followers were based on the castle at Bristol. After a considerable amount of confused fighting Stephen finally won and it was agreed that he should remain king providing that on his death he should be succeeded by Matilda's son Henry.

Henry II came to the throne in December 1154 and with peace restored, William Crassus I, now the main power locally, looked about him and decided to do what other property owners were doing and decreed that a new town should he founded to help in restoring the state of the countryside by providing a focal point for trade. As a side effect, of course, various tolls and charges would also flow into his coffers. For a site he chose a slight rise at the western end of his lands, which could have been where a previous settlement had been destroyed and started work in about 1158.

He was fortunate because two routes crossed at a spot within his Manor where there was also a good supply of water and reasonably dry ground. One route was the ancient Salt Way running roughly north to south along the ridge from the Midlands and the other was the main line of communication between Bristol and Tetbury, Cirencester, Oxford and beyond.

How the latter route reached Sobburi is not known but certainly it left by what is now Hatter's Lane, crossing the brook and then going east towards the hills.

The plan for the new town appears to have been on the grid principle although it was never entirely completed. A visit to Sherston or Wotton under Edge will show that the idea of two parallel main streets linked by burgages in between was not unknown.

Since William Crassus I had died by 1179 his plans must have been put in hand before or in that year. It is from that date a document, translated in 1904 by a Miss Salisbury of the Gloucester Records Office, reads as follows:

To all who shall see or hear the present charter greetings from William Crassus, the elder. Know ye that we have given to our burgesses of Sobburia all the liberties which belong and pertain to the laws of Breteuil. To have and to hold to them and their heirs, freely and quietly, as any very free town which is of the law of Breteuil better and more freely holds or may hold (the same). So that neither we nor our heirs may exact any other thing from the aforesaid burgesses or their heirs except according to the tenur of the charter fore-rehearsed. Furthermore we have given to every one who has a burgage in Sobburia aforesaid licence to

38 *The Three Sodburys – An Introduction*

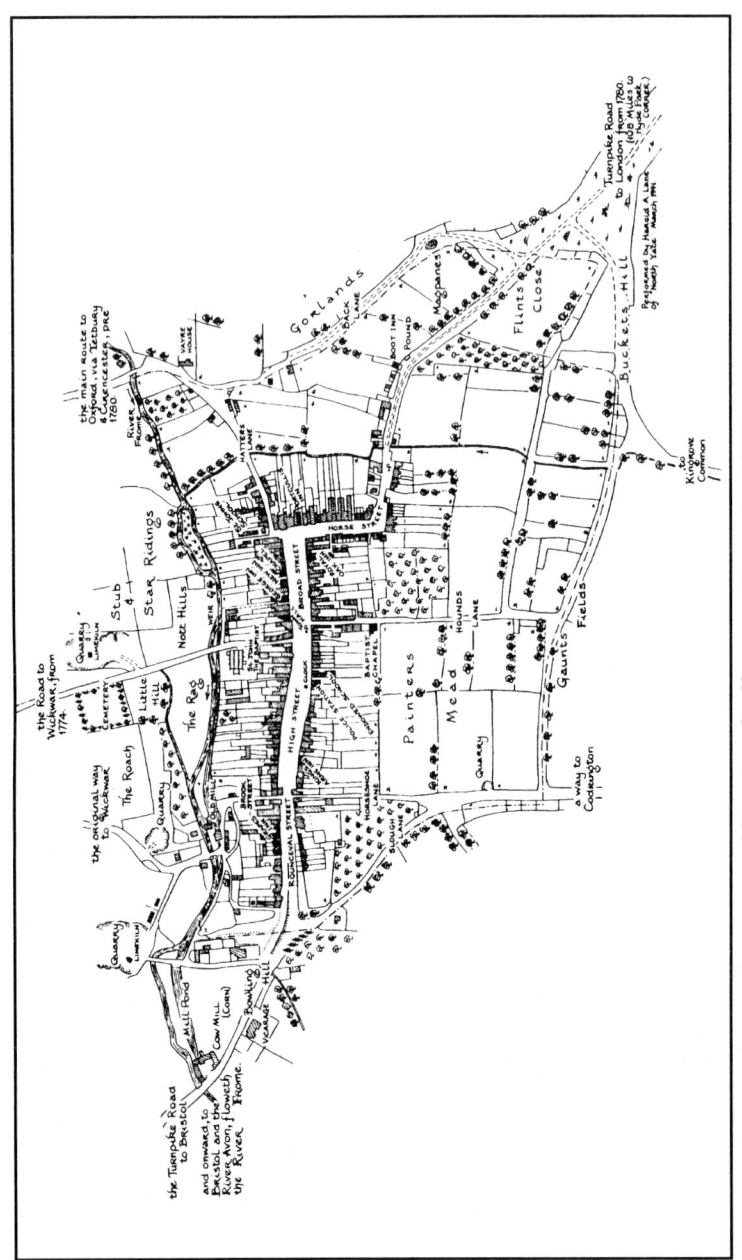

have a cow in our common, freely and quietly to them and their heirs of us and our heirs. These being witnesses. William Marshall, Earl of Pembroke, William de Mandeville, Earl of Essex, etc., as before, Walter chaplain or headman of Sobburia, John de Greinvill, Hugone, the clerk who wrote this charter, and many others.

The often quoted right to have a cow on the common appears in this document but the word 'vaccam' which has been translated here as 'cow' can also mean more generally 'a beast of burden' which is the more likely version as cows had not become as common as they were to do later. It should also be noted that the burgesses were granted the right to run a beast of burden on the common of the manor quite separate from any lands associated with the town.

It was once thought that Sobburia was granted the same liberties as those accorded to the citizens of Bristol by Prince John in 1188 or 1189 and that the founding of the town must thus be after one or other of those years. It is now known that this was not so. Among the testators of William Crassus I's Charter is William de Mandeville whose name also appears at the foot of the document applicable to Preston, thought to date from between 1175 and 1185. Another testator of the Sobburia document was William Marshall, Count of Pembroke who took the surname from his office as Lord Mareschal of England and was also, or

Chipping Sodbury main street in 1989 looking west towards Yate

became, Earl of Chepstow.

To encourage settlers (burgesses as occupiers of some three hundred burgages) William Crassus I stipulated that the town should be governed under what was known as the 'Laws of Breteuil'. Breteuil was a small town in Normandy whose customs formed the basis for the founding of some seventeen new towns in England and Ireland in the twelfth century. The implications of this were only realised after a great deal of research had been carried out by a Miss M. Bateson whose conclusions were published in the English Historical Review at the beginning of this century. The rules are listed in detail as set out in the Custumal of Preston in Appendix A to this book.

After William Crassus I died in 1179 he was succeeded as owner of the manor by his nephew, William Crassus II. This gentleman undertook to go on the Crusade with King Richard but withdrew on health grounds (folklore says it was because he had become too fat). He was convinced, however, that his future lay with Prince John. To start with luck was on the side of the conspirators and Prince John seemed to be winning when Richard was imprisoned in Germany while on his way home. The people of England ransomed Richard, however, and John and his friends were toppled from power and their estates, including Sobburia, were seized by the King's Escheator. The accounts for Sobburia at the time the estates were seized are contained in the Pipe Rolls for 1195. According to the Transactions of the Bristol and Gloucestershire Archaeological Society Volume 59, page 205 they were as follows:

Sobbury £9. 8s. 8d. no details. Again at Sobbury for the half year in 1195 we find three items, Scutage £1, Hidage £1 and auxilium, or aid, £2, presumably taxes in connection with raising the King's ransom, like the tallage on royal demesnes.

Corn from Sobbury sold at £6. 6s. 8d, cows 10s, oxen and cart horses 4s each, sheep 6d (but once only 2¹/₂d), sows 1s, pigs 6d (8d in Henry's reign), ploughs 24s, carts 20s to 24s.

At Sodbury too, pannage (payment for the right to pasture pigs on the acorns) brought in 10s. 2d, passagium caretarum 8s. 6d (this would usually be translated as payment for ferrying carts over a stream, but there is no stream at Sobburi where a ferry would be needed). Sale of small stuff 4s (there was also comprehensive 'Perquisitones' i.e. small profits which at Sobburi brought in no less than £5. 7s. 8d). At this time the new town was part of the Forest of Kingswood forming, with other places, a 'Liberty' bearing its name. It is possible, therefore, that 'passagium caretarum' relates to passage through the forest. The new town had become a successful addition to the manor and was doing very well as a market town.

The Arrival of the Normans

As can be seen from the map of the three Sodburys at the beginning of the book, the new town was an urban centre of one hundred acres within, but separate from the rural remainder. Although modern building schemes have blurred the original boundary lines somewhat, Harry Lane's map of Chipping Sodbury as it was in 1882 on Page 38 show them quite clearly.

King Richard was mortally wounded at the siege of a castle at Chalus and died in April 1199 having held the throne for almost ten years. Prince John then became king but as a result of his misrule was eventually brought to book by his Barons at Runnymede where he was forced to set his seal to the Magna Carta in 1215.

Meanwhile, as he was now on the winning side, Sobburia was restored to William Crassus II and in 1205 he was made Seneschal of Normandy. In 1227 he obtained a confirmation of the Market Charter. He died during the next five or six years and his son, William Crassus III, nephew of Crassus I, succeeded to the manor and the borough.

Crassus III immediately gave the burgesses of Sobburia an undertaking that the privileges conferred by his uncle would continue. To clarify what follows, a part of the Crassus' family tree is shown on the next page. The following is the first part of the document translated by Miss Salisbury:

> *To all who shall see and hear this present writing William Crassus, the eldest son of William Crassus junior, gives greeting. Know ye that we have granted and by this our present deed have confirmed to our Burgesses of Sobburia and their heirs the gifts which William Crassus the elder, our uncle, made to the same, and by his deed confirmed, that is to say, that they shall have and hold all liberties which belong and appertain to the laws of Breteuil to them and their heirs of us and our heirs freely and quietly for ever, in the same manner as any other town which is of the laws of Breteuil better or more freely doth or may hold (the same) and that everyone who hath a burgage or any liberty to a Burgage belonging, in the aforementioned Sobburia may have one vaccam (cow or beast of burden) in our common freely and quietly to himself and his heirs of us and our heirs as the deed of the aforesaid William Crassus, the Elder, our uncle, which they have, thereon witnesseth. We have granted also for us and our heirs to the said Burgesses of Sobburia and their heirs that the courts in the aforesaid Sobburia be held as they were in the times of our ancestors held, and that is on the Saturday only and upon no other day contrary to the will of the aforesaid Burgesses or their heirs without contradiction or impediment. So that neither we nor our heirs at any time may be able to extort or demand*

anything from the aforesaid Burgesses or their heirs contrary to the tenor of this present deed. And the above confirmation, grant and donation we and our heirs will warrant and defend to the said Burgesses and their heirs against (all mortals). And for this confirmation, grant and donation the said Burgesses have given to me four marks of silver in hand paid, And because I am willing that this my grant, donation and warranty shall obtain the force of perpetual firmness and stability we have strengthened this our deed by the apposition of our seal. These being witnesses: Ralph de Wiliton, Roger de Lokinton, John de Saltmarisco, Knights. John de Aketon, William Crassus, junior, Jordano Bissop, William le Cingtelo de Freinton, Stephen de Aketon Turvile, Radulpho le Cu de Parva Sobbiria.

Note: It is only right to point out that in the Latin copy the place name 'Breteuil' looks as much like Bristol as Breteuil, but this is not the case in respect of the earlier charter where it is obviously Breteuil. In both copies the phrase used is "leges de" and Miss Bateson points out that she has not found this to be used in conjunction with Bristol where the phrase usually is "sicut in villa nostra de B" or "sicut civitates de B".

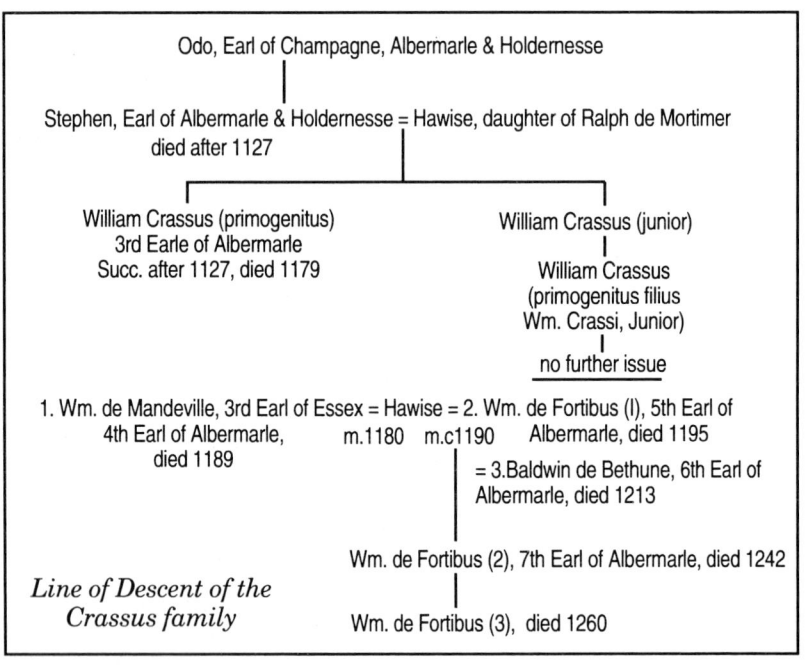

```
                Odo, Earl of Champagne, Albermarle & Holdernesse
                                    |
    Stephen, Earl of Albermarle & Holdernesse = Hawise, daughter of Ralph de Mortimer
              died after 1127                |
                         ┌──────────────────────┴──────────────────┐
         William Crassus (primogenitus)              William Crassus (junior)
             3rd Earle of Albermarle                            |
           Succ. after 1127, died 1179                  William Crassus
                                                      (primogenitus filius
                                                       Wm. Crassi, Junior)
                                                              |
                                                      no further issue

    1. Wm. de Mandeville, 3rd Earl of Essex = Hawise = 2. Wm. de Fortibus (I), 5th Earl of
         4th Earl of Albermarle,        m.1180   m.c1190    Albermarle, died 1195
              died 1189                             |
                                          = 3. Baldwin de Bethune, 6th Earl of
                                               Albermarle, died 1213

                                    Wm. de Fortibus (2), 7th Earl of Albermarle, died 1242
         *Line of Descent of the*                  |
            *Crassus family*        Wm. de Fortibus (3), died 1260
```

The document, unfortunately, is undated and has probably survived several copyings but it is thought that the original could not be later than 1225 and that somewhere about 1214 is likely. Obviously, therefore, by 1225 a town existed which had been established some fifty years earlier complete with burgesses and the usual accessories. It will be noted that those attesting the charter include Radulpho le Cu of Little Sobburia, confirming that this place too already existed. It also describes the beginnings of the 'Ridings'. The following was written by Rudge when he wrote his *History of Gloucestershire* in 1803.

> *The estates called the Stub Riding and Meadow Riding were anciently granted by two lords of the manor, in the reigns of Henry II and John, to the bailiff and bailiff-burgesses for the following purposes: The former consisting of about one hundred acres is granted for summer pastures under certain regulations for sixty-eight cow beasts, to as many persons as have been inhabitants of the town for fourteen years. The latter is divided into eighty-one lots besides two others called the Bailiff's and Hayward pieces. Each of these containing rather more than a statute acre, is held by a leasee for his own life and the life of his widow. Out of these estates the Lord of the Manor receives an annual payment of £5 and the Vicar of Old Sodbury £1. 13s. 4d in lieu of tythes. The bailiff is entitled to 50s. yearly for which, by ancient custom, he provided an ox and two barrels of ale, on St. Stephen's Day for the inhabitants.*

When an acre changed holders an on-site Investiture Ceremony was called which read:

> *The piece of land upon which we are now standing (commonly called an acre), has lately fallen into the possession of the Bailiff and Bailiff-Burgesses of Chipping Sodbury and in pursuance of their direction, I invest you therewith, in delivering to you this twig and turf, to hold the said land for your life and the life of any woman that may be your lawful wife and survive you, as long as you and your wife shall reside in this town. Subject and chargeable with all manner of waste, particularly waste in felling or cutting any tree or trees whatsoever growing on it that may hereafter grow on the said piece of land. And also subject to the present rules and orders of the said Bailiff and Bailiff-Burgesses respecting the grounds called the Ridings, as well of those that may be, from time to time made, relating thereto.*

William Crassus was not the only one making grants. His fellow benefactor was one of the testators to his Charter, Jordano Bissop, who then or later was Lord of the Manor of Little Sobbiria. During his lifetime

he made an agreement as follows:
> THIS INDENTURE shows the agreement between Jordano Bissop of one part and Thomas Hulla, John Wickened, Thomas Mulls, William Watership and all the other burgesses of the town of Sobiry of the other part that is to say that the above mentioned Jordano hath granted it for him and his heirs and assigns to the said Thomas, Thomas, William and all the other burgesses of Sobiry that they shall have and hold common pasture for cattle in my woods named Dymeshed and Norwood in Parva Sobbiria and they shall hold them according to the decree of the freeholders of the foresaid town. To have and to hold for the said Thomas, John, Thomas, William and all of the other burgesses of the town of Sobiry the common pasture in my woods aforesaid to them their heirs and assigns without challenge or disturbance from me the aforesaid Jordano or from my heirs and assigns and I the above mentioned Jordano my heirs and assigns grant the above mentioned common pastures to the aforesaid Thomas, John, Thomas, William and all other burgesses of the town of Sobiry which all people must pledge and support and defend. As a witness of these grants they are here sealed by my hand and seal.

This is a copy several times removed which it is impossible to date, although obviously it must have been during Jordano's lifetime, who was an adult when he witnessed the deed of William Crassus. The concession was later confirmed by Jordano's son who calls himself Lord of Sobiry, presumably meaning Little Sobiry.

At about this time Sobburia again appears in ecclesiastical history. As stated previously, the church at what is now Old Sodbury had been conferred upon the Abbey at Tewkesbury. This had been done by a certain Simon, Bishop of Worcester from 1125 to 1150. This was not approved of by a later Head of the See who, in 1218, bestowed it upon the Benedictine Monastery at Worcester, giving rise to an appeal to Pope Honorius III, who confirmed possession to Tewkesbury in 1221.

Before passing on from the last quoted charter it should be noted that the grantor was William Crassus III and that the testators include what was probably William Crassus IV.

William Crassus III appears in another deed believed to date from 1225 or before, translated from the Latin by Miss Salisbury as follows:
> Know all men present and future that I, William Crassus, eldest son of William Crassus, the younger, lord of Sobburi, have given, granted and by this present charter confirmed to Adam Alba of Sobburi two fields, to wit, Galoneffeld, which contains twenty acres of arable land and Tyrianesinding which contains eight

acres of arable land, and one meadow which is called Rochemed
and contains four acres. To have and to hold the said two fields
with the said four acres of meadow and all their appurtenances
to the said Adam Alba his heirs or assigns, freely, quietly, well
and in peace, by hereditary right for ever, of me, my heirs or
assigns, rendering yearly for the same to me, my heirs or assigns,
one penny at the feast of St Michael for every secular service
exaction or demand. And I (truly) the said William Crassus my
heirs or assigns will warrant, acquit, and for ever defend the
aforesaid fields with the foresaid meadow and all their appurtenances to the aforesaid Adam Alba, his heirs or assigns, for the
aforesaid service against all mortal men and women. But for this
gift, grant, and confirmation of the present charter the said
Adam Alba has given me forty marks of good money and one
palfrey in hand paid. In witness whereof I have affixed my seal
to the present charter. These being witnesses: domino Stephano
archidia (cono), Olivero la Gras, domino Waltero le (Gras),
Reginaldo de Welun, Willelmo de Fromtona, Willelmo .... ?,
Roberto capellano, and many others.

'Archidia' has been interpreted as archdeacon and 'capellano' has become 'chaplain'. Waltero le Gras, is one of the five sons of the Earl of Pembroke where 'le Gras' is the phonetic rendering of the family name 'le Grace'. His brothers were William, Gilbert, Richard and Anselm and one of these may have been misread as Oliver. The translation of a further deed by Miss Salisbury of about the same period is as follows:

To all the faithful in Christ who shall see or hear the present
writing, the lord William Crassus, eldest son of William Crassus
Crassus junior, greeting in the Lord. Know ye that I have
inspected the charters which I made to Adam Alba, whose heir
Robert le Fayre is, in these words.

Know all men present, and future, that I, William Crassus eldest
son of William Crassus junior, have given granted and by this
my present charter confirmed to Adam Alba of Sobburi, half a
virgate of land in the territory of Sobburi with all its appurtenances; and three parts of one acre which lie near the great road,
between the road and the croft which Richard, son of Ralph,
sometime held; and two acres of land in the field which is called
Mershe, to wit those which John, son of Margery, sometime held
in the place of his croft, and those which lie next Holemede; and
one acre of meadow which is called Wrokehememede between the
meadow of Adam Gardner and the meadow of Reginald de
Broke; for which the said Adam Alba, his heirs or assigns, shall

render to me and my heirs or assigns 2s 10d. yearly, to wit at the feast of St. Michael 12 pence, at the feast of the Purification of the Blessed Mary 12 pence, and at the Nativity of the Blessed John the Baptist 10 pence for every secular service, exaction or demand and truly I, William and my heirs, will warrant, acquit and for the aforesaid service for ever defend the said lands with the said meadow and all appurtenances to the said Adam, his heirs and assigns against all men and women. And that this indeed my gift and grant and the confirmation of the Present writing may endure firm and stable for ever I have affixed my seal to the present writing; these being witnesses; John de la Legrave, Ralph le Chamberlain, Richard, the clerc, Henry de Lecrinton, William de Frompton, Roger de Wyke, Andrew de Wappeleyghe, Robert, the chaplain, who wrote this writing, and others.

Which gift, grant and confirmation of the present writing holding verily firm and acceptable, as better and more fully in their charters, with all their appurtenances as in the common of pasture with all manner of beasts, as well horses as oxen, cows, steers, pigs, sheep without number, as in woods, plains, feedings, pastures, waters, and in all other places within the town and without, for me and my heirs or assigns, I grant, confirm and will for ever warrant the same to him and to his heirs or assigns for ever. In witness whereof I have affixed my seal to this present writing of my confirmation. These being witnesses: the lord Stephen, the archdeacon, Lord Oliver le Gras, domino Waltero le Gras (junior), domino Reginaldo de Dalun, Willelmo de Frompthona, Silvestro pincerna, Willelmo de la Legrave, Andrea de Wappelyghe, Ricardo, clerico de Sohburi and many others."

These two deeds do not represent the full total of Adam Alba's acquisitions. There is a third document of about the same date which when translated reads:

Also another charter. Know (all men) present and future that I, William Crassus, eldest son of William Crassus, the younger, have given, granted and by this my present charter confirmed to Adam Alba all that croft by the old ditch, with the ditches, and hedges, and all its appurtenances, to wit, which Richard le Tanyur formerly held of that land which was Richard de Roche's and for which afterwards the said Richard accepted in exchange the land which Roger de Quarreria formerly held; and all that towards my meadow at the head of that croft which lies between the meadow which John de Roache held and that meadow which Walter Gynegove held, according as the bounds and ditches of the aforesaid meadow show. I have also given and granted to the same Adam Alba two acres and a half in my southern field of Sobburi, to wit, those which lie between that land which Hugh Sercherons held, and extend to the road which leads to Estgrave coming from le Legrave. To have and to hold all the aforesaid to the said Adam Alba and his heirs and assigns for ever, freely and quietly, wholly and honourably, well and in peace, with all their appurtenances and liberties and free customs which may come to the said tenements. And the aforesaid Adam Alba and his heirs and assigns may enclose and hold in defence the said croft and the aforesaid meadow on all days of the year for ever; paying therefor yearly to me and my heirs five pounds of wax or 30 pence at five terms, to wit, at the Conception of the Blessed Mary one pound of wax or six pence, at the Purification of the same one pound of wax or six pence, at the Annunciation one pound of wax or six pence, at the Assumption one pound of wax or six pence, at the Nativity one pound of wax or six pence for all services and every secular demand pertaining to me or my heirs. I, truly, and my heirs will warrant all the aforesaid tenements with all the aforenamed appurtenances and liberties to the said Adam Alba and his heirs or assigns for the aforesaid service against all mortal men for ever, and will acquit them of all services which may ever arise for the same. And that this my gift and grant may remain firm and stable for ever, I have affixed my seal to this writing.

(The testators are the same as on the previous document.)

As will become apparent later, these deeds concern properties which later belonged to the Town or the Church. Copies of them, in Latin, appear in the Charity Commissioners Report, No. 48234, of the 22nd March 1897.

The properties involved are listed again below for reference purposes:

1.	Galoneffeld	20 acres	arable
2.	Tyrianesinding	8 acres	arable
3.	Rochemed	4 acres	meadow
4.	Mershe	2 acres in	
5.	Wrokehemede	1 acre	
6.	Half a virgate	15 acres	
7.	Near the Great Road	3/4 acre	
8.	Croft by the old ditch		
9.	Meadow		
10.	Land in the South Field of Sobburi	2½ acres	extending to the road which leads from Legrave to Estgrave .

It is reasonable to assume that Galoneffeld is the origin of Gaunt's Field. 'Gallina' is the Latin for 'hen' and 'Gallus' was a Roman surname but the meaning of 'Galone' will always, perhaps, be a mystery. The acreage used to be nearly correct.

'Tyrianesinding' could be a Celtic word which when translated could mean 'the clearing of the house of Ryan'. Just where it was, like the others, is anyone's guess. A number may have been along the town side of the brook (the old ditch) from near Blanchards Farm to an extension eastward from Hatter's Lane represented by the Great Road. 'Rochemede' may have been on the far side of the brook along the northern edge of the town. 'Mershe' could probably, be 'Marsh' but 'Wrokenemede' could be anything, except for the 'mead' or 'meadow' portion. Whether 'croft' in the third deed was a farm is unclear but this is the only one in which tenements are mentioned.

The location of the 2½ acres in the south field of Sobburi is even more interesting because it referred to the road from Estgrave to Legrave, the only occasion on which either of these two names are mentioned.

If there was a south field, it is logical that at least one other field was named from the compass. While East and West are unlikely, to the north there are the Ridings. It is not until some centuries later that they appear in the records under that name, but it is known that in other towns each burgage plot was endowed with a sizeable area of cultivated land outside the borough. It is quite possible, therefore, that the origin of the Ridings is from one or more of the provisions mentioned and were at this time the north fields of Sobburi.

Silvestro who appears as one of the testators as the 'pincerna' would probably be known later as the steward.

Re-quoting from the second deed, "which I made to Adam Alba, *whose heir Robert le Fayre is*, in these words" gives invaluable information as the ownership of the lands is traced through the later generations. In some of the town records 'Adam Alba' appears as 'Adam White' the anglicised version of his name. The same thing happens with William Crassus who becomes 'le Gros'. At no time, however, does he appear in the records as other than Crassus and he is so named in the following grant. This is from the year 1227 and can be found in the Charter Rolls II, Henry III, part I. Mem.3, No.22. Before giving the details, however, Professor Maurice Beresford in his book, *New Towns of the Middle Ages* quotes a source which says a market was first granted in 1218 which was confirmed in 1227. He also says the town was represented separately from the rest of the manor at an Assize in 1221. Here then is the charter:

> *For Sir William Crassus, King etc., greeting. Let all men know that we have granted and by this our charter confirmed unto William Crassus, the elder, for himself and his heirs for ever each*

Thursday in his manor of Sobyre a market and in connection therewith a fair each year for eight days, anything to the contrary notwithstanding, on the day of St. John the Baptist and for seven days next thereafter. As is testified by:

Mr. Fineberg gives the dates of the fair in his *Gloucestershire Studies* as the 24th June – 1st July.

The granting of this charter meant that the borough could now assume the role of a market centre officially and from this time on it was known as Sobyre Mercato (Sobyre Market) to distinguish it from the rest of the manor.

In 1228 after the local inhabitants had made a general petition and paid £150, King Henry III agreed to de-forest a large area of land, details of which are given in Charter Roll 12 of his reign. It was an event which was to have far-reaching repercussions. The appropriate part reads:

Concerning that part of Gloucestershire disafforested. King Henry, etc., his salutation. The king has for himself, and his heirs, granted that all the woods, towns and lands, which are between the wood of Furches near Bristol and Huntingford, and between the river Severn and Rudgeway, on the hill of Sobbury (montis de Sobiry) as the hill stretches itself to Lansdown to the river Arleleigh ? be for ever disafforested, excepting the park Alweston, lately enclosed. All persons who have hitherto had any woods within the forest may now use them as they please – make parks, fell and sell timber, and grub up as they please – without hindrance from the verderer, and chimiage or tolls for passing through the forest. Dated 6th May at Westminster, etc.

When the Sheriff proclaimed the success of the petition throughout the area, there was probably a great deal of relief felt because the need for timber for building and fuel was growing. But then as now it is impossible to please everyone all of the time. The head of a religious order near Wapley complained about losing his local monopoly of pannage for their pigs.

By 1242 the relationship between the Kings of England and France were very strained and that autumn the King of France ordered that English merchants trading in France should be seized and a reciprocal order was made regarding French traders in England by an angry Henry III. The situation continued to deteriorate and in 1244 the King of France at a meeting in Paris announced:

Whatever inhabitant of my realm has estates in England, seeing that he cannot fitly serve two masters, must completely and irrevocably attach himself to me or to the King of England.

This resulted in estates and revenues both in England and France being abandoned by their owners who preferred to live wholly in either country. In England, when Henry found out about it, he ordered that the lands of all those who had elected to remain in France should be confiscated. Whether this affected any land owned locally is not known.

The Laws of Breteuil, on which the town charter was based, required a Great Port-mote or Court to be set up which met twice a year. This became known as the Court for the View of Frankpledge together with the Court of the Baron.

The details of what frankpledge was can be found elsewhere but very simply it meant that each adult male had to belong to a group of ten, each of whom was responsible for the good behaviour of the others. So when a young man became twelve years old, he had to appear before the Lord of the Manor, or his steward, to take certain oaths to prove his allegiance to such a group. These courts eventually became Courts Leet.

As well as the lord, or his steward, Sobburi was governed by a Bailiff and twelve bailiff burgesses. The list for 1247/48 has survived and reads:

Rad. Mercator	Ad. Blundus	Sim. Pistor
Rad. Carney	Ric. Clericus	Godep. Pistor
Benedic de Sobburi	John de Kinegrave*	Ph. Summoniter
John le Graunt	Peter Juvenis	John de Holebrok

* this name could be a clue to the origin of Kingrove.

At the October session of the Court the various officials for the next year were appointed by a jury consisting of the bailiff burgesses. Assuming that the system in use in the 1600s, for which records survive, was still the same as earlier, the order of business would have read:

1. Citing of absentees with reasons, if any, and infliction of fines for contempt where appropriate.
2. Appointment of Bailiff for the next year, to be selected by the presiding official from three names submitted by the jurors. (In 1854 it was resolved that the same person should not serve in successive years.)
3. Report by the petty constable and his election.
4. Report by the 'carnarii' (two persons responsible for the quality of all meat offered for sale in the town) and their election.
5. Report by 'gustators' (two persons responsible for the quality of all ale offered for sale in the town) and their election,.
6. Report by 'scrutatores corarium' (two persons required to examine all leather produced in the town and to suitably mark that which was of required quality) and their election.

7. Report by scavengers (two persons whose duties seem to have been very wide. Apart from the obvious they were responsible for the maintenance of the 'ducking stool', the rope for 'bull baiting' and the removal of heaps of manure which householders, who retained draught animals at the rear of their residences, were allowed to accumulate in the street).
8. Any other business.

Mr. Tufton Beamish in his book *Battle Royal* quotes from a contemporary author of this time, Matthew Paris, on conditions in the country generally, as follows:

Shame to the wretched English, who are trampled under foot by every foreigner and do not blush at suffering the ancient liberties of their realm to be extinguished, nor model themselves on the pattern of the Welsh... O England! Justly art thou reckoned the handmaid of nations, and the last of them in rank. What thy inhabitants produce, strangers plunder and carry away.

Mr. Beamish pointed out that the situation was made worse by a bad harvest in 1257 followed by a severe winter which resulted in famine. In London alone it is said that 15,000 people died and even if this claim was exaggerated, certainly the whole country suffered hunger and misery, made worse by the King, who when corn was imported from Germany, seized it to sell for his own profit at famine prices.

Other places in the locality besides Sobburi were being developed. In November 1252 the Abbot of Pershore was granted a market at Hawkesbury on Mondays with a fair from August 28th – 30th and Richard de la Ryvere obtained a similar grant for Tormarton in February 1254. His market was on a Friday with a fair also from August 28th – 30th.

At some time before 1270, the Crassus family negotiated an exchange of their lands in this area for lands at Tulleron and other places in Ireland and the new Lord of the Manor here became William de Weyland who sought and was given a fresh market charter for Sobburi in November 1270. The market day was changed from Thursday to Monday and the fair from June to August 28th – 30th, the same as those at Hawkesbury and Tormarton. William de Weyland also claimed his rights of 'Infangeth', allowing him to pass sentence of death, and also use of the pillory, the ducking stool and the assize of bread and ale. The assize fixed the quality of the loaf which always sold at a fixed price, similarly the ale. The ale was tested by two 'tasters' appointed at the great port-mote. The court concerned in fixing the quality was known as 'The Court of Assize' which was something quite different from an

'Assize Court'.

Records called the Hundred Rolls show that in 1273 there were problems with merchants both in Bristol and Sobyry who were using other than standard weights. Any corrective action appears to have been ineffective, however, because the complaint comes up again in 1275.

Reported in the Hundred Rolls for 1275 there is the story of a thief who escaped from custody in Magne Sobiry and was caught again in Bristol. The Bailiff of Sobiry went to Bristol and, by some judicious bribery, got the prisoner back and had him hanged in Sobiry. Also reported for that year is that Thomas de Weyland had now succeeded his father, William, as Lord of the Manor.

In 1280 Thomas de Weyland changed the market arrangements yet again and the market day became Thursday with the fair from June 23rd – 25th.

In the early 1100s a church had been established at Old Sodbury. The distance from the new town to the church is two miles and as the church was very much the centre of activity in those days, the journey must have caused a lot of grumbles, especially during the winter. These so influenced the Lord of the Manor and other responsible people in the town that a Chapel of Ease was built in the new town on the site where the present church stands and was brought into use on 9th May 1284 when it was dedicated by Godfrey Giffard, Bishop of Worcester.

When one thinks of just how much of our local history has been lost forever, it seems silly to say that it is possible to state that on this important occasion the Bishop's text was from Psalm 93, part of the last verse, reading, "holiness becometh thine house, O Lord, for ever". The chapel which it is believed was in Early English style, was small and very little of it now is still recognisable.

More market charters were being granted locally. The Charter Rolls for September 1284 mention that Pucklechurch received a grant which, however, may be a confirmation of a general grant in 1227. Wickwar also received a market charter in January 1285, the market day being held on Tuesdays with a fair on the Monday, Tuesday and Wednesday after Whitsun.

1285 was the year when Edward I brought in the 'English Statute of Winchester' the opening paragraphs of which commented on the state of the country at that time, an extract of which was:

> Every day robbery, homicide and arson are committed more frequently than used to be the case.

The Statute ordered that there should be a cleared area on either side of the highway so that evil doers had nowhere to hide and it called for stronger policing in towns and villages.

The Arrival of the Normans

Church of St. John the Baptist, Chipping Sodbury c.1912 (above) and in 1989 (below)

The Three Sodburys – An Introduction

In the same year, Thomas de Weyland gave the right to appoint the clergy of the new Chapel of Ease to the Prior of the Church of St. Mary at Worcester for which in return he was promised perpetual remembrance in the prayers there.

The next year not only Thomas but his wife Margareta and their son Ricardus appear in the Assize Rolls (15.Ed.I. No.279). Apparently, some difficulty had arisen about the right to the market and fair and their attorney, while asserting that it existed, could not produce written evidence. The problem rumbled on for another two years before it was finally resolved.

As well as improving the spiritual facilities available, de Weyland also encouraged rabbit culture which had by then become popular in the countryside. The following appears in the Close Rolls for 15th November 1280:

> *Grant to Thomas de Weyland and his heirs of free warren in all demesne lands in Old Sobbire, Little Sobbire and Sobbire Marche.*

The warren was a long low mound in which stone lined burrows were sometimes built for the animals to live in. There are still many traces of these warrens, now known as 'Pillow Mounds', which at one time were wrongly thought to be barrows. One such can be found at Little Sodbury.

Contemporary drawings show ladies hunting the rabbits with ferrets. No doubt too, poaching in a neighbour's warren was also a less reputable occupation!

At some time before September 1289 Thomas de Weyland fell from grace and was imprisoned in the Tower. In 1290, however, Edward changed his mind and on the 20th February, he issued the following instruction:

> *Commission to R. Malet and Wm. de Giselham and G. de Thorneton to deliver the Tower of London of Thomas de Wey(land) with power to grant him life and limb if he will confess his felony and abjure the realm.*

Thomas seems to have agreed to his exile. Meanwhile, the King seized Thomas's lands although it would appear that in fact Thomas held them from the tenant in chief, Gilbert de Clare. When, shortly afterwards, it was brought to the King's notice that Thomas's wife and son, Richard, had been jointly enfeoffed of the manor, the following order was issued on the 2nd March 1291:

> *To the Sheriff of Gloucester, order to restore to Margery, wife of Thomas de Weyland, who abjured the realm for felony, the manor of Sobbur(y) which the King caused to be taken into his*

The Arrival of the Normans

hands by the Sheriff, as the King has restored it to Margery under certain conditions which he enjoined upon her before his council.

To record the end of the association of the Weyland family with the manor, it is necessary to move forward a few years out of sequence. In the Calendar of Charter Rolls for 3rd December 1308 the following testimony appears:

Enrolment of release from Richarde de Wellonde, son of Sir Thomas de Wellonde, knight, to Gilbert de Clare, Earl of Gloucester and Hertford of his right in the manors Sobbury, Legrave, and in the borough of Sobbury, co, Gloucester, and in all the lands held by the said Gilbert that belonged to the said Sir Thomas in the said county. Dated at London on Friday the Feast of St. Nicholas II. Edward II.

In April 1290, Gilbert de Clare, Earl of Gloucester and Hertford whose second wife, Joan, was the daughter of King Edward I, fell out with his father-in-law who promptly seized his lands which, for some reason, did not include Gilbert's lands at Sobbiri. He was however forgiven by June seemingly after subscribing to the following:

Enrolment of Gilbert de Clare, Earl of Gloucester and Hertford whereby he promises to the King that he will cause himself and Joan his wife, the King's daughter, to be enfeoffed jointly of all the lands that he may hereafter acquire.

Up to 1291 nearly successive ownership can be established, first of the manor of Sobburi and then of the borough and manor as follows: pre-conquest Brictric, 1066 Queen Matilda, 1080 Count Odo, Stephen Earl of Albemarle, William Crassus I (elder son of Stephen), William Crassus II (second son of Stephen), William Crassus III (son of II), probably William Crassus IV (son of III), by 1270 William de Weyland, by 1275 Thomas de Weyland jointly then, or subsequently, with his wife and son Ricardus.

The reason for repeating this information is that after 1291 for several centuries it is not clear just who was the Lord of the Manor although the overlordship continued to be part of the honour or earldom of Gloucester but the more rural manor, as distinct from the borough, was divided and sub-divided during this time.

According to evidence to be shown later, the lower part of the main street of the town, now known as Broad Street, was not always as wide as it is now, because a third row of houses was built in the middle from the Cross up to Hounds Road.

Whether these houses were part of the original plan or were a later brainwave of the then ruling Lord of the Manor is not known. What is known is that the market space in several other towns was encroached upon. In 1279 at New Thame, for instance, it was reported that the Bishop of Lincoln had raised a hundred feet of houses in the middle of the market place so that his rights might increase.

In 1296 revenues at Sobburi were:

	£	s	d
Burgage and other rents	9	11	7
Tolls of markets & fairs	2	0	0
Profits of justice	1	0	0

There were 176 burgages and the town was prosperous.

Undoubtedly the people living in the three Sobburi's were no different to those elsewhere. The peasant spent more of his time growing various crops rather than herding animals. Most of his hard work went to supporting himself and his family, except for a little wheat which was generally grown for sale to provide a small amount of cash.

Both food and drink came mainly from barley and oats augmented by peas, beans and onions. Meat and cheese, which was made generally from ewe's milk, varied in quantity according to the livestock owned, while eggs were probably fairly readily available. A lot of dietary evidence is available from the records of the religious houses.

The obligation to look after aged parents is stressed in tenancy agreements. For instance, if an heir took over a half yardland with the consent of his widowed mother, she was to have twelve bushels of rye, one of barley and a quarter of oats each year and be lodged on the holding.

The more important 'home farm' servants who would have made up part of the populations of Old and Little Sobburi probably received a wage of four shillings a year, together with a quarter of mixed grains every twelve or thirteen weeks.

Even in those days it was possible to provide for old age as long as you were not too badly off. The system was to buy, either in cash, or by making over property to take effect on death, what was known as a 'corrody' from a local priory or abbey for which the monks undertook to look after that person to certain defined standards for the rest of his, or her, life.

CHAPTER FOUR

MEDIEVAL TIMES

In 1300 Sobburi made the headlines in church affairs again when the dispute of seventy years previously was revived. It was considered so important that it was brought before King Edward I at Carlisle.

The ownership of the church at what is now Old Sodbury had been disputed by the heads of the Worcester and Tewkesbury establishments and in 1221 the Pope had decided in favour of Tewkesbury. Jocelin, Bishop of Bath and Wells, had reversed this in 1252 but now the King decided in favour of Tewkesbury. It was never implemented, however, and Worcester continued to make the appointments, currently a monk called Nicholas. He was appointed as a perpetual curate, as had been those before him of whom is known Walter (1277), Nicholas (1290) and William (1297).

In this year too, the first surviving and noticed ecclesiastical reference to Little Sobburi is made. It is contained in the Hockaday abstracts from church records held at Gloucester Library and reads:

1300 AD November 12th. John of Sywardely acolyk was instituted to the chapel of Little Sobburi by the Bishop of Worcester on the presentation of Sir John, called Byssop, Knt.

A record of 1305 shows that John was ordained as a priest.

It is not known whether this was a new or an established chapel, nor is it known to whom it was dedicated. Much later it was dedicated to St. Adeline, the patron saint of the Flemish weavers, something which is very rare in this country.

The ruins, traces of which are still on the hillside at the rear of the manor house, show that it was a small building. Also, whilst the Chapel of Ease in what was to become Chipping Sodbury appeared to have a burial ground, those who died in Little Sobburi were buried at Old Sobburi, a situation that continued for many centuries.

The mention of Sir John Byssop in the abstract is also of interest. He

58 *The Three Sodburys – An Introduction*

appears to be the grandson of Jordano Bissop who made a grant to the burgesses of Sobburi. He was mentioned in the Placita de Quo Warranto (p.25, 2–5. 15 Edward I 1286), when he was summoned to answer for his refusal of suit for his lands in Little Sobburi. He eventually acknowledged suit and paid half a mark in arrears.

We thus have one family of standing holding Little Sobburi Manor for at least a century and probably living here. First grandfather Jordano, then his son, whose name is not known, then grandson Sir John.

When an important person died an 'Inquisitione Post Mortem' was held. The following, which is a report of that held on the death of Gilbert de Clare, who was the son-in-law of Edward I is a good example. It is not clear whether the de Weylands had fallen from grace or whether they held the manor under the de Clares.

Inquisition made at Solbury on Monday next after the Feast of the Epiphany of the Lord, 24 Edward I.(1296) of the lands and tenements which were of Gilbert de Clare, Earl of Gloucester and Hertford in Solbury, by John de Chalkeleye, Geoffrey Wynebold, Ralph de Westcote, Robert le Eyr de Badmynton, Hugh de Bury, William Deveneys, Henry de Kyllycote, William Batyn, Ralph Caumbrey, John de Boxstede, John de Sale and Nicholas de Gurdino, who say that:

"Gilbert de Clare and Joan, his wife, held the manor of Solbury jointly of the gift and feoffment of King Edward, and they held it of the same king in chief, but by what service is not known, and nothing of others in the same manor.

There is a Capital Court with gardens, dovecotes, curtilages and barton at La Leyegrave, and the easement of the houses which are worth per annum 13s. 4d. There are in the demesne 454^1/2 acres of arable land and the acre is worth, by the year, 3d. Sum 113s. 7^1/2d. Also of meadow that can be reaped 58 acres, and the acre is worth, by the year, 3d. Sum 4s. 9d. Also two parks which contain in themselves 69 acres and the profits of the same are worth, per annum clear 13s. 4d. Also two watermills, and they are worth 26s. 8d. Also of the rent of Assize of the freemen at the Feast of the Purification of the Blessed Mary, Easter, the Nativity of St. John the Baptist and Michaelmas £8 13s. 7^1/2d. Also at Michaelmas 1lb. of pepper of rent and it is worth 12d. Also 3 capons of rent at the same term and they are worth 4^1/2d. Also 1 quarter of salt at the same term and to be taken at Wych and is worth 16d. Also 5 hens of rent at the same term and they are worth 5d. Sum 3s. 1^1/2d. Also of cert money at the View of

Frankpledge half a mark. Sum 6s. 8d. The pleas and Perquisites of the court are worth per annum ^{1}/₂ a mark. Sum 6s. 8d. There are four virgates of land in villeinage, whereof the rent and services are worth, per annum, clear 23s. 2^1/₂d. Also eight half virgates of land in villeinage whereof the works and customs, with rent, are worth per annum 48s. 10d. Also 28 cottars and the rent and services of the same are worth, per annum clear 108s. 7^1/₂d. Also of the same of Notepenny at the Feast of St. Martin 2s. 6d. There is also rent of Assize in Solbury Mercatit £9 11s. 7d. at 4 terms of the year, viz, at Michaelmas £8 16s. 1d. at Christmas 4s. 10d. at Easter 5s. 10d. and at Midsummer 4s. 9d. The Pleas and Perquisites of the court of the borough are worth per annum 20s. The tolls of the market with the fairs of the said borough are worth per annum 40s. Grand total £41 5s. 5d.
Gilbert, son of the said Gilbert is his next heir and is aged 4 years and 9 months.

Note: There were two daughters by a previous marriage.

The above appears in Chan. Inquisitiones Post Mortem. 24. Edward I. No.107 p.184, etc., in the Gloucestershire Collection at the Central Library in Gloucester.

The widow, Joan, then married Ralph de Monthermer and he became the Earl of Gloucester while the heir, Gilbert, was still a minor. Joan died in 1307 shortly before her father, Edward I. The Inquisitione reported:

Extent made before the King's escheator at Sobbury, 24 May. 35 Edward I (1307) of the lands and tenements which Gilbert de Clare formerly Earl of Gloucester and Hertford, and Joan, his wife held of the feoffment of the King, by oath of ‡Robert le Ferre, Robert Cambrey, Philip Rauf, William de Kenegrave, †Peter Clericus, William le Chepnon, Nicholas Opdoune, Adam Molend, John de Boxstede, John de Hynewyke, John le Dicare, and †William Clericus, who say that:

Gilbert de Clare held the manor of Sobbury in his demesne as of fee on the day that he died, of the King in chief, in which Joan, his wife, was not joined, by the service of 1 knight's fee. There is a CAPITAL MESSUAGE, which, with a garden, curtilage and 2 dovecotes are worth per annum 10s. There are there 299 acres of arable land, which are worth per annum 74s. 9d price of the acre 3d. Also 399 acres and half a farndal of arable land which are worth per annum 56s. 7^1/₂d price of the acre 2d. Also 90 acres of meadow, which are worth per annum £6 price of each acre of 30 acres 2s. and of

60 acres 12d; also 57 acres of pasture, which are worth per annum 19s. price of the acre 4d. There is a certain park with wild beasts the herbage whereof is worth by the year 13s. 4d, beyond the sustentation of the beasts. Also another park at La Leigrave without beasts, the undergrowth whereof is worth per annum ...?. Also a certain foreign wood containing 6 acres, which is worth nothing per annum because it is common to all tenants. There are 2 water mills, which are worth per annum 20s. Sum of the demesnes by the year £15 16s. 8^1/2d.

The pleas and perquisites of the said manor with the view of la Hockeday, are worth 20s. There is a certain market town, in which are (?)10 burgesses, who hold 176 burgages and a half, and pay per annum £9 14s. 0^1/2d to wit at Christmas... at Lady Day... at Midsummer 5s. 10d. and at Michaelmas £7 5s. 1^1/2d. There is a fair on the day of the Nativity of St. John the Baptist, which is worth.... The toll of the market is worth per annum 30s.

The pleas and perquisites of the said borough with the view of Hockeday, are worth 40s.

Sum of the value of the whole extent by the year £49 6s. 7d. The said manor by inheritance to Gilbert de (illegible) Clare... (?)... Gilbert...(?) ... said Gilbert descended by escheat after ...(?) ...

‡Probably Robert le Fayre.
†Clericus probably refers to someone in holy orders.

Note: The above were taken from Chan. Inq.P.M. Edward I No.47. The '...(?)'s' are where the original could not be read.

The young Gilbert duly came into his inheritance and in 1314 was with Edward II's army near Bannockburn where Robert Bruce waited with his Scottish army. The Scots were well placed and the young Gilbert de Clare tried to persuade Edward to put off joining battle for a day to allow the English troops to get some much needed rest. The King taunted him with cowardice and the battle started. Thoroughly annoyed, Gilbert launched himself into the thick of the fray. He was brought down from his horse and died from a number of spear wounds and a crushed skull. His defeated companions were allowed to recover his body which was then brought back and buried at Tewkesbury. The necessary Inquisitione Post Mortem was held at Ryndecombe on the 24th August 1314 and read:

The Jurors say that they understand that Matilda, who was the wife of the said Earl is pregnant, and if she be not pregnant then the next heirs of the said Earl are Alianor, wife of Sir Hugh le Despenser (junior), Margaret who was the wife of Sir Peter de Gaveston (put to death by the barons) and Elizabeth de Burgo, his sisters. The said Alianore is aged 22 years, the said Margaret 20 years and the said Elizabeth 18 years.

Some of the properties listed include Campden, Fairford (value £78 8s. 2d), Thornbury, Tewkesbury, and Stoke Archer but Sodbury does not appear but appears later in the possession of one of the heiresses. Alianor seems to be a version of Ellenore or Ellen.

Nothing is known of what happened to the young widow, Matilda. It is possible that she died in childbirth and the baby with her because the inheritance was divided among the three sisters of the late Gilbert.

Alianor acquired a third and became Countess of Gloucester while her husband, Sir Hugh le Despenser, was made Earl of Gloucester. Unfortunately the Earl supported Edward II who was fighting a Civil War with his wife Isabella and Roger Mortimer. After Isabella had won, the king and Hugh were captured in South Wales. Hugh was hanged, drawn and quartered at Hereford in November 1326, some months after his elder brother had suffered the same fate at Bristol. Maurice de Berkeley became caretaker of Sobburi until they were restored to Alianor by King Edward III on the grounds that it was part of her inheritance in 1327. Alianor then married William le Zouch, who thus became Lord of Sobburi.

In 1336 a certain John de la Welde was his tenant who, for some unknown reason made the following grant, found in Chan. Inq. P.M. 10 Edward III. No. 74:

Inquisitione taken at Alueston before the King's escheator, 26 September 10 Edward III (1336), by the oath of John de Alkele and twelve others who are named.

It will be no damage to the King or any other to allow John de la Welde to assign 52 acres of pasture in Great Sobburi to the Priory of Bradenstoke in part satisfaction of 20 marks worth of land and rents they have licence to acquire under letters patent of Edward II.

The pasture is held of William la Zouch, which is of the inheritance of his wife by the service of 13s. 4d. per annum. It is worth beyond the said rent 2s. 8d. yearly, 1d per acre. William la Zouche is the only intermediary between the King and the said John. There will remain to John 40s. rent in Sobburi, likewise held of the said William by knight's service.

This property was the bigger part of a sub-division of the main manor known as Hamstede, now Hampstead Farm, and adjacent land alongside the road from Chipping Sodbury to Wickwar. Bradenstoke Priory was not far from Lyneham and John de Lyneham figures in the deeds of 1308 and 1315. Perhaps it was because of him that the Prior of Bradenstoke acquired property so far from Lyneham.

In 1308, we have the first surviving record which deals with people other than the nobility within the town. This is a deed, originally in Latin, but again translated by Miss Salisbury:

Know all men present and future that I, Walter Faber of Irenactone and Julia my wife by unanimous assent and consent have given granted and by this our present charter confirmed to John le Skynnere of Fromptone, son of William le Skynnere of the same town, one burgage built in the town of Sobbury Mercato; which said burgage is situated and lies between the burgage of Adam Attemulne on the east, and a certain road which is called the Church Lane on the west, and abutts upon the King's highway on the south and upon the Were on the north to have and to hold etc., etc.,

Testators: Johanne de Brugges, then mayor of the town; Adam Attemulne, Willelmo de Keynsham, Willelmo de Radford, Waltero de Hamstede, Willelmo de Cromhale, Ricardo de Alkeberwe, Johanne de Hynewikes, Radulpho Sely, all burgesses of the aforesaid Sobburi; Henrico de Mareys, Roger Attesnede, free foreigners; Johanne de Lynham, clerico, and many others.

The plot of land referred to was on the corner of Church Road which was probably much the same as it was until the 1960s when the road was widened. At that time it would have just been the access road to the church and not the road to Wickwar which it became several centuries later.

Walter Faber of Iron Acton appears in some records as Walter Smith which is only one of a number of possible translations of his name, which meant 'an artisan'.

In 1315 John le Skynere subdivided the burgage, disposing of the land on the west of the holding which now would be part of the road. It was a fortunate decision because we now have the names of yet more burgesses.

The plot was granted to Roberto le Sherreve (or le Sherrevile) son of Willelmi of that name from Little Sobburi. The testators were:

? Attemulne, then mayor of the town, Waltero de Hamstede, then his sergeant, Willelmo de Keynsham, Johanne de Brugges, Johanne Drawesper, Stephano Danyel, Nicholae Philipson, Robert Packet, Johanne & Thomas Attemulne, Willelmo, clerico, Willelmo Fabro, Andrea ?, Petro Fabro, Willelmo le Proute,

Medieval Times

Ricardo atte Nasshe, burgesses, Johanne de Lynham, clerico, and many others.

In both documents the first testator is the mayor of the town, which shows that from 1308 until 1315 at least the leading townsman was of a higher rank than a bailiff.

Although there is only seven years between the two documents there are several differences in the wording. Fromptone becomes Fromptone Cotel, Sobbury Mercato is Cheping Sobbury and La Were is the Rochebrook.

The majority of the testators were burgesses and some of them were lords of neighbouring manors, which is not unusual. Johanne de Lynham, described as 'clerico' could have been the incumbent with Willelmo in the second deed his assistant or curate.

The following also appeared in the Chanc. Inq.P.M. Edward I No.47 (1307) for Gilbert de Clare:

Freemen on the Manor	Holding Virgates	(equiv. Acre)	Rent pa £.	s.	d.
Bischop John	1 pasture			13	4
Carpenter le John	tenement in Bridenwike			11	6
Cambrey Ralph*	4	96		4	–
Cotel Elias	1 carcucate			5	–
Drawpper John	1	24		5	1
Emelot Richard	½	12		3	1½
Faber Nicholas	2	48	1	3	2
Faire le Robert	1	24		9	5
Gardeford ? John	1	24		10	–
Herm Henry	?			1	8
Hynewyke de John*	1	24		9	–
Kenegrave William de*	5	120	1	12	3
Leigrave de la John	3	8			6
Leygrave at Thomas	1	24		15	–
Moland de Adam*	–	8		3	5
Northarde att Richard	1	24		10	–
Opedonoe Nicholas	–	12		5	–
Perys John	1	24		11	–
Radulp/Rauf Phillip*	1	12			1?
Chepon le William*	3	8		8	–
Total 20					

* Also appears as a member of the Jury.
24 acres = 1 Virgate

Sum of the rents of the free tenants by the year were £8 12s 2½d, and 1lb. of pepper. Payments were due at different times in differing amounts.

So far as the freemen are concerned the foregoing represents an analysis of some twenty items two of which read thus:

> John Bischop holds one pasture, and pays by the year 13s. 4d. at two terms of the year, viz, at the feasts of St. John and St. Michael. Adam de Moland holds the third part of a virgate of land, and pays per annum 3s. 5d., and one pound of pepper, price 12d at the feast of St. Michael.

A similar analysis is given below for the villeins. The following items are quoted as examples:

> John Husee holds 1 virgate of land in villeinage, and pays per annum 5s. 3d, to wit, at Lady Day 16d, at Midsummer 16d and at Michaelmas 2s. 7d and shall do 3 bind days in the autumn which are worth 6d price of each 2d.
> William Sperit holds the third part of a virgate of land, and pays at the Feast of St.Michael 5d. And shall do between the Feast of the Purification up to the feast of St. John the Baptist 70 works, which are worth 35d price of each $^1\!/_2$d. And between the nativity of St. John and the gule of August 10 works which are worth 15d price of each $1^1\!/_2$d. And from the gule of August up to the feast of St. Michael 26 works which are worth 52d price of each 2d.

Name	No. Acres	Rent pence	Payable at	No. Bind days	No. days other work	Period/s
Broke atte Roger.	12	72	1,2,3	16 @ 2d.		
Bourne William	8	24	1,2,3		70,10,26	E,F,D
Copere ?				3	35,7,8.	J,G,H
Copere Robert	8	24	1,2,3		70,10,26.	E,F,D
Cumba de John	12	41	1,2,3	3		
Denys John				3	35,7,8	J,G,H
Denys Thomas	24	65	1,2,3	3		
Emelot Richard	12	37$^1\!/_2$	1,2,3	16		
Gardiner William	8	24	1,2,3		70,10,26	E,F,D
Hullme John	8	24	1,2,3		70,10,26	E,F,D
Husse John	24	63	1,2,3	3		
Legh de Walter	12	29$^1\!/_2$	1,2,3	3		
Molend Richard	8	24	1,2,3		70,10,26	E,F,D
Molend Walter	2	14$^1\!/_2$	1,2,3	2		
Panel Nicholas	$^1\!/_2$	31$^1\!/_2$	1,2,3			
Russell Radulpus	24	63	1,2,3	3		
Sperit William	8	24	1,2,3		70,10,26	E,F,D
Swon le Richard	8	24	1,2,3		70,10,26	E,F,D

... de Hammond	12	53½	1,2,3	3		
... John	8	24	1,2,3		70,10,26	E,F,D
...reves John	8	24	1,2,3		70,10,26	E,F,D
... Richard	8	24	1,2,3		70,10,26	E,F,D
W...nd Roger	12	7½	3		32,15,26	K,L,D
... Hugh			3		35,7,8	J,G,H

Total Males 24

Females 6

Alward Christiana	8	24	1,2,3		70,10,26	E,F,D
Emelot Alice	6	30	3			
Medstile atte Joan	4½	?			44,7,12	P,N,O
Nashe atte Juliana	24	63	1,2,3	3		
... Matilda	½	29½		3		
... atte Matilda	12	7½	3		32,15,26	K,L,D

Grand Total 30

Explanation of symbols – Extra Work

                                                                                    Per day

D From Gule of August till Feast of St. Michael 26 days to value 2d
E Feast of Purification – Feast of St. John   70 days to value ½d
F Feast of St. John till Gule of August   10 days to value 1½d
G Feast of St. John till Gule of August   7 days to value 1½d
H Gule of August till Feast of St. Michael   8 days to value 2d
J   Feast of St. Michael till Feast of St. John   35 days to value ½d
K Feast of St. Michael till Feast of St. John   32 days to value 1½d
L Feast of St. John till Gule of August   15 days to value 1½d
M Gule of August till Feast of St. Michael   26 days to value 2d
N Feast of St. John till Gule of August   7 days to value 1½d
O Gule of August till Feast of St. Michael   12 days to value 2d
P Feast of St. Michael till Feast of St Michael 44 days to value ½d
Gule of August probably Lammas.
Rent payable: 1. Lady Day; 2. Midsummer; 3. Michaelmas

    With regard to some middle class people living in Old Sodbury, this fragment of a grant has survived:

> *John le Yonge granted and confirmed to Richard* (le Yonge) *and his heirs* (the same house and lands probably as in the next extract). *To hold to the said Richard and his heirs; rendering yearly to the chief lords a red rose at the Feast of the Nativity of St. John the Baptist, for all secular services exactions and demands, except royal services and attendance at the View of*

Frankpledge held on Hock-day. Warranty of the premises by John le Yonge to the said Richard against all people. For which grant, confirmation and warranty the said Richard has given a certain sum of silver. Witnesses John le Boxstede, Lawrence Cambray, William le Chepman, John Drawsper, Robert le Fayre, Richard de Gardino, William de Kenegrave, John de Lynham (clerk), Henry atte Mulle, Nicholas Rolues, Nicholas Uppedonne. Dated at Olde Sobury (Gloucestershire) on Monday next after the Feast of the Apostles Philips and James, in the 10th year of the reign of King Edward, son of King Edward (1317).

What appears to be a more comprehensive version of the above is:

John le Yonge of Olde Sobbury, son of John le Yonge of the same place gave, granted and quitted claim to Richard le Yonge, son of John le Yonge and his brother, his right and claim in a house called 'Le Nywehous' and a piece of land for a yard (Cartella) within the manor of Olde Sobbury; he also granted and quitted claim to the said Richard, his brother, his right and claim to 5 acres of land within the said manor. And he also gave granted quitted claim to the reversion of an acre of land called 'Douneswelles Aker' and also of an acre of meadow in 'Babenhames Mead' which two acres Agatha le Yonge held for her life. To hold the same to the said Richard le Yonge his heirs and assigns; rendering to the chief lords thereof yearly all services as appeared in the charters feoffment between John le Yonge, the father, and the said Richard le Yonge.

The witnesses are as before and it is dated at Olde Sobbury on Sunday next after the feast of the Nativity. Another lease reads:

Richard le Yonge of Great Sodbury granted and demised to Thomas atte Hulle and Matilda his wife three acres or arable land in the fields of Great Sobbury; to hold to the same Thomas atte Hulle and Matilda, his wife, for the term of the life of them or the longer liver of them, of the chief lords of the fee, by the services therefore due and right accustomed. Warranty against all persons. Witnesses Jordano Bisshop, John de Berkele, Laurence de Cambrey, John le Fayre, Richard de Gardino, Henry atte Mulne, Reginald de Stanford. Dated at Great Sobbury the Monday next after the Feast of the translation of St. Thomas the Martyr in the fifth year of the reign of King Edward III (1334).

Yet another document survives which reads:

Richard le Yonge confirmed to Thomas atte Hulle and Matilda his wife six acres of arable land in the fields of Old Sodbury to

Medieval Times

hold of him or his heirs and assigns to the said Thomas and Matilda as long as they or either of them shall live. Rendering therefor yearly a red rose within the octave of John the Baptist for all services. Warranty against all persons. Dated at Great Sobbury on Friday in the feast of St. John the Baptist in the eighth year of the reign of King Edward III (1334). Witnesses, Laurence Cambrai, Roger Cambrey, John le Faire, Richard atte Orchard, Robert Large and others.

Matilda atte Hulme (widow of Thomas) made certain dispositions including:

those three acres and a half of my land in Oldesobbri which I formerly had of the gift and enfeoffment of John son of Peter Le Yonge.

The family of le Yonge in the above records appear and then disappear leaving two questions unanswered. Did they die out in the years of the plague? Were they at some time the occupiers of the 'Court' whose ruins are mentioned by Leland in 1540?

As it was agreed between King Henry VII and the widowed Countess of Warwick, Sobbury passed into royal hands when she died in 1487. This could account for the appearance of the three lions on the Borough seal.

For obscure legal customs at the time and for some unknown reason, the following Inquisitione (Chan. Inq. aqd File 269 No.9. Gloucester Library Inq. PM p.303) took place.

Inquisitione taken before Simon Bassett at Sobburi, 21st April 18 Edward III (1344) by the oath of Nicholas Phillippes, Richard atte Orcharde, Thomas Adams, Robert Watership, William Watership, Ralph Blakeneye, John le Fayre, Roger Camercy, Robert Paket, Nicholas Brown, John Logtihale, Hugh Hammond who say that:

It will be no damage, etc., to allow Hugh le Despenser to enfeoff Edmund de Grymesby, John de Hamslape and William de Oseberstone, clerks, with the manor of Sobburi to hold them and their heirs for ever. The manor is held of the Earl of Gloucester by the service that the lord of Sobburi, for the time being, or his bailiff, on receiving notice shall go to meet the said earl on the west side of the said manor and shall bring him to the east side thereof. It will be no damage for the said clerks to grant the said manor to the said Hugh and Elizabeth his wife, to hold to them and the heirs of the said Hugh.

The said manor is worth £50. per annum.

The Black Death came to England in 1348 and was to sweep the country at intervals for several centuries. Before it was finished it had killed about one third of the craftsmen in the country and reduced the population from four million to two and a half million. Almost certainly Sobburi suffered as much as anywhere else and it is believed that the plague was responsible for delaying the work of enlarging and completing the 'Chapel of Ease'.

One of the victims in Sobburi may have been Thomas atte Hulle because a deed of 1349 exists which shows how his widow, Matilda, disposed of some of the family property:

- *All the burgage in Cheping Sobbury which is situate in the corner of the High Street which she had received from her brother John, the son of Henry Hynewykes.* (property on the corner of what is now Horse Street and Broad Street – Broad Street was still called High Street at that time.)

- *All the arable land which lies in Chepyng Sobbury in a certain enclosed croft in Fore Street near the good cross next to the close sometime Henry Danyel's.* (This appears to have been somewhere in Horse Street. The mention of the good cross implies that a market cross already existed, pre-dating the remains incorporated in the present one by two hundred years or more.)

- *All the land in her croft situate in the boro of Sobbury in Houndustrete which had come to her from John and Edith Brugges in an exchange.* (This is the earliest mention of Hounds Lane.

- *Three and a half acres of her land in Olde Sobbury which had come to her from John son of Peter le Yonge.* (There is no way of positively identifying this land.)

The next deed which has survived is dated 1357 and is quoted in full:

William Hodder grants to Thomas le Fayre and Miliencie, his wife, all his tenement with a place for putting stalls; which said tenement is situated between the tenement which Thomas already rents on the east and the burgage of Nicholas Broun on the west, and one end stretches to the King's Highway, the place on the road however lies opposite to the said tenement in the market place in the town of Chepynge Sobbury. To have etc.

Again it is difficult to identify its location but was probably close to what is now the Royal Oak public house. If this is the case it would point to there being a gap in the row of houses in the middle of the street which is exactly what later evidence shows. The mention of the market place and stalls is significant.

The property on the corner of Church Lane which had belonged to Robert le Sherreve, eventually came into the ownership of 'Sir' Thomas Fox, the curate at Horton. Some curates were called 'Sir' but it did not mean that they were a knight. In 1375 he died and left it to John and Denyse Puttoc of Chepyng Sobbury.

Alianor died in 1357 and the necessary I.P.M. was held at Fayreford 20th July II Edward III. The report, to be found in Chan. Inq. P.M. Edward III. File 51. in Gloucester Library, reads:

The said Eleanor held the manor of Sobburi of the King in chief by the service of one knight's fee. In this manor there is a capital messuage, worth nothing per annum beyond the keeping up of the houses, because the houses cost more than they yield; a dovecote, worth 3s. 4d per annum; 460 acres of arable land of which 307 acres were sold before the said Eleanor's death, worth 102s. 4d per annum 4d per acre; 153 acres cannot be valued because they lie fallow and in common. There are 125 acres of meadow, worth £8 6s. 8d. per annum, 16d per acre, 90 acres of which were mown before the said Eleanor's death. There are 50 acres of pasture worth 12s. 6d, 3d per acre. There is a park with wild animals, with no underwood, and the pasture there is worth nothing beyond the maintenance of the said animals. There is a windmill, worth 6s. 8d per annum, and no more, because it is in a bad state and broken down; and rents of assize of free and customary tenants £11 14s. 10³/4d, viz., at the Feasts of St. Mark 2s. 6d of the Purification 53s. 8¹/2d, of Easter 12s. 4d of the Nativity of St. John Baptist 64s. 9¹/2d and of St. Michael 101s. 6³/4d. There is rent of the burgesses £9 18s. 6¹/2d, viz., at the feasts of St. Thomas the Apostle 5s. 9d of Easter 6s. 4¹/2d of the Nativity of St. John the Baptist 6s. 9d and of St. Michael £8 19s. 7d. There is a rent of the chymenagium* of carts 2s., at the feasts of Christmas the Annunciation, the Nativity of St. John the Baptist and St. Michael equally. There are 2 fairs yearly, viz., one on the feast of the Assension, worth 40s. by estimation, and the other at the feast of the Nativity of St. John, worth 40s. by estimation. There is a toll of the market place there, worth 5s. per annum by estimation. There are 15 customary tenants each of whom works, from Michaelmas to the feast of the Nativity of St. John the Baptist, every week two works⸸ excepting 2 weeks at Christmas and the weeks of Easter and Whitsuntide. And from the said feast of St. John to the Gule of August they do 2 works weekly, worth 1¹/2d each work; and then to Michaelmas 3¹/2 works per week, each worth 2d. And each of them does 3 boon works with one man in Autumn, worth 2d each work. The pleas and perquisites of the court there are worth 10s. per annum. Hugh le Despenser, son of the said Eleanor (by her first marriage) is her next heir and is aged 28.

*This conflicts with the de-afforestation quoted earlier which stated that passage was to be without chimiage.
‡Breaks at specified Holy Days.

It will be remembered that Eleanor (Alianor) was married to Sir Hugh le Despenser and had a son by him and that Hugh was hanged, drawn and quartered at Hereford in November 1326. His lands had been seized by Isabella but were eventually given back to Eleanor by Edward III. Eleanor was then married again, to William le Zouch but her lands passed to the son of her first marriage, another Hugh le Despenser, who granted it to an Alice Burnell, the wife or widow of Edward de Burnell for her lifetime. Alice died in 1363 and the resulting I.P.M. (Inq.P.M. Edward III file 177. Gloucester Library. p31) includes:

Inquisitione taken at Sobburi before the aforesaid escheator 10th. June 37. Edward III (1363) by the oath of John le Parkere, William Fox, Thomas Hampstede, William atte Hulle, Nicholas Brown, William Bryce, William Kyngstone, Richard Coteliche, William Peytefyn, John Puttick, Richard Brugge, John Waget who say that:

The said Alice held the manor of Sobburi from the King in chief by knight service by the grant of Hugh le Despenser, to hold for her life, the licence of the king having been granted thereupon by letters patent to the said Hugh. There is in the said manor a capital messuage worth nothing by the year beyond the reprise; a garden worth 12d. 2 carucates of land worth 13s. 4d, 60 acres of meadow worth 50s. a pasture worth 26s. 8d. There is some land lying fallow, the pasture of which is 6s. 8d. There is a wood with undergrowth valued at 6s. 8d per annum. There are £12 15s. 8d of the rents of free and bond tenants, payable at the feast of the Annunciation and St. Michael. The pleas and perquisites of the court there are worth 40d a year beyond the reprise.

There is a borough there in which there are two fairs, one on the feast of the Invention of the Holy Cross and the other on the feast of the Nativity of St. John the Baptist, worth 26s. 8d a year. There are 9s. 18d. of rents of Assize there, payable at Michaelmas. the pleas and perquisites there are worth 30s. The said manor, with the borough and all other appurtenances, ought to revert to Edward le Despenser, cousin and next heir of the above said Hugh, who is aged 30 and more. The said Alice died 17th May last.

The original is written in Latin with the generous use of a form of shorthand.

Edward would have been somewhere around forty-two years old when he died in 1375. This time the description in the I.P.M. (Inq.P.M. Edward III – Henry IV Gloucester Library p.65) was:

Inquisitione on Edward le Despencer taken at Tewkesbury 49.Edward III (1375). The said Edward held in like manner the manor of Sobburi and the borough of Chepyn Sobburi to the same manor annexed. There is a capital messuage in the manor, worth nothing by the year beyond the reprises; 3 carucates of arable land, two thirds of which are worth 26s. 8d when sown and the remaining third nothing (as above). 60 acres of meadow worth 60s., 160 acres of several pasture worth from Michaelmas to the Feast of the Invention of the Holy Cross 40d and thence to Michaelmas 36s. 8d. There is a pasture called Mansmede, which is in severalty from the Feast of the Purification to Michaelmas, during which time it is worth 13s. 4d. and from Michaelmas to the Feast of the Purification it is worth nothing because it lies in common. There is a close called Leigrave, the pasture of which is worth 20s. yearly; and a park, the pasture of which is worth nothing beyond the upkeep of the game. There is underwood worth 40d, £16 rents of free and bond tenants payable at the Feasts of the Purification, St. John the Baptist and St. Michael, in equal portions. The pleas and perquisites of the courts are worth 40d. In the said borough there are rents of assize of £10 payable at Michaelmas, and two fairs, to wit on the Feasts of the Ascension and St. John the Baptist, worth 26s. 8d beyond the reprises. The pleas and perquisites of the borough court are worth 20s. The said Edward died 11th November last. Thomas, his son and heir was aged 2 on the 22nd of September last past.

After the young heir had grown up, like earlier members of the family, he supported the wrong side. King Richard II was a prisoner in the tower and Henry Bollingbroke had been declared king in his place as Henry IV. Despite this, Thomas and others tried to stir up trouble by attempting to seize Cirencester. This was foiled by the bailiff and townspeople and the Earls of Kent and Salisbury were beheaded in the market place. Thomas got away and tried to escape by sea but he was caught, brought to Bristol and beheaded. In Gloucester Library, (F.491) there is the following writ:

in the loaf. It could also fix the strength of the ale for which the standard price was one penny per gallon.

The fairs were frequented by peddlers selling little fineries to the local ladies, and chatting with the peddlers gave the chance for those so inclined to learn something about the world beyond the borough boundaries.

There is no real indication at this time of what was the town's main livelihood. There must have been some industries and tanning and weaving could have been included.

Gough's map, which is one of the earliest surviving, shows a road running from Oxford to Bristol, apparently through Cirencester, although this and another town on the route are not named. Such a route would have passed through Sobbury as it did centuries before. As well as this east-west road there was still the north-south highway. Both of these linked the various monastic establishments such as those at Tetbury, Bristol, Tewkesbury, Worcester, Kingswood (Wotton), Keynsham and Glastonbury. Such roads would be used by pilgrims, church dignitaries, monks and friars and many others.

A reasonable living could no doubt be made from providing accommodation for these travellers, hence the number of hostelries which crop up in later records. As now, these roads would have been used also for distributing goods with the traffic increasing year by year, so anyone with a wagon or a string of pack mules would do very well in a market town at the junction of two busy highways.

Regarding the pilgrims, it was customary for abbeys to set up places at intermediate points to give at least basic accommodation for them. The George's at Glastonbury, Norton St. Philip and Tewkesbury are good examples of this practice. In a deed of 1439, preserved at Gloucester, a tenement in the high street at Sobbury is mentioned, next to "the Great Hospice", a reference to what became The George, now unfortunately closed. The other inns which might also have existed at that time are The Bell, subsequently the home of the British Legion and now also closed, and The Swan. The fact that Willelmo de Keynesham appeared as a testator to the deed of 1315 may indicate that the abbey at that place had some establishment in the borough.

The battle of Agincourt, fought in 1415, has been well documented both in the history books and in Shakespeare's *Henry V*. Even Chepyng Sobbury has some small claim to fame from that battle because John Codrington, who lived nearby was Henry V's standard bearer on that day. His tomb can still be seen in Wapley Church which states that he died at the astounding age of 111 years although there are those cynics who think that the mason cut 'CXI' instead of 'XCI'. If John Codrington was there it is almost certain that men from the Sodburys were also part

Chipping Sodbury Town Hall c. 1910.
To the right of the Town Hall with the horse and cart outside is Pontins Drapers and to the left is a grocers shop. Note on the left end of the rank Allens the saddlers shop, demolished in the 1960s to widen Church Road.

of Henry's army on that day. When he died he was Sir John, his knighthood possibly arising from how he conducted himself at Agincourt.

In 1415, whilst John Codrington was with King Henry, his father, Robert, and his mother, Juliane, secured a lease on some large properties in Sobbury. The Gloucestershire historian, Rudder, thought that they could have been living in a house at Lyegrove at this time. Perhaps this was the Legrave to which the road led from Estgrave as mentioned in the thirteenth century deed between William Crassus and Adam Alba (page 47).

In the second of the three deeds from about 1225, covering the transfer of lands from Crassus to Adam Alba, Robert le Fayre was Adam's heir (page 45). Robert's surname was to crop up in documents for more than two centuries in a variety of spellings, as was common right up to Victorian times, settling finally for the variation 'Vayre' as the correct spelling. Certainly in 1415 there was a William Vayre or le Fayre in Olde Sobbury and Chepyng Sobbury, who was the direct descendant of the heir of Adam Alba. Some time previously, he had, by gift and enfeoffment, passed over all his lands except a close called Prowtecroft and a croft adjoining Fayremead for one life at a rent of one red rose to William atte Naysshe and Thomas Godestounde, described elsewhere as 'procuratores'. In 1415 they leased the lands in turn to the Codrington family.

Among the testators was a certain John Doughton. When these lands were mentioned again in 1428 when William Fayre had died, his heir, another Fayre, "gave, granted and confirmed to Thomas Doghton of Chepyng Sobbury and Robert Barbour, dyer, burgess of the town of Bristol, all the lands and tenements and rents, etc., which he had in Olde Sobbury and Chepyng Sobbury".

Just what lay behind these deeds is not now known but they amounted to the gift, in part to the church and in part to the town, of the following:

Galoneffeld (i.e. Gaunts Field)	20 acres arable
Tyrianesinding	8 acres arable
Rochemead	4 acres meadow
Mershe – therein	2 acres meadow
Wrokehememede	1 acres
Half a virgate of land	15 acres
Three parts of an acre	
All that croft by the old ditch	
All that meadow	
Land in south field of Sobbury	
Burgage on corner of High Street	
Arable land in Fore Street	
Croft in Houndestrete	
In Olde Sobbury	$3^1/_2$ acres
Tenement in street with right to stalls.	

The deeds which have been quoted to date show that all the above belonged to the Fayre family and included Gorefurlong, Prowtecroft and Fayremead, which cannot be identified and may indeed represent what Rochemead, etc., had become.

John Codrington cropped up again in 1437 when he and the current procurators, Thomas Glover and John Puryman, arranged an exchange of properties. John Codrington owned a property to the left of the Town Hall and he agreed to exchange that for a tenement which the borough owned in another part of the town. Three or four years later the tenement, which had passed back to the town, was granted to Thomas Boucher (or Bocher) as a shop, the first to be mentioned in Sobbury.

The transactions in both deeds show that even as early as this the borough owned a number of properties, several of them near to the present Town Hall.

A deed of 1443 contains several interesting items and so is produced here in full:

Know all men present and future that we Simon Cotesbrook and Thomas Wynter, otherwise known as Vycary, have given granted and by this our present charter confirmed to John Doughton a certain void piece of land in the town of Chepyng Sobbury situated between the King's highway on the east and the tenement of Nicholas Stanshawe on the west, and the land sometime William Kyngon's on the north and the tenement sometime John Godstone's on the south which same piece of land we lately had by the gift and legacy of John Hagod (?) chaplain. To have and to hold etc., Witnesses. Walter Lye, the bailiff of the borough, Thomas Godstone, John Burnell, John Brugge, Thomas Boucher and others.

This shows that the day to day running of the town was in a bailiff's hands as opposed to the mayor of the century before. There is also a mention of the Stanshawe family who were very big landowners in the area at this time.

In February 1446 Robert Barbour signed a legal document breaking up the partnership between him and Thomas Doughton when Thomas died and releasing his interest to John, brother and heir of Thomas, described as a 'clerk'.

Henry VI, noted for founding Eton and King's College, Cambridge, obviously knew of Chepyng Sobbury's existence because in the thirteenth year of his reign, 1452, he granted a licence for the foundation of a Fraternity or Guild in the town as follows:

Pro Canteria Fundanda in Sobbury.
Know ye that of our certain knowledge and special favour to the praise and honour of Almighty God and of the Glorious Virgin Mary, We have given and granted licence and our Heirs as far as in us lies to Thomas Hampton, Richard Bocher, Thomas Bocher, William Burnell, William Adams and Thomas Burnell of Chepyng Sobbury in the County of Gloucestershire. That they, in the said vill or parish of Chepyng Sobbury, one Fraternity or Perpetual Guild of one warden (bailiff or master) and his brethren and sisters of the same vill and other who by their solemn vow and promise were desirous to be of the same Fraternity or Guild may have power to begin, found, erect and unite, create and establish to continue for all future times for ever. And that the Warden or Master and his brethren and sisters of the same Fraternity or Guild or at least the major part of the same of the more noted estimation in the same Vill then present and their successors every year on the Eve of the Feast of the Assumption of the Blessed Virgin Mary create and make out of

themselves one Warden or Master to support the burdens touching, incumbent upon and concerning the Fraternity or Guild. Out of the profits and revenues of the said Fraternity or Guild after the best manner that may be besides we have granted that the said Warden or Master and his brethren and sisters of the Fraternity or Guild aforesaid when it shall have been thus founded, erected, united and established be in reality and name one body and one perpetual community and may have a perpetual succession and a Common Seal to save for the business of that Fraternity or Guild. And that they and their successors for ever may be persons fit and capable in the law to purchase for themselves and their successors in fee and perpetuity Lands and Tenements, Rents and other possessions whatsoever which are not held of us in chief within our kingdom of England of any of our liege subjects whatsoever. And that the same Warden or Master and his successors for ever by the name of Warden or Master of the Fraternity or Guild of St. Mary of Chepyng Sobbury may plead and be impleaded before whatsoever Judges in the King's Court and in whatsoever action. And further out of our more abundant favour we have granted and given licence for ourselves and for our heirs as far as in us lies that the Warden or Master of the Brethren or Sisters of the said Fraternity or Guild when the said Fraternity or Guild shall have been founded, erected, united, created and established a certain chantry of two chaplains to perform divine service for the wholesome state of us while we live and for our souls when we shall depart from this life and for the souls of all our forefathers deceased as also for the wholesome state of Richard Andrews, our secretary and the warden or master, the brethren and sisters of the same Fraternity or Guild whilst they live and for their souls when they shall depart from this life and for the souls of John Doghton and Thomas Doghton and for all the faithful deceased at the altar of St. Mary in the Chapel or Church of Chepyng Sobbury aforesaid in the County aforesaid according to the appointment of the aforesaid Thomas, Richard, William, William, Thomas and Thomas or their exors or assigns in their behalf to be made may create found and establish and purchase Lands, Tenements and Rents to the value of ten pounds per annum which are not held of us in chief of whatsoever persons they please. To be had or holden to the same Warden or Master this brethren and sisters of the Fraternity or Guild aforesaid and their successors for the relief and support of the same Fraternity or Guild aforesaid and their successors and the maintenance of the two chaplains aforesaid for ever the statute made concerning Lands and Tenements not to be placed at Mortmain or any other statute to the contrary notwithstanding. Whilst nevertheless by Inquisitions in this behalf to be taken and rightly returned into our, or our heirs, Court of Chancery it be found that the same may be done without the loss or prejudice of ourselves our heirs and of all other persons whatsoever. IN WITNESS whereof we have caused these our Letters to be made Patent. Witness myself at Westminster the sixteenth day of May in the thirtieth year of our Reign.

No apology is made for quoting the document in full because it is a good example of a licence to found a Guild and deserves to be placed on record. The details are taken from a translation of a copy of a confirmation given by Henry VIII but there is no reason to doubt its validity because of that.

As can be seen, this was a religious Guild which, in addition to prayers for the dead, Christian charity was freely exercised. There was mutual assistance for Guild brothers and sisters in their old age and every imaginable sort of distress.

One final point to be noted is that the Fraternity or Guild was to have a common seal.

The church was responsible for education at this time, regarding it as a religious duty. Among the Guild's objects was help for poor scholars, maintaining schools and paying schoolmasters. It is possible that among the duties of the two priests mentioned was the instruction of a number of boys and this could mark the beginning of what was to become the Grammar School.

For the day to day running of affairs there had to be at least some literate people and literacy brought some fringe benefits. Indeed, special privileges could be granted in the Courts by claiming

This very old door was found beneath the plaster in the second house into Broad Street from the corner of Church Road.

'benefit of clergy' where to qualify, the claimant had to read aloud a passage from the Bible.

For some time the chief lordship of the manors of Sobbury Borough and Olde Sobbury, had been in the hands of the Despenser family, the last being Isabel Despenser. She married her first husband, Richard Beauchamp, Lord Bergavenny and afterwards Earl of Worcester in 1412. Her second husband, by a special dispensation from the Pope, was yet another Richard Beauchamp, this one being Earl of Warwick. The daughter of this marriage, Anne, married Richard Nevil, Earl of Salisbury, who, when his brother-in-law died, became, because of the marriage, Earl of Warwick. He was such a forceful and efficient person that during the Wars of the Roses he was known as 'Kingmaker'. His luck finally ran out on him, however, and he was killed at the Battle of Barnett in 1471 fighting for the Lancastrian cause. The battle was a triumph for the Yorkists led by Edward IV, who procured an Act of Parliament to strip Anne, the widowed Countess, of her possessions.

This building in the High Street, Chipping Sodbury, could have been the site of a Weaver's Guild. It could also have been used as an early school by the priests. The building was presented to the town by Mr. F. Fox as an Institute and Reading Room which it remained for many years until it was converted to business premises.

When the future King Henry VII won the Battle of Bosworth in 1485, however, he gave Anne back the lands which she had lost for her lifetime with the rider that they should be left to him on her death. Anne died in 1487 and the manor of Sobburi passed into royal hands.

Before she died, Anne presented Sobbury with an article that is generally classed as a mace. At a Meeting of the Society of Antiquaries

Medieval Times

in February 1889 the assistant secretary, W.H. St. John Hope Esq., showed the mace of the Borough of Chipping Sodbury. He is reported as saying:

> By the kindness of John D.B. Trenfield Esq., the last bailiff of Chipping Sodbury, I am able to exhibit a mace. The example has been looked upon as a seal and the two ends have been actually used for the purpose of sealing. On receiving a print of the insignia from Mr. Trenfield, I at once saw the real nature of the so-called seal.

A mace was usually carried on an official's shoulder during a procession but the 'mace' quoted above is made of an iron shaft with silver gilt and is only 11½ inches long. There is a decorative top and inset in circular base is the arms of the Beauchamp family. Its short length would make it impossible to carry it on an official's shoulder with any degree of dignity and so it must be a seal.

Both the ruling body of the town and the Guild would have needed a seal and the Countess could have given it to either of them. The Guild was especially empowered in its Charter to acquire a seal and such a gift would be very appropriate.

Not everyone in Sobbury were able to enjoy any benefits from the founding of the Guild for long. The Wars of the Roses broke out in 1455 and as the Earl of Warwick was active on the Yorkist side, the two manors would have had to provide a number of armed men.

After Henry VI had re-appeared briefly, the throne was occupied by Edward IV in 1461 and it is in this year that Samuel Rudder, in his history of 1779, reported:

> (Lyegrove is a considerable estate in this parish where was a good house now in decay and a park.) John Gotherington and Alice his wife levied a fine of lands in Lyegrove to the use of themselves for life, the remainder to Humphry, John and Thomas successively in taille, the remainder to Margaret Basile, late wife of Sir Peter Basile, in taille.

As has been said before, spelling was a lot more uncertain at that time and Gotherington is one of more than a dozen variations of the Codrington name. This is the same Sir John, of Agincourt fame, who some fourteen years later was buried in Wapley church. The son John mentioned married into the Poyntz family of Iron Acton whilst Humphrey became the King's Escheator in 1467.

Three years after this the Earl of Warwick turned against Edward IV, whom he had helped to win the throne and drove him from the kingdom, reinstating Henry VI. This situation only lasted until 14th April 1471 (Easter Sunday), when Edward IV again became King after the Battle of Barnett, in which the Earl of Warwick was killed.

Yet again, Sobbury looked like being on the losing side and the inhabitants must have been very worried. Although Henry VI had died in May of that year, his queen, Margaret, and son, Prince Edward, were still trying to maintain the Lancastrian cause. They had landed with a small force at Weymouth on the very day the Battle of Barnett took place and their numbers grew as they advanced on Bristol via Taunton and Wells with the object of joining up with the Earl of Pembroke.

To do this they had to cross the River Severn, which could only be done at Gloucester. Meanwhile, King Edward IV was hurriedly marching east from London to intercept Margaret, believing that she was at Bath and intended to move towards Gloucester.

This seems to have been a feint on her part to prevent the King from marching directly to Gloucester and she succeeded. He arrived at the Camps at Little Sobbury on the 1st May and prepared for battle. Some scouting troops on the flank of the Lancastrian army came into Sobbury and a skirmish occurred at the entrance to the town. Margaret's army, however, successfully avoided the King who was forced to chase her to Tewkesbury where her complete defeat ended the conflict. Anne, widowed Countess of Warwick, lost her vast estates which she was made to pass on her daughters.

Hatters Lane c.1910. At this time Tudor House was a common lodging house.

Apparently, when things had settled down, someone decided to modernise his house since it is the opinion of experts that part of what is called Tudor House in Hatter's Lane dates from this time.

Tudor House in 1989. In 1956 it was bought by Mr.Mark Harford, was renovated and became the Headquarters of the South Gloucestershire Conservative Association, for which it is still (1994) being used.

CHAPTER FIVE

THE TUDORS

Although the manors of Sobbury Borough and Olde Sobbury came into the hands of Henry VII in about 1486, Little Sobbury Manor next door was owned by a Richard Forster. How it had come to him from the Bissop family is not known. In 1485 his daughter, Elizabeth, married John Walshe of Alveston, an important gentleman as he and Sir Robert Poyntz were King's Receivers for the Berkeley lands. The manor was part of Elizabeth's marriage settlement and it was then that the house was extensively rebuilt.

John Walshe of Alveston, died in 1502. His will was proved on 7th May, having been drawn up in January 1498–99. Parts of it read as follows:

...I bequeath to the marriage of Alice Walshe, my daughter, so that she be married after the advice of Elizabeth, my wife, and the more part of her co-executors £100. To every of my younger daughters Elizabeth, Anne and Margaret in like manner 100 marks. My feoffees of my lands in Hanham in Gloucestershire and of the manor of Charlton in Somerset and of lands etc., elsewhere in those counties shall levy the issues thereof till all my debts and legacies be fully contented and performed provided this my will be in no way prejudicial to any covenants or bargains made between Sir Robert Poyntz and me by indenture concerning the marriage between Anne, daughter of the said Robert and John Walshe, my son and heir apparent and my feoffees shall make an estate to my seconde sonne James of my lands in Somerset excepting the manor of Charlton, etc., Whereas a fine was levied by John Stanshawe and Humphrey Stanshawe to William Freme of certain lands etc., in Olde Sobbury and elsewhere in Gloucestershire to ...? of me and mine heirs, the said William shall make a lawful estate thereof to Nicholas Poyntz and to her of my said daughters whom it shall happen the said Nicholas to take to wife.

84

The Tudors   85

Whether Anne Poyntz and John Walshe (the second) were already married at the time the will was proved is not known but certainly they did marry at about this time.

John Foxe (1516–1587) wrote his book *Acts and Monuments etc.*, more widely known as the *Book of Martyrs* in which an account appears of a woman being burned at the stake in Chipping Sodbury (P.315 of Vol.I of the 1803 edition) which reads as follows:

A Faithful Woman Burned

But among all the examples of God, whereof so many have suffered from time to time for Christ and His Truth, I cannot tell if ever any martyrdom was more admirable wherein the plain demonstration of God's mighty power and judgement hath at any time been more evident against the persecutors of his flock than at the burning of a certain godly woman put to death in Cheaping Sobbury, about the same time, under the reign of Henry VII.

The constancy of which blessed woman, as it is glorious for all true godly Christians to behold; so again the example of the bishop's chancellor, who cruelly condemned the innocent, may offer a terrible spectacle to the eyes of all papistical persecutors to consider and take example which the living God grant they may.

The name of the woman is not known, but the name of the Chancellor who condemned her was Dr. Whittington. After this godly woman, and martyr of Christ, was condemned by the wretched chancellor, above named Dr. Whittington, for the faithful profession of the truth, which papists call heresy, and the time now come when she should be brought to the place and pains of her martyrdom, a great concourse of all the multitude both in the town and country about, were gathered to behold her end; among whom was also the aforesaid Dr. Whittington, the chancellor.

Thus this faithful woman and true servant of God constantly persisting in the testimony of truth, committed her cause to the Lord gave her life over to the fire refusing no pains or torments to keep her conscience clear and unreproveable in the day of the Lord.

The sacrifice being ended the people began to return homeward, coming from the burning of this blessed martyr. It happened, in the meantime, that as the Catholic executioners were busy in slaying this lamb at the town's side a certain butcher was busy within the town slaying of a bull, which bull he had fast bound in ropes to knock him on the head. But the butcher (belike not so skilful perhaps in his art of killing beasts as the papists are in murdering Christians) he was lifting his axe to strike the bull, failed his stroke and smote a little too low; the bull, not stricken down, put his strength to the ropes and brake loose from the butcher into the street, the very same time the people were coming in a great press from the burning. Who seeing the bull coming towards them, and supposing him to be wild, gave way for the beast, every man shifting for himself as well he might. Thus the people giving back, and making a lane for the bull, he passed through the throng of them, touching neither man or child till he came where the chancellor was against whom the bull, as pricked with a sudden vehemency, ran full butt with his horns, and taking him upon the paunch, gored him through, and so killed him immediately, carrying his intestines and dragging them with his horns all over the street, to the great admiration of them that saw it.

Although the carnal sense of man be blind in considering the works of the Lord, imputing many times to blind chance the things which properly pertain to God's only praise and providence yet in so strange and so evident example, what man can be so dull or ignorant who seeth not a plain miracle of God's mighty power and judgement both in punishment of this wretched chancellor and also in admonishing all other like persecutors by his example to fear the Lord and abstain from like cruelty.

While interesting, the whole thing could have been made up by Foxe and it would have helped if he had named the victim who supposedly had died less than fifty years earlier. At the time of the incident Sobbury was part of the See of Worcester which would have made Dr. Whittington the Chancellor of that Bishop. The Records Office at Worcester, however, has no documents which mention him but Sir Robert Atkyns, writing in 1712, said that the story was confirmed by local people living at that time.

The burning is reported as taking place "at the side of the town", which could have been just past the church on what later became known as The Rag. Besides being much narrower then, compared with now, there was a row of houses opposite the Church Road exit in the middle of the main street, known as the Shambles, inhabited by the butchers. A frightened animal could have charged down Church Lane until it met the chancellor who was probably wearing a brightly coloured cloak. Whoever told Foxe the story knew the town's layout but it is only when evidence is discovered of how Dr. Whittington really died can the story be proved true or otherwise.

When John Walshe the younger married Anne Poyntz he gained an estate as well as a bride and at some time he also acquired a knighthood. While these things were happening to him a young man, by the name of William Tyndale, was proving himself something of a scholar. William was born between 1490 and 1495 near Slimbridge with the family name of Tyndale but with an alias of Huchyus, which had been adopted when his forebears had fled from the north during the Wars of the Roses. He went to Oxford at the start of the Easter Term in 1510 under the name of Huchyus and became a Bachelor of Arts in 1512 followed by a Master's Degree in 1515. He then moved to Cambridge until 1521 when Sir John Walshe brought him to Little Sobbury as his chaplain and tutor to his children.

His duties were light as he found time to preach in the surrounding villages including Little Sobbury itself, the pulpit of which was transferred to the later erection and can still be seen.

His unorthodox views brought him into conflict with the establishment. William Knight, a Doctor of Laws and Prothonotary of the Holy See, had married Sir John Walshe the younger's sister and had come to live at Horton Court. Whilst visiting his brother-in-law at Little Sobbury it is popularly believed that there was an argument between him and

Remains of the ancient church at Little Sodbury. A church is first mentioned in 1300 and was in use during Tyndale's time as tutor at the Manor. It was abandoned in 1859 when the present church was built.

William Tyndale during which Tyndale, pointing out the window at a boy in the fields said the immortal words, "If God spare my life, ere many years I will cause a boy that driveth the plough to know more of the scripture than thou doest".

By the middle of 1523 his views had provoked so much anger he found it impossible to stay in Little Sobbury any longer and he went first to London and then to Flanders on the continent where he completed translation of the New Testament into English from the original Greek. This was not the first translation to have been made, at least two having been completed previously. But by now Caxton had introduced printing so Tyndale's work could be circulated to a much wider population.

Copy of an old engraving of Tyndale

Copies of the translated New Testament were soon circulating in England, of which many were subsequently collected by the authorities and burned. A fifth edition of this New Testament was printed in 1529 and Tyndale then started to print the first four books of the Old Testament. Two copies of his New Testament still exist, one in the library of St. Pauls, the other in the Baptist College at Bristol.

Having failed to lure him back to England, his enemies had him arrested on a trumped up charge of heresy and on Friday 6th October 1536, at Vilvorde, he was chained to a stake, strangled and burnt. His last words are reported as, "Lord, open the King of England's eyes".

In 1537 his last prayer was answered. The translated bible was published and put in every church throughout the country for the free

The Martyr's Pulpit, Little Sodbury Church

The pistle of paul
vnto Titus.
The fyrst Chapter.

Paul the servaunt of god and an Apostle of Jesu Christ/ to preache the fayth of goddis electe/ and the knowledge off the trueth/ which trueth is in servynge god in hope of eternall lyfe/ which lyfe god that cānotlye/ hath promysed before the worlde began: but hath at the tyme appoynted opened his worde by preachynge/ which preachynge is committed vnto me/ by the commaūdement of god oure saveoure.

To Titus his naturall sonne in the commen fayth.

Grace mercie and peace from God the father/ and from the lorde Jesu Christ oure saveoure.

For this cause left J the in Creta/ that thou shuldest performe that which was lackynge ādshuldest ordeyne senioures in every citie as J apoynted the. Jfeny be soche as no man can complayne on/ the husbāde of one wyfe/ havynge faythfull children/ which are not sclandred off to pote/ nether are disobediēt. For a bisshoppe must be soche as no man can complayne on/ as it be commeth the minister off God. not stubborne/ not angrye/ no dronkarde/ no fyghter/ notgevē

Copy from the "Reproduction by F. Fry 1862" of Tyndale's New Testament

use of the people and as more people learned to read, Tyndale's boast made some sixteen years earlier was fulfilled.

Because he was living in the area at the time, Richard Colymore must have at least known of Tyndale. He and his wife, Edith, are commemorated on a stone in Chipping Sobbury church. He died early in 1522–23, his will being proved on 14th February. It read:

> *Richard Colymore to be buried in St. John Baptist Chepyng Sobbury by the glass window which I made in same. I bequeath to the mother church at Worcester 2s. to the high altar of Sobbury 3s. 4d. To the altars of St. Clement, the Trinity and St. Nicholas 6s. 8d. To the altars of St. Katherine and our Lady 3s. 4d. To son John £20, daughter Margaret £20; residue to wife Edith; eldest son Richard to be overseer and to receive £3 6s. 8d for his trouble.*
> *Witnesses: Maurice Berne (Sir) Curate of C.S.*
> *Thomas Tailer, Bailiff.*

Sir John Walshe became Sheriff of Gloucestershire in 1525, again in 1529 and yet again from 1534 to 1535. During that last period King Henry VIII and his current Queen, Anne Boleyn, were at Thornbury from where they intended to go to Bristol but as plague had broken out again in Bristol they changed their minds and visited Little Sodbury instead.

For many years the border territory between England and Wales had belonged to the Lords Marchers. The area was being fought over

Little Sodbury Manor
Photo by Murray Dowding

continuously as each Lord Marcher sought to extend his holding and they treated the Welsh people particularly badly with murder and rape often going unpunished. While successive rulers had been aware of these problems, Henry VII was the first to do something positive about them. He established a court of law, meeting in different places in the area at different times, whose power stretched not only over North and South Wales but also the three English counties of Shropshire, Herefordshire and Gloucestershire.

In 1538, as the result of Sir Nicholas Poyntz mis-managing the Gaunts Fields, representatives from Chepynge Sodbury appeared at Montgomery where the Court was sitting that year to make a formal protest. The journey to Montgomery must have been quite an undertaking in those days. The following is a modernised version of what happened from a transcript of the time of Edward VI. Apologies are offered for the gaps but the writing was somewhat faded:

The Vestibule, Little Sodbury Manor

> This order was made as here appeareth at the suite of the commoners and poor inhabitants of Sodbury Market who from ...? poverty being right ...? with the consent of ...? whereupon at the ...? would have enclosed ...? so that Given at Montgomery 30th day of July in the thirtieth year of King Henry VIII.
>
> At which day Thomas Smith and Lawrence a Brugge for themselves and others the tenants and inhabitants of Sodbury, complainants, and Richard Frankome and John Andrews (could be John a Deane), defendants, appeared before the King's Commissioners, by whom the matter within specified was deliberately examined and the depositions of sundry witnesses there sworn, whereby it was proved and also upon hearing of the matter confesses by the defendants in open court that the ground within specified called Gaunts Field hath been used, had and occupied in common as well to the said tenants and inhabitants of Chepyn Sodbury as to others of Olde Sodbury in manner

> *following: Two years several and the third year common that is to wit, the years that the same ground is sown with corn to be cast open and kept in common immediately after the reaping of the corn there, and if it be kept in pasture then to be common at Lammas, and the year that the same lieth fallow to be common during the whole year; and it is therefore ordered that the said co-plaintiffs shall have common in the said ground of Gaunts Field according to the said proof and confession of the defendants without any interruption of the defendants or of the said John (a Deane) or of any other ... without the said defendants shall have showed and proved before the Counsel good matter to the contrary; and for the charter of Chepyng Sodbury, which the co-plaintiffs appearing confess to have in their custody, it is ordered that the said co-plaintiffs shall deliver the same charter of Chepyng Sodbury to the bailiff thereof ... ...? by them the said council that the said defendants shall suffer the plaintiffs and other the tenants and inhabitants of Chepyng Sodbury foresaid for this present year to enter and common in the said Gaunts Field ...? day next coming ...? and after that by the defendants (to cast open) the (hedges) and so to suffer the plaintiffs to common the same thereafter (until the year then following).*

The scribe then confirms that the foregoing is correct by adding the words "Copia concordant cum originali" (copy agrees with the original).

Sir John Walshe was made High Sheriff of the County again in 1539. This was also the year when, after quarrelling with the Pope, Henry VIII dissolved the monasteries, an act which was to affect the local area quite considerably over the next ten years. Despite the See of Gloucester being founded at this time, the King still conferred the advowson of the church at Sodbury on the Dean and Chapter of the Cathedral Church of Worcester in 1542.

In the early 1540s a man called Leland came to our area who was making detailed notes of what he saw so he could make a complete record of the realm for the King. He died before he had finished his work but some of his notes on the area have survived as follows:

> *Thence to Cheping Sodbyri and a mile from thence to Little Sodbyri. The double ditched camp thereby on the hill containeth 2 acres. King Edward IV's army kept this camp here going to Tewkesbury Field. Old Sodbyri and Chepinge Sodbyri were the Earl of Gloucester's lands and since Beauchamps, Earls of Warwick, Gilbert de Clare possessed them. The Manor place stood hard by the west end of the church, now clean down.*

And again:

Walshe is Lord of Little Sodbyri and hath a fair place there in the side of Sodbyri high hill and a Park. Old Sodbyri is a mile from it and there appear ruins of an old manor place belonging, as the town did, to the Earl of Warwick now to the King. To the Earls of Warwick belonged also Chepinge Sodbyri a pretty little market town and through thence to Brighstow. There is a park of the kings by this town, sometime the Warwicks. Little wood is full right nigh to the south parts of the country soil Sodbyri. There is great plenty by South Sodbyri of wood in a large valley sometime thence clearly to the Severn lying in the Forest of Kingswood. The crests of the hills that lye by Sodbyri cloaketh one way to Gloucester.

He also made notes about the brook which in 1214 was called the "Old Ditch". These were in his notes on the course of the Acton river:

"This brook by some is called Loden, but commonly Laden, and riseth above Dodington where Master Wiks' house is and so to Acton, Master Poyntz house a four miles off and thence towards Brightstow takynge the name Frome. There meet two waters one half mile beneath Acton at a mill. Sodbyri water cometh from the hills thereby

Leland also said about Dodington:

A glass with bones yn a sepulchre found by Dodington church yn the highway.

The Romans used to bury their dead by the highway and this find could indicate the presence of a dwelling and a trackway from the Roman period nearby.

Sir John Walshe decided to prepare a will in August 1547, a wise decision on his part because he died the following spring. This is an extract of the will:

I bequeath to my wife Anne all my household goods excepting what is at my manor place at Olveston which I give to my son Maurice. To my said wife my leases of the farm and borough of Old Sodbury and the parish church there. I bequeath my lands in tenure of various tenants (named) *in manors of Northwicke and Redwicke co. Glous. and lands in Chepyng Sodbury and the lordship of Old Sodbury and lands called Raysfield, Bellmede and the Christopher in the lordships of Yeate, Dodington and Old Sodbury and in Hasill to my wife for 15 years and after as I have directed her verbally. Legacies to servants. John Grought, Nicholas Came, Nicholas Parsonage, John Shatterley, Robert Stanbourne, Overseer Mr John Soper of Codrington, Executrix*

The Three Sodburys – An Introduction

my Wife ....Signed. John Walshe (knight)
Witnesses: David Broke Esq., Richard Ivye., Thomas Ivye gent,
William Frenche, vicar of Haukysbury, Nicholas Came.

For whatever reason, between Sir John's death and his own death later in the year, Henry VIII conferred the manors of Old and Chipping Sodbury upon the heir, Maurice Walshe. These, it will be remembered, had been inherited by Henry VII when the Countess of Warwick had died. So for the first time the lordship of all three manors rested with one family.

As a continuing action in the dissolution of the Monasteries, the first active steps were taken against the Religious Guild in Sodbury in 1549 during the second year of the reign of Edward VI. Three years earlier the accounts read:

	Dr.		**Cr.**
Income	£18 19s 0d	Stipend 2 priests	£12 4s. 0d
		For 4 omits	8s. 0d
		For an organ player	13s. 4d
		For a steward's fee	13s. 4d
		For keeping of a clocke	6s. 8d
		For keeping of the ornaments	8s. 8d
		For rents	11s. 9d
		Balance	£3 13s. 3d
	£18 19s 0d		**£18 19s 0d**

Eventually the plate and other ornaments were sold for £11 13s. 4d. The last incumbent was John Glover who received a pension of £4 per annum in 1553.

In the break-up of the Guild, 24s. of the income was first to go which had been the rent for one tenement, one burgage, and one plot of land on which the current tenant was Robert Browne and previously had been Richard Cullymore. The ownership passed by King's letter patent to Anthony Borchid Esq., his heirs and assigns for ever.

The next beneficiaries were Sir Miles Partriche and his brother Hugh. Sir Miles was one of the nine royal commissioners appointed to enquire into the chantries of Bristol and Gloucestershire. They acquired:

(a) All that messuage and tenement and one garden with the appurtenances, now, or late, in the tenure of Thomas Summers formerly belonging to the Guild of the Blessed Virgin Mary,

(b) One messuage and all the chambers and buildings adjoining belonging to the Guild and being in the occupation of the priests of the same.

(c) All that messuage, house and building vulgarly called the Guild house, or otherwise also called the Church house and one garden adjoining the same.

Which same messuages and other premises are together situate between the tenement wherein Thomas Holder now dwells on the west and the communal hostel called The George on the east and the King's highway on the south and towards the Rouche weir on the north.

The properties involved appeared to be the present Town Hall and the two properties to the left of it. A century before the property detailed in (b) above was a shop let to Thomas Boucher. Its size and the fact that it was where the priests lived could mean that it was the site of the earliest school.

Before the end of 1549 all the three properties were owned by Richard Pate of Gloucester, another of the King's commissioners, having been sold to him for £34 5s. 8d. During this period, actually in 1544, among other possessions which changed hands, was a "capital messuage" at Old Sodbury which had belonged to the Collegiate Church at Westbury-on-Trym which went to Sir Ralph Sadler.

It was around this time that for no apparent reason the name 'Sobbery' became 'Sodbury' in documents and so today's spelling will be used for the rest of this book.

Once Maurice Walshe had succeeded his father in 1547 he began to make a number of changes in the use of the land which had been conferred on him by the late king. This restricted the rights both of the Old Sodbury inhabitants and the Chipping Sodbury burgesses who both sent representatives to plead their cases before the Court of the Marches, this time at Ludlow during 1551-1555. The following sets out their complaint and the decision so far as Old Sodbury was concerned:

It appeared to the arbitrators that before this time there were certain grounds enclosed in the meadows and marshlands, which severally and particularly were limited and appointed to the copyholders, which grounds at this present still remain enclosed and are occupied in several by the same copyholders, whereof there was very little in quantity and limited to any cottager, cottageholder, or half yard-land with Old Sodbury aforesaid, by reason whereof the same cottagers were impaired by loss of such common as they pretended to have in the meadows and marshlands aforesaid, and the copy-holders thereby much bettered and amended. It is therefore ordered by the said arbitrators and by the assent of Maurice Walshe, and also his assent for his tenants as much as in him lieth, or may do, that the copy-

holders of the said manor of Old Sodbury herein named, and all such as shall hereafter have and hold such copy-lands as they now have, shall not at any time after the Feast of St. Michael, the Archangel, which shall be in the year of our Lord 1553 use, have and enjoy any common for any manner of cattle in the said waste ground called Horwood: and that the cottagers of the manor of Old Sodbury, which now be, or hereafter, shall be dwelling in the cottages of half-yard lands, in which they now dwell, shall have reasonable communion after the rate of their cottages or half-yard lands in the waste ground called Horwood, anything before expressed to the contrary notwithstanding. It was further agreed between the two parties that a Hayward should be appointed with authority to take and impound all such cattle which shall be taken in or upon Horwood or Kingrove aforesaid of all such persons as have not common there, and the same to be impounded in the lord's pound at Old Sodbury for the same; and shall have yearly half the profits of the pound.

The copy holders of the manor of Old Sodbury for terms of lives, who were concerned were John Woodward, John Saunders, John Aldridge, Maurice Aldridge, Thomas Hopkins, Richard Francombe, John Coxe, each of which held a messuage with yard-land and its appurtenances. From details actually applying to Leicestershire but which were probably similar in Sodbury, a Yard-land represented a holding of about thirty acres and generally speaking conferred rights to common for the following: three or four oxen, one or two cows with calves, two horses, about 30–35 sheep with their lambs, a sow with its young for a short period and four to ten geese.

The following Old Sodbury Manor cottagers were appointed to have common upon Kingrove and Norwood according to the rate of their cottages:

Two cottages: John Bishop.
One cottage: Thomas Tiley, William Dack, John Martin, W. Francombe, Henry Saunders, John Jervice, William Balle, William Colls, John Hill, Thomas Anstee, Francis Codrington, William Whiting, Robert Barrow, John Yeoman, Nicholas Wickson, Robert Hopkins, John Adams.

This information shows that at this time Old Sodbury consisted of at least seven small farms and nineteen cottages. It is appropriate at this moment to look at what food the occupants of the cottages normally lived on.

Generally speaking, in normal times, the daily diet would have been one pint of milk, one pint of whey, two ounces of cheese, one ounce of bacon, two pounds of bread and two ounces of peas. The bread would probably have been made from either maslin, a mixture of rye and wheats or drage, a mixture of barley and wheat, or even from rye alone. In times of shortage, beans, peas, lentils and oats were used. In Chipping Sodbury the burgesses and townsfolk probably had a slightly higher standard of living.

The dispute between the burgesses of Chipping Sodbury and the Lord of the Manor, Maurice Walshe, was more involved and went on longer than the dispute involving the Old Sodbury inhabitants.

Around 1551 John Wyrriett, thonger, Richard Mories and Thomas Smythe, all burgesses of Sodbury, complained to the Privy Council that Maurice Walshe's servants, had interrupted the exercise of their rights of common in the marshes and meadows of Old Sodbury by impounding their cattle and enclosing stretches of land with hedges and ditches and that they were no longer permitted pasturage in the Leyes, the Kenleys, the Nokes and the Hangers as had been their practice after the hay had been mown or corn cut.

The Privy Council decided in favour of the burgesses and instructed a Thomas Throgmorton to do all that was necessary. Unfortunately for the burgesses, this gentleman was a close friend of Maurice Walshe and so did nothing at all to rectify the matter as he had been instructed to do.

After another two years, their patience exhausted, the burgesses laid the same complaint before the Court of the Marches, making it plain that because of "the special favour and affection by hyme borne towards the said Maurice Walshe, Thomas Throgmorton had failed in his duty".

At first the Court appointed Sir John Veynlow, John Welch and Thomas Throgmorton of Tortworth to arbitrate but this time Throgmorton declared his interest and declined to act as also did the other two. Eventually Sir John Dennis agreed to act provided he had the help of an able lawyer called David Broke, sergeant-at-law.

Sir John's award was that:

> The burghers of Chipping Sodbury were to enjoy all their old rights in the waste ground called Horwood, outside the hedge of the ground called Little Sodbury Park, lately disparked, and in the lane leading to the Yate that divideth and encloseth the said waste grounds from the common meadows of Old Sodbury, and shall also use for their cattle the ground called Kingrove Wood also Gaunts Fields.

However, their claim to the grounds called the Hangers, the Nokes, the Kinleys, the Leys, the marshes, and meadows lying east of Horwood was not allowed.

The Court of the Marches approved this award which was a considerable set back for the people of Chipping Sodbury. At some point John Wyrriett appears to have been guilty of a serious misdemeanour, perhaps perjury or falsification of evidence, because the Attorney General to the King, Henry Bradshaw, felt it necessary to issue the following indictment:

> *That the plea of the aforesaid John Wyrriett is not sufficient in law for claiming or having the liberties and franchises aforesaid, to which the same attorney of the said Lord King has no need nor is bound by the law of the land to answer for the same Lord King. Therefore the said attorney for the said Lord King seeks judgement by reason of the insufficient plea and claim aforesaid, and that the franchises and liberties aforesaid may be seized into the hands of the said Lord King. And that the same John Wyrriett be imprisoned for the usurpation aforesaid upon the said Lord King, and make fine and redemption with the aforesaid Lord King for his usurpation aforesaid.*

The above makes more sense when it is remembered that the manors had been in royal hands for some years previously and perhaps John Wyrriett had attributed to King Henry one or two grants for which he had no proof. What happened as a result of the indictment is not known but John obviously survived it as will be seen later.

In 1552 massive frauds came to light regarding the activities of some members of the Commission responsible for disposing of the property of the late Guild and other similar organisations in Gloucestershire and in February 1552–53 Sir Miles Partriche was hanged for felony.

Even though the death of King Edward VI, the overthrow of Lady Jane Grey and the subsequent crowning of Queen Mary during 1553 must have caused some local excitement, time was still found to replace the old market cross upon which the sculptures of the saints had aroused the anger of the local inhabitants. Parts of the one which replaced it have survived to the present day in the shaft of the present War Memorial above the inscriptions. It probably stood in the same spot as the present War memorial.

The open mouth in this hideous face in Little Sodbury Manor was used as a peep-hole from the Ladies' Gallery into the Banqueting Hall. It is a rare specimen dating from about 1500.

The Tudors

Having married Dame Elizabeth Hartcorte, a widow, on 9th November 1547, Maurice Walshe decided in June 1556 to make his will. Considering what was to follow, it was very fortunate that he did. The following is the relevant section of it, dated 7th June.

> *I bequeath to my mother, Lady Anne Walshe, for life, the lease of Little Sodbury Park, which I have assigned my brothers-in-law Edmund George and George Huntley Esquires for her, and I desire my mother to bring up my five daughters Jane, Cicelye, Joan, Lucie and Elizabeth Walshe and my sons Nicholas and Henry until their ages of 24. To my said mother the site of the manor called the Farm of Old Sodbury and the farm called the Hayelygrove and all the fines, heriots and rents of the said manor, the borough of Cheping Sodbury and the lease of the Park at Little Sodbury. To each of my daughters on marriage £400. To my son Walter, all my household stuff in the lodge in Old Sodbury Park, the lease of the dayhouse there, several pieces of pewter and so forth. To my nephew and servant John Norton £10 and the profits of the toll of the two fair days in the borough of Sodbury for life, to my nurse, Edy Bowton, a cow. Bequests to servants... To my son William the household stuff in my house at Olveston. To my mother my lease of the parsonage at Aylburton, for life, with reversion to my son Nicholas. Executrix my Mother. Witnesses. Thomas Payne, Robert Frankcombe, John Norton (gent), William Frankcombe of Hyland, Nicholas Canne, the writer, William Walshe, Walter Walshe, Hugh Dabbeham.*

A fortnight later he added a codicil:

> *Should my son William die without heirs male the bequests made to him to go to my son Nicholas with reversion to my son Walter.*
> *Witnesses. John Norton, Andrew Hathewaye, Nicholas Came.*

Maurice Walshe's second wife, Dame Elizabeth Hartcorte, had obviously died previously as she is not mentioned in his will. In June 1556, therefore, the family consisted of the following: Maurice Walshe, Lady Anne Walshe his mother, older sons Walter and William (whose health was perhaps uncertain), daughters Jane, Cicely, Joan, Lucie, Elizabeth, and two younger sons Nicholas and Henry.

Some time between 21st June and 18th July 1556, there was a very bad thunderstorm which caused the greatest local tragedy so far recorded. In the words of an old history:

> *In 1556 during a severe thunderstorm while Maurice Walshe was seated at dinner in the manor at Little Sodbury, a sulphurous*

The Three Sodburys – An Introduction

globe entered the open door, and traversing the room passed out by the opposite window killing one child on the spot. Others were so injured that they died within two months.

The full impact of what happened is summed up in the brief codicil that Maurice added to his will on 18th July 1556:

My daughters Jane, Cicely, Joan and Elizabeth and my son Walter are now dead therefore my son Nicholas to have Walter's portion.
Signed, Maurice Walshe.
Witnesses, Nicholas Canne, John Canne.

By 28th September 1556 Maurice Walshe had also died. Nicholas, having inherited Walter's portion, was now the Lord of the three Manors. The remaining members of the family were his grandmother, Lady Anne, brother Henry and sister Lucie.

Although fortunately rare, proof that events such as the above do occur is given in a report in the Daily Mirror for 9th April 1979 of an incident near Newport (Gwent):

A freak ball of lightning mowed down eleven soccer players yesterday. Their match had just been abandoned because of a severe hailstorm when the lightning struck. The ball of fire flashed into a metal fence and bounced off, bowling over the players. Last night a 23 year old player was critically ill with severe shock and burns.

Fortunately, the result was less severe than that at the manor.

On 14th May 1557 the will of Richard Colymore, son of Richard and Edith Colymore who were commemorated by the stone in Chipping Sodbury church was proven of which the following is a part:

To the high altar of my parish church 5s. 0d, to every spinner of mine having no plough 12d, to every weaver 3s. 4d, to every poor householder 12d. To the poor householders in Marshe Street, Bristol 20s. 0d. To my son Edward £60. To my son George £100 at his age of 21. To my son Jasper £40. To my daughter Edith £20. To my niece Jane Colymore dwelling with Thomas Shipman at Bristol £50 at her age of 18. To my sons Thomas and Jasper my lease of Stanshalls to be divided between them and the cattle there and the household stuff in my house at Sodbury. Legacies to my servant Elen Adams, to Denys Browne, Jackelyne Colymore, father-in-law Christopher Browne. To my sons Thomas and Jasper the lease of the new mills at Kingswood.
Executors, Son-in-law Thomas Shipman of Bristol and son Thomas Colymore.

The Tudors

This is the first time that the weaving trade is mentioned in the town. The reference to the new mills at Kingswood, which would have been near Wotton, not Bristol, shows that the movement north to the Wotton and Stroud areas had already started. Stanshalls is almost certainly Stanshawes and as such is an interesting reference.

In December 1557 the two messuages and the Guild or Church House, originally bought by Richard Pate from the Partriche brothers, changed hands again, being bought by John Bisshope and Henry Somers for £24 13s. 4d "on behalf of the inhabitants of Chippinge Sodbury otherwise called Great Sodbury" with the intention of applying any profits arising from the ownership to the benefit of the poor of the town. There were two qualifications needed to receive benefit, they had to be of 'good report' and to have resided in the town for three years. A number of burgesses were enfeoffed to hold the property, initially John Bisshops, Henry Summers, John Colymore, Richard Norrys, John Walker, Edward Browne, Richard Boxe, John Wyrriett, Edmund Hill, Edmund Taylor, John Hill, Thomas Colymore and Thomas Taylor.

When, by death or other causes, the number of those surviving had been reduced to three or four, another group was to be enfeoffed. The appearance of John Wyrriett's

The Cross shown above was removed c.1770 and placed in the garden of Trotman's Mill in Brook Street. It was recovered in the 1800s and placed at the entrance to the Catholic Church in Broad Street.

name is interesting because it shows he came to no great harm from his indictment in 1553.

Around about this time, also, Hampstead, which had been granted to Bradenstoke Priory, passed into the hands of Anne, widow of Sir Adrian Fortescue under the title of "The Manor, Grange or Farm of Hampstead".

In 1572 the position regarding properties belonging to the town was regularised when John Wyrriett, who was now Bailiff, together with fourteen others were made the owners on behalf of the town by Thomas Evans (alias Taylor) and others, of the following properties:

1. One tenement in Chipping Sodbury called "Vayre (Fayre) House".
2. One close of pasture and meadow called "Vayre (Fayre) House leaseholds".
3. One parcel of land situated in a meadow called "Hole Mead" (Dolemead?) in the parish of Old Sodbury.
4 & 5. One close called "Brand Ashe" and "Hulkynge Close" situated in the said parish (i.e. Old Sodbury).
6. Certain lands called Gorlands in the same parish.
7. A piece of land called the Splotte.
8. A burgage in "Flint Close" in the borough of Chipping Sodbury.
9. A tenement and meadow in Chipping Sodbury outside the Bar Gate on the east.
10. A tenement and orchard outside the Bar Gate.
11. A tenement and orchard outside the Bar Gate.
12. A burgage adjoining Gaunts field.
13. A tenement and orchard in Horse Street in the said borough.
14. A burgage in Rounceval Street.
15. A shop in the street called the Butcher's Shop.
16. A tenement in the place called the "Garrett".

These properties were to be held to their proper use with the intention that the rents and profits should be used to maintain and repair the roads in Chipping Sodbury and "to sustain the virtuous and deserving poor" living in the town "in accord with the custom from time out of mind and to no other purpose whatsoever".

It is believed that the Thomas Evans, alias Taylor mentioned, was the last master of the Guild and that these properties and others had been administered on behalf of the townsfolk by the Guild officers. "Fayre" has been inserted in brackets after "Vayre" in Items 1 and 2 because it is believed that they are the tenements, burgages, etc., which were given

The Tudors 103

as a gift by one of the Fayre family to Thomas Doghton and Robert Barbour in 1428. It will be remembered that they came to the le Fayre family from Adam Alba at some time after 1225.

Fayre House would not have been on the site of what is now called Vayre House, because it had to be in the Borough of Chipping Sodbury.

Flint Close was near Bucketts Hill. The mention of the Bar Gate is interesting because it is the first time it has been mentioned and was probably just beyond the present post office, halfway along Horse Street which was not the main road as now, and leading only to various burgages in open country. A gate was probably needed, therefore, to stop animals straying into town.

Horse Street c.1910.
In Medieval times there was a gate across the road where the pavement buts out on the left hand side of the road.
(A photograph from the Sodbury Historical Society collection)

The Shambles or Butcher's Shop and the Garrett were both in the centre of what is now Broad Street, the Garrett being at the bottom near to the War memorial and the Shambles, as indicated before, opposite the Church Road and Hounds Road exits.

There must be a reason for the name of 'The Gorlands' referred to in item 6 and the most likely explanation is that it became known by the name of the family who owned or leased it. In 1572 the will of a certain Mary Gore, widow of Chipping Sodbury, was proven showing that a family of that name lived in the town. The custom was to let lands for the term of a number of lives, generally three, or for ninety-nine years. If that part of the Town Lands had been leased for that period to a member of the Gore family it would explain why it became known as "The Gorlands" if only for ease of reference. This is exactly what happened later when a part became known as "Norris Gorlands" as the result of being let for a long period to a family of that name.

By April 1575 Anthony Somers had become bailiff instead of John Wyrriett. Some parts of the town lands were let for a period of three lives to Nicholas Packer, his wife and son with a down payment of £8 and a yearly rent of 7s. 0d. The property was described as:

All that tenement of house called Denes Wattes and seven burgage grounds thereunto adjoining containing, by estimation, two acres, be it more or less, situate and being in Chepinge Sodbury aforesaid in the street there called Horse Street without the barre gates there now in the occupation of the said Nicholas Packer and late in the tenure of Ellen Packer, widow.

The original document was endorsed later with "House & Hopyard". Several names that are still familiar now appear for the first time in another document of the same date as the one above:

Two parcels of pasture called Brande Aysshe and Hawkyns Close containing, by estimation, two and a half acres lying in the parish of Old Sodbury between a close called Gorlands, now in the tenure of John Blanchard, on the south side and a close called Standell or Standuff, now in the tenure of Robert Warner, on the north side, and extendeth from Godsons Lane on the west part eastward unto the said Close called Gorlands.

These were first let to John Cam for one year and then for the three lives of Alice, Clement and Thomas Merrick. The down payment was 40s. 0d with a yearly rent of 6s. 8d.

The lawyers must have been very busy on 12th April 1575 because there is also another agreement with that date. This one covers part of the Gorlands known as Cowlands which extended themselves between the park of Old Sodbury on the north east and the Queen's highway on the south west and bounded on the north and south by other portions of Gorelands. The recipients were John Cam for one year and then Jane Wyrriett for three lives, her own, her son Thomas and then daughter Mary. It had to be Jane Wyrriett because John Wyrriett, probably the son of the first John, was one of those responsible for the leasing. The down payment was £11 with an annual rent of 8s. 4d.

Whatever the reason for it, there was a rash of enfeoffments in Sodbury at that time. For instance, in 1576, Robert Warner and John Hellyer, "procurators" of the church, made over to the bailiff and burgesses a number of properties in the town, the income from which was to be used solely for repairing and sustaining the church. The properties concerned were:

1. One messuage or tenement and the garden adjoining to it on the south side; which said messuage is situate and is "the corner house" on the south side of the high road opposite the high cross there and is occupied by Thomas Edwardes.
2. A burgage ground in Hounds Lane containing two burgages more or less.
3. A messuage situated between "The Bell" now in the tenure of Anne Walker, widow, on the west (left) and the tenement of Thomas Evans, alias Taylor, on the east (right) the high road on the south and the church on the north.
4. One burgage ground lying next the road in Rounsevall Street containing half an acre held by William Somers.
5. One meadow in Chipping Sodbury containing two acres called Pyrle Mead, held by George Wyrryet.
6. Two acres of meadow in Dolemeade in Old Sodbury.

The "Corner House" had passed from Matilda atte Hulle to Thomas le Fayre together with certain lands in Houndustrete in 1349. Almost immediately after the bailiff and burgesses had received the above property in Item 1 from Robert Warner and John Hellyer, they let it to a Richard Turner for a long period at an annual rent of 16s. 0d.

It is probable that Pyrle Mead lay on the left towards the lower end of Hatter's Lane.

Also in 1576 there is a record of the letting of three burgages, Little Flints ¾ acre and two pieces called Splatts or Splotts of 1½ acres.

The "Corner House" c.1918.
The house in question is on the corner of Broad Street and Horse Street just to the right of the telegraph pole in the photograph above.

'Splatts' and 'Splotts' are alternatives for 'Rag' and in old Bristol slang mean 'a parcel of land' . The land referred to was on the far side of the brook behind the church.

After the tragic thunderstorm, Nicholas Walshe had inherited the manors in 1556, but then had died in 1578. The properties were then inherited by Henry Walshe, said by some to have been the son of Nicholas but who might just as easily have been his brother.

Henry must have been a short-tempered man who was involved in at least one other duel before being killed in a mysterious duel with Edward Wintour who, if he was a member of the Dyrham family, could be the one said to have been a secret agent. The Walshe family had trading connections with the Lowlands and it could be that some incident in the run up to the sailing of the Spanish Armada might have caused it.

In this same year the letting of yet another part of the town lands is recorded. This time it was a tenement, a garden and three quarters of a burgage ground in "Horestreete without the Barriattes", that is, outside the gates previously mentioned, halfway along Horse Street.

In 1580 there is one of the earliest mentions of a definite tradesman when John Bircombe (or Burcombe), his wife Alice and son, another John, are mentioned. He is described as a cutler who takes the lease of the town property between the Church House (Town Hall) and the George. The property is described as:

All that messuage now containing two upper chambers and two lower chambers, with a pair of stairs and entry leading into the said upper chambers and also one garden and backside adjoining to John Winter's tenement on the west side (left) *containing by estimation nine lugges and a half in length and twenty feet in breadth situate between the said church house on the one side and a messuage there called the Sign of the George on the other side.*

On the 20th October 1582 Sir Nicholas Poyntz, Sir Richard Berkeley, Thomas Throckmorton, William Rede, Matthew Poyntz, Walter Dennys, John Seymore and Nicholas Thorpe formed a consortium to leasing the ex-Guild or Town house for twenty-eight years. Why they leased it at all and why the period was limited is not known but it could have been to provide a school. Indeed, there is no evidence that the agreement was ever implemented and the whole transaction is something of a mystery. Whatever the purpose, the document does provide us with a description of the Town Hall as it was at that time, as follows:

The Loftes or Hyer Roomes of all the messuage in Sodbury known by the name of the town house lying on the north side of the street there. *The dwelling house of John Burcombe on the east side* (right) *and the dwelling house of John Winters on the west side* (left). *And also one little void place, or lower room, where a double pair of stairs is fixed at the time of this demise going up into the said lofts or hyer rooms. And one little house, being ruinous, at the entering into of the said void place. And all those inner rooms, or dwelling places, wherein certain poor people and others are now dwelling, adjoining at the north end. And also all that void piece of ground lying at the north end of the dwelling houses extending on to the pale of the garden of one John Burcombe, cutler, and other grounds not already granted to John Burcombe or John Wynter. Also free egresse and regresse downe to the watercourse or river called the Church Brook.*

All the above is contained in a very long document which goes on to name the poor people living in the houses at the north end and to make provision for their transfer without hardship to alternative accommodation in Rounceval Street. The rent for the property was to be 26s. 8d per year.

In 1586 a transaction took place which explains why part of Gorlands was known as 'Norris' and mentions the tanning industry for the first time. The indenture of the lease reads:

A parcel of meadow called Gorlands containing, by estimation, five acres or thereabouts now in the occupation of the said Richard Norris, tanner, being in Old Sodbury. Which five acres extendeth itself from the park of Old Sodbury on the east part, the Queen's highway on the west part, one other part of the said grounds called Gorlands, now in the tenure of John Wiriat on the north part and one paddock of meadow now in the tenure of Thomas Longe of Old Sodbury on the south part.

The mention of the Queen's highway is interesting because it was the extension of Hatter's Lane eastwards and was the main Bristol to Oxford road via Tetbury and Cirencester which was becoming steadily more important.

The tenement on the west (left) of the Bell changed hands in 1592 when it passed to Agnes Taylor. She was a widow of the family known as 'Evans alias Taylor' and after her it was held by Edmund Taylor.

One event which probably caused little comment in either Sodbury or anywhere else in 1593 was that the standard mile was changed to 1760 yards instead of the previous figure of 2,428 yards. It would have made little impact until maps began to be drawn in 1675 but it does explain how Chipping Sodbury suddenly became twelve miles from Bristol instead of the original nine.

108 *The Three Sodburys – An Introduction*

The footbridge and ford in Hatters Lane on what was the main exit road from Chipping Sodbury to Oxford. The flooding used to be an annual event. The Sodbury Common gate used to be just the other side of the bridge resulting in wet feet even if you had a horse and cart. After many protests it was moved in the late 1800s to the entrance to the common on the road to Little Sodbury where there is now a cattle grid.

CHAPTER SIX

THE STUARTS

The record of the burial at Old Sodbury in 1605 of John Neale of Boukete Hill gives a clue to the origin of Bucketts Hill. It could have begun as Bouquette, a Flemish family name. The same records show that there were other families with continental forebears in several items relating to "Blauncharde" who are the family mentioned in the deed of 1575 quoted earlier. Since the Gorlands were neighbours they could have lived at the farm, still under that name, midway between Chipping and Old Sodbury. They are also remembered in the name of the group of council houses built in one of the farm's fields. Some years ago an architect identified some sixteenth century work in the farm building.

By 1608, during which there was a very severe winter, Walter Walshe owned the properties consisting of the following:

The manor of Old Sodbury, Chipping Sodbury, alias Burgus de Sodbury, Kingrove, Little Sodbury, and a capital messuage and lands called Camer's Race.

These were divided up into some twenty messuages and five hundred acres of land, meadow, pasture and wood. A few years later they were bought by Thomas Stephens, Attorney-General to Prince Henry and Prince Charles.

Also in 1608, John Smith, steward to the Berkeley Family, made a list of all the able bodied men in Gloucestershire showing their ages and trades. In Old Sodbury there were 2 bakers, 1 clothier, 5 coal drivers, 1 glover, 11 husbandmen (small holders), 9 labourers, 1 lime carrier, 1 mason, 1 mercer, 2 millers, 7 servants, 1 shepherd, 2 smiths, 1 tailor, 1 tinker, 5 weavers, 5 yeomen, 6 unidentified, Total 58.

In Little Sodbury there were 4 carpenters, 9 husbandmen, 4 weavers, 2 unidentified, Total 19

The 4th Earl of Worcester bought Badminton Manor in 1609, beginning the association that the Beaufort family has had with Badminton to this day.

In February 1609–10 one of the messuages bequeathed by le Fayre, together with several parcels of land is again mentioned in an indenture. This was the tenement on the left of the entrance to Church Lane. If it was not the original Fayre house then it could well have been on the same site because one of the parcels of land mentioned in the same deed was a barn called the Vayre (Fayre) house in the parish of Old Sodbury together with two closes and a meadow called Vayre (Fayre) house leaseholds. The same indenture also mentions the separate Manor of Kingrove which appears in the details of the Walshe estate where a meadow there called Pynnes Meade had been held in lieu of a holding in Dolemead.

Another acre previously held by Edward Rowles but currently leased to Synnyffe Rowles is also mentioned. The forename needs to be said aloud before it is realised that it is "Sniffy". It is to be hoped that Mr Rowles would never think that the trouble he had with his nose would be commented on nearly four hundred years later.

Another deed in the same year mentions George Webb, a clothier of Old Sodbury, Edmund White, a tyler, and Thomas Browne, the constable for that year.

As mentioned previously, the property known as Hampstead, originally owned by Bradenstoke Priory, had passed to Lady Anne Fortescue in 1557–58. Interest was shown in the property again in 1612 when Sir Henry Hobart, H.M. Attorney-General, filed a charge in the Court of the Exchequer against John Smith, Bailiff of the Borough of Chipping Sodbury, and others that the Ridings belonged to the Crown as part of the possessions of the dissolved monastery of Bradenstoke. The defendants replied with a well researched answer which reads:

And first therefore as touching the parcels in the said information mentioned called the Ridings or Mead Riding and Stub Riding these defendants say that the same grounds are (as these defendants verily believe) parcel of the Lordship or Manor of Sodbury in the County of Gloucestershire in which grounds certain Burgesses and poor inhabitants dwelling and inhabiting in certain Burgages in the town or borough of Sodbury (which Town or Borough, or the greatest part thereof also these defendants verily believe to be parcel of the said Manor of Sodbury) have been used, time out of mind, to the maintenance and relief for Kine and Cattle in sort as followeth (that is to say): On or at the third day of May yearly the said Burgesses and inhabitants of the said burgages within the said borough of Chipping Sodbury do, by the licence, consent and appointment of the Bailiff, of the said town or borough for the time being, put into the said pasture ground called the Riding a certain number of Kine to the number of three score or thereabouts which are then fed or depastured until or about the feast of All Saints then next following in the same year at which time the former Kine or Cattle and some others are put to feed and depasture in the said ground called the Meade Riding where the Kine or Cattle are, or may be, fed and kept until the purification of Our Lady commonly called Candlemas Day then after following at which day and time the same is tyned and rid of cattle and in such sort the said inhabitants and Burgages do have and take the herbage and profit of feeding of the said ground time out of mind. And; these defendants further say that (for the most part) the Bailiff doth appoint and allow yearly the pasture and feeding of the said grounds to several persons to the number of three score persons at least so that for the most part any Man or Woman put one cow there for one year and few or none have two Kine or Cattle there. And the pasture or first cutting or crop of the grass in the said meadow ground called the Meade Riding is yearly from time to time taken by and amongst the said burgesses and inhabitants an acre by one person and few or none have or hath two acres of meadow there. For which pasture and meadow everyone having a cow pastured in the said pasture ground doth pay for the same unto the said Bailiff of the said town or borough, for the time being, yearly for every cow the sum of 2d and every one having the cutting of an acre of grass or meadow, doth pay to the bailiff yearly for every acre of meadow sixpence and the bailiff who is made and appointed yearly from time to time by the Lord of the said town or borough or his steward for that year of his bailiwick to gather and collect the same and doth pay therefore yearly to the Lord of the said borough for the said Ridings the sum or yearly rent of five pounds per annum and what is by the winter pasture so otherwise raised out of the profits of the said grounds called the Ridings is allowed yearly unto the said bailiff towards his great care and charges in governing of the said town and in paying for the Lord's stewards coming there to keep Court and for and towards his other great expenses. And these defendants do not claim other right or interest or estate in the said grounds called the Ridings than as aforesaid but do think and believe that the soil and inheritance thereof (as well of the Manor of Sodbury) belong unto Thomas Stephens Esq., the Prince's Attorney General unto whom the said bailiff of the said borough or town payeth yearly for the said premises five pounds and if any trespass be done in the said grounds or any estrayes or other *casualties or profits there happen to come (other than only for the feeding and taking the grass pasture and herbage of the same ground in sort as aforesaid and taking estovers thereby the Bailiff (only for the time being) the same are answerable and belong to the said Thomas Stephens without whom these defendants cannot directly answer touching the title of the same grounds and do therefore leave the same to him.*

In the following Hilary Term the charge was dismissed, the appropriate part of the dismissal reading:

It is ordered by the Court that the said Cause shall be absolutely dismissed out of this Court and that the defendants shall and may continue in the quiet possession of the premises and every part and parcel thereof as they have done before the said bill exhibited into this Court until the said defendants shall either upon an Information or Injunction to be brought by His Majesty's Attorney General or upon some other action to be commenced in the Office of Pleas of this Court be evicted out of the premises by verdict and judgement of this Court.

Strangely there is no mention of the Crassus family. Unfortunately the original charge has not survived as it may well have given some clue to the real origin of the Ridings of which this case gives the first mention by name.

The purchase of the manor by Thomas Stephens is confirmed by this document but apparently Walter Walshe did not part with the right to appoint the priest at the same time because:

In 1613 a certain George Boswell B.A. was instituted to the rectory and parish church of St. Adeline of Little Sodbury, vacant by the resignation of Thomas Hook, on the presentation of Walter Walshe, patron.

The record above from the Hockaday Abstracts is the first time that the dedication to St. Adeline is mentioned, although the church existed in 1300. St. Adeline was the patron saint of the Flemish weavers and the dedication is believed to be unique in this country. This, with the personal names like Blauncharde, Bouquette and Bocher (or Boucher) and places like Dunkirk and Petty (Petite) France shows that weavers from the continent probably came to this area at some time previously.

Records at Old Sodbury Church mention the burial, on 14th March 1613–14, of Thomas Blauncharde. In the September of 1614 George Webb and the other feoffees of the Chipping Sodbury town lands let Brande Ash and Hawkins Close to Bartholomew Merrick, shoemaker. The lease was to run for ninety-nine years or the duration of the lives of his wife Mary and sons John and Anthony. In defining the holding a portion of Gorlands is mentioned which was in the possession of Thomas Blanchard deceased and currently held by his widow Anne. Blauncharde and Blanchard are thus shown to be the same family. Godsonnes Lane is mentioned again in the definition.

In 1615 the Wyrriett family appear briefly again. The males are all dead leaving only the widow, Jane, and daughter, Marie who is married to Richard Warner. Because of this the feoffees grant him the lease of lands previously held by the Wyrrietts. The highway on the west and the parks of Old Sodbury on the east are again mentioned as boundaries.

With regard to the weather at about that time, no doubt the severe winter of 1615–16 brought the usual degree of suffering in its train, alleviated perhaps by the mild winter the following year. Any relief that brought was probably offset by the cold summer of 1618 which had hardly faded from memory before 1621 and 1622 renewed the chilly spell.

Charles I succeeded to the throne in 1625 and on the 11th January in the third year of his reign a decree was issued showing the uses to which the charitable funds in Chipping Sodbury were to be put in future. From the revenue on lands belonging to the town which were specially limited to church use, £4 was to be used annually for road mending in the town with any money left over being used for poor relief of those inhabitants who had lived in the town for at least three years. From the other rents and revenues from the town lands not being used in some other way, £20 was to be distributed among the poor of the borough annually, a further £20 was to be paid for binding out apprentices of the poor town-born children to handicraft trades with no more than £4 being given with each apprentice and, finally, £20 per annum was to be paid to a schoolmaster.

During the previous two centuries at least, priests had been running small schools and since some education was essential in any business community it is reasonable to assume that Sodbury would be no exception. The decree quoted above shows that shortly after 1628 a more formal arrangement was entered into with a proper school being provided.

For some time previously there had been premises in Chipping Sodbury High Street which had been occupied by Robert Peaslie and his son Joseph who were saddlers. These now passed to John Williams, a mercer, and his wife Jane and daughter Sara. Together with the messuage there was one close of pasture ground in Chipping Sodbury known as Buckettes Hill which contained four burgage grounds.

There had been properties in Wickwar for a long time from which the profits were used for the benefit of the Chipping Sodbury inhabitants. They were re-enfeoffed on 20th August 1632 to the Bailiff, Robert

114   *The Three Sodburys – An Introduction*

Haynes, and the Bailiff Burgesses and then on the 31st August they became responsible for:
1. A tenement in Chipping Sodbury held by Henry Boxe.
2. A barn called the Faire House in Old Sodbury.
3. Two closes of pasture called the Fairehouse Leazes.
4. One parcel of land in a meadow called Dolemead in Old Sodbury.
5. A close of pasture called Brandash and Halkins Close in Old Sodbury.
6. Certain lands called the Gorlands in Old Sodbury.
7. A piece of land called the Splotts.
8. A burgage in Flints Close within the borough of Chipping Sodbury.
9. A tenement and a meadow in Chipping Sodbury beyond the Bargates on the east.
10. A tenement and orchard beyond the Bargates held by Law. Farr.
11. A burgage against Gaunt's Field.
12. A tenement with an orchard in Horse Street.
13. Two burgages in Rounceval Street.
14. A shop in the street called the "Butcher's Shop".
15. A tenement in the street at Chipping Sodbury called the Garrett.

As previously the income from all these was to be used for the upkeep of the highways, the relief of the poor and the other specific purposes already spelled out.

One of the burgages listed was leased in March 1634–35 to Robert Coole and from that document it is learned that Robert Haynes was a clothier.

The re-enfeoffment of properties continued in 1635 when the following were made over to the Bailiff, Robert Davis, and Bailiff Burgesses:
1. The corner house on the south of the street over against the Cross.
2. A burgage in Hounds Lane containing, by estimation, two burgages held by Thomas Browne.
3. A messuage between the tenement called the Bell, held by Samuel Webb on the west and a tenement occupied by Henry Boxe, joiner, on the east.
4. A burgage ground, half acre, in Rounceval Street held by Martha Pill.
5. A plot of two acres of meadow called Pyrle Mead held by Tobias Davis.

The Stuarts 115

6. Three and half acres in Dolemeade in Old Sodbury.

The intention this time was that the Bailiff and Bailiff Burgesses of the borough should use the income from these properties solely for repairing the church.

It will be remembered that in 1582 the ex-Guild House had been let for a period of twenty-eight years. The lease must have expired in 1610 but the only news of the building during this time is the mention of re-enfeoffment at some time in 1592. Another re-enfeoffment in 1636, however, provides the following description:

All those three tenements and two garden grounds situate in Chipping Sodbury between an inn called the George on the east part, a tenement in the possession of William Turner, on the west part. One of which said three tenements lies next to the George Inn, with a garden ground and a back side extending down to the brook there and is occupied by William Caurbridge. The middle tenement of the three is used as the Town House, and the other of the three, with a garden ground, is in the possession of James Wineard.

The income was to be paid by themselves their heirs and assigns, to two burgesses appointed to receive it and then used partly for the support, relief and maintenance of the Town of Chipping Sodbury, the other part being used for a weekly or monthly distribution of alms to the poor.

Meanwhile, on a wider front, Thomas Stephens who had bought Little Sodbury Manor had died and been succeeded by his son Edward who was High Sheriff of Gloucestershire 1634–35. He was responsible for extensive renovations to the Manor building with many of the rooms being panelled and stone fireplaces being fitted bearing coats of arms and initials.

Trouble had been brewing between Charles I and Parliament for some time and eventually this resulted in open war with a battle at Worcester on 23rd September 1642.

Edward Stephens was a firm supporter of the Parliamentary side as shown by the following précis of letters in the Gloucester Records Office (D.2510/22). The Smyth mentioned is the famous steward at Berkeley.

5.10.1642. Letter from John Seymour, John Codrington, and Edward Stephens requesting him to attend meetings of gentlemen supporting Parliament at Chipping Sodbury and to supply horses for cavalry.

Again on 25th November 1642:

Summons from John Seymour, Edward Stephens and Anthony Kingscote, Justices of Gloucestershire to Smyth to meet at Chipping Sodbury with all Berkeley dragoons for the defence of the County.

Although no record survives which mentions any attack on or skirmish at the Manor, Edward's position must have been precarious at times.

Whilst organising his forces the King told Prince Rupert that there was a supply of cloth, canvas and locharame in several places in South Gloucestershire including Chipping Sodbury. He was instructed to obtain these supplies exchanging them for a ticket which could be redeemed at Oxford. If the Prince carried out these orders it would not have endeared the local inhabitants to the Royalist cause. His Majesty knew that the borough existed because in the accounts for January 1642–43, the sum of £1 11s. 0d. was allowed to the bailiff for expenses "when the king passed through the town". This could have happened more than once as Chipping Sodbury was on the direct route from Bristol to Oxford.

Bristol fell to Prince Rupert in 1643 but before this Colonel Massey, the Parliamentarian commander at Gloucester, had placed a garrison in Yate Court, a fortified manor house belonging to the Berkeley family two miles north of modern Yate. Prince Rupert's success in Bristol placed the Yate garrison in jeopardy and a relief column was sent from Gloucester. When the local Royalist commander learned of this, he placed his considerable forces, as he thought, to the best advantage and waited for the Roundheads to arrive.

Unfortunately, the Roundheads, probably helped by local sympathisers, arrived unexpectedly from a completely different direction and routed the Royalists, capturing twenty prisoners, including two captains, eighty horses and a quantity of arms, before relieving the men at Yate Court and withdrawing in good order.

On another occasion a local Royalist Commander, Colonel Strange, was told that an enemy force was approaching and started to fortify the town. He subsequently decided that discretion was the better part of valour, however, and withdrew to Berkeley.

While Prince Rupert was holding Bristol he decided to strengthen the defences and a number of men were conscripted from the Sodburys and other places as labourers. It was wasted effort, however, because in 1645 the Prince was persuaded to surrender the city. The rest of the war seems to have passed by the Sodburys, the only other connection with it being through a member of Edward Stephens of Little Sodbury Manor's family. Nathaniel Stephens at Chavenage ten miles to the

The Stuarts

north, after considerable persuasion, added his signature to the warrant for the execution of Charles I which took place on 30th January 1648/9.

Around about 1645 a young man from Wrexham, in Denbighshire, named William Davis arrived in Chipping Sodbury. He courted and married the daughter of a well-to-do inn keeper and father-in-law did not let him down because he was set up in a farm at Old Sodbury where he prospered and raised a family.

By 1648 the local weaving trade had deteriorated so much that a lad had to go to Bristol to become a bound apprentice. The apprentice books for Bristol show that William, son of Thomas Trotman of Sodbury, yeoman, was bound to William Barnes, weaver, and Susanna for seven years from July, 1648.

Legend says that after the second battle of Worcester in 1651, Prince Charles made his escape disguised as a servant attending on a lady called Lane, crossing Gloucestershire with him riding behind her on one horse. On their way they passed through Sodbury, Winterbourne and Stapleton.

On the wall in Chipping Sodbury church there is an inscription which reads, "Tobias Davis his charge". Tobias appears once or twice in surviving records and died in or about 1653 either during, or shortly after he was Bailiff. He owned, or held on lives, considerable properties in Codrington, Dirham, Hinton and Wapley, including a house, garden and orchard near Wapley Church. He also had two granddaughters, Mary and Ann Davis, to whom he left his possessions in equal parts with the proviso that each of them gave 20s. each year towards the apprenticing of one poor boy from Chipping Sodbury.

How long there had been a Baptist Chapel in Chipping Sodbury is not known but in 1656 it had a minister of its own, namely Rev. James Nobbs.

In the year that Tobias Davis died, Oliver Cromwell became Lord Protector, a post which he held until his death in 1658. This was the same year that a stage coach running between London and Bath was established. The journey took three days during which twelve hours of each day were used in travelling and cost 25s. The body of the coach was suspended on heavy leather straps and held six people with some seats on the roof for outside passengers.

John Stephens the son of Edward Stephens of Little Sodbury, was elected as Recorder for the City by Bristol Council in March 1659. Edward was one of the current members of Parliament for Gloucestershire. John had also been a strong supporter of the Roundhead cause.

Richard Cromwell, who had succeeded Oliver, decided to stand down and the monarchy was restored on 8th May 1660 with Charles II. It was decided to ignore the Commonwealth and to date the reign of the new king from the death of his father, so 1663 was regarded as his fourteenth year on the throne.

It was during this year that the "Act of Uniformity" was passed which, among other things, required schoolmasters and others to sign a declaration and subscribe to certain articles of faith. Because of this it is possible to give the names of the headmasters of the school at Sodbury from this time, referred to at different times as a free, public or grammar school. The master in 1663 was Thomas Godwin but one master between 1628 and this time had been William Russell who was born in Wickwar. He went on to become the master of a school at Gloucester where he died in 1659.

Although there is nothing in the records to show that the Sodburys were affected by the plague which ravaged London in 1665, there is a note that a collection was made for those who suffered in the great fire the following year.

William Davis, who had settled down as a farmer in about 1645, had done very well for himself by this time with his family totalling eighteen. He seems to have been regarded as a success story and was known locally as the "Golden Farmer".

It is fortunate that Chipping Sodbury records of the proceedings of "Curia Visus Franc Pleg. cum Curia Baron" or Court Leet and Baron's Court have survived for a number of years starting with those for 1669. This court descends directly from those mentioned in the Laws of Breteuil and was held twice a year, in March and late September or early October. The Autumn Court was more important and as the name indicates, one of the original purposes was the View of Frankpledge (see page 50).

By this time, however, View of Frankpledge had virtually disappeared and it was the business of the Baron's Court which took the time when the Lord of the Manor or his seneschal were given written reports by a number of burgesses known collectively as the jurors.

Although the same bailiff could not be elected for successive years, he could stand again later. This system eventually broke down, however, and one man could continue for a number of consecutive years as can be seen from the list of Bailiffs in the Appendices.

In 1669 the scavengers reported to the Baron's Court:

We present that if Richard Cabbell Senr. and Richard Cabbell Junr. shall after the date hereof throw any more tan into the back brook adjoining to their backsides they shall pay for each offence ten shillings as often as it shall by them or either of them or their agents be committed and likewise that they shall throw no dead carcasses in the said brook and also that they shall take a bay lower to let the water have free passage from the ...? Well and also before the first day of November next on pain of paying a forfeit of ten shillings in case of neglect.

A report was received on the condition of the pillory and the ducking stool and on at least one occasion two ladies were sentenced to the stool because they were "perpetual scolds".

The first turnpike was created on the Great North Road in 1670, the first in many such experiments all over the country.

On 19th May 1671 Nathaniel Ridley was licensed to teach boys in Chipping Sodbury, taking over from Thomas Godwin. At the Court Leet in October of the next year the people of Sodbury were ordered to repair the lane leading to the Stub Riding without delay.

The Court of October 1673 was presided over by Sir Thomas Stephens' seneschal, Daniel Burcomb, gentleman. The jury found it necessary this time to restate the right of everyone living in Chipping Sodbury to set up stalls for the fairs and markets according to ancient custom before his own door out as far as the King's Highway. The schoolmaster changed again with Robert Smith replacing Nathaniel Ridley.

The surviving 1675 records are for the Spring Court of 10th April with the following being of greatest interest:

The difference between John Skinner, bayliffe of the borough, and Margaret Davis, widow, is referred to Mr. Stokes, John Barnes and George Browne on behalf of ye widow Davis, and Samuel Burcombe, Henry Wickham and Maurice Neale on the behalf of the bailiff to view the mounde in difference after dinner this court day and make peace between them if they can.

Whether the difference was resolved was not recorded but the reference to the dinner is interesting. Presumably it was provided after the court by the Lord of the Manor's steward. There are two other items worthy of note:

We present that no householder within the said borough shall entertain any journeyman within his house without sufficient certificate for return to the place of his last habitation upon pain of a fine of 20s. for each person.

We present that no person, be he habitant or foreigner, shall forstall the market upon pain of a fine of 3s. 4d.

The second paragraph is interesting because it shows that like many other places, Chipping Sodbury suffered from those who 'forestalled' the market. These were people from outside the area who approached the local farmers and their wives on their way to market to buy all their produce, or made a bulk purchase as soon as the market opened.

The Three Sodburys – An Introduction

Normally a bell was rung twice during market day, the first to show it was open to residents and again after an interval, to show that anyone could trade. There are several references to the ringing of the bell in Chipping Sodbury which was one of the duties of the Town Crier. Although no specific reference to a Town Crier has come to light, there must have been one, the most likely person being the assistant bailiff who was always appointed by the bailiff immediately after his own election and was his general 'dogs-body'.

At some time during the previous three or four years some of the Chipping Sodbury inhabitants must have watched with surprise while a man marched through the town pushing a large light wheel in front of him, followed by a soldierly looking horseman making notes.

The horseman was John Ogilby who was collecting data for his book on road routes within England and Wales published in 1675. This was the equivalent of the AA or RAC Year Book and contained one hundred routes from London and other important cities and towns. Chipping Sodbury was shown on the route from Bristol to Banbury.

The Bristol to Oxford road was now via Tormarton and Malmesbury. Probably, by this time, there was some sort of road through Old Sodbury to join up with this, although at first it might have taken the modern Kennedy Way route from the top of Horseshoe Lane and Hounds Road rather than Horse Street past the Boot. Several of the routes make it obvious that Aust Ferry was fully operational at this time.

In 1676 a lad called Thomas Bussell took part in an 'Ambulation of the Borough Boundaries'. Some sixty years later he recalled the excursion:

We began our walk at an ash tree growing on the Bowling Hill and walked along the side of Barley Close after Slough Lane to

The road from Chipping Sodbury to Old Sodbury c.1910, taken from what is now the Smarts green roundabout.

the boundage stone on Culverhill and from thence on down over Gaunt's Field Lane and Lower Gaunt's Field Lane to a boundage stone about twenty yards from the corner of Flints Close on the causey that leads from Old Sodbury; from thence we walked along Catshol or Back Lane to another boundage stone on Greenhill and from thence to the mouth of Trinity Lane and then on to the Stub Riding and so on into the Ridings a considerable way and the persons that were with us said that the whole Riding was in Chipping Sodbury. We came from thence to the Ridings Lane that comes down to Weare's Hill and came down to the highway from Ridings Lane through the brook and up the hill to the place where we began on the Bowling Hill where the tree stood.

Culverhill comes from the Latin *Columbarium*, meaning a place where doves are kept but why it should be so called is lost in the mists of time. The Bowling Hill was the name applied to the rise at the north end of the Parade.

Bull baiting was one of the townsfolk's pastimes. This is confirmed in the record for the Court Leet for 1677 when for some reason the overseers of the poor were required to provide the necessary rope and collar. At the same Court butchers John Skinner, George Bingham, William Hellier, John Somers and John Tovey junr., were in trouble concerning their market stalls. It shows what the volume of trade must have been if at least five butchers could make a living from it.

Just how long Lord of the Manor, Edward Stephens lived into the Cromwellian period and the Restoration is not known but by 1677 his son, another Thomas, had succeeded him because in that year he signed a warrant to send a pauper back to the parish where he had been born. Some idea of what happened to someone without a visible means of support is shown in that order signed by Thomas. This is one of a number that have survived and is the second, at least, concerning William Garrett for whom Chipping Sodbury seems to have held some attraction. He had been similarly deported two years earlier on the order of Christopher Cole.

Glou. To the Constable, tithingmen, Churchwardens and overseers, ye poore of Chipping Sodbury.
Whereas complaint hath been made unto us by ye churchwardens and overseers of ye poore of your said towne yt (that) William Garrett within forty days last past came into the said towne with an intent to settle there. He not renting there to the value of ten pounds yearly nor otherwise giving security to ...? the said towne harmless contrary to ye statute in yt case provided. Thus and

therefore in his Ma'tes name I do require you, ye constable, tithingmen, churchwardens and overseers of ye poore of Chipping Sodbury aforesaid yt on sight hereof you take and convey ye said William Garrett with his wife unto ...? in ye County of Middlesex where, as we are informed, he had his last legal settlement and to deliver him to ye churchwardens and overseers of ye poore there or to one of them who are hereby required him to receive and to set to work or dispose of according to ye law and this shall be your sufficient warrant given under our hands and seales this 12th day of September, Anno ...? Caroli Scdi nunc Anglia ...? non Ano Dom 1677.

signed. Tho. Stephens.

At the Court in 1678 Mrs. Anna Berkeley was fined 2s. for doing something which was a bad example and Henry Werrall had to pay 10s. for striking a juryman.

Up until this time and for a further seventy or so years, the year ended in March rather than December. This meant that January, February and March 1680 were followed by April 1681 and the convention has generally been adopted that dates falling in the first three months are now shown as, for example, 1680–81. So Charles I was beheaded on 30th January 1648–49 and Charles II dated his reign from that date. On 31st January 1680–81, therefore, he had completed 32 years and the following 10th February he was in his 33rd year as quoted at the end of the extract from the following proclamation:

Charles, the Second, by the Grace of God, of England, Scotland, France and Ireland, King, defender of the Faith, etc., to all to whom these present letters shall come, Greeting.
Whereas our town or borough of Chipping Sodbury, in our County of Gloucester, is an ancient and populous town or borough; and whereas the inhabitants of the same town and parish of Chipping Sodbury aforesaid have humbly besought us, that we should graciously vouchsafe to incorporate the said borough or town by the same name, and to give and grant to the inhabitants thereof such liberties and privileges, as, for the publick good and common utility of the said town or borough, to us it shall seem good and expedient.
Know ye therefore that we, at the humble petition of the said inhabitants, do, will, and by these presents, for our self, our heirs and successors, do ordain and grant, that the said town or borough of Chipping Sodbury aforesaid is, and shall be, a free borough for the future for ever; and we do make, create, ordain

constitute and declare, the said town or borough to be a free borough for the future for ever. Etc., etc.,
In testimony whereof we have caused these our letters to be made patents.
Witness our self at Westminster, the tenth day of February in the thirty-third year of our reign.

The full charter is several large pages long on a roll and is held by the Gloucester Records Office. When this dispensation was granted, it seems to have taken many of the inhabitants by surprise, despite what is said about it having been humbly besought and there is nothing in the surviving records to show that any such petition was made. According to Fox the following officers were elected, beginning with a Mayor. This was not the first time that the chief townsman had been called 'Mayor', of course, John de Brugges held the distinction in 1308 and ...? Attemulne in 1315. By 1437, however, the head man was once again the bailiff:

Mayor	Burcombe Samuel	(not to be confused with Daniel of that name who was the Steward of the lord of the manor.)

Aldermen:
Cabell Richard (Senr.)	By trade a tanner. He became the next mayor and seems to have died in office in 1681.
Skinner John	Had been bailiff in 1674 and became mayor in 1684–85.
Orchard Bernard	Became Mayor 1683–84.
Legg Nicholas	Bailiff 1669. Mayor 1685–86.
Smith Stephen	Bailiff 1676 and again in 1683–84.
Wickham John	Bailiff from 1677 to 1683.

Burgesses:
Barnes John, Stokes Richard, White Walter, Webb Daniel, Wickham Henry, Russell John, Dorrington Th., Elliott R., Tily Thomas, Sawbridge John, White Henry, Edwards R.

High Steward:
The Marquis of Worcester (shortly to become the first Duke of Beaufort)

Under Steward:
: John Powell Learned in Law

Town Clerk:
: Hawkesworth Richard

The introduction of a mayoral system did not make the old system redundant as one might have expected so the office of bailiff was still occupied and the courts were held as usual. Although some of the records of these courts have survived there is no mention of the Mayor or Corporation. This must have led to a great deal of discord and several prominent people were fined for contempt of court.

On the 13th May 1680 Robert Davis of Little Sodbury had an Indenture drawn up. For the consideration mentioned in it, he granted and confirmed to Richard Thynne, Thomas Walker, Thomas Ody, and Giles Manning:

> a newly erected messuage in Little Sodbury in which he lived and which he had lately built upon, or near, a certain close of ground called Farmers Leaze, and several other lands therein also mentioned lying in Little Sodbury; and also all other lands therein mentioned which he had purchased from Mary Roswell, to hold to the said feoffees for forty years. And after the determination of that term to several uses therein mentioned, subject to the payment of an annuity of £10 per annum, formerly granted out of the said premises by the said Robert Davis to the bailiff and burgesses for the use of a free school to be kept within the same borough.

It was agreed that the executors were to raise the £10 annually for a grammar school master appointed by the bailiff and burgesses of Chipping Sodbury. Alternatively he could be appointed to teach two poor boys, each of them aged ten years and upwards, born in Chipping Sodbury, for a period of five years.

The money was paid for a number of years but there is no record as to how it was used. Possibly a supplementary teacher known as a 'writing master' could have been employed in the already existing free, or grammar school.

The records at Broadmead Baptist Church in Bristol show that the Baptist Chapel in Chipping Sodbury still existed in 1681, despite attempts to stifle it. On 13th September of that year Sister Sylvester, a member of Mr. Nobb's church at Sodbury, was admitted to communion there. The Rev. Nobb's ministry extended over twenty-five years until he was succeeded by Rev. Jennings, who some years before had been thrown out of the Rectory of Brimsfield, Glos.

Some time during their existence the Mayor and Corporation decided to adopt a coat of arms using the old town seal. Earlier, when Anne, Countess of Warwick had died, the manors of both Old and Chipping Sodbury fell into the hands of Henry VII and whatever seal had existed previously was probably superseded by a new one bearing the royal 'three lions'. Although Henry VIII later bestowed both manors on Maurice Walshe, the seal was not altered and became the arms of the borough. Those responsible overlooked the need to make this official despite a visit by representatives from the College of Heralds to the area giving them the opportunity to do so. The representatives, however, still made an official record of the seal's existence. The Heralds' report on their visitation can be found at Gloucester in *Visitation of Gloucestershire 1682-3*, page 214. Under a small reproduction of the badge an extract reads:

The Town Seal

This is the common Seal of the Borough of Chipping Sodbury in the County of Gloucester created by his present majesty King Charles the Second by his Charter under the Great Seal of England, and a body politique and corporate by the name of Mayor, Aldermen and Burgesses in perpetuate succession, with the power of purchasing lands to the value of £40 per annum, and that the number of the Aldermen shall be six, and the Burgesses twelve, constituting Samuel Burcombe, the first Mayor...

Other officers were named in the document which at the same time regularised the use of the seal.

Among the business dealt with by the Heralds was the entitlement to a Coat of Arms put forward by Messrs. Legg, Webb, Nicholas and Henry Wickham. Their claims were rejected but the reasons for this are not known which has been very disappointing to descendants of a Thomas Wickham who followed the Pilgrim Fathers to America from Chipping Sodbury.

The family were prominent in the town for a considerable time and members held the office of Bailiff on several occasions. In 1711 a draft of a letter written by John Wickham addressed to various relatives at Sodbury was discovered in America. This shows that he had left England because of money problems but now wanted to repay his main creditors. The Wickham family have formed a thriving society in

America and one of these, Mrs. Hale, came to Chipping Sodbury in May 1984 when local historian, Percy Couzens showed her around the area pointing out the various places associated with her family. There is now a Wickham Close off St. John's Way in honour of that family.

The first Duke of Beaufort was created in 1682 and in September of the same year the Corner House and the Town House properties were re-enfeoffed.

The headmastership of the free school changed in 1684 when John North, BA took over from Robert Smith.

When Charles II died in 1685 and James II was crowned, a period of national uncertainty began, including a rebellion led by the Duke of Monmouth. Although the rebel forces reached Keynsham the Sodburys seem to have avoided any closer involvement.

For some reason, Robert Smith, whilst he was the mayor, decided in September 1687 to buy two houses in the High Street and four burgages called Bycketts Hill from John Atwood of Doynton for £125 on behalf of the townspeople. The transaction was financed in a somewhat dubious way as follows:

From the stock of the poor of the town	£45.
Left by George Russell for the poor*	£10.
Given by Mary Stiles	£10.
Said property mortgaged with Mrs. J. Burcombe	£60.
	£125.

* At some much earlier date a George Russell of Tormarton had left £10 each to Marshfield, Tormarton, Old and Chipping Sodbury, to be disposed as stocks for the good of the several poor.

The church records at Gloucester mention the following under this year of:

> *Matthew Pritchard, literate, now to be admitted to practice the art of Chircurgery in the parish of Sodbury Chipping and throughout the diocese of Gloucester.*

On 11th December 1688, James II abdicated and on 13th February following, William and Mary came to the throne. Locally during 1689 Robert Smith who had been mayor two years before, completed a deal with Thomas Hooper an extract of which is quoted here because the inn mentioned has since disappeared:

> *...All that messuage or tenement with a garden and backside situate in Chipping Sodbury heretofore in the tenure of William Horwood, the elder, and now in the possession of Henry Wickham lying between a messuage or inn called the Goat now in the possession of Henry Wickham on the west part and a tenement*

heretofore of William Butt and since of Nathaniel Skinner and now, or late, of Robert Deek on the east part and extending on the south part to a backside parcel of ground heretofore of Jane Butt and since of Thomas Baynham...

The disagreements about the Mayor and Corporation finally came to a head at the October meeting of the Court Leet in 1689. It began with the election of four burgesses, Christopher Ludlow, John Hodges, Jacob Pitt and Edward Clarke. Three other new burgesses, George Browne, William Higgs and Stephen Webb had been sworn in at the previous Court in April. This is the first time a Ludlow appears in Chipping Sodbury and Christopher probably arrived with the advent of William and Mary as the name of Ludlow was out of favour with the supporters of both Charles and James. Later records show that he was an apothecary and a Baptist Minister and he probably came to Chipping Sodbury to take over from Rev. Jennings. Christopher Ludlow was elected Mayor, probably by the rival group seeking to take control of the town, and his election as a burgess was perhaps part of the ploy to make his election as mayor more acceptable.

Three things certainly happened at this Court. John Skinner was appointed bailiff, for some reason thirty-seven people are cited as residents and fined three pence each and the following petition was prepared:

We the grande jury sworn for the Court Leet held for the manor of Chipping Sodbury alias Sodbury the eleventh day of October in the first year of the reigne of our Sovereigns Lord William and Mary now of England King and Queen etc., of which manor Thomas Stephens, Esq., is lord. Being sensible by sad experience that the charter granted by our late Sovereign Lord King Charles the second in the three and thirtieth year of his reign for incorporating this town without the knowledge of most of the inhabitants hath been very prejudicial to this manor in general and to most of the inhabitants in particular occasioned by the ill management of such as were the pretended members of the Corporation, who, for the most part, have been very liberal in their impositions and abuses of their neighbours whereby our trade is lost, our poore increased and our town almost ruined. We therefore humbly desire the Lord of the said manor that in case the said charter is not already vacated that he will use his endeavours, by such ways and means as he shall think fit and be advised to vacate the said charter and not only we but most of the trading men of this place shall have great cause to render him our most unfeigned thanks.

By 28th April the following year it was known that it was only a matter of time before the charter was officially cancelled and the Court Leet acted as if it had already happened. Jacob Wickham and Daniel Webb were elected as burgesses. It was also agreed that all the old customs and responsibilities of the bailiff and burgesses should be restored, including that the Ridings should be "stemmed by the bailiff and burgesses in accordance with ancient practice". Although it is repeated regularly in later documents, this is the first time that an entry concerning the administration of the Ridings appears in the surviving Court records.

It was decided at this time also that the mace should be carried before the bailiff when he came to the Court and it was ordered that it should be returned to the bailiff. The Royal assent to withdraw the charter was actually signed on 30th May 1690 and the bailiff and bailiff burgesses resumed their full former status officially. A list of those persons known to have held the post of mayor will be found in the Appendices.

Something else happened at this time which must also have set the tongues wagging. William Davis, better known as the 'Golden Farmer' at Old Sodbury, now aged 63 or 64, wanting to buy some more land, went back to his original profession to raise the necessary money. Perhaps age had slowed him down because he was recognised while holding someone up as a Highwayman! He managed to escape capture by shooting a pursuing butcher and fled to London. He was eventually caught, tried and hanged at the end of Salisbury Court, Fleet Street on 22nd December 1690. At his trial it came out that the source of his wealth all along had been highway robbery. As his father-in-law kept an inn, he was in a very good position to get information from the staff on what 'clients' were worthy of his attention, the staff being suitably rewarded later. Having reaped a good harvest he "retired" to live as a respected and envied farmer until his final adventure. Full details can be found in the Dictionary of National Biographies in which he is the first Sodbury person to appear.

During all the excitement, first with regard to the running of the town and then with the scandal of the 'Golden Farmer', few were probably even aware of the appointment of Charles Parry to teach the children in the public school.

An Act of 1691 highlights the state of the highways generally. Not only were the surfaces in a shocking state but the roads were very narrow. The new law required local surveyors to make highways between market towns at least eight feet wide and the minimum width for causeways for horses was fixed at three feet. Frequently, up to a dozen horses or oxen had to be called for to pull a coach out of the mud and people only travelled any distance in the winter when it was absolutely necessary.

The Stuarts

For the next few years nothing of any great importance is found in the records until 1694. when the authorities decided to investigate the way in which the charitable funds and properties in Chipping Sodbury were being handled.

The following Commissioners were appointed under the Great Seal in September: John Delabeer, Samuel Codrington, Nathaniel Wade, Edward Stephens, Thomas Edwards, Thomas Oldfield and Thomas Davis, with Joseph Jackson and Samuel Trueman as clerks. The investigation took several months and their report was submitted the following January. It was clear that whoever had brought about their visit had been fully justified in his suspicions.

When the Commission examined the various feoffments they found that the funds arising from them had not been limited to the proper uses. In the case of the legacy left by Tobias Davis, for instance, they found that the grand-daughters had married and still had an interest in most of the property described but the two pounds per annum had not been paid by them since 1661 even though the ladies in question had sufficient means to both pay the annual sum and meet the arrears. The grant of £10 per annum from Robert Davis was also in arrears to the tune of £20.

The Commissioners took a poor view of the way in which the purchase of the house and land from John Attwood had been financed. They concluded that a number of the bailiffs and bailiff burgesses who were responsible for the monies, fines, rents and revenues coming from the town lands, had not used them as laid down, contrary to the donors' wishes, to the great detriment of the town.

They then cited misappropriations amounting to £105 18s. 6½d and named those responsible. Among them was the annual rent of 10s. from Dolemead which had been kept by the respective churchwardens for the past 34 years. They also found irregularities in the last series of enfeoffments and ordered the properties to be re-conveyed to Christopher Ludlow, Bailiff, Peter Hardwicke and James Wickham, town masters, etc. On the method of leasing on lives they said that:

It appeared to us that oftentimes abuses happened by letting out lands, etc., for lives or years, for fines, in diminishing the full rent by letting the same to friends and acquaintances at an under-value.

To stop this abuse they ruled that when current leases expired renewal should be at a rack rent of the full yearly value.

The Commissioners also noted that on 5th January each year it was a long standing custom that the bailiff, bailiff burgesses and town masters elected two important inhabitants of the town as town masters for the next year. These would be responsible for letting and receiving rents from charitable lands and tenements and were authorised to use them, as laid down, recording the details in a ledger book. A great strong chest was kept in a public room in which the ledger book was kept. The idea was that several different keys to the chest should be held by different individuals but they found that unfortunately this business-like practice was not now being followed and the Commissioners blamed this as one of the reasons for the abuses they had uncovered. It was decreed that the ancient custom was to be reinstated immediately with a new ledger book which had headings covering the various uses to which monies had to be put. Four locks were fitted to the chest and the keys were to be held by the bailiff, the two current town masters and one of the preceding town masters. The Commissioners also ordered that the rents and revenues of church lands left for the maintenance of St. John the Baptist Church should be used only for that purpose. In accordance with the conditions set out in 1628 with regard to those revenues not specifically limited, the church had to find £4 each year towards the cost of repairing the highways in the town with any money left over being donated to the poor. The other earlier provisions were also confirmed and in particular that a master be appointed by the bailiff and bailiff

The Town Strong Chest, shown in its position inside the main front door at the foot of the stairs before the Town Hall was renovated in recent years. The chest can still be seen in the Town Hall.

burgesses to teach the townsmen's children their grammar. He was to be paid £10 each half year plus the sum of £10 annually which had been bequeathed by Robert Davis. Rents and revenues from the properties bought from John Attwood were to be used to repay the mortgage. The report then goes on:

> ...and further noticing that there was within the said town a certain house, some part of the lower part whereof had been for a long time past made use of by the Lord of the Manor of Chipping Sodbury, to take his toll at all markets and fairs; and another part of the lower part whereof had been made use of as a prison; and the overpart whereof had been made use of as a school house; and the townsmen of the said town, and also the lord of the said manor, had each of them claimed the whole house, but neither of them had made appear any other title than the usage aforesaid...

The Commissioners achieved a compromise between the contending parties and it was agreed that things should continue as before with the over-part to be used as a school-house, maintained out of the town stock. The house concerned was the Garrett which, as has been said before, stood in what is now the middle of the road roughly opposite the Royal Oak and was about 50 to 60 feet long and 20 to 25 feet wide.

Before leaving the Commissioners ordered that restitutions were made in cases of neglect and payments brought up-to-date. It was also laid down that any surplus was used to buy more town lands.

In the following March the church lands were re-enfeoffed as directed; they were:

1. The corner house and land. This had now been divided and formed two holdings.
2. The house on the right of what in this century used to be the Bell and later belonged to the British Legion and currently (1994) is empty, then held by Daniel Webb, who also held the house on the right again.
3. A parcel of burgage ground in Rounceval Street on the right of what later became Hill House. The latter was held by William Tily.
4. Pirlemead.
5. A burgage in Hounds Lane.
6. Three and a half acres in Dolemead.

This indenture is of great interest in as much as it gives the trade, profession or standing of the new feoffees as follows:

Christopher Ludlow, Mayor and now Bailiff
Peter Hardwick, the elder   tanner

Daniel Webb	mercer
John Dorney	saddler
Richard Thresher	merchant tailor
Stephen Edney	maltster
Nathaniel Ogbourne	joiner
William Higgs	butcher
James Wickham	yeoman
Stephen Webb	mercer
Joseph Bingham	cordwainer
Daniel Burcombe	baker
Thomas Wickham	merchant tailor
Robert Burcombe	gent'n
Peter Hardwick (the younger)	
John Champines	

On the next page is a copy of the record of presentments at the Court of 1696.

The bailiff and other office holders for the year then ending would have to state on oath that all was well in their particular spheres or lay any charges they wished to make.

A church parade in the main street in 1909. In the background, left of centre, is the Bell Inn which, like a number of the inns in Chipping Sodbury, had a large double-doored entrance for vehicles with a yard behind, in this case to the left of the building. To the left again is the awning of what is now (1994) Nelson's butcher shop.

October 30th (Friday) 1696

Sodbury Borough	The presentment of the grand jury of the said Borough to be delivered at the Court Leet holden on Friday being the 30th of October A.D. 1696.
We present	Daniel Burcombe constable for year ensuing. ... Alden and John Naish, Ale tasters Edward Tanner and William Stiff, Carners Edward Bowman and ... Curtis, Scavengers George Alimand and John Tyler, Sealers of leather
	That all ancient customs which were formerly presented by the Bailiff and Burgesses according to the decrees and likewise all ancient customs in the last presentment we elect to stand.
We elect that	The Ridings shall be steined by the Bailiff and Burgesses according to the ancient customs and that no man of the borough in the Ridings shall feed but is their own proper goods and if it doth not appear that any person or persons shall have any more sheep than his own the owners thereof shall pay two shillings for each sheep to the Bailiff and he that shall take in or detain any such goods shall lose his privilege in the Ridings for seven years.
We elect that	The Bailiff of our borough shall receive the profits belonging to the said Ridings according to ancient customs.
We elect that	Every inhabitant of the said borough shall set forth every market and fair day standings and sheep cubs before his own door so far forth as the King's Highway, according to the ancient custom.

Bayliffe for the year ensuing (signatures of:-)

Thomas Tily,	Sam. Stiff,	Wm. Jones,
Christopher Ludlow,	Jerome Chapp, jun.	Nich. Legg,
Daniel Webb	John Somers,	Thos. Wickham,
William Higgs	W. Burcombe,	Thos. Hellier,
Jerome Chapp sen.,	Dan. Smith,	Geo. Browne

The Three Sodburys – An Introduction

In 1700 a member of the Stephens family was still lord of all three manors and the populations of the three Sodburys were:

Chipping Sodbury	650 incl.	30 freeholders	140 houses
Old Sodbury	200 incl.	16 freeholders	
Little Sodbury	90 incl.	5 freeholders	24 houses

In the Court report for October 1700 there is another complaint about the lack of a collar and rope for the bull baiting. The current price of the collar was 6s.

At the same Court further reference was made to the desirability of carrying the mace before the bailiff on formal occasions in accordance with ancient custom. The impression is that the sceptre used before the office of mayor had been introduced had still not been returned to the Bailiff. It had still not been returned by October 1702. There is a gap in the surviving records after this date. The true mace, which still exists, carries the inscription "Wm. Higgs, bailiff". He held office in 1704–05 which makes it probable that it was then finally accepted that the old mace had vanished and a new one was bought.

Trade with France had been re-established in 1696 and as a result foreign silks and other light fabrics were replacing woollen cloth for women's clothes. The clothiers in the Southwest, including locally, complained bitterly to their MPs that their industry would be ruined and the volume of protest forced the Government to take action. An Act of Parliament was brought in on 29th September 1701 which banned the use of foreign made silks and calicos. Inevitably, smuggling of the banned materials became very lucrative and continued to be so while the law remained in force.

The next two items are quoted from the records of 1702:

> *Presentment of William Tanner Jnr. and Thomas Tyler, Carners, given in the Court Leet and Court Baron held this 28th day of October 1702. We present that all meat that has been killed in the town or brought to market have been good and wholesome to the best of our knowledge.*

This shows the type of certificate that the officers had to give. The Scavengers made a similar report:

> *We present the ditch from Painter's Mead Gate to the end of Hounds Lane and also the ditch on the right hand of Gauntsfield Lane to the lead ore pits and that the occupiers do scour and clean same ditch by the fifth of January next.*

Painter's Mead covered the area behind the High Street properties from Horseshoe Lane to Hounds Road up to what is now Kennedy Way, hence the name of the primary school on the site. Where the lead ore pits were is an intriguing question. This was the first of only two known references. Some traces may have disappeared when the railway was built and there was a deep hole in the side of the cutting near Lilliput. There was also an old quarry in what is now the playing fields of Chipping Sodbury Comprehensive School. The second reference to lead ore is in a book by Rev. Thomas Rudge published in 1807 which reads:

Yate
Riding End *a good estate was the property of Thomas Russell, gent, who died 1803. Considerable veins of lead have been discovered on this estate and some attempts made to work them but not with success. Lead ore and calamine are found in other parts of the parish, but no mines are worked.*

William III died in 1702 to be succeeded by Queen Anne. In 1703, at the time of the Great Storm, a great fire took place at the Manor House, fortunately without loss of life. An entry in the Parish Register reads:

Thomas Stephens, esq., patron of this Church, his wife, his son and wife, were wonderfully preserved from being burned, and the house also; an infinite number of trees torn up by the roots; brought in by the ocean upon a spring tide broke the walls and overflowed the country; £100,000 damage to Bristol.

This catastrophe has always been remembered as "The Great Storm". The rain was torrential and the hurricane was accompanied by thunder and lightning. Tremendous damage occurred all over the country. Bristol was flooded and Bishop Kidder and his wife, in the palace at Wells, were killed by a chimney-stack being blown down and falling through the roof. The Eddystone lighthouse was entirely demolished.

In 1704 the bailiff and burgesses decided to alter the period of residence needed to qualify for an acre in the Ridings. In 1558 this had been set at seven years, increased to twenty-one years in 1663. This time a compromise was decided upon with the period set at fourteen years.

Turnpike Trusts were set up throughout the country in 1706 with the idea that new roads could be constructed and existing ones improved from the tolls paid by the users while still allowing a certain amount of profit for the organisers. A separate Act of Parliament was needed for each Trust and some years were to go by before it affected the people of the Sodburys. A number of people in the area probably ran transport businesses using both wagons and pack animals. Some idea of transport rates at that time can be seen from those laid down at the quarter sessions by the Justices at Bristol in May 1707 for the carriage of goods between Bristol and London:

The Baptist Church in Hounds Road c.1910. The burial ground with some monuments showing can be seen to the left. In the foreground left is part of Painters Mead, now the site of the school of that name.

By pack animal	Summer	Winter
Above 28 lbs:	5s. per cwt:	6s. per cwt:
between 14–28 lbs:	1d per lb:	1d per lb:
between 5–14 lbs:	1½d per lb:	1½d per lb:
small parcels	6d each.	6d each.
By wagons		
Heavy goods	5s. per cwt:	4s. per cwt:
Light goods*	5s. per cwt:	6s. per cwt:

(*those which were of considerable volume but little weight)

Little Sodbury parishioners were summoned to worship from 1707 onwards by a new bell hung in the tower of the church behind the manor.

The Baptist cause was thriving in the borough in 1708. Under the leadership of Rev. Christopher Ludlow the members were able to increase the size of their premises, the land in question being the site of the older chapel still standing now used for general purposes and the burial ground attached to it described as:

> *All that plot of garden ground containing, by estimation, 48 feet in length and 31 feet in width, with a lane called Hounds Lane on the east side, with a ground commonly called Paynter's Mead on the south side and the garden of Anthony Wickham on the west.*

The person who sold it was William Alden, a farrier, and both Josiah Weare, tailor, and Henry Ford, clothworker, are mentioned.

The Court Leet record for October of that year contains the following report from the scavengers:

> *We present that if any person shall fail or neglect to carry his or her dung out of the street within thirty days after notice given them by the scavengers, for the time being, then the said scavengers shall have liberty to take it for their own use or benefit.*

It appears that it was customary to clear out the stables at the rear of the dwellings and pile up the manure in a heap in the street until it could be removed to the holding on the Ridings or elsewhere. It perhaps is just as well not to dwell on what the High Street must have been like on a hot summer day.

Some examples from the Church Accounts for the period 1681–1719 below give some idea of ordinary affairs in the Sodburys at that time:

1681 Paid to a man that brought a fox, 1s.
1682 Court Fees and expenses when we returned concerning who received the Sacrament at Easter, 9s.
Paid when we cited about the bells, 4s. 6d. (This entry occurs in several years).
1683 Spent at visitation 16s. 8d.
To Mr. North for his dinner 2s. 6d. (Vicar).
1684 Cloth for pulpit cushion 14s. 6d.
13½ oz. silk fringe 18s. 4d.
Thomas Clark for making 3s. 8d.
John Watts for a pound of feathers 2s.
1685 Laid out for an order brought from the Chancellor for irreverent behaviour at Church and not coming to Divine Service, 1s.
1686 Paid to one that had a petition from the Privy Council for the redemption of a minister taken by the Turks, 1s.
For an Hour glass, 8d. (Hour glasses were, as a rule, placed on the pulpits of Churches to measure the sermon by, and also to remind the people how fleeting a thing time is.
For a bottle of wine that was spilled by accident, 2s. 6d.

In the reign of William and Mary:
1695 William Lingin for ringing the bell at Queen Mary's death, 2s. 6d.
1700 Paid to the Apparitor for a proclamation against immorality and profaneness.

In the reign of Queen Anne:
1705 To William Powell for a prayer book for the victory in Bavaria (thanksgiving for Blenheim).

1713 Thomas Sumsion, for mending the tower, a dial on the porch, and other work about the Church £17 15s.
Mending the Communion Cup, 3s.
Going to Bristol with the Cup, 2s.
Plank to make a weathercock, 4s.
For fetching the rope from Colerne, to draw the lead up the tower and for carrying it back 1s. 6d. Spent at a parish meeting, 5s. 6d.
John Monk for altering Mr. North's desk 3s. 6d. (Reading Desk).
For a warrant to distrain upon Tobias Walker 1s. 6d. (9d for non-payment of Church Rate)
Pint of linseed oil, ochre, and red lead, to colour the weathercock 9^1/$_2$d.

Reign of George I.
1714 For the Coronation Day, 5s.
1718 Ringing on the fifth of November, 2s.
1719 John Monk for mending the ringing loft floor, 1s.
Nathaniel Hignell, for mending the bells, and timber, 3s. 4d.

CHAPTER SEVEN

THE EIGHTEENTH CENTURY

Either the records have not survived or nothing in particular happened locally during the next ten years. Nationally, Queen Anne died and George I was crowned in 1714. In 1719 there is a mention of a J. White in Chipping Sodbury who was a coal miner and it is likely that there were a number of people in the area by this time whose livelihood depended upon coal and its distribution.

The Rev. J. North who had been the incumbent for a long time passed away in 1721 and was succeeded first by Rev. Allen Sherwood in 1721 and then by Rev. W. Hughes in 1722 at Old Sodbury Church. It was in 1721 that Walpole became prime minister.

Newspapers were by now becoming a regular feature and the Sodburys came within the territory of the Gloucester Journal, distributed by Walter Nelmes of Frampton-on-Severn.

On May 27th 1721 the Baptist congregation lost their pastor, Rev. Christopher Ludlow at the age of 75. He had also been the last mayor and also a bailiff of the town. He was succeeded by his son, Rev. Ebenezer Ludlow.

Although a coach service could be operated from Gloucester to Bristol and on to Bath, the general state of the roads was terrible. By ancient law every farmer who paid at least £50 rent annually also had to supply a wagon and team for six days a year for road work in his parish while the poorest labourer or tradesman gave six days in each year of his own labour. This was often ignored and even when enforced was not enough to make good the damage from the increasing traffic.

In 1726, having noted the shocking state of the roads leading into the city, the authorities in Bristol petitioned Parliament for permission to erect turnpike gates. Several highways near Sodbury and Wotton-under-Edge were singled out because, it was alleged, they were not wide enough to allow two horses to pass each other and one witness testified that his horse had suffocated in the mud.

The Bill received Royal Assent in April 1727 the same year that George I was succeeded by George II.

A number of trusts were set up with the power to levy tolls. The authorised charges in part of Yate were:

Wagons with six horses or oxen	1s. 0d
Wagons with four horses or oxen	8d
Wagons with two horses or oxen	4d
Wagons with one horse or ox	2d
Pack horse laden with general goods	1d
Pack horse laden with coals	1d

These charges were meant to take effect from 26th June 1727 but the reaction of the miners of Kingswood had not been taken into account, who were angered by the levy on animals carrying coals. Over the next few years they repeatedly demolished various turnpike gates, creating a state of anarchy.

Those responsible for the care of the poor at Chipping and Old Sodbury decided to set down the monthly contribution required from each resident for the poor rate. This was based on the value of the property at so many pence in the pound. Fortunately a list showing the inhabitants and the amount due from each has survived and is shown in full in Appendices C and D. The twelve inns together with their monthly rate which were included were:

Inn	Landlord/Lady	Rate
Bell	Robert Burcombe	8d
Crown	Widow Tily (see Appendix N)	5d
George	Robert Allaway (prob.)	6d
Goat	Sir Wm. Codrington	4d
Hat & Feather	Wm. Russell	2d
Horseshoe	Wm. Dorrington	5d
Portcullis	John Roden	5d
Queens Head	Edward Bayly	5d
Star	Nicholas White	2d
Swan	Widow Jones	4d
White Hart	Wm. Tanner	4d
White Horse	Henry Edwards	4d

The Bell and the George are now closed (1994) but their location and that of the Portcullis were as they are today. The Crown is now Hill House on the Parade which was made from three houses with a facade built across the front. The Goat is now the Beaufort Hunt while the Hat and Feather, apparently named after the Cavaliers, became the Cap and Feather before finally disappearing from its position in the set back portion of Horse Street on the right-angled bend. The Swan stood on the site of the Catholic Presbytery until about 1830 when it was transferred to the corner of Hatter's Lane. The White Hart was in Horse Street somewhere opposite to the present Melbourne House whose facade probably covers the site of the White Horse. The Horseshoe, was in Horseshoe Lane and the Queen's head became the Bunch of Grapes in Rounceval Street. The location of the Star is still not known.

It is also known that there was the Three Crowns in 1719, kept by F. Cross and a person of that name appears on the main list (see Appendix C). The rateable value was only 1d, so perhaps he had gone out of business by 1727. Finally, in 1725, the Mitre was kept by Widow Pocock who is not mentioned in 1727 so perhaps she had died and the business lapsed. One inn not mentioned in the list is the Royal Oak which was known to exist in October 1736 when it was stated that it had been lately occupied by Cecily Smith. Widow Smith appears on the main list in 1727 with a rating of 6d so perhaps the business was temporarily suspended.

The Turnpike at the junction of the Wickwar Road and Love Lane. It was demolished in the 1960s.

It is difficult to pick out any one factor that made Sodbury so successful at this time. There was definitely one, if not two, tanneries at the rear of premises at about the centre of the High Street on the left hand side looking towards the cross and the leather was used, in part, by a number of local shoemakers and saddlers. The clothing trade still existed and a good deal of coal and lime was being transported over a wide area by pack horse and wagon. Whatever the reasons, the Sodburys must have been very prosperous as most of the houses date back to around this time or a little earlier. After the Civil War was over it occurred to someone that gunpowder could be used in quarrying and the cost of stone fell very considerably. One of the earliest sites of a large quarry was on the left of the road at Lilliput. It was closed and filled in when the railway line was built and is now the site of a school playing field.

There is also a mention in 1727 of Stephen Clarke who was a cheese factor and it does seem that the Sodbury area had quite a reputation for producing and marketing cheese, as attested to by the following extract from *A Tour of Great Britain* by Daniel Defoe (1724–27):

> *By the way we visited some friends at a Market Town, a little out of the road, called Chipping Sodbury. A place of note for nothing that I saw, but the greatest cheese market in all that of England or, perhaps any other, except Atherstone or Warwickshire.*

Perhaps there may be some significance in the fact that on the list of inhabitants (Appendix C) is a William Cheddar!

When Edward died in 1728 the Stephens family became extinct on the male side and the Lordship of the three manors went to a Robert Packer whose mother had been the daughter of a Richard Stephens. Either then or later, Robert married the daughter and sole heiress of Sir Richard Winchcombe, Baronet, of Bucklesbury in Berkshire.

Some idea of the esteem in which the Stephens family was held can be seen on the memorial in Old Sodbury church:

> *Here lyeth the remains of Edward Stephens of Little Sodbury. Esq., Who had all the Virtues that adorn a gentleman, a Magistrate and a Christian. In his sincere Piety to God, In his impartial Justice and Benevolence to Mankind. In his Fidelity and Zeal for his friends. In his instructive conversation and a peculiar Happiness of address which never failed to gain him the Goodwill of all that approached him. In short in every Social Virtue. He was a pattern equalled by few. Excelled by none. He died the 6th. day of April MDCCXXVIII, in humble hope of a glorious Resurrection Through him who is the Resurrection and the Life.*

While on the subject of memorials the following sad item, also from Old Sodbury, cannot be left out:

> *In Memory of Mary, the wife of Nathaniel Horwood, who departed this life the 25th. day of October A.D. 1726.*
>   *In Darkness long I Lived by God's decree*
>   *No Glymspe of light or sun returned to me*
>   *Yet you the Least of my misfortune knew*
>   *Some brutal hand gave me my fatal blow*
>   *A crime so horrid who doesn't grieve to tell*
>   *Yet grieve not for in Bliss with Christ I dwell.*

The Eighteenth Century 143

This photograph shows the position of Old Sodbury Church in relation to the village. According to Leyland, who wrote in 1542, the remains of a manor house were then to be seen at the foot of the promontary on which the church stands. The stones were probably used for building the cottages and other buildings in the vicinity.

Old Sodbury Church. The clock was installed to mark Queen Victoria's Jubilee.

While no age is given, her husband died in 1705 aged 36. Mary was blind but could still carry on her business as a shopkeeper. She was murdered by an unknown person who afterwards robbed the house.

In 1729 John Isaac ran a school of some kind in Old Sodbury because it is recorded that he was paid 8s. by the parish for schooling a lad named Cowle. The same accounts show that a sack of coal cost 9d and a few years later the price had gone up to 1s. 2d.

Two mysterious items crop up regularly in the Old Sodbury accounts. From 1730 until 1746 there are entries covering payments for hauling the King's Carriage. Nothing indicates what this was or why the work was necessary. Generally the journey is to Bristol or to Tetbury and the payment is 10s. The other puzzle is an annual outgoing known as County Bridge Money which started before 1723, in which year it was £1 11s. 4d. It stayed at about this figure until 1754 and then doubled. The amount is too nearly the same each year for it to have been 'toll' money and is more like to a County Rate.

In 1731 the re-enfeoffment of the church property throws a little light on some of the trades in the town. The new feoffees were:

David Clarke	bailiff
Joseph Power	baker
Daniel Burcombe	baker
Thomas Hulbert (senr.)	cooper
Thomas Hulbert (junr.)	cooper
William Sargent	saddler
William Harvey	tallow chandler
William Wickham	woollen draper
James Wallis	apothecary
Thomas Winter	butcher
James Wickham	butcher
Thomas Prewett	joiner
John Watts	rope maker
Francis Cross(senr.)	tailor
Henry Hellier	tailor
Thos Burcombe	carpenter
Robert Burcombe	gent.
Daniel Burcombe (of Old Sodbury)	gent.

Peter Hardwicke, doctor in physick, of Bristol.

The descriptions of the properties are a mine of information. The house on the right of the Bell was the home of Ebenezer Ludlow and the houses between that and Church Lane were occupied by John Bence and James Watts. Two buildings had now been built on a burgage in Rounceval Street, occupied by William Winstone and John Barrett.

These were on the right of what is now Hill House and was then the Crown Inn, the previous tenant being William Tily and now his widow, Elizabeth Tily. Since the last deed had been drawn up the corner burgage on the south of the street near the cross had been developed and was now two messuages occupied by John Clarke and William Harvey. Details are also given about the rest of the properties, namely Purlemead, two burgages in Hounds Lane and 32 acres in Dolemead.

Another deed of about the same time mentions the Town House or Hall and shows that there was a pavement in that area at least. It also shows that the house on the left of the Hall was occupied by William Sargent and that on the left again by Sarah Dorney. The house on the right of the hall was occupied by Andrew Cummings.

Mrs. Martha White drew up her will in July 1731 with £140 being applied at the discretion of her trustees for the relief of the poor of Sodbury and Yate.

Although the list of inns for 1727 show that Sir William Codrington was responsible for the rates on the Goat, he appears in a rather more important role some four years later. On page 155 of Vol.2 of the Annals of Bristol, John Latimer wrote:

In the State Papers is a letter from Sir W. Codrington to the Duke of Newcastle dated 14th July 1731, stating that the house of Mr. Blathwaite, of Dyrham, who had made himself obnoxious by attempting to defend the turnpikes, had been attacked by four hundred colliers, who threatened to demolish it. The writer rode to the spot with twenty of his tenants and servants; but was forced to release four of the rioters previously captured, and to give the rest a hogshead of ale before they would depart. Nearly all the gates were then down. The following is highly significant:

'I am afraid my lord, these wretches would never have been so impudent if they had not been prompted by men of some fortune and figure; and we have been informed that two or three bailiffs, as we call them, to some gentlemen were seen to be a-drinking with the colliers the evening before they were at Mr. Blathwaite's.'

A week later, in a letter from Bristol, Sir William reports that 'the insolencies of the rioters are greater than ever, they having cut down some of the gates even at noon-day, and are now collecting money of travellers where the gates stood... The remaining part of the inhabited turnpike house at Yate was burnt down last night.'

Despite troops being sent to Bristol the rioters continued to defy the law even though the charge for horses carrying coals having been abolished.

The Three Sodburys – An Introduction

This cottage on the left near the top of Dog Hill survived until relatively recently. It is typical of the cottages that once made up Old Sodbury village. Such buildings were sometimes semi-detached and housed two families. The church tower can be seen in the background.

A typical homestead in Church Lane, Old Sodbury. It was said that it was difficult to move about upstairs because of the lowness of the main beam.

The Eighteenth Century

While it had long been the custom for a local 'Assize' to fix the details for the sale of bread and ale, at some time before 1732 a similar practice had been adopted for fixing the wages of personal servants and agricultural workers. In this case however the Assize was at Gloucester and the findings applied to the County which for 1732 were:

Every head servant
not exceeding £5 p.a.
Every second servant
not exceeding £4 p.a.
Every driving boy
not exceeding £1 p.a.
Every head maid servant & cook
not exceeding £2. 10s. p.a.
Every second maid servant
not exceeding £2 p.a.

Presumably the above were in addition to keep and uniform.

In the hay harvest every mower, without drink, had to receive not more than 1s. 2d, with drink 1s. per day. In the corn harvest 'with diet' the rate was 1s. per day; labourers with drink received 8d but with diet only 4d. If they took neither drink nor diet they received 10d. Carpenters, wheelwrights and masons were paid 1s. 2d per day 'without drink' but only 1s. if drink was supplied.

The Assize order was comprehensive and laid down all kinds of penalties if either the servants or the employers failed to obey it. If any master, either directly or indirectly, paid more than the scheduled rate he was to be imprisoned for ten days without bail and forfeited £5. The servant helping him spent twenty-one days in prison without bail. At the end of his period of service, no servant could transfer from one town or parish to another unless he took with him a certificate over the seal of the town or the signature of the constable and two other honest householders. Failure to produce such a document within twenty-one days of arrival in a new area could end in a whipping and being treated as a vagabond.

All artificers and labourers hired by the day or week from the middle of March to mid-September were to be at work at or before 5.00 am and not leave until between 7.00 or 8.00 pm. They were allowed 2½ hours off altogether for breakfast, dinner and drinking. In winter they had to work from dawn to dark.

The Gloucester Journal shows that in February 1733–34 Natham Corbett occupied Raysfield Farm and in the following April a Chipping Sodbury inhabitant, Tobias Luton, currier, was in difficulty because his wife had absconded.

There was still trouble when collecting tolls on the roads. In 1732 the men from Kingswood had marched as far as Ford, near Chippenham, and destroyed the gates there. Two years later in June 1734, every gate between Bristol and Gloucester was destroyed by armed bands. According to Latimer, in August 1735 Sir William Codrington informed the Duke of Newcastle that the colliers still held the roads, sometimes extorting 50s. in a single day, and if the government would not render more help, "God knows how it may end". He added that a bailiff named Pritchett, at Westerleigh, was "at the bottom of the whole affair".

Almost the last of the surviving Court Leet records is for October 1736 when Daniel Burcombe, gent., presided as the steward of the Lord of the Manor. The following is one of the presentments:

> *The said jury of homage do present that it has been the custom and usage for the owners and occupiers of the Royal Oak, lately in the occupation of Cecily Smith to put out sheep cubs before the depth of her house to the King's Highway that leads from Hatter's Lane up High Street by the Garrett towards the sign of the Swan and against the house now occupied by John Wilkins, blacksmith, as far as the breadth of the said Royal Oak extends and the said Cecily Smith have enjoyed this privilege etc. ...* (torn)

It is this item which shows that at this time High Street stretched from the Cross to Rounceval Street.

Around about this time, too, there was a big row among those responsible for the poor rate about whether the amounts payable on the Ridings should go to Old or Chipping Sodbury. It was decided in favour of Chipping Sodbury but the interesting part is that in support of that claim the perambulation of the boundaries carried out sixty years previously (see page 120) was quoted.

The Rev. Francis Gold became headmaster of the Grammar School in succession to the Rev. Edward Shellard in 1737. The following year the bailiff and burgesses decided to alter and repair the front of the Town Hall. The Sodbury Fairs at this time were held on 24th June and Holy Thursday, i.e. the fifth in Lent.

The struggle over the turnpikes still carried on and in 1739 Ralph Allen of Bath, in giving evidence for a local turnpike bill, deposed that the Bristol Acts were still inoperative "by reason the colliers have pulled down, and do constantly pull down the turnpikes".

Walpole, prime minister since 1721, left office in 1742. The following is a description of his life and times:

> *He resolutely promoted the prosperity of the country; agricultural methods were improved; farming flourished; manufactures increased and towns grew rapidly in size. Social and moral*

advance, however, did not accompany material progress. There were three sections of society, an intelligent aristocracy lacking in religious belief; a prosperous middle class inclined to puritanism; and the vast majority, the ignorant and brutal poor. Savage penalties did not serve to reduce crime and pestilence spread in the overcrowded prisons. The spirit of the century was highly material and religion, often administered in the country by dissolute clergy, sank to a mere formal observance.

The method of recruiting members of the medical profession was highlighted by an advertisement in the Gloucester Journal for 19th October 1742. It read:

Any youth qualified to be an apprentice to an apothecary and surgeon in the County may hear of a good master by enquiring of the printer hereof. N.B. All letters on this account must be post paid.

Some idea of the cost of living in 1744 is shown by the prices per bushel at Gloucester which were: corn 2s. 8d to 3s. 4d; oats 1s. 6d to 1s. 10d; beans 2s. to 2s. 8d.

Living in Chipping Sodbury at this time was an apothecary named Wallis who was probably at least the second of that profession and name locally. This one deserves to be remembered because it was he who persuaded the authorities to establish a 'pest house' on the Stubb Riding in a nook there called the 'Fryding Pool'. (A later map shows a building roughly opposite the old turnpike.) It was meant to be an isolation hospital for smallpox victims and was based on the same idea as the lazar house which was used in the eleventh, twelfth and thirteenth centuries to fight leprosy. Smallpox was first reported in England in 1514 and it wrought havoc for nearly three centuries.

The payment of £6 to Mr Wallis in 1744 was probably an annual allowance in return for which he treated the poor of the parish as necessary, showing that they were not entirely neglected. In 1753 £3 was paid out so that Francis Stone could go into the infirmary at Bath.

In the year of the rebellion, 1745, the traffic through Sodbury increased slightly when an additional mail coach was introduced between Bristol and London via Oxford and Cirencester.

When the Guild had been in existence a number of poor people had been accommodated in tenements at the rear of the Guild Hall which later became the Town Hall. It was then leased to certain gentlemen for 28 years for some unknown reason, the poor people being moved to Rounceval Street. The hall then reverted to the town after the lease expired because the bailiff and burgesses at that time decided to build a workhouse for the poor people that had settled in the lower parts of the

Town Hall. The accommodation might have been provided somewhere near the Hat & Feather Inn in Horse Street.

For a while around this time Thomas Chatterton worked as a writing master at the Grammar School assisting Rev. Francis Gold. Eventually he went to another school at Redcliffe in Bristol. He returned to Chipping Sodbury to marry Sarah Young of Stapleton in 1749 and died in 1752 before his son, another Thomas who as an adolescent became the tragic boy poet, was born.

It was in this year that two major alterations were made to the calendar. Previously the year had ended on 25th March. The first clause of the Act changed what would have been January 1751 to be the first month of 1752 and was a popular measure. The second clause, which was necessary to bring the calendar up-to-date, decreed that the day following 2nd September was to be 14th September. This provoked opposition which was kept up for a number of years and the cry, "Give us back our eleven days!" was raised at the elections in 1754.

A deed, dated two years earlier, shows that there was a salt pan originally erected by one Thomas Hooper behind the houses on the left of the Town Hall. This deed and another of 1731 are quoted in full in the hope that someone may be able to explain them.

AD 1731 All those three tenements and two garden grounds with all backsides pavements and other appurtenances situate in Chipping Sodbury borough one time in the possession of George Smith then in the possession of Richard Legg since that Nicholas Legg and now William Ambrose on the east part and tenement and land in the holding of one Robert Edwards and now Sarah Dorney on the west part. One of the three tenements lying next to the George with garden ground extending down to the Brook side in the possession of Mary ...? since in the tenure of William Cambridge now in the tenure of Andrew Cummings and the middle of the said three tenements being used as the Town House or Town Hall. The other of the three tenements with garden and backside adjoining next to the other said tenement called Town Hall was in the occupation of Thomas Hooper and now in the occupation of William Sargent.

AD 1750 All that messuage or tenement with the Salt Houses and one garden and back side thereunto belonging situate in Chipping Sodbury between the Town Hall and Church House on the east and a tenement of Sarah Dorney on the west whereof which said messuage and premises hereby described were formerly parcel of the possession of the said Guild are now in the possession of Samuel Sargent and also all that other messuage or tenement called the Lower House wherein one Thomas Hooper formerly erected a salt pan wherein Levy Weare formerly inhabited with a Little Court belonging to the same and that part of the garden extending as far as the arbour with the bounds pertaining to the same and also a little stable thereunto adjoining which was formerly a pigsty with free liberty of egress etc., and also free liberty at any time to make use of the arbour and shops, cellars, etc.

By now turnpike roads were firmly established and an Act is mentioned for repairing and widening the road leading from Chippenham Bridge to the top of Old Sodbury Hill.

In 1758 Thomas Blanchard held office as one of the town masters. Ebenezer Ludlow, the Baptist pastor, died on 6th March 1760. He was Christopher Ludlow's grandson and was survived by a number of Ludlows who were to become well known in several other spheres of influence.

There appears to have been some difficulty at this time in finding anyone willing to become bailiff, to the point that the following was resolved:

The Bailiff and Bailiff Burgesses do order and agree that if any person, chosen a burgess of this borough and who hath not at any time served the office of bailiff of the same, shall refuse to take upon himself the said office when called upon by the lord's steward. He shall upon such refusal be immediately deprived and forfeit such privileges which would belong to him as a burgess besides paying a fine to the lord of £5.

This seems to have worked but was two-edged because several of the subsequent bailiffs could not sign their names but were not prepared to give up their privileges and forfeit £5.

Among other important families in the town at this time were the Hardwickes, one of whom, Samuel, prepared his will in 1762. He bequeathed to the churchwardens and Vestry of Sodbury the sum of £40 on which the interest was to be used to distribute sixpenny loaves to the poor of the parish yearly, on the Sundays after Michaelmas and Christmas.

Another lease of 1763 reads:

All that plot or piece of now void ground situate in the Borough of Chipping Sodbury whereon several tenements called Church Houses lately stood containing in breadth about 33 ft. and in length about 36 ft. (Condensed) *Town Hall on south – on west land belonging to town leased to Josiah Higgs. Stables belonging* to Bailiff and Bailiff Burgesses now in possession of Josiah Higgs and the other in possession of Thomas Slade on the north and a lane or way leading down to River Frome on the east. (Known as Churchhouses Lane). *This property was purchased by Josiah Higgs.*

So the brook, in some quarters at least, was now being referred to as the River Frome.

There were those who felt that the dignity and facilities of the church at Old Sodbury should be improved and the following is a quotation from the Church Records:

> At a Vestry meeting held in the Parish Church of Old Sodbury, in the county of Gloucester; on Friday the sixth day of January, 1764 in pursuance of notice given in the said Parish Church on Sunday preceding; it is ordered and agreed that the present Churchwardens, John Parker (Jun), and William Cam shall forthwith sell the old bells which are cracked and of no use to the Parish; also all the old bell-metal; and out of the moneys arising by the sale thereof pay all the charges and expenses of new casting and hanging the new bell; and afterwards to lay out the remainder as shall be appointed at some future meeting. (Signed). W. Codrington, W.H. Hartley, W. Hughes (Vicar), Danl. Ludlow, Ed. Shellard, John Parker, Sen., John Parker, Jun., F. Holborrow, James Wickham, Henry Gingell, Jonathan Godwyn, Robert Andrews, Robert Watts.

Some of the detailed expenses in connection therewith read:

> Takeing down the Old Bells etc., 10s. 0d
> For weying her (15 cwt 2 qrs.) and hauling to the boat, 4s. 6d
> Went to Bristol with waggon to fetch the Bell by order and disappointed: ye 15th. went and fetcht the new Bell from Bristol to Sodbury; ye 16th. hald him to Church, £1 0s. 0d
> Paid the bell-founder in part for casting and hanging, £26 5s. 0d
> Paid Mr Phillips, Proctor, for obtaining Faculty pursuant to order of the Vestry, £5 3s. 4d
> Paid the bell-founder the remainder of his demand, £6 15s. 10d
> Taking the old bell metal to Bristol, £1 10s 0d
> Paid Mr. White for beer for the men that helped unload her, 2s. 6d
> For beer when the bell was pulled up and hanged, 5s. 6d
> (The total cost of recasting and hanging the bell, and repairing the frame work was £55 1s. 11d.)

The vicar at the time was Rev. William. Hughes.

More attention was beginning to be paid to providing an education for those children whose parents could pay a fee leading to the growth of private schools known often as 'Dames Schools'. Frequently these were run single-handedly or by two members of a family. The work provided a living for those who could not, for whatever reason, follow any other occupation. As in all things there was a mixture of good, bad and indifferent but the fees were low and they did meet a need.

The bailiff and burgesses decided that their meetings were not being conducted with the appropriate dignity and adopted today's equivalent of 'Standing Orders' as follows:

We, the Bailiff and Bailiff Burgesses, having taken into consideration and duly weighed the inconveniences that attend meeting on Public Business when good order and decorum are not duly observed and being desirous that all meetings shall as much as in us lies and the Publick good, do agree, that at all future meetings according to notice given to the Bailiff's officer, one hour's grace only shall be allowed, and whoever neglects to attend within one hour after notice given shall forfeit the sum of one shilling unless some excuse to be admitted by a majority of the Brethren and be excluded from acting on that day unless by a majority of members present. And if anyone of the Brethren shall leave the hall without some very material business before the books are signed he shall be liable to the above forfeiture. And in order to prevent disputes we do agree that one of the Brethren previous to entering on business be appointed chairman to whom all matters in dispute shall be referred and in case of any indecent behaviour or contests arising he shall call to order, and shall be immediately obeyed under the forfeiture of one shilling. When any matter is to be noted, particularly the giving away of acres and the like, the Chairman shall put the question and after taking exact minutes shall declare the majority. Whoever has any motion to make shall address himself standing to the Chairman who shall on all occasions when one or more are talking call to order and shall be immediately obeyed.

Josiah Higgs. Bailiff, etc.

In December 1766 Thomas Morgan was paid 15s. for pitching the causeway leading to the Boot. This is the only early mention of this inn and from the use of the word 'causeway' there was probably a marshy area at the foot of the hill.

By 1770 the population of the three parishes had become: Little Sodbury 115, Old Sodbury 200 (with 48 houses), Chipping Sodbury 800.

The Baptists in Chipping Sodbury had now chosen Thomas Ferebee as their minister.

The workhouse set up by the bailiff and burgesses was now well established and Daniel Woodward bequeathed £50 towards its upkeep.

A copy of a plan of Chipping Sodbury in 1771 has survived in a book setting out the Codrington estates which clearly shows the position of the Garrett and the Shambles. Originally there were more such houses in the High Street but by this time only the two remained. The market cross also appears on the plan as this was the year before it was moved to Weare's mill in Brook Street. This was done to prevent it being damaged by passing traffic and although there is no doubt that the move did take place the only record of it is in Fox's book.

In 1772 it was recorded that the bailiff and burgesses agreed to contribute ten pounds towards building a bridge over the Broad Brook and mill stream in accordance with the plan and proposal put forward by the Commissioners of the Turnpike. This represents the first move in a proposal to bring the road from Wickwar into Chipping Sodbury via Church Lane instead of Brook Street. The actual payment was made in 1774, so presumably the work was completed by that time. Whilst on the subject of roads it is interesting to note that in 1772 the Lord Mayor of

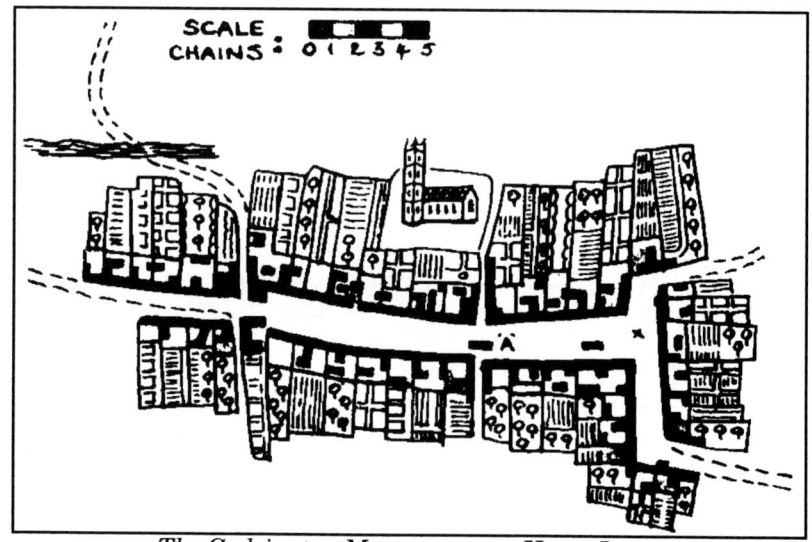

The Codrington Map – courtesy Harry Lane.
The Shambles (marked 'A') and the Garret are shown but there is some question as to whether the relative size of the buildings is correct or whether they are shown for position only.

The junction of Hounds Road with the main street c.1930. The Shambles was opposite this junction.

London made a by-law that all traffic using London Bridge was to keep to the left. This had been done before but, unlike his predecessors, he made sure that it was obeyed. It was such a good idea that it spread rapidly throughout the country.

An advertisement in the Bristol Journal of 13th February 1773 shows that a private traveller from Bristol to Chipping Sodbury would have had to pay 9s. to hire a post chaise with two horses. This represents a big increase on what was being charged some twelve years earlier.

Parson Woodeford, a well-known traveller of his time, confirmed how the general condition of the roads was improving when he recorded in 1774 that he was able for the first time to journey from Oxford to Ansford near Castle Cary in one day. He used the post chaise service and covered the one hundred miles in $14^{1}/_{2}$ hours. The normal coach from Oxford to Bath took fifteen hours to cover the seventy miles but there were breaks for breakfast at Burford, dinner at Cirencester and tea at the Cross Hands.

A list of the freeholders from the Sodburys who voted in the election in 1776 is reproduced in Appendix E. There were 41 from Chipping, 12 from Old and 2 from Little Sodbury. A prominent name was Higgs of which there were four.

There are two Ludlows, Ebenezer, who was a well-known surgeon, and Daniel. There were other Ludlows who either did not qualify or chose not to exercise their franchise. Ebenezer had a son Christopher, who was also an apothecary and surgeon, and who in June of this year married Elizabeth Maria Blanchard.

156   The Three Sodburys – An Introduction

Brook Street c.1909. This was the original route from Chipping Sodbury to Wickwar over the bridge shown left of centre. This was a postcard sent to Percy Couzens when he was in the Bristol Children's Hospital. It was postmarked 4th November 1915.

Brook Street in the 1920s. This view shows the steepness of the hill up to the main street which probably influenced the decision to open an alternative route to Wickwar via Church Road. The house in the photo now (1994) belongs to Mr. R.W. (Dick) Tily. Note the absence of Dando's sheds on the skyline above the house.

There is an interesting document from 1776 showing how a pew in the church was conferred upon a family. It reads:

Chipping Sodbury Borough.
Be it remembered That we the Church Wardens of the aforesaid Borough Do vest Ratify and confirm Thomas White of the same Town or Borough, Tiler and Plasterer, in a Seat or Pew in the Church of and belonging to the said Borough and which said Seat or Pew is situate and being near the South Great Door of the said Church. And is the first Seat or Pew on the Right hand on entering the said Church.

And so the said Thomas White in consideration of his being so Seated as aforesaid therein and his Family to hear Divine Service; hath paid us the said Church Wardens one shilling of Lawful British money. And we have given him the said Thomas White the full and Sole possession of the said Seat or Pew TO HOLD to him, his Heirs and Assigns for ever. Witness our Hands this 16th day of October in the year of our Lord 1776.
Witness.
N.B. The above is a true copy as entered in the Church Book.
James Wickham, Geo. Hicks   Churchwardens.

Isaac Taylor produced his map of Gloucestershire in 1777 on which the previously mentioned pest house is shown together with the Windmill which stood near the present Golf Club House. He shows one large house in Horse Street, together with Buckett's Hill, Blanchards, Frome Bridge and Common Mead Lane. Besides the windmill shown on Taylor's map, there are signs of another having existed at some time on the top of the hills between Old and Little Sodbury in an area known as Windmill Field.

This was not a good year for carrier Thomas Clarke of Chipping Sodbury who had to eat humble pie by publicly apologising in the Gloucester Journal for maligning the character of Charles Rodway, a waggoner of Little Sodbury. This is the first time these two professions have been mentioned.

In other editions of the same newspaper from time to time, the following advertisement appeared:

The Subscription Assembly and Ball Will be at the Bell Inn (date given). *Non-subscribers admittance 3s. Tea and coffee included.*

From time to time some of the able bodied inhabitants, selected by means of a draw, had to join the local Militia and spend a month in a training camp. For obvious reasons this was very inconvenient and so those likely to be involved took part in a kind of insurance scheme. This was run by a local businessman on a profit making basis into which a

Subscription of 5s. 6d was paid, hence the name. In return the guarantee was given that if the subscriber's name was drawn a substitute would be found to do the training or if the subscriber decided to go himself anyway, he received £5. The militia was called by an order from the Commanding Officer and from later newspaper items there were a lot of defaulters.

Another advertisement in the Journal, for October 1778, was with regard to a State Lottery. It read:

> STATE LOTTERY TICKETS and shares of tickets are now selling in variety of numbers at the prices below by Wm. and Robert Clement, Linen drapers, at their licensed Lottery Office in Wade's Passage, Bath.
>
> | Sixteenth | 1. 0. 6. | 1250 L. |
> | Eighth | 2. 0. 6. | 2500 L. |
> | Quarter | 4. 0. 0. | 5000 L. |
> | Half | 7.17. 6. | 10000 L. |
>
> This Lottery is very advantageous for adventurers as there are only forty-eight thousand tickets and seventy-five capital prizes. Not two blanks to a prize. All their shares are stamped according to Act of Parliament and the full money will be paid as are prizes as soon as Government begins paying. Numbers registered at sixpence each. Scheme given gratis. The most money given for prizes as soon as drawn.

The ladies' tongues in the Sodburys must have been set wagging when the news broke that Mrs. Christopher Ludlow, née Blanchard, had eloped with a handsome recruiting officer from a Scottish regiment. Christopher Ludlow himself went to America later and became the garrison surgeon in New York.

A decision was made in 1788 on what the money was to be used for from what was left over after the Old Sodbury Church bells were replaced by a single new bell:

> At a Meeting held this day it was agreed that the £24 arising from sale of the bells in the Parish Church of Old Sodbury, and the remaining part of £55 and odd shillings, be laid out to erect a gallery. And that we have agreed with William Higgs of Old Sodbury to build the same for the sum of four and twenty pounds according to a plan then produced.
>
> (signed) *Edmd. Chapp, James Ludlow, John Parker, Henry Gingell, Richard Hall, Robert Andrews, Cyrus Cadell, James Hatherell, Edward Godwin, Daniel Ludlow.*

The Gallery was duly built for the price named. It was demolished again, presumably when the Church was renovated in 1858/9.

Samuel Rudder published his book on Gloucestershire in 1779. His description of Chipping Sodbury which is quoted here is likely to be quite accurate because it was written as the result of a questionnaire he had sent to a local resident but the details he gives about the families owning the manor are more questionable:

> CHIPPING SODBURY. *This is a small market town consisting of two streets lying somewhat in the form of a letter 'L' on the route from Bristol through Oxford or Abingdon to London and is lately much improved in its buildings. The market which is held on Thursdays is very little frequented, being nothing more than a few neighbouring people gathered in the public houses. The town lies in a great dairy country and formerly the market is said to have been very considerable for cheese. But things are diverged from their proper point and markets in general are reduced to almost nothing owing to factors, jobbers and forestallers buying up great measures at the farms and dairy houses. This pernicious, if not illegal, practice fraught with many evils is particularly unjust to market towns which are taxed higher than villages and as such subject to many charges unknown to the latter but are thus more and more deprived of the means of bearing them.*
>
> *There are two fairs in the year held on Holy Thursday and on 24th June for cattle and peddlary.*
>
> *There is a good deal of travelling through to Bristol and carts are continually passing through it to the coal pits which lie two or three miles further westwards whence many parts in Gloucestershire, Wiltshire and even some places in Berkshire are supplied with coal and the whole district or country from Salisbury and London westward as far as the City of Bristol. Here also is a sort of limestone called the white leys, of a blue cast very compact which breaks into strong lime as white as snow. Considerable quantities of this lime are sent into various parts of the country not only on account of its goodness but it is relatively cheap also from the low price of coal.*
>
> *There is no large manufacturer present; one master clothier employs a few hands but the women and children receive sufficient work from elsewhere.*

He then goes on to relate how the town first achieved and then gave up its mayor and corporation in the 1680s.

It will be remembered that the Lordship of the three manors had passed to Robert Packer. The marriage of Robert Packer of Donington to the daughter of Sir Richard Winchcombe produced four sons, all of whom died childless, and a daughter Elizabeth who became his sole heiress. She was described at the time as a young lady with a fortune of £6,500 and a very amiable quality. Elizabeth became the second wife of David Hartley, a well known philosopher-physician of Bath. David Hartley died on 28th August 1757 aged 52 and his wife Elizabeth on 19th February 1778 aged 65. Their son Winchcombe Henry Hartley inherited property at Bucklesbury in Berkshire as well as the local property. He made Bucklesbury his main residence when not in London as an MP and was buried there when he died in August 1794 aged 54. As a result, both the manor house at Little Sodbury and the house at Lyegrove were neglected with a resulting decay. Although there is nothing recorded locally, he must have had at least one son who in turn married and produced a son, Winchcombe Henry Hartley, in 1811, who subsequently came to live at Lyegrove.

In Old Sodbury church there is a tablet to the memory of another David, who appears to have been another son of David and Elizabeth Hartley and brother to Winchcombe Henry Hartley. He was a Fellow of Merton College, Oxford, MP for Kingston-upon-Hull and Plenipotentiary to the Court of Versailles where peace with the United States was negotiated in 1783.

Although a Manor Court would have been held for the Parish of Old Sodbury from the 12th and 13th Centuries, only scanty records have survived for the years from 1770 to 1793 and, after an interval, fuller details for some later years. The meetings from 1770 to 1793 were concerned mainly with appointing the Parish Constable for the year starting at the end of October. Until 1776 they met at the Dog Inn where the current landlord was Thomas Hayes and from 1777 they met at the Cross Hands which at that time was still a private dwelling. The people appointed were:

> 1770/1 Edward Isaac, shoemaker, 1772 Nicholas Barker, 1773 Thomas Hayes, 1774 Thomas Dowding, 1775/6 John Light, 1777 John Shugar, 1778 Robert Light, 1779 Edwin Godwin, 1780 not shown, 1781 Wm. Iles, 1782 not shown, 1783 John Dike, 1784 Elias Isaac, 1785 not shown, 1786 James Shugar, 1789 Wm. Pritchard, 1790 Wm. Clarke, 1791 John Parker, 1792 John Darke, 1793 Wm. Golding.

A quarry at Buckett's Hill, the original name of Smart's Green is mentioned.

In 1743 the muddy track from Bath to Tetbury which passed through

The Eighteenth Century

the Manor from south to north along the edge of the hill had been transformed into a Turnpike Road. This had led to endless repercussions, especially later when a similar road was added which enabled people to travel to Gloucester via Nympsfield, and the Chippenham road was upgraded. Stage and private coaches became a common sight. Whilst the roads above were still tracks they joined up with another from the west through Old Sodbury at the Cross Hands (see page 19). At some time during the years a substantial building had been erected which served as the site for the Petty Sessions Court. The need for an hostelry was met by the Plough Inn, now Plough Farm, which was a little further up the road towards Stroud. For a long time there was also a smithy on the right going towards Bath.

The following notice appeared in the Gloucester Journal in November 1778:

> *Notice is hereby Given that a Meeting of the Trustees of Sodbury Pike commonly called Yate Elm Pike and of the Trustees of the Sodbury Hill District of Road will be held at the sign of the Cross Hands in Old Sodbury on Friday, 4th December next, at 10.00 in the forenoon of the said day agreeable to their respective adjournments. When the new Trustees for the said Sodbury Hill District of Road will be chosen in room of such as are dead or have declined to act.*
>
> *Geo. Hicks.*
Clerk to the Commissioners

Commissioners were also appointed who were responsible for repairing the road from Cirencester to Lansdown, their clerk being Stephen Ludlow. By this time Chipping Sodbury had achieved the distinction of being a 'post town'.

In a 'for sale' advertisement in 1780 a close of ground near the workhouse of Chipping Sodbury is mentioned, let to John Watts and held for 99 years from Lady Bampfylde. The poor people were obviously still getting some degree of care and protection. In the same advertisement there is a glowing blurb for the town:

> *Sodbury is an healthy, airy Market Town lying within eleven miles of the City of Bristol and 14 of Bath, has the high road from Bristol and the western counties by way of Oxford to London through it and is within fifteen miles of Chippenham and Tetbury, two exceedingly good market towns.*

While there is nothing specific in the records, it seems that by this time the Hatter's Lane route had declined and the high road out of town was now via Horse Street to Old Sodbury where it joined with the turnpike road from Bath to Cirencester at the Cross Hands.

When the bailiff of the borough assumed office he had to give a receipt for items he received from the previous bailiff. A number of these have survived, but the receipt for 1780 is a good example:

> 5th Jan. 1780. Received of Mr. Josiah Higgs, late bailiff of the Town and borough of Chipping Sodbury. Two maces, keys of the Town or Guild Hall, keys of the Town Chest, racks for toasting meat, received in trust for the Town and in pursuance of an order made for that purpose.
>
> Thomas Higgs.

It is not now known whether the date for appointing the bailiff had been moved from October to January or whether there was simply a delay in handing over the articles or providing the receipt. Earlier examples of receipts were puzzling, with the outgoing bailiff handing over 'two dogs' until it was realised that these were the 'dog-irons', or racks for toasting meat. These would have been used for the feast which the bailiff had to provide for every male resident in the town on St. Stephen's Day.

The bailiff and some of the burgesses obviously felt that the time had come in 1781 to make some economies because on the 17th April the following is recorded:

> At a Vestry this day in the church belonging to the borough 'tis agreed that in future there shall be no allowance to the Ringers for their ringing on the King's proclamation day. It not being observed in other places.
>
> James Wallis, bailiff, James Wickham jnr., Wm. Tily, Wm. Wigg, Robert Alder.

The reference was presumably to the observance of the anniversary of the King's coronation.

Having mentioned the turnpikes before, it is useful to note what the charges for the use of the highways were in 1782. Although they varied from trust to trust, those for the Minchinhampton area were:

For every Horse, Mare, Gelding, mule or other beast or cattle drawing any carriage	4d
For every Horse, Mare, etc. not drawing	1d
For every drove of oxen or other neat cattle	10d per score
For claves, sheep or swine	3d per score
For broad wheeled wagons or carts	3d per horse
For narrow wheeled carriages	$3^{1}/_{2}$d per horse
For narrow wheeled vehicles with four horses, from 1st Nov. to 30th April	2s. 0d
For the remainder of the year	1s. 6d

The Eighteenth Century

Initially the tolls were let to contractors by public auction to the highest bidder but this gave rise to such a high level of fraud by the bidders, who made a ring among themselves to keep the prices down that the Trustees collected the tolls themselves and the gate-keepers were sworn to give an honest account of all tolls taken.

In the town accounts there is a very interesting entry for this year:

> *Feby.7th. Paid to Mr Eb. Ludlow for inoculating the Poor belonging to this borough by order of the Committee appointed for that purpose............ £45.*

Ebenezer Ludlow was a surgeon with a considerable reputation and Jenner had been apprenticed to him some twenty years earlier, perhaps in response to an advertisement similar to the one already quoted. Throughout this century the people in the Sodburys were served by members of the Ludlow and Wallis families as apothecaries and doctors. Doctor Hardwicke of Bristol was also a local man and between them it is possible that they perfected a serum for vaccination against smallpox.

After being the headmaster of the Grammar School for over 45 years, the Rev. Francis Gold resigned at the end of 1782. He also held the livings of Wapley and Rangeworthy. In the last years of his headship there was again an assistant or writing master and for a while this was a Mr. Ferebee. With such an unusual surname it could be that this was the Rev. Thomas Ferebee, the minister of the Baptist Chapel.

With the need to appoint a new headmaster, the bailiff and burgesses decided to restate the rules under which the school was to operate. The two opening paragraphs were brought forward from a much earlier document as, perhaps, have some of the rules. The document reads:

> *The Bailiff and Bailiff Burgesses having taken into their serious consideration the great importance of attending to the morals and affording improvement to children born in the town whose fathers are townsmen. Resolved that a part of the overplus arising from the improved rents of the town lands shall be apportioned according to the direction of the decree (for such good purposes) to the payment of twelve guineas annually to a schoolmaster to be appointed for that purpose subject to the following Rules and Regulations to be improved or varied from time to time by direction of the Bailiff and Burgesses.*
>
> *Rule No. 1 That the school hours from Lady-day to Michaelmas shall be from eight in the morning to twelve, and from Michaelmas to Lady-Day at the same hours and from such time as the master shall judge right in the afternoon.*

2 That neither the Christmas or Whitsun recesses shall exceed three weeks or Easter one week.
3 That the roll shall be called every morning and afternoon at such hour after opening the said school as the master shall appoint.
4 That every defaulter shall be subject to correction by the master, and shall be, by him, reported to the Committee at their next visitation.
5 That the Committee shall have power to expel on the complaint of the master and to re-admit when they think right.
6 That each boy shall be able to read the bible before admission and that no boy be admitted without a ticket signed by three of the Committee.
7 That it be an invariable rule to attend to the cleanliness of the boy admitted .
8 That the master shall instruct all boys after admission in reading, writing and arithmetic, and he shall frequently practise them in spelling.
9 That strict attention shall be paid to the morals and particularly that lying and swearing shall be punished by the Master and be afterwards reported by him to the Committee .
10 That all boys neglecting to attend the church, or some place of public worship, on Sundays shall be liable to expulsion by the Committee.
11 That the Church, and no other catechism, shall be publicly taught in the school by one of the masters at least once in every week, and the boys shall be obliged to learn and repeat to the Master every Monday morning the Collect of the preceding day and twice at least in every Lent shall be obliged on such days as the minister of the Parish shall appoint to appear in the Church and be examined in the Catechism.
12 That the Grammar Master be expected, from time to time, to report, and to make such observations to the Committee for their reflection as to him shall appear proper for the better regulation, order and improvement either of the said Grammar or Writ-

The Eighteenth Century

    ing School, and that he be at all times considered as having a superintending power in the School.
13 That these rules be written or printed in large characters and affixed up in the school and that parents or guardians applying for admission tickets to be made acquainted with them.
14 That the Master be appointed for one year only.
15 That no greater number of Country boys than twelve be admitted.
16 That the Churchwardens be apply'd to set apart a seat in the church or one part of the gallery for the Schoolboys to sit in.
17 That the pay shall commence from St. Thomas' Day and the school be opened on Monday 20th day of Jan. 1783.

Rule 6 shows that there was an entrance examination inferring that there were other schools where reading, at least, was taught. Rule 16 confirms that there was a gallery in the church prior to re-construction.

Rev. Edward Davies, the new head, arrived from Wales in time for the re-opening. He was a bachelor 27 years of age. His sight had been somewhat weak since the age of six as the result of an accident but before he was twenty he had become known as the writer of a number of hymns and poems in Welsh. He obviously felt more secure with this appointment because he married a Miss Margaret Smith of Whittington. By the next year he had brought out the first of his chief works, *Aphtharte, the Genius of Britain*, a poem written in a sixteenth century style.

There was great excitement in Bristol and surrounding areas in April 1785 when a Mr. Decker advertised his intended ascent in a 'hot air' balloon from a field at St. Philips, Bristol, on the 19th of that month. This was to be a repeat of the ascent he had made in London the September before. When daylight dawned on the 19th, crowds of people were either in, or on their way to, Bristol. A successful ascent was duly made and the balloon came down at Chippenham some sixty-seven minutes later, somewhat to the irritation of all those people from that direction who had paid inflated prices for horse and coach hire to be present at Bristol. For a long time after this balloons kept appearing in the designs on crockery, glass and fans.

Travel by road was becoming more popular with each succeeding year as the roads themselves improved and in 1786 a man named Paterson brought out a road book giving routes and mileages to a number of places. The three quoted here have been selected as being of local interest.

The Three Sodburys – An Introduction

Route: Bristol to Banbury

to	Stapleton	3	C. Sodbury	11
	Hambrook	5	Petty France	16
	Wiblet (Nibley)	9	Didmarton	19
	Yate	10 etc.		

The fact that the distance between Chipping Sodbury and Petty France is shown as 5 miles confirms that the route was now via the Cross Hands.

Route: Bath to Birmingham & Derby

to	Monument on Lansdown	4	Nympsfield	26.
	Tollhouse	9	Frocester	27½
	Cross Hands	12	Whitminster	31
	Petty France	14½	Cold Arbour	22

The distance to the Cross Hands was 12 miles because at that time the route from Dodington Ash was via Tormarton. Even at this late date the ancient track along the hills to cross the Severn at Arlingham was still partly being followed until it joined the Gloucester-Bristol road at Whitminster. It is worth noting that at this time the river was still fordable from Arlingham to Westbury.

Route: London to Sodbury

to	Chippenham	93½	Nettleton	102
	Yatton Keynell	97½	Acton Turville	107
	Castle Coombe	99	Cross Hands	109

A lady called Mary Russell looked after the workhouse occupants in 1788. In the next year yet another member of the Ludlow family was bailiff of the town as shown by his signature to this resolution:

Whereas it appears that the road through this town hath of late been much improved by the removal of the houses called the Shambles and whereas it hath been represented that the several persons who contributed to the purchase of such houses made their respective contributions that the building used as a school house would also be taken down for the greater improvement of the road. And the lord of the manor having been pleased to relinquish that part of the building which hath hitherto been used by him or his tenants and whereas the whole of the said building is now in a very ruinous condition and it is judged expedient that the same be taken down for the advantage of the said road and accommodation of the inhabitants of this town.

Resolved that the same be taken down, accordingly resolved also that a commodious schoolroom and a proper...? be provided under the direction of the bailiff and burgesses to be substituted in place of those intended to be removed.

D. Ludlow, Bailiff

The Rev. Edward Davies at the Grammar School had by now completed his second literary work, *Vacanalia*, which consisted of essays in verse. Now the school house had been demolished, he no longer had anywhere to live and from subsequent reports it seems that he was allowed to occupy one of the houses belonging to the charities rent free. For at least part of his time as headmaster, however, the Rev. Francis Gold had lived in Hill House on the Parade. A deed in connection with Hill House shows that a felt maker called William Withers was living in Sodbury in 1790.

It was not long after the Garrett had been knocked down that a new school together with a house for the headmaster was provided on the site where the Old Grammar School now stands. This had been the site of the Lamb Inn which by this time was derelict. This is the only time that an inn of this name is mentioned. The dwelling house part of the new building was paid for, in part at least, by donations of £40 each from Peter and Samuel Hardwicke and £50 from Rev. Thomas Shellard.

At the time the town bought it, the Lamb Inn was owned by Ebenezer Ludlow. The Ludlows were still one of the important families in the town and they had now gone into banking at a time when such business was largely conducted by family concerns. Their premises were on the site of the house with the double front on the right, looking towards Bristol, at the top of High Street. A specimen of one of their bank notes has survived and is held in the Institute of Bankers archives. The note is thought to be pre-1793 because in the Gloucester Journal it is obvious that many of these small family banks ran into trouble so their notes were not acceptable to the ordinary traders. To keep up confidence in them prominent people were persuaded to make a public avowal, through the newspaper, that they were willing to accept the cash notes of their local bank. Sodbury was no exception and the following appeared in the Gloucester Journal for 27th March 1793:

> *We, whose names are hereunto subscribed in consequence of the responsibility of the Sodbury Bank under the firm of Ludlow, Wallis Ludlow and Co., do agree to take the cash notes of the said Bank as usual.*
>
> *Josiah Higgs, bailiff. Geo. Hardwicke, MD, Arthur Tanner, Daniel Higgs, Joseph Hiatt, Josiah Higgs, brewer, (& 33 others)*

The bank is here quoted as Ludlow, Wallis and Ludlow, whilst the bank note shows all Ludlows. Perhaps, having run into difficulties, the

Ludlows persuaded Wallis to join them and then had the notice of confidence published.

Earlier in that same March the possibility of building a waterway through part of the Manor of Old Sodbury was being discussed. With Christopher Codrington, High Sheriff of the County, as chairman, a meeting was called at Tetbury to consider the construction of a Navigable Canal starting at the City of Bristol and passing as near as possible to the coal mines in Bristol and in the parishes of Westerleigh and Pucklechurch before going on to join the Thames and Severn Canal at Thames Head. An examination of the terrain to be crossed probably resulted in it being nothing more than talked about.

The Inclosure Act. 34 George III (1794) recited Articles of Agreement from 1791. These were between W. Henry Hartley Esq., Lord of the Manor of Old Sodbury and Little Sodbury, and the Duke of Beaufort, Chapter of Worcester and other Land owners in the North and South Common fields of Old Sodbury, White's Tyning, Grickstone, and Great Fields of Old Sodbury making 698 acres in all and in the Common Mead or Dole Mead consisting of 106 acres. These were made up into separate parcels by Commissioners of the Commonable Lands and awarded to the appropriate owners. The Act confirmed the award and directed it to be enrolled at Westminster or Gloucester, with a copy to be kept in the Parish Church at Old Sodbury.

The North and South fields were on those sides of the road running from Cross Hands to Chippenham after it had climbed the hill. Grickston(e) is the farm of that name some distance to the north. Common Mead is commemorated by the lane of that name leading from Old to Little Sodbury. The map is not now in Old Sodbury church but it is possible that one is with the Beaufort papers at Gloucester Record Office, but is not available except by special permission.

Survived from 1795 is a form issued by the Chief Constable for the area requiring the Petty Constable of Chipping Sodbury to appear at the dwelling house of Thomas White in Old Sodbury commonly known as the Cross Hands. The purpose, on this occasion, was to brief the Chief Constable prior to the General Quarter Sessions at Gloucester. In Gloucester Records Office details are preserved of proposed alterations in 1797/8 to the roads near "the House by the name of the Cross Hands".

The year 1795 is an important one in the history of Chipping Sodbury because in that year the Vestry decided to commission Mr. J.P. Sturge to survey the parish and to prepare a plan so that the Poor Rate could be estimated. An analysis of the available details gives some idea of how things stood in Chipping Sodbury at this time.

The Eighteenth Century 169

Dwellings
Houses	154
Tenements	78
Cottages	5
Inns, current	5
Inns, late	1
	243

Connected with the above there were:

Courts 50; Stables 46; Yards 28; Brewhouses 11; Bakehouses 6; Malthouses 4; Coach houses 2; Greenhouse 1.

The tenements were small houses at the back of the larger houses with frontages on the street. They were reached by a side entrance and formed three sides of a square. They were probably the dwellings of drovers and waggoners. Many of them have still survived.

Inns

Sign value	Proprietor	Occupier	Rateable
Bell	G. Hardwicke	Jn. Hancock	£22½
George	Eliz. Hawkins	Eliz. Hawkins	£20
Swan	Mary Cox	Mary Cox	£22½
Portcullis	Wm. Tily	Wm. Tily	£15
Royal Oak	Thos. Watts	Thos. Watts	£12
Duke William*	W.H. Hartley	John Hancock	£12

*This was on the site of the present Police Station.

There are fifteen shops indicated without the particular trade being shown. The identified premises were:

Shops (Total 18)
Apothecary	1.	Hyatt, J.
Bank	1.	Ludlows
Butcher	2.	Alden Th.
		Alding I.
Cabinet & watch maker.	1.	Miles G. and/or
		Weeks J.
Chandler	1.	Harvey R.
China	1.	Wright Wm.
Stationer	1.	White J.
Collar maker	1.	Thompson W.
Draper	4.	Wickham Wm.
		Chilcott Wm.
		Naish Sarah
		Bruton Moses

Tenements in Alleluyah Alley in Rounceval Street between the Grapes and The Parade before they were renovated by the late Les Tily and renamed Southview. They are currently (1994) under further renovation by his son, Peter Tily.

Grocer	1.	Philips Th.	
Sadler	1.	Bailey Jonathan	
Shoemaker	2.	Courtier S.	
		Short G	
Clothier	1.	Tanner A.	

Trades (Total 20)

Braziers	2.	Wood J.	
		Neal J.	
Brandy merchant	1.	Higgs Dan.	
Brewer	1.	Higgs Jos. I	
Carpenters	4.	Tily Th.	
		Rice W.	
		Higgs W.	
		(not known)	
Currier (leather dresser)	2.	Taylor S.	
		Watts T.	
Miller	1.	Tandy J.	
Salt ref'r	1.	Muffett R.	
Slaughter house	1.	Wickham J.	
Smith	3.	Tily S.	
		Beams M.	
		(not known)	
Tanyard	1.	Higgs W.	
Tiler & plasterer	1.	White J.	
Cooper	1.	Amos M.	
Maltster	1.	Higgs, Josiah II	

The system applied was first to decide a value for the land and houses. The land was then charged at 1s. in the pound on the full figure and the houses paid 1s. on two thirds of the value. The total rateable value is recorded as £1,088 16s. 4d giving a total return of £54 9s 2½d

The fact that "The Island" was excluded as being in Old Sodbury gives some indication of the care with which the work was carried out. The Island was in the brook at the back of what is now the Old Bank House. Although north of the brook, the Ridings were taken to be part of Chipping Sodbury. The total population was 1,087.

Although the highest rateable value was £35 for a house on the south side of Rounceval Street, the other valuations varied between one and ten pounds. One item, a footnote to the report, is really worth noting.

> *A cottage in the Stub Riding built to be used for the smallpox but now used as a pest and poor's house and since occupied by two poor families. Not rated.*

172   *The Three Sodburys – An Introduction*

To appreciate just what this meant, the following is quoted from Latimer's *Annals of Bristol,* Vol.2, first published in 1893:

> *Readers of the present day (i.e.. 1893) are unable to realise the devastation committed a century ago by small pox. In spite of attempts to check the malady by inoculation every town in the kingdom was repeatedly swept by outbreaks of the scourge during the reigns of the three Georges. The mortality in Bristol in 1758 and other years is known to have been great. The disease was never so rife or so destructive as during the last ten years of the century when 92 per 1,000 of the population – nearly 1/10th – are recorded to have died of smallpox alone whilst at least twice that proportion narrowly escaped from the scourge and were disfigured for life.*

That was Bristol in 1795. By contrast, in the same year the cottage on the Ridings was no longer needed for its original purpose! It is certain, therefore, that the local inhabitants must have had some form of protection. All the available evidence indicates that this immunity had been brought about by Ebenezer Ludlow and/or Josiah Wallis. Edward Jenner, who published the results of his researches and came to fame in 1798, was Ludlow's former pupil.

Those who carried out the survey must have found the work tiring, to the landlady of the Swan's benefit who after submitting her account gave the following receipt:

> *The 17th of September 1795. Received of the Overseers of Sodbury the sum of ten pounds ten shillings and fivepence for expenses of eating and drinking upon parish business while making an Equal Poor rate as per Bill.*
>
> Mary Cox.

The survey was carried out by Jacob Sturge and Richard Hale, with J. Symons as clerk. The first two received fourteen guineas for their work and the clerk three guineas. Mr. Sturge received a further five guineas for drawing the plan. The total cost of this exercise was quite heavy and it was decided to pay for it from revenue.

Some idea of how justice was maintained can be seen in the following form used to summon the petty constable to report to the Chief Constable for the area. The items that are in italics have been written in on the original while the rest is printed.

Margin Hundred of

Grumbald's Ash
County of
Gloster

To the Petty Constable or Tithingman of *Chipping Sodbury* in the said Hundred
These are to will and require you personally to be and appear at the dwelling house of
Thomas White in *Old Sodbury* commonly known by the sign of the *Cross Hands* on the *21st* day of this *Instant* at *09* of the clock in the *fore*noon, there to give me the meeting and to deliver to me in writing, under your hand, a presentment of all felonies, rescues, escapes, nuisances, disorderly houses, and all other matters and things within your district which have come to your knowledge, and which you are bound in virtue of your office to present in order that I may take and deliver the same at the next *General Quarter Sessions* to be holden at *Gloucester* for the County of *Gloucester* on the 6th of *October next*

Hereof fail not at your peril. – Given under my hand this *5th Sept. 1795*
Henry White
CHIEF CONSTABLE
Constables Returns
NB. With your Bridge Money ...£2. 2s. 9^3/$_4$d.

Early in 1796 someone was needed to take charge of the workhouse and the following advertisement appeared in the Gloucester Journal for 28th January with the same advertisement appearing in several subsequent issues:

Whereas there is a mistress wanted to take care and management of the workhouse of Chipping Sodbury in the County of Gloucestershire. Whoever is inclined to become a mistress of the said workhouse are requested to give in their proposals immediately to us the undernamed churchwardens and overseers of Chipping Sodbury aforesaid.
James White, James Neal, Church Wardens; Rob. Rowland, Geo. Short, Overseers.

In March the same year the Bell Inn changed hands and the new landlord put the following announcement in the Journal for 25th April and several subsequent issues:

Bell Inn, Chipping Sodbury
T. COX

Having taken and entered upon the above inn, most respectfully informs the Nobility, Gentlemen Travellers, his friends and the Public in general, that he has neatly fitted it up, and laid in a good choice of Liquors. He humbly solicits their support, and at the same time assures them that his utmost endeavours shall be exerted to render their accommodation agreeable. Neat POST CHAISES. Excellent stabling with good attention. He continues his new and elegant POST COACH from the Golden-Hart, Stroud, every Monday, Wednesday and Friday at eight-o-clock in the morning to the George Inn, Castle Street, Bristol, calls at the White Hart, Minchinhampton, Three Cups, Tetbury, and Bell and Swan, Sodbury, and arrives at Bristol at three-o-clock the same day. Returns Tuesdays, Thursdays and Saturdays at nine-o-clock in the morning. Fare inside 10s. 6d. Outside 5s. 6d. Extra luggage 1d per pound.

N.B. No parcels above £5 value will be accounted for unless entered as such and paid for accordingly.

By December the coach operators had become Cox & Co., and the vehicle ran over the same route but starting now from Gloucester.

A tax known as 'Game Duty' was levied on those who were better off and a list was published annually. The list in October of 1796 included Brooke Fitzherbert Esq., and Tanner Thomas, gent, of Chipping Sodbury, Higgs Thomas, gent, of Little Sodbury and Ebenezer Ludlow of Stanshawes Court, Yate. The last entry demonstrates how much the Ludlow family had prospered.

It appeared to be sensible in those days to form local associations against Burglary, Felony, etc.,

Melbourne House, Horse Street in 1976
The photograph is from the Sodbury Historical Society Collection.

and Chipping Sodbury had followed suit, confirmed by a notice of the annual meeting to be held at the Bell Inn on 8th December. Dinner was to be on the table prompt at 2 o'clock. The members included Daniel, Thomas and William Higgs, James and William Ludlow, Arthur Tanner, Joseph Wallis, Richard Tovey, Thomas Brooke, Geo. Hardwicke, John and William Wickham, Robert Cam, John Hancock, John Godwin and John Parker.

A proposal was made in 1797 to divert an old road and build a new one in the area between Cross Hands and Tormarton. There are not very many details available but it could be in relation to building a direct section of highway from Cross Hands to Dodington Ash.

The Chipping Sodbury accounts were heavily in the red at this time, probably because of the cost of the 1795 survey. The situation was saved, however, by a number of local gentlemen who made a £100 loan to the borough.

The Rev. Edward Davies gave up the headmastership of the Grammar School in 1799 to take up a curacy at Olveston. Some four years earlier he had finished his third book, a novel called *Eliza Powell, or the Trials of Sensibility*. During his last years at the school one of his pupils was local born Philip Bliss who was to become famous as a bibliographer. It was said of him in later life, "The punctuality of his habits and the method with which he kept the muniments entrusted to his care became a proverb at Oxford, while the sweetness of his disposition and the courtesy of his manners were the delight of all with whom he came in contact." The new head of the school was another Davis, this time Rev. John Davis.

Some of the many trades and professions in which residents of the three Sodburys were employed before 1800 are given in Appendix F. The list is by no means an exhaustive one, nor does it mean that the particular trade or profession did not exist before the date mentioned; it is simply that this is the first time it was mentioned in the records for the area.

This was a time of great hardship with the poor being particularly badly affected. The harvests had failed for a number of years and 1799 had been even worse, with 1800 proving to be no better. The price of wheat soared higher and higher until the average in the markets of Bristol and Gloucestershire reached 159s. 10d per quarter. General malnutrition made the majority of the people an easy target for diseases and the death rate crept higher and higher each month.

CHAPTER EIGHT

THE NINETEENTH CENTURY

The first census returns were introduced in 1801 and the figures for the three Sodburys were: Chipping Sodbury 1090, Old Sodbury 687 and Little Sodbury 89. At around this time part of the Chipping Sodbury records were destroyed by fire and those which were saved were deposited in a bank for safe keeping. A number of the records bear the marks of rough handling.

The harvests were still failing and all through the late autumn and winter 1800–1801 the overseers of the poor had to buy what corn they could. They stored it at the home of John Andrews where the poor could buy it at the normal price. A loss was made over the period of £55 with a further £9 loss for a similar subsidy on two barrels of rice. Ten sacks of potatoes at 15s. 9d each and a further three at 15s. 6d were also bought. Payments out to the poor from Easter 1800 to Easter 1801 exceeded £450 and the overseers were £22 in the red.

Subsidies are not a new concept and neither was the 'Home Guard'. In 1804, with the threat of a French invasion, Isaac Light was paid £4 5s. 0d for drilling the volunteers. In Old Sodbury, the village stocks were repaired, first in 1802 when three new locks were fitted and again in 1805 when some woodwork was renewed.

The County Bridge Money still cropped up in the accounts and by this time had increased to a sum varying from £5 15s. 7½d to £6 18s 9d per quarter. This rose to £9 5s 0d per quarter in 1810 and in 1815 three quarterly payments of £24 5s. 7½d were made. What these payments were actually for is still not known.

Payment was made for maintaining the water supply in 1803 with work done on the pumps in the High Street, Brook Street and the road leading to the Riding, together with the new pump put up in Horse Street.

While the main roads run by the Turnpike Trusts were now in a reasonable condition there were still many miles of secondary roads for which the parish authorities were responsible although Chipping Sodbury was lucky because there were few such roads within its boundaries and a number of charitable bequests existed specifically for repairing them. Elsewhere in the countryside, a specially strengthened large plough was usually parked in some convenient spot. Then, in the spring, the local farmers jointly provided a team of up to eight horses and restored the minor roads by ploughing them up and then harrowing them down to a fairly level surface. In Old Sodbury a scraper was used rather than a plough. Responsibility for the work was centred on the Church and two residents were appointed each year as surveyors, in 1809 those being Oliver Morton and John Hatherell. This sort of work was paid for out of a rate levied on the inhabitants of the parish. Everyone had to either pay cash, provide teams and labour, or work themselves for an appropriate number of hours.

The Old Sodbury Statute Labour books for the early 1800s show that the inhabitants were divided into two groups, those whose valuation was above £50 and those below. In 1808 there were 14 paying more and 49 paying less, the highest figure being £249 and the lowest £2. Stone was quarried from Horwood Common and from quarries near the Chippenham and Tormarton roads, for which gunpowder was used, and the stone was then carried to the required site by sledges rather than wheeled vehicles. The rate for the job was 1s. 6d per day for men and 9d for women but the length of the day is not reported. During the next few years the following items were noted:

Scraping Parsons Lane and Scots Hole Lane. 122 3/4 lug. @ 3s. 4d.
Eleven days making a new road King Grove Common side of Mill Lane.
Eighteen days making and mending a Bridle road in Portway Lane 18d per day .
Paid Robert Light for scraping the Church Lane and Scots Hole Lane.

Old Hill and Dog Lane are frequently referred to while Trinity Lane and Saltwell Lane are also mentioned. Dog Lane was probably what is now Chapel Lane before the chapel was built and Saltwell Lane was probably the lower end of this, as there is a house there called Saltwell House. Parsons Lane is a mystery as is Scots Hole which might now be Cotswold Lane. Another lane in the Old Sodbury area was Fattinghouse Lane, now Mill Lane. This was a corruption of Vattinghouse and shows that there was some connection with the tanning industry and the soaking or vatting of hides for which, because of the smell, an isolated spot was needed.

Just how close the Bristol Turnpike Trust was to the Sodburys is not clear, but in 1815 the Trust employed Macadam, whose road-making ability was widely acknowledged, to resurface their roads. When building a new road Macadam worked on what he called the "three times" principle. A bottom layer of stone four inches thick was first laid and then worked down well with rollers. Two successive layers were then laid but no binding material was used. As the first requirement in road making was toughness Macadam preferred whinstone flint, limestone and pebbles. Limestone tended to absorb moisture and to break up under frost but it was cheap.

Small stones were broken down on site by men with hammers, for which they received 9d per day. This practice continued into the 1920s and it was once common to see a man sat at the roadside breaking up a large heap of stones with a long-handled light hammer and a strip of wire netting on stakes to stop chips flying into the road.

The 1811 Census showed slight increases in the populations of Chipping and Old Sodbury and a small decrease at Little Sodbury. There was an election in this year and a list of those who voted are listed in Appendix E. The Swan Inn was bought in 1811 by Mr. Hall for £2,000.

In 1812 rioting brought a night of terror to Bristol and to restore order the East Middlesex Militia was called in from Chipping Sodbury. How they came to be here is not known but perhaps they were in the area on a training exercise.

In this year a school was established in Horse Street by Mr. E.H. Parker. School teaching was not too highly thought of in those days, as can be seen in an application preserved in the Gloucester Record Office. It was from a lady applying on behalf of her husband who had "been necessitated to teach school, the only resource for honest poverty that has not been brought up either to trade or labour".

No doubt some Sodburys residents were among those who flocked to Bristol in September 1814 to watch yet another balloon ascent. This time the bag was filled with hydrogen obtained from more than three tons of iron filings and 25 large casks of sulphuric acid. The aeronauts were Messrs. Sadler and Clayfield who, having taken off successfully, came down in the sea off Lynmouth where they were rescued by a boat.

Various people had left sums of money to be invested and the interest distributed to the poor in bread and other comforts over the years and they were not forgotten in other ways. At a Vestry meeting in March 1816 Mr. Joseph Hyatt, a local apothecary living at that time in what is now Vickers Electronics on the corner of Horseshoe Lane, was reappointed as medical officer for the poor within an area of four miles for a fee of ten guineas (£10.50). Two guineas were also subscribed to Bristol Infirmary.

The London based firm of Messrs. Christy & Co., built a factory at Frampton Cotterell in 1818 to take advantage of the local skill in making felt hats and a much cheaper labour force than in London. This was close enough for some Sodburys inhabitants to get their first taste of factory life. In the following year the employment of children under nine years of age was forbidden and schools began to spring up everywhere supported by various societies.

Matches were invented in 1820 and life must have become a little easier everywhere. This was also the year when George IV came to the throne. The next year saw yet another census and this time there were slight increases at Old and Little Sodbury, but a decrease of nearly 200 at Chipping Sodbury.

It was around this time that the present road from the Cross Hands to the top of Dog Hill was built along the side of the hill as an alternative to the old more direct but very steep road which is now a bridle path. For some reason the Codrington family would not allow the spoil from the corner to be tipped on their estate and so it was brought into the village and spread to the north of the road between the Turnpike and the Green.

There was now a Turnpike road between the Cross Hands and Yate with a purpose-built house for the tolls collector. It was a transport café for a number of years run by Mr. & Mrs. H. Gough and is now a restaurant. The new length of road had a turn-off on it on the long bend, which led to Dodington and by-passed the Turnpike, so the Trust employed a boy with a collection box to sit there and the site is still known as 'Catch Box' Corner.

The private residence known as the 'Cross Hands' was now rebuilt and took over from the 'Plough' as an Inn, which then became a farm.

While there must have been a post office of some sort in Chipping Sodbury at an earlier date, the earliest record the Postal Authorities can find is for 1823. At that time mails for this area travelled via Bath and then on the Bath to Oxford mail which was met at the Cross Hands by a postman on foot. At this time there was a 'penny post' reaching from Bristol to Iron Acton and for equal distances in some other directions. This covered small parcels as well as letters and had started in July 1793. The selection of the parishes included was somewhat hit or miss leading to some anomalies. For instance, a packet was carried eighteen miles for one penny to an address within the scheme while the charge for a similar distance to an address outside the scheme could be as much as 6s. 8d.

In the early years of the nineteenth century the Hartleys, of which Winchcombe Henry Howard (born 1811) was to become the head, moved from Bucklebury in Berkshire to Lyegrove House, giving it a new lease of life. They altered the house extensively and at the bottom of the drive, in 1835, they built the little Gothic entrance lodge near a set of Georgian gateposts. They also transferred a magnificent fireplace, bearing indications of Stephen's ownership, from Little Sodbury Manor.

The Cross Hands Hotel, Old Sodbury

The Toleration Act of 1689 gave Dissenters the legal right to worship publicly once they had registered the address of their place of worship in the Bishop's Court and abolished the penalties for disobedience.

The Hockaday Abstracts at Gloucester show the following:

> *1807. June 2nd. Certificate to the Bishop of Gloucester by James Reed, Samuel Arthurs, Thomas Ferebee, Charles Powers, Stephen Sallis, Arthur Warner and John Wick, that the dwelling house of James Reed in the parish of Old Sodbury is to be used as a place of religious worship by Protestant Dissenters. Which certificate they request may be registered in the Bishop's Court persuant to Statute Registered June 3rd 1807.*

On 17th September 1819 a similar application was made for a room in the house of John Garroway. The residence of James Reed was registered in 1827. By 1835 the congregation had built a Chapel in the lane leading to Dodington which was still used until the 1970s when it was converted into a private house.

The Baptist Chapel in Hounds Road was built in 1819 on the site of what was apparently known as the Baptist Meeting House and there was a Sunday School from before the new chapel was built. This was probably run after the example of Robert Raikes and taught the 'three R's' as well as religious knowledge. The school rules have survived and clearly show that membership was not a matter to be treated lightly:

RULES FOR THE SUNDAY SCHOOL ESTABLISHED AT BAPTIST MEETING HOUSE, SODBURY

1. THAT the school shall be opened at nine o'clock in the morning and one in the afternoon, precisely, and as it is commenced and closed with singing and prayer, it is expected that all the Children will be then present, and to stay during Public Worship.
2. That any Scholar who shall be absent from School four successive Sabbaths, without a sufficient reason being given, shall be dismissed; but with liberty of appealing to the President.
3. That the children be entitled to Rewards as below.
4. That if any scholar does not come clean, washed and combed; or if guilty of lying, swearing, pilfering, Sabbath-breaking, talking in an indecent manner, or otherwise misbehaving, to be subject to the forfeits below; and if, after repeated reproof the Scholar shall not be reformed, he or she shall be excluded from the School.
5. That no book shall be taken away from the School on any pretence.
6. That on changing their places of abode, the Parents or Friends of the children must send notice of the same to the President.
7. That no scholar, who shall have left or been dismissed from the School, shall be re-admitted without leave of the President.

FORFEITURE OF TICKETS

Each child, on coming to School with dirty hands or face, or hair not combed, shall forfeit one Ticket; for not coming in proper time, one Ticket; for playing on the Sabbath, three tickets; for swearing, three tickets; and for stealing, five tickets.

REWARD OF TICKETS

Each child, for early attendance at School, shall receive one Ticket each time; and one for their attendance and good behaviour at the Evening Meeting. For repeating the Text, one each time; and a large Ticket for learning and reciting the Verses on the Tickets, when exchanged on the last Sabbath every month.

N.B. It is earnestly recommended to the Parents and Friends of the Children to set them proper examples at home, and especially to keep holy the Sabbath day, and attend a Place of Worship, without which no blessing can be expected on their labours. Parents are required to be punctual in their observance of these Rules, as it will materially assist in the instruction of their

Children; and to insure such observance, it is recommended to fix up a copy of the above Rules on some conspicuous part of their dwelling.

The last entry in the book used in the Poor Rate Survey of 1795 and brought up-to-date each year is for 1823. It reads:

This year in the spring was 8 new bedsteads had, eight new beds and change of bedding new for the workhouse and new wall in front of the house for a Court and the poor lett or farmed to a Mr. Roberts at £383 per year and the next year £440 and the bastard money also gave him.

The heyday of coaches had now arrived with improved roads and shorter routes and journeys could now be made in much more comfort than was possible only ten years before. The Commissioners of the Sodbury Division of Turnpike Roads were responsible for the local highways and they held regular meetings at the Swan Inn. Their clerk was Mr. J. Fowler.

A coach was operating between Gloucester and Bristol via Sodbury in 1796 and the postal arrangements show that there was a mail coach from Bath to Oxford via the Cross Hands, and return, in 1823.

Anyone living on the 'top road' during 1824 to 1826 would have seen "The Alert", "The Mercury", "The Original" and a Post Coach travelling daily from Gloucester to Bath. The fares were, Inside 12s. 0d, Outside 6s. 0d.

Passengers from Cheltenham to Bath were carried daily by "The Invincible" and there was also "The Surprise" which left Bath for Gloucester on Monday, Wednesday and Friday, returning on Tuesday, Thursday and Saturday.

Chipping Sodbury itself was served, among others, by "The Champion", which ran daily from Bristol to Oxford, arriving there at 6.30 pm and meeting coaches to Buckingham, Northampton, Cambridge and all parts of the North.

The volume of traffic can be assessed by the fact that in 1825 the Didmarton and Dunkirk Turnpikes collected £1,020.

The Lord of the Manors' benevolence is recorded in the Gloucester Journal for 2nd January 1826 as follows:

Rev. W.H.H. Hartley's annual Christmas donation of beef and bread was last week distributed to the poor of the parishes of Little Sodbury and Old Sodbury and to his tenants in Chipping Sodbury.

A bitter dispute now began between the Bailiff and Bailiff Burgesses with their legal representative Mr. Whittington and the head master of the Free School, Rev. Thomas Smith with his legal representative Mr. Hetling.

Mr Whittington, who was living in Hill House, had two pamphlets printed and circulated putting his point of view, of which a copy only of the second has survived, making it difficult to be sure of what the row was about.

The Rev. Edward Davies had been succeeded in the headship of the school by Rev. John Davis in 1799 who continued until 1815 when Mr. Edward Parker became head until 1818. The Rev. Thomas Smith was then appointed by the bailiff and licensed by the Bishop of Gloucester. Possibly, the Rev. Smith believed that because he had been licensed by the Bishop, he was no longer bound by certain conditions of employment which had existed between the Bailiff and his predecessor, even though those conditions had been made clear to him by Mr. Whittington in an interview, prior to his selection. Among other things these terms laid down the salary, the number of pupils and the subjects in which they were to be instructed. The matter reached the courts as the following brief note indicates.

> *The Petitioner Thomas Smith prayed. Firstly that an Action of Ejectment then brought against him by the Bailiff and Bailiff Burgesses may be restrained which was by order of the court accordingly done. – Secondly that it may be declared that the said school was intended and ought to be a Grammar School for the purpose of teaching the learned languages – that it may be referred to one of the Masters of the Court to settle and approve a scheme for the government of the said school – And to enquire whether or what increase in the rents and revenues of the said Town Lands, not appointed or appropriated for the repair of the church or otherwise limited before the said decree of 3rd. Charles I to any particular use, has taken place and what are the estates from the rents and revenues of which the salary of the master of the said school ought to be paid – and what ought to be the amount of such salary – And also to enquire into and report as to the said ten pounds per annum given by the said Robert Davies and the lands charged with the same. And that the said Petitioner Thomas Smith's costs may be paid or provided for.*

There is no date on this extract so it is not certain whether this dispute led directly to a visit from the Charity Commissioners in 1827 but such a visit took place and their examination was thorough.

They appeared satisfied that the town's affairs had been conducted in a proper manner in regard to the various properties except that they were still being let by lives instead of rack rents and an undertaking was given that this would be put right. The Commissioners found that the Toby Davis charity had not been paid for many years and the same applied to a bequest by Robert Davies for £10 per annum. They pursued their enquiries into the latter at some length but finally came to the conclusion that both must be regarded as having lapsed. They rapped the knuckles of certain people over the distribution of relief and then reported on the school as follows:

The school is conducted on the premises already stated to have been erected on the site of the Lamb Inn, whereon now stands a good dwelling house for the master and behind it and next to it, a schoolroom, about 30ft. by 15ft. to accommodate about 50 boys. There are 20 boys instructed in this school by the Rev. Thomas Smith, perpetual curate of Chipping Sodbury, to whom instruction is given in grammar, reading, writing and accounts; and the master declares himself ready to teach the classics if desired. Whether this may be considered a grammar-school in the strict sense of the word may be doubtful. We recollect from the earliest entries in the Minute Book of the Corporation that the master was expected to teach grammar, and also to write and cast accounts, and read in the Bible. Mr Smith is allowed to take boarders, but he has not been able to avail himself of that privilege to any extent, as such boarders do not choose to associate with boys of inferior condition. On consideration of this subject it has been resolved by the Bailiff and Burgesses, in concurrence with the inhabitants of the town, that the salary of the master shall be doubled, and that he shall be required to teach no more than 20 boys and further more that the house shall be put and kept in comfortable repair.

The Rev. Smith then continued as head for many years. The reference to him as the perpetual curate, a post to which he had been promoted by the Bishop in 1822, marks the point when the Chapel of Ease at Chipping Sodbury officially became a Church with its own parish instead of being served mainly by the priest from Little Sodbury, although the living, the perpetual curatory, remained in the gift of the Vicar of Old Sodbury. There was an oversight regarding this matter, however. There is no record of an announcement in the London Gazette as was the usual practice and, as a result, an alternative date in the 1850s has also been quoted.

The Commissioners also questioned the use of revenue from the Town Lands for the improvement of the Ridings "which have been in the possession of the town from time immemorial". They approved a resolution that this should stop and "leave the Ridings to be maintained out of their own proceeds". Some ten years previously Mr. Whittington had tried to find out how the town came to own the Ridings but even though he went as far as employing a searcher in London no answer could be found.

Details are given of the Church properties amounting to eight messuages, two of which were smith's shops. These, together with the burgage in Hounds Road, Purlemead and Dolmead, were all covered by enfeoffments let on lives.

The Town properties consisted of fifteen messuages with various gardens etc., all of which were let on lives, with some 40½ acres of land, in various lots, let at rack rents. There was also property in Wickwar.

There is the only reference to what might have been a pack horse or mule train in 1828 when the baptism of John, son of William & Eliza Phelps of Chipping Sodbury is recorded. William's trade is given as 'Bristol Caravan Proprietor'. A caravan in those days meant a string of pack bearing animals. William Phelps obviously owned such a string and operated between Sodbury and Bristol.

A large number of travellers must have passed through the town and used the various hostelries. The milestones placed from Hyde Park Corner to Sodbury and from Sodbury to Aust show the use of this route from London to South Wales. The Severn ferry crossing could be much more dangerous than might be thought. In September 1839 the ferry boat *Dispatch* went down in mid-channel with the loss of thirteen lives together with five horses and two carriages and there was another similar accident four years later.

When the Poor Law Amendment Act of 1834 was passed, it relieved the parishes of the greater part of their official functions regarding the poor. They were grouped into Unions under one central authority and Sodbury was the focal point of one such union. This is the origin of what is now Ridgeway, a much more dignified name than 'The Spike' as it was once known. Another act covered Municipal Reform and its effects were to be eventually profound locally. The story of the local Union has been very well told by Pat Alcock in her book, *Whispers From The Workhouse* published in 1992. It is recommended reading.

The year 1838 saw the return of the Roman Catholic faith to the town when a church was consecrated at the rear of what had once been the Swan Inn. The latter moved to the end of Broad Street and survived until 1913 when Mr. Powell took over the premises and maintained the name as the 'Swan Cycle Shop'. About this time too the Cap & Feathers went out of business. Records mention an H. Williams and a Henry Alford Sergent as schoolmasters but there is nothing to show where they did their teaching. Henry Williams had come to the town in about 1800 and bought Melbourne House. He was a brandy merchant by profession as

The interior of the Catholic Church of St. Lawrence, Chipping Sodbury, c.1920. The Catholic faith was re-established here in 1838.

shown in the 1851 Census but in the 1841 Census he is indeed shown as a schoolmaster. This is made all the more mysterious because in 1838 he was 72 years old, having lost his wife two years earlier, and had been Bailiff on four separate occasions (see Appendix B).

Sir Robert Peel's police appeared for the first time in Gloucestershire in 1839 but were not universally accepted as for a number of years there were petitions seeking to return to the previous system. Sir Robert was also responsible for the repeal of the Corn Laws which led to these years being known as the hungry forties. All over the country there were reports of great hardships and privations but in Gloucestershire the labourers seem to have done a little better than average. Their wages at this time were 9s. 0d per week with cottage and garden, and extra at harvest. Tradesmen such as masons, blacksmiths, carpenters and plasterers made from 15s. 0d to 17s. 0d per week.

In 1839 it was ordered that a detailed map was to be drawn for each parish showing the fields names etc., their owners and the amount due from each to the church by way of tithe (see Harry Lane's reproduction in the preliminary pages).

The maps are a mine of information as individual acreage and usage were recorded. Some of the more outstanding items for Old Sodbury are:

> Grand total including premises, commons, waste and roads, 3,617 acres. This included 940 acres of arable, 1,952 acres of

meadow and pasture, 272 acres of common and waste and a churchyard of 3 roods.

The undermentioned persons owned in excess of 50 acres:

Winchcombe Henry Howard Hartley, Lord of the Manor,	1,067 acres
Sir Christopher Bethel Codrington,	650 acres
Elizabeth Dorney,	236 acres
Dean & Chapter of Worcester Cathedral (leased to Dorney),	96 acres
Rev: Israel Lewis*	195 acres
Rev: W. Dixon *	104 acres
Morton M. Anne	52 acres

* It does not appear that either of these gentlemen held local livings.

The rest was taken up by a large number of owners of in some cases single cottages.

The Little Sodbury parish consisted of 1,071 acres. There were 145 lots of which W.H.H. Hartley (again Lord of the Manor) held 72, the Duke of Beaufort 3, and the parish 5. The remainder were held by some 11 individuals with in some cases only a cottage being involved.

The manor house was let to a farmer called William Hatherell who also rented some 25 other lots including the Camps.

An item in the Old Sodbury Parish Book reads:

1841, Paid the carriage of Old Sodbury map. 1s. 0d.

Kelly's Directory was published in 1842 and gave details about the Sodburys. The item reads:

Sodbury or Chipping Sodbury (the prefix to its latter appellation being to distinguish it from the other two Sodburys in the County) is a market town and parish in the super division of Grumbold's Ash 108 miles west by south from London, 28 s.s.w. from Gloucester 11 n.e. from Bristol and about 14 miles from Bath, the last two named cities being the nearest railway stations. Situated at the foot of the hill and on the roads leading from Malmesbury and Cirencester to Bristol and near the line of the projected railway from Bristol to Stroud and Gloucester. The town owes its chief support to markets and fairs, the former are noted for the sale of wheat and cheese, to the carriage of lime and coal and the malt trade to which may be added considerable advantages derived from the passage of travellers for whose accommodation there are some excellent inns. By Charles the second the town was incorporated but at the request of the inhabitants the charter was annulled in 1690, since which period it has been governed by certain officers elected annually at the court of the lord of the manor, Winchcombe Henry Harold Hartley Esq. Sodbury is a polling station at the election of members for West Gloucestershire. The places of worship are the parish church of St. John the Baptist, a large structure for Baptists and others for Roman Catholics and the Society of Friends. The living of Sodbury is a perpetual curacy annexed to the vicarage of Old Sodbury in the gift of the vicar. The present curate is the Rev. Thomas Smith. The market is on Fridays, the fairs are on May 23rd and June 24th for cattle. The statutes for hiring servants on Fridays before Lady Day and Michaelmas. (The latter are the 'Mops'.)

There was a post office of which the master was Edward Higgs. Letters from London, and the south and east arrived each morning from Chippenham at 7.45 and letters out were sent every evening at 7.15. A Royal Mail from Stroud called at the Portcullis every morning at 8.45 on its way to Bristol, and at 5.45 every evening en route to Stroud, providing a passenger service to and from Bristol.

Educational needs were met by:

The Free Grammar School,	Rev. T. Smith, headmaster (he was also the curate)
Boarding Schools,	maintained by Hariet and Elizabeth Knox and Mary Parker
Four day schools,	operated by Agnes Howes, Caroline Porter, John Parker and Thomas Ward.

If you needed a lawyer, then one of the attorneys, Alfred Cox, John Trenfield or William Bush-Parker could have helped you. The manager at the National Provincial Bank (hence Old Bank House) Richard Arnold would have welcomed your account. It is not known what happened to the Ludlow's Bank but it is interesting that in the early part of the century, Joseph Hyatt, one of its sponsors, ended up owning a lot of Ludlow property.

Seven bakers, nine butchers and five grocers would have ensured that you were properly fed. If you needed new shoes or boots any one of the five boot and shoe makers would have sold them to you. Two watch makers, James Frewin or Samuel Collings, would have been delighted to ensure that you kept your appointment with your choice of the four surgeons, Thomas Atkinson, Henry Moreton, Hugh Brookman, or Paul Downton Leman and your horse would be well looked after as well by one of the two blacksmiths or the veterinary surgeon, Isaac Limbrick. Serving the ladies were seven milliners and dressmakers while the gentlemen had five tailors to choose from. Three straw hat makers looked after both sexes as did the hair dressers, Louis and William Ball. All other tradesmen and shop keepers were represented at least once.

Wheat, salt and lime are mentioned in the description and these were the stock in trade of the millers, Stanley Trotman and Edmund Chapp Dudfield, the maltsters, John Godwin and Thomas Watts, or the lime burners, James Hanock, John Watts and Ann Love.

Accommodation and food were available at three inns, The Bell, The George, or the Portcullis, or refreshments only at three taverns, The Grapes, Royal Oak and New Inn. If you were simply thirsty there were three 'retailers of beer'.

The following carrier services were available:

Alden I.	Badminton & Dodington – Mon., Wed., Thurs.
Ambridge R.	Bath – Mon., Wed., Sat.; Wotton – Thurs.
Amos	Bristol – Mon., Wed., Sat.
Higgs	Bristol – Mon., Wed., Sat.
Hazell	Bath – Mon., Wed., Sat.
Harris	Bristol – Tues., Fri.; Malmesbury – Wed., Sat.
Lock	Bristol – Mon., Thurs., Sat.: Cirencester – Wed., Sat.; Tetbury – Wed., Sat.
Short	Bristol – Thurs., Sat.

These probably carried passengers as well so the less well-to-do could get from place to place. 'Post horses' were available for hire for those who could afford them.

The picture is one of a small thriving market town where out of a total population of 1,269 over a hundred were engaged in trade apparently as mastermen. The wind of change was beginning to blow, however. Some twelve years before, tramways had been constructed between the pits at what is now Coalpit Heath and the River Avon at Bristol and Keynsham. At first the wagons were pulled by horses but in 1844 the Bristol to Gloucester Railway was finished and took over the route to Bristol. A station was opened at Yate with all due ceremony and little by little horse transport died, except for purely local purposes.

As with the borough of Chipping Sodbury a Court Leet and Baron's Court was held for the Manor of Old Sodbury. Although it was at least as old as the Court for Chipping Sodbury, the only records to survive are for 1842 onwards and even they are not complete.

Among them is the notice convening the annual meeting for 1844, issued by the Steward, J. Trenfield, to the constable of the manor, Samuel Isaac, the younger. It read:

> You are to give notice wit in the said manor that the Court Leet and Court Baron of Winchcombe Henry Howard Hartley Esq., will be held at the Dwelling House of Mr. William Foreman, commonly called the Plough Inn, within the said manor on Tuesday the twenty-second day of October instant at eleven-o-clock in the forenoon precisely. And you are to summon and warn the several Freeholders, Copyholders, Leaseholders and Residents within the said manor from the age of twenty years to sixty to be and appear at that time and place aforesaid to do and perform their several suites and services. And you are also to summon and warn proper Persons to be at the time and place aforesaid for the Jury and Hommage. And be yourself then and there present with a list, fairly written, of all the Freeholders, Copyholders, Leaseholders and residents aforesaid. Given under my hand and seal the seventh day of October 1844.
> (signed) J. Trenfield.
> Steward of the said manor.
> You will be pleased to return this precept at the siting of the Court and pay the common fine.

A large number of presentments were made in subsequent years about manure heaps, the bad state of footpaths and bridges and handrails, sewerage in ditches and encroachments on Common Land, many of them repeated year after year.

In Chipping Sodbury the bailiff and bailiff burgesses continued to reign supreme. The form of oath taken by the bailiff on assuming office has been preserved and probably the only change in the wording through the centuries was the reference to the appropriate monarch. It read:

> You shall swear that you well and truly serve our Sovereign Lady the Queen and the lord of this leet in the office of bailiff and for this borough and manor, until you be thereof lawfully discharged according to due course of law; you shall well and truly do and execute all things belonging to your office according to the best of your knowledge. So help you God.

Allocating an acre in the Mead Ridings still rested with the bailiff and burgesses and there was keen competition for the privilege. In 1849 there were ten applicants for two vacant lots. The proper ceremony had to be followed and a proper form of investiture was laid down though whether it was always carried out is open to question.

> The piece of land on which you are now standing (commonly called an acre) has lately fallen into the possession of the bailiff and bailiff burgesses of Chipping Sodbury, and in pursuance of

their direction, I invest you therewith, by delivering to you this twig and turf, to hold the said piece of land for your life and the life of any woman that may be your lawful wife and survive you, so long as you and your wife shall reside in this town. Subject and chargeable with all manner of waste, particularly waste in felling and cutting any tree or trees whatsoever growing or that may hereafter grow on the said piece of land. And also subject to all the present rules and orders of the said bailiff and bailiff burgesses respecting the grounds called the Ridings, as well as those that may be, from time to time, made relating thereunto.

The sum of 10s. 0d was payable upon investiture. There were eighty three acres in all.

The Stubb Riding was 'stemmed' or divided and allocated by the bailiff and bailiff burgesses annually.

The 38 rules covering the Ridings were consolidated in 1849. Among them was one which laid down that the person chosen as bailiff, provided he had not previously served in that office, should be entitled to the crop of grass on the bailiff's piece during his year of office. This was to help pay for the annual dinner he gave when quitting office. An adjustment was made if the person concerned held the position for more than one year.

The Court Leet was now only held annually in the autumn and it was then that the outgoing bailiff gave a dinner to invited guests. This was still expected of him even if he was re-appointed. The feast for the male inhabitants on St. Stephen's Day for which the bailiff had also been responsible came to an end in 1837.

Rules 33 and 34 are of some interest. The first orders that the bailiff shall name the person to act as his under-bailiff immediately after election, the second describes the under-bailiff's duties and reads:

That the duties of the under-bailiff appear to be to attend and wait upon the bailiff at all meetings of the bailiff and bailiff burgesses to serve all notices, precepts, and other documents relating to the office of bailiff, or town business, to assist the hayward in collecting the dues, and to do and perform all acts which may be required of him in relation to his office.

As can be seen the occupant of this post was the Town Crier in all but name and a hat and coat suitable for his position were provided by the town.

Two items from the Old Sodbury Baron's Court in 1850 are worth special notice.

We present that for the securing of idle and disorderly persons and drunkards there ought to be a pair of stocks erected and kept

> *in good repair within this parish and manor and within the jurisdiction of this court and we find that such stocks ought to be provided at the charge of this parish and we order the parish officers of this parish to provide such stocks within two calendar months under of 40s.*
>
> *We present all horses and cattle found on either of the Commons or wastes within this manor and within the jurisdiction of this Court without being pitch marked on the hind quarter, or burnt on hither hoof with the initials or the names of the owners to be deemed trespassers and thereupon impounded by the hayward and not released until payment of 1s. 4d per head.*

The Court annually appointed one 'Hayward' for Horwood Common and a separate one for the other commons. A list of persons summoned to serve on the juries for 1845 is given in Appendix I.

At some time between 1842 and 1852, the Grammar School stopped functioning and the only education available was in private schools of which there seems to have been enough and both church and chapel Sunday schools, would have taught some secular subjects. In 1852 action was taken to set up a regular elementary school under the auspices of the Church of England. The Lord of the Manor, W.H.H. Hartley granted and conveyed to the church authorities:

> *All those two messuages or tenements with the shops and garden ground thereunto adjoining and belonging situate at the corner and in the north side of Hatter's Lane in the town or borough of Chipping Sodbury.*

This condition caused some difficulty more recently when the school closed, the family reclaimed the site and then sold it to the Free Masons. These premises in 1795 consisted of a house, shop (unspecified), offices, gardens, yards, orchard, etc., owned and occupied by Elizabeth Watts. A John Watts lived there in 1820 holding the property on a term of lives which probably expired about this time when it would have 'fallen into the hands of the lord'.

The new school was to be run by a committee consisting of:

> *The principal officiating Minister for the time being of the said Chapelry, his licensed Curate or Curates, if the Minister shall appoint him, or them, to be a member, or members, of the said committee and five other persons of whom the following shall be first appointed, that is to say, the said Winchcombe Henry Howard Hartley, Thomas Hetling of Chipping Sodbury, gentleman, Hugh Brookman, doctor of medicine, John Trenfield, gentleman, Rev. E.J.C. Hasluch of Little Sodbury. and to con-*

tributors in every year of the amount of 20s. 0d each at least to the funds of the said school.

Sufficient subscriptions came in from a variety of sources to meet the account for £523 14s. 0d covering the building of the National School Room and the Master's house. There is a record of a payment to a Mr. Freeman Morris and his sister of £70, which was their salaries for one year as schoolmaster and schoolmistress. According to an old directory these posts were held by Francis Eardley and Caroline Porter in 1852.

At Old Sodbury by 1857 a National School also existed in a building in what is now the churchyard at the top of Cotswold Lane. It may well have been founded earlier than that but that it was there in 1857 is confirmed by a grave in the churchyard on which is an iron memorial inscribed: "Herbert Edward Reeve, son of W.H. Reeve, 24 years master of National School. Died June 28th, 1881, aged 19." Some years later it was decided that the school site was unsuitable, it being on the slope, and the school was moved to a purpose built building on the opposite corner. A detailed history of the school appears in Appendix H.

The schools at Old Sodbury somewhere around 1905 to 1910.

In 1858 a two year programme started to renovate Old Sodbury Church. The work did not, however, include the tower. The balcony, to pay for which the church wardens had sold the metal from several of the bells some hundred or so years before, was demolished and disposed of.

The Three Sodburys – An Introduction

The people of Little Sodbury were more ambitious. They took their church down and rebuilt it on the spot where it now stands. They kept the plan of the old edifice except for the roof which had been flat. Enough of the old building was left behind to show where it had been previously (see photo on page 87).

Chipping Sodbury meanwhile rebuilt the Town Hall. Arthur Mee, in his book on Gloucestershire says every child in the town was given a bun and a mug of beer to celebrate the event but, strangely, no record of the work or of the re-opening has survived. The front of the building was altered previously in 1738. Originally it was a very late Perpendicular building. Before the alterations in 1858 it consisted of a long hall on the first floor with a fine old 15th century timber roof dating from when it became the Guild Hall. The floor of the hall was supported by strong moulded beams so the space below was not just cellars but was at one time probably open to the street and used for holding markets. The street frontage could be called modern Gothic. At one time there were a number of almshouses at the rear and there was also a lane at the side which ran down to the brook known as Church Houses Lane.

Chipping Sodbury Cricket Club was founded in 1860 with a pitch on the Ridings.

The census in the following year revealed decreasing populations at Chipping and Old Sodbury with a slight increase at Little Sodbury.

In 1862 the borough is still written about as having a great market for corn and cheese. Quarrying was being carried on around the fringes of the Ridings and probably at Yate Rocks, from where there was a trackway to a lime kiln next to the Midland Railway lines and to which it was connected by a siding. Coal mines were active in Yate and Rangeworthy and iron ore was being extracted in the Frampton Cotterell/Iron Acton area by the Chillington Iron Co. Some 5,000 tons of ore were produced in the first year and this figure steadily increased annually.

This year also saw the Police Station built in the main street on the site that in 1795 had been the Duke William Inn, yards, stables, bakehouse, garden, etc., owned by the Lord of the Manor and occupied by John Hancock. Somewhat later, in 1878, the Petty Sessional Court was transferred from the Cross Hands where it had been held for over a hundred years, to next door. Much more recently the Court was transferred to its present location in Kennedy Way, Yate.

The market cross was moved again from where it was put some ninety years before in the vicinity of a mill in Brook Street, known by this time as 'Trotman's Mill'. Why there was the sudden interest is not known but the cross was duly re-erected at the rear of what had been the Swan Inn and was now the Catholic Church.

This photograph was taken before 1910. The building behind the telegraph pole is the Old Grammar school. Next to it(centre) is the Police Station while to the right again is the former Petty Sessional Court. The clock was built as a memorial to Lt. Col. George W. Blathwayt of Dyrham in 1871.

The Rev. Thomas Smith, who had been locked in legal combat about the Grammar School with the Bailiff and Burgesses some years before, died in 1857 and the school was closed.

The heyday of the Turnpike Trusts was now over and 1865 saw them beginning to disappear until quite rapidly they were gone altogether. The sites of many of the toll houses however, can still be identified.

The church cemetery was getting uncomfortably full at Chipping Sodbury so the church authorities acquired a new area for a cemetery at its present site on what had been The Roach. At the same time the church was scheduled to undergo extensive renovations.

Although at the time few if any people in Sodbury knew about it, there was a development in the saga of Mrs. Ludlow and her lover, James Campbell who, after Christopher Ludlow's death lived in Scotland until Campbell died in 1806. Their eldest son was born in 1788 and he, in turn, had a son who in 1867 was declared by the House of Lords to be Sixth Earl of Breadalbane and Holland, Viscount of Tay and Paintland, Lord Glenorchy, Benederaloch, Ormelie and Weick, an imposing list which fails to point out that his grandmother was a Blanchard of Sodbury in the County of Gloucestershire. Her great grandson married a daughter of the Duke of Montrose, was created a peer of the realm as Baron Breadalbane of Kenmare and held office in the Queen's Household.

Mr. W.B. Bacon took over the National School in Chipping Sodbury in 1867 and, as was usual in those days, his wife took charge of the infants. Some four months earlier the government had laid down that a log book was to be kept in all such schools. Luckily the book started by Mr. Bacon and continued by his successors has survived. It was found at a local Jumble Sale, recognised as being of value, purchased and passed to the then head teacher, Miss Bannister, and has since been deposited in the Gloucester Records Office. It shows that the school had been closed for a short while and that when it re-opened in April 1867 there were 74 pupils. By the end of the month this had increased to over 100, all of whom were called upon to pay threepence per week, a large amount in those days. There are references from time to time in the log book to monitors and pupil teachers and it seems that when a pupil reached the leaving age of nine, they served as a monitor for four years. After that, if they showed sufficient talent, they became a pupil teacher and then later sat an examination to enter a training college. The other side of the coin is illustrated by this entry in the log book:

Henry Love away this week for want of shoes.

Towards the end of September attendances fell because the children were out picking up potatoes. Nevertheless a holiday was given for the whole day on Friday 26th September as this was "the occasion of the Mob or Mop Fair, which it is said answers to the Statute Fair of the past".

At the National School Mr. Bacon extended the educational facilities towards the end of 1867 when he opened a night school, attended initially by sixteen scholars.

Following an application by the bailiff and bailiff burgesses in 1861, the Charity Commissioners in 1867 worked out a scheme for re-opening the higher school. It covered not only the school but all the charities for which the bailiff and burgesses were responsible.

After all expenses had been paid the income was to be divided into three parts. Two thirds were to be for the school and one third for the benefit of the poor. The school was to be called the Chipping Sodbury Endowed School and the head master had to be a member of the Church of England and a graduate of one of the English Universities. His salary was to be £100 per annum payable half-yearly and he had to sign a contract. If there were enough funds an assistant master or masters could be employed. Children between the ages of eight and sixteen could be accepted and with the Trustees' approval the master could have a limited number of boys in his house as boarders. Reading, writing, spelling, English grammar and composition, general history, geography, Latin, French and German were to be taught, together with Greek if specifically demanded. Arithmetic, algebra and elementary mathematics, land mensuration and surveying and general knowledge subjects were also to be included as the Trustees considered appropriate. Everything was to be rounded off with religious instruction and the principles and doctrines of the Church of England but exemption from the latter could be claimed. The capitation fees payable were:

For every boy from the parish under 14	£3 per annum
For every boy from the parish over 14	£4 per annum
For every boy from any other parish or place	£6 per annum

These fees were to be paid quarterly in advance and half of them were to be paid half-yearly to the headmaster to boost his salary. The other half was to be used to help pay for assistant teachers and other expenses.

There was to be an annual exam, taken in front of the Trustees, in June, conducted by a graduate of Oxford or Cambridge selected by the Trustees. Prizes could be awarded up to a total cost of £15. The Trustees were the bailiff and bailiff burgesses together with the incumbent of the Parish.

The school re-opened in January 1869, the headmaster being Mr. J.P. Wills, BA, London. Both he and Mr. Bacon, from the National School, were keen and proficient cricketers and the records show they often played in the Sodbury team.

The building of the new school at Old Sodbury was also finished at this time and the old premises in the corner of the churchyard were demolished.

The choir at Chipping Sodbury Church was thriving and the idea of an annual outing was catching on. In September 1869 they went to Knole Park. The previous May the school children had enjoyed a holiday for the festivities at Badminton in honour of the coming of age of the Marquis of Worcester, heir to the Duke of Beaufort.

The year 1869 saw the renovation of Chipping Sodbury Church completed. The work had been carried out so thoroughly by Mr. G.E. Street that it almost amounted to a re-building and cost £3,000. During the course of the work an unusual pulpit was discovered. It was thought to have been built in the 15th century but later it had been blocked up, plastered over and hidden behind a 'double-decker' pulpit. Mr. John Russell, one of the Churchwardens, with the help of a few others, managed the whole of the business and raised enough money by mortgaging the Church and Town Trust properties to pay the money as it became due to the contractors. While the work was being done Sunday Services were held in the Town Hall. Mr. Russell was a Warden for many years and did not resign until the whole of the borrowed money was repaid.

There are several mentions in the school log book of a day off for

'Sodbury Races' which were explained by Mr. J. Mills, who became a prominent member in the town at the end of the century and who had his reminiscences published in the Dursley Gazette in June 1936. The first real race meeting was held in 1869 and the venture was started by Dr. A. Grace, Messrs. F.J. and W. Vizard, Fred Godwin and others. The course was at Codrington, starting near Down Farm and running towards Hamwood, round by Lyddes Farm and finishing in a long field between Down Farm and Hamwood Cottages. Mr. Mills says he was eleven at the time and left school at mid-day to hurry off to watch the Races. Two things remained in his memory. Dr. Grace ran a horse called 'Blaze Chestnut' which was ridden by Mr. J.D. Lloyd. At the fence leading into the finishing field the first time round, 'Blaze Chestnut' fell and threw Mr. Lloyd. Dr. Grace, who was near the fence, caught the horse and vaulted into the saddle and finished the race. Although he came in second, he could not claim the prize money as he was not carrying the correct weight.

The pillar pulpit in Chipping Sodbury Church c.1910.

In the next two years the meeting was held over a course between Raysfield Farm and Stanshawes Court. At one of these meetings a horse named 'Vendetta' won three races, one of three miles and two of two miles each. Unfortunately the Races were not profitable and so were allowed to lapse.

Mr. Mills continued, "by the time I was twelve the cricket team fell off, owing chiefly to Mr. J.D.B. Trenfield getting too busy and too corpulent to play much. Dr. A. Grace was captain for a time, but he was not so keen on cricket as he was on hunting and racing. Also his profession made him an uncertain player, consequently the club got slack." He then gave details of various matches and the eventual revival of the Club.

Lyegrove House was at the peak of its importance around 1870 when the Lord of the Manor, W.H.H. Hartley, was living there and was one of the Deputy Lieutenants for the County. He was described by Mr. Mills as:

> ...a little feeble man who walked with short quick steps and with the aid of a stick. He married a lady much younger than himself. She was a fine dashing woman very fond of society and consequently spent most of her time in London. Occasionally, in her absence, the old gentleman would amuse himself in his own way. They kept a large number of servants and outdoor workers, numbering twenty-five to thirty. The old gent would cause the Butler to assemble as many as could be spared at the long table in the servant's hall. Beer flowed copiously and there was singing. At Christmas all the cottage tenants were requested to be at Lyegrove at a given time. A bullock was killed and cut up into small joints and each person was given a portion. A plum pudding was also made and distributed.

The Dog Inn flourished in Old Sodbury in the capacity of shop as well as that of an inn. The post office was in the care of Peter Stinchcombe.

A number of the public houses ran Sharing Out Benefit Clubs and Mr. Mills talked about some of their individual fête days:

> At the White Lion, Yate, there was a strong club and their fête day was the 29th May. The members assembled about 10.00 am and headed by their large silk banner and a good brass band, marched in procession, each with a coloured rosette and carrying the club stick, through Goose Green up to Yate House, then occupied by Rev. Randolph, owner of the estate. Then they would come from there down the Riding Road into Sodbury, and stop at the Oak Inn and refresh themselves. After that they would form up again and walk to the Bell Inn on the road to Old Sodbury. More refreshment was taken and then they returned through Sodbury to the Lion to dine. In the evening they enjoyed themselves with coconut shies, skittles and dancing.
>
> On Whit-Monday, the Club at the Oak Inn held their annual day. Much the same formula was gone through, the great difference being that every member had to wear a top hat, and the show of hats was remarkable. On Whit-Tuesday the Club at the Bell Inn, Old Sodbury had their day with the usual marching and adjournment for dinner.

He goes on to outline general conditions.

From Whitsun until Christmas there were no holidays but continuous work. The hay harvest in the district used to be a very busy time as all the grass was cut with a hand scythe. There was a good number of skilled mowers who worked 'piece work' and earned a good sum during the season. It was hard work, they would start at daybreak and work until 10.00 or 11.00 am and then rest until four or five in the afternoon and work until dark. They were paid so much an acre and three gallons of beer each day. Beer in those days was the general drink for the workers; the farm hands had an amount allowed them each day which they drank for breakfast, dinner and at their work. The death knell of the mowers was sounded when Mr. Thomas or Mr. John Arnold brought a mowing machine from Wickwar and gave it a try out in the field between the Riding and the cemetery. A few years later most of the farmers had their own machines.

On Christmas, Mr. Mills says:

At Christmas there were several parties of rival singers consisting of four voices which professed to sing quartet, Christmas carols, etc. They began operations six or seven weeks in advance and would go to all the big houses and farms within a radius of five or six miles. They were well known and almost certain of being well received, often partaking of plenty to eat and drink and taking away a contribution to their fund which was shared out at the end of the season. The Town was generally left until Christmas Eve when the others, who carried a Wassailing Bowl about with them, paraded. They only bawled one refrain which ended as follows:

> *"Butler come fill us a bowl of your best,*
> *I hope your soul in heaven will rest.*
> *But if you fill us a bowl of your small*,*
> *Down goes bottle, bowl and all."*

*Small beer, i.e. of inferior quality.

Others came from Horton bringing what they termed the 'Horton Bull' which consisted of the skin and horns of a bull's head fixed on a dummy which they carried with them. This lot used to visit each Inn and take the Bull into any room where there were customers. Each party did themselves well at quenching their thirst. Boxing Day was 'Mumping Day' when several old women, well known characters, visited the houses for their Christmas Boxes.

Life was made a little brighter and easier for the people of Chipping Sodbury with the introduction of a gas supply. Mr. Mills recalled the Chipping Sodbury Gas Light & Coke Co. being formed on 26th January 1871:

> *Previous to this the street was lighted in winter by a few oil lamps. Mr. John Trenfield was the moving spirit and aided by other tradesmen formed the company. The Gas Works (which stood on the site of what is now Bennetts Court the other side of the river at the foot of the Bowling Hill) was built and mains laid down each side of the street. On completion the Town Hall was illuminated with a large star and crown with the letters 'V.R.' on each side of it. The occasion was suitably marked by the distribution to the school children of buns and oranges.*

There is no mention of beer this time, as was the case when the Town Hall was re-opened explained, perhaps by the entry in the National School log for July 1872:

> *Teetotal fete, half holiday as nearly all the children are teetotallers.*

The following August the addition of a room for the infants on the north of the original school building in Hatters Lane was finished. It was found, however, that this led to a considerable loss of natural lighting and so the skylights, which many ex-pupils will remember in the 'big room' were added.

In September the branch line between Yate and Thornbury was opened with intermediate stations at Tytherington and at Iron Acton where a siding was provided to link up with the iron mines at Frampton Cotterell. These were now being worked by Messrs. Brogden & Sons and in that year produced 9,201 tons. This was provided by three pits, Burgess, Red Gin and Roden Acre, and the ore was sent to works at Seend, Westbury (Wilts) and South Wales.

Flower Shows had become very popular by this time becoming firmly established as an annual feature of village life with those at Old Sodbury and Iron Acton appearing in the records of this period.

In 1875 Mr. and Mrs. Bacon left the National School to be succeeded by Mr. and Mrs. Freeman. For some reason the number of pupils had fallen to 55 but in 1876 the Managers offered prizes of 1s. 0d for regular attendance and this brought the figure back to 100. As well as the 'Dames' Schools' and other private schools, there was a boarding school in the town for young ladies in Hill House with Mrs. Robert Good in charge.

By 1876 Little Sodbury also had a school in a purpose built building, still to be seen near the church, the teacher in charge being Miss

Prescott. It was closed as a school, however, a considerable time ago.

Public transport was provided by Mr. H.J. Bees who at about this time began running a bus which met every train at Yate station.

The market at Chipping Sodbury was now held once a month on a Tuesday while the fair and mops continued as before. The residents had the services of a 'cow-keeper' available, Edward Holliday, who these days would be known as a dairyman.

The members of the Baptist faith at Old Sodbury now had their own minister, the Rev. W. Hutchings Butler. The Rev. A.K. Davidson officiated at Chipping Sodbury chapel, which must have been a little confusing because another Rev. Davidson was the C of E vicar.

Old Sodbury is fortunate because some truly local history has survived. A number of copies of *A Record of Passing Events in the Parish of Old Sodbury* of which the official title was *The Fly Leaf* were discovered in the roof space at Ian Edgar's home, the Hayes. Number one is missing but number two, issued on Thursday 1st November 1877 and some later issues were found. They consist of four pages printed on foolscap size paper folded over. While the Editor is not named he was prompted to break into verse in the second edition:

> *So now, O ye Herald, strike up a mighty flourish of trumpets:*
> *Likewise, ye drummers, perform a glorious fantasia;*
> *For here is presented to the world, the great and priceless boon,*
> *The second number of THE FLYLEAF.*

The latest issue was for May 1880 and there is nothing to show what happened to it after that. In the 1890s village news was included in the Chipping Sodbury Church Magazine.

Another interesting feature on the Tithe Map is the steam mill on the right hand side of the road coming from Chipping Sodbury at Frome Bridge. It is not known when it was built but it belonged to Stephen Burcombe Dutfield. Its fate was reported in the Parish Magazine for October 1878.

> *A characteristic feature of this village has disappeared during the last week or so. Everyone who knows the least about the place, has seen the old steam mill, with its tall chimney, forming quite a conspicuous object in the surrounding landscape. The property has been bought by Mr. J. Hatherell (senior) who is having the engine house etc., converted into four cottages. The great chimney has been pulled down. During the progress of the latter operation, a large stone accidentally fell from the top, striking a workman named Thomas Uzzell, breaking his arm.*

It was then a farm for a number of years until all the buildings were finally demolished around 1950 when the road was widened and a replacement farm built on the other side of the road nearly opposite.

Another report in the Parish Magazine, this time for December 1877 was:

> *Great excitement was caused in this village, the other week, by a traction engine travelling along the highway. Many people went flocking to see a sight which was so strange to them; as it was preceded by a signalman bearing a red flag, one or two persons were not quite clear whether or not it had some mysterious connection with the war in the East.*

There was a crisis at the National School in Chipping Sodbury in the autumn of 1877, it was broke! The situation was so bad that the teacher's salary, due in November, was not paid until nearly the end of January 1878 after a rescue operation.

On the first day of January 1878 a new Education Act came into being and the Editor of the Parish Magazine went to great pains to make its provisions plain to the parishioners. It was made clear that children under ten were not allowed to leave school and dispensations were only allowed for those who lived more than two miles from a school and during six weeks of Harvest and other necessary farming operations. This education was not free. Children began at the National School at the age of 3 years. The payments for tradesmen were 4s. 0d per quarter for one child, 7s. 0d for two children, and 2s. 0d each for the rest. Labourers had to pay 3d per week for one child, 5d for two children and 1d each for the rest. All fees were payable in advance and no debts were allowed. Scholars who had been absent for less than twelve times during a quarter had a penny returned for each week that the school was open in that quarter.

In the nineteenth century the lot of the majority of the people, especially agricultural workers, was hard but alleviated somewhat by organisations like the Old Sodbury Friendly Society which came into being in 1862 and dealt with incidents like the following reported in the March 1878 issue of the Church Magazine:

> *It is our painful duty this month, to record the deaths of two members of the Old Sodbury Friendly Society Edward Willis and William Bennett, the former of which took place under extraordinary circumstances. Willis, who for some little time past had been residing in the neighbourhood of Berkeley, had, on the day of the fatal event, been to Charfield with a waggon and two horses. On his return he had to pass a brook, which being much swollen by heavy rains, was flowing several feet deep, over the roadway. The horses were carried off their feet by the strong current; and both they and their driver were drowned.*

In June of the same year it was reported that the membership was now 103. The Anniversary was commemorated on Wednesday 31st July in the following way:

> The members assembled on the Vicarage lawn at 10.30, and, after electing officers for the ensuing year, attended Divine Service in the Church. Dinner was afterwards served in the National Schoolroom, there were 87 persons present. The Company then adjourned to the Vicarage Field. During the afternoon and evening the Didmarton Brass Band was in attendance and played a good selection of music. Tea was taken in a tent on the lawn, after which the members and their friends amused themselves with dancing, cricket, quoits etc., which were kept up with spirit, until darkness set in.

A similar event was organised in July 1879 when the accounts were gone through by the treasurer:

> It appears that the amount paid into the Sick Fund, during the year, was £60 18s. 0d with Honorary subscriptions of £15 16s. 0d, outpayments to members amounted to £46 2s. 6d. This time the Old Sodbury Brass Band was in attendance.

A branch of the club was now formed to cover those boys at work who were under seventeen years of age. The contributions were 3d fortnightly if admitted under fifteen years of age and 4d if admitted over

The Swan Inn on the corner of Broad Street and Hatters Lane before it became The Swan Cycle Shop in 1913.

fifteen. The weekly allowance when sick was 2s. 0d for members under twelve years, and 3s. 0d if over.

A Magic Lantern lecture was advertised for 8th January 1879 and this, no doubt, was only one of many such increasingly popular events. In 1879, and for some time afterwards, there was a 'Coffee House Club' in Broad Street, managed by Mr. Joseph Chandler.

The postal services available are reproduced as they appear in the directory for that year.

POST OFFICE AND POSTAL TELEGRAPH OFFICE
Miss Elizabeth Caradine Postmistress

DELIVERY

Lines of Road & principal places from whence mails are received	Delivery by Letter Carriers begins at	Delivery to Callers begins at
London, General Night Mail	7.00 am	7.00 am
Bristol, London, etc.	2.30 pm	12.15 pm

DISPATCH

Lines of Road & Chief Places of Destination	Letters etc. can be posted without extra charge	with additional stamp	Letters etc. can be registered until
Town and Rural Posts	6.45 am		
Chippenham & Badminton	7.00 am	7.55 am	8.00 pm
Bristol, Bath, London, Eastern Counties and Foreign	10.20 am	10.30 am	10.15 am
North of England, Midland Counties, Wales, Scotland, Ireland	6.20 pm	6.30 pm	6.00 pm
London Gen. Night Mail	7.30 pm	7.50 pm	7.0 pm

The records of this period mention two inns, the Swan now in its new position on the corner of Broad Street and Hatters Lane whose landlord was Mr. Cooper and the Bell Hotel, not the one in the main street but the one on the road to Old Sodbury at the entrance to what was to become Chipping Sodbury railway station whose landlord was Mr. A.J. Carter. In those days these premises had a tall tree each side of it and looked very different from today.

This year was remembered for a very long time as the Black Summer. It was the wettest and worst on record. The harvest rotted in the fields and sheep died of liver fluke by the thousand, faster than they could be buried, so that some farmers were left almost without livestock or crops and were ruined.

The Mop Fair was a direct descendant of the fairs granted centuries before. As the result of legislation in the reign of Queen Elizabeth it had now become a Hiring Fair. All ranks of servants paraded wearing some emblem showing their particular calling and were signed up by an employer on a printed contract form. The employer usually paid a shilling as 'earnest' money to seal the contract. Although regarded with some nostalgia the event had deteriorated as is shown by the following entry in the Old Sodbury Parish Magazine for February 1878:

> Every one in these parts has, of course, heard of Sodbury Mop. On that day Susan dons her most elaborate costume, Johnny dresses up in his best and they wend their way to Chipping Sodbury. The ostensible reason for the fair being held at all is, as we have said, the hiring of servants; but besides this, there are cake and orange stalls, shows, round-abouts, fiddling, dancing, and all manner of high jinks going on. We would be the last in the world to say a word against Johnny and Susan enjoying themselves after their hard life of toil; but too often, they spend at such places what they can ill afford; excessive drinking (that curse of all who indulge in it) plays a most conspicuous part at these gatherings, bringing in its train a vast amount of vice and immorality; and very many have cause to wish they had stayed at home. Many Clergymen, and other benevolent gentlemen, are now endeavouring to provide more wholesome employments and amusements for young people in the rural districts; choirs, guilds, bands, ringing, reading rooms, cricket clubs etc., are doing a great work in that direction. Mops are declining in all parts of the country, and every young man and woman would feel it a degradation to be at such scenes of dissipation.

For the benefit of those who today speak in doom-laden tones of the changes in the weather and such things as global warming and a new ice age, the following is quoted from the July 1878 issue of the Old Sodbury Parish Magazine:

> On Sunday evening, June 30th., this village and neighbourhood were visited by very violent storms of rain, accompanied by wind, thunder and lightning. So heavy was the down-pour, that in many places the earth was washed away, leaving long and deep furrows; great trouble was also caused by the water flowing into many of the houses.

The issue for August 1878 lists not only the vicars and curates but those usually unsung servants, the Parish Clerks, listed here:

1678 John Watts, eight years. 1686 William Lingrin, thirty-seven years. 1723 John Isaac, forty-five years. 1768 Samuel Vizard, thirty-two years (who probably wrote the report about the bells). 1800 Robert Light, nineteen years. 1819 William Bennett, one year. 1820. William Curthoys, twenty-four years. 1844 Thomas Curthoys, three years. 1847 Samuel Isaac thirty-one years (up to present time).

Until 1880 candles had been the main source of artificial light for those who lived outside the range of a gas works but in this year the oil lamp was invented and came into general usage.

By this time, too, a major feature in the town had appeared, namely the Clock. Originally it was a plain tower with steps around the base and was erected as a memorial to Lt. Col. George W. Blathwayt of Dyrham who had served in the Waterloo campaign and died in 1871. It was some time during the ten years after his death that the idea of a memorial to him in the form of a clock, was carried out.

An item in the National School log for December 1880 highlights the prevailing conditions for people at the time:

Re-admitted Emily X. Mrs. X. called and said what a difficulty she had to raise nine pence per week out of 10s. 0d weekly wages.

The weekly rate was 3d. per child so presumably she had three at the school. For those without proper clothing or heating the next month must have been difficult. Mr. Freeman wrote:

1881, Jan.18th Tuesday, a day to be remembered for the most severe weather within recollection.
19th Roads blocked up – buildings covered with snow drifts – no school.
24th Monday, weather still severe and very cold.

From the 1881 Census, there were 714 people living in Old Sodbury consisting of Males – 257, Females – 248, Children – 209.

The main occupation was agriculture with Farmers 15, Labourers male 60 female 14, Servants Domestic 21 farm 5, and there were 10 people who were unemployed. The overall numbers were steadily decreasing, 1861 – 809, 1871 – 804. The usual supporting trades were represented by individual or one or two operators. The village now is occupied mainly by people from the professional classes. Farmers are few and labourers still less. For Census purposes it is paired with Chipping Sodbury.

At this time the population of Little Sodbury was 132 for which a breakdown is not available but again it would have been almost exclusively agricultural.

The Three Sodburys – An Introduction

The Lord of the Manor, Winchcombe Henry Howard Hartley was alive when the Census was taken in 1881 but he must have died soon afterwards because on Friday 28th July 1882 a large number of lots on the estate were sold by auction at the George Inn on the behalf of Elizabeth Ann Hartley de Palatiano to meet the various bequests.

A copy of the sale bill is included with the deeds of quite a number of properties in Chipping and Old Sodbury of which several are of particular interest:

> *No.10. The old established and fully licensed Public House known as the Royal Oak Inn situated in the best part of High Street occupied by Mr. Pullin, etc., etc., with side entrance from Horse Street.*

Obviously the clerk who compiled the details was not a local man and copied information from the distant past quite unaware that the lower half of the main street was now known as Broad Street. No.30 is described as

> *...a piece of valuable accommodation pasture land known as the 'Roaches' with warm early garden and quarry of the finest limestone situate close to the town of Sodbury on the east side of the road leading from Brook Street to the Mead Riding.*

In an earlier deed John de Roache is mentioned as the landowner and his name survived down through the centuries. It was the land that once lay beyond the cemetery. The very large hole on that site now shows just how true was the remark about the limestone.

No.31 was a farm house, buildings and orchard together with the Home ground and three other fields. Known as Smart's Farm, it was finally demolished and disappeared beneath Greenhayes. It is still remembered in Smart's Green roundabout on what was originally known as Buckett's Hill.

No.47 was a property at Old Sodbury consisting of a carpenter's shop and corner premises next to the Dog Inn. It was occupied by Peter Stinchcombe who also ran the Post Office on the opposite side of the road where he also had a saw pit. The Dog Inn which was fully licensed and well used, with newly built brew-house, two stables, coach house, piggeries, etc., was item No.48.

The notice convening the Court Leet and Court Baron of the Manor on 6th November 1882 reads:

> *The Court of Elizabeth Ann Hartley de Palatiano, Nina Katherine Webley Parry, Frances Oxenham, Henrietta Santa Russell, Olivia Fanny White, Ladies of the above manor will be held at the dwelling house of Messieurs George Francis Blackmore & Charles Sheppard commonly called the Cross Hands.*

The Nineteenth Century 209

The Green, Old Sodbury. The heart of the village as it appeared in the early years of this century. The church can be seen on the left, one road to it being the lane in the foreground that leads off to the left, now known as Cotswold Lane but known around 1800 as Scot's Hole Lane. The square building in the centre of the photograph was the engine house of the West Gloucester Water Company. It is probable that the stocks once owned by the village were here on the Green.

Old Sodbury Post Office and old cottages on Dog Hill

The Steward was J. Trenfield and the Constable Samuel Isaac. The same ladies are listed in 1886 and 1901 after which there are no more records.

There was a brewery at Old Sodbury which was bought by James Perrett, together with Hill House, Old Sodbury, in 1884. Trading under the name of James Mason Perrett & Sons, they supplied over twenty

The Old Brewery
Photo courtesy Ray Pearce

The J.M. Perrett & Sons Off-licence next door (to the right) of Murray Dowding's hardware shop c.1909.

public houses in the neighbourhood and owned an off-licence next to Murray Dowding's shop in Chipping Sodbury. Having been a landmark on the right at the top of Dog Hill for many years, the premises were sold in the 1960s and demolished but the expected planning permission for rebuilding modern housing was not received so the land remains empty. For those interested, the grandson of James Perrett, Mr. R.C. Pearce, who lives in Yate, has produced a small book on the Perrett family.

In 1885 the bailiff and burgesses decided that the feast given by the bailiff after his election or re-election to office, should no longer continue. In fact they had little choice in the matter because after 29th September 1886 the Corporation ceased to exist and those holding office became caretakers pending a new scheme for local government being implemented nationally.

In 1886 the Baptists in Chipping Sodbury built a New Hall next to the Old Grammar School This has become, much more recently, the place of worship for the Baptists while the original chapel, built in 1819, has been put to other uses by them. The children of the town enjoyed a free entertainment when the New Hall was opened although there is no

The New Hall, built by the Baptists, to the left of the Old Grammar School

mention of either buns or beer! Their Minister was the Rev. Aquila Lemon whose bearded patriarchal face against the background of the windows behind the pulpit in the old Chapel was once a familiar sight.

The Jubilee of the Great Queen occupied people for most of 1887 and the occasion was commemorated at Old Sodbury with a clock being installed in the church tower.

Mr. Freeman, headmaster of the Chipping Sodbury National School, reported in 1888 that the children were entertained with a 'Magic Lantern' show. This is the first time that he mentions an invention that was to be a popular evening entertainment for the next thirty or forty years. At the same time he records that several children had left to go as free scholars to the Grammar School which he properly should have called the Endowed School. It seems that at about this time, membership of the church choir was the passport to going into the higher school as some five years later there is a record that a child had to attend the Grammar School because he was a member of the choir.

The final dissolution of the Turnpike Trusts came with the introduction in 1889 of the County Councils who took over the responsibility for maintaining the highways in their area. Elections were duly held and the first chairman of Gloucestershire County Council was Sir John E. Dorrington, MP, who held the office until 1908. With this change in local government the wind of change began to freshen.

The Baptists living in Little Sodbury built their own place of worship in 1890. Meetings had probably been held in a cottage before that, as happened elsewhere. In the census of the following year Little Sodbury was the only one of the Sodburys to show an increase in population.

This was the year that saw a further step forward when the legal age for employing children was raised from nine to twelve. In September school fees in elementary schools were abolished and mothers, like Mrs. X., needed to struggle no longer to find ninepence per week. One pupil, whose education would have been free anyway, left the lower school to become a 'boots' scholar at the Endowed School. He received free tuition in return for carrying out menial tasks for the boarders.

In June 1891 yet another Society arrived in Old Sodbury, a branch of the National Sick & Burial Association. They too celebrated their Anniversaries and in 1893 the members assembled at 11.00 am and, after parading through the village to Dodington House headed by the Downend Military Brass Band, dined together in the National Schoolroom.

The way in which the members of Chipping Sodbury Church provided local entertainment to brighten people's lives is illustrated by the following extracts from the Church Monthly magazine.

The building in these photographs was built as a Chapel by the Baptists in Old Sodbury in 1835. It was very well attended until the 1960s when it was converted to the private house shown below. For many years the village was about equally divided between church and chapel and there was considerable co-operation between them.

February 1892
Church of England Temperance Society (CETS)

We have had two entertainments in connection with our CETS here during the present month. On the 12 inst. we had the second of a series of Free Concerts which Mrs Harvey, Miss. B. Leman and Miss. K. Short have kindly undertaken to arrange monthly for us. The programme was a good one consisting of vocal and instrumental music, and some readings. There was also a pleasing variety – a nigger troupe, consisting of six of the juvenile members, who had been trained for the occasion by Miss. E.O. Limbrick. We hope to have another concert before Lent commences on 21st instant. Mr. A.W. Bodger delivered in the schoolroom an Instructive Lecture, illustrated by a first rate lantern, on 'The Native Races and the Spirit Traffic in Africa'. This entertainment was provided at considerable expense by the Society, and was one which young and old alike could enjoy, therefore we regretted that a greater number did not avail themselves of it. We should be very glad of some fresh helpers in this CETS work and at the close of our next concert we would gratefully take the names of any who would signify their readiness to help us. The Working Class is held in the schoolroom every Saturday at 2.30 and we look forward to a small sale at Easter.

As an illustration of how much can change in a hundred years, the use today of the word 'nigger' is totally unacceptable. After some considerable thought the author of this book decided to leave it in only because it came in a direct quotation from a document, for historical veracity. The extracts from the Church Monthly continue:

April 1892
CETS

On Thursday April 21st, we have made arrangements for a Sale of useful and fancy articles in the Schoolroom, which we hope will be well attended. There will be a 'Doll Show' among the entertainments and concerts in the smaller schoolroom. Doors open 2.30 to 9.30 admission 3d.

May 1892

On Thursday 21st Ulto. we held, in the National Schoolrooms, the second annual sale of work in connection with the CETS, consisting of fancy and useful articles made by the juvenile members. The day was a bright one both out of doors and in the schoolroom and the attendance was excellent. At the door Mr. Thomas Iles took £1 0s. 6d, Miss Laura Freeguard 10s. 0d at the

Lower Stall, Miss Ethel Critchley at the 'dip' 5s. 2d, Mrs. Thomas Iles and Miss. Boyce £2 at the stall for useful articles; Loftus Reade £1 6s. 4d. Fancy stall, Miss. Rita Iles, Miss G. Critchley 15s. 5d, Miss. K. Short refreshment table £3. 11s. 0^1/₂d, Concerts 14s. 1d, Weighing machine 5s. 6d. Miss Emily Morgan held a most interesting 'Doll Show' the dolls representing various Nations, Seasons, Groups, etc. A large doll dressed as an Irish Peasant girl was much admired and the Vicar's little daughter became the happy possessor of it. £1 14s. 0^1/₂d. was made by the show. A general and social afternoon tea was partaken of at 5.00 o'clock, and the several concerts which were presided over by Miss Leman added much to the pleasure of the day. Special thanks are due to Mr. Thomas Iles, and Miss Blanche Leman, as well as to all the other workers, for the trouble and interest they took in the cause. The balance exceeded that of last year by nearly £4.

July 1892
The dedication to St. John the Baptist was celebrated on Friday July 24th in the following manner. 8.30 am Holy Communion, 9.30 am Guild of St. John social breakfast, 11.00 am matins, 5.00 pm tea in schoolroom (120 present) followed by concert, 8.00 pm Evensong.

1893
On Dec. 5th 1892 a Concert in aid of Church needlework was held in the town, balance £7 12s. 3d. After the Concert a Dance was held in the Hall in aid of cloakrooms for our National Schools, balance £3 3s. 6d.
Jan. 3rd. CETS tea and concert in National Schoolroom.
On Thursday April 6th was held the third annual sale of work in connection with the CETS. A novel feature was a General Post Office, where a brisk business was done, also a Basket stall, Garden Trugs, Stable, fruit, work and knitting, baskets from the celebrated Trug Basket Works at Herstmonceaux. These baskets were the gift of the Vicar's sister Mrs. Robert Bush, who has always taken a very active interest in the work of the Church of England Temperance Society. The sale was a success.
Celebration of St. John the Baptist Day June 24th.
July 6th. Celebration of Royal Wedding Day (Duke of York and Princess May). The town was gaily decorated with flags, etc and on the Ridings there was a large gathering to witness a cricket match between the 'married' and 'single' men.
The Vicar and Mrs. Harvey gave the Annual Fête to the Sunday

> School children on that day. After a prizegiving in the schoolroom all adjourned to the Church where a short service was held. After which a large contingent of adults and children marched through the town and proceeded to the Ridings headed by Yate Brass Band. The Vicar entertained at tea 160 children with the adults, the arrangements for which were carried out by Mr. and Mrs. Sweatman. On the grounds were various amusements, cricket, racing (and prizes), swing boats, coconut bowling, etc.
> Later on the adults danced to the stirring music of the local band. God's blessing was asked for the Royal Bride and Bridegroom.
>
> **1893 September**
> Last month we held our Annual Choir Fete; the day began, as was fitting, with Matins at 8.00 o'clock, at which there was a good attendance of the choir. A large number of us left Yate station at 9.30 am accompanied by well-filled hampers containing materials for dinner. Tea was partaken of at Messrs. Huntley's. The weather was perfect and everyone seemed bent on thoroughly enjoying themselves. The pier with its numerous amusements proved most attractive and several enjoyed a trip to Cardiff and back. No contretemps occurred to mar the day's pleasure and we returned safely to Yate about 9.30 pm.

A further more detailed report from a different source on the celebrations of the marriage of the Duke of York and Princess May read as follows:

> There was a cricket match between teams captained by the churchwardens. Afterwards the school children and cricketers etc., had tea on the Vicarage lawn. In the evening there were various races for all comers for which Mr. Jacoby gave numerous prizes, and he also presented to the school children medals commemorating the auspicious event...

Mr. & Mrs. Jacoby were now living at Lyegrove House and gave annual treats for the school children as well as providing hot soup in the winter. The Treat for 1893 was reported as follows:

> The children of Old Sodbury, with their teachers started from the schoolroom at 2.00 pm with more than forty of the younger children being driven in a wagon decked with flowers and evergreens. On arriving at Lye Grove they found swings, roundabouts, and other amusements provided for them and at 3.30 pm they sat down to a very substantial tea. After a very enjoyable afternoon they left Lye Grove, giving hearty cheers for the donors of the Treat.

Mr. Mills in his reminiscences about these times was very informative on the subject of the Town Lands Charity, the Ridings Charity and the Church Lands Charity and how they were managed in 1893, when the Act was passed creating the Parish Councils, to come into operation in 1894. He said that:

> The first and last consisted of houses and lands but the Ridings consisted of lands only. They were governed by the Bailiff and Bailiff Burgesses who exercised complete control. This body had three servants: the newly elected Bailiff would choose his own Under-Bailiff to act for a year. His duties were to attend and wait upon them at their meetings and act as messenger when required. For this service he received two stems, one spring and one fall stem. If he had not an acre already he was given the first that fell vacant. The other two servants were paid a salary besides having stems and an acre each as their duties were more numerous. Mr. Samuel Matthews held the office of Hayward for many years until his death. His duties were many; he collected all dues paid on stems and acres, marked all cattle and horses turned on the Ridings, impounded any stray cattle and generally supervised the Ridings.

Mr. Charles Wilkins was the first Town Crier that Mr. Wills could recall. He held the office until he died and was succeeded by his son who held the office till it ceased. He wore a very smart uniform on state occasions.

The Ridings consisted of about ninety acres of pastures. These were called 'acres' although this was less than accurate in actual measurement, the piece called the Bailiff's acre, for instance, was over three acres in size. Each one of the Bailiff Burgesses had an 'acre' allotted to him and his wife, and at his death the widow held it for her life.

After the officers had been allocated their 'acres' the rest was allotted to those inhabitants of the town as the Burgesses saw fit and were held by a man and his wife for life. The owner could, if he liked, make his hay and sell that, or let his 'acre' to anyone at a yearly rent.

In those days the 'acres' were valuable, as most of the town's tradesmen had one or more horses to be fed so the 'acre' holders could always find a ready market for their hay.

When one or more 'acres' became vacant, notice was given that a meeting would be held in the Town Hall to allot it. Any inhabitant who had lived in the town for three years was invited to apply personally. After questioning the applicants and discussing their relative merits the choice was made and the new owner(s) invited to be at the Ridings at a given time when the Bailiff, etc. would attend to make an investiture.

The spring stem was the right to pasture on the Stub Riding, one cow or horse or five sheep from 20th May to the end of August. Anyone wanting a stem had to ask a Burgess to put their name on a list. Then, at a meeting convened for the purpose, each Burgess produced the list of the people he would like to have a stem and after comparing lists the recipients were decided on, a final list then being handed to the Hayward. The next day he, and the Under-Bailiff would go around and notify the lucky ones and collect dues of 3s. 6d each. In those days a spring stem was worth 18s. 0d or 25s. 0d each and in a special season when grass feed was scarce as much as 30s. 0d was paid. The owner of the stem, if he did not want to use it himself, had the right to sell it to any other inhabitant but not an outsider.

The autumn stem was the right to pasture on the Mead Riding after the crops were gathered, from 1st September to December. After that date the Riding was common for some weeks during which any inhabitant could turn out any number of cattle or horses by paying 2d per animal. The same method was used to allocate these stems, the dues being 1s. 6d and raising from 8s. 0d to 15s. 0d depending on the demand for keep.

The Town and Church Lands were let by tender, the rent being paid twice a year in March and September. Mr. J.B.D. Trenfield collected the rents at the Portcullis and in the evening the tenants sat down to a good dinner presided over by the Bailiff or the clerk. After dinner tobacco and pipes were laid on the tables and bowls of hot punch ladled out when the toasts were drunk.

The Dole Charities, i.e. bread and blankets, were managed by the Vicar and Churchwardens, the recipients going to the Church Vestry to receive their tickets.

One of the most important functions of the year was the Court Leet when two juries were summoned to attend at the Town Hall. The Grand Jury, was made up from the leading inhabitants and tradesmen whose primary duty was supposed to be to elect the Bailiff for the year. In fact, the only part they took was to sign as duly elected the gentleman whose name was written on the form. If anyone dared to ask any questions or make any suggestions, he was a marked man and future invitations would not arrive.

The Petty Jury's duties were to walk around the Parish bounds and give their report. After that everyone adjourned until the evening when the banquet was given at the Portcullis, attended by the Lord of the Manor, the newly elected Bailiff and all the leading Burgesses. The evening was spent in speeches, toasts and songs.

On the following Sunday afternoon the new Bailiff, attended by all the Burgesses, met at the Town Hall and formed into procession, marched to the Church to the tune of the Church bells.

Considering the flagrant favouritism and the autocratic secrecy in which the old body carried on ruling the town, it was natural that many of the rate-payers were quietly wondering if the new Act would bring any differences.

The first thing that happened was that a public meeting, not a Parish meeting, was called in the Town Hall. The business of the evening was to consider how the new Act would affect the town and to make arrangements for carrying on under it.

Mr. R.H. Hooper, of Stanshawes Court, Yate, attended to explain the powers of the new Act. He pointed out that the Charities of Sodbury were so ancient and had been handed down from Corporation bodies even when Sodbury was a Borough, that he doubted if the new Parish Council would have the power to deal with them. He was very vague and would not say anything outright, but his aim was to imply that there would be very little change. Although Mr. J and Mr. J.D.B. Trenfield were both Lawyers neither of them tried to explain the powers of the new Act. What they did acknowledge, however, was that a Parish Council would be elected to take over some duties which the Act would define. The meeting finally closed with nobody being much wiser than before except that it was obvious the old body hoped to predominate in the new Council.

The next day Mr. Hooper's speech was severely criticised in the leading article in the Bristol Mercury and a quite different opinion was expressed about the powers under the new Act. This article caused excitement and a lot of quiet talk among a number of rate-payers. They could see that if they wanted a change, now was the time to get it and it soon became obvious that the objective of the public meeting had failed. The Rev. A. Leman, non-conformist Minister, together with Dr. T.C. Leman and others had declared their willingness to contest the election. Mr. Wills decided to stand and he and Rev. Leman held a number of well attended public meetings.

Rounceval Street, Chipping Sodbury, c.1910. Note the paving slabs over the drain at the entrance to the cottages on the right hand side with the pump at the end of the row and the carts outside the Grapes opposite.

The Boot Inn on the road out of Chipping Sodbury towards Old Sodbury. This photograph gave rise to one of Murray Dowding's favourite jokes because just out of the photograph on the right was the town Pound. So Mr. Dowding used to say that this was the only public house in Britain where beer could be bought by the pound.

CHAPTER NINE

THE LAST HUNDRED YEARS

The elections having taken place in December 1894, the Bailiff and burgesses were finally phased out as 1st January 1895 saw the birth of the Parish Council. The results had staggered the old body. It came out like this:
Dr. T.C. Leman (top of the poll), J.W. Trenfield, J. Mills, Dr. A. Grace, Rev. A. Leman, E.O. Limbrick, J.W. Savory, R.W. Arnold, R. Jones and Rev. T. Pullen (jnr.) In February they were joined by A.H. Vizard who was co-opted onto the Council.

This result gave the old guard four members. Dr. Leman was elected Chairman by five votes to four. The position of Vice-Chairman was offered to Mr. J.W. Trenfield but he refused and Mr. Mills took the post. Meetings were held in the Church of England School in Hatters Lane, necessary because the bailiff and burgesses still held on in the Town Hall, obstructing the new Council in every way they could. The first meeting must have been a heavy session. The next day the master recorded:

Found an iron standard of one of the desks broken – done at Parish Council meeting on previous evening.

Mr. J. Mills concluded his memoirs:

Unfortunately for me I was the target of the old body and blamed for their downfall. One of their number told me plainly it would ruin me. Ten years after, that came true. I held the Vice-Chair for ten years.

In 1895 *Gloucestershire Notes and Queries* started publishing reports on individual Parish Council meetings. One such for Chipping Sodbury reads:

Two resolutions were unanimously carried; (1) that a letter be written to the Charity Commissioners asking them to make or sanction under the Municipal Corporation Act 1883 for the town pastures. And that the said scheme shall provide that the Parish Council, as representing the rate-payers, shall in conjunction with the present trustees, manage the charity. Also that for the future a register of applicants shall be kept, who shall be considered in order of entry; and that if the applicant be qualified to receive the benefit he shall receive it. Also that those who receive gifts of acres shall not be called upon to pay money for drink to those who may be refused, or for any other purpose. Also, that the dues on the acres and stems shall be abolished.

The second resolution referred to the government of the Grammar School.

The plea did not pass without a struggle. An inspector eventually came to hold an enquiry into the whole matter and things became very acrimonious but most of the allegations made by Mr. Mills and others were more than justified. Eventually things were set on a proper footing by the Charity Commission Report 311/99, sealed 27th January 1899.

A Parish Council was elected for Old Sodbury also at a parish meeting chaired by Mr. Jacoby at which the following members were elected:

Canon R.S. Nash (vicar), Messrs: James Hatherell, Job Chandler, J.M. Perrett, A.J. Parker, J. Grivelle and J. Collins.

Little Sodbury had too few inhabitants and so was entitled only to an Annual Parish Meeting.

When the councils were formed it highlighted that one could not enter Chipping Sodbury without passing through some of Old Sodbury parish, something which had existed for centuries without comment. This originated, of course, from when the market borough was founded in the twelfth century within the Manor of Sodbury and its boundaries defined within which any special privileges applied and the bailiff held the reins. This situation was by no means unique. In Wotton-under-Edge, for instance, the town was separated from the market (or Chipping) portion at one time, which went by the name of Wotton Foreign.

Following the establishment of the Parish Councils, the Rural District Council was formed in 1895 and the three Sodburys, with some twenty or so other adjacent parishes were combined to make up the area of Chipping Sodbury Rural District. The name was changed to Sodbury Rural District Council in 1935. The first chairman was Sir Gerald W.H. Codrington and for many years the offices were at the Ridgeway.

There was a disagreement between the newly elected Parish Council and the Trustees of the Town Trust as to who should be responsible for maintaining the town fire engine. There was a call-out to a fire at Mr. Shipway's farm for which he was asked to pay £2. This was less than the expenses of the turn out of £2 2s. 0d, part of which was for horse hire.

The Last Hundred Years

Other expenses for the year were the Superintendent's salary of £1 and £2 2s. 0d rent for the engine house, a stone built shed in Horse Street. The appliance consisted of a pump operated by the see-saw motion of two handles on the part of several men. The original hose was made of leather as were the buckets.

The Diamond Jubilee of Queen Victoria in 1897 was commemorated by the inhabitants of Old Sodbury with a fountain installed on the Green.

Looking east along the A432 before the road was widened at the far end. The Dog Inn is on the right and is still in business after several centuries. At one time it was also a shop. The sign shows a dog and a gate, the caption being, "This gate hangs well and hinders none, now down/up the hill before you pass step in and take a cheerful glass." The fountain on the left commemorates Queen Victoria's Diamond Jubilee.

In that year the market was again being held fortnightly on the first and third Tuesday in the month in Chipping Sodbury, a practice which continued for a number of years.

Mr. H.J. Bees with a business in Broad Street continued to run an omnibus to meet every train at Yate station but both he and the railway had a competitor in Messrs. Jones & Son, also of Broad Street, who ran an omnibus daily to Bristol. It was this year, too, that a pumping station was erected at Old Sodbury by the West Gloucestershire Water Co., and within the next twenty years the old wells and pumps fell into disuse

224 The Three Sodburys – An Introduction

throughout the three parishes. The station stood on the east of the Green, looked after by the Gleed family. The engine exhausts were a commonplace feature for some sixty years.

This photograph, taken c.1912, shows Mr. Gleed and his family. He looked after the water pumping station which, together with his house, was on the eastern edge of the Green at Old Sodbury.

A very important event took place on 29th November when the Duchess of Beaufort cut the first sod to start the construction of a new length of railway. This was undertaken by Messrs. Pearson on behalf of the Great Western Railway and was designed to provide a direct route between South Wales and London with an easier gradient for coal trains. A newspaper of the time details the reasons for the work and then continues:

> *The ceremony of cutting the first sod was performed in Blanchards field which abuts on the road from Chipping Sodbury to the Cross Hands. At mid-day the place presented an animated aspect. Hundreds of visitors had arrived from adjacent villages, and the number was increased by the fact that the Great Western Railway Company had invited all those who owned or farmed*

> The Chairman and Directors of the
> Great Western Railway Company
> request the pleasure of the company of
> _W. Henry Slade_
> at the Ceremony of cutting the first sod of their
> South Wales and Bristol Direct Railway,
> by Her Grace The Duchess of Beaufort,
> at Chipping Sodbury, on Monday, the 29th instant, at 12 noon.
> Luncheon will be provided at 1.0 p.m.
>
> Paddington Station, Nearest Station, YATE, MIDLAND R? G. K. Mills,
> November, 1897. (2½ miles distant.) Secretary
>
> AN EARLY REPLY IS REQUESTED, ON RECEIPT OF WHICH A LUNCHEON TICKET WILL BE FORWARDED.

land through which the intended line will run, and also the parsons of the various parishes affected by the scheme, to take part in the proceedings and be present at a lunch to be served in a large marquee erected on the ground. The day was beautifully fine, but cold and windy. Flags were flying and the Bristol City Band was playing, and fresh arrivals were adding to the throng. The chairman of the Company, Lord Emlyn, a number of members of his board, and many officials had come down from Paddington by a special corridor train which left at 8.50 and reached Bristol at 11.05. At the terminus it picked up a number of railway people from this district, and then running on to the Midland Railway quickly reached Yate. Vehicles awaited the train and the party drove to the ground. The sod cutting ceremony was performed beneath a tent, an enclosure being railed off so that the throng might not impede the proceedings. The Duchess of Beaufort, who was accompanied by the Marchioness of Worcester, was received with hearty applause on her arrival, and a very handsome spade was presented to her by the company for the task. The blade was of silver and bore the Great Western Railway Company's arms engraved upon it; the handle was carved and ornamented with silver enrichments and the top was of silver. Cutting up turf is not easy work, and the ground had been made ready so as to lighten the Duchess' duty. Her

> *Grace dug up several sods, placed them in a barrow, and wheeled it out into the field, and she was again cheered for the thoroughness with which she performed her part. Lunch followed, and a company of three hundred persons were catered for by Mrs. Codrington of the Portcullis Hotel, Chipping Sodbury, the arrangements being under the supervision of Mr. Buott of the GWR hotels and refreshment department. During the gale of Sunday night it was a moot point whether the marquee would weather the storm, but happily it did so, and very pretty it looked when all was ready for the visitors. Lord Emlyn occupied the chair.*

The original intention had been for the railway to follow a route slightly north of that which it eventually took but a deviation was made to carry it further away from Badminton House.

Mr. A.W. Matthews, son of a village shopkeeper and himself a life-long resident in the area vividly recalled his observation of the procedure and went on to say:

> *The navvies who worked on the railway were a tough lot. I have seen them fighting outside the Dog Inn many a time. Mrs. Ralph kept the inn at that time when the long room was added. We had a lot of huts about the village and at the Cross Hands. In a field near Plough Farm there were about fifty huts also repair shops and a small Mission Hall where services and St. John's Ambulance Classes were held. There were also about fifty huts at Lyegrove.*
>
> *There were seven ventilation shafts, the one you see at the top of the hill was No.6. No.7 was near the Dog Inn, and was filled in when the work was complete. The other five shafts were towards Badminton. I remember walking through the tunnel before ever a train went through it.*
>
> *When the railway was being built there was a wooden bridge, which was called a gantry, over the road near Mr. Aggs (house with motto to east of road at the turn at the top of the hill). This was used to take goods to No.6 shaft, mainly bricks, from the brickworks in Chapel Lane. For a long time there was a very high chimney at the works which was later demolished.*

Miss. M.R. Isaac, who was a niece of Murray Dowding, visited the village in her childhood. She also has recollections:

> *It was a wonderful engineering feat and travelled in a dead straight line from end to end. I remember seeing the steam navvies at work on the cutting, forerunners of our present "Bulldozers". Also men with red flags warned of the blasting of*

rock. We children were scared to play in the fields. A sort of cable railway carried trucks up over the hill to the first shaft over the house roofs!

Mr. A.W. Matthews left so many recollections that they cannot be quoted in full but the following is a selection, edited as necessary:

In 1895 there were many more thatched cottages than there are to-day (1955). There was little other work than on the farm. A man's wages at that time for a seven day week starting at 6 am and working until 6 pm would be 11s. 0d and his house. His wife very often worked as well doing such things as hoeing in the fields. At home she baked her own bread. The flour was obtained from corn gleaned in the fields after harvesting and ground at the mill. Some had their own ovens others had to take it to a large bakehouse. They used to get two pennyworth of 'Barm' (a form of yeast) at the local brewery. Boys nearly always started work early and were paid 2s. 6d weekly by farmers for scaring crows or leading horses.

Canon Nash was the vicar, he was also a J.P. and kept a coachman and a gardener.

To get to Bristol before July 1903 you had to go to Yate station or take the horse bus which came through the village from Sherston three times a week. You could also get a horse bus from Chipping Sodbury to Yate station.

The police had bull's eye lanterns, you did not have anything but candle lamps for vehicle lights. I well remember the oil lamps in the street at Old Sodbury, my father brought the pillars and lamps from Bristol. Today we have all amenities such as tap water and electric light. In my early days there were only pumps and wells. I well remember a pump in Cotswold Lane near the school.

Mr. Matthews was born at Old Sodbury and went to the Merchant Venturers School in Bristol after which he helped with his father's bakery. He then set up as a travelling supplier of oil, soap and similar goods in the area before he worked, finally, at Chipping Sodbury railway station as checker during World War I. He was prominent as a District and Parish Councillor for many years.

The manor house at Little Sodbury was reported at this time as being in a very bad condition but Lyegrove became the property of the Beaufort family at about this time and so, once again, was receiving the care and attention it deserved.

The village emporium where Mr. F. Matthews and his staff looked after the needs of the people of Old Sodbury. Home-made bread and bacon was also produced and was much appreciated. Deliveries were made by cart and there were eighteen horses on the payroll. Passenger vehicles could also be hired. The shop's greatest period of prosperity was during the construction of the railway (1897–1903) and it faded out during the 1930s. The son, Arthur Matthews, ran a mobile 'shop' for many years selling oil, soap, etc., and he was active also in local government.

The Boer War is mentioned in the Chipping Sodbury National School log book in 1900 when the children gathered at the Portcullis to welcome back Captain Codringon on his return from South Africa.

The census figures for 1891 and 1901 illustrate the effect of the construction of the new length of railway.

	1891	**1901**
Chipping Sodbury	1,028	1,177
Old Sodbury	690	1,332
Little Sodbury	143	139

It was a time of great prosperity for Old Sodbury with a large temporary population in residence while the tunnel was being built and because of the brickworks which provided bricks not only for the tunnel but for other buildings as well. The brickworks was in the field on the left of the mouth of the railway tunnel looking towards Bristol. The clay came from the cutting excavation. Although all traces of the kilns have long gone bricks and pieces of brick can be found just below the field surface. One or two cottages had rooms specially built on to accommodate lodgers. Work went on by day and by night and in some cases the beds were rarely empty.

At different times several tokens have come to light that were issued by the landlords of the Cross Hands at Old Sodbury and the Portcullis in the town. They were about three-quarters of an inch in diameter for values of 2d and 3d and the traditional explanation is that they were introduced for navvies working on the railway to use. As they could only be changed at the inns in question they were less likely to be taken by landladies or wives from the men's trousers while they slept.

The tunnel is responsible for the castle-like tower on the hill above the village. It is a ventilation shaft and there are several more on the way to Badminton.

The whole length of railway from Patchway to Wootton Bassett was completed in five and a half years. During that time the workers enjoyed at least two celebrations, the first being the Coronation of Edward VII. This also gave rise to the ceremonial summoning of a final Court Leet

The mouth of the tunnel, the construction of which brought prosperity to Old Sodbury from 1897 to 1903. It allows a direct route from South Wales to London, emerging at Badminton, a distance of two miles. Now, trains from Parkway Station to London use this line.

230   The Three Sodburys – An Introduction

Leaving the tunnel en route to Bristol. Because of the springs encountered during construction of the tunnel, the tracks always flood after heavy rain. The photograph shows a train negotiating the floods in the early years. The problem has never been entirely solved to this day leading occasionally to the closure of the line until the flood water subsides.

Chipping Sodbury Station, opened to all traffic in 1903. Its distance from the town and an increasing bus service eventually made it uneconomical to keep open and it was closed to passengers on 3rd April 1961, and to goods on 20th June 1966.

at Chipping Sodbury at which Mr. J.D.B. Trenfield, the last person to hold the office of bailiff, read the proclamation. The last petty constable was Charles Wilkins and the last under-bailiff (or town crier) was William Watkins whose uniform, consisting of a large black coat decorated with red and a cocked hat, still existed in 1916.

The second event was the passage of the Prince and Princess of Wales, later King George V and Queen Mary, through the area on their way from Badminton to Yate station on 5th March 1902, having arrived at Badminton on 3rd March via Chippenham Station. The following is a précis of the account which appeared in the South Gloucestershire Chronicle:

The day was observed as a holiday throughout the area and several arches and other decorations were erected at selected spots along the route. Some of these were in the form of banners bearing inscriptions such as 'Welcome' and 'God bless the Prince of Wales'. The decorations commenced at Lyegrove where the workmen employed on the new railway made a feature of their especially burnished tools. There was a concourse of people at the Cross Hands and numbers lined the roadside until Chipping Sodbury was reached. Here there were two or three of the arches and a vast gathering of people who had taken up their places in good time. Around the clock tower local school children had assembled, their number being swollen by contingents from adjoining parishes to make up 1,000 in all. They were each equipped with a miniature Union Jack. The Yate band was in attendance and the church bells pealed happily. The reporter comments that it was very noticeable how ready the Prince and Princess were to recognise the enthusiastic cheering of those members of the working classes that in certain places were a good deal in evidence. When the Royal carriage arrived in the main street there was a great burst of enthusiasm which his Royal Highness acknowledged by bowing. The children, accompanied by the band and conducted by Mr. A.J. Foxwell, sang 'God bless the Prince of Wales', waving their flags meanwhile. The 70 inmates of the workhouse were paraded for the occasion and are said to have cheered lustily as the cavalcade passed. The roadside continued to be lined with spectators until Yate station was reached. The children received suitable refreshments in the New Hall, some buildings were illuminated at dusk and there was a well attended dance in the Town Hall. The Sodburys had indeed been 'en fête' as never before.

Mr. Foxwell, who had conducted the children, was well known and a much respected figure in local music and non-conformist circles for many years. He was a bank manager but as a young man in Wotton-under-Edge he had been a teacher at Sir Isaac Pitman's school. His bust, on a pedestal, now stands just inside the entrance to the New Hall but its original position was just beyond the clock towards Bristol.

As has already been shown, the market charter was granted in 1227 and throughout most of its long existence it was as much a market for produce as for animals.

In July 1902 the government intervened in a way that could have brought the market to an abrupt and untimely end. On the afternoon of 19th August, a well attended meeting in the Town Hall considered the crisis. The Bristol Times and Mirror reported the meeting in full and published the following leading article:

> *The inhabitants of Chipping Sodbury are much concerned at the possibility of the abolition of their old established market, which is held on the sides of the wide street that forms so conspicuous a feature of the town. The danger arose through the intervention of the Board of Agriculture who demanded that the space used for the market should be properly paved and drained, adding the plain intimation that if this was not done to their satisfaction, the market would be condemned. It is obviously in the interest of the town that the market should be preserved and fortunately there appears to be no insuperable difficulty in the way. The course which is suggested is that the District Council should delegate to the Parish Council their rights over the sides of the street; and that the latter body should, with the permission of the County Council and of the Local Government Board, borrow the money necessary to comply with the requirements mentioned. The market would then be in the hands of the Parish Council and a serious danger to the prosperity of the town averted.*

During the public meeting Mr William Higgs produced an original copy of the notice convening a meeting on Friday 22nd September 1837, to establish a market in the town of Chipping Sodbury. From this it would seem that by that time part, at least, of the market had either lapsed or until then had not been used for cattle.

The Parish Council took over the District Council powers as proposed and formed themselves into a Committee to operate the market. Approximately 1,750 square yards more had to be paved. Part of that which was already up to standard extended from the front of the Royal Oak to the corner of Horse Street and was part of the area where pigs were sold. The Ladies of the Manor gave permission for the work in

Market Day in Chipping Sodbury, c.1915/18.

return for an annual fee of £1 and a loan provided the necessary finance.

Records show that before the re-organisation, on 17th September 1902, the following were sold:

    21 calves   70 beasts   980 sheep.

This was above the averages, which were:

    20 calves   65 beasts   500 sheep.

The confidence of those who worked hard to make the new scheme a success was fully justified and the paved area still exists although its use for market purposes stopped in June 1954. The cattle markets at the time were held in the street on the 1st and 3rd Tuesday in the month and were the scene of great activity. Pens were erected on both sides of Broad Street, one side of the first part of Horse Street and up to the Clock in High Street. Some of the pens were made up from wooden hurdles while others consisted of iron stanchions which fitted into sockets in the pitching. These were stored in a shed on the side of Church Lane which disappeared when the road was widened in the 1960s. They were taken from the shed and back again on a trolley with iron wheels and the clatter was considerable.

Around Christmas each year prizes were awarded for the best animals and there was considerable competition among the butchers to buy them. Subsequently they exhibited the winning rosettes with the meat in their shops.

This year saw the last stage of the changeover in the form of local government taking place. There were already County, Rural District and Parish Councils, and now finally, so far as Chipping Sodbury was concerned, three bodies were called into being. They were:

The Trustees of the Town Trust
13 members
Trustees of Town Lands & Grammar School Trust
11 members
Trustees of Church Lands
6 members

The Town Trust Scheme was amended on 31st December 1959 and a new scheme for the Chipping Sodbury Endowed School was introduced on 9th March 1967. There are still thirteen trustees to the Town Trust and seven trustees to the Chipping Sodbury Endowed School Foundation.

The constitutions of the Town Lands Charity and Church Lands Charity are unchanged except that some of the properties mentioned in the various enfeoffments have been sold.

The bailiffs, under-bailiffs, leather sealers, ale tasters, meat examiners, scavengers, petty constables, and their Court Leet are gone for ever but the part they played in managing local affairs through seven or more centuries make them worth remembering.

With the internal combustion engine beginning to make its presence felt together with the imminent opening of another railway station in the neighbourhood, the outlook for horse transport operators was not good. Messrs. Jones & Son still operated their daily omnibus to Bristol whilst Mr. Bees was still meeting every train at Yate. This station could also be reached by villagers on most days of the week using services operating from Hawkesbury, Sherston and Luckington.

The Endowed School at Chipping Sodbury now had Rev. Dumas as headmaster while Mr. E.A. Freeman was Head of the National, or C of E school, and Mr. Millership was Head at Old Sodbury. Little Sodbury had now lost its separate school and the children went either to Old Sodbury or Horton .

By the summer of 1903 work on the new railway was finished and on 1st May goods trains between Patchway and Badminton were operating, followed by full working throughout on 1st July with some five or six trains calling at Chipping Sodbury daily in each direction and many expresses and coal trains passing through. The first station master at the new station of Chipping Sodbury, which was, in fact, in the parish of Old Sodbury, was Mr. F. Savage.

The coming of the railway to the countryside had a wide reaching effect well beyond the realm of transport especially after Parish Councils were formed. Until then, life in the villages could still be expressed in the words of the verse that is tactfully omitted to-day, of the hymn 'All things bright and beautiful' namely:

> *The rich man in his castle,*
> *The poor man at his gate,*
> *God made them high and lowly*
> *And ordered their estate.*

Previously most people had worked for local employers and rented their houses from them or some other local land owner, so even if they became Parish Council Councillors they had to watch their step. With the coming of the railways employment and often housing was far away from the local scene and men in this position were able to speak their mind in a way that would have been impossible earlier. Two local examples were signalmen Bacon and Backe. It was also laid down that Parish Council meetings could not be held before 6.00 pm so allowing Councillors to be elected who otherwise would have been excluded by their employment.

A common sight at a country station in those days was the milk churns waiting to be collected by the various farmers whose names were engraved on plates attached to the lids. Each evening around 6.00 o'clock, a number of carts could be seen hurrying to the station with three or four full churns for the evening train to which a special wagon was attached. On their return journey the carts carried away the empties. Chipping Sodbury station was soon as busy as the others with this traffic and with stone from the quarries carried to it in horse drawn carts. Well-to-do passengers and commercial travellers used a 'Fly' provided by Mr. Bees to carry them to Chipping Sodbury. The driver, named Butler, was well skilled in using his whip to dislodge any small boys who tried to ride on a bar at the back of the vehicle.

According to the Chipping Sodbury National School Log, 1908 had one thing in common with 1971, there was snow at the end of April! Mr. Penglaze had been head since August 1905 and Mrs. Penglaze the infants' teacher from 1906. The log also records a ceremony which it was becoming a nation-wide custom held annually on 26th May and continued for about a quarter of a century:

> *Today is being observed as 'Empire Day'. In the morning the Managers, parents and others interested in school are invited to attend while the children will salute the Flag, sing patriotic songs, and listen to an address by Rev. D. Wrigley, Vicar of Old Sodbury, on the 'British Empire, with special attention to Australia'. The afternoon will be a half-holiday.*

For many years, on a Friday in March and September, the school had a holiday for the Sodbury Mop. The last such entry in the Log is for 23rd September 1910. Due, it is said, to a fatal accident the Mop was moved from the street to the 'Rag' behind the church. By this time, however, it had lost its original significance and was simply an excuse for the presence of Messrs. Coles' roundabouts and various side shows. It stopped when the First World War started in 1914 and was re-introduced in the 1930s. More recently the Rogers family has provided the fairground rides and sidestalls.

Tudor House in Hatters Lane was at this time what was known as a lodging house. It provided accommodation for tramps who did not wish to lodge in the workhouse. Answering a knock on one's door in those days often meant being confronted by a very scruffy individual asking for hot water for his tea can, followed by a plea for a piece of cake or bread.

At the rear of Tudor House were Mr. Stanley Ball's livery stables. He also had several horse drawn vehicles which could carry about a dozen people and were known as 'brakes'. They were very popular for such things as Sunday School outings. At this time, Down Leaze House was the private residence of Capt. Nell who owned a pack of hounds and often drove a spick and span dog cart. Later the house became the home of the Sodbury Rural District Council and it was finally demolished in the 1980s by Northavon District Council when it became too expensive to maintain.

George V was now on the throne and Little Sodbury Manor had fallen into disrepair with the north wing almost in ruins and the sound parts

Down Leaze House, c.1910/12.

being used as a farm. In 1911 the Hartleys sold it to the ninth Duke of Beaufort who sold it in turn to Lord Hugh Grosvenor who commissioned Mr. Harold Brakspear to restore it.

Sodbury Rifle Range was in full swing in a long temporary building in Hatters Lane and the Golf Club was also in existence. Like the rest of the country the Sodburys were shocked by the disaster to the Titanic and responded to the appeal for funds.

May 1912 was a month to remember at the C of E School. Two choirs took part in the Bristol Eisteddfod and the Boys' Choir came second in their class as did the mixed choir which ended up only two marks behind the winners.

The roads, although firm, were still dusty in summer and muddy in winter but the traffic using them had changed out of all recognition. Motor cars and buses were now common and cycling was a popular pastime. Mr E.H. Powell had established the first cycle shop in the town on the corner of Broad Street and Hatters Lane on the site of the former Swan Inn. It was quite usual then to be able to hire a cycle when the proposed journey was too long for walking and in many places there were people like Mr. Powell willing to oblige. The charge was per hour and was quite reasonable.

It was about this time that the first 'moving pictures' came to Chipping Sodbury, shown in a tent on the Rag. One of the epics showed a shepherd on a hillside and the fact that the match could be seen to flicker when he lit his pipe caused considerable com-

Old Sodbury villager, Mrs. Annie Walker. The photograph was taken c.1911 by Murray Dowding, who in his caption said that she had nearly one hundred descendants.

ment for several days afterwards. A year or so later a film-making company came on location to the Sodburys and used a number of the local youth as extras to whom the result was demonstrated in a room at the rear of the Portcullis.

Eyes were now turning skywards when an aeroplane passed over. Although they were increasing in numbers it was still a rare enough event to be mentioned in the Gazette.

Some years previously Sir Robert Baden Powell had started the movement that will always be associated with his name, 'Scouting for Boys' and two public spirited young ladies, the Misses Burgess, daughters of Col. Burgess of the Ridge House, founded the Chipping Sodbury troop of Scouts.

No story of these times would be complete without mentioning George Dickson who was the unfortunate possessor of two wooden legs and drove around in a small donkey cart. When roused to fury, which happened often when he had been drinking, he used to unstrap one of his legs and use it as a club, somewhat to the dismay of the local constabulary.

Both the Superintendent of Police and the Surveyor of the Roads went about their duties on horseback and Constable Winn could often be seen exercising the Superintendent's horse.

When the Rev. Dumas died around 1906 the Endowed School died with him and there was a gap of some seven years or so before the Board of Education implemented a scheme worked out in October 1912. The premises were re-opened as a Grammar School in January 1913 with Mr. C.D. Waters, BA as headmaster and Miss Irene G. Verney, BA as headmistress. The appointment of a headmistress was necessary because it was now a mixed school with girls being admitted for the first time. The governing body consisted of seven representatives; two appointed by the County Council, one by the Rural District Council, three by the Parish Council and one by Bristol University. There were also to be six co-opted members of whom two had to be ladies. The first chairman was Mr R.N. Hooper JP but he died within a year or so and was succeeded by Rev. W.E. Blathwayt. The Board decided that the type of education available should be geared to an agricultural and partly urban district and a number of scholarships were established. To start with there were 24 pupils, but that number steadily increased.

The memoirs of Mr. (later Army Captain) C.G. Colwill provide a great deal of information on Chipping Sodbury and its personalities between 1900 and the Great War. Let him tell the story:

> *I was born in March 1894 in Hatters Lane next door to what was then 'The Lodging House'.*

Pound House, Old Sodbury (not to be confused with the one next to the Boot Inn at Chipping Sodbury).

Jimmy Dixon

One of my earliest recollections is being taken up the Church Tower on the relief of Mafeking and seeing pictures in the 'Black and White Magazine' and the 'London Illustrated' of Gen. Roberts (Bobs), Gen. Kitchener, Kruger and De Wett, Spion Kop, Bloomfontain and the Modder River. We sang 'Dolly Gray' and 'Soldiers of the Queen'. I remember seeing the Sodbury contingent of the Gloucestershire Yeomanry parade in front of the Portcullis in which Clare Freeman (one of E.A Freeman's sons and Bill Davery were present going off to Africa.

Then there was the school under E.A. Freeman (Daddy Freeman) whose wife taught the infants and Miss. Critchley. Our first lesson was knitting squares, the boys as well as the girls! Mr. Freeman taught in the Big Room assisted by Mr. Bazeley and his daughter Hetta. When Mr. Freeman retired we were taken over by Mr. John Penglaze, who became organist and choirmaster. Practically his first words were, "stand up the choir boys. You will come round the harmonium at a quarter to eleven, at twelve and again at four o'clock" and from then on he gave us a thorough musical training from breathing to sight reading until we were almost Cathedral standard. He formed an operatic society and we did several cantatas and Gilbert and Sullivan works and visited neighbouring Churches.

He also ran a football club and instituted school sports which was frowned upon by many people in the town who thought we should be learning not playing. He was also a pioneer of motoring, owning a four cylinder FN motor bike which many enthusiasts will remember as one of the first. I remember seeing Mr. Tom White walking in front of one of the first motor cars carrying a red flag. Mr. Penglaze eventually gave up teaching and opened a garage which was regrettable as he was a born teacher, if somewhat cruel. At that time there was a large choir with ten or twelve men and a good many boys, a band of ringers who were E.J. Tily, Reg. Freegard, Jack Alway, Leonard Hewitt, Frank Robins, Harry Lewis and myself and Albert Vizard. There was at one Christmas time a strike of the ringers because W.H.P. Harvey, who was the Vicar at the time, would not allow them to have beer in the tower. Once when training a young band we tied the clappers of the bells to save making a din by bells crashing together. Several people living near the Church became almost hysterical on hearing noises from the belfry and no sound of bells and went to the Vicar in a panic. Amongst some of the outstanding characters I remember are Mr. Tom Short, a very big man who owned a string of horses which hauled stone from the local quarries and used us boys to tell him the time. There was old Mr. Greenaway who was very proud at having acquired false teeth and when my father asked him how he was getting on with them he said, "fine Harry, fine, I only takes them out to have me meals!" There was Jimmy Bees who owned the livery stables, whose son Bert drove the Fire Engine and Ernest drove the two-horse bus to and from Yate Station. Jimmy Dixon who lost both legs in an accident on the line and who periodically got sent to Gloucester Gaol for being drunk, when he would drive his donkeys at a stretch gallop up and down the street. Poor Jimmy must have suffered a lot from frustration as he was obviously a powerful man before his accident. It was said of him that once when serving a sentence, the warden came into his cell where Jimmy was picking oakum and said, "Come on Dixon, the man in the next cell has finished his". Jimmy replied, "Take him some of mine then". There was Mr. J. Slade, the carrier, whose one and only outing was to drive his wife and family to Sherston Races from which he always returned slightly inebriated but never drank at any other time.

Dr. A.H. Grace, doctor to the Beaufort Hunt who never missed a meet and insisted on jumping until well past seventy. When there was no meet he would call for me to go down to the Reading Rooms and play billiards with him. He used to say, "Have a go at the red boy! It might go down". Then there was Mr. Harry Gerish, an auctioneer, a real old Edwardian character, always elegantly groomed and always with a rose in his button hole. If he was drunk after the market he would never walk up the street but along what we used to call the Back Brook, which is a narrow path between two streams, the one on the left being about four feet deep. One market day I saw him weaving an unsteady course along this path when he suddenly fell in. He scrambled up onto the path, got up and walked off as sober as a judge.

The Mop fair used to be held in the middle of the street annually. On one occasion I was watching Jimmy Amos's roundabout when I saw my friend Charlie Morgan coming round with blood in the middle of his forehead. He had been shot from the shooting booth close by. It must have been in the spring of 1904. He was carried over to his father's shop, which is kept now by Jack Sandells and we heard later that he had died. The Mop was never held in the street again but in a field called 'The Rag'.

I remember the visit of the Prince of Wales when we school children were assembled near the Town Clock and sang 'From

Out Our Ancient Mountains' under the direction of the late James Foxwell, whose statue once stood outside the Reading Room but now stands at the entrance to the New Hall.

About the autumn of 1914 we were invaded by the 5th Battalion Loyal North Lancs Territorials under the command of Lt. Col. Hesketh, a Bolton mill owner. They were welcomed and entertained by almost every family in the town. Later, in early 1915, while serving in the BEF in the second Battalion Gloucestershire Regiment I met them coming out of the front line in Courmetiers. [Referring to one of Percy Couzen's books] *I see one of the photographs shows the house where we lived for many years. It was between Mr. J.B. Trenfield's and Mr. E.J. Tily's house which was then the King's Arms Inn kept by the late Charlie Wilkins who supplemented his living by selling coal and clipping horses, which he did with hand clippers until later getting a machine. We boys of course, never missed any of this and were proud of being asked to help by holding the horses' heads. I was delighted to renew acquaintance with my old friend Murray Dowding. We spent many happy hours together on long walks visiting Churches and places of interest. At that time he was much misunderstood by the majority of the people of Sodbury and for many years unappreciated.*

Mr. Colwill also wrote another letter which in places repeats some of the first one. It reads:

Even now after all those years the date, August the fourth, still wrings my heart. I think of all my school mates, Percy Dash and George Vizard who were killed early in '14, Leonard Andrews, and several of those I served with so young and bright.

*I shall never forget as I was driving the men to work on the Badminton Estate as we passed Mrs. Williams' paper shop, the one word in giant letters '**WAR**' on the placard outside. It marked the end of an era of peace and security, when the Church of England and the British Navy were dominant. When you could put your sons and daughters into the banks or on the railways or Civil Service and know they would be there until they were presented with their gold watch and pension. When authority, the police and parents were respected, we were just beginning to enjoy life. We were free of the sadistic tyranny of John Penglaze (National School Master). There was the thrill of that first wage packet and that ride to Bristol on your bicycle to buy your first suit of clothes. There were whist drives and dances and concerts we arranged ourselves, and those long walks on a Sunday*

The top classes of the St. John's C of E School, 1914. The headmaster (back row left) was Mr. John Penglaze. Third left back row is Mr. Frank Colwill and front row far left is Mr. Percy Couzens.

afternoon over the Ridings in cowslip time, or to stand under that red chestnut tree in the Churchyard in full bloom. What fragrant memories!

Mr. Colwill served with distinction throughout the Great War and was promoted to the rank of Captain. Later he lived in Barnstaple for some time and then emigrated to Australia where he died.

The Declaration of War on 4th August 1914 came as a shock to the Sodburys as indeed it did to the whole country and the common belief that it would all be over by Christmas was also shared. One widely held belief was that the Germans were going to use spies for acts of sabotage with the railways being a major target and the railway staff were set to guard the mouths of the tunnel and the ventilating shafts immediately, armed with pick-axe handles. Very shortly their places were taken by fully equipped soldiers of the 5th Loyal North Lancashire Territorials who set up guard posts also at bridges and stations.

In those days the railway lines were laid so that there was a small space between the joints to allow for expansion. When this had happened during a hot summer day it was not unusual for a loud clang to be heard when the rail cooled and contracted again. The territorials

244 *The Three Sodburys – An Introduction*

came in August and they came from the industrial north so they found it a bit strange to be alone on a bridge over the railway in the heart of the country on a dark night. More than once rifles were fired off when the rails contracted. On 11th November 1914, with the cheers of the school children ringing in their ears, the territorials marched to the station and left for Seven Oaks for further training before going to France where a large number of them became casualties. By this time the spy scares had become fewer.

Camp Kitchen by the Town Pump on the corner of Hounds Road and Broad Street, 5th Battalion N. Lancs. Regiment, "The Terriers", c.1914.

From 1915 onwards the various battalions of the 'Bristol's Own' continued training in the area and for a long time the sides of the main street were filled with the vehicles of 494th Company Mechanical Transport Army Service Corps under the command of Capt. B.T. Taperall. Meanwhile, the Royal Flying Corps had built a small aerodrome in nearby Yate. Aeroplane frames and wings were made and covered at Parnalls, now Jacksons (Creda) factory in Yate and engines were built and tested at Newmans factory, now the site of B&Q and Safeway supermarket. The big house at Newmans, Poole Court, was the Officers' Mess. The other ranks lived in a camp on the left hand side at the entrance to Yate common.

There was a factory for filling smoke shells at the rear of the Cow Mills. A test once caused considerable alarm when it went slightly wrong and a column of black smoke rose high in the air.

The Cow Inn and Cow Mills c.1910 (above) at the bottom of the Bowling Hill. The River Frome running at the back of these buildings, on the left, is the boundary between Old Sodbury and Yate. The much later photograph below (1990) shows the back of the Cow Mills and the River frome where the smoke bombs were tested in the First World War.

Avro biplanes were frequently flown over the area by Australian pilots training at Leighterton aerodrome.

Entertainment was provided by a cinema in a tent on the corner of Eggshill Lane and the main road.

As a result of German submarine attacks on merchant ships in the Atlantic and elsewhere, food began to be scarce through 1916 and 1917 but the Government did not introduce rationing for a long time. The queues that formed at shops with supplies in the Cities were enormous. Eventually the Government reluctantly gave in but as a result of that delay malnutrition was rife. The introduction of rationing ensured that the available food was fairly shared out even if, at times, the bread and other items were far from appetising The final outcome of the initial malnutrition was a 'flu' epidemic in 1917 and 1918 which carried off considerable numbers of old and young alike. The only 'cure' that scientists could come up with was ammoniated tincture of quinine which tasted terrible, making it most unpopular.

In 1917 Parliament introduced a Daylight Saving Bill under which the clocks were advanced one hour during the summer, a measure still practised today as 'British Summer Time'. When it was first introduced it caused quite a bit of confusion, not least because communications were much poorer then, and on more than one occasion people turned up for Church or Chapel at nearly the end of the Sunday service.

Everyone was urged to grow as much food as possible and it was pointed out from the church and chapel pulpits that under the circumstances it was no sin to till the land on the Sabbath.

A Flying Visit, c.1916.

Haymakers at Old Sodbury, c.1916. There are so many women in the photograph simply because the men were away in the War.

Even the hedgerow fruits were utilised and in 1917, on nine occasions, the elementary school children had a half holiday so they could gather blackberries. Others were urged to collect horse chestnuts (conkers). No-one knew what they were to be used for but one of the rumours was that they were to be ground up to supplement the flour in the bread.

Although Zeppelin airships never came as far west as the Sodburys, the threat of raids ensured that a rigorous blackout was maintained at night. If anyone needed a reminder that there was a war on, there was a Camp for German prisoners of war on the left at the bottom of the Bowling Hill, now covered by part of the Elms Estate.

In the last years of the war with so few able bodied men left at home, a Training Corps was

Believed to be Mr. Short of Old Sodbury, c.1916. He also appears among a group of haymakers of about that time.

formed to use the older men on guard and other duties. Locally, a Unit was raised at Old Sodbury led by the current schoolmaster, Mr. F. Iles.

When peace came on 11th November 1918 the traffic on the roads increased considerably as ex-army vehicles were turned to commercial activities. The improvements in the internal combustion engine meant that lorries, cars and motorcycles were capable of a high standard of performance and rapidly took over from the horse. By now, too, the aeroplane was such a familiar sight that people no longer took much notice when one flew over.

Anticipating an increasing demand, Mr. J. Penglaze left the C of E School in September 1919 to run the garage business he had established in Broad Street at what became Dunkerleys. This was the first garage in Chipping Sodbury. At the back of the premises he achieved another first when he opened the first permanent cinema in the town. Mains electricity had not yet reached the town so a dynamo was used and in the winter there was always some worry in the waiting queue about whether the engine would start.

Broad Street, Chipping Sodbury, c.1925.
On the left is one of the petrol pumps for Mr. Penglaze's Garage.

Throughout the country thoughts now turned to perpetuating the memory of the millions who had lost their lives in the War. Someone remembered the old Market Cross at the rear of the Presbytery and parts of the main shaft were built into a newly-designed purpose-built memorial which was erected on the same spot from which the original cross had been removed a hundred and fifty years before. The new memorial was dedicated in a service held from the memorial steps on 31st March 1920.

Dedication of the Memorial Cross in Chipping Sodbury, 31st March 1920.

A later, more ambitious project was the founding of the War Memorial Cottage Hospital by a committee of which Mr. W.H. Williams was the hard working honorary secretary. The Cottage Hospital was downgraded from general purpose use to become a Maternity Hospital some time after World War II and since then, despite a vigorous and long campaign, has been down-graded yet again although remaining in the National Health Service.

For a long time an ex-German field gun was parked on the Bristol side of the clock where it rusted quietly away. At Old Sodbury a lynch gate was erected at the entrance to the churchyard and a tablet placed in the chapel listing those from the area who had lost their lives. For many years after British Legion Parades were held to Old Sodbury Church in the morning and the Chapel in the evening on Armistice Day.

Thought was also put into helping to rehabilitate those who were fortunate enough to come back home resulting, amongst other things, in recreational Institutes being opened in towns and villages all over the country. At Old Sodbury some of the out-buildings at Home Farm were modified to provide facilities for billiards and cards until a purpose built Institute could be erected some five or so years later. At Chipping Sodbury the Reading Room or Literary Institute was modified to provide similar facilities.

250   *The Three Sodburys – An Introduction*

Among the casualties on the battlefield was Lord Hugh Grosvenor, the owner of Little Sodbury Manor and in 1919 this was bought by Baron de Tuyll, the dowager Duchess of Beaufort's son by her first husband. He started to restore the Manor but unfortunately did not live long to enjoy it. On his death it passed to his cousin Mr. Mark Harford and then to his son Gerald.

Lyegrove, too, was given a new lease of life when it became home to Lady Westmorland. In the early twenties, also, Dodington House was rented by the Lyon family who had two cricketing sons, M.D. Lyon who played for Somerset, and Beverley who was a member of the Gloucestershire side. Both of them sometimes turned out for the Old Sodbury village team.

With the population on the increase, housing was becoming an acute problem and to resolve it, local councils began to build housing estates, such as that at Blanchards at the Smarts Green roundabout. These were among the first but were soon followed by Colts Green and Westmoreland Terrace and since then, of course, many others.

Fortunately, by this time roads were being given a tarmacadam surface so doing away with the mud which in winter made even the main street in Chipping Sodbury difficult to negotiate. The demand for the new material together with the increasing demand for ordinary roadstone brought in a period of prosperity for the quarries in the area which has

An early garage in Hatters Lane – Beard & Colwill.

continued nearly to the present day. An area just past the church on the right hand side of the Wickwar road was quarried and eventually left as a large hole in the ground. This flooded and as late as the 1940s was used as an open air swimming pool with water polo matches on Bank Holidays and a 'safe area' was fenced off for non-swimmers. With a combination of an increased awareness of the general health risk involved coupled with an unfortunate drowning incident when a swimmer got caught up in the weed, the quarry was condemned and filled in.

Soon after the First World War a regular bus service was set up between Bristol and Chipping Sodbury and was quickly extended to Tetbury and Malmesbury. Despite the competition from the two local railway stations, Mr. Slade was still operating a successful carrier business between Chipping Sodbury and Bristol.

Both the Church and the Baptist Chapel at Old Sodbury were well attended. In 1927 the chapel opened a Sunday School of some thirty-five children, the mainstay being the Misses Haward. There was a resident minister who was in charge of a small circuit of local chapels. Money was tight but there were still annual Sunday School Outings, usually to Weston super Mare.

In the middle twenties a new feature started to appear at the rear of many of the houses in the district. It consisted of one single, or two parallel, lengths of wire with one end attached to a chimney and the other to a tall pole and a connecting wire running into the house. This was the status symbol of the decade since it showed the ownership of a wireless set. This area was just within crystal set range of the Cardiff

Old Sodbury Baptist Chapel Sunday School, September 1927.

broadcasting station. In this form of receiver no battery was required but everyone had to be very quiet because the signal strength was only sufficient to operate special earphones.

A little later valve sets became available for those who could afford them and before a mains supply was available, accumulators, which were large liquid filled batteries had to be used. It was a common sight to see all sorts of people carrying an accumulator to and from a charging station.

Generally only the husband and older children went out to work. Labour saving devices in the home were few and far between, so Mother had as much as she could cope with in the family home. The household needs were catered for by a milkman, who called at the door with a large can and measured out the milk with a dipper into a jug. The baker called regularly as did the travelling oil man and the fishmonger. Horses and carts were still used, that of the baker being of a special high wheeled type. Some grocers sent a man around for orders which were then delivered, as did some butchers. For ordinary people there was no such things as refrigerators so homes had a larder with a pennant stone shelf to keep things cool, if they were lucky, or else a 'safe' which was a cupboard with a metal gauze door placed in a shady place if not. In the summer the milk often needed to be scalded to prevent it going sour.

The Sodburys suffered during the industrial slump, like the rest of the country, from 1925 to 1936. There was very little money to spare but somehow life went on.

There was a brief buzz of excitement on 1st May 1931 when the area had a very minor earth tremor.

In the thirties both mains electricity and a sewerage scheme were introduced in Chipping Sodbury and the local area. The gas lamps which had lit the streets and approach roads to the town for over sixty years disappeared. At one time these had reached nearly to Chipping Sodbury railway station to the benefit of many nervous walkers on a dark night. With their going, of course, went the lamplighter who, with his pole, did his rounds lighting and putting out the lamps as necessary. The last man to be employed locally was Mr. H. Higgs.

King George V and Queen Mary's Silver Jubilee was celebrated with the proper ceremony, as was the coronation of George VI following the brief appearance of Edward VIII.

With the growing threat from Germany now at last being recognised, frantic efforts were being made to catch up with the appropriate armaments and some prosperity began to return. Chipping Sodbury still had a market every other week and kept its position as a trading centre. There were now several more garages and the 'Cozy Cinema' was thriving in a hut at the top of Hounds Road under the proprietorship of

Chipping Sodbury main street in the 1930s.

Mr. Watts Williams. This gentleman also ran a milk round and it was possible to book seats at the cinema by leaving a note in the top of an empty milk bottle.

The Chipping Sodbury Rural District Council was now called Sodbury RDC and had moved from Ridgeway to Down Leaze House. The Grammar School having outgrown the building in the High Street moved to a brand new building on Cotswold Road, now part of Kennedy Way.

The Misses Brooks, daughters of A.C. Brooks of Hayes Farm, formed the Old Sodbury Troops of Boy Scouts and Girl Guides which flourished for a while.

Mr. Robert Wilson, who had been Clerk to the Sodbury District Council, gave two fields on the hill side at Old Sodbury opposite Home Farm as Playing Fields for children in memory of his late wife, Annie Margaret. They were handed over to the National Playing Fields Association with due ceremony with the local Guides and Scouts in attendance. Unfortunately, being on a slope, they proved unsuitable and were not much used. Eventually they were sold after fifty years and the money was used to buy part of the field opposite the present post office.

Chipping Sodbury Parish Council put forward proposals to extend the boundaries of the former borough, largely at Old Sodbury's expense, which naturally were opposed and led to a public enquiry. The Inspector decided that the solution was to join up Chipping and Old Sodbury to form one civil parish with two wards but before this could be implemented World War II broke out.

In preparing for the war Civil Defence organisations such as the Air Raid Precautions (ARP) and Auxiliary Fire Service (AFS) were set up and personnel were recruited and trained in their respective duties. It was accepted that aerial bombardment would play a great part in the German attack and that poisonous gas could also be used so one of the duties taken on by the ARP wardens was to give everyone a gas mask. The local chief warden was Major D. Brown and ARP posts were set up at the RDC offices in Chipping Sodbury and at the old chapel near the entrance to Chapel Lane at Old Sodbury.

Meanwhile, knowing that incendiary bombs would probably be used, AFS personnel were trained in how to deal with them and suitable equipment was provided.

On 3rd September 1939 the storm broke. In general terms the Sodburys had to endure the same privations, trials and dangers as other country areas. Many of the local warnings were caused by enemy bombers passing overhead on their way to bomb Liverpool, Birmingham and other places in the Midlands. At least one bomber was shot down, crashing near Falfield. When Bristol was badly bombed, the individual flames from the burning city could be seen in Chipping Sodbury. Although no bombs actually fell on Chipping Sodbury itself, the Old and Little Sodbury parishes were not so fortunate. Two high explosive bombs fell on Parks Farm and several others fell between Cross Hands and Dodington together with clusters of incendiaries at other places, fortunately with no casualties. In all the siren on the roof of Chipping Sodbury police station sounded its warning 548 times.

A number of the inhabitants were among the heavy casualties caused by the afternoon bombing raid on Parnall's works at Yate in 1941. The author can remember, having been in the air-raid shelters at the back of the C of E School in Hatters Lane all afternoon, watching the workers walking back up the Bowling Hill in the late afternoon, many pushing their bicycles, and seemingly all covered in blood and bandages.

The juvenile population of the district was considerably increased when 'evacuees' from the Midland Cities were billeted on the local population but when Bristol came under heavy attack a number of them went home again.

A section of the Local Defence Volunteers, later known as the Home Guard, was formed in the area under the command of Major L.M. Harris. From about the middle of the war onwards members of the US Army and their vehicles were billeted in the area, some in the old Quakers Meeting Place in Brook Street and the majority under canvas in part of Painter's Mead fields.

Having learned the lesson from the First World War, rationing was introduced very early on and although not generous, the rations proved adequate. Employers had to provide staff canteens and National Restaurants were built in some cities and towns.

The Princesses Elizabeth and Margaret and their grandmother, Queen Mary, spent a lot of time at Badminton during the war and Queen Mary became a familiar sight as she was driven to and from some function in her distinctive car.

When peace was restored in 1945 time was found to implement the decision made before the war that Chipping and Old Sodbury should become the wards of the civil parish of Sodbury and on 16th April 1946 the new parish council was elected, the members being:

Chipping Sodbury Ward
H.J. Dando, S.H. Hobbs, T. Lediard, W.E. Thompson, E.J. Tily, C.D. Waters.

Old Sodbury Ward
E. Seymour-Williams (chairman), A.E. Batten, H.R. Gough, T.L. Bennett, E.J. Hughes, Mrs. M.J. James. Mr. P.A. Couzens was co-opted on when Mr. Hughes left the area.

Meetings had to be held alternately at Chipping and Old Sodbury and a similar arrangement was made for the annual parish meeting.

In mid 1947 Mr. C.D. Waters died and the Sodburys lost a much respected figure. He came to Chipping Sodbury in 1913 as headmaster of the Grammar School when it was re-opened with 25 pupils. By the time he died it was a thriving establishment in new premises with several hundred scholars.

The Old Grammar School in the High Street, having been used for a number of purposes had now become an annex to the C of E School which was outgrowing the buildings in Hatters Lane. In 1946 one of the old classrooms was used to house a branch of the County Library, run by Mrs. P.A. Couzens. The County Library still uses a room in the building and continues to be very popular. Previously, books had been available at the private house of Mrs Champion.

In the early 1950s the Chipping Sodbury Football Team, by a series of machiavellian moves inspired by Major L.M. Harris, became members of the Western League. The team proved not to be up to it, however, and they only lasted in the League for two seasons.

January 1953 saw big changes in local education. The Old Grammar School, had a number of extra classrooms built at the rear of the premises and became the Secondary Modern School providing education for those children over 11 who had not qualified for the Grammar School. What had been the Elementary School at Hatters Lane now became a Junior School for children from 5 to 11 years of age.

On 2nd June 1953, having mourned the passing of King George VI, the people in the Sodburys, with the rest of the country, gathered to celebrate the coronation of Elizabeth II. Television sets were spreading

The Proclamation of Queen Elizabeth II, February 1952.

in a boom industry and this was the very first time that cameras, television and otherwise, had been allowed to record a coronation from within the abbey itself. Those who still had no television set imposed themselves on those neighbours who did and so millions throughout the country were able to witness the ceremony of the crowning as it actually took place. Despite the disappointing weather on the day, there were well attended sports, teas and dances and all the school children received a coronation mug.

Old Sodbury was "Dressed over all" as a result of a competition for the best decorated residence and there was a tea for all in the Institute, the day ending with a dance. In the autumn a professional film of the coronation was hired and shown with the aid of a projector loaned by Mr. D. Matthews.

Locally, in August 1953, Michael Toghill discovered some remains of old pottery at the quarry of Wilson & Turner which was on the left hand side of the road from Sodbury to Wickwar, about a mile out of the town. Murray Dowding, who had a great interest in such things, had the fragments and the site examined by Mr. L.V. Grimsell from Bristol Museum, who decided that the fragments were, in part at least, Roman in origin. Unfortunately, further quarrying prevented any further examination of the site.

The Last Hundred Years

After over 700 years, the market at Chipping Sodbury came to an end in June 1954. It had been held alternately in the street and at Yate Sale Yard near Yate railway station for some time and the new regulations coming into effect were such that the Market Committee were unable to meet them. It was with regret, therefore, that the business was transferred completely to Yate. At this point, strictly speaking, the ancient borough forfeited its right to the prefix 'Chipping'.

Rev. H.N. Burgess, who had been the vicar at Old Sodbury since 1928, died in 1955. During his time at Old Sodbury he had earned everyone's respect and liking.

On Tuesday, 21st October 1958 the radio competition 'Have a Go' run by Wilfred Pickles and pianist Violet Carson recorded an instalment in the Grammar School. A number of 'locals' were invited to take part, including Miss Pratley, Miss Short, Mr. Fred Trotman and Percy Couzens who won the star prize of £2. Things took a more than usually hilarious turn when a lady, who shall remain nameless to save her and her family's blushes, was asked to name all her children. The family was a very large one and in the stress of the moment, the lady was quite unable to do so.

Chipping Sodbury lost its railway station in April 1961 when passenger services stopped and Yate followed in January 1966. The Thornbury branch was closed completely in December 1967 there having been no passenger service since 1944 but the track was replaced as far as Tytherington to provide a rail link to the Quarry. Two main lines still cross the area but the locomotives are diesel powered. The shrill whistle of the steam engines and the heavy thump-thump as a heavily laden coal train pulled away towards the tunnel after taking water is no longer heard and the oldsters can no longer state that it will rain soon because the clank of the Midland engines can be heard at Old Sodbury!

King Edmund, whom it will be remembered died at Pucklechurch in 946 AD, was remembered by the authorities when a new secondary modern school was opened on the new Stanshawes Estate in Yate in 1965. The new school replaced the one which had occupied the Old Grammar School at Sodbury and for a while the premises were occupied by a Technical School from Kingswood. When Comprehensive Education was introduced throughout most of the country, both King Edmunds and Chipping Sodbury Grammar School became Comprehensive Schools. With the housing developments in the north of Yate a new Comprehensive School, Brimsham Green, was built, bringing the number of such schools in the area to three. The Junior section of St John's C of E School was transferred from Hatters Lane to the back of the Old Grammar School buildings in January 1966. After a time, new buildings were built fronting onto Hounds Road in one of the Painter's Mead fields, and in moving into them the old St. John's C of E became Painter's Mead School. When the Technical School closed, the emphasis on the use to which the Old Grammar School was now put shifted from formal education to community activities. The empty buildings in Hatters Lane were reclaimed by the Hartley family and sold by them to the Free Masons who still own them today. It is here that the Sodbury Historical Society now meets.

When Major L.M. Harris, or "Monty" as he was more familiarly known, died in 1961, one of the town's more notable characters was lost. He used to find considerable pleasure in mentioning "The Ancient Borough of Chipping Sodbury" and was associated with a movement to explore the possibilities of re-establishing the mayor which for a number of reasons was found to be impracticable. His position in the town as a solicitor and Clerk to the Court and his membership of numerous other bodies, ensured a place for him in the memories of all who knew him.

Murray Dowding has been mentioned in several places and a few words about him is appropriate. He died in 1964 and will always be remembered as the local photographer and historian. Before the invention of the cinema and wireless, his magic lantern lectures regularly entertained people throughout the area on winter evenings. He also owned a general store which stood on the left of Arnold's Stores of which it eventually became a part.

His photographs of local scenes were taken over half a century and show people and places as they were years ago. The vast majority of the photographs in this book were taken by him. The original glass plate negatives are now held by Bailey's who own the Gazette newspaper group.

Murray Dowding and his family in the 1920s.
Photo courtesy Ray Pearce.

Since the 1950s Old and Chipping Sodbury have developed almost beyond recognition. The churches are now combined again but centred this time on Chipping Sodbury. The vicarage is located in a more modern building in Horseshoe Lane, replacing the more pretentious building which was demolished to make way for the offices of the Midland Electricity Board at the bottom of the Bowling Hill and both Churches are covered by means of a Curate.

Also at the bottom of the Bowling Hill but on the opposite side to the old Vicarage is Rock House, the one-time home of Mr. J. Mills and now a Nursing Home. A large car park for shoppers appeared just beyond the Church but is not well patronised, people preferring to jostle for space in the streets which have become more and more taken over by cars.

Houses and housing estates have been built all round the town except the north where there is a huge hole created by the quarrying activities of Amy Roadstone Corporation. While no more stone is being removed, what to do with the hole is still being debated. No doubt, in time, a decision will be reached.

At the present time (1994), visitors will find that the hamlet of Little Sodbury is divided into two sections. The part which includes the church and the manor nestles in the lee of the Cotswolds and the building that for a number of years was the school, run by Miss Prescott is now a private house.

As a glance at Harry Lane's map at the beginning of this book shows, the other section lies about a mile to the west and is called Little Sodbury

The Bowling Hill and Chipping Sodbury Vicarage in the 1960s. The gasometer for the gas works is just visible to the right of the Vicarage.

Rock House, at the junction of the Bowling Hill and Quarry Road.

End. It is located mostly at the entrance to the Common and is probably the larger of the two. In 1890, a small Baptist Chapel was built there.

There has been one more change in the boundary between the wards of the parish of Sodbury. Chipping Sodbury now extends to the entrance of the former railway station by the Bell Inn on the A432. The main boundaries of what was Old Sodbury and those of Little Sodbury, remain the same as they have been for hundreds of years.

Lyegrove House continues to thrive as a private residence but Little Sodbury Manor, though well maintained, has fallen somewhat in status. Dodington House, which for a time was open to the public, has been sold by the Codrington family into private hands and is again no longer available to the general public.

A new Charity Scheme has allowed the town lands to be sold. The sale price was considerable and this had to be invested with only the interest being available to spend. The Trust used much of the money to modernise the Town Hall to very great effect. Many will remember the dances held in the old Town Hall to the sounds of the Arcadians Dance Band, and while the Palais Glide was going on in the dance hall upstairs, those taking refreshments downstairs used to watch the old ceiling beams flexing. The modernisation, of course, was long overdue and the new Town Hall is very heavily used by all sorts of groups, not least by those putting on plays, musical shows and classical music evenings, for which the new premises are well suited.

There is still a Post Office in the town although with the building of a new Crown Post Office and Sorting Office on the new shopping centre

The Last Hundred Years

in Yate, its status has been reduced to that of a sub-post office similar to those at Old Sodbury and Station Road, Yate. There has been a Post Office in Chipping Sodbury since the middle of the 1700s on three known sites; on the south side of Broad Street between what is now the NatWest Bank and what used to be the Swan Cycle Shop (see the photograph on page 204), on the north side of Broad Street near the Royal Oak and, since 1907 or so, in its present position in Horse Street. Here it was run by Mr. and Mrs. Turner. In those days one means of communication was by telegram. These were delivered by boys on bicycles and it was a much sought after first job. It is worth noting that at one time, if a card with a ½d. stamp on it was posted early in the morning in the town, addressed to a friend at Old Sodbury, it would be duly delivered the same day.

On 9th May 1984 the Church members commemorated the 700th Anniversary of the Chapel of Ease being founded in Chipping Sodbury. Through the generosity of the ARC the church bells were overhauled and there was a special service at which the Bishop of Worcester preached as the then holder of the Office had done so long before.

Changes are taking place in the three Sodburys at an ever increasing pace and the present day Chipping Sodbury is very different from that of only fifty years ago. Many shops and family businesses, which existed from the last century, when a farthing was legal tender, have disappeared or changed with some of the old premises changing hands many times.

For nearly a thousand years the Sodburys were in the County of Gloucestershire. This changed in 1974 when they became part of the new County of Avon. Now, twenty more years on, the boundaries are under discussion again with various options being put forward. The final outcome will be known after this book has been published but almost certainly it will not please all of the people.

The three Sodburys, while changing rapidly, are still growing rather than declining and, with time, there will be a lot more history to record but that must be left to our children and our children's children. Perhaps it is appropriate to close with Percy Couzen's words:

TO BE CONTINUED.

APPENDICES

APPENDIX A

THE LAWS OF BRETEUIL

This is the law of Preston in Aumundrenesse which came from the Breton Law. The following translation represents the "Laws of Breteuil" as they applied to the townspeople of Preston, and according to the charter of William Crassus the liberties of the town of Sobbeburia were to be modelled on them.

Including the two just mentioned, some seventeen towns in England and Ireland were similarly endowed, including Hereford, Shrewsbury, Bideford, Ludlow and Welshpool. The laws varied in some degrees from place to place but the appearance of 12 pence (xii denarii) as a rent and a fine is universal.

The original is not sub-divided into paragraphs, each new feature being preceded by the word "item". For ease of reference these have been given numbers:

1. *So that they shall have a Guild mercatory, with hanse, and other customs and liberties belonging to such Guild; and so that no one who is not of that Guild shall make any merchandise in the said town, unless with the will of the Burgesses.*
2. *If any nativus (born bondman) dwell anywhere in the same town, and hold any land and be in the forenamed Guild and hanse, and pay loth and scoth with the same burgesses for one year and one day, then he shall not be reclaimed by his lord but shall remain free in the same town.*
3. *The Burgesses of Preston in Aumundrenesse shall have soc and sac, toll and them, and infangthef, and they shall be quit throughout all our land of toll, lastage, passage, pontage and stallage, and from Lenegeld and Danegeld, and Gaithwite and all other customs and exactions throughout all our land and dominion, as well in England as in other our lands; and that no sheriff shall intermeddle within the borough of Preston in Aumundrenesse concerning any*

plaint, or plea, or dispute, or any other thing pertaining to the aforesaid town, saving the pleas of the king's crown.

Miss Bateson was of the opinion that the three classes quoted above were not part of the original but were added later from some royal charter. Number three, in part, agrees with what are known as the Laws of Bristol later introduced by Prince John when Count of Mortain, and it may be significant that he once held Preston but forfeited it in 1194. Most Norman charters, however, contained a clause whereby a bondman could earn freedom by residence of a year and a day in a borough, so some such stipulation would appear in the original. The Liberties continue:

4. If any one wish to be made a burgess, he shall come into court and give to the Mayor (bailiff or reeve) 12d and shall take the burgage from the Mayor; afterwards he shall give to the Mayor's servant one penny, that he may certify him to have been made a burgess in court.
5. When any burgess shall receive his burgage, and it shall be a void place, the Mayor (bailiff or reeve) shall admit him, so that he shall erect his burgage within forty days, upon a forfeiture; if he does not erect it he shall be fined 12d.

(**Note**: The building required to be erected would be largely of wattle and daub; completion within the time specified would therefore not be impossible.)

6. When any burgess shall challenge his burgage against another and shall prove it to be his right, and the tenant who holds it shall prove that burgage to have been held without challenge several years and days, and by name for one day and one year shall prove him self to have been possessed thereof, and shall prove the same in court by the oath of two of his neighbours, or several witnesses, to have been so held; he who has proved by these may also make his own oath and hold it. Also he who shall by them so prove shall hold without contradiction of the claimant, whoever that claimant may be, for one year and one day within the realm of England.
7. If any burgess complain of any matter, and another shall challenge against him, the plaintiff for judgment shall name two witnesses, and shall have one of them at the day and term, and he may have any law worthy person for witness and another burgess; but the defendant against a burgess shall be put to his oath at third hand by his peers.

(**Note**: Shall have two witnesses beside himself).

8. No fine in the court shall exceed 12 pence, unless for toll evaded when it shall be 12 shillings.
9. A burgess shall be bound to come to no more than three port-motes yearly, unless he shall have a plea against him, and unless he shall

come to one great port-mote he shall be fined 12 pence.
(**Note:** The port-mote was a court held frequently by the burgesses for the regulation of town matters. The great port-mote became the court-leet held twice in the year only, about Easter and Michaelmas.)

10. *The steward shall collect the lord's rent at the four terms of the year, and shall go once for the rent, and another time if he pleases and shall pull down (or displace) the door of such burgage, and the burgess shall not replace his door until he have paid his debt, unless at the will of the steward.*

11. *If any burgess shall buy any bargain or any merchandise, and shall give earnest (deposit), and he who sold it shall repent of his bargain, he shall double the earnest; but if the buyer shall have handled the goods, he shall either have the merchandise or 5 shillings from the seller.*

12. *If any burgess shall have drink for sale, he shall sell according to the assize (i.e. fixed price) 'nisi in tonello reponatur'*
(**Note:** What the penalty was is not entirely clear).

13. *A burgess shall not come to the Mayor (or bailiff) after sunset for any claim, if he is unwilling, unless the claim is made by a stranger.*

14. *If a burgess shall allow credit to his lord, the lord shall pay within 40 days; but if he doth not, the burgess shall not further accommodate him until he shall pay.*

15. *No one can be a burgess unless he has a burgage of 12 feet in front.*
(**Note:** Miss Bateson was of the opinion that this represented a subdivision or a possible minimum; frontage being in multiples of a 12 ft. perch.)

16. *If a burgess shall sell for more than the assize, he shall be fined 12 pence but the purchaser shall not be punished. A burgess of the aforesaid court shall have duel (or) fire and water to make judgment.*
(**Note:** The translator gives the following notes on the second paragraph. In this clause we have two methods of purgation, or arbitrament of a quarrel, – the Anglo-Saxon one of ordeal, or great judgment, by fire or by water; and the Anglo-Norman one of the duel or judicial combat. Of the former there were chiefly two kinds. That of fire was either to pass barefoot or blindfold over nine glowing hot ploughshares, or to carry burning irons of specified weight in their hands; and as they escaped or suffered, they were adjudged innocent or guilty. The fire ordeal was chiefly reserved for freemen, and persons of better condition. The water ordeal was for bondmen and the servile classes. It was by either hot or cold water. In cold water (a great test of witches), the person floated if guilty, sank if innocent. In the other trial the accused plunged their bare

arms, or legs, into scalding water, and if, when withdrawn, the limbs were unhurt the parties were declared innocent. The judicial duel, or trial by combat, between the accuser and the accused, or two champions appointed in their places, was a Norman institution, and the original belief was that God would give victory to the right. It was sometimes continued until one killed the other. In the higher ranks the combat was usually with swords; in the lower with batons or staves an ell long. Before engaging the combatants made oath that they had neither eaten nor drunk, "nor done anything else by which the law of God may be depressed and the law of the devil exalted".)

17. *If anyone be taken for theft or breach of trust, and be condemned, he who sued shall do justice.*
(**Note:** The real intent of this clause seems to have been lost in the copying or translation.)

18. *The (?) of the said court may take for his toll, for one cart (or cart load) twopence; for one horse load one penny; and for a pack or bundle on a man's back one halfpenny; and for a man's load or burden one halfpenny; for a horse sold twopence; for an ox or a cow a penny; for five sheep a penny; for five swine one penny.*

19. *If a burgess wound another and they shall be willing to agree amicably, friends appointed between them may require for every out of sight cut the breadth of a thumb 4d, and for every visible wound 8d; and whoever is wounded may prove that he has lost by the wound, and the other shall pay him, and in like manner what the wounded has paid to the leech for healing the wound he shall repay; and the arms shall be brought to him, and he shall swear upon his arms that he has been wounded and such things have been done to him, so that, if his friends consent and approve; he may take what is offered to him.*
(**Note:** This item must be taken as it stands, the explanation being long and involved; suffice it to say that the clauses are thought to be of high antiquity.)

20. *If a burgess complain of another that he owes a debt to him, and the other shall acknowledge the debt, the Mayor (or Bailiff) shall command him to settle within eight days, upon pain of forfeiture 8 pence for the first week, 12 pence for the second, and so for every week until he shall settle. But, if he shall deny the debt, and the plaintiff hath witnesses, the other may deny by third hand upon oath, and then the plaintiff shall be fined 12 pence. And if the defendant shall come with his witnesses, and the plaintiff shall not come, the defendant shall be quit and the plaintiff in mercy; and if the plaintiff shall not be able to come and shall place anyone in his stead before,*

he may take or receive the defendant's oath. And no other plaint or forfeiture shall be set on any burgess in the court aforesaid in excess of 12 pence unless he shall be vouched to duel, and the duel may be adjudged to him but if the duel shall be adjudged to him and waged he shall be fined 40 shillings.

(**Note:** It was usual for the victor to fine the beaten man who survived.)

21. *If a burgess marry his daughter or grand-daughter to anyone, he may marry her without the licence of anyone.*
22. *A burgess may make a bake-oven upon his ground, and take for his baking; for one horse load of flour or meal one halfpenny, and he whose meal or corn it shall be shall find the wood to heat the oven.*
23. *The burgesses shall not go to the oven, or to the mill, or to the drying kiln, unless they please.*

(**Note:** It was not unknown for the lord to specify that drying, milling and baking should be carried out only at establishments owned by him for which he received a fee.)

24. *If anyone shall set another's 'turrellum' on fire, and it shall have one door, he shall give 40 pence, and if it shall have two doors half a mark.*

(**Note:** The consensus of opinion seems to be that a 'turrellum' was a drying place for grain.)

25. *If Burgesses by the common council of the neighbours shall travel for any business of the town, their expenses shall be rendered to them when they return.*
26. *If anyone cometh into the town, who ought to give toll, and if he shall withhold it beyond the market, he shall be fined 12 pence.*
27. *A stranger may not participate in any merchandise with the burgesses of the town.*
28. *When any burgess shall be desirous to sell his burgage, his next of kin is to buy that burgage of him before any other, and when it shall be sold and he hath not another burgage, when the buyer has taken possession he shall give 4 pence from the issue, but if he hath another burgage he shall give nothing.*
29. *If any burgess shall have offended in the matter of bread and ale (not having sold according to the fixed weight or measure or price), the first, second, or third time, he shall be fined 12 pence, but the fourth time, unless he pay a larger fine, he shall go to the cuck-stool.*

(**Note by the translator:** Three times an offender, as to bread and ale, escaped punishment by paying a fine of 12 pence, but the fourth time unless he paid a heavier fine, fixed by the Court-leet, he had to suffer the punishment of being ducked in a pond of filthy water by means of the cuck, or ducking, stool. This was a punishment imposed by law for great offenders against the assize of bread and ale, especially the latter, as ale was brewed chiefly by women and the ducking stool was used mainly for that sex. The bakers were more commonly punished by the pillory.)

30. If a burgess of the town shall die a sudden death, his wife and heirs shall quietly have all his chattels and land; so that neither his lord nor the justices may lay hands on the houses and chattels of the deceased, unless he shall have been publicly excommunicated, in which case, by the council of the priest and of the neighbours, they are to be expended in alms. The widow may marry whosoever she pleases.

31 & 32. If anyone shall demand a debt of another before the Mayor (or Bailiff), if he will not pay, the Mayor shall render to the plaintiff his debt from the community purse, and shall distrain the other by his chattels that he pay the debt or he shall seize the house into his hands.

33. The burgess shall not receive a claim from the Mayor (or Bailiff) on a market day unless the claim be made from a stranger.

34. A burgess gives no transit (i.e. does not pay transit toll on beasts passing through the town).

35. A burgess hath common pasture everywhere, except in corn fields, meadows and hayes.

36. If a burgess shall strike the mayor (or bailiff), or the mayor a burgess in court, and shall be convicted, he shall be liable to be fined.

37. If the mayor (or bailiff) shall strike anyone out of court he shall be in mercy of his own acknowledgment.

38. If a burgess shall strike the mayor (or bailiff) out of court he shall be liable to a fine of 40 shillings.

39. If a burgess overcome another, if he confess it, he shall forfeit 12 pence, if he deny he shall clear himself by his sole oath against witnesses; if beyond the court nothing.

40. If anyone bearing false coins shall be taken, the mayor (or bailiff) shall render to the king the false pennies, as many as there are, and shall account in the rent of his town for the goods, and deliver his body to our lord the King for judgment to be done, and his servants shall take quitance and have the pledges.

41. It shall not be lawful for regrators to buy anything which shall be sold on a market day to a regrator until the vesper bell shall be rung in the evening nor in any day of the week until that which he bought shall have been in town for one night.

42 & 43. A burgess shall not go in any expedition, except with the lord himself, unless he may be able to return the same day.
(2) If he shall be summoned when the justice of the town shall be in

the expedition (or circuit) and shall not go, and shall acknowledge himself to have heard, he shall give amends 12 pence, if he denies to have heard the edict, he shall clear himself by his own oath.
(3) But if he shall have ession (excuse for non-appearance) to wit, either by siege or his wife's lying in childbed of a child, or other reasonable ession he shall not pay. If he is going with the person of our lord the King he cannot have ession.

44. It is the custom of the borough that no burgess ought to be taken for an accusation by the lord or by the mayor (or bailiff) if he shall have sufficient pledges. In the case of a claim made of a burgess by a knight, whoever the knight may be; if duel be adjudged between the burgess and the knight, the knight may not find a champion unless it be found that he ought not to fight.
45. If the mayor (or bailiff) command any burgess by another than his own servant, and he shall not come, he shall make no amends.
46. No justice shall lay hands on the house or chattels of any deceased.
47. If anyone shall call a married woman a whore, and complaint be made there-of and witnesses be absent, he may clear himself by his own (or sole) oath, and if he cannot make oath he shall pay three shillings; and he by whom it was said shall do this justice, that he shall take himself by the nose and say he hath spoken a lie, and he shall be pardoned. There is the same judgment as to a widow.

APPENDIX B

SOME LEADING INHABITANTS OF CHIPPING SODBURY

Year	Canellano				
c.1179	Waltero	1653	Davis Tobias	1685	Legg Nich.
c.1225	Roberto	1654	Ellery William	1686	Smith Robt.
1247/8	see page 50	1662	Tilly Thomas	1687	?
		1663	Burcombe Sam.	1688	?
1275	**Bailiff** mentioned but not named	1664	Skinner Zach.	1689	Ludlow Chr.
		1665	Weare Thomas	**Bailiff**	
		1666	Trotman Thom.	1691	Ludlow Chr.
1308	**Mayor** John de Brugges	1668	Howles or Rowles John	1692	?
				1693	?
1315	– Attemulne (or Attehulle)	1669	Legg Nicholas	1694	Ludlow Chr.
		1673	Jones William	1696	Legg Nich.
1437	**Bailiff**	1674	Skinner John	1699	Wickham J.
	Brugge John	1676	Smith Stephen	1704	Higgs Wm.
1443	Lye Walter	1677	Wickham John	1705	Prout Dan.
1466	Bolatre William	1679	Wickham John	1706	Bingham Jos.
1522	Taylor Thomas	1680	Wickham John	1707	Hooper Th.
1546	Peres Robert	1681	Wickham John	1708	Webb Jos.
1572	Wyrriett John	1682	Wickham John	1709	Watts Jn.
1575	Summers Anthony	1683	Smyth Stephen	1710	Bingham Jos.
1576	Baynham Thomas	1684	?	1711	Ogborne Rob.
1530	Harris Robert (P)	1685	?	1712	Ogborne Rob.
1581	Welsh Maurice (P)	1686	?	1713	Ogborne Rob.
1582	Somers William	1687	?	1714	Ogborne Rob.
1583	Box Robert	1688	Skinner J.,	1715	Blake Rich.
1584	Edwards Thomas	1689	Webb Stephen	1716	Blake Rich.
1585	Collins Thomas (P)	1690	Webb Stephen	1717	Blake Rich.
1592	Warner Robert	**Mayors**		1718	Edwards Hy.
1629	Webb William	1680		1719	Edwards Hy.
1632	Haynes Robert (P)	Oct.	Burcombe S.	1720	Burton Rob.
1635	Wickham William	1681	Cabell R.	1721	Harvey Rob.
1636	Cabbell Richard	1682	Tily T. (P)	1726	Allaway Rob.
1642	Wickham James	1683	Orchard B.	1727	Allaway Rob.
1643	Legg Richard	1684	Skinner J.	1729	Clarke David

270

Appendices

1730	Clarke David	1780	Wallis Joseph	1823	Watkins C.
1731	Hillier Hy.	1781	Nash Isaac	1824	Higgs Will.
1732	?	1782	Ludlow Eben.	1825	Higgs Will.
1733	Hillier W.	1783	Tovey Rich.	1826	Higgs Will.
1736	Roden M.	1784	Hopkins Jos.	1827	Bruton C.
1737	Bence John	1785	Wallis Jos.	1828	
1739	Bence Rich.	1786	Tovey Rich.	to	Dutfield S.B.
1740	Aldin Will.	1787	Hopkins Jos.	1837	
1741	Higgs Dan.	1788	Ludlow Dan.	1846	Arnold J.
1742	Bence Rich.	1789	Wickham J.	1847	Trenfield J.
1744	Hulbert Th.	1790	Ludlow Eben.	1862	Limbrick I.
1745	Roden Jno.	1791	Tanner Arthur	1866	Higgs Will.
1746	Boddily J.	1792	Higgs Josiah	1869	Arnold Rich.
1747	Knapp John	1793	Harvey Will.	1874	Grace Alfred
1748	Tily Will.	1794	Tovey Rich.	1879	Morgan Geo.
1749	Bence Rich	1795	Higgs Dan.	1880	Limbrick E.O.
1750	Boone Th.	1796	Ludlow Dan.	1881	Greenman R.
1751	Pike John	1797	Hiatt H.	1883	
1752	Pike John	1798	Wickham J.	to	Trenfield J.D.
1756	Wallis James	1799	Tily T.	1886	

Under Bailiff

1757	Ludlow Daniel	1800	Tily Will.	1851	Holborrow G.
1758	Adey Henry	1801	Harvey Rob.	1854	Roberts J.
1759	Ludlow Daniel	1802	Bruton Moses	1858	Amos I.
1760	Wickham J. (Jnr)	1803	Williams H.	1859	Caradine Chas.
1761	Harvey Will.	1804	Whittington G.	1860	Thompson W.A.
1762	Hardwicke George	1805	Whittington G.	1861	Alsop J.
1763	Tanner Arthur	1806	Williams H.	1864	Carter J.
1764	Winstone Will.	1807	Williams H.	1866	Caradine Jos.
1765	Higgs Josiah	1808	Harvey Rob.	1867	Short James
1766	Higgs Thomas	1809	Tily Will	1873	Morgan A.
1767	Brooke Thomas	1810	Wickham Ja.	1875	Trotman Will.
1768	Wallis Joseph	1811	Hiatt Jos.	1876	Tily Th.
1769	Nash Isaac	1812	Hiatt Jos.	1877	Tily Th.
1770	Ludlow Eben.	1813	Williams H.	1878	Chandler J.
1771	Brooke Th.	1814	Arnold R.	1879	Sweatman W.
1772	Wallis Joseph	1815	Knight Th.	1882	Ball J.
1773	Ludlow Daniel	1816	Knight Th.	1883	Tily Will.
1774	Wickham James	1817	Watkins Chas.	1884	Matthews W.
1775	Harvey Will.	1818	Tily John	1885	Russell G.
1776	Tanner Arthur	1819	Limbrick I.	1886	Wilkins Ch.
1777	Winstone Will.	1820	Limbrick I.		
1778	Higgs Josiah	1821	Fowler J.		
1779	Higgs Thomas	1822	Fowler J.		

APPENDIX C

POOR RATE 1727
Chipping Sodbury Borough

A monthly pound rate made by us whose names are hereunto Subscribed for collecting of money for the relief of the Poor of the said Burrough this 8th day of May, 1727.

		£	s	d
1	Robert Allaway, Bayliffe			2
2	The same for the George or landlord			6
3	Wm. Russell for ye Hat and Feather			2
4	Henry Edwards for late White's			3
5	The same for Adams Leaze			4
6	The same for a burgage			2
7	The same for ye White Horse			4
8	Wm. Tanner for Packer's Leaze			3
9	The same for his own			2
10	The same for ye White Hart Inn			4
11	The Widow Richards			2
12	Stephen Ludlow's Executors			1
13	Daniel Flower's do.			3
14	John Somers			1½
15	Henry Savage for his house			1
16	Tho. Winter for his house and burgage			3
17	Nicholas White			1
18	The same for ye Star			2
19	Jn. Clark for late Naishes			2
20	Tobias Walker or tenant			3
21	The Widow Smith			6
22	Robert Deek for ye house and burgage			3
23	Robert Tanner			2
24	The Same for Humphreys			1
25	Sir Wm. Codrington for ye Goat Inn			4
26	The same for Flint's Closes			5
27	Thos. Musgrove for Toveys			2

Appendices 273

28	Jn. Roden	1
29	The same for Portcullis Inn	5
30	James Dorrington or tenant	2
31	Daniel Burcombe	4
32	Mr James Bush or tenant	3
33	Tho. Hulbert	1
34	Isaac Hulbert	1
35	The same and Aaron Isaac	1
36	Wm. Audlin	2
37	The same for his late father's	1
38	Robert Wallington	1
39	Samuel Wickham or Tenant	2½
40	James Neale or Tenant for Painter's Mead	2½
41	James Wickham	1
42	Andrew Hellier	2
43	Robert Ogborne or Tenant	6
44	Daniel Prout's Executors-	7
45	Charles Beams and for his own	2
46	John Russell	2
47	Wm. Cheddar	1
48	Henry Pierce or tenant	4
49	Joseph Power	2
50	James Neale for his late father's	2
51	Wm. Dorrington for late Bishop's	2
52	The same for his own and the Horseshoe	5
53	The Widow Walter	3
54	John Barkley	1
55	Thos. Hellier	1
56	The Widow White	1
57	Mr. Robert Burcombe	8
58	The same for his own and Long Leaze	7
59	The same for ye Bell Inn	8
60	Peter Hobbs or tenant	2
61	Jn. Wickham or tenant for a burgage	1
62	The Widow Tilly for ye Crown (*now Hill House*)	5
63	Wm. Smith or tenant	1
64	Geo. Iles for part of Warners	1
65	Gabriel Amos for the other part	1
66	John Clark	1
67	Hannah Tilly or tenant	1
68	Stephen Clark	4
69	The same for late White's	1
70	The Widow Weare for ye Mill (**N.B**. *Brook St.*)	3

71	Ed. Bayly for ye Queens Head	3
72	Wm. Belshire late Darks	1
73	Stephen Clarke late Stiff's	1
74	Ju. Pritchett for ye New House	1
75	The same for ye houses at Brook & Ludlows	3
76	The Widow Champney's	2
77	Joseph Welch	1
78	David Clark	2
79	Hester Tilly or tenant	1
80	John Curtis	2
81	Nath. Hopkins for a burgage	1
82	Samuel Blake for part of late Baynhams	2
83	Thomas Neale for the other part	1
84	Edward Bowman	5
85	The Widow Powell or tenants	3
86	Thos. Flower for part of late Long's	1
87	Thos. Flower for late Stiff's	1
88	The same for a burgage late Skinner's	1
89	Arthur Sargent	2
90	Ben. Hardwicke – Peter Hardwicke – Jo.Hardwicke	5
91	Ebenezer Ludlow	2
92	Daniel Webb's administrators	1
53	Jn. Bence for late Henry Webb	2
94	Henry Hillier	2
95	Richard Tresher	6
96	Henry Wickham and Edith Barton's Executors	3
97	Joseph Dorney's Executors	3
98	Henry Cummins	1
99	Henry Allsop's Administrators	1
100	Mary Wickham or tenant	4
101	Edward Pinyon	3
102	The Widow Jones for ye Swan	4
103	Wm. Wickham	8
104	Edmund Chapp or tenant	4
105	James Wallis	4
106	Francis Cross	1
107	The same for late Hellier's	1
108	The same for his own	2½
109	Josiah Weare	2½
110	John Watts	3
111	Jn. Russell for late Collin's	2
112	Daniel Tanner	2
113	Joseph Webb's Executor or Tenant	5

Appendices

114	Peter Weare or tenant	2
115	The Widow Dorney and others	4
116	The same for Mag Payne's	2
117	The Widow Harvey	2
118	Thos. Prewett for Webb's Burgage	1½
119	Thomas Musgrove for late Skinner's	2½
120	Mary Cowley or tenant for a burgage	1½
121	John Hulbert	2
122	John Barnes	3
123	Cicily Dowling	1
124	Nathaniel Bennett (abated by age)	1½
125	Nehemiah Naish	1
126	Robert Naish	1
127	John Tovey	1
128	The Widow Coombs	1
129	Wm. Winstone	1
130	Wm. Harvey	1
131	Wm. Emmett	1
132	Thos. Blanchett	1
133	Solomon Roberts	1
134	William Higgs	1
135	Arthur Watts	1
136	Philip Niblet	1
137	John Prout	1
138	Abraham Tanner	1
139	Thos. Burcombe	1
140	Griffith Gwynn	1
141	Simon Smith	1
142	James White	1
143	Solomon Davis	1

£1   7   11½

This rate on the foregoing pages is allowed by us.
Robert Allaway, Baylliffe.   Solomon Roberts, Church warden
                                    Henry Alsop, Church warden
Charles Beams, Andrew Hellier, Overseers
P. Hardwicke, Dan. Burcombe, Robert Wallington,
Wm. Tanner, Richard White.

APPENDIX D

POOR RATE 1727
Old Sodbury

	£	s	d
Edward Stephens Esq.,		17.	6½
Mr Richard Stokes, or tenant		3.	0
William Hughes, Vicar		5.	0
William Stephens		6.	8
John Parker, for the Parks		14.	6
Richard Adey, for the Crews		2.	
for his dwelling house		2.	4
for the Marsh Leazes and the land in the fields that belong to them			10
for Burcomb's Grounds			6½
for the lease land			3
for the Leys part of Kingrove farm			9
William Sainsons for Combsend		8.	3
Mr. Dolling		4.	11
Richard Sanders or tenant		2.	0
Mr. Oakey for Hamstead		8.	0
Daniel Watts for ? Rickholds			7
Robert Skinner for ? Edpeans			8
John Parker for Trumans		3.	5½
James Smart for the Parsonage		7.	0
Henry White		1.	4
Jeremiah North		1.	2
Edmund Chapp		5.	6
John Garraway		1.	5
Robert Tanner for Barnetts			7
Ralph Walker			4
John Mead			8
Robert Webb, for the Mill			8
Jeremiah Russell		1.	2
Edward Watts		1.	0
Charles Power			3
Mrs. Waller, or tenant, for Bucketts Hill		4.	3

The Widow Woodward		1.	3
do.			5
James Smart			11
John Clarke			2
Nicholas White			2
John Cadle		1.	3
Robert Ogborn		2.	0½
Daniel Burcombe		1.	3
Daniel Burcombe, for Trinity			9
Jane Biggs			7
The Widow Nichols or tenant			6
Thos Bishopp		1.	6
Mrs. Ludlow			8
Thomas Burcombe			6½
Samuel Hardwicke			2
Peter Hardwicke	for Trinity	1.	0
	for the footbridge		3
Nathan Corbut for Bellmead			4
William Tanner		2.	9
Samuel Ellory			2
David Clarke for Emmotts			1½
William Hignoll & Hester			9
John Dowey			4½
Peter Hardwicke for Pinsmead			1
Tobias Walker for Mensmead			8
Joseph Higgs for the ffairy grounds		1.	6
The Widow Prout for the Roach		1.	0
Robert Alaway for the Notthills (*Nottles*)		1.	4½
Tobias Walker for the Notthills (*Nottles*)		1.	3
Sir Wm. Codrington		1.	0
Henry Cummings for Stanly			4
Robert Tanner for Brandashes			6
Joseph Hardwicke			8
Henry Edwards			1½
Robert Webb for Barley Close		1.	10
Joseph Higgs for Norris' Gorlands			7
John Shellard			9
Wm. Dorrington for Culverhill			7
Robert Burcombe			1½
Kingrove Farm divided			
	John Bennet	3.	9½
	Mrs. Waller or tenant	1.	7
	Wm. Harvey for Howmead	1.	0

James Wickham for Kenly		8
James Wickham (see also Rich. Adey)		4
Blanchards Farm divided		
Wm. Wickham		9¾
Ed. Watts		11
David Clarke		6½
Chas. Power		8
John Parker for Gorlands	1.	1½
£8	**1.**	**2¼**

As far as can be seen this represents a weekly rate paid quarterly.

APPENDIX E

VOTERS AT ELECTIONS IN 1776 AND 1811
Old Sodbury

The undermentioned freeholders from the Sodburys voted at the Election in 1776.
Chipping Sodbury

Alden Thomas	Hardwicke John	Pearce Thomas
Beams William	Harvey William	Rice William
Belsere Xr.	Hellier John	Short George
Blanshard Thomas	Hicks George	Smith Jeremiah
Burcomb William	Higgs David	Smith William
Clark James	Higgs Josiah	Tovey R.
Clark Robert	Higgs Thomas	Wallis Joseph
Cox Thomas	Higgs William	Walter John
Crew Thomas	Hopkins Nath.	Warner William
Day John	Jones William	White Thomas
Dorrington Thomas	Ledyard William	Withers Walter
Dyke Thomas	Ludlow Daniel	Withers William
Fletcher William	Ludlow Ebenezer	Wood Joseph (Senr.)
Hardwicke George	Nash John	
		(41)

Old Sodbury

Brown James	Gingell Henry	Parker John
Burcomb Thomas	Holbrow Francis	Shellard Edward
Cadell Cyrus	Jones Thomas	White Henry
Chapp Edmund	Ludlow James	Wickham James
		(12)

Little Sodbury

Coates Rev. R.	Walker Toby	(2)

279

This is a record of those who exercised their franchise and not necessarily a complete record of those entitled to vote.

The undermentioned freeholders from the Sodburys voted at the Election in 1811.

Chipping Sodbury

Alden William	Hook Edward	Simons John
Alden James	Hulbert Thomas	Smith John
Arnold Richard	Iles John	Tanner Arthur
Beams William	Isaac Samuel	Tiley William
Carpenter William	Isaac William	Tovey John
Clarke Thomas	Morgan Joseph	Tovey R.
Clarke Thomas	Morgan George	Vizard William
Cox Thomas	Morgan Samuel	Warner Thomas
Courtier Samuel	Parry Robert	Watts Thomas
Crew Thomas	Phillips John	Wickham James
Hiatt Joseph	Rice William	Wickham William
Higgs Daniel	Short George	(35)

Old Sodbury

Burcomb Thomas	Higgs John	Parker Philip
Codrington John	Holborrow Francis	Rodway Richard
Dixon Rev. William	Jages Edward	White James
Dutfield Joseph	Moreton Oliver	(11)

Little Sodbury

Hall Richard	Rice Edward	Slade William
		(3)

Although some of the names may be the same as those appearing on the list for 1776 it must be remembered that it was common practice to give the eldest son the same Christian name(s) as his father, a system that still applies in the New England States in America.

APPENDIX F
TRADES AND PROFESSIONS IN CHIPPING SODBURY

Some of the trades, professions and callings followed by the inhabitants of the Sodburys before 1800 with the year when they are first mentioned. No doubt they existed before the date given and there were many more that have not been recorded.

Apothecary	1708	Ludlow Christopher	
Attorney/Solicitor	1681	Powell John	
Baker	1545	Burley Edward	
Bankers	1795	the Ludlows	
Brazier	1707	Osgood Philip	
Butcher	1677	Six are named	
Carpenters and Joiners	1603	Boxe Henry	
Chandler tallow	1731	Harvey William	
Cheese Factor	1731	Clarke Stephen	
China Shop	1795	Wright William	
Clothier	1609	Webb George	
Coach Operator	1796	Cox Thomas	
Coal Miner	1719	White John	
Cooper	1731	Hulbert Thomas	
Currier	1795	Taylor S. Watts T.	
Cutler	1580	Bircombe John	
Draper and Mercer	1592	Webbe George	
Felt maker	1682	Hooper Thomas	
Grocer	1795	Philips Thomas	
Inn-keeper	1576	"The Bell" Walker Anne	
Maltster	1694	Edney Stephen	
Miller	1682	Brook St. Weare Thomas	
Sadler	1625	Peaslie Robert	
Salt refiner	1795	Muffett Robert	
Shopkeeper	1437	Bocher Thomas	
Shoemaker	1545	Wrighte John	
Smith	1708	Aldin William	
Tailor/merchant	1694	three mentioned	
Tanner	1557	Norris Richard	
Tiler	1609	Wite Edmund	
Weaver	1520	Colymore Richard	

APPENDIX G

SOME OF THE 687 PEOPLE LIVING IN OLD SODBURY IN 1805

Andrews John (Hays Farm)
Arthurs Sam.
Arthurs Tho.
Ayliffe James
Ayliffe Tho.
Ayliffe Wm.*

Batchelor Ann
Beazer Wm.
Belshire Chris.
Bennett Anthony
Bennett David
Bennett Sarah
Bennett Wm.
Bishop Wm.*
Bowley Wm.
Boy Thos.
Brett Chas.
Brooke Mrs. (Brooke House)
Brooke Philip

Cam James
Carpenter Wm.
Carter John
Chappey John
Cleter John (Mill O.S.)
Coates James
Codrington John
Cole Robert (Parks Farm)
Cooper Isaac
Cowley Isaac

Dee Joseph

Dobson Nathan
Dowding Thos. Senr.
Dowding Thos. Jnr

Farr D.
Field Joseph
Ford Joseph
Frankcomb Thos.
Fry Henry

Garraway Anne
Garraway Hannah
Garraway Richard
Garraway Jane
Godwin Charles
Godwin Edward
Goulding Thos.
Griffin Thos.*

Hall Job
Hanks John
Harford Thomas
Hartley David (Lyegrove)
Hatherell James ¥
Hatherell John¥
Hayward William
Hewitt Daniel
Higgs Lewis (shopkeeper)
Higgs Mary
Higgs William
Hitchings R.
Holborow Francis Sr.
Holborow Francis Jn.

Holloway James

Iles James
Iles Thomas
Isaac Elias

Jacques Edward
Jones Thomas

Keepen John
Kilminster William
King Vincent
King William

Lait Thomas
Langley Giles
Lemon Richard
Leonard William
Light Charles
Light Hester
Light Robert
Limbrick John*
Lockstone Guy
Lockstone Reuben
Lovegrove Joseph

Matthews William
Messenter John
Morton Oliver

Neale John
Nelson Mary
Neve Chas. Rev.

Appendices

Orchard David	Reeves William	
	Roach Arthur	Thompson Richard
Parker John	Rodway Richard	Tily Samuel
Parker William	Rumming John	Tily William
Powney William	Rumming William	Titcombe John
Prior Thomas (Cow Mill)		Tyler William
Pitchard William	Search Moses*	
Pullin William	Shell Martha	Watts Mrs.
	Shell - Miss	Watts Thomas
Raggot Jacob	Shuggar James	Whitchell Robert
Raggot Shupannah	Simmons Sarah	White James
Raggot William	Skeates Thomas	Wilkins Richard
Higgs Daniel	Smith Thomas	Woodward John
Rallings W. (Rawlings)	Stafford Jacob	
Redwood Robert	Sturge Toby Walker	Young Wm.
Reed J.	(Trinity Est.)	(pt Trinity Estate)

¥Lyegrove Farm
*It is probable that Limbrick John occupied Blanchards Farm and the others marked * lived in the adjoining cottages.

APPENDIX H

OLD SODBURY C OF E SCHOOL

When this school was founded it was held in a building which stood in what is now the churchyard on the corner of Cotswold Lane. There was only one room of any size and this was long, narrow, ill-lit and had a stone floor. It was cold and difficult of access for the infants.

In 1857 the head master was Mr. H.W. Reeve. Whether he was the first to hold the post and when he took up his duties is not known.

After complaints by HM Inspectors and others, it was decided to build a new schoolroom, 50ft. x 18ft. on land given by the lord of the manor. The existing large room came into use on 13th September 1869 and the old building was demolished.

In 1864 the oldest pupil was less than nine years of age. George Gowen could not have been much older when he was withdrawn to keep Combsend Turnpike Gate, wherever that was, in 1866. A little time before a young girl left to go to Lady Codrington's school.

Every year the children had a holiday on the occasion of the dinner held by the Old Sodbury Sick & Burial Club, who also organised an annual procession and fête. These events continued into the present century.

It is to be assumed that quill pens began to go out of use after the master received a box of steel nibs in June 1868.

In October 1869 Mr. Reeve organised evening classes for those adults who had not had the opportunity to attend a school in their childhood.

The staff in 1871 consisted of the headmaster, a pupil teacher in his second year (W.J. Bishop), a monitor (J. Gowen) and Mrs. Reeve, who took charge of the sewing instruction. Their salaries for the year totalled £78 2s. 6d and the total cost of running the school for that period was £110. Elementary education was not free and all those attending were required to pay in accordance with the following scale, which represents the revised figures applicable from April 1873.

Farmers & Tradesmen		Labourers	
One child	4s. 0d per qtr.	one child	2d per wk.
two children	7s. 0d per qtr.	two children	4d per wk.
rest each	2s. 0d per qtr.	rest each	1d per wk.

These are different from the charges in Chipping Sodbury where there seems to have been a flat rate of 3d per child per week irrespective of the position of the parents. There is no record of an allowance in respect of a long family.

Prizes were given for regular attendance at the correct times and throughout the records emphasis is laid on the correct marking of the registers. Some rewards were in cash as is revealed by the following rules:

> *Each child attending 10 times during the week will receive a ticket marked 'A', ten such tickets will at the end of the quarter be worth threepence. Each child attending nine times will receive a ticket marked 'B', ten such tickets being redeemed by master by payment of one penny at the end of the quarter.*

The school had a holiday on 22nd July 1884 because the choir went on an outing as far away as Bournemouth! They no doubt went by horse brake to Yate station and must have spent a number of hours in travelling.

Jonathan Pearce, who had succeeded in getting part time work as a postman, was sufficiently interested to continue at school where he was unable to arrive before 10am and in consequence did not receive a 'mark'.

There was quite a modern touch in 1888 when the children were photographed. One wonders whether a print still survives hidden away somewhere.

School fees in elementary schools were abolished in September 1890 but strangely enough this does not earn a mention in the log book.

Mr. Jacoby, who was living at Lyegrove House in 1895, displayed a considerable degree of benevolence by providing hot soup for the children on Tuesdays and Fridays during the winter.

By 1898 arrangements had been made to divide the large room into two and there was also an external addition made of wood and measuring 30ft. x 16ft.

During the construction of the new stretch of railway and the tunnel the number of children attending the school increased substantially. Many of the workmen brought their families with them and they lived in what was termed the hutments.

In 1909 there was considerable concern when a case of smallpox was discovered in the village and there was a rush to be vaccinated. Fortunately an outbreak did not occur.

There are echoes of the Great War in the following entry for 2nd November 1914:

> *Admitted the family of Fermont, Belgian refugees, also family of Sargent.*

At some time the temporary wooden building was replaced by a more substantial building and the school became as it is today, with the addition of yet another temporary structure in April 1966 to accommodate the increase in numbers brought about by the transfer of the children from Tormarton.

The following have filled the position of head teacher:

1857	–	Sept. 1882	H.W. Reeve
Oct. 1882	–	July 1883	W.J.G. Boole
Aug. 1883	–	Aug. 1885	H. Coleman
Sept. 1885	–	Aug. 1889	F.E. Child
Sept. 1889	–	June 1896	H. Rowe
June 1896	–	Feb. 1897	C.B. Hardy
Feby. 1897	–	July 1912	G. Millership
Aug. 1912	–	Aug. 1927	J.D. Iles
Sept. 1927	–	Aug. 1942	A.J. Ridler
Nov. 1942	–	Dec. 1946	E.J. Hughes
Jan. 1947	–	Aug. 1952	C.G. Stokes
Sept. 1952	–	April 1954	Miss G. Parker
May 1954	–	1981	Mrs. V. Slocombe
1981	–		Mr. K. Harris

APPENDIX I

MANOR OF OLD SODBURY
Jurors on the Court Leet, 1845

List of persons summoned to serve on the Jury of the Court Leet and Court Baron of Winchcombe Henry Howard Hartley Esq., to be holden Tuesday 21st October 1845.

Name	Residence	Calling
James Hatherell	Lyegrove	Farmer
Moses Higgs	Hampstead Farm	Farmer
Isaac Holberrow	Old Sodbury	Farmer
William Higgs	Horwood Gate	Farmer
William Cole	Parks Farm	Farmer
George Till	Old Sodbury	Farmer
Daniel Park	Old Sodbury	Farmer
James Adams	Old Sodbury	Mealman
George Smith	Old Sodbury	Farmer
Joseph Iles	Old Sodbury	Farmer
Guy Leonard	Old Sodbury	Farmer
Thomas Dowding	Old Sodbury	Farmer
John Orchard	Old Sodbury	Farmer & Wheelwright
Robert Collins	Old Sodbury	Inn Keeper
George Dowding	Old Sodbury	Malster
Joseph Ralph	Old Sodbury	Mealman
Thomas Brookes	Old Sodbury	Carpenter
Thomas Curthoys	Old Sodbury	Baker
Edward Isaac (the younger)	Old Sodbury	Cordwainer
Thomas Eyles (the younger)	Old Sodbury	Quarryman
Moses Higgs	Bucketts Hill	Farmer
Stephen Sugar	Bucketts Hill	Thatcher
James Cam	Bucketts Hill	Coal Haulier
Isaac Hatherall	Lye Grove	Farmer
William Russell	Lye Grove	Blacksmith

In respect of 1846 add:-

Josiah Ballinger	Old Sodbury	Innkeeper v. Robert Collins
Nathaniel Hughes	Old Sodbury	Farmer v. ?

APPENDIX J

DESCENT OF THE MANOR AND BOROUGH

Descent of the Manor:

Saxon Days	Sopanbyrg – Cheopan (place of selling) Byrg (strongpoint).
Doomesday	Sopeberie – Cheopan (place of selling) Byrg (strongpoint).
By 1170	Sobburia – founding of New Town.
	Sobburia Mercato. Chipping Sodbury (prefix from Cheopan above).
About 1500	Sodbury.

Owners or Tenants:

c.750	Eanbald (part) then Eastmund (part).
888	Eanoth, Aelfred, Aelstan. (part).
	Eanoth (rented part).
1066	Brictric.
1066	Matilda, Queen to William the Conqueror, steward Humfrid.
1080	Count Odo, Earl of Holderness, Earl of Albemarle.
1096	Stephen Crassus, Earl of Holderness, Earl of Albemarle, also known as "Le Gras" and "Le Gros".
1127	William I. (son of Stephen) Earl of Holderness, Earl of Albemarle, founder of the New Town of Sobberi, dead by 1179.
by 1195	William II Crassus (brother of William I).
By 1127	William III Crassus (son of William II, nephew of William I).
by 1285	William IV Crassus. Exchange Sobburi with De Weyland for lands in Ireland.
1296 died	De Clare Gilbert (in chief, De Weyland could have been tenant).
1307 died	De Clare Joan (son Gilbert a junior).
1314 died	De Clare Gilbert II, killed in Battle of Bannockburn.
1314	Ellinore, wife of Hugh le Despenser executed for treason.
1326	Lands confiscated but returned to widow as they were inheritance.

1337 died	Ellinore.
	Hugh le Despenser, her son by first husband uncertain.
1363 died	Alice Burnell.
1375	Edward le Despenser
	Thomas son of Edward then aged 2. Executed for treason.
1400/1	Lands forfeited but returned to widow Constance.
	Isabella (daughter) married second husband the Earl of Warwick.
	Anne (daughter) married Earl of Salisbury. On the death of her brother he became, in her right, Earl of Warwick. Killed Battle of Barnett.
	Anne Countess of Warwick. Lands forfeited to Edward IV returned by Henry VII on condition she willed them to him.
1487	Henry VII.

APPENDIX K

DESCENT OF LITTLE SODBURY MANOR AND COMBINED MANORS

Descent of Little Sodbury Manor
Name: Pre-conquest unknown. Around 1066 Sobburi Parva then Little Sodbury.

Owners or tenants:
Pre-conquest   Aluuward, Saxon nobleman.
1066   Bishop Maminot let to his nephew, Hugh.
               Hugh Maminot. No record, as far as writer knows.
1220 approx.   The Bissop family.
1300   Sir John Bissop.
1398   Richard de Alerdine & Edith his wife.
               Stanshaw family
               Richard Forster
1491   John Walshe
1547/8 died   Sir John Walshe. Henry VlII granted Sodbury manor including the borough.
1556 died   Maurice Walshe.

Combined manors Great Sodbury (including borough) Little Sodbury
1547/8   Maurice Walshe (died from injuries received in thunderstorm).
1556   Nicholas Walshe (son).
1578   Henry Walshe killed in duel ? date.
               Walter Walshe sold property to
               Thomas Stephens.
c.1630   Edward Stephens.
by 1677   Thomas Stephens.
1728 died   Edward Stephens, manor passed to niece whose son was Robert Packer, who married daughter & heiress of Sir Richard Winchcombe.
               Elizabeth (daughter) married David Hartley.

1757 died	David Hartley.
	Winchcombe Henry Hartley (adopted mother's maiden name as Christian name). Resided at Bucklebury, Berks.
c. 1835	Howard Winchcombe Henry Hartley came to live at Lyegrove.
c. 1880 died	Howard Winchcombe Henry Hartley.
	? ?
early 1900's	Duke of Beaufort. Several tenants
Around 1927	Earl Westmoreland
	Countess Westmoreland
	Private Person

APPENDIX L

INCUMBENTS IN THE PARISH CHURCHES

Incumbents Of Old And Chipping Sodbury
What is now Old Sodbury was founded, or perhaps refounded, about 1120

1225 Ricardo
1277 Walter

Chapel of Ease founded at what is now Chipping Sodbury AD 1284, Thereafter these priests were officiating at one or the other or both. The context in which they appear does not make it clear.

1290 Nicholas	1330 Richard (son of Simon) Uppedowne
1297 William	? to 1401 Philip Scherer
1300 Maurice	1401 Thomas Baker
1308 John de Lyneham (P)	1522 Maurice Berne (Curate)
1314 John de Hampstede	1525 Henry Jones

January 1542/3 PRO Pat: Roll 33 Henry VIII. Rectory of Old Sodbury and advowson thereof granted to Dean & Chapter of the Cathedral church of Worcester previously belonged to Priory of St. Mary, Worcester.

1543 Thomas Sargeant, Hy Dawson	1676/1721 John North
1545 John Glover	1721 Allen Sherwood
1546 HumphreyWebley, Wm.Ramsey	1722/68 Wm.Hughes (also Rector Dodington from 1750)
1547/57 John Bawle	
1568 Wm. Ramsey	1768/69 Wm. Harley also Rector of Everley)
1568/1600 Thomas Howell (alias Powel)	
1601/45 Marmaduke Chapman	1769/86 Philip Duval
1645/59 Edward Potter	1786/95 Chris. Nicholls
1659/76 William Sheen (P)	1795/1822 Chas. Neeve

Robert Coates, Rector of Little Sodbury 1720-83 was Curate at Chipping Sodbury for at least part of that time.

It appears Chipping Sodbury became a separate ecclesiastical parish in 1822.

Old Sodbury
1822/29 Charles Neeve
1829/31 John Davidson
1831/33 Godfrey Faussett
1833/37 Thomas Blofield
1837/51 Robert N. Raikes
1851/55 Allen Wheeler
1856/1905 Robert S. Nash
1905/16 Daniel Wrigley
1916/21 William C. Curtis
1921/28 Chas. H. Gough
1928/55 Henry N. Burgess
1955/61 Sidney Thomas
1962/68 Reginald Barry Jupp
1968 Peter H. Thorburn, MA

Chipping Sodbury
1822/57 Thomas Smith
1857/59 Henry Clelan
1859/61 John Clifford
1861/66 Wm. R. Lawrence
1866/77 Jonas P.F. Davidson
1877/1918 William H.P. Harvey
1918/20 Fred. C. Townson
1921/25 Albert E. Addenbrooke
1926/31 Thomas Longley
1931/37 Alex. G. Robinson
1938/46 Ralph H. Charlton
1946/9 James Gilchrist
1949/53 Derrick M. Brookes

Combined
1955/61 Sidney Thomas
1962/68 Reginald Barry Jupp
1968/74 Peter H. Thorburn, MA
1974/89 Barry Finch
1989 Neville Jacobs, LTH

Incumbents Of Little Sodbury
*AD 1300 12th Nov. John of Sywardley acolyk was instituted to the Chapel of Little Sodbury by the Bishop of Worcester on the presentation of Sir John, called Byssop, Knt.

*1305 John of Sywardley ordained priest.
*1375 John Buthe
*? John Caas
*1542 John Clerke
1584 John Savage
1600 Thomas Hook, MA
? John Dutton
1612/3 George Boswell, MA
1619 ?
1661 Paul Hartman
1673 Marmaduke Sealey
1696 Henry Bedford, MA
1717 Jeremiah Horter, MA
1724 Thomas Lodge, MA
¥1740? Robert Coates, BA
1783 Nathaniel Booth
1788 Henry Willis, BA
1794 Richard Coxe, MA
1819 Gaius Barry
1851 James G.E. Hasluck, MA
1901 Henry H.J. Golledge

With Old Sodbury
1934/54 P.F. Boughey

With Horton
1957 J.B. Airton
1965 K.U. Ensor

*from Hockaday Abstracts.
¥also Curate at Chipping Sodbury.

APPENDIX M

BENEFACTIONS AND CHARITIES

Date	Grantor	Grantee	Details
c.1179	W. Crassus I Earl of Albemarle	Town	Charter according to laws of Breteuil. Common rights.
c1214	Jordano Bissop	Town	Rights to common.
1227	Sir W.Crassus III	himself	Charter for market.
1403	Dionisia Puttoo	Church	3½ acres in Dolemead.
1428	**Le Fayre	Church	Lands & properties.
1653	Tobias Davis	Town	Apprentices.
1680	Robert Davis	Town	£10 pa for schoolmaster.
c.1687	George Russell	Poor	£10.
1731	Mrs. Martha White	Poor	£140 between Chipping Sodbury and Yate.
1765	*Samuel Hardwicke	Poor	£40, interest for bread.
		Town	£40 house for schoolmaster.
?	Peter Hardwicke	Town	£40 house for schoolmaster.
?	*Richard Blake	Poor	£50 interest for bread.
1771	Daniel Woodward	Poor	£50 for use of workhouse.
?	James Wallis	Poor	£50 to assist.
1790	Rev.Tho. Shellard	Town	£50 house for schoolmaster.
1792	W. Winstone	Church	£20 interest to be paid to six poor householders, churchgoers, not paupers. £10 interest for sermon on Good Friday.
1792	*Geo.Hardwicke, MD.	Poor	£40 interest for bread.
1807	*William Harvey	Poor	£40 interest for bread.
1807	*Thomas Brookes	Poor	£40 interest for bread.
?	Samuel Isaac	Poor	£30 interest for bread.

1821	Sarah Hewitt	Poor	£800 interest for bread. At Christmas distribution of beef & bread to poor of Old and Little Sodbury & tenants in C. Sodbury.
No. of years	Lord of Manor	Poor	
1836	*Lt. C.J.H.Ollney, JP	Poor	£300, interest for bread and blankets.
1890s	C. Jacoby of Lyegrove	Children	Provided hot soup for children at Old Sodbury school twice weekly in winter.

* £36. 18s. 8d continues to be received annually in respect of these items. The money used to be distributed in bread and blankets by ticket system, now goes to deserving cases for diverse purposes at discretion of a representative committee.

** This is the origin of much of the Church & Town property.

APPENDIX N

LAST WILL & TESTAMENT OF ISABELLA TILY (NEE CLARKE)

Isabel is the 'Widow Tily' referred to in the poor rate assessment of 1727 (Page 140). She died in 1733 and the Crown Inn passed to her daughter, also Isabel, who had by that time married the Daniel Burcomb who witnessed the will.

It will be noted that the will was written in 1702. This is almost certainly due to the fact that Isabel's husband, William, had died unexpectedly in this year and, to judge by the paperwork at Gloucestershire Record Office, the problems caused by a close relative dying intestate are not a modern one. She chose not to visit the same problems on her own descendants.

In the name of God Amen. I Isabella Tilly of Chipping Sodbury in the County of Gloucs widow being sick and weak in body but of sound and perfect mind and memory thanks be given to almighty God for it do make this my last will and testament in manner and form following that is to say. First of all I commend my soul unto the hands of Almighty God that gave it hoping to be saved by the — — of Jesus Christ my Saviour and Redeemer. This my body I commit to the earth from whence it came to be decently interred in Christian like burial by mine Executrix hereinafter named. As for my worldly estate which God hath blessed me with all I dispose thereof as followeth.

First I give and bequeath unto my son William Tilly all his father's wearing apparell both woollen and linen, his silver George, silver buttons, silver buckles and silver seals, the silver cad—, two silver wine dishes one of them plain and the other nurled, one silver spoon besides his —. Also I give unto him the little box and the half of twenty shilling piece of old broad gold and the several piece of silver money therein which was his brother John's. Also I give unto him a twenty shilling piece and a half of twenty shilling piece of old broad gold, the old clock and the iron grate,

——, and tongs in the hall chamber and two small gold rings. Also I give and bequeath unto my daughter Hannah Tilly the messuage or tenement in Chipping Sodbury which I bought of Daniel Pill of the City of Bristol, Grocer, for —— and nineteen years if she the said Hannah Tilly, Isabell and William Tilly her sister and brother shall — long live and all the estate te— of years right and title therein. Also I give and bequeath unto her the said Hannah Tilly the little silver tankard, two silver wine dishes, one silver porringer, two silver spoons besides her own. Also I give unto her the two beds and bedsteads with the curtains and vallaines [valance?], rugs and blankets and appurtenances thereto belonging in the hall chamber. And two table boards and five leather chairs and window curtains in the same chamber. Also I give unto her one flockbed with the curtains and vallains, rugs and blankets and appurtenances thereunto belonging in the kitchen chamber, one oval table, six leather chairs, the brass and iron — and tongs and one — and three window curtains and one carpet cloth in the parlour chamber. Also I give and bequeath unto her the said Hannah Tilly two pairs of the best sheets and two pairs of the best pillow drawers, one diaper tablecloth and half a dozen of the best — napkins. Also I give unto her twenty pounds in money to be paid by my Executrix to my friends in trust for her use within one month after my decease and therefore one of their receipts shall be a sufficient discharge to my Executrix for the same. Also I give unto her one — and one twenty shilling piece of broad gold and two gold rings one with the p— I — my choice and the other to be chosen by my said daughter. Also I give unto my daughter Isabell the large silver — two silver wine dishes two silver diane [?] dishes and three silver spoons and one bed and bedstead curtains and vallains rugs and blankets with the appurtenances thereunto belonging six leather chairs and oval table board and one carpet cloth in the parlour chamber. And also one flock bed curtains and vallains rugs and blankets with the appurtenances thereunto belonging, six black matted chairs and two little table boards one pair of brass — and one form in the kitchen chamber. And all the linen that is not before bequeathed. Also I give and bequeath unto my brother Edward Clarke one guinea piece of gold and to his daughter Isabell half a guinea piece of gold. Also I give and bequeath unto my sister Susan, the wife of Henry Box half a guinea piece of gold and my grey crape gown and pettycoats and — cloth under pettycoats my best hat and my best shoes and stockings. And her daughter Isabell a half guinea piece of gold. And all thereof of my money goods and personal estate whatsoever not by me before bequeathed my debts and funeral expenses paid and discharged I give and bequeath unto my said daughter Isabella Tily whom I make Executrix of this my last will and testament. Also I desire — and appoint my loving friend William Prigg of Westerleigh in the County of Gloucs gent, Joseph _ingham of Chipping Sodbury aforesaid cordwainer and my loving brother Edward Clarke of Chipping Sodbury aforesaid trustees of this my last will and testament and see that this my will be performed. And to be assistant to my Executrix and my other children and do desire that they do agree and live lovingly together and if any difference do arise between them that they my said trustees do end and determine the same. And that my said children do abide and stand to their award and determination thereon. In witness whereof I have hereunto set my hand and seal this four and twentieth day of March in the second year of the reign of our sovereign Lady Ann by the grace of god of England, Scotland, France and Ireland, Queen, defender of the faith Anno Domini 1702

Isabell Tilly

Sealed delivered and published in the presence of
?
Danl Burcomb
? Burcomb

Index

A
Act of Uniformity 118
Akerman Street 18
Alba, Adam 46, 48
Alianor 61
Allocating an acre 190
Alterations to Calendar 150
Aluuard 34
Ambulation of the Boundaries 120
Anglo-Saxon Chronicle 22
Ascent in a 'hot air' balloon 165
Augustine, St. 24
Aurelianus, Ambrosius 20

B
Badminton Manor 109
Bagenden 16
Bailiff 50
Bailiff burgesses 50
Baptist Chapel 117, 124, 180
Baptist Church 136
Bar Gate 103
Baron's Court 118
Barrows and tumuli 14
Bateson, Miss M. 40
Battle of Dyrham 23
Battle of Hastings 31
Beaufort, Duke of 126
Bede 20, 23, 24, 25
Bees, H.J. 202
Bissop, Jordano 43
Black Death 68
Black Summer 206
Blanchards Farm 48
Blauncharde, Thomas 112
Book of Martyrs 85
Boot Inn 220
Bordarii 35
Bosel, Bishop 24
Bowling Hill 121
Bradenstoke Priory 62
Brewery at Old Sodbury 210
Brictric 30, 32, 34
Bristol to Gloucester Railway 189
Broad Street 55, 68
Brook Street 12, 16, 194
Brown Hematite 11
Bucketts Hill 103, 109
Buckett's Hill 160
Bull baiting 121, 134
Burgred 27
Burnell, Alice 70
Bussell, Thomas 120
Byssop, Sir John 57

C
Caerleon 17
Caerwent 18
Caesar, Julius 16
Carnarii 50
Catch Box' Corner 179
Celestine 11, 20
Ceolwulf II 27
Ceorl 26
Chapel of Ease 52, 57, 68, 184
Charitable funds, usage 113
Charity Commission Investigation 129
Charles I 113
Charles II 117
Chatterton, Thomas 150
Chessels 17
Chipping Sodbury Church renovated 197
Chipping Sodbury Cricket Club 194

Chipping Sodbury Endowed
   School   196
Church cemetery   195
Church Lands Charity   217
Church Lane   69, 86
Church Monthly magazine   212
Church of England Temperance
   Society   214
Clare, Gilbert de   54, 58, 60
Coal mines   194
Coat of arms   125
Codrington, John   74, 76
Codrington, Sir William   145
College of Heralds   125
Colymore, Richard   90, 100
Common Seal   125
Constantine   20
Construction of a Navigable
   Canal   168
Corio   16
Corner House   105, 126
Corner house   131
Corporation ceases to exist   211
Cotswolds   12
Council of Arles   20
County Bridge Money   144, 176
County Councils introduced   212
Court Leet   118
Court of Assize   51
Court of the Marches   97
Courts Leet   50
Crassus   35
Crassus, William   35
Cromwell, Oliver   117
Cromwell, Richard   117
Cross Hands   160, 179
Cross Hands Hotel   19
Cross Hands to Dodington
   Ash   175
Culverhill   121
Cuthwulf   22

D
Dames Schools   153

Danes   27
Dark Ages   20
Davies,
   Rev. Edward   165, 167, 175
Davis, Tobias   117
Davis, William   117, 128
De Palatiano,
   Elizabeth Ann Hartley   208
Despenser, Isabel   80
Dissolution of Monasteries   92
Dobunni   16
Dodington House   11
Dog Inn   11, 160, 199
Domesday Book   34
Doughton, John   76
Dowding, Murray   16, 211
Druids   21

E
Eanbald   25
Eanulf   24
Eastmund   25
Ecqwine   24
Ederestan(e)   35
Edmund I   29
Education Act 1878   203
Edward II   60
Edward IV   80
Edward the Confessor   30
Endowed School   212
Enfeoffing   33
Ethelflaed   28
Ethelred   28

F
Faber, Walter   62
Faithful Woman Burned   85
Fattinghouse Lane   177
Fayre, Robert le   60
Ferebee, Thomas   154, 163
Fiefs   33
Forestalling the market   119
Forster, Richard   84
Frankpledge   50
Fullers Earth   11

G

Garrett   103, 131, 154, 167
Garrett, William   121
George I   139
George II   140
George IV   179
George, The   74
Gildas   20
Gloucester Journal   139
Gloucestershire   29
Godwin, Earl   31
Golden Farmer   118, 128
Gorlands   113
Gorlands, The   103
Grace family   35
Grammar School   79, 192
Great Hospice   74
Great Storm   135
Greek traveller   16
Grickstone Farm   13, 19
Grumbold's Ash Hundred   35
Grundy, Mr. B.   22
Guild, foundation of   77
Guild, Religious   94
Gustators   50

H

Hampstead Farm   61
Hartley, Winchcombe Henry   160
Hartley, Winchcombe Henry Howard   208
Harvests failure 1800-1801   176
Hatter's Lane   37, 48, 83, 161
Hauling the King's Carriage   144
Hawise   35
Hawkesbury   28
Heathwred, Bishop   25
Henry I   36
Henry II   37, 43
Henry III   49
Henry IV   71
Henry V   74
Henry VI   77, 81
Henry VII   84
Hide   35
Highways Act of 1691   128
Hilary Term   112
Hinton   18
History of Gloucestershire   43
Hockaday Abstracts   112, 180
Hockaday abstracts   57
Horse Street   68, 161
Horton   13
Hounds Road   103
Hundred   26
Hundred Courts   30
Hundred Rolls   52
Hundreds   30
Hunfrid   33
Hwicci   23, 24
Hyatt, Joseph   178, 188

I

Inquisitione Post Mortem   58
Introduction of a gas supply   201
Iron Age   15
Isolation hospital   149

J

Jacoby, Mr. & Mrs.   216
James II   126
Jordano Bissop   58
Justices of the Peace   72

K

Kelly's Directory   187
King Alfred   27
King Edward I   57
King Ethelbert   24
King Ethelwald   25
King Henry III   49
King Henry VII   67
King Henry VIII   90
King Ine of Wessex   26
King Oswy   24
King Richard   41
King Richard II   71

King's Escheator   40, 81
King's Feorm   26
Kingswood, Bristol   16

L
Lady of the Mercians   28
Lane, Harry   41
Lanfrac   32
Latimer   148, 172
Laws of Breteuil   40, 50
Le Despenser, Hugh   67
Le Despenser, Sir Hugh   61
Le Fayre, Robert   48, 75
Le Gras   35, 45
Le Gros   35
Le Yonge, John   66
Le Zouch, William   61
Legio II Augustus   19
Leland   19, 92
Little Sodbury Camp   16
Little Sodbury Church re-built   194
Lords Marchers   90
Ludlow, Christopher   127, 136
Ludlow, Ebenezer   167, 174
Lugbury   14
Lyegrove   75
Lyegrove House   199, 216

M
Macadam   177
Mace   80, 134
Magic Lantern lecture   205
Magic Lantern' show   212
Magna Carta   41
Maintaining secondary roads   176
Maminot, Hugh   34
Market at Chipping Sodbury   202
Market cross   68, 98, 154, 194
Marketing cheese   142
Massey, Colonel   116
Matilda   30
Mayor   123

Mayor and Corporation   127
Melbourne House   174
Mercia   27
Mesozoic rocks   11
Mills, J.   198
Millstone Grit   11
Milred   25
Milred, Bishop   25
Miners of Kingswood   140
Monastery at 'Geate'   24
Monastery at Westbury   25
Mop Fair   196, 206
Mortimer, Ralph de   35

N
"Nan Tow's" tump   14
National School   203
National School Log Book   196
National School Room   193
Nettleton   14
New Hall   211
New town   37
Nobbs, Rev. James   117
Normandy   30

O
Odo   33
Odo, Count   35
Offa   25
Ogilby, John   120
Old Ditch   93
Old Grammar School   167, 211
Old Sodbury Church bells   158
Old Sodbury church bells   152
Old Sodbury Church renovated   193
Old Sodbury Friendly Society   203

P
Packer, Robert   142
Painter's Mead   134
Parish Council   219
Passagium caretarum   40
Pershore Abbey   28

Index

Pest house   149
Petty Sessional Court   194
Petty Sessions Court   161
Pew in the Church   157
Picts   20
Plough Inn   161
Police Station built   194
Poll tax   72
Poor Law Amendment Act of 1834   185
Poor Rate 1795   168
Post office   179, 188, 199
Postal services available   205
Poyntz, Anne   85
Poyntz, Sir Robert   84
Prince John   40, 41
Prince Rupert   116
Pucklechurch   29

Q
Quarrying   142
Queen Anne   135
Queen Matilda   33

R
Rabbit culture   54
Rag, The   86
Records destroyed by fire   176
Renovations to the Manor   115
Repeal of the Corn Laws   186
Rev. Aquila Lemon   212
Ridgeway   185
Riding   27
Riding, Meade   111
Riding, Meadow   43
Riding, Stub   43
Ridings   43, 48, 110, 128, 135, 148, 171, 172, 184, 191, 217
Ridings Charity   217
Rights of 'Infangeth'   51
River Avon   12
River Frome   11, 152
Roman Camps   15
Roman coins   20
Romanised Celts   17

Rounceval Street   107
Roundheads   116
Royal charter 1681   123
Royal Oak   131
Royalists   116
Rudder   75
Rudder, Samuel   81, 159
Rudge   43
Rufus, William   35, 36

S
Saxon Charters   23
Saxons   20
Scavengers   51
School Rules restated   163
Scrutatores corarium   50
Servii   35
Sextary   35
Shambles   103, 154
Shambles, the   86
Sharing Out Benefit Clubs   199
Shire Courts   30
Silvanius   19
Sir Robert Peel's police   186
Sobyre Mercato   49
Sodbury   95
Sodbury Bank   167
Sodbury Fairs   148
Sodbury Races   198
Sopanbyrg   25, 26, 28, 30
Sopeberie   30
St. Adeline   57, 112
Standing Orders   153
Starveal   14
State Lottery   158
Staters   16
Steam mill   202
Stephens, Edward   115
Stephens, John   117
Stephens, Thomas   112, 115
Stonehenge   14
Stub Riding   218
Stubb Riding   191
Sturge, J.P.   168

Sturge, Jacob   172
Subscription Assembly and Ball   157
Sunday School   180
Synnyffe Rowles   110

T
Tacitus   16
Taylor, Isaac   157
Tenements   169
Tesseri   17
The Clock   207
The Court of Assize   51
The Fly Leaf   202
The Green, Old Sodbury   209
Three times principle   178
Throgmorton, Thomas   97
Tog Hill   22
Toleration Act of 1689   180
Town Crier   120, 191
Town Hall   95, 106
Town Hall rebuilt   194
Town House   126
Town House or Hall   145
Town Lands Charity   217
Town Strong Chest   130
Tribal Hideage   33
Tudor House   83
Turnpike   119
Turnpike Trusts   135, 212
Tyndale, William   87

U
Unusual pulpit discovered   197

V
Vaccination against smallpox   163
View of Frankpledge   50, 118
Villein   35
Visitation of Gloucestershire 1682–3   125

W
Waerfrith, Bishop   28

Wages in 1732   147
Wallsend Lane   14
Walshe, Henry   106
Walshe, John   84
Walshe, Maurice   94, 99
War Memorial   98
Wars of the Roses   81
Water supply in 1803   176
Weaving trade   101
Wessex   25, 27
West Littleton Down   14
West Saxons   23
Westerleigh   18
Weyland, Thomas de   52, 54
Weyland, William de   51
Whitby   24
Whittington, Mr.   182
Wickham, Thomas   125
Wickwar Road   11
William and Mary   126
William Crassus I   37, 40
William Crassus II   40, 41
William Crassus III   41, 44
William Crassus IV   44
William I   31
William III   135
William the Conqueror   31
Wintour, Edward   106
Witan   30
Workhouse   166, 173
Workhouse for the poor   149
Wulfstan   30, 32
Wyrriett, John   97, 98, 102

Y
Yard-land   96
Yardland   35
Yate   12
Yate Court   116
Yatton Keynell   16